Services Industries
and the Knowledge-Based Economy

THE RESEARCH PAPERS ASSEMBLED IN THIS VOLUME are the product of work undertaken by academic researchers and a few researchers, with governmental and international organizations, writing in a personal capacity. In addition, several of the commentators on the research papers were employees of governmental or international organizations, writing in a personal capacity, at the time this volume was compiled. Industry Canada staff formulated and managed the project, and provided constructive feedback throughout the process. Nevertheless, the papers and comments ultimately remain the sole responsibility of the authors and do not necessarily reflect the policies and opinions of Industry Canada, the Government of Canada, or any other organization with which the authors or editors are affiliated.

GENERAL EDITORS:
RICHARD G. LIPSEY & ALICE O. NAKAMURA

Services Industries and the Knowledge-Based Economy

The Industry Canada Research Series

University of Calgary Press

ISBN 1-55238-149-8
ISSN 1700-2001
IC 54407

University of Calgary Press
2500 University Dr. N.W.
Calgary, Alberta, Canada T2N 1N4

Library and Archives Canada Cataloguing in Publication

Services industries and the knowledge-based economy / general editors, Richard G. Lipsey & Alice O. Nakamura.

(Industry Canada research series, ISSN 1700-2001 ; 13)
Co-published by: Industry Canada.
Includes bibliographical references.
ISBN 1-55238-149-8

1. Services industries--Canada.
I. Lipsey, Richard G., 1928-
II. Nakamura, Alice
III. Canada. Industry Canada
IV. Series.

HD9985.C32S468 2006 338.4'7'000971 C2006-900731-4

Canadä We acknowledge the financial support of the Government of Canada through the Book Publishing Industry Development Program (BPIDP) for our publishing activities.

We acknowledge the support of the Alberta Foundation for the Arts for this published work.

Published by the University of Calgary Press in cooperation with Industry Canada and Public Works and Government Services Canada.

EDITORIAL AND TYPESETTING SERVICES: The Summit Group

COVER DESIGN: Paul Payer/ArtPlus Limited

Printed and bound in Canada

 This book is printed on acid-free paper.

Table of Contents

ACKNOWLEDGMENTS *xiii*

1. INTRODUCTION *1*

RICHARD G. LIPSEY & ALICE O. NAKAMURA

Endnotes 15
Bibliography 16

2. CONCEPTS AND MEASURES OF PRODUCTIVITY: AN INTRODUCTION *19*

W. ERWIN DIEWERT & ALICE O. NAKAMURA

Introduction 19
Different Types of Productivity Measures 22
Productivity Measures for the One Input-One Output Case 23
The Two Input, One Output Case 27
The General N Input, M Output Case 29
Conclusions 32
Appendix 34
Endnotes 35
Acknowledgments 37
Bibliography 37

3. POLICY CHALLENGES IN THE NEW ECONOMY 39

RICHARD G. LIPSEY

What is the "New Economy?" 39
General-Purpose Technologies 41
New Economies Throughout History 43
How Do We Know a New Economy When We See One? 44
Key Characteristics of the New Economy 49
Disbelievers in the Importance of the New Economy 54
Two Views of the Economy 55
Policy Challenges 59
Conclusion 69
Endnotes 70
Bibliography 73

4. THE SERVICES ECONOMY IN CANADA: AN OVERVIEW 77

RAM C. ACHARYA

Introduction 77
The Services Sector in G-7 Countries 79
Real Growth in Services in Canada 82
Employment in Services 84
Productivity and Wages in Services 91
Interdependence between the Goods and Services Sectors 96
Capital Intensity in the Services Industries 101
International Trade and Foreign Direct Investment in Services 105
Innovation in Services 110
ICT and Services 117
Conclusions 118
Appendix A 122
Appendix B 125
Appendix C 126
Endnotes 127
Acknowledgments 129
Bibliography 129

5. RELATIVE WAGE PATTERNS AMONG THE HIGHLY EDUCATED IN A KNOWLEDGE-BASED ECONOMY 131

RENÉ MORISSETTE, YURI OSTROVSKY & GARNETT PICOT

Introduction 131
Data and Concepts 134

Employment Trends: 1981-2001 137
Exploring Gender and Age Differences 140
Disaggregating the Data by Industry 144
The Evolution of the "Field" Premium 150
Conclusions 151
Appendix 153
Endnotes 157
Bibliography 158

PANEL: KNOWLEDGE-ECONOMY AND SERVICES: PERSPECTIVES AND ISSUES

WILLIAM WATSON

A Policy for Services? Don't Tilt 159

6. LOCATION EFFECTS, LOCATIONAL SPILLOVERS AND THE PERFORMANCE OF CANADIAN INFORMATION TECHNOLOGY FIRMS 167

STEVEN GLOBERMAN, DANIEL SHAPIRO & AIDAN VINING

Introduction 167
Review of the Literature 169
Sample and Data 176
Estimation Model 179
Estimation Results 182
Conclusions and Implications 192
Appendix 1 195
Appendix 2 197
Endnotes 199
Acknowledgments 200
Bibliography 200

COMMENT 205

AJAY AGRAWAL

7. LIBERALIZATION IN CHINA'S KEY SERVICES SECTORS FOLLOWING ACCESSION TO THE WORLD TRADE ORGANIZATION: SOME SCENARIOS AND ISSUES OF MEASUREMENT *211*

JOHN WHALLEY

Overview 211
Trade Liberalization in Key Services Categories 212
China's Banking, Insurance and Telecoms Sectors and the Implications of China's WTO Accession 216
Analytic Structures for Evaluating Chinese WTO Commitments in Services 222
Quantifying the Effects of Services Liberalization in China 226
Concluding Remarks 229
Endnotes 230
Acknowledgments 231
Bibliography 231

COMMENT 233

JOHN MCHALE

8. CANADA'S EXPERIENCE WITH FOREIGN DIRECT INVESTMENT: HOW DIFFERENT ARE SERVICES? *237*

WALID HEJAZI

Introduction 237
Canada's FDI Position in a Global Perspective 241
Changes in Canada's Industry Level FDI 247
The Estimating Equation 257
Empirical Estimates 259
Policy Implications and Conclusions 265
Endnotes 267
Bibliography 268

COMMENT 269

JOHN RIES

9. PRODUCTIVITY GROWTH IN THE SERVICES INDUSTRIES: PATTERNS, ISSUES AND THE ROLE OF MEASUREMENT *277*

ANITA WÖLFL

Introduction 277
The Role of the Services Sector in the Economy 278
Productivity Growth and the Specific Characteristics of Services Industries 294
The Role of Measurement 305
Conclusions 319
Endnotes 320
Acknowledgments 322
Bibliography 322

COMMENT *323*

ALICE O. NAKAMURA

10. INNOVATION IN THE CANADIAN SERVICES SECTOR *329*

PETR HANEL

Introduction 329
Innovation in Services — Concepts, Measures and Statistics 330
Canada's Innovation in Services — an Overview 337
Canadian R&D in Services 356
Concluding Remarks 361
Appendix 363
Endnotes 366
Acknowledgments 371
Bibliography 372

COMMENT *375*

STEVEN GLOBERMAN

11. TECHNOLOGY AND THE FINANCIAL SERVICES INDUSTRY *379*

EDWIN H. NEAVE

Trends in Financial Services 379
E-finance in the Financial Services Industry 385
E-finance and Financial Markets 390
Implications for Public Policy 392

Conclusions 397
Endnotes 398
Bibliography 399

COMMENT 400

ERIC SANTOR

12. LIBERALIZATION OF TRADE AND INVESTMENT IN TELECOMMUNICATION SERVICES: A CANADIAN PERSPECTIVE 405

ZHIQI CHEN

Introduction 405
An Overview of Canada's Telecommunications Services Industry During the 1990s 406
Quantifying the Relationship Between Telecommunications Services and Economic Growth 417
Liberalization of Trade and Investment in Telecommunications Services 424
Conclusions 436
Endnotes 437
Acknowledgments 438
Bibliography 438

COMMENT 439

SUMIT K. KUNDU

13. THE RURAL/URBAN LOCATION PATTERN OF ADVANCED SERVICES FIRMS IN AN INTERNATIONAL PERSPECTIVE 445

C. MICHAEL WERNERHEIM & CHRISTOPHER A. SHARPE

Introduction 445
Previous Studies 447
Descriptive Analysis 451
Location and Agglomeration: A Stochastic Approach 465
The International Evidence on Services Location 470
Conclusions 478
Appendix A 481
Appendix B 482
Appendix C 483

Endnotes 484
Acknowledgments 485
Bibliography 485

COMMENT 491

MARIO POLÈSE

14. PRODUCTIVITY GROWTH IN SERVICES INDUSTRIES: A CANADIAN SUCCESS STORY 503

SOMESHWAR RAO, ANDREW SHARPE & JIANMIN TANG

Introduction 503
Comparison of Output and Employment Shares and Labour Productivity Levels in the Canadian and U.S. Services Sectors 506
Productivity Growth in the Business-sector Component of Services in Canada and the United States 521
Sources of Real Output and Labour Productivity Growth in Canadian and U.S. Business-sector Services Industries 525
Contributions of Business-sector Services Industries to Business-sector Output and Productivity Growth in Canada and the United States 535
Factors Accounting for the Relative Success of Business-sector Services Productivity Growth in Canada 539
Conclusions 544
Appendix 546
Endnotes 548
Acknowledgments 552
Bibliography 552

COMMENT 553

RICHARD G. HARRIS

15. SERVICES AND THE NEW ECONOMY: DATA NEEDS AND CHALLENGES 557

W. ERWIN DIEWERT

The North American Industrial Classification System and Services Sector Data Deficiencies 557
The Importance of Accurate Services Sector Price and Output Measurement 558
The Measurement of Industry Output and Productivity 562
Preliminary Considerations on Measuring Services Sector Output Prices 563

Services 1: Communication, Storage, Information and Entertainment Services 564
Finance and Insurance 567
Services 2: Leasing Services, Real Estate Services and Other Business Services 569
Education, Health and Social Assistance 571
Services 3: Live Entertainment, Sports, Cultural, Recreational, Travel, Restaurant and Personal Services 572
Summarizing Measurement Difficulties in the Services Sector 574
The General Structure of a Proposal for Better Services Measurement in Canada 575
Conclusion 576
Endnotes 576
Acknowledgments 578
Bibliography 579

COMMENT 581

PHILIP SMITH

16. SERVICES INDUSTRIES IN A KNOWLEDGE-BASED ECONOMY: SUMMING UP 583

PIERRE SAUVÉ

Introduction 583
The Services Economy: Salient Facts 584
Are Services Exceptional? 584
Summing Up What We Know (and What We Know We Don't Know) 586
A Policy Research Agenda for the Future 603
Endnotes 605
Bibliography 605

ABOUT THE CONTRIBUTORS 607

Acknowledgments

THE GENERAL EDITORS WOULD LIKE TO THANK all those involved in the preparation of this volume and of the conference. Renée St-Jacques, Someshwar Rao and Prakash Sharma from the Micro-Economic Policy Analysis Branch of the Policy Sector at Industry Canada planned and organized the conference in close collaboration with Chummer Farina, John Lambie and Lee Gill of the Industry Sector and Keith Parsonage of the Spectrum, Information Technologies and Telecommunications Sector. First drafts of the papers published here were presented and discussed at the conference in Winnipeg. Varsa Kuniyal, Rachelle Boone and Natalie Popel provided valuable assistance in the organization of the conference. Joanne Fleming and Varsa Kuniyal coordinated the publication of the volume. McEvoy Galbreath and her team at Summit Group provided the English editing, page setting and the French translation; Véronique Dewez proofread the French version. We would also like to thank Walter Hildebrandt and John King of the University of Calgary Press for their support in the publication of the volume. Finally, we wish to thank the authors for participating in the project and the conference, as well as for their own excellent contributions and commentaries to the volume.

Richard G. Lipsey & *Alice O. Nakamura*
Simon Fraser University *University of Alberta*

1

Introduction

IN BUSINESS AND INDUSTRY, reputation is an important basis for making decisions in matters of finance and human capital investment. Many studies, including some in this volume, report that services industries are performing poorly in terms of productivity growth. Being branded this way can channel public and private investment away from those industries. This may be unfair if a negative judgment was based on facts that are wrong because the data were inadequate, or if findings are outdated, or if the theories used to interpret the facts are inappropriate. As explained in greater detail, the studies in this volume question the reputation for poor productivity performance ascribed to services industries in Canada.

Computing the usual productivity measures requires data on the value of transactions and either prices or quantities. In the final research study of this volume, Erwin Diewert notes that Canada lacks direct price and quantity measures for many important services industries. Other nations also have this problem. As a result, the usual productivity indexes cannot be evaluated properly for those services industries, nor can we get a complete picture of productivity performance for the economy as a whole. Recognizing this, the United States has now committed significant resources to improving services sector measurement.

The study of productivity and the 'new economy' also requires a proper theoretical framework.

The papers in this volume illustrate the evolutionary nature of services, and the pervasive importance of context. In the large body of research that he draws from in his keynote address, "Policy Challenges in the New Economy," Richard Lipsey makes the point that the existing neoclassical paradigm largely ignores context.[1] Even if we had all the data that we could wish for, interpreting it within the neoclassical theoretical framework would greatly restrict our ability to interpret this information effectively. He introduces a new intellectual technique for understanding the long-term economic growth process: structuralist-evolutionary (S-E) theory. Lipsey explains that S-E theory emphasizes the importance of a detailed knowledge of technologies and the process of technological change. His keynote address is intended to provide an intellectual framework for the research studies in this volume. These studies do not focus just on productivity indexes. In addition, they provide empirical evidence and institutional detail for a wide assortment of activities, inputs and outcomes believed to be associated with innovation, technological change and economic growth.

Lipsey uses the term 'new economy' to refer to the economic, social and political changes brought about by the revolution in information and communication technologies (ICTs). The studies in this volume help us to understand the evolution and functioning of the new economy. Lipsey describes the new economy as a knowledge-based economy because its total capital stock is embodied in human rather than in physical capital to a greater degree than ever before. Lipsey focuses especially on general-purpose technologies (GPTs) that he terms "transforming technologies," of which ICTs are an important example. Among their many important effects, new GPTs enable goods and processes of production that were technically impossible with older technologies. Lipsey's address introduces the reader to the issues surrounding the measurement of economic growth and technical progress, and includes reasons why conventional measures do *not* measure technical progress.

If the usual productivity measures do *not* measure technical progress, then what do they measure? And what are the relevant differences among the different productivity measures used in several of the studies in this volume? These questions are taken up in "Concepts and Measures of Productivity: An Introduction" by Erwin Diewert of the University of British Columbia and Alice Nakamura of the University of Alberta. This brief study constitutes a methodological introduction to this volume and productivity indexes.

Diewert and Nakamura distinguish labour, multi- and total-factor productivity indexes. They explain that these indexes each measure the conversion of some component of input, or total input into the measured output. They explain the difference between measures of productivity levels and productivity growth, and why price measurement matters for the measurement of productivity. They also illustrate Lipsey's point that the usual productivity measures do not measure technical progress, though technical progress can affect the values of these indexes. They show that anything that reduces the rate of transformation of real cost outlays into real sales revenues will pull down measured productivity. This can even include the diversion of funds into social programs.[2]

The empirical research studies that make up the main body of this volume begin with the paper titled, "The Services Economy in Canada: An Overview," by Ram Acharya of Industry Canada. Acharya examines the size of the services sector over time as well as changes over time in real gross domestic product (GDP), shares of industry employment, and hourly wages for both the services and the goods sectors in Canada. He also explores the interdependence among the services-producing and goods-producing industries, the capital intensities of these two sectors as well as their relationship to foreign trade, direct investment and research and development (R&D) spending.

Acharya finds that services industries are doing better than in the past. He concludes that:

> In overall sectoral comparisons, the services sector still seems to lag behind manufacturing.... However, the overall performance of services-producing

> industries has improved over the years, whether performance is examined in terms of employment, the use of machinery and equipment (M&E), the employment of highly skilled workers, innovation or participation in international markets. There are some areas where the services sector is leading manufacturing. This is the case, for example, in the production and the use of information and communications technologies and skill-intensity. There are also some services industries that are outperforming manufacturing even in productivity growth and investment in research and development.

In their study, "Relative Wage Patterns among the Highly Educated in a Knowledge-Based Economy" René Morissette, Yuri Ostrovsky and Garnett Picot of Statistics Canada extend previous work on the education premium. They investigate divergence over time in the university/high school earnings ratio for different industries in the knowledge-based economy. They also investigate the changing demand for high-skilled workers by comparing relative wages for university graduates holding degrees in "applied" fields with the wages of other university graduates ("field" premia). Their main finding is that even though employment grew much faster during the last two decades in industries classified as high-knowledge, trends in relative wages and real wages of university and high-school graduates have displayed remarkably similar patterns across industries.

In the next study, "Location Effects, Locational Spillovers and the Performance of Canadian Information Technology Firms," Steven Globerman of Western Washington University, and Daniel Shapiro and Aidan Vining, both of Simon Fraser University, examine how one aspect of business context — location — affects firm performance and innovative behaviour. The authors note that little research has been conducted into location effects for Canadian businesses, despite growing policy interest in the topic. For example, policy concerns have been raised about the limited number of "high-tech" clusters in Canada as compared to the United States.

The authors estimate the effects of location on the growth of high-tech firms in Canada. To do this, they create a base model of firm growth that does not include locational variables. They then augment this model with variables for firm location. They find that firms that are located closer to Toronto grow faster than firms located further away, all else being equal.

The authors report that the existing literature focuses attention on a number of other factors that might contribute to the growth of clusters of firms. One of these is the scientific infrastructure of a region, such as the presence of universities with research and teaching capabilities in science and engineering. This possible factor in stimulating clusters might be good news for Canadian localities that are far from major metropolitan areas. The authors note that research institutes and universities are relatively dispersed when compared with, for example, leading Canadian corporations.

In his comments on the Globerman-Shapiro-Vining study, Ajay Agrawal of the University of Toronto agrees that the authors offer compelling empirical evidence that "location matters." He cautions, however, that it is precisely because this study offers a compelling argument in favour of some radical rethinking of public policy that we should examine its limitations.

Agrawal notes, for example, that while the study suggests reasons why regions may vary in their ability to support economically successful information technology (IT) firms, the question actually documented is whether or not there *is* regional variation in the growth of the sales of Canadian IT firms.

Agrawal points out that the dependent variable they use (sales growth) does not take account of costs. He notes that if labour costs are significantly higher in bigger cities and labour comprises a significant portion of total software development costs, then software firms in larger cities must sell more than their smaller-town rivals in order to generate the *same* profits. Thus Agrawal sharpens the contextual focus of the Globerman-Shapiro-Vining study by calling attention to additional aspects of the context that could affect the interpretation of the results.

As is the case for many of the studies in this volume, the results of the Globerman-Shapiro-Vining study are interesting, but more work seems called for before they can be used to inform policy.

John Whalley of the University of Western Ontario begins his study, "Liberalization in China's Key Services Sectors Following Accession to the World Trade Organization: Some Scenarios and Issues of Measurement," with a strong assertion about the scope and importance of its subject matter. Whalley writes:

> ...over a five-year period from 2002 to 2007, China will open all of its markets to full international competition from foreign service providers in a series of key areas: distribution, telecommunications, financial services, professional business and computer services, motion pictures, environmental services, accounting, law, architecture, construction, and travel and tourism. China will remove all barriers to entry in the form of discriminatory licences to operate and all conduct-related barriers in the form of differential regulation for domestic and foreign entries.

Whalley documents policy changes in three key service categories in China: banking, insurance and telecoms. He notes that the starting point for the Chinese reform effort leaves a lot to be accomplished and raises doubts about the feasibility of the Chinese carrying through as promised. Whalley discusses different scenarios about how this liberalization might unfold.

He also discusses the literature on trade liberalization in services and observes that very little of it takes account of the individual characteristics of the services under discussion. He compares this literature with the larger one that treats all services as analytically equivalent to goods and considers the liberalization of services in a conventional trade-policy framework. Whalley then outlines an alternative theoretical framework for analyzing the impacts of services liberalization.

Throughout his study, Whalley pays attention to how economic development depends on the path being pursued and the importance of having detailed knowledge of the context. He argues for a new theoretical framework for analyzing services liberalization that would take more account of the specific characteristics of services.

In his comment, John McHale of Queen's University describes Whalley's study as a wide-ranging review of services sector liberalization in China. Based on his own understanding of the economic development context, McHale is more optimistic than Whalley about both the credibility of the Chinese commitments and the gains that are likely to follow.

McHale expects that China will follow through on its commitments because doing so is an important part of the government's strategic plan to move forward with market-based institutional reforms. McHale notes that over the past decade, China has used its high savings rate to support fast growth but China has also diverted a substantial amount of capital to state-owned enterprises through the state-dominated banking system. McHale argues that reformers in the Chinese government realize that sustaining high growth rates will require a shift to allocating capital based on market principles. McHale notes that foreign investment in the banking system could allow for the recapitalization of existing banks together with the emergence of a well-capitalized, non-state dominated banking sector, operating according to market principles. He feels that policy makers in China know that they must pre-emptively strengthen their financial system and that removing investment restrictions offers a shortcut to achieving this goal.

As in the Whalley study, McHale pays attention to the path dependence of development and to context, as recommended in the S-E approach.

Walid Hejazi of the University of Toronto takes foreign direct investment (FDI) as the subject of his study: "Canada's Experience with Foreign Direct Investment: How Different are Services?" The study has three purposes. First, it places Canada's FDI position within a global context. Second, Canada's performance is benchmarked against other major economies. Third, the study identifies factors that help to explain changing patterns in FDI.

Hejazi assembles the factual context needed for a fuller consideration of FDI policy choices. He notes, for example, that Canada has been transformed from a host economy for FDI in the 1970s to an important source country for FDI by 1997. Whereas in 1970 Canada's inward FDI stock was four times its outward, today outward FDI stock exceeds inward. He notes that Canada has been able to maintain its share of the rapidly growing stocks of world outward FDI but its share of global inward FDI stocks has been falling. He observes too that the data indicate that the surge on the outward side is largely attributable to a surge in services FDI.

In contrast to the outward side, Hejazi does not find an increasing trend toward FDI in services on the inward side. Rather, the apparent source of the surge in Canada's inward FDI in the last half of the 1990s is the investment flowing into manufacturing.

Hejazi's study illustrates that context is important for judging the benefits of alternative policy options. He notes, for example, that if Canadian FDI is moving abroad to exploit firm specific advantages, perhaps such investments should be encouraged. On the other hand, to the extent that firms are moving abroad because of disincentives such as relatively high taxes or a lack of skilled labour, then such investments are a bad sign for Canada. Hejazi argues that to assess the policy implications properly, we must first understand what impact these changing FDI patterns have had on the Canadian economy and what is driving the changes.

The study's discussant, John Ries of the University of British Columbia, comments that any assessment of whether Canada's FDI experience is "unusual" first depends on developing a benchmark of what we might expect for Canada in terms of FDI levels and growth. Ries notes that Hejazi has chosen the member countries of the Organisation for Economic Co-operation and Development (OECD) as his benchmark. Ries proposes to augment this by examining the FDI of OECD countries relative to a theoretical benchmark that relates FDI shares to gross national income with an adjustment for country size. Thus Ries argues for taking account of additional aspects of the context in judging Canadian FDI performance.

"Productivity Growth in the Services Industries: Patterns, Issues and the Role of Measurement" by Anita Wölfl of the OECD, Directorate of Science, Technology and Industry, examines the empirical evidence on services sector performance across OECD countries.

Wölfl explains Baumol's Cost Disease theory and examines whether it is an appropriate framework for productivity policy analysis. She notes that Baumol's theory was purportedly motivated by empirical observation of an economy that consisted "of a growing (manufacturing) sector characterized by technological progress, capital accumulation and economies of scale and a relatively stagnant (services) sector" consisting of services such as education, performing arts, public administration, health and social work. Wölfl explains that the main idea behind Baumol's Cost Disease is that the tendency to unbalanced growth across sectors will induce resource re-allocation toward the slowly growing or stagnant sector, eventually slowing down aggregate growth.

In the empirical portion of her study, Wölfl finds measured productivity growth to be low or negative in many services industries, including social and personal services as well as some business services. Wölfl claims that this confirms the characterization of much of the services sector as "stagnant" — a key prerequisite for the Baumol Cost Disease framework. She does, however, report that some services industries are exceptions to this generalization. She also concedes that the low or negative measured productivity growth rates for some services industries might be linked to problems with measurement.

In her comments on Wölfl's paper, Alice Nakamura of the University of Alberta offers two primary reasons for not accepting some of Wölfl's conclusions and recommendations. One, Wölfl's study and others that she draws on rely on measures of labour productivity. Nakamura argues that measures of labour productivity are fatally flawed for making productivity comparisons between the services and other sectors because there are systematic differences between services and other sectors as well as among different service industries. These differences pertain to the proportion of total costs that are comprised by labour costs. Two, Nakamura argues that there are serious problems — some of which Wölfl briefly acknowledges — with the productivity measures for many services industries. Among them are the fact that outputs are being measured by inputs for some industries because direct output measures are lacking. This leads by construction to a finding of no or low productivity growth. When analysis is based on poor measures, policy makers have no sensible rules for how to use that information or any recommendations based upon it. Wrong facts can lead policy makers to take initiatives that are counterproductive.

The study by Petr Hanel of the University of Sherbrooke and the Centre interuniversitaire de la recherche sur la science et la technologie addresses "Innovation in the Canadian Services Sector." His objective is to review the empirical evidence for innovative activities in Canadian services industries and to assess how Canada's innovation in services compares with that of its competitors.

Hanel notes that in spite of the economic importance of the services sector, innovation and technical change have been much less studied in services than in manufacturing. He begins by discussing the concepts relevant to, and the measurement of, R&D and innovation in services industries. He argues that much of the innovation in services is not well captured by the traditional indicators of innovation inputs (R&D activities) and outputs (such as patents). Insofar as innovation policies are geared to larger industrial firms, the small services innovators may not qualify for the benefits of those policies and their innovation activities may not be measured by data that is gathered from programs set up to encourage innovation.

Mirroring some of the themes in Lipsey's keynote address, Hanel draws attention to the interactive character of most services and the fact that many services cannot be separated from the competence of the persons who provide them. As a result, he suggests that personal contact, training and tacit knowledge are also important aspects of innovation in the services sector. According to Hanel, these aspects are ignored when using the predominantly 'industrial' focus of traditional measures and studies of innovation.

In his comments on Hanel's study, Steven Globerman of Western Washington University notes that a general conclusion to be drawn from the literature reviewed by Hanel is that services firms introduce innovations at rates that are comparable to manufacturing firms. He finds this surprising given the traditional reports of lagging productivity performance for services compared to manufacturing industries — as found, for example, by Wölfl in the contribution noted above.

Globerman speculates that factors promoting innovation and technological change in the services industries may be fairly idiosyncratic to specific industries. His observation suggests that achieving an understanding of how to promote R&D in services may require detailed case studies to complement the broad statistical surveys and analyses of the sort that Hanel's study discusses. This is in line with the recommendations made in Lipsey's address.

In his study, "Technology and the Financial Services Industry," Edwin Neave of Queen's University examines the importance of technology and innovation to Canada's financial system.

Neave argues that today's financial service providers (FSPs) are innovative developers of products and services. He discusses numerous recent innovations in this sector: automated banking machine networks, Internet banking, portals and aggregators, credit scoring, securitization and risk management, networks such as Interac and Cirrus, a variety of clearing systems for settling inter-bank payments, securities and derivatives transactions, and non-bank forms of payment including credit cards.

Neave claims that the Internet and other technological advances have shrunk economies of scale in the production of financial services that can now easily be unbundled and commoditized. Examples of this include payment and brokerage services, mortgage loans, insurance, and some forms of trade finance. He argues that reduced economies of scale have lowered barriers to entry and thus increased competition in delivering those kinds of financial services. In contrast, he argues that for services characterized by sunk costs and low commoditization potential — services such as corporate advisory services, underwriting and facilitating mergers and acquisitions — there have been fewer new entrants.

Neave also suggests that recent changes in how financial services are provided raise questions about the adequacy of the current approach to financial sector regulation. He wonders if the traditional reasons for regulation and supervision remain valid and if policy areas such as competition and consumer protection deserve increased emphasis. According to Neave, the need for a financial sector safety net arises from the perceived need to treat deposit-taking institutions differently from other economic agents. He asks if the recent emergence of substitutes for bank deposits and alternative payment mechanisms are eroding the nature of what made banks special over the past 70 years.

Neave argues that the main issues facing competition policy in financial services include determining what market definitions to use, what constitutes market power, what constitutes barriers to entry and exit, and what are allowable vertical and horizontal ownership structures within the evolving financial services industry. Thus Neave suggests that there is considerable flux in certain aspects of the context that is important for any analysis of public policy toward financial services.

In his commentary on the Neave study, Eric Santor of the International Department at the Bank of Canada acknowledges that Neave provides an excellent summary of how technological and financial innovation is leading to new financial products and services as well as to more efficient financial markets of different kinds. Santor also notes that Neave highlights important policy issues raised by these innovations.

Santor goes on to raise several questions and concerns. He asks if innovations such as credit scoring models now used by banks reduce the importance of the bank-borrower relationship. He then speculates about the potential importance of this declining relationship.

"Liberalization of Trade and Investment in Telecommunication Services: A Canadian Perspective" by Zhiqi Chen of Carleton University reports on the results of his study of the telecommunications services industry in Canada during the 1990s. Chen notes that advances in technology led to substantial reductions in the costs of communication services and widespread adoption of new channels such as wireless communication and the Internet. He also notes that reforms of telecommunications policy in many countries allowed the entry of new services providers, giving consumers unprecedented choice. Chen observes that a significant development in telecommunications services during the 1990s was the rapid penetration of mobile services throughout the world. He notes too that in many OECD countries, the penetration rate of mobile phone units has exceeded the rate for fixed units.

Chen uses data from 20 OECD countries to quantify the contributions of telecommunication services to economic growth. He constructs an econometric model of fixed and mobile telecommunication services and uses it to estimate the effects of barriers to trade and investment in telecommunications infrastructure. This then allows him to estimate the impact of trade liberalization.

The general picture that emerges from Chen's analysis is that while the performance of Canada's telecommunication services industry during the 1990s was very respectable in absolute terms, it was poor relative to the OECD average in a number of areas. Chen finds that shortcomings in the cellular mobile services area are responsible for the poorer outcomes in Canada. He argues that this is worrisome since, according to his econometric analysis, telecommunications infrastructure is a significant driver of economic growth.

In his comments on Chen's study, Sumit Kundu of Florida International University points to the following as its main contributions. First, it documents the importance of the telecommunications industry in the economic development of OECD nations with a focus on Canada in terms of growth, size, infrastructure and productivity. Second, it investigates the effects of barriers to trade and investment in telecommunication infrastructure. Third, it measures spillover effects of telecommunication services across countries. And fourth, cellular services, mobile services and fixed network services are included in the analysis.

Kundu draws attention to the fact that the Chen study provides a detailed contextual background for a key Canadian service sector industry. Kundu questions, however, if it is appropriate to use the OECD figures as a benchmark for comparing Canada's performance. Kundu suggests, for example, that it might be more meaningful to make comparisons for clusters of countries that are comparable in terms of market size, policies towards foreign competition, and the extent of liberalization.

"The Rural/Urban Location Pattern of Advanced Services Firms in an International Perspective," by Michael Wernerheim and Christopher Sharpe, both of Memorial University of Newfoundland, shows that over the past decade, employment growth in professional, scientific and technical (PST) services in Canada has been especially robust in rural localities close to urban agglomerations.

They ask whether externalities associated with the urban core of metropolitan areas exert an attraction on PST firms outside that core, or whether there are other reasons why some of these firms huddle on the fringes of urban agglomerations. They also speculate on the related issue of whether advanced producer services can serve as growth poles for regional development.

In the empirical part of their study, they look for patterns in the spatial distribution of PST establishments. They develop data sets for PST establishments in the core and the non-core areas outside the metropolitan centre. They map this spatial data and then test the so-called 'dartboard theory' of plant location. The results extend what had been known about the spatial pattern of PST activity in Canada.

In his comments, Mario Polèse of the Institut national de la recherche scientifique (INRS) Urbanisation, Culture et Société in Montreal explains that Wernerheim and Sharpe draw on data that allow them to decompose information for urban areas spatially into three classes ('urban core', 'urban fringe', the undeveloped 'rural fringe'), dividing the rest of Canada into two classes: 'small towns' and 'rural areas'. Polèse notes that outside of the urban core, Wernerheim and Sharpe show that growth in PST employment was more rapid in the 'rural fringe' than for small towns, which leads him to conjecture that much of the non-core growth is taking place just beyond the outer limits of large metropolitan areas and is stimulated by them.

Polèse also notes that, unfortunately, the data that Wernerheim and Sharpe use do not allow them to decompose the PST sector, and thus to separate out 'modern' (scientific and technical) tradeable services from more traditional professional services. He takes the analysis one step further himself, working together with Richard Shearmur, William Coffey and other colleagues at INRS and the University of Montreal. They look at knowledge-intensive services in Canada using a different data set that permits decomposition of the PST sector by type of service and introduction of a distance variable.

The study titled "Productivity Growth in Services Industries: A Canadian Success Story" by Someshwar Rao of Industry Canada, Andrew Sharpe of the

Centre for the Study of Living Standards and Jianmin Tang of Industry Canada provides an in-depth analysis of output and productivity performance for services industries in Canada relative to other Canadian industries and their U.S. counterparts. Their main conclusion is that in the Canadian services sector, both labour and multi-factor productivity showed an impressive acceleration in growth between the 1981-1995 and 1995-2000 periods. Retail trade and business services were the largest contributors to the acceleration in labour productivity growth. However, the level of Canada's services sector labour productivity in 2000 was still about 15 percent below that in the United States.

The superior performance of the Canadian services sector stands in marked contrast to the performance of Canada's manufacturing sector, which experienced a widening gap in measured labour productivity when compared with the U.S. manufacturing sector.

Rao, Sharpe and Tang report that in both the 1981-1995 and 1995-2000 periods, the services sector was the most important contributor to growth in Canadian business sector labour productivity. In terms of business sector multifactor productivity growth, the services sector went from being only the third most important contributor in 1981-1995 — behind both manufacturing and the primary sector but ahead of construction — to being the most important contributor in the 1995-2000 period, with a contribution almost twice that of manufacturing.

The contribution of the services sector to U.S. business sector productivity growth has been smaller than in Canada. Manufacturing remained the largest contributor to both business sector labour and multi-factor productivity in the United States in both the 1981-1995 and 1995-2000 periods.

The authors conclude that the performance of the Canadian services sector in terms of productivity growth is a success story both relative to other Canadian industries and relative to the U.S. services sector. They suggest, however, that if the Canadian services sector is to close the remaining productivity gap with the United States, Canadian industries need to make significant progress in narrowing gaps in human and physical capital intensity as well as catching up to their U.S. counterparts in R&D intensity and the share of ICT capital in total capital.

In his comments, Richard Harris of Simon Fraser University notes that the Rao-Sharpe-Tang study provides a wealth of information on productivity levels and trends. He goes on to observe that his own interest lies in trying to understand what it was about the 1990s that produced relatively poor measured growth performance for Canada.

Harris raises the possibility that the superior performance of the Canadian services sector and the poor performance of the manufacturing sector both reflect country differences in the mix of activities within the two sectors. He speculates that low productivity growth service activities in manufacturing firms may have been outsourced in the United States, but not in Canada. If that is the case, such a trend would tend to shift measured productivity growth toward manufacturing in the United States and toward services in Canada. He speculates that if outsourcing trends accelerate in Canadian manufacturing, we may start to see the same patterns in Canada that have already occurred in U.S. manufacturing.

Harris feels that there are some obvious questions raised by this study as to timing and patterns of productivity change. For example, it would be instructive to see whether the same patterns emerge in provincial data. He notes that there is a general presumption that growth has been stronger in the 1995-2000 period in Central Canada than was the case in the resource intensive provinces. He wonders if we would see a parallel trend in services sector growth across provinces. He notes too that in 1995, Canada started at a much lower point in the business cycle than was the case in the United States, where there was a much larger output gap.

In the final research study, "Services and the New Economy: Data Needs and Challenges," Erwin Diewert of the University of British Columbia lauds Statistics Canada for the overall quality of the services they provide and notes a number of important steps that Statistics Canada has taken recently to improve their services data. Nevertheless, he argues forcefully that statistical information on the outputs produced and inputs used by services sector industries remains poorly developed in all OECD countries and is inadequate for the needs of public and private decision makers. He explains that the current system of national accounts came into being about 70 years ago when services sector industries were a smaller part of the economy, and the statistical system did not have sufficient resources to develop information for services, comparable in quality or coverage to that for goods.

Diewert notes that by 1996, services industries accounted for about 66 percent of Canadian output, but only 24 percent of the industries for which productivity statistics were published. He notes that Statistics Canada has a monthly publication on industry price indexes, but the entire publication is devoted to goods prices. Diewert also observes that detailed monthly consumer price indexes are available for approximately 160 commodities, but only about 40 of these represent the services sector.

Canada, the United States and Mexico are in the process of switching from the old Standard Industrial Classification system (SIC) to the North American Industry Classification System (NAICS). Unfortunately, however, the price indexes needed to deflate outputs, using these new industrial classifications, will not be available unless resources are allocated to developing them.[3] Diewert notes that without good price indexes, it will not be possible to provide accurate measurements of the real output of industries grouped under the new NAICS categories. Without real output measures, it will not be possible to measure the productivity of many new economy NAICS industries with any degree of accuracy.

Diewert explains why having price information for services industry outputs is important for productivity measurement and for economic management. He then goes through the NAICS services sector industries, classifying them according to their importance and the difficulties involved in producing constant quality prices for their outputs.

He concludes with the hope that conferences (and this conference volume) will help to stimulate more research interest into these difficult but important measurement problems.

In his comments, Philip Smith of Statistics Canada provides a context for Diewert's study. Smith explains that:

> For the benefit of those not already familiar with the background, Diewert's study is part of a broad initiative led by Renée St-Jacques and her colleagues at Industry Canada aimed at expanding and improving Canadian statistics related to services sector prices and output.

Smith goes on to say that the Diewert study makes a strong case for regular and frequent measurement of services sector price and output trends, noting that the services sector accounts for two-thirds of Canada's GDP and that productivity advances in the sector cry out for better measurement. Smith very much agrees with Diewert on this issue and also with his suggestion that Statistics Canada is the right institution to undertake this challenge.

The concluding chapter of this volume is a rapporteur's overview. In his "Services Industries in a Knowledge-Based Economy: Summing Up", Pierre Sauvé of the Groupe d'Économie Mondiale of the Institut d'Études Politiques de Paris captures the essence of this collection of studies and adds greatly to its value.

Sauvé states the purpose of his concluding chapter is to:

> take stock of some of the key policy challenges emerging from the research done to-date and to identify a range of issues where further research might be expected to yield strong public policy dividends, helping Canadians reap the full benefits of a knowledge-based economy.

He begins by examining some salient facts about services in Canada, noting the large size and central importance of services within the overall economy as well as the fact that services have become an important driver of growth in employment, exports and FDI. He also observes that services hold the key to spreading and realizing the full benefits of a knowledge economy. He reminds us that services generally place fewer strains on the global commons and can play a central role in enhancing environmental stewardship. He suggests that services are an area where efforts to achieve structural reform typically raise some of the most complex policy challenges and can encounter the fiercest political resistance.

Sauvé groups the studies in this volume into those addressing horizontal challenges and those presenting sectoral perspectives. The studies offering sectoral perspectives (Chen, Neave and Whalley) focus attention on core groups of infrastructure industries. Sauvé then lists the six issues addressed by the studies that take horizontal perspectives: (1) labour market performance (the initial conference roundtable discussion and the Morissette, Ostrovsky and Picot study); (2) locational determinants (Globerman, Shapiro and Vining, as well as Wernerheim and Sharpe, together with the discussions of these studies);[4] (3) the FDI performance of services sector firms (Hejazi); (4) confronting the productivity paradox and the issue of whether or not Solow and Baumol got it wrong (Rao, Sharpe and Tang, as well as Wölfl); (5) innovation and R&D in services (Hanel); and (6) the data needs of the new economy (Diewert).

With respect to the fourth issue, Sauvé seems to be in the camp of those who think there is a significant issue here. He notes that two of the conference studies measured strong performance in services, presumably, he argues, showing that the productivity paradox may be in the process of being resolved by acceleration in the growth of service productivity. In contrast, Lipsey in his keynote address debunked the expectation of a productivity bonus and hence the idea of a productivity paradox. After a lengthy analysis, Lipsey concluded:

> My points, however, are (1) the fact that we are in the later stages of a general purpose technologies (GPT) driven new economy (this time the GPT is an ICT) provides no reason to expect a productivity acceleration; (2) neither the presence nor the absence of such an acceleration tells us anything about whether or not we really are in a new economy driven by a new GPT; (3) the concept of a productivity bonus is not well defined, since there is no stated precise comparison to which it refers; (4) the expectation of a bonus, however it is defined, is only a vague impression being derived from no tight theory; and (5) the expectation is not stated in any testable form such that at some specific time in the life cycle of each 'new economy' we can say that the productivity bonus theory is either refuted or consistent with the facts.

Sauvé goes on to note that, as the research studies make clear, productivity trends in the services sector and not manufacturing are and will increasingly be the driving force behind aggregate productivity growth and hence real income growth in Canada. He argues that these studies also make clear that, because of the growing interdependence between manufacturing and services, productivity improvements in services will loom increasingly larger in the competitive position of Canadian manufacturing firms. Sauvé argues that these trends explain why it is crucial to policy that attempts be made at correcting our knowledge gap about the sources of productivity growth in services and overcoming still acute measurement difficulties in a number of sub-sectors the output of which tend to be less tangible.

Sauvé notes that the Wölfl study and Nakamura's comments on it allowed for a candid discussion of the measurement headaches that plague empirical analyses of services and especially cross-border productivity comparisons. He echoes Nakamura's concern that policy conclusions deriving from erroneous measurements are likely to be socially harmful. Sauvé especially picks up on

Nakamura's concerns about reported productivity measures for education, arguably the sector that should occupy the most prominent place in preparing workers for the requirements of a knowledge economy. The productivity of the educational sector is generally found to be quite low when measured by traditional methods.

Sauvé depicts Erwin Diewert as performing the "Herculean task" of drawing attention to the current limitations of statistical information on the knowledge-based economy. The descriptive adjective Sauvé applies to Diewert's efforts seems appropriate to the task he tackles and also brings to mind a visual image of Diewert at the conference podium. This is a matter about which Diewert cares passionately. Sauvé notes that conference participants agreed strongly with Diewert's assertion that there are large spillovers to be gained from better economic measurement of services sector activity.

This is a volume dedicated to increasing our knowledge of the services industries and the new economy. In carrying out our editorial responsibilities, we did not impose our own views as a filter on the material in these studies. The authors are an experienced group of scholars. We felt they should be free to convey their own observations and judgments. We found the material stimulated our thoughts even when, occasionally, we were not fully convinced. The authors have been ingenious in making use of a wide assortment of evidence, with careful attention to context and evolutionary processes as is the hallmark of the S-E approach Lipsey recommends. The studies challenge how we think about the productivity of the services industries and raise many questions for future research. How can we best measure services productivity given the current limitations of official statistics data? How does productivity in services affect the productivity measurements for Canada as a whole? How does this relation between the whole and its services part compare with the same relationship in other countries such as the United States?

We believe that these studies will influence policy and research in Canada for years to come, and will also help to encourage the development of new data for the services sector — data which is critical to the further progress of research into that sector.

ENDNOTES

1 The second author, Alice Nakamura, felt that readers of this introduction and volume should have the following list of references to the body of research that Richard Lipsey draws on in his keynote address which provides a context for the volume as a whole: Bekar and Lipsey (forthcoming); Carlaw and Lipsey (2002) and (forthcoming); Lipsey (1993, 1994, 1997a, 1997b, 2000, 2002); Lipsey and Bekar (1995); Lipsey, Bekar and Carlaw (1998a, 1998b); Lipsey and Carlaw (1996, 1998a, 1998b, 2002, 2004); and Lipsey and Wills (1996).

2 For example, Corak and Chen (2003) document the large magnitude of the diversion of resources away from some of the services sector industries that takes place through the Canadian Employment Insurance (EI) program:

> At the industry level, UI funds were transferred from the services and the public administration industries to the construction industry, the latter receiving an average net transfer of $1.58 billion annually and the former contributing $1.79 billion. The largest contributor was the service industry in Ontario, being surcharged $805 million per year, on average....

Surprisingly, no one yet has looked at the impacts of industry level cross subsidization through EI on the measured productivity of the services industries or sector.

3 Most of these "new" industries are not really new in the sense that they did not exist a decade ago. They are new in the sense that they have been singled out for disaggregation from larger groupings of industries.

4 Sauvé also notes that, "...in his masterful keynote address, Richard Lipsey reminded participants that governments could not (and should not) be expected to abdicate their support for new economy applications, even outside Ontario!"

BIBLIOGRAPHY

Bekar, Clifford, and Richard G. Lipsey. (forthcoming). "Science, Institutions, and the Industrial Revolution," *Journal of European Economic History.*

Carlaw, Kenneth I., and Richard G. Lipsey. 2002. "Externalities, Technological Complementarities and Sustained Economic Growth," *Research Policy*, Special Issue Honouring Nelson, 31 (Winter): 1305-1315.

————. (forthcoming). "GPT-Driven, Endogenous Growth," *The Economic Journal.*

Corak, M., and W.H. Chen. 2003. "Who benefits from unemployment insurance in Canada: Regions, industries, or individual firms?" Ottawa: Social Research and Demonstration Corporation, Working Paper 03-07.

Lipsey, Richard G. 1993. "Globalisation, Technological Change and Economic Growth," *Annual Sir Charles Carter Lecture.* Ireland: Northern Ireland Economic Council, Report No. 103, reprinted in Lipsey (1997b).

————. 1994. "Markets, Technological Change and Economic Growth," Quaid-I-Azam Invited Lecture, in *The Pakistan Development Review*, 33: 327-352; reprinted in Lipsey (1997b).

————. 1997a. "Globalization and National Government Policies: An Economist's View," in John Dunning (ed.). *Governments, Globalization, and International Business.* Oxford: Oxford University Press, pp. 73-113.

————. 1997b. *The Selected Essays of Richard Lipsey: Volume I: Micro-economics, Growth and Political Economy.* Cheltenham, UK: Edward Elgar Publishing.

————. 2000. "New Growth Theories and Economic Policy for the Knowledge-Economy," in Kjell Rubenson and Hans G. Schuetze (eds.). *Transition to the Knowledge Society: Policies and Strategies for Individual Participation and Learning.* Vancouver, BC: UBC Press, pp. 33-61.

————. 2002. "The Productivity Paradox: A Case of the Emperor's New Clothes," *ISUMA: Canadian Journal of Policy Research*, 3: 120-126.

Lipsey, Richard G., and Clifford Bekar. 1995. "A Structuralist View of Technical Change and Economic Growth" in *Bell Canada Papers on Economic and Public Policy* Vol. 3, Proceedings of the Bell Canada Conference at Queen's University, (Kingston: John Deutsch Institute), pp. 9-75.

Lipsey, Richard G., Clifford Bekar, and Kenneth I. Carlaw. 1998a. "What Requires Explanation?" Chapter 2 in Elhanan Helpman (ed.). *General Purpose Technologies and Economic Growth.* Cambridge, MA: MIT Press, pp. 15-54.

————. 1998b. "The Consequences of Changes in GPTs," Chapter 8 in Elhanan Helpman (ed.). *General Purpose Technologies and Economic Growth.* Cambridge, MA: MIT Press, pp. 194-218.

Lipsey, Richard G., and Kenneth I. Carlaw. 1996. "A Structuralist View of Innovation Policy," in Peter Howitt (ed.). *The Implications of Knowledge-Based Growth for Micro-Economic Policies.* Industry Canada Research Series. Calgary: University of Calgary Press, pp. 255-333.

————. 1998a. "Technology Policies in Neoclassical and Structuralist-Evolutionary Models," *OECD Science, Technology and Industry Review*, Special Issue, 22: 31-73.

————. 1998b. *A Structural Assessment of Technology Policies: Taking Schumpeter Seriously on Policy*. Working Paper No. 25. Ottawa: Industry Canada.

————. 2002. "Some Implications of Endogenous Technological Change for Technology Policies in Developing Countries," *Economics of Innovation and New Technology* (EINT), 11: 321-351.

————. 2004. "Total Factor Productivity and the Measurement of Productivity," *Canadian Journal of Economics*, 37 (4): 1118-1150.

Lipsey, Richard G., and Russel M. Wills. 1996. "Science and Technology Policies in Asia Pacific Countries: Challenges and Opportunities for Canada," in Richard G. Harris (ed.). *The Asia-Pacific Region in the Global Economy: A Canadian Perspective.* Industry Canada Research Series. Calgary: University of Calgary Press, pp. 577-612.

W. Erwin Diewert
University of British Columbia

&

Alice O. Nakamura
University of Alberta

2

Concepts and Measures of Productivity: An Introduction

INTRODUCTION

THIS VOLUME IS FILLED with estimates and analyses of productivity. But what is productivity? It seems to be like love in that everyone knows they want it, but few have a good definition of it. As the following quotations demonstrate, several different types of productivity measures are used in the studies in this volume:

> Even more striking is the growth of labour productivity in telecommunications services....
>
> (Chen, Chapter 12)

> The factor driving Canada's superior business sector services labour productivity growth has been better multifactor productivity growth....
>
> (Rao, Sharpe and Tang, Chapter 14)

> [Information communications technology (ICT)] contributes to economy-wide total factor productivity growth.
>
> (Wernerheim and Sharpe, Chapter 13)

This study defines different types of productivity measures and draws distinctions among them. A production process can be thought of as a black box with purchased inputs taken in on one side and outputs sold out the other. Measures of productivity assess how well the black box is doing at turning quantities of inputs into quantities of outputs. Different productivity measures standardize for and provide a basis for different types of comparisons. In this study, we demonstrate the importance of distinguishing between measures of productivity level and productivity growth.

Also, some authors flip between discussing productivity and remarks about prices and price indexes. We explain the connection. We address these and other issues while introducing the reader to the language and formulas of productivity measurement. In other areas of life, everyone recognizes the difference between "levels" and "growth," the latter being a comparative assessment.

"I love you" is a "level" type of declaration. The declaration itself is unconditional and neither limits nor recommends standards of comparison for the declaration. The recipient of the declaration, however, can choose to compare it with things the other person said the day or year before, or is reported to have said to others, or things others have said to them. In contrast, statements such as "I love you more than anyone before" or "I've grown to love you" specify a basis of comparison. Similar considerations hold in differentiating between measures of productivity level and productivity growth.

In this volume, there are discussions of various aspects of production and the circumstances that may affect productivity. For instance, mention is made of "resource allocation improvements" (Whalley, Chapter 7); of "poor R&D performance" linked to "Canada's productivity gap" (Hejazi, Chapter 8); of "agglomeration economies that offer productivity enhancing opportunities" (Globerman, Shapiro and Vining, Chapter 6); of how "ICT contributes to economy-wide total factor productivity growth" (Wernerheim and Sharpe, Chapter 13); and of how "innovativeness has improved… operating efficiency" (Neave, Chapter 11). It is important to keep in mind that these are not alternative forms or definitions of productivity. Lipsey is right in the keynote address that is included in this volume when he cautions that the usual productivity indexes such as total factor productivity (TFP) are not measures of technological change:

> [A]s it is measured in practice, changes in TFP emphatically do not measure changes in technology, in spite of the common belief that they do.
>
> (Lipsey, Chapter 3)

Historically, industries with strong productivity growth have often had rising wages. Interest in understanding the interrelationships between productivity growth and wage-rate changes is reflected in many of the studies in this volume such as Acharya's:

> [W]e combine the insights on output and employment and discuss productivity growth and the wage distribution.
>
> (Acharya, Chapter 4)

Indeed, some researchers (Wölfl, Chapter 9) imply that observed relative wages or wage trends might be used to support or question reported productivity results for specific industries. However, results in other studies in this volume point to the fact that productivity growth, employment growth and wage growth do not always go together:

> Our main finding is that even though employment grew much faster in high-knowledge industries than in other sectors during the last two decades, trends in relative wages and real wages of university and high school graduates have displayed remarkably similar patterns across industries. In other words, the acceleration of employment growth in high-knowledge industries

> has not been accompanied by an acceleration of real and relative wages of university graduates in this sector (relative to other sectors) …
>
> (Morissette, Ostrovsky and Picot, Chapter 5)

Examinations of relative wages or wage trends cannot substitute for productivity analysis.

Yet for many industries we lack the price and quantity information needed for productivity measurement. This reality is driven home in several of the studies:

> [T]he work presented in this conference volume is a useful reminder of how little we still know about the services economy — how poor and too highly-aggregated (if nonetheless improving) services sector data continues to be relative to manufacturing; … how difficult it is to measure labour and total factor productivity in fields where output takes intangible forms, such as in health care and education.
>
> (Sauvé, Chapter 16)

> Without proper price indexes, it will not be possible to measure the real output of these new [National American Industrial Classification System (NAICS)] industries with any degree of accuracy. This in turn implies that it will not be possible to measure the productivity … with any degree of accuracy.
>
> (Diewert, Chapter 15)

> Diewert and Fox (1999)… argue that the proliferation of new products and new processes could have led to a systematic underestimation of productivity growth. This measurement problem could be the reason that we even see negative productivity growth in some services industries for a long period of time!
>
> (Acharya, Chapter 4)

This study is a methodological introduction to the studies in this volume. It constitutes a crash course on the measures of productivity level and growth used in these research studies. There is an emphasis on measures of total factor productivity (TFP) and total factor productivity growth (TFPG) in part because the other measures commonly used can be viewed as special cases of these two fundamental indicators. We use them to describe the production scenario under consideration in relationship to a comparison scenario ("*s*"). The comparison scenario could represent an earlier time period for the same production unit or a different production unit for the same time period.

Basic definitions are introduced in the following section.

Formulas for the productivity measures are first introduced in the simplest possible context of activities embodying one input and one output. Of course, most production units have multiple outputs, and virtually all use multiple inputs. Nevertheless, it helps to begin with a 1-1 process before moving on to a general production process with N inputs and M outputs. That is because in the 1-1 case, there is no need to add up the quantities of different types of inputs or outputs to form total input and output variables.

This study then proceeds to present an analysis that is broadened to include two inputs that are used to produce one output. This introduces some of the problems that must be faced with multiple inputs or outputs.

There are different sorts of formulas that can be used for adding up the quantities of different inputs and outputs. All of the common ones involve using price information (or value share, which embodies price information) to calculate weightings for the quantities to be added. This includes the Paasche, Laspeyres and Fisher formulas introduced later. The Paasche and Laspeyres formulas are the ones most commonly mentioned in general economics, business statistics and accounting textbooks. We demonstrate by example how a Laspeyres-type productivity index controls for price change and, by analogy, how the Paasche productivity index does this as well. This is followed by a demonstration of how the Fisher formula relates to the formulas of Paasche and Laspeyres.[1] An appendix describes the Törnqvist formula which is widely used by productivity researchers including a number of the authors in this volume. The Törnqvist formula approximates Fisher's.[2]

The study concludes with a summary of key points for understanding productivity measures.

DIFFERENT TYPES OF PRODUCTIVITY MEASURES

THIS VOLUME CONTAINS REFERENCES to the following productivity level indexes:

- Single factor productivity (SFP) defined as the ratio of a measure of output quantity to the quantity of a single input used.
- Labour productivity (LP) defined as the ratio of a measure of output quantity to some measure of the quantity of labour used, such as total hours worked.
- Multifactor productivity (MFP) defined as the ratio of a measure of output quantity to a measure of the quantity of a bundle of inputs often intended to approximate total input.
- Total factor productivity (TFP) defined as the ratio of a measure of total output quantity to a measure of the quantity of total input.[3]

Most of the usual productivity growth measures can be defined in terms of the growth[4] or change from s to t in an associated productivity level measure, where t denotes the production scenario of interest and s denotes the comparison scenario.[5] Thus, we usually have

(1) $SFPG^{s,t} = SFP^t / SFP^s$,

(2) $LPG^{s,t} = LP^t / LP^s$,

(3) $MFPG^{s,t} = MFP^t / MFP^s$, and

(4) $TFPG^{s,t} = TFP^t / TFP^s$.

All of the productivity indexes we consider have some measure of output quantity or change in the numerator and some measure of input quantity or change in the denominator. A key issue in the construction of variables of input and output quantity is that they should only change in response to changes in *quantity*. If a factory produces a constant 10 widgets a day as its output, the output quantity measure should reflect this constancy in output quantity, even if the price for the widgets and the revenues generated change daily. If only one good is under consideration, quantity data can be used directly, without any price or value share information. In contrast, "constant" relative price or value share information is needed when multiple inputs or outputs are involved. In the section on the general *N* input and M output case below, we demonstrate how this adding up problem is handled in productivity measurement.

PRODUCTIVITY MEASURES FOR THE ONE INPUT-ONE OUTPUT CASE

MOST PEOPLE WOULD PREFER that mathematical notation, like taxes, be kept to the minimum needed to accomplish the objectives desired. Hence our notation for the 1-1 case is chosen so that we can continue using the same conventions with multiple inputs and outputs. The quantity of input 1 for production scenario *t* is x_1^t. Following the same conventions, the price for input 1 is w_1^t, and the quantity and price of output 1 are y_1^t and p_1^t.

When labour is the only input, the whole collection of productivity level measures — *SFP, LP, MFP* and *TFP* — are the same. We have:

(5) $SFP = LP = MFP = TFP = (y_1^t / x_1^t)$.

For this 1-1 case, the productivity growth measures are also the same. We have *SFPG*=*LPG*=*MFPG*=*TFPG*, which is the case dealt with in this section. It is a convenient starting point for establishing some productivity measurement basics.

Even when labour is the only input — so that the single factor, labour, multifactor and total factor measures are all the same — it turns out that there are still several ways of thinking about productivity growth. These different concepts lead to measures that can be shown to be rearrangements of the same thing. Such different concepts, however, are useful when thinking about different sorts of policy problems.

Examples can be helpful for understanding the meaning of formulas. We have set up some hypothetical car-wash production scenarios to clear up misunderstandings about productivity measurement.

In the first scenario, we use the following small-town hand car wash operation:

> Two new operators were hired at $8 per hour for 8-hour days. The first day, they each washed 1 car per hour. They did 2 an hour on days 2 and 3. Customers paid $10 for a car wash. The specifics of the scenario are summarized in rows 1-4 of Table 1.

Labour productivity level values are shown in row 6 of Table 1. Labour is the only input, so these are also *TFP* values. Measured productivity rose from day 1 to day 2, but there was no technological change. The new operators simply got faster at doing a job that has been carried out in much the same way since the days of the Model T. This illustrates Lipsey's point that these indexes should not be viewed as measures of technological change.

Productivity level measures do not dictate standards of comparison. It is up to those using the results of these measures to be sensible about the comparisons they choose to make. In contrast, productivity growth measures build in a standard of comparison. This is the key difference between productivity level and growth measures. Suppose some standard of comparison — comparison scenario *s* — has been selected. Then, there are several ways that a productivity growth index can be conceptualized. The first is as the rate of growth for the corresponding productivity level index. *TFPG*, defined conceptually as the rate

TABLE 1

SMALL-TOWN HAND CAR WASH

	DAY (T)		
	T=1	T=2	T=3
1. Operator Hours: x_1^t	16 hours	16 hours	16 hours
2. Operator Wage: w_1^t	$8	$8	$8
3. Cars Washed Per Day: y_1^t	16 cars	32 cars	32 cars
4. Price Per Car Wash: p_1^t	$10	$10	$10
5. Revenue/Cost: R^t / C^t	$160/$128=1.25	$320/$128=2.5	$320/$128=2.5
6. LP=TFP: y_1^t / x_1^t	16 cars/16 hours=1	32 cars/16 hours=2	32 cars/16 hours=2
7. TFPG with s=Day t-1	—	$\frac{32\text{ cars}/16\text{ hours}}{16\text{ cars}/16\text{ hours}}=2$	$\frac{32\text{ cars}/16\text{ hours}}{32\text{ cars}/16\text{ hours}}=1$
8. TFPG with s=Day 1	$\frac{16\text{ cars}/16\text{ hours}}{16\text{ cars}/16\text{ hours}}=1$	$\frac{32\text{ cars}/16\text{ hours}}{16\text{ cars}/16\text{ hours}}=2$	$\frac{32\text{ cars}/16\text{ hours}}{16\text{ cars}/16\text{ hours}}=2$

of growth over time for *TFP* and denoted here by $TFPG(1)$, can be represented for the 1-1 case as:

$$(6) \qquad TFPG(1) = \left(\frac{y_1^t}{x_1^t}\right) / \left(\frac{y_1^s}{x_1^s}\right).$$

Alternatively, *TFPG* could be conceptualized in terms of how the growth in output compares with the growth in input. *TFPG* could be defined as the ratio of the output growth rate, y_1^t / y_1^s, and the input growth rate, x_1^t / x_1^s. Thus, for this second concept of *TFPG* we have:

$$(7) \qquad TFPG(2) = \left(\frac{y_1^t}{y_1^s}\right) / \left(\frac{x_1^t}{x_1^s}\right).$$

Expressions for revenue and cost are needed to implement a third concept of *TFPG*: the ratio of the growth rates for real revenue and real cost. For the 1-1 case, revenue and cost are given, respectively, by

$$(8) \qquad R^t = p_1^t y_1^t \text{ and } C^t = w_1^t x_1^t .$$

Thus, the third concept of *TFPG* can be represented as

$$(9) \qquad TFPG(3) = \left[\frac{R^t / R^s}{p_1^t / p_1^s}\right] / \left[\frac{C^t / C^s}{w_1^t / w_1^s}\right].$$

Diewert and Nakamura (2003, 2005) have shown that the formulas for $TFPG(1)$, $TFPG(2)$ and $TFPG(3)$ are equal even for the general case of *N* inputs and M outputs when they are applied to the types of functional forms introduced below in the discussion of this general case. Hence the same productivity numbers will result no matter which of these three concepts of *TFPG* is adopted. In contrast, the nature of a *TFPG* measure will differ greatly depending on the choice of a comparison scenario *s*. This is even so in the simple 1-1 case.

Past performance can be used as a standard of comparison. Comparisons to the previous period are common in applied research, with the previous period often being the previous year.[6] In our car-wash example, if we let $s=t-1$, then the *TFPG* values are the ratios for the current to the previous day's productivity. These productivity growth values are shown in row 7 of Table 1.[7]

Alternatively, we could compare the performance in period *t* with the performance for some fixed choice for the comparison scenario *s*. For instance, a series of productivity comparisons could be made with some base year. In our car-wash example, we might use a fixed day — say, day 1 — as the standard of comparison. Then we would get the *TFPG* values in row 8 of Table 1.

The *TFP* figures in Table 1, row 6, which are also the labour productivity figures for this example, and the *TFPG* figures in Table 1, rows 7 and 8 all confirm that productivity rose from day 1 to 2.[8] However, from day 2 to 3, the figures in Table 1, rows 6 and 8 stay the same but those in row 7 fall. Depending on the selected basis of comparison, the *TFPG* values move differently. A value of 1 in row 7 means no change in productivity from the previous day, in accordance with the results in rows 6 and 8.[9] The choice of a standard of comparison has implications for addressing different sorts of questions about productivity.

Interest in productivity often stems from an interest in maintaining or improving the revenue return on cost expenditures. The third concept of productivity growth is useful for examining this. Equation (9) representing the third concept of *TFPG* can be rewritten as a formula that breaks down growth in the revenue/cost ratio into two terms: a productivity growth term which is the growth in the rate of conversion of input into output, and a term for the output versus input price growth:

$$(10)\qquad \frac{(R^t/C^t)}{(R^s/C^s)} = \left[\frac{y_1^t/x_1^t}{y_1^s/x_1^s}\right]\left[\frac{p_1^t/p_1^s}{w_1^t/w_1^s}\right] = TFPG^{s,t}\left[\frac{p_1^t/p_1^s}{w_1^t/w_1^s}\right].$$

Suppose we would also like to compare the productivity of the small town car wash with a hypothetical larger-volume city operation that has the following specifics, which are also shown in rows 1-4 of Table 2:

> On days 1, 2 and 3, the city car wash has 4, 5 and 6 operators, respectively, working at $12 per hour for 8-hour days. They washed an average of 3, 2.5 and 2 cars per hour over the period of days 1-3. Customers paid $20 a car wash.

TABLE 2

CITY CAR WASH

	DAY (T) T=1	T=2	T=3
1. Operator Hours: x_1^1	32 hours	40 hours	48 hours
2. Operator Wage: w_1^1	$12	$12	$12
3. Cars Washed Per Day: y_1^1	96 cars	100 cars	96 cars
4. Price Per Car Wash: p_1^1	$20	$20	$20
5. Revenue/Cost Ratio: R^1/C^1	$1920/$384=5	$2000/$480=4.2	$1920/$576=3.3
6. LP=TFP: y_1^1/x_1^1	96 cars/32 hours=3	100 cars/40 hours=2.5	96 cars/48 hours=2
7. *TFPG* for s=Day t-1	—	2.5/3=.83	2/2.5=.8
8. *TFPG* with s=Day 1	—	2.5/3=.83	2/3=.67
9. *TFPG* with the small town car wash figures used as the standard of comparison	3/1 = 3	2.5/2 = 1.25	2/2 = 1

The figures in row 5 of Tables 1 and 2 show that the city operation earns more per dollar of cost expenditure. Also, the figures in row 6 show that the daily labour productivity levels — the cars washed per operator-hour — are as high or higher on all days for the city operation. Yet, the *TFPG* figures in rows 7 and 8 are lower for the city operation.

The figures in row 9 of Table 3 were computed using the small-town car wash as the standard of comparison for the city car wash. These show that the city car wash was more productive on days 1 and 2, and equally so on day 3. This information could not be gleaned from just the figures in rows 7 and 8 for productivity growth over time for the two different production units.

The figures in rows 7-9 of Table 2 illustrate that estimates of productivity growth over time cannot be used to examine the *relative* productivity levels for different production units.[10] When there is interest in making comparisons for different productive units such as different industries, then productivity level measures must be used or two-way comparisons must be made using one production unit in each pair as a standard of comparison for the other one. This is why Industry Canada often produces and often focuses on measures of productivity levels.[11]

THE TWO INPUT, ONE OUTPUT CASE

WE NEXT USE A SLIGHTLY MORE COMPLEX production process as the context for introducing choices that must be faced with multiple inputs or outputs.

> Our small-town car wash company rents a car-wash machine for \$100 per day, with a first day introductory rate of \$50. Suppose this machine can handle up to 100 cars per 8-hour day with 1 operator. Hence, operator hours are 8 per day less than before.

Input costs at current prices are higher than the costs without the machine (days 1-3 shown in row 3 of Table 1). The machine rental is more than double the cost of the operator who was fired, and the remaining single operator pushed for and got a raise to \$12 per hour on day 6. However, the owner plans on being able to increase volume, so the machine may save money over time.[12] This illustrates Lipsey's point that a change in technology will not necessarily increase the measured productivity at that time.

> Suppose 32 cars are washed on day $t=4$, which is the first day for the new machine. On day $t=5$, the car wash has a half price sale which brings in 40 cars to wash. On day $t=6$, there are also 40 cars to wash even though the sale has ended.[13]

Notice that the labour productivity numbers (cars washed per operator hour) in Table 3, row 7 are higher than the old figures for the small-town car wash (Table 1, row 6). Give a worker a machine and that worker will produce more! However, the operation is not more profitable. The revenue/cost figures in row 8 of Table 3 are mostly lower than the Table 1 figures.

A common reason given for using labour productivity measures is that the data are lacking to compute a more comprehensive productivity measure. But this is not a good reason for making inappropriate comparisons that could yield misleading results and wrong choices.[14]

This example, however, also makes it clear why looking just at the profit rate, or the revenue/cost ratio, is not satisfactory either. The revenue/cost ratio figures in row 8, Table 3 change greatly from day to day. This effect could be attributable to either a productivity change or a price change. To find out which, we need a way of measuring productivity that takes account of both inputs — operator time and machine time — but controls for the effects of price change.

One way to form a total input quantity measure when there are two inputs is to use current-period price weights for the quantities. An advantage of current-period price weights is that they represent the current opportunity cost of using one more unit of each associated input. Notice that the numerator and denominator of the revenue/cost ratio are current price-weighted sums of the quantities of the outputs (1 in this case) and the inputs (2 in this case). However, as is clear from our example, the revenue/cost ratio also reflects the *price*

TABLE 3

LABOUR AND TOTAL FACTOR PRODUCTIVITY FOR A SMALL-TOWN AUTOMATIC CAR WASH

		DAY (T)	
	T=4	T=5	T=6
1. Cars Washed per Day	32	40	40
2. Price per Car Washed	\$10	\$5	\$10
3. Operator Hours: x_1^1	8 hours	8 hours	8 hours
4. Operator Hourly Wage: w_1^t	\$8	\$8	\$12
5. Car Wash Machine: x_2^t	1 machine	1 machine	1 machine
6. Car Wash Machine Daily Rental: w_2^t	\$50	\$100	\$100
7. Cars Washed per Operator Hour: y_1^t / x_1^t	32/8 = 4	40/8 = 5	40/8 = 5
8. Revenue/Cost Ratio: R^t / C^t	\$320/\$114 = 2.81	\$200/\$164 = 1.22	\$400/\$196 = 2.04
9. Sales/Total Input Evaluated at Day 4 Prices: $p_1^4 y_1^t / (w_1^4 x_1^t + w_2^4 x_2^t)$	\$320/\$114 = 2.81	\$400/\$114 = 3.51	\$400/\$114 = 3.51
10. $TFPG_L^{4,t}$	—	3.51/2.81 = 1.25	3.51/2.81 = 1.25

changes from period to period. It can change even when there are no changes in input or output quantities. For example, from day 5 to 6 in our example in Table 3, there is no change in either the output or the input quantities. Hence, there should be no change in the productivity level measure. But from Table 3, row 8 we see that the revenue/cost ratio almost doubles because of the price changes.

To deal with the problem of changing price weights, we could instead use the prices from some fixed comparison scenario such as a previous time period for the same production unit. In row 9 of Table 3, we use day 4 as the comparison scenario; that is, we let $s=4$. This embeds the relative price values of that particular time period into the resulting productivity measures: the time period was one when the relative prices were similar but not the same as in period t. In row 9 of Table 3 we show values for the ratio of output to input, all evaluated at day 4 prices. That is, we show values for the following type of productivity level expression that we will refer to as a Laspeyres-type measure since Laspeyres indexes use comparison scenario weights:

$$(11) \qquad p_1^s y_1^t / (w_1^s x_1^t + w_2^s x_2^t) .$$

For our Table 3 example, if we divide the day 5 row 9 value by the day 4 value, this gives the value of the Laspeyres productivity growth index for $t=5$ and $s=4$. And if we divide the day 6 row 9 value by the day 5 one, this gives the value of the Laspeyres productivity growth index for $t=6$ and $s=4$. These are the values shown in row 10 of Table 3.

If we chose some other comparison period — such as $s=6$ — then the resulting productivity and productivity growth measures would embed the relative prices of that period. In particular, they would embed the opportunity costs/gains or changes in the relative amounts used or produced for the inputs and outputs. These choices are made in different ways in the productivity index formulas introduced in the next section. It is necessary first to define the time period over which productivity level comparisons are to be made, or for which productivity growth measures are to be computed. Once this is selected, the Laspeyres approach is to use the price weights from the start of that time interval. By contrast, the Paasche approach is to use the price weights from the end of the period. The Fisher productivity index uses a geometric average of the Laspeyres and Paasche results.

THE GENERAL N INPUT, M OUTPUT CASE

THE SIMPLEST SORT OF PRODUCTION PROCESS is one with a single input and single output. In that simple context, we were able to introduce the distinction between level and growth (or comparison) measures of productivity as well as three different concepts of *TFPG* that can be useful in policy analysis and that all can be evaluated using the same computational formula. We also discussed the significance of the choice of the comparison scenario for productivity growth measures. Next we added one more input. This introduced the adding up issues that must be confronted as soon as there is more than one input or output.

It can be seen from the material in the previous section that the weights for the input and output quantity aggregates can greatly affect the computed productivity measures.

For a general production process involving N inputs and M outputs, the Laspeyres, Paasche and Fisher productivity measures can be defined using eight price-weighted sums of quantity data for the production scenario of interest (t) and the one used as the base line comparison (s). The first four of these sums are the total costs and revenue for t (C^t and R^t) and for s (C^s and R^s):

$$(12) \qquad C^t = \sum_{n=1}^{N} w_n^t x_n^t \,, \; R^t = \sum_{m=1}^{M} p_m^t y_m^t \,,$$

$$(13) \qquad C^s = \sum_{n=1}^{N} w_n^s x_n^s \text{ and } R^s = \sum_{m=1}^{M} p_m^s y_m^s \,.$$

Four hypothetical quantity aggregates are also needed.[15] The first two result from evaluating period t quantities using period s price weights:

$$(14) \qquad \sum_{n=1}^{N} w_n^s x_n^t \text{ and } \sum_{m=1}^{M} p_m^s y_m^t \,.$$

These sums are what the cost and revenue would have been if the period t inputs had been purchased and the period t outputs had been sold at period s prices. In contrast, the third and fourth aggregates are sums of period s quantities evaluated using period t prices:

$$(15) \qquad \sum_{n=1}^{N} w_n^t x_n^s \text{ and } \sum_{m=1}^{M} p_m^t y_m^s \,.$$

These are what the cost and revenue would have been if the period s inputs had been purchased and the period s outputs had been sold at period t prices.

A Laspeyres-type TFP index can be defined as:

$$(16) \qquad TFP_L^{t|s} = \sum_{m=1}^{M} p_m^s y_m^t \Big/ \sum_{n=1}^{N} w_n^s x_n^t \,.$$

Equation (11) in the previous section is a special case of this formula. Values for this productivity level index can be meaningfully compared over the time interval of period s to t provided that relative prices have not shifted too much over that time interval.

The corresponding productivity growth measure is given by:

$$(17)\qquad TFPG_L^{s,t} = \left[\frac{\sum_{m=1}^{M} p_m^s y_m^t}{\sum_{n=1}^{N} w_n^s x_n^t}\right] \Bigg/ \left[\frac{\sum_{m=1}^{M} p_m^s y_m^s}{\sum_{n=1}^{N} w_n^s x_n^s}\right].$$

Suppose that values for the Laspeyres type productivity level index defined in (16) are computed for period $t = s, \ldots, T$. The measure embeds period s relative prices over the entire time interval of s through T. The longer this time interval is and the greater the amount of relative price change there was over this interval, the less satisfactory the productivity level index given in Equation (16) will be. This is why it is common to use $s=t-1$ for the Laspeyres productivity growth index, so that the price weights are only being held fixed for a two-period stretch. For a longer time interval, a series of period-to-period productivity growth estimates can be computed.

Along the lines of the concept 3 form of the *TFPG* index for the 1-1 case given in Equation (9), it has been shown that the Laspeyres productivity growth index given in Equation (17) can also be defined in terms of revenue and cost totals converted to period s dollar terms using the Paasche output and input price indexes.[16] Thus we have:

$$(18)\qquad TFPG_L^{s,t} = \frac{(R^t / R^s) / P_P^{s,t}}{(C^t / C^s) / P_P^{s,t}}.$$

The output and input price indexes are given, respectively, by:

$$(19)\qquad P_P \equiv \sum_{i=1}^{M} p_i^t y_i^t \Big/ \sum_{j=1}^{M} p_j^s y_j^t \text{ and}$$

$$(20)\qquad P_P^* \equiv \sum_{i=1}^{N} w_i^t x_i^t \Big/ \sum_{j=1}^{N} w_j^s x_j^t.$$

There is no satisfactory Paasche-type counterpart of the Laspeyres-type productivity level index.[17] However, the Paasche *TFP* growth measure controls for price change by fixing the price weights at their period t values. That is, we have:

$$(21)\qquad TFPG_P^{s,t} = \left(\frac{\sum_{m=1}^{M} p_m^t y_m^t}{\sum_{n=1}^{N} w_n^t x_n^t}\right) \Bigg/ \left(\frac{\sum_{m=1}^{M} p_m^t y_m^s}{\sum_{n=1}^{N} w_n^t x_n^s}\right).$$

A Paasche productivity growth measure embeds period t relative prices for both periods s and t. As with the Laspeyres productivity growth index, when there is a need to assess productivity growth over a longer time span, say from $t = s, \ldots, T$, it is common to compute the productivity growth measure for each successive value of t taking the comparison period for that "chain link" productivity estimate to be period t–1. Hence the price weights for each productivity growth calculation are just held fixed over a two-period time span.

It has been shown that this same Paasche productivity growth index given in Equation (17) can also be defined in terms of revenue and cost totals, converted to period s dollar terms using the Laspeyres output and input price indexes.[18] This alternative formulation of the Paasche productivity growth index is given by:

$$(22) \qquad TFPG_P^{s,t} = \frac{(R^t / R^s) / P_L^{s,t}}{(C^t / C^s) / P_L^{*s,t}} .$$

The Laspeyres output and input price indexes are given by:

$$(23) \qquad P_L \equiv \sum_{i=1}^{M} p_i^t y_i^s / \sum_{j=1}^{M} p_j^s y_j^s \text{ and}$$

$$(24) \qquad P_L^* \equiv \sum_{i=1}^{N} w_i^t x_i^s / \sum_{j=1}^{N} w_j^s x_j^s .$$

A Paasche-type productivity measure embeds period t relative prices for both periods s and t. Rather than choosing between the Laspeyres and Paasche productivity growth indexes, Diewert (1992b) recommends using a geometric average of the two. This is the Fisher index and it is given by:

$$(25) \qquad TFPG_F^t = (TFPG_P^t \times TFPG_L^t)^{1/2} .$$

CONCLUSIONS

OUR FINDINGS can be summarized as follows:

- Most production processes involve multiple outputs and virtually all involve multiple inputs, in which case the choice of the productivity measure matters. Indeed, even with just 1 input and 1 output, it matters whether a productivity level or growth index is used.

- Productivity growth indexes build in a standard of comparison but productivity level indexes do not. With productivity growth measures, it is important to notice whether the standard of comparison is suitable for the intended uses of the productivity estimates. For instance, if a comparison over time is built into a productivity growth measure, it will not usually be appropriate to compare the resulting estimates with figures for other production units. Productivity level index values can be compared in whatever ways are deemed sensible. In this respect, they can be used more flexibly than the productivity growth figures.

- The fact that the value of productivity *growth* is higher for one production unit than for another (e.g. for a particular industry or sector or nation as compared with another industry, sector or nation) says nothing about which one has the higher productivity level.
- For a productivity growth index, a value of 1 means that, relative to the standard of comparison built into the productivity growth index, productivity is unchanged, whereas a value greater than (less than) 1 means that, relative to the standard of comparison scenario, productivity has increased (decreased).
- A productivity growth index can take on a value different from 1 with, or without, any change in technology over the time interval for which the index is calculated.
- Productivity level measures that embed relative price information from some given comparison period should not be used for computing productivity level or growth estimates in production scenarios where the actual relative prices are very different from those in the selected comparison period.

APPENDIX

THE TÖRNQVIST (OR TRANSLOG) INDEXES

TÖRNQVIST INDEXES ARE WEIGHTED GEOMETRIC AVERAGES of growth rates for micro-economic data (the quantity or price relatives).[19] These indexes have been widely used by national statistical agencies and in the economics literature. The formula for the natural logarithm of a Törnqvist index is the one that is usually shown. For the output quantity index, this is

$$\text{(A-1)}\qquad \ell n Q_T = (1/2)\sum_{m=1}^{M}[(p_m^s y_m^s / \sum_{i=1}^{M} p_i^s y_i^s) + (p_m^t y_m^t / \sum_{j=1}^{M} p_j^t y_j^t)]\,\ell n(y_m^t / y_m^s) .$$

The Törnqvist input quantity index Q_T^* is defined analogously, with input quantities and prices substituted for the output quantities and prices in Equation (12).

Reversing the role of the prices and quantities in the formula for the Törnqvist output quantity index yields the Törnqvist output price index, P_T, defined by

$$\text{(A-2)}\qquad \ell n P_T = (1/2)\sum_{m=1}^{M}[(p_m^s y_m^s / \sum_{i=1}^{M} p_i^s y_i^s) + (p_m^t y_m^t / \sum_{j=1}^{M} p_j^t y_j^t)]\,\ell n(p_m^t / p_m^s) .$$

The input price index P_T^* is defined in a similar manner.

The implicit Törnqvist output quantity index, $Q_{\tilde{T}}$, is defined by $(R^t / R^s)/P_T \equiv Q_{\tilde{T}}$,[20] and the implicit Törnqvist input quantity index, $Q_{\tilde{T}}^*$, is defined analogously using the cost ratio and P_T^*. The implicit Törnqvist output price index, $P_{\tilde{T}}$, is given by $(R^t / R^s)/Q_T \equiv P_{\tilde{T}}$, and the implicit Törnqvist input price index, $P_{\tilde{T}}^*$, is defined analogously.

Diewert coined the term "superlative" to describe an index number functional form that is "exact" in that it can be derived algebraically from a producer or consumer behavioural equation that satisfies Diewert's flexibility criterion: it can provide a second-order approximation to twice continuously differentiable linearly homogeneous function. Diewert (1976, 1978) and Hill (2000) established that all of the commonly used superlative index number formulas, including the Fisher, the Törnqvist and implicit Törnqvist, approximate each other to the second order when evaluated at an equal price and quantity point. This is a numerical analysis approximation result that does not rely on any assumptions of economic theory.

ENDNOTES

1 The Fisher formula is increasingly being used for official statistics purposes in Canada and the United States. Diewert (1992b) provides an analysis of the properties of the Fisher index.

2 For example, in the data Appendix to their study in this volume, Rao, Sharpe and Tang write: "The data source for the U.S. data is Jorgenson, Ho and Stiroh (2002). For their study, they have developed such a dataset for 44 industries, which are collapsed into 34 common industries using Törnqvist aggregation indexes. The Canadian data are obtained from the Canadian Productivity Accounts that provide a consistent set of detailed industry (122 industries) and aggregated data on inputs and outputs (current prices and chained Fisher indexes) for productivity measurement and related economic performance analysis."

3 It is almost never the case that *all* inputs are included in a productivity study. This is why official agencies tend to prefer the terms multifactor productivity (MFP) and multifactor productivity growth (MFPG) instead of total factor productivity (TFP) and total factor productivity growth (TFPG). However, the TFP and TFPG terminology has caught on in the economics literature and the popular press. Also, there are useful relationships between TFPG and the total revenue and cost. Thus we focus on MFPG and TFPG. To the extent that the MFPG indexes are approximations of TFPG ones, the properties developed for the latter are also relevant to the former.

4 A "G" added to the name of a productivity level index denotes the corresponding growth index.

5 This is not the case for the Törnqvist formula, as explained in Diewert and Nakamura (2005).

6 In fact, indexes with $s=t-1$ are used so much, there is a special name for them: chain indexes.

7 The interested reader can verify that formulas (6) and (7) yield the same TFPG values as formula (9): the Table 1, row 7 values when s is taken to be the previous day, and the Table 1, row 8 values when s is day 1.

8 Perhaps the workers learned on the job. Or the station manager might have made suggestions, in which case there is one more factor of production that is not being accounted for. Moreover, either way, the knowledge of how to do the job faster becomes embodied in the workers; they become "experienced" and this change in their status could be thought of as another output of this production process. These more complex issues are outside the scope of this technical introduction, but some of these issues are taken up in studies in this volume.

9 In general, a value of 1 means that the rate of conversion of input into output was the same in period t as in s, whereas a value greater than 1 (less than 1) means the rate of conversion was greater (less) in period t than in s.

10 This is also why there is literature on the proper methods of international and intersectoral or industry comparisons. See Diewert (1987); Caves, Christensen and Diewert (1982); and Diewert and Nakamura (1999) for an introduction to some alternative approaches for making multilateral comparisons among production units as well as the presentation of additional references on that topic.

11 Statistical agencies and researchers often prefer the productivity growth indexes to the levels ones because it seems likely the growth measures can be estimated more accurately. However, when confronting policy questions, productivity growth measures are of little help, however accurately measured, if levels measures are needed.

12 Also, the machine will not threaten to go on strike for higher wages at peak business times the way the operators did sometimes, and it could be operated by the owner if need be without a loss of business.

13 So perhaps the sale was an investment in more business for the future. This complication, having to do with the proper treatment of advertising services, is also ignored in this technical introduction. But advertising services are one of the service industries in need of improved price and quantity measurement.

14 We are not trying to argue that labour productivity indexes are never useful. They can be used for monitoring the productive performance of labour for the same productive unit over periods when it is known that there was little change in the use of other factors of production. For an individual production line, office or plant, or even a firm, management would know when there were changes in capital equipment. Also, comparisons of labour productivity may make sense between production units with similar production processes, plant and equipment.

15 Formally, the first two of these can be shown to result from deflating the period t cost and revenue by a Paasche price index. The second two result from deflating the period t cost and revenue by a Laspeyres price index.

16 See Diewert and Nakamura (2003, 2005).

17 The Paasche counterpart of the Laspeyres-type measure in Equation (16) is just the revenue/cost ratio, and it is not a good productivity measure because the values from period to period will reflect relative price changes as well as the changes in the rate at which input quantities are being transformed into output quantities.

18 See Diewert and Nakamura (2003, 2005).

19 Törnqvist indexes are also known as translog indexes following Jorgenson and Nishimizu (1978) who introduced this terminology because Diewert (1976) related Q_T^* to a translog production function. For a study of the properties, see Balk and Diewert (2001).

20 See Diewert (1992a).

ACKNOWLEDGMENTS

THIS RESEARCH WAS SUPPORTED in part by research grants from the Social Sciences and Humanities Research Council of Canada (SSHRC) to Alice Nakamura and Erwin Diewert. All errors are the sole responsibility of the authors.

BIBLIOGRAPHY

Balk, B.M., and W. Erwin Diewert. 2001. "A Characterization of the Törnqvist Price Index," *Economics Letters* 72: 279-281.

Caves, D.W., L.R. Christensen, and W. Erwin Diewert. 1982. "Multilateral Comparisons of Output, Input and Productivity using Superlative Index Numbers," *The Economic Journal* 92 (March): 73-86.

Diewert, W. Erwin. 1976. "Exact and Superlative Index Numbers," *Journal of Econometrics* 4 (2): 115-146, and reprinted as Chapter 8 in Diewert and Nakamura. 1993. *Essays in Index Number Theory*, vol. 1. Amsterdam: North-Holland, pp. 223-252.

————. 1978. "Superlative Index Numbers and Consistency in Aggregation," *Econometrica* 46: 883-900, and reprinted as Chapter 9 in Diewert and Nakamura. 1993. *Essays in Index Number Theory*, vol. 1. Amsterdam: North-Holland, pp. 253-273.

————. 1987. "Index Numbers," in J. Eatwell, M. Milgate, and P. Newman (eds.). *The New Palgrave: A Dictionary of Economics*, Vol. 2. London: Macmillan Press, pp. 767-780.

————. 1992a. "The Measurement of Productivity," *Bulletin of Economic Research* 44 (3): 163-198.

————. 1992b. "Fisher Ideal Output, Input, and Productivity Indexes Revisited," *Journal of Productivity Analysis* 3: 211-248.

Diewert, W. Erwin, and Alice O. Nakamura. 1999. "Benchmarking and the Measurement of Best Practice Efficiency: An Electricity Generation Application," *Canadian Journal of Economics*, 32 (2): 570-588.

————. 2003. "Index Number Concepts, Measures and Decompositions of Productivity Growth," *Journal of Productivity Analysis* 19 (2/3): 127-160.

————. 2005. "The Measurement of Aggregate Total Factor Productivity Growth," in J.J. Heckman and E. Leamer (eds.). *Handbook of Econometric Methods*. Amsterdam: North-Holland.

Diewert, W. Erwin, and Kevin J. Fox. 1999. "Can Measurement Error Explains the Productivity Paradox?" *Canadian Journal of Economics*, 32 (2): 251-280.

Hill, R.J. 2000. "Superlative Index Numbers: Not All of them Are Super," Sydney, Australia: School of Economics, University of New South Wales, September 10.

Jorgenson, Dale W., and M. Nishimizu. 1978. "U.S. and Japanese Economic Growth, 1952-1974: An International Comparison," *The Economic Journal* 88: 707-726.

Jorgenson, Dale W., Mun S. Ho, and Kevin J. Stiroh. 2002. "Growth of U.S. Industries and Investments in Information Technology and Higher Education," Boston, MA: Harvard University.

Richard G. Lipsey
Simon Fraser University

3

Policy Challenges in the New Economy

IN THIS CHAPTER, I DISCUSS INSIGHTS into long-term economic growth that are provided by what my colleagues and I call structuralist-evolutionary (S-E) theory.[1] I also explore the concept of general-purpose technologies (GPTs) and the enormous economic, social and political transformations that GPTs induce. I first look at the meaning of the term 'new economy,' the name given to the latest of these economic transformations — one that has been brought about by the GPT of the electronic computer and a few related technologies. I then discuss the concept of a GPT in more detail and look briefly at those that have occurred in the past. This gives rise to the question of how we can know a GPT when we see one. In particular, I look at the generally held myth that a new GPT must be accompanied by a "productivity bonus." I then lay out a list of some of the main transformations that have accompanied the current new economy and use that list to refute those who argue that its alleged importance is much overrated. I then go on to contrast the two views of how the economy works that are implicit in the neoclassical and S-E theories. This leads to a section contrasting the policy implications of each. The most important of these is that neoclassical theory derives a set of policy prescriptions that are meant to apply to all economies at all times, whereas S-E theory implies that the performance of most policies depends on the detailed contexts in which they are instituted. I end on an optimistic note that I hope heralds the demise of economics as the dismal science.

WHAT IS THE "NEW ECONOMY?"

MUCH CONFUSION HAS BEEN CAUSED because various writers have used the term 'new economy' to mean different things.

- Initially, the term was often used, particularly by financial journalists and others writing in a more popular vein, to mean an economy that had been totally transformed by new technologies so that standard relations no longer held. Some claimed, for example, that both business cycles and inflation would no longer be experienced. Although this extreme view was naive, new technologies do alter many economic relations. This happens, for example, when "natural monopolies" are turned into highly competitive industries and vice versa.

- Dale Jorgenson (2001) defines the new economy as that sector which produces computing power and related items. Statistics Canada and the Department of Finance are often tempted to do the same thing. When this approach is used, the new economy appears to be only a small fraction of the whole economy. Jorgenson's definition leads him to argue that if technological progress stopped in the computer sector, the growth attributable to the new economy would also stop. This is similar to assuming that the electronic revolution that followed on the invention of the dynamo in 1867 could be measured by the developments in the electricity generating industry and would have come to a halt if electricity prices had been stabilized!
- Most growth economists use an aggregate production function in which technological change is visible only through its effects on productivity. Such models equate changes in technology with changes in productivity, a view I will return to later. Following in this tradition, Robert Gordon (2000) defines a new economy as occurring when the rate of improvement in new products and services is greater than in the past and there is thus an acceleration in the rate of productivity growth.
- I use the term to refer to the economic, social and political changes brought about by the current revolution in information and communication technologies (ICTs). That revolution is being driven by the computer, lasers, satellites, fibre optics, the Internet and a few other related communication technologies, many of which were developed with the assistance of computers. It is an economy-wide *process* not located in just one high-tech *sector*, any more than the new economy initiated by electricity was confined to the electricity-generating sector.

The computer started as a single-purpose technology used to calculate the trajectories of shells and to break codes in the Second World War. It gave rise to a research program that improved the GPT itself and applied it across the whole economy in new processes, new products, new organizational forms, and new political and social relations. Decades were required for it to be improved and diffused through the whole economy. Its effects became increasingly visible in the 1970s, which was the transitional decade between an old order dominated by mass production and forms of communication and organization based on paper and hard copy, and a new economy dominated by the computer. By the 1980s, deep structural adjustments were occurring rapidly in response to the ICT revolution. Today we are living through a profound, ongoing, economy-wide transformation of economic, political and social structures driven by this cluster of new technologies, amplified by changes in biotechnology and incipient changes in nanotechnology.

In his contribution to this volume, William Watson takes issue with the term "knowledge-based economy" to describe the new ICT-driven economy. He is right in arguing that technological ideas have been the driving force in all long-term economic growth throughout history. In my view, the term "knowledge-based economy" used to describe the current new economy refers to the phenomenon that much more of the economy's total capital stock — capital that embodies new technological knowledge — is embodied in human rather than in physical capital. That may or may not be correct — I think it is — but it is clearly a testable hypothesis about one of the distinguishing characteristics of the current new economy in relation to all the others that preceded it.

GENERAL-PURPOSE TECHNOLOGIES

THE ELECTRONIC COMPUTER IS AN EXAMPLE of what has come to be called a general-purpose technology (GPT). These are technologies that typically start in a relatively crude form for a single or very few purposes. They increase in sophistication and efficiency as they diffuse through the economy and when they mature, they are used throughout most of the economy for many different purposes, while causing myriad spillovers in the form of externalities and technological complementarities.[2]

It is important to note that many of the responses to a new GPT cannot be modelled (for measurement or any other purpose) as the consequence of price changes in the flows of factor services produced by the previous GPT. This is because most of the action is taking place in the technological structure of capital. The new possibilities depend on how one technology is related to another, not on how a given technology can respond to a change in price.

For example, the most profound effects of electricity came not from a fall in the price of power, but from the fact that it made possible new products, new processes and new forms of organization that were technically unavailable with steam. There was a revolution in the layout of factories in which machine tools, each with its own independent power source (the unit drive), were rearranged on the shop floor according to the logic of production rather than their power demands. This caused a major increase in productivity. This new layout could never have been adopted in steam-driven factories, even if the price of steam power had fallen to zero. Electrically powered machine tools, in turn, enabled the assembly line with its extensive restructuring of all manufacturing production and further large gains in productivity. In addition, the household machines that revolutionized domestic work and freed women, or their servants, from millennia of drudgery were all enabled by electricity. No steam engine could have been attached to the carpet sweeper to turn it into a vacuum cleaner, to the ice box to turn it into a refrigerator, or to a washing tub to turn it into a clothes-washing machine. Indeed, none of these changes would have occurred if the steam engine had remained the main source of power, even if the price of its power had fallen to zero.

Similar comments can be made about all GPTs. Most of their really transformative effects arise because they enable goods, processes and forms of organization that were technically impossible with the technologies that they supplanted. The iron steamship, equipped with refrigeration, could do things that transformed agriculture worldwide but that could never have been achieved with sailing ships, even if the price of transport by sail had fallen to zero. Similarly, the internal combustion engine could do things that the steam engine could not.

Nonetheless, measures of equivalent price changes are often used. For example, we might think of comparing the steam engine and the electric motor with a hedonic index that relies on horsepower or BTUs produced by each motor for equivalent amounts of inputs. But as just noted, the major economic gains that came when the electric motor replaced the steam engine were the result of its ability to reorganize production in ways that were *technically impossible* with steam power. Similarly, the principal gains from a practical quantum computer will not be measurable by a hedonic index comparison with electronic computers because its gains will mainly come from allowing such procedures as predicting the results of genetic engineering of proteins that could not be performed on any conceivable conventional computer.

This has important implications when we come to measure the consequences of new GPTs.[3] Measures of contemporaneous externalities capture only a small part of the transformative spillover effects that spread geographically over the whole economy and temporally over decades and even centuries. It is enough to consider, for example, how many of the new things that were recently invented would have been impossible without electricity.

Most GPTs are what we call transforming technologies — technologies that induce major changes in the structures of society's economic, social and political arrangements. Any technological change requires alterations in the structure of the economy, but such changes are often small and proceed incrementally, more or less unnoticed. However, most major new GPTs cause extensive structural change in areas such as the organization of work, the management of firms, skill requirements, the location and concentration of industry, and supporting infrastructure — all of which are part of what we call the economy's "facilitating structure."[4] In addition, GPTs often have major impacts on the political structure, as when television transformed the way elections were fought in the United States. They can exert an impact on the social structure, as when the factory system turned the majority of people in the West into urban rather than rural dwellers and when lean production and the robotization of factories eliminated most of the well-paid, relatively unskilled jobs that used to exist in assembly plants. We call such GPTs transforming technologies and I shall concentrate on this sub-class in the rest of my study, a subclass that includes most but not all GPTs.[5]

NEW ECONOMIES THROUGHOUT HISTORY

INTERESTINGLY, IN ALL OF HISTORY from the Neolithic agricultural revolution up to the end of the 19th century, we can identify fewer than two-dozen transforming GPTs. The 20th century is a bit more problematic as innovations followed each other thick and fast, and there are several technologies that are right on the border of inclusion or exclusion from the GPT category. Although other readers might expand or contract our list by a few items, its order of magnitude is unlikely to be changed. So history has not seen 200 GPTs, nor has it seen just two: GPTs are not an everyday occurrence but neither are they so rare that their effects fail to permeate most economies most of the time.

Here is our list of transforming GPTs from 10,000 BC to 1,900 AD. The dates indicate not when they were first discovered but approximately when they began to exert transforming effects on the economies of the West.[6] For example, iron had been produced for millennia before it came into general use and began to transform Western societies, both economically and militarily, in the latter part of the second millennium BC.

1. The domestication of plants — *10,000 BC;*
2. The domestication of animals — *8,000 BC;*
3. Smelting of ore — *8,000-7,000 BC;*
4. Pottery[7] — *6,000 BC;*
5. The wheel — *5,000 BC;*
6. Writing — *3,400 BC;*
7. Bronze — *2,800 BC;*
8. Iron — *1,200 BC;*
9. The principle of mechanical advantage incorporated in such tools as the lever, fulcrum and the pulley[8] — *Greek Civilization;*
10. The water wheel — *early medieval period;*
11. The heavy plough[9] — *early medieval period;*
12. The three-masted sailing ship — *15th century AD;*
13. Printing — *15th century;*
14. The steam engine — *18th century;*
15. Automated machinery (originally in textiles) — *late 18th century;*
16. The factory system — *18th century;*

17. The railway — *19th century;*
18. The iron steam ship — *second half of the 19th century;*
19. The internal combustion engine — *second half of the 19th century;*
20. The dynamo — *second half of the 19th century.*

These technologies fall into six main classes: materials technologies, power, information and communication technologies, tools, transportation and organization. Notice that at any one time, there may be several GPTs in existence and even more than one in one particular class (e.g. the dynamo and the internal combustion engine).

William Watson says that he is "not wholly convinced the world is changing more rapidly than it has in recent centuries." This is an interesting research issue on which I think neither of us have the last word. But I would point out that the time between GPTs has diminished over the millennia and the time that elapses between the original invention and the transforming impact of each GPT has diminished over the past few centuries. The rate of technological change has clearly accelerated between the past two centuries and everything that had gone before. But the question: "has the rate of change accelerated within the last two centuries?" is a more difficult issue, and casual observations will not settle it.

How Do We Know a New Economy When We See One?

In the immediate aftermath of the Second World War, both the computer and atomic power were commercialized. Few expected the computer to become a transforming GPT while most expected that atomic energy would. These mistaken expectations illustrate the difficulty of predicting the course of new innovations, particularly potential GPTs. More than anything else, this is due to the uncertainty attached to their development and diffusion. We might wonder then if we can predict anything about future GPTs.

Potential GPTs Identified

Often, a new technology can be identified as a potential GPT solely on the basis of its technological characteristics. For example, if one were told that a new technology would permit the altering of the gene structure of plants and animals by direct intervention into the mechanism of inheritance, rather than by the hit and miss procedure of selective breeding, it could be confidently said, as it was soon after Crick and Watson's momentous discovery of the structure of DNA, that the technology had a clear potential to develop into a GPT. No one could predict how such a technology would evolve in detail or whether it would encounter insurmountable cost obstacles to its commercialization, but it would clearly be a prime candidate for close attention from economists and policy makers. The same was said about the dynamo and nanotechnology very early in their lifetimes.

All Potential GPTs Not Identifiable Early On

It is easier to identify some emerging technologies as potential GPTs than to rule out others as not having the necessary potential. The history of technological development is replete with surprises that no one could possibly have anticipated. When the first commercial computers were introduced at the end of the Second World War, they were estimated to have a world market of between 5 and 10 machines. At the time, few would have foreseen the place of computers in our lives in 1985, let alone in 2005. Thus, there is no way of knowing if there is currently some seemingly modest technology occupying some small niche that is waiting to burst forth as the next GPT that will transform our entire economy.

Later Identification of GPTs

Although it may not have been identified as such at the outset, a technology can often be seen to be developing into a GPT well before it reaches full maturity. For example, the computer's potential to change the way we did many things was becoming clear long before the emergence of the desktop computer. Identifying a GPT, even after decades of development, can be useful in helping policy makers to understand, facilitate and smooth out the structural adjustments that must accompany its diffusion.

Predictions Based on Common Characteristics

Although every GPT has unique characteristics and its own development path, they do share certain common characteristics that can be used to make some limited predictions about their evolution. All start as fairly crude technologies with a single purpose or a small range of purposes. All tend to follow two paths, each of which can be approximated by a logistic curve. One path is the efficiency with which the GPT carries out its primary major function (e.g. delivering electricity or making computations). The other path is the range of additional applications of the GPT and the new technologies that it enables. There tend to be few of these initially but they then expand rapidly after which their diffusion slows down as the full potential of the GPT is developed. This slowing, however, may occur at any time from several decades to several centuries, and occasionally even millennia, after the GPT is first introduced. For example, the steam engine lasted less than a century as the economy's prime source of power after the development of the high-pressure engine at the beginning of the 19th century turned it from a useful technology into a fully-fledged GPT. In contrast, iron and steel are still with us more than two millennia after iron became a transforming GPT and electricity is still with us more than a century and a half after its emergence and shows no signs of being replaced by a superior alternative.

CAN NEW GPTS BE IDENTIFIED BY ACCELERATIONS IN PRODUCTIVITY GROWTH?

IT SEEMS THAT ECONOMISTS have been waiting for the expected productivity bonus, assumed to be associated with the new ICT-based economy, almost as long as others have waited for the Second Coming. The absence of the bonus was often taken throughout much of the 1990s as an argument against the existence of an ICT-induced GPT revolution.

My colleagues and I have argued elsewhere that there is no valid reason to expect that the introduction of every transforming GPT will be accompanied by a "productivity bonus."[10] Growth economists typically have these expectations because their intuitions are honed on models that use an aggregate production function. Stated generally this is:

$$(1) \qquad Y = AF(x_1,\ldots,x_n),$$

where Y is a nation's gross domestic product (GDP), $x_1,\ldots,x_n$ are quantities of n factor service inputs and A is a constant. Technology is not modelled explicitly in this formulation but it presumably helps to determine the form of the function and hence is hidden in the black box of F and A. In this model, a change in technology can only be observed as either a change in A or a change in the efficiency embedded in the units in which one or more of the inputs are measured. Both of these are used in theoretical exercises but empirical work typically uses only the former. In practice, the measurement of technological change takes the form of measuring the residual amount of Y that cannot be associated with changes in measured inputs. In Equation (1) this implies a change in the parameter A that is then interpreted as a productivity parameter. Such a change is called a change in total- or multi-factor productivity.[11]

Note three critical problems with this formulation.

One, it equates changes in technology with changes in total factor productivity (TFP). There cannot be one without the other. So the formulation is ill equipped to deal with situations in which independent evidence suggests that technology is changing rapidly while productivity is not. Furthermore, it should be noted that changes in one must be contemporaneous with changes in the other. So waiting decades for the observed changes in technology to produce a productivity bonus can at best be described as implicit theorizing. There is nothing explicit in any growth model based on an aggregate production function that would predict anything but a contemporaneous acceleration of the rate of change of productivity in response to an acceleration in the rate of change in technology.

Two, it does not explicitly model the structure of the economy that supports any technology, new or old. The facilitating structure needs to be modelled separately if we are not to risk confusing changes in that structure with changes in technology. This is important because the extent to which a new technology comes to pervade the economy has no simple relationship to the extent of the induced changes in the facilitating structure. Yet dramatic changes in the facilitating structure are obvious events and are often confused with big changes in technology. For example, one of the most profound transformations in facilitating structure in all of technological history was the move of production out of cottages into factories that took place in England in the first half of 19th century. Yet this was accompanied by only modest productivity gains, as shown by the fact that factories coexisted for decades with hand-loom weavers and other forms of cottage industries, as was documented by Crafts (2003). The big technological advances came in the 18th century with the mechanization of textile production and the development of the steam engine. The big changes in the facilitating structure came well into the 19th century when these two technologies, well-developed by that time, were combined to replace water power in factories, freeing them from the need to locate near fast moving water. This enabled the shift of production to the new industrial cities of the British Midlands. Such events give rise to an apparent paradox if neoclassical growth theory is used to interpret them, since that theory cannot distinguish between changes in technology, the facilitating structure and productivity.[12]

Third, as it is measured in practice, changes in total factor productivity emphatically do not measure changes in technology, in spite of the common belief that they do. Our argument as to why this is so is detailed in Lipsey and Carlaw (2004) but the position has been argued, albeit in much less detail, by many other authors, including Jorgensen and Griliches (1967) and Hulten (2000). One of the many reasons for this is that conventional measures of the quantity of capital ensure that much of the technological change that is embodied in new capital equipment will be measured as changes in the quantity of capital rather than as changes in technology. For example, Jorgenson (2001) states that "capital investment has been the most important source of U.S. economic growth throughout the post-war period." This needs to be understood as referring to capital as it is measured, which includes much embodied technological change.

In common with a body of theorists who study technological change from an evolutionary perspective (about which more later), we argue that the aggregate production function is at best a tool of very limited value for studying issues concerning economic growth. Since technological change is the most important driver of long-term growth, it is not desirable to have that driver impounded in a black box instead of being out in the open where it can be studied directly. Nor is it desirable to leave the facilitating structure unmodelled, since its characteristics undergo many induced changes when innovative technologies are introduced.

We argue that there is no reason to expect a new economy to be accompanied by a productivity bonus. The real effect of GPTs is to rejuvenate the growth process. If no further GPTs were invented to provide new research programs, the number of derivative technological developments would eventually diminish. There would be further innovations using existing GPTs, but their number and their productivity would be much less than if further GPTs were to become available. Consider, for example, what the range of possibilities for new innovations would now be if the last GPTs to be invented had been the steam engine for power, the iron steam ship for transport, steel for materials (no man-made materials), the telegraph for communication (the voltaic cell but no dynamo) and the mid 19th century factory system for organization. New GPTs such as computers, electricity and mass production stop the number of efficiency-increasing innovations from petering out. They avert a steady decrease in the return on investment and opportunities for innovations that increase productivity. Each new GPT brings with it an implicit research program that evolves as the GPT grows in efficiency and range of use. One GPT may introduce a rich program that brings large changes in products, processes and organizational arrangements, and perhaps eventually productivity. Another may introduce a program that is less rich. The gain to the economy is to be measured by what would have existed in their absence, not by what they do compared with what previous GPTs did. Indeed, there is no reason to expect that each successive GPT will increase the average rate of productivity growth over all previous GPTs. If each did, we would see a secular trend for productivity to rise as each GPT succeeded its predecessor.

Furthermore, duration matters as much as overall magnitude. Consider an example in which one new GPT brings an average gain in productivity of 2.5 percent per year and its main influence lasts 20 years while its successor brings 2 percent per year but lasts 50 years. The second has a bigger overall productivity impact, and will probably lead to more transformations than the first, but it will lower, not raise, the average rate of productivity growth in the economy. Assuming that the first GPT had reached the limit of its exploitation, the new one rejuvenates the growth process and prevents it from petering out, although it is associated with a lower rate of productivity increase than its predecessor. In this connection, notice that many of the effects of the ICT revolution on new design and production methods that are listed below occurred between 1975 and 1990, taking place long before most economists were even willing to contemplate the existence of a new ICT-based economy.

Finally, notice that an apparent "productivity bonus" may arise out of lags associated with the introduction of a new GPT. Several decades are typically required for a GPT to make a major impact both because many structural adjustments are needed before its full potential can be realized and because it takes decades for the research agenda that the GPT brings with it to get into full swing. As argued by Paul David (1991), electricity offers a prime example. Thus for some GPTs, there may be a slowdown in productivity growth in its early stages, followed by an acceleration to the average rate that will be achieved over the life time of that GPT. But this is not a real productivity bonus in the sense that the GPT has brought more productivity growth than previous new technologies; it is only a return to whatever underlying rate of growth the particular GPT in question will produce. Neither is it a phenomenon that is necessarily associated with all new GPTs. The possibility of a slowdown is problematic both because at any one time, there are likely to be several GPTs, at least one in each of the categories listed above, each at various stages of its development, and because the existing GPT in any one category typically has not been fully exploited when another challenges it.

The conference rapporteur, Pierre Sauvé, raises the issue of the 'productivity paradox'. He does not mention my analysis, but he seems to be in the camp of those who think there is a substantive issue here. He notes that two of the conference studies measured strong performance in services, presumably showing that the productivity paradox may be in the process of being resolved by an acceleration in the growth of service productivity. Of course, I would welcome a rise in productivity in any sector and especially services since they are such a large part of the total economy. My points, however, are: (1) the fact that we are in the later stages of a GPT driven new economy (this time the GPT is an ICT) provides no reason to expect a productivity acceleration; (2) neither the presence nor the absence of such an acceleration tells us anything about whether or not we really are in a new economy driven by a new GPT; (3) the concept of a productivity bonus is not well defined, since there is no stated precise comparison to which it refers; (4) the expectation of a bonus, however it is defined, is only a vague impression being derived from no tight theory; and (5) the expectation is not stated in any testable form such that at some specific time in the life cycle of each 'new economy,' we can say that the theory of a productivity bonus is either refuted or consistent with the facts.

KEY CHARACTERISTICS OF THE NEW ECONOMY

IS THERE REALLY A NEW ECONOMY or is it just a figment of the more lurid imaginations of literary economists? To answer this question, I offer a sampling of the many changes that the new economy has ushered in over the past 30 or so years. The list is a somewhat expanded and modified version of the list in Lipsey (2002). These changes are grouped loosely under the headings of process, product and organizational technologies, and social and political implications, although the categories clearly overlap. Goods (G) are distinguished from services (S) where relevant.

Process Technologies

- Computerized robots and related technologies have transformed the modern factory and eliminated many of the high-paying, low-skilled jobs that existed in the old Fordist assembly line factories. (G)
- Computer-assisted design is revolutionizing the design process and eliminating much of the need for "learning by using" in ways that were analyzed for the aircraft industry by Rosenberg (1982). (G&S)
- Surgery on hips, knees and other delicate parts of the body is increasingly performed with the aid of computers, which will soon facilitate surgery at a distance. This will allow specialists working in major urban hospitals to operate routinely on patients in remote parts of the world. (S)
- Instead of flying to Ottawa, lawyers in many distant cities make teleconferencing submissions to the Supreme Court of Canada, turning a two-day slog into a two-hour effort. (S)
- Research in everything from economics to astronomy has been changed dramatically by the ability to do complex calculations that were either impossible or prohibitively time-consuming without electronic computers. This is both a process technology in which old things are done in new and more efficient ways and a product technology that allows things to be done that were hitherto impossible. (S)
- Computer-age crime detection is much more sophisticated than it was in the past. Here the biological and the ICT revolutions complement each other as is so often the case with co-existing GPTs. (S)
- Traffic control in the air and on the ground has been revolutionized in many ways. Navigation at sea is now so easy that lighthouses, the sailor's friend for several millennia, are being phased out. They are unnecessary since ships can determine their positions to an accuracy of several yards using satellites and computers. (S)
- Technologies are just coming online that will eliminate the danger of workers breaching existing underground cables and pipes when digging to install new ones. Computers linked through satellites to detailed maps can provide the workers wearing appropriate glasses with virtual images of all existing buried cables and pipes. (G&S)

Organizational Technologies

- The management of firms has been reorganized as direct lines of communication opened by computers eliminated the need for the old pyramidal structure in which middle managers processed and communicated information. Today's horizontally organized and loose structure bears little resemblance to the management structure of the 1960s. (G&S)
- Firms are increasingly disintegrating their operations. Virtually no firm in Silicon Valley now produces physical goods. In other industries, the main firm is increasingly becoming a coordinator of sub-contractors who do everything from designing products, through manufacturing them, to distributing them. (G&S)
- The growing e-lance economy allows groups of independent contractors to come together for a single job and then disperse. It is also, incidentally, becoming difficult for authorities to track. (S)
- Just as the First Industrial Revolution took work out of the home, the ICT revolution is putting much of it back, as more people find it increasingly convenient to do all sorts of jobs at home rather than "in the office." (S)
- ICTs have been central to the globalization of trade in manufactured goods as well as the market for unskilled workers. This has shifted the location of much manufacturing and allowed poor countries to industrialize. It has also created new opportunities and challenges for both developed and developing nations. (G&S)
- Digitalized special effects have changed the movie industry in many ways. For example, they have reduced the need for shooting on location or for hiring myriad extras who can now be produced digitally. (S)
- The music industry has been changed in many deep ways, including the introduction of the virtual band: several different sung and instrumental outputs can all be produced by one singer and one instrumentalist whose varied performances are then amalgamated digitally. (G&S)

Product Technologies

- Many goods now contain chips that allow them to do new things or old things more efficiently. New applications continue to be developed. For example, cars will soon be equipped with systems that warn drivers of oncoming dangers and take over control if the driver fails to take evasive action. (G)

- The pilotless aircraft is now a military reality and will soon be available for civilian purposes. This will eventually remove the major bar to having a family aircraft parked in every garage since the only skill needed to operate it will be to punch in the destination. (G)
- Automated teller machines have enormously facilitated access to bank accounts and funds in any currency in almost any part of the world — in sharp contrast to the major difficulties experienced in the past when one was caught short of cash on a weekend or while travelling. The convenience of this wonderful, computer-driven innovation is hard to measure, but those who have travelled in earlier times know just how great it is. (S)
- Subscriber long distance dialling has replaced operator-assisted calls that were expensive, slow to complete, and all too often interrupted. (S)
- E-mail has largely replaced conventional mail with a large increase in volume and speed of transmission. Messages that used to take days or weeks in the past can now be received in minutes. (S)
- Computerized translation already exists. It will evolve from its present crude form to higher degrees of sophistication within our lifetimes. We are near to realizing Douglas Adam's vision in *The Hitch Hiker's Guide to the Galaxy*: the ability to hear in one's own language words spoken in any other, and to be understood in any other language while speaking one's own. The only difference is that instead of inserting a fish into one's ear, a small computer will be attached to one's body. (S)
- Children do school work by consulting the Internet. Instead of hearing only the received wisdom from their teacher and prescribed texts, they are now exposed to a wide array of diverse knowledge and opinion. They will have to learn how to cope at a very early age with more than one view on any subject. (S)
- Distance education is growing by leaps and bounds and many are enrolled in educational courses where they never (or only rarely) set foot inside the institution that they are attending. (S)
- Cars can receive real-time information on routes and traffic conditions at all points in their journey. (S)
- Smart buildings and factories already exist and will grow rapidly in number. Among many other things, power consumption can be adjusted continually in response to real-time price signals sent out by the electricity supply company and calculated in response to current loads. (G&S)

- The electronic book looks like it might do an end run around consumer resistance to reading books on screen. The book's blank pages fill up on demand with any one of a hundred or more books stored in a chip that is housed in its cover. A touch of a button, and one is reading a Physics 101 text on what looks like a conventional book; with only another touch, a Chemistry 202 text replaces the other on the book's leaves. **(G)**
- Looking into the future, the computer is enabling most of what is happening in the biological revolution and will do so during the forthcoming revolution in nano-technology and nano-electronics. These technologies will transform our society at least as much as the ICT revolution already has. **(G&S)**

POLITICAL AND SOCIAL

- The computer-enabled Internet is revolutionizing everything from interpersonal relations to political activity. Chat rooms are the basis for new forms of communication, making interpersonal relations possible on a scale never seen before. Non-governmental organizations are able to organize activities to protest clear-cut logging or to work against political initiatives such as efforts by the World Trade Organization to reduce trade barriers or by the Organization of American States to establish a Free Trade Area of the Americas. Never again will trade negotiations take place in the relative obscurity that they enjoyed from 1945 to 1990.
- Dictators find it much harder to cut their subjects off from knowledge of what is going on in the outside world.
- Driven by the Internet, English is becoming a *lingua franca* for the world and, unlike Latin in the Middle Ages, its use is not limited to the intelligentsia.
- In former times, a physical presence was required from virtually everyone providing a service. With computers, e-mail links and a host of other ICTs, this link between physical presence and provision has been broken in many services with profound social and political effects on such things as place of residence and the ability to regulate and tax many activities.

Although some of these changes are minor, others are revolutionary. Examples include globalization and its many ramifications, the total reorganization of company management, the end of mass production and the automation of factories, alterations in the structure of political power, the emergence of the civil society and its effects on the conduct of international negotiations. As I said at the end of the related discussion in Lipsey (2002):

> I cannot help but marvel over how many economists can assert, first, that all of these rich events can be adequately summarized in one series for productivity (usually total factor productivity) and, second, that the existence or non existence of this entire ICT revolution depends on how this number is now behaving in comparison with how it behaved over the past couple of decades!

DISBELIEVERS IN THE IMPORTANCE OF THE NEW ECONOMY

TWO MAIN ARGUMENTS HAVE BEEN USED to downgrade the importance of the new ICT-driven economy. The first relies on productivity figures while the second compares the current transformations with those induced by GPTs earlier in the century (particularly electricity).

The first criticism stems from the formulation of most growth models in terms of an aggregate production function that we discussed above. Many economists have argued that technological change must be associated with, and measured by, changes in productivity, in particular in TFP. Total factor productivity grew rapidly in the post war period then slowed in the latter half of the 1970s, remaining low through most of the rest of the century just when the new ICT revolution was supposed to be taking place. Thus the revolution, so goes the argument, is mainly an illusion. Such is the strength of this way of thinking that many North American economists were sceptical of the existence of the new economy until U.S. productivity picked up in the mid-1990s. That scepticism was reactivated when the U.S. economy slowed in 2001. But we have already argued that there is no reason to expect variations in the rate of technological change to be associated with variations in the rate of growth of some measured index of productivity.

Another way of casting doubt on the existence of an ICT revolution leading to a new economy comes from Robert Gordon. He observes that it has not given rise to anything like the range of new goods that transformed people's lives in the previous 50 or so years, such as the flush toilet, the automobile, and the range of electric appliances that transformed household work. I accept this position with respect to consumers' durables but observe that, as is illustrated by my own list quoted in the previous section, some of the most important changes initiated by the ICT revolution have been in process technologies and in consumer services. There are few goods and services produced today that are not made with the aid of computers at some stage in their production processes. Also, the new communications services have transformed people's lives in ways that are possibly just as fundamental as did the new consumers' durables introduced in the first half of the 20th century. I have argued that the technologies of the current new society are increasingly embodied in the human capital that provides services rather than in physical capital that produces goods. In doing so, I do not mean to imply that the broad category of services constitutes a meaningful distinction upon which to base policy that is focused exclusively on them instead of on manufactured goods. In this I am in agreement with William Watson. But the distinction is important for many measurements, since we are so much better at measuring productivity in the production of goods than in services. Erwin Diewert argues in his important study in this volume that the accurate measurement of service productivity is essential for any reasonable assessment of the performance of the economy. Yet, according to his expert opinion, this is almost impossible without major reforms in many relevant measurement procedures.

Although not advanced in the debate about the existence of the new economy, there is another criticism of the GPT story that is based on discontinuities that are assumed to be necessarily associated with new GPTs. If these technologies transform the economy so dramatically, the argument goes, why do we not see discontinuities in the statistical series for the rates of growth of output and of productivity? We have dealt with this criticism in detail in Carlaw and Lipsey (2002) and here we merely note two of the many points that address this concern. One, even though a new transforming GPT does alter almost everything in the socio-economic order, this usually happens incrementally over several decades during which time the new GPT slowly replaces the old, firm by firm, industry by industry, and sector by sector. Two, discontinuities only apply in models in which there is only one operative GPT, which is true of all published GPT models so far, but not true of the models developed in Lipsey, Carlaw and Bekar (forthcoming 2005). When several GPTs are in existence at the same time, each one at a different stage of its evolution, there is no reason why changes in the trajectories of production and output, associated with one existing incumbent GPT and its challenger, should dominate the statistics for the whole economy.

Two Views of the Economy

Understanding the kinds of growth and transformations that I have been discussing requires a theoretical framework. Indeed, there are two competing frameworks for doing so, the neoclassical and the structuralist-evolutionary. These involve very different views of the functioning of the economy and carry distinctly different policy implications.

Neoclassical

In the canonical general equilibrium (GE) version of the neoclassical micro-economic model, tastes and technology are the two exogenous variables. This theory presents an idealized form of all market systems. There is nothing in the general models that distinguishes one economy from another such as different specific technologies, different institutions and different stages of development. Given all the other standard assumptions, a welfare-maximizing equilibrium exists. Departures from this equilibrium are caused by market failures, which take three general forms: externalities, imperfect information and non-convexities. The removal of these market failures is the main object of neoclassical micro-economic policy advice, which is totally non-context specific, applying at all times and in all places.

Neoclassical theory works well in many already well-established market economies, in situations in which technology can be taken as exogenous and in which the forces at work can be expected to work quickly towards at least a local equilibrium. Indeed, in the majority of policy issues that I face, such as predicting the consequences of a radical change in the exchange rate or of effective price controls, I reach for my neoclassical tool-box. But when I come to issues involving economic growth, the limitations of neoclassical micro-economics become very clear. Neoclassical theory does not think of technological change as endogenous. It has no dynamic to handle situations in which an equilibrium is never achieved or even closely approached because the conditions assumed constant, such as technology and tastes, are, in fact, continually changing. It lacks any explicit modelling of technology or the facilitating structure that gives it practical effect. Finally, it lacks any specific context to temper its policy advice.

STRUCTURALIST-EVOLUTIONARY

STRUCTURALIST-EVOLUTIONARY THEORIES emphasize the importance of a detailed knowledge of technologies and the process of technological change. This is something that is not required by neoclassical theory, which does not seek to master all of the complexities of aggregate growth theory, regardless of whether it treats technical change as exogenous or endogenous. Structuralist-evolutionary micro treatments go inside that neoclassical black box, seeking to understand how technological change actually occurs. Much has been discovered by such analyses, but for present purposes, the most important characteristics are endogeneity and uncertainty.

Because research and development (R&D) is an expensive activity that is often undertaken by firms in search of profit, innovation is partly endogenous to the economic system, altering in response to changes in perceived profit opportunities.[13] Indeed, much inter-firm competition in non-perfect markets takes the form of competitive innovations. A firm can survive a mistake over prices or over capacity (the two main variables handled in most conventional theories of the firm), but falling behind in innovation is often disastrous. Dertouzos, Lester and Solow (1989) and Chandler (2001) provide excellent examples of this important insight, one that is all-too-seldom emphasized in courses on industrial organization.

Long ago, Frank Knight (1921) distinguished between risk and uncertainty. Risky events cannot be foretold with certainty but they have well-defined probability distributions and hence well-defined expected values. Economic analysis has no trouble handling risk. Agents merely maximize expected values — rather than the actual values that they would maximize in a world of perfect certainty. Uncertain events have neither well-defined probability distributions nor well-defined expected values. Because innovation means doing something not done before, it always involves an element of Knightian uncertainty. When engaging in R&D, it is impossible in advance to specify all the possible outcomes, and when something new has been discovered it is not possible to know what its range of applicability will be, how much it will be improved over time and how long it will prove to be economically useful. No one knows, for example, when some superior alternative will end the useful life of internal combustion or electric engines, just as no one knew in 1850 how long it would be before the steam engine would be dislodged from its position of being the industrialized world's most important source of power. The basic uncertainty surrounding invention, innovation and diffusion does not arise from a lack of information but from the nature of knowledge itself. Until new sought-after knowledge is obtained, no one can know what the nature of that knowledge will be.

A key characteristic of risky situations is that two agents possessed of the same information set, and presented with the same set of alternative actions, will make the same choice — the one that maximizes the expected value of the outcome. A key characteristic of uncertain situations, however, is that two equally well-informed agents presented with the same set of alternative actions may make different choices. If the choice concerns R&D, one may back one line of attack while the other backs a second line, even though both know the same things and both are searching for the same technological breakthrough. No one can say which agent is making the better choice at the time that the decisions are being made.

Because many firms are constantly making R&D choices under uncertainty, there is no unique line of behaviour that maximizes their expected profits. If there were, all equally well-informed firms would be seeking the same breakthrough made in the same way. Because of the absence of a unique best line of behaviour, firms are better seen as groping into an uncertain future in a purposeful and profit-seeking manner, instead of maximizing the expected value of future profits.[14]

Contrast in Desirable Characteristics

So far, we have contrasted many characteristics of market behaviour as seen in the two approaches. We now present how the two approaches consider which of these characteristics contribute to, and which detract from, the efficient functioning of the market. We give the market characteristics that seem desirable from the viewpoint of neoclassical theory in Roman type and the contrasting desirable characteristic as seen by S-E theory in italics.

- The perfectly competitive equilibrium describes the optimal configuration of the economy. *Path dependent evolutions brought about by new technologies are preferable to static equilibriums.*

- No firm should have market power so that price taking is the typical situation. *Market power gives firms the opportunity to exploit temporary advantages brought about by their own or other's research. Perfectly competitive industries rarely innovate. It is rather oligopolies that do the most innovation and that hence are a desirable market form.*

- Prices should be equal to opportunity costs and do not, therefore, allow for any pure profits. Thus, rents associated with the market power of oligopolies and monopolies or other forms of market power should be minimized. *Rents from innovation drive the system and really large ones are the carrot that induces agents to attempt leaps into the unknown and to make many more modest innovations under conditions of uncertainty.*

- Sources of non convexities such as scale effects and high entry costs should be minimal or non-existent since they are causes of market failure. *Non convexities are a key part of the desirable growth process. Scale effects, rather than being imperfections to be offset, are some of the most desirable results of new technologies. Entry costs for new products and new firms that cause non-convexities are the costs of innovation and the sources of some of the rents that drive innovating behaviour.*

- One of the main objects of economic policy is to remove market imperfections that prevent the attainment of an optimal allocation of resources. *Although the special case of an entrenched monopoly that does not innovate is regarded as undesirable, most other market "imperfections" are the very driving force of economic development. In any case, given the uncertainties associated with innovation, the optimal allocation of resources (either statically or dynamically) is an indefinable concept.*

It is apparent from the above set of contrasts that the characteristics S-E theory sees as driving the economy towards desirable results are the very characteristics that neoclassical economics sees as undesirable sources of market imperfections. The contrast could hardly be more stark. Yet neoclassical theory, in one form or another, is what provides the world view, and hones the intuitions of many, if not most, economic policy analysts.

POLICY CHALLENGES[15]

FOR THIS DISCUSSION, I follow Lipsey and Carlaw (1998b) in distinguishing two types of policy.[16]

> *Framework policies* provide general support for one specific activity across the whole economy. In practice, they are usually single-instrument policies. They do not discriminate among firms, industries or technologies. They do not judge the viability of recipient firms or the specific projects in which they are engaged. Instead, to be engaged in the covered activity is both a necessary and sufficient condition for obtaining benefits under the policy. Examples are patent protection for the owners of intellectual property and R&D tax credits. *Focussed policies* are designed to encourage the development of specific technologies, such as nuclear power, specific products, such as unmanned undersea craft, and particular types of R&D, such as pre-commercial research. They are usually sufficiently narrowly focussed to make falling within the focus a necessary and sufficient condition for receiving benefits under the policy.

NEOCLASSICAL POLICY IMPLICATIONS

NEOCLASSICAL POLICY ADVICE TO REMOVE 'market imperfections' wherever possible is quite general, applying to all times and all places. Kenneth Arrow (1962) provided the basic rationale for this policy advice with respect to technological change. He argued that because of positive externalities arising from any new technological knowledge, its production will be sub-optimal. It follows that it is welfare enhancing to encourage an amount of R&D beyond what would be provided by the free market.

There are two policy instruments that are typically recommended to encourage R&D. The first is to tighten intellectual property laws, which will internalize at least some of the social benefits that now accrue externally. The second is to give direct support to R&D in the form of subsidies and/or tax relief.[17]

When the neoclassical aggregate production function is used, technological knowledge is assumed to be measured by a single scalar value. There is then no distinction between framework policies such as R&D tax credits and focused policies such as support for innovation in some particular industry. Dissagregation is needed to compare these types of policies. If there are no externalities or other sources of market failure, and if all situations of less-than-perfect knowledge are risky and not uncertain, the unaided price system yields an optimal allocation of resources among all lines of activity, including R&D. This is because maximizing agents equate the expected returns from a marginal unit of expenditure everywhere in the economy, including along all lines of research and development.

Now let the only source of market failure be the externalities created by the non-rivalrous aspect of new knowledge. There is now a potential for welfare-enhancing policies that increase R&D toward the socially optimal amount. If the externalities are uniform across all lines of R&D, a generalized R&D subsidy is appropriate and, in principle, can restore a first-best optimum. It is neutral with respect to private incentives since the expected value of the payoff for the last dollar's worth of R&D is the same in all lines of activity both before and after the introduction of the non-distorting R&D subsidy. This, in the neoclassical, risk-only world, is *the optimal way* to counteract the externality that arises from the under-production of knowledge as a result of its public-good aspects.

In contrast, focused policies such as support for research into some specific aspects of biotechnology, or special support for R&D undertaken by small firms, are non-optimal because they selectively distort the price and profit signals that are generated by competitive markets. Although such policies may sometimes yield a positive net benefit, more benefit can always be achieved by devoting the same amount of tax-expenditure to a "non-distorting," economy-wide policy such as general R&D tax relief.

Structuralist-Evolutionary Policy Implications

Structuralist-evolutionary theories are designed to deal with the non-equilibrium, evolutionary, path-dependent, dynamic situations that characterize technological change. In contrast to neoclassical policy advice, S-E advice is context-dependent because it assumes that there is no simple set of universally applicable policy rules.

The theoretical underpinnings of this S-E position follow from its analysis of innovation. Firms that innovate are seen as profit seeking in the presence of uncertainty, rather than profit maximizing in the presence of risk. Because there is no unique best line of activity in such circumstances, there is no unique optimal allocation of resources in general and no unique optimal amount of R&D in particular. It follows that there is no unique set of scientifically determined, optimal public policies with respect to technological change and R&D. It also follows that there is no such thing as the neutral, non-distorting set of policies so beloved by textbook writers and many policy analysts, since there is no optimum to distort. Because there is no unique best policy for all times and places, it follows that good policy advice must be context-specific. The sections that follow offer several illustrations.

Accepting these conclusions has important consequences for how S-E theorists view economic policy in the area of growth and technological change. If there are no unique optimal rates of R&D, innovation or technological change, policy with respect to these matters must be based on a mixture of theory, measurement and subjective judgment.

When William Watson writes that his overall policy prescription is "not to tilt," he is working from the neoclassical position. He must live in an imaginary world of a flat, billiard-table economy in which any government intervention is a tilt — and usually a bad one at that. S-E theorists hold that we live in a messy, uneven economy, that is already full of what Watson would regard as "tilts." This is an economy in which the injunction "do not tilt" has no definable meaning. The relevant injunction is, instead, "try to change some of the many existing tilts in ways that are productive rather than counterproductive."

Context Specificity with Respect to Development

Joseph Stiglitz (2002), and other critics of the International Monetary Fund, have disapproved of its one-policy-fits-all approach, which is rooted in neoclassical theory. In contrast, S-E theory recognizes many country-specific influences, one of the most important of which is the country's current level of development.

Very poor countries often do not have a minimal set of working institutions that would allow a market economy to grow up and function effectively. This is an issue that cannot be discussed within the confines of the neoclassical general equilibrium model, which is featureless. Developing countries with established market economies that are trying to catch up to advanced countries face sets of problems that are different than those confronted by countries trying to stay on the cutting edge of technological progress. For one thing, they have the advantage of dealing with already established technologies. Adopting and adapting existing technologies is an activity that differs from advancing technologies at the cutting edge. Different policies are required to support each set of activities.

One key example of the importance of seeing development policies in context concerns import substitution, a policy originally followed by three of the four original Asian Tigers. For example, South Korea's early industrial policy was biased towards exports but neutral among firms. Capital and intermediate inputs could be imported without tariffs, quotas or indirect taxes, provided that the resulting production was export-oriented. Exporters could borrow from state-controlled banks in proportion to their export activity. Quarterly export targets were set and failure to meet them led to withdrawal of specific supports. A government "export situation room" helped to resolve problems and the most significant export achievements were eligible for additional benefits.[18]

According to its advocates, export promotion had several advantages over the older policy of import substitution. One, it forced industries to learn about the requirements of international markets in areas such as quality of product, delivery times and after-sales service. This entailed a high fixed cost of learning how to manage international competition in place of serving the soft domestic market. Without financial incentives to make this adjustment attractive and without financial assistance to make it possible, firms might never have made the jump, as they failed to do in many other 'developing countries' at that time. Two, it provided a bottom line, in that if firms failed in the tough international market, their support was terminated. Three, it did not allow firms to collect rents from a protected home market. Four, it encouraged endogenous technological change by forcing domestic firms into competition with the most innovative of foreign firms.

Controversy surrounds the issue of what export promotion accomplished. Neoclassical economists tend to argue that because it pushed the economies away from specializing in products in which they had a comparative advantage, it lowered their incomes. For example, Lawrence and Weinstein (2001) use statistical analysis of the relation between TFP growth and trade data to argue that during the period 1964-1985 neither import restrictions nor export promotion contributed positively to Japan's TFP growth. They conclude: "Our results call into question the views of both the World Bank and the revisionists and provide support for those who advocate more liberal trade policies." Their analysis does provide some support for those who argue that Japan might have gained from more liberal trade policies in that decade but it hardly supports those who advocate liberalizing trade at all times and at all places — which a literal reading of their conclusion seems to imply. Their results have little direct bearing on the question of whether or not export promotion helped the Tigers to get off the ground when they were attempting to turn from producing unsophisticated products for the home market to addressing the challenges of the global marketplace. The Tigers' context was one of very backward economies led by business people who were inexperienced in export markets and where capital and entrepreneurship were limited. In contrast, by 1964 Japan was a sophisticated economy with much higher living standards and much more experience in international markets. Its experience with import protection and export promotion during that period is just not relevant to the issue of how much such policies helped the Tigers in their initial phase when they turned away from the old development model to embrace the new one. In judging policies, context specificity matters!

A different approach is taken by those who hold that export promotion created new comparative advantages that did not exist at the outset. They argue that there is no way that the exports of the Tigers around 1980 could have been predicted by a study of their comparative advantages in 1955. Nor could a *laissez faire* policy have produced wholly new industries such as Taiwanese electronics. Instead, these industries, and the human capital that supported them were created by government intervention with an eye to creating comparative advantages that did not yet exist rather than exploiting those that already did.

Rodrik (1993) surveys four cases of export promotion in Korea, Brazil, Turkey and Kenya. Contrary to his original hypotheses about the conditions favouring success, he concludes that the most successful promotions were "...highly complex and selective, differentiated by firm, subject to frequent changes, gave bureaucrats enormous discretionary powers, and entailed close interaction between bureaucrats and firms. On the other hand, the least successful programs in my sample, those in Kenya and Bolivia, consisted of simple, across-the-board, and non-selective subsidies" (Rodrik 1993). This agrees with our S-E analysis that context specific policies are potentially superior to non-selective, universal policies — provided that rent seeking and other counter productive exploitation of such policies can be kept under control. The empirical lessons contained in Lipsey and Carlaw (1998a) give some indication of how this might be done. Of course, an important caveat is that: "...these successful experiences cannot easily be replicated in settings characterized by weak states" (Rodrik 1993).

Misreading the Lessons of Failed Policies

The neoclassical view that one policy fits all situations causes some serious errors of interpretation whenever some context-specific policy that once worked begins to fail because the context has changed. The neoclassical economists' interpretation is often: "We said this was a mistaken policy all along and now, at last, we see we were right because it is failing." In contrast, the correct response is more likely to be: "We may now be able to isolate some of the contexts in which this policy is likely to work by comparing situations in which it did work with those in which it failed." Since no focused policy will work in all contexts, opponents can always find a context in which a specific one did not work and draw the conclusion that this is a mistaken policy in general. A case in point has already been provided by the example of how Japan's attempt at import substitution is interpreted.

Context Specificity with Respect to Types of Innovation

Civil servants are not entrepreneurs and should not be required to take entrepreneurial decisions. But what has succeeded in many catch-up countries is cooperation between the private and public sectors at the stage of pre-commercial research. The public sector created the institutions in which private and public sector agents could pool their knowledge and come to a consensus on where the next technology push should be. Acquiring such knowledge is often beyond the financial capabilities of individual private firms. The Singapore government, for example, spent several millions of dollars identifying software as the next wave of computer development at a time when it was hard coded into computers and given away free. The parties then jointly financed the required research. This became one of the main contributors to the great success of Singapore's economy in the 1980s. For further discussion of this issue, see Lipsey and Carlaw (1996) and Lipsey and Wills (1996).

Another example of context specificity is offered by the cooperative-consultative policies that worked so well in the early stages of development among the Asian Tigers. They still work well when all private agents are pushing for a *fairly well defined* modest advance in pre-competitive knowledge and where cooperation can reduce wasteful duplication of research. But when major breakthroughs are being sought, inherent uncertainties argue for a multiplicity of investigations, each pursued with the minimum required resources. Concentrating effort has often been demonstrated to be worse than the apparent "wastefulness" of uncoordinated experimentation that occurs in the free market.

Context Specificity with Respect to Externalities

Neoclassical theory sees little difference between subsidizing R&D and protecting its results through better patent laws. Structuralist-evolutionary theory emphasises the differences. An R&D subsidy lowers costs equally for everyone doing R&D, whether their efforts succeed or fail, and whether or not success creates externalities. In contrast, better intellectual property rights do not raise returns for everyone equally. Many people doing R&D fail to find patentable inventions. In addition, the ability to extract value from patents on successful inventions varies greatly across different types of innovation. In some lines of activity, patents are relatively easy to enforce. Firms in industries such as chemicals and pharmaceuticals are able to internalize enough of the value that they create to provide them with strong incentives to innovate. In the case of innovations such as differentiated consumer goods and processes, patents are of little value in protecting markets. It follows that any given amount of aggregate R&D will be allocated differently among firms depending on whether it is induced by an effective patent system or by an R&D subsidy. An ideal policy would give support that was inversely correlated with the ability to internalize externalities through private efforts. This might be an unattainable ideal but it shows that it is by no means "neutral" policy to support all equally with no consideration to the amount of externalities created and internalized.

Context Specificity with Respect to Pre-Commercial and Commercial R&D

Lipsey and Carlaw (1996) argue that the ability to keep results of pre-commercial research secret varies greatly among industries. Where this is difficult or impossible, there is a tendency to do less R&D than is socially desirable. Where it can be kept secret, there may be more R&D than is socially desirable if all firms are seeking the same more or less well defined research goal. A focused policy that effectively discriminates between these two situations is potentially superior to a framework policy that merely encourages more of whatever is already being done. For example, where individual firms find it difficult or impossible to maintain the secrecy of their research, focused policies can create commitments among firms that encourage them to do pre-commercial research from which they all benefit.

Context Specificity with Respect to Types of R&D

Not only will a framework policy cover some activities that do not need support, it will miss some that do. For example, because there is no clear distinction between innovation and diffusion, much activity that is related to the development and use of new technologies may not appear to be basic R&D, at least as it is defined by Canada Revenue Agency (formerly Revenue Canada). John Baldwin has many times pointed out that small firms do little recognizable R&D but spend a lot of time monitoring what larger firms are doing and adapting what they find to their own uses (e.g. Baldwin and Hanel 2003.) From a growth point of view, this activity may be as important as more conventionally defined R&D. Typically, however, it is not covered by such framework policies as R&D tax credits or subsidies, which support only R&D as it is defined by the Canada Revenue Agency.

Acquiring workable knowledge about new technologies often requires fixed costs that small firms cannot rationally bear. Government bodies can assist with the dissemination of technological knowledge by operating on a scale that spreads the sunk costs over many different applications. The Canadian Industrial Research Assistance Program (IRAP) operates along these lines and has apparently been successful. It is described and evaluated in Lipsey and Carlaw (1998b).

Canadian firms have recently expressed concern about the unfortunate effects of Canada Revenue Agency's tightening of eligibility criteria for R&D tax credits. This illustrates the fact that any policy is interpreted and administered by civil servants. As a result, neutrality is much harder to achieve in practice than on the theoretician's drawing board. This is not a quibble: once one accepts that there is no unique optimal set of policies, context-specificity must include the nation's institutional capabilities and the biases of those who administer any specific policy — what elsewhere we call the policy structure.

Technologies Can Be Singled Out

Neoclassical theory is opposed to policies that focus on specific sectors or technologies. Indeed economists are fond of saying that governments cannot pick winners. The facts, however, are otherwise. Governments the world over have picked winners and some of these have been spectacular successes. At the same time, others have been disastrous failures. Success has been particularly apparent when public assistance has encouraged new technologies in their early stages of development. U.S. policy provides many examples of such successes.[19]

Virtually every modern Western industrialized country, including the United States, went through the early stages of its industrialization with substantial tariff protection for its infant industries.[20] Indeed even in the United Kingdom, the subsequent home of free trade, the prohibition on the importation of Indian cotton goods was critical in the development of the machines that produced the first industrial revolution.[21] Publicly-funded U.S.

land-grant colleges have done important agricultural research from their inception in the 19th century. The 20th century "green revolution" was to a great extent researched by public funds. In its early stages, the U.S. commercial aircraft industry received substantial assistance from the National Advisory Committee on Aeronautics (NACA) that, among other things, pioneered the development of large wind tunnels and demonstrated the superiority of retractable landing gears. The airframe for the Boeing 707 and the engines for the 747 were both developed in publicly funded military versions before being transferred to successful civilian aircraft. Electronic computers and atomic energy were largely created in response to military needs and military funding. For many years, support for the U.S. semiconductor industry came mainly from military procurement that enforced rigid standards and quality controls which helped to standardize practices and to diffuse technical knowledge. The U.S. government's heavy involvement in the early stages of the U.S. software industry produced two major spin-offs into the commercial sector. One was an infrastructure of academic experts, built largely with government funding; the other was the establishment of high and uniform industry standards.

The post-war Japanese automobile industry was prevented from becoming a branch of the U.S. industry, as did the Canadian, by government policies that prohibited foreign ownership and protected the local market. Fierce competition among too many firms for too small a home market led to one of the great examples of policy-induced endogenous innovation when Toyota invented lean production to cope with the absence of sufficient scale to make U.S. practices efficient. After two decades of experimentation, techniques were perfected that were better than those in North America and Europe. On the other side, without government protection, many U.S. and European firms would have succumbed to Japanese competition.

The Taiwanese government literally created its electronics industry from scratch using government-owned firms that were transferred to private owners once they had become successful.

The list can be extended almost indefinitely. Such examples show that at least in some areas, knowing when and how to use public funds to encourage really important new technologies in their early stages is an important condition for remaining technologically dynamic. I hasten to add that this is no easy task.

When presented with evidence of this sort, neoclassical economists typically resort to bluster. For example, William Watson tells us that "...a social institution (government) that cannot properly maintain the windows on a public school is unlikely to be much use in helping commercialize deep uncertainty." But, as the above discussion illustrates, governments (national not local) have succeeded in assisting the development of many technologies in their early stages and the U.S. government has registered many such successes. So have some of the newly industrialized countries. Slogans will not help, nor will analogies with windows, nor will the confusion of national with local governments. What we urgently need to know is: "Will it matter if other governments, particularly the United States, persist in encouraging new technologies while we do not?" and, "If we do decide to do this, how can we do it while avoiding the many catastrophic failures that Carlaw and I, among others, have chronicled" (Lipsey and Carlaw 1996).

Surveying such focused públic polices, Rodrik (1993) agues in much the same vein:

> In thinking about policy, academic economists alternate between theoretical models in which governments can design finely tuned optimal interventions and practical considerations which usually assume the government to be incompetent and hostage to special interests. I argue in this study that neither of these caricatures is accurate, and that there is much to be learned by undertaking systematic, analytical studies of state capabilities — how they are generated and why they differ across countries and issue areas.

When William Watson says "...leaving things to the market is the lesser of two inefficiencies," he is reacting just as Rodrik predicts. We know that there are market failures, and that there are government failures. We need to go beyond slogans about which of the two are to be the *only* ones to be considered and find out how each of these may be overcome in each of a very specific set of circumstances.

Context Specificity with Respect to Alterations in the Facilitating Structure

Neoclassical policy analysis recognizes only R&D as a suitable object for the encouragement of innovation. Tests of policy effectiveness tend to concentrate on the amount of R&D encouraged or the new technologies established. In contrast, S-E studies of innovation reveal other areas where policy can be helpful (Lipsey and Carlaw 1998b).

Policies may indirectly target technological change by altering elements of the facilitating structure. Examples include integration of relevant university, government and private sector research activities, creation of technology information networks, and changing private-sector attitudes toward adopting new or different technologies. A government can give funds to firms to develop technologies that they would have developed in any case but then attach structural conditions to the assistance. More than one government has done this to encourage the development of long-range research facilities. This includes the Canadian government's Defence Industry Productivity Program (Lipsey and Carlaw 1998b). Such initiatives often arouse the ire of neoclassical economists who focus on direct results and correctly point out that spending in such areas led to no inventions or innovations. But that is not the point. The objective is to alter the facilitating structure in ways that would not have occurred without government pressure. A prime example, already referred to, is U.S. military procurement policy that virtually created the U.S. software industry.

Is Market Orientation Enough?

MANY NEOCLASSICAL ECONOMISTS ARGUE that creating a market-oriented environment is a sufficient goal for public policy. Create that environment and the magic of the marketplace will do the rest: the actions of domestic agents and foreign multinationals will bring growth and development without any need for a more pro-active policy. Furthermore, where pro-active polices are used, they are likely to do more harm than good.

Others argue that it is not enough simply to set up policies reflecting the market-oriented consensus that developed after the fall of the planned economies. They also suggest that newer theories in the S-E tradition show the need for more focused policies — always on the understanding that these are in addition to, not substitutes for, a basic market-orientation. Voltaire once observed that magic can kill whole flocks of sheep if accompanied by sufficient doses of arsenic. Similarly, the magic of the market can do everything that is needed if it operates in the context of the necessary set of created institutions and is accompanied by a sufficient number of policies designed to spur innovation.

Long ago, I predicted a conflict between those who argued that market orientation alone was sufficient for growth and those who argued that it was necessary but not sufficient (Lipsey 1994): "The consensus [on the importance of market orientation] has been followed not by 'the end of history' but, just as one should have expected, by a new battle of ideologies. Both of the ideologies that are now in competition accept the...[value of] the price system, but they divide over the importance, and policy-relevance, of the views on technological change I have reported on in this lecture." These views were similar, although much less fully developed, to those I have expressed here, 10 years after the quoted comment was published.[22]

The fact that technological change is endogenous to the system creates scope for influencing it. The fact that there is no unique set of non-distorting, scientifically determined policies shows that policy must be based on a mixture of empirical knowledge, theory and judgment. The fact that governments have picked great winners and terrible losers shows that there is no single approach to this issue that is reducible to a simple slogan. The real problem is to determine the conditions that maximize the chances of success and minimize those of failure in focused policies, something that I have tried to do in a series of publications of which the most detailed is Lipsey and Carlaw (1998b).

As I have said elsewhere (Lipsey 1997a):

> These ideas are both powerful and dangerous. They are powerful because they suggest ways to go beyond neoclassical generic policy advice to more context-specific advice. They are dangerous because they can easily be used to justify ignoring the market-oriented consensus, accepting only the interventionist part of the S-E policy advice (forgetting that this is meant to supplement the advice of the consensus, not to replace it).

CONCLUSION

THE WORKING OUT OF THE FULL IMPLICATIONS of endogenous technological change, particularly at the micro-economic level, is an ongoing research project. This project has revolutionary implications for how we view the workings of the economy and for the role we assign to government policy. Some of these implications are profoundly upsetting for economists trained in the orthodox neoclassical tradition. They worry, correctly in my view, that the advocates of the new theories may discard the large amount of truth that lies with the old when they set about discarding those things that are in error, or at least misleading.

But the possibility of some excess of revolutionary zeal is no excuse for avoiding a revolution when the old order is seen to be dysfunctional in many ways. And when it comes to understanding the forces that drive long-term growth, the market conditions and the public policies that encourage it, the old order is, if not dysfunctional, then at least resting on very shaky foundations and often profoundly misleading.[23] Caution is required not to lose major insights about the advantages of a market-based economy but caution is also needed not to worship that economy as if it came into being by immaculate conception and functions so perfectly that it needs no policy assistance, only adoration.

In conclusion, let me point out the good news that is implicit in the new ways of understanding technological change and economic growth in a largely knowledge-driven society. Economics need no longer be the dismal science that it was when growth theory from Adam Smith to Robert Solow was dominated by considerations of diminishing returns from the accumulation of capital. As I have put it elsewhere (Lipsey 1994):

> Economic analysis will no doubt be used in the future to analyse many dismal economic events [and no doubt there will be many]. But the days when the underlying basis of the subject justified the title 'dismal science' are over. The modern title should become 'the optimistic science' — not because economics predicts inevitable growth or the arrival of universal bliss, but because its underlying structure, altered to incorporate the economics of knowledge, implies no limit to real income-creating, sustainable growth, operating in a basically market-organized society. If we cannot achieve sustained and sustainable economic growth, the fault dear Brutus must lie with ourselves not with some iron-clad economic law that dictates failure before we start.[24]

ENDNOTES

1 This chapter is based on the keynote address given at the Winnipeg conference in November 2003. The ideas discussed here are much more fully elaborated in Lipsey, Carlaw and Bekar (forthcoming 2005). Since my address was intended as a report on how I saw the challenges, there are, of necessity, more self-references than would normally be seemly.

2 For further discussion of the meaning of GPTs and issues surrounding its definition, see Lipsey, Bekar and Carlaw (1998).

3 These implications are elaborated in some detail in Carlaw and Lipsey (2002).

4 The full set of elements of our facilitating structure are (1) the stock of physical capital, (2) the stock of consumers' durables and residential housing, (3) people: who they are, where they live, and all human capital that resides in them and that is related to productive activities, including tacit knowledge of how to operate existing value-creating facilities, (4) the actual physical organization of production facilities, including labour practices, (5) the managerial and financial organization of firms, (6) the geographical location of productive activities, (7) industrial concentration, (8) all infrastructure, (9) all private-sector financial institutions and financial instruments, (10) government-owned industries and (11) educational institutions. We also distinguish a policy structure, which consists of the institutions and people who give effect to public policy.

5 Since not all GPTs require great structural changes to become effective, we distinguish two types: "transforming GPTs" lead to massive changes in many, sometimes most, characteristics of the economic, social and political structures, as mentioned in the text. Other GPTs do not. Lasers provide one example of the later type of GPT. They are widely used for multiple purposes: to measure inter planetary distances in astronomy, to read bar codes at check out counters, to facilitate numerous types of surgery in hospitals, to support many forms of communications, to cut diamonds, for milling materials in new machine tools and for welding plastics. In the future, they will facilitate the usage of nanotechnology. Lasers, do not, however, qualify as a transforming GPT because they fit well into the existing social, economic and institutional structure, causing no major transformations.

6 We confine all of our discussions to the West, which in ancient times includes the civilizations of the Tigris and Euphrates. In Chapter 1 of Lipsey, Carlaw and Bekar (forthcoming 2005), we explain our reasons for adopting this more or less Eurocentric viewpoint.

7 This was the first of a series of technologies that created what has been called a "pyrotechnic revolution," that included the invention and increasing use of pottery, glass, terra-cotta, lime plaster and cement, all of which would eventually become important building and engineering materials technologies. The basic technology was the discovery of the transforming effects of heat.

8 My colleagues and I are never quite sure whether or not to include this as a GPT. The principle itself is a scientific, not a technological discovery but its many uses were technological. Although the principle had been used in practice for

millennia, it was the Greeks who understood it and turned it into a systematic body of useful knowledge rather than just an empirical knowledge of what worked and what did not.

9 The second half of the first millennium AD witnessed a European agricultural revolution whose technological foundations were the heavy plough, the three-field system, and the harnessing of horse power. The basic GPT was the heavy plough which created the pressures that led, on the one hand, to changes in the layout of fields and, on the other hand, to the development of efficient horse harnesses, horse shoes and other new technologies related to powering the ploughs. Similar technologies would not be regarded as GPTs in a modern economy. They had a restricted variety of uses, and today's agricultural technologies only affect a limited segment of the entire economy. They were, however, general purpose with respect to virtually all agricultural commodities and, at the time, agriculture constituted the vast majority of contemporary productive activities (probably over 90 percent).

10 We advanced an early version of our argument in Lipsey and Beker (1995) and I elaborated it fully in Lipsey (2002).

11 Taking the Cobb-Douglas version of the aggregate production function and assuming only two factors, L and K:

$$Y = AL^{\alpha}K^{\beta},$$

and with a little manipulation we get a measure of the change in TFP as:

$$\frac{\dot{A}}{A} = \frac{\dot{Y}}{Y} - \alpha\frac{\dot{L}}{L} - \beta\frac{\dot{K}}{K} = \frac{T\dot{F}P}{TFP},$$

(where the dot superscript denotes the time derivative). This equation defines total factor productivity as the difference between the proportional change in output minus the proportional change in a Divisia index of inputs. We have discussed the issues surrounding this and other methods of measuring TFP in Lipsey and Carlaw (2004).

12 We give our full interpretation of these events and those that led up to them in Bekar and Lipsey (forthcoming).

13 The study of endogenous technical change has a long history in micro-economics. In a volume first published in 1834, John Rae (reprinted 1905) studied endogenous technical change and pointed out that it undermined the case for complete *laissez faire* in general and free trade in particular. In 1912 Joseph Schumpeter made the innovating entrepreneur the centrepiece of his theory of growth (English version 1934). Schumpeter did not, however, study the process of technical change in detail and, as a result, he developed a theory that made too sharp a distinction between innovation (whose perpetrators were his heroes) and diffusion (done, according to him, by "mere copiers"). In the early 1960s, Nicholas Kaldor — one of the greatest of the economists who were passed over for the Nobel Prize — developed models of endogenous growth (see especially Kaldor and Mirrlees 1962). His work influenced a generation of European scholars. Also in the 1960s, the historian Schmookler (1966) provided detailed empirical evidence that innovation was endogenous. Nearly two decades later, Nathan Rosenberg (1982) established endogeneity in his classic work, *Inside the Black Box.*

After that date, there could be no doubt that technological change was endogenous at the micro-economic level, in the sense that it responded to economic signals. Rosenberg (1982, Chapter 7) also made a persuasive case that pure scientific research programs respond endogenously to economic signals. All of this happened long before macro-economists discovered endogenous technical change.

14 This approach to the behaviour of firms has a long lineage going back at least to the work of Herbert Simon (1947). A seminal book by Richard Nelson and Sidney Winter (1982) later pioneered its application to growth and technological change.

15 Ken Carlaw and I have addressed these issues, along with their theoretical background presented in the previous section, in a series of articles including Lipsey and Carlaw (1996, 1998a, 1998b, 2002) and Lipsey (2000).

16 They actually distinguish and study three types of policy but for the purposes of this discussion, we do not need to consider their third type, blanket policies.

17 Notice that in the neoclassical model, in which the expected payoffs from all lines of R&D expenditure are equated at the margin, there is no distinction between encouraging the inputs into the advancement of technological knowledge and encouraging the output of the new technological knowledge. Increasing one increases the other. The policy prescription, therefore, does not differentiate between lowering the costs of generating new technological knowledge and raising the payoff to that knowledge.

18 For fuller discussions see Lipsey and Wills (1996) and Westphal (1990).

19 Lipsey and Carlaw (1996) studies about 30 cases in which focused policies either succeeded or failed, and attempts to isolate some of the circumstances that tend to favour either result.

20 It is worth noting, although there is no space to go into it in detail here, that the standard infant industry argument for tariff protection is altered when technology is recognized as being endogenous. In the standard model with known technology, the only reason for subsidizing an infant-industry tariff is to assist it to move along a downward sloping long-run cost curve (i.e., to exploit scale economies) when capital markets are imperfect. With endogenous technology, tariff protection serves many purposes, including providing time to develop many activities that confer major externalities and to develop the kinds of structures that are conducive to technological diffusion and technological advance. The object is to create circumstances in which the relevant cost curves will shift downwards, and continue to do so over time, rather than to move outwards along a pre-determined cost curve.

21 A recent detailed argument that Britain's success owed a great deal to its mercantilist polices can be found in Ormrod (2003).

22 See also Lipsey (1993) for an earlier similar statement.

23 Long run equilibrium analysis is profoundly misleading in situations in which endogenous technological change responds to the shock being investigated: one response comes from given technology and a quite different response if technology changes in response to the shock.

24 Lipsey 1994, p. 351.

BIBLIOGRAPHY

Arrow, Kenneth J. 1962. "Economic Welfare and the Allocation of Resources for Innovation," in *Rate and Direction of Economic Activity*, NBER Conference series. Washington, D.C.: National Bureau of Economic Research.

Baldwin, John, and Petr Hanel. 2003. *Innovation and Knowledge Creation in an Open Economy: Canadian Industry and International Implications*. Cambridge: Cambridge University Press.

Bekar, Clifford, and Richard G. Lipsey. (forthcoming). "Science, Institutions, and the Industrial Revolution," *Journal of European Economic History.*

Carlaw, Kenneth I., and Richard G. Lipsey. 2002. "Externalities, Technological Complementarities and Sustained Economic Growth," *Research Policy*, Special Issue Honouring Nelson, 31 (Winter): 1305-1315.

Chandler, Alfred D. Jr. 2001. *Inventing the Electronic Century*. New York: The Free Press.

Crafts, Nicholas F.R. 2003. "Steam as a General Purpose Technology: A Growth Accounting Perspective," LSE Working Paper No 75/03. London: London School of Economics.

David, Paul. 1991. *Computer and Dynamo: The Modern Productivity Paradox in a Not Too Distant Mirror*. Paris: Organisation for Economic Co-operation and Development.

Dertouzos, Michael L., Richard Lester, and Robert Solow. 1989. *Made in America*. London: MIT Press.

Gordon, Robert. 2000. "Does the 'New Economy' Measure up to the Great Inventions of the Past?" NBER Working Paper No. 7833. Washington, D.C.: National Bureau of Economic Research.

Hulten, Charles R. 2000. "Total Factor Productivity: A Short Biography," NBER Working Paper No. 7471. Washington, D.C.: National Bureau of Economic Research.

Jorgensen, Dale W., and Zvi Griliches. 1967. "The Explanation of Productivity Change," *The Review of Economic Studies*, 34: 249-83.

Jorgensen, Dale W. 2001. "Information Technology and the U.S. Economy," *American Economic Review*, 91: 1-32.

Kaldor, Nicholas, and James A. Mirrlees. 1962. "A New Model of Economic Growth," *The Review of Economic Studies*, 29: 174-192.

Knight, Frank Hyneman. 1921. *Risk, Uncertainty and Profit*. New York: Houghton Mifflin Co.

Lawrence, Robert Z., and David E. Weinstein. 2001. "Trade and Growth: Import-Led or Export-Led? Evidence from Japan and Korea," in Joseph E. Stiglitz and Shahid Yusuf (eds.). *Rethinking the East Asian Miracle*. Oxford: Oxford University Press.

Lipsey, Richard G. 1993. "Globalisation, Technological Change and Economic Growth," *Annual Sir Charles Carter Lecture*. Ireland: Northern Ireland Economic Council, report no. 103, reprinted in Lipsey (1997b).

————. 1994. "Markets, Technological Change and Economic Growth," Quaid-I-Azam Invited Lecture, in *The Pakistan Development Review* 33: 327-352, reprinted in Lipsey (1997b).

————. 1997a. "Globalization and National Government Policies: An Economist's View," in John Dunning (ed.). *Governments, Globalization, and International Business*. Oxford: Oxford University Press, pp. 73-113.

————. 1997b. *The Selected Essays of Richard Lipsey: Volume I: Micro-economics, Growth and Political Economy.* Cheltenham, UK: Edward Elgar Publishing.

————. 2000. "New Growth Theories and Economic Policy for the Knowledge Economy", in Kjell Rubenson and Hans G. Schuetze (eds.). *Transition to the Knowledge Society: Policies and Strategies for Individual Participation and Learning.* Vancouver, BC: UBC Press, pp. 33-61.

————. 2002. "The Productivity Paradox: A Case of the Emperor's New Clothes," *ISUMA: Canadian Journal of Policy Research,* 3: 120-126.

Lipsey, Richard G., and Clifford Bekar. 1995. "A Structuralist View of Technical Change and Economic Growth," in *Bell Canada Papers on Economic and Public Policy,* Vol. 3, Proceedings of the Bell Canada Conference at Queen's University. Kingston: John Deutsch Institute, pp. 9-75.

Lipsey, Richard G., Clifford Bekar, and Kenneth Carlaw. 1998. "What Requires Explanation?" Chapter 2 in Elhanan Helpman (ed.). *General Purpose Technologies and Economic Growth.* Cambridge, MA: MIT Press, pp. 15-54.

Lipsey, Richard G., and Kenneth I. Carlaw. 1996. "A Structuralist View of Innovation Policy," in Peter Howitt (ed.). *The Implications of Knowledge-Based Growth.* Industry Canada Research Series. Calgary: University of Calgary Press, pp. 255-333.

————. 1998a. "Technology Policies in Neoclassical and Structuralist-Evolutionary Models," *OECD Science, Technology and Industry Review*, Special Issue, 22: 31-73.

————. 1998b. *A Structural Assessment of Technology Policies: Taking Schumpeter Seriously on Policy*. Working Paper No. 25. Ottawa: Industry Canada.

————. 2002. "Some Implications of Endogenous Technological Change for Technology Policies in Developing Countries," *Economics of Innovation and New Technology* (EINT), 11 (4/5): 321-351.

————. 2004. "Total Factor Productivity and the Measurement of Productivity," *Canadian Journal of Economics,* 37 (4): 1118-1150.

Lipsey, Richard G., Kenneth I. Carlaw, and Clifford Bekar. (forthcoming 2005). *Economic Transformations: General Purpose Technologies and Long Term Economic Growth.* Oxford: Oxford University Press.

Lipsey, Richard G., and Russel M. Wills. 1996. "Science and Technology Policies in Asia Pacific Countries: Challenges and Opportunities for Canada," in Richard S. Harris (ed.). *The Asia-Pacific Region in the Global Economy: A Canadian Perspective.* Industry Canada Research Series. Calgary: University of Calgary Press, pp. 577-612.

Nelson, Richard, and Sydney Winter. 1982. *An Evolutionary Theory of Economic Change*. Cambridge, MA: Harvard University Press.

Ormrod, David. 2003. *The Rise of Commercial Empires: England and the Netherlands in the Age of Mercantilism, 1650-1770.* New York: Cambridge University Press.

Rae, John. 1905. *The Sociological Theory of Capital.* New York: Macmillan. First published in 1834 as *A Statement of Some New Principles on the Subject of Political Economy Exposing the Fallacies of the System of Free Trade and of Some Other Doctrines Maintained in the Wealth of Nations.*

Rodrik, Dani. 1993. "Taking Trade Policy Seriously: Export Subsidization as a Case Study in Policy Effectiveness," NBER Working Paper No. 4567. Washington, D.C.: National Bureau of Economic Research.

Rosenberg, Nathan. 1982. *Inside The Black Box: Technology and Economics.* Cambridge: Cambridge University Press.

Schmookler, J. 1966. *Invention and Economic Growth.* Cambridge, MA: Harvard University Press.

Schumpeter, Joseph. 1934. *The Theory of Economic Development, English Translation.* Cambridge, MA: Harvard University Press. First published in German, 1912.

Simon, Herbert. 1947. "Some Models for the Study of the Effects of Technological Change," Cowles Commission, DP 2132. Chicago: University of Chicago.

Stiglitz, Joseph, E. 2002. *Globalization and its Discontents.* New York: W. W. Norton & Co.

Westphal, Larry E. 1990. "Industrial Policy in an Export-Propelled Economy: Lessons from South Korea's Experience," *Journal of Economic Perspectives,* 4: 41-59.

Ram C. Acharya
Industry Canada

4

The Services Economy in Canada: An Overview

INTRODUCTION

SERVICES ARE ECONOMIC ACTIVITIES that include the provision of human value in the form of labour, advice, managerial skill, training, entertainment, sale and distribution of goods, intermediation and the dissemination of information. It is a heterogeneous group of activities that are not directly associated with manufacturing of goods, mining or agriculture. In recent years, there is growing policy interest in the services economy, as countries become more service-oriented and as the services sector's contribution to aggregate production and employment grows. Furthermore, the industries that are most intensive in their use of information and communication technology (ICT) and the knowledge-based industries that are believed to be crucial to Canada's future prosperity fall into the services sector. As Lipsey (Chapter 3, in this volume) reminds us, many of the most important changes brought about by the ICT revolution have been in consumer services.

Realizing this fact, both academics and government officials are increasingly interested in understanding the services sector. Compared to the research available on manufacturing, there is a dearth of research that focuses on the services sector and Canada is no exception to this. Among the very few studies that address the Canadian services sector is the book by Grubel and Walker (1989) which provides a detailed account of Canadian services industries up to the mid 1980s. Needless to say, very important changes in the services sector may have occurred in the late 1980s and the 1990s in light of the ICT revolution. Using data from a survey of services industries, Baldwin, Gellatly, Johnson, and Peters (1988) develop profiles of innovative firms in financial services industries. Despite its usefulness, this study is of limited help in understanding what is happening in sectors other than financial services. More recently, Mohnen and Raa (2000) analyzed the services sector in Canada, exploring the seemingly inconsistent phenomena of exploding costs and persistent demand in some industries within this sector. Since their focus was mostly on this paradox, they do not cover many other aspects of the important changes that are taking place in the services sector. Ultimately, there is no comprehensive recent analysis of the services sector in Canada. One area where there has been some recent research is on the measurement of productivity growth. This has been part of a general surge of interest in the methodology and the findings of empirical studies of productivity measurement.[1] This study builds on this research and sets out to satisfy, at least partially, the need for a current and comprehensive services-sector analysis. As a result, the study not only examines the productivity performance of services industries but also provides an overview of Canada's services industries over roughly the past two decades.

This study uses data from the North American Industrial Classification System (NAICS) which has replaced the Standard Industrial Classification (SIC) that was used prior to 1997.[2] In many cases, the data are available only at the sectoral (2-digit) level, which is why much of our analysis in this study is at that level, though analysis at the 3-digit level is presented where possible. Appendix A contains detailed industry lists at the 2-digit and 3-digit levels. The data are not available at any finer level of disaggregation. It should be added that even the most disaggregated input-output table for Canada, at the worksheet level, presents only 300 industries, 206 of them goods-producing, 81 services-producing and 13 non-business and fictitious industries.[3]

Growth in services industries should not be seen as coming at the expense of other sectors in the economy. Rather it reflects ongoing structural changes in a dynamic economy. In many cases, services complement the outputs of other sectors. This is especially so for manufacturing. For example, a well functioning economy needs well-established financial, transportation and distribution services. Similarly, although services are not as widely traded internationally as are manufacturing goods, they are associated with and support every international transaction. In recent years, the distinction between manufacturing and services has become more blurred since services are often bundled into the sale of many manufactured goods.

In overall sectoral comparisons, the services sector still seems to lag behind manufacturing in many respects. However, the overall performance of services-producing industries has improved over the years, whether performance is examined in terms of employment, the use of machinery and equipment (M&E), the employment of highly skilled workers, innovation, or participation in international markets. There are some areas where the services sector is leading manufacturing. This is the case, for example, in the production and the use of information and communications technologies and skill-intensity. There are also some services industries that are outperforming manufacturing even in productivity growth and investment in research and development (R&D). Indeed, one point of this study is that the services sector comprises a huge and heterogeneous group of industries: generalizations for the entire sector can sometimes hide more than they reveal.

The rest of the study is organized as follows. The first section provides a comparative overview of the services sector in the G-7 countries. This is followed by a section on the role of services in the Canadian economy. The next section highlights the role of the services sector in employment creation. The section after that combines insights on output and employment, and discusses productivity growth and wage distribution. This is followed by an examination of the interdependence of the services and the goods-producing sectors, looking at input requirements for both goods-producing and services-producing industries. This section also decomposes the use of gross output into intermediate input and final demand components. The study then proceeds to an examination of the capital intensity, skill intensity and ICT investment-intensity of services industries. There is an account of international trade and foreign direct investment which calculates revealed comparative advantage for Canada's services industries vis-à-vis those of the United States, the United Kingdom and Japan. Then there is a discussion of innovation in the services industries after which there is a brief section on the ICT sector and the role of services in ICT, followed by the study's conclusion.

THE SERVICES SECTOR IN G-7 COUNTRIES

THE SERVICES SECTOR PLAYS A KEY ROLE in G-7 economies, accounting for 66 to 77 percent of total value added. Figure 1 shows that the share of services in value added has increased steadily from 1970 through 2002 in all G-7 countries except Canada. In the other six G-7 countries, the average share of services at current dollar gross domestic product (GDP) was higher in the latter half of the 1990s than it was in the first half. In Canada, however, the share of services increased from about 60 to 70 percent over the period from 1970 to 1992, but then declined to about 66 percent in the latter half of the 1990s. The average share for the period between 1996 and 1999 was 66.5 percent as compared with 67.7 percent for 1990-1995. Once we get the data for 2001 and 2002, we may find that the share of services at current prices increases, as it did in real terms.[4] But, with the data available to us at this point, it seems evident that the importance of services in Canada's GDP relative to other G-7 countries has declined. However, this is not the pattern that emerges when the figures are in real terms. As we will show in the next section, in real terms, the share of services for Canada was constant throughout the 1990s.

Figure 1 shows that until the United Kingdom overtook Canada in 1979, Canada's services sector share of value added was the second largest in the G-7. From 1979 till 1993, Canada had the third largest share of services among G-7 countries. Since then the share of services in Canada has been consistently lower than in almost all of the other G-7 countries, and in 1999 it was the lowest of all. If the relative prices of goods to services in all G-7 countries were changing at the same rate, then the falling relative share of services (at current prices) in Canada would imply that service sector activities in Canada, expressed in real terms, were not advancing at the same pace as in the other six countries. The lack of data on real value added for G-7 countries makes it impossible to check this hypothesis.

Table 1 shows the drastic difference in the importance of the services sector to Canada as compared to the United States. In 2000, the share of services in Canada was significantly lower than it was in the United States in terms of value added (a difference of 9 percentage points), gross production (10 percentage points), total employment (4 percentage points), number of employees (4 percentage points) and hours worked (6 percentage points). The largest gap was in gross fixed capital formation where the Canadian services sector accounted for 57.4 percent and the U.S. services sector contributed 75.6 percent, a difference of 18 percentage points.

Over the past two decades, the share of services in total value added has been higher in the United States than in Canada and the gap is widening. Though shares of both the business and non-business sectors are higher in the United States, the widening gap has been primarily driven by

FIGURE 1

SERVICES SECTOR SHARE OF TOTAL VALUE ADDED AT CURRENT PRICES FOR G-7 COUNTRIES

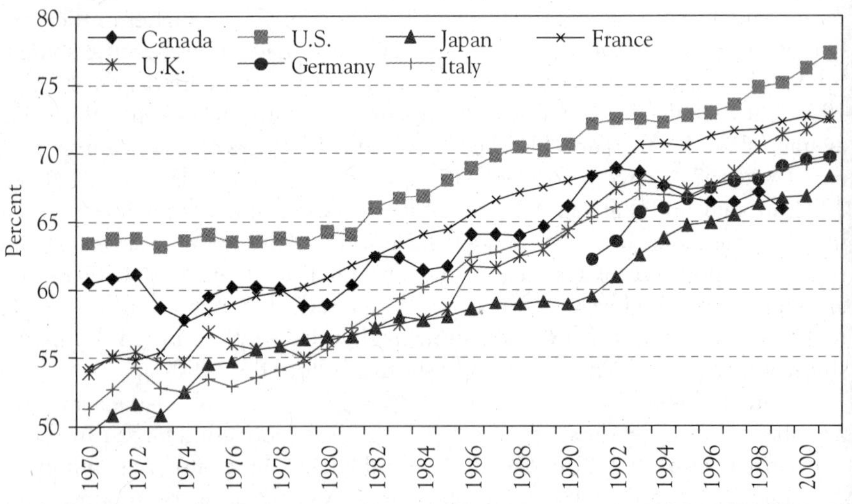

Source: Organisation for Economic Co-operation and Development (OECD), Structural Analysis (STAN) database.

TABLE 1

SHARE OF SERVICES-PRODUCING INDUSTRIES IN CANADA AND THE UNITED STATES (PERCENT)

	CANADA			UNITED STATES		
	1980	1990	2000	1980	1990	2000
Value Added at Current Prices	58.9	66.1	65.9	64.2	70.6	75.1
Gross Production at Current Prices[a]	46.7	54.8	55.0		60.1	65.2
Total Employment, Number Engaged	67.0	71.4	74.2	70.2	75.5	78.3
Number of Employees	68.7	72.7	74.6	70.9	76.2	79.0
Hours Worked	64.2	68.3	70.9	67.6	72.7	75.7
Gross Fixed Capital Formation at Current Prices	43.4	57.0	57.4	57.9	68.8	75.6

Note: a. The figures labelled for year 2000 are actually for year 1999, as the data on gross production for year 2000 in Canada are not yet available.

Source: OECD, STAN database.

TABLE 2

INDUSTRY SHARE IN VALUE ADDED IN CANADA AND THE UNITED STATES (PERCENT)

	CANADA			UNITED STATES		
	1980	1990	1999	1980	1990	1999
TOTAL SERVICES	**58.9**	**66.1**	**65.9**	**64.2**	**70.6**	**75.1**
Business Sector Services[5]	*39.5*	*44.4*	*46.2*	*44.0*	*48.4*	*53.8*
Trade	11.7	11.9	11.3	16.8	16.4	17.2
Hotels and Restaurants	2.6	2.7	2.4	0.7	0.8	0.9
Transport and Storage	5.2	4.2	4.3	3.7	3.1	3.3
Post and Telecommunications	2.8	3.0	2.8	3.2	3.2	3.4
Financial Intermediaries	4.8	6.0	6.9	4.6	5.9	8.1
Real Estate, Renting and Business Activities	12.3	16.7	18.5	15.0	19.0	21.0
Non-business Sector Services	*19.5*	*21.7*	*19.8*	*19.9*	*22.0*	*21.1*
Public Administration and Defense; Compulsory Social Security	6.6	6.9	5.7	13.1	13.2	11.7
Education	5.6	5.5	4.9	0.6	0.7	0.8
Health and Social Work	5.1	6.5	6.1	4.4	5.9	6.2
Other Community, Social and Personal Services	2.2	2.8	3.0	1.9	2.2	2.4

Note: The industries are arranged according to the International Standard Industrial Classification (ISIC).

Source: OECD, STAN database.

changes in the business sector. Table 2 shows that shares of value added for all U.S. business sector services were higher in 1999 than in 1990. In contrast, in Canada, shares of trade, hotels and restaurants, and post and telecommunication industries fell over the same period. Furthermore, even among industries where the share of total value added has grown in both countries, growth rates are higher in the United States than in Canada. This is the case for financial intermediaries and real estate.[6]

The share of non-business sector services industries has remained relatively flat in both countries and it is of roughly the same importance to the economy in both countries: the huge share that public administration and defence accounts for in the United States is offset by the relatively large educational sector in Canada.

Real Growth in Services in Canada

In real as opposed to nominal terms, Canada's services sector growth has outpaced overall economic growth for decades. As a result, the share of services in total economic activity has increased over time.[7] The share of services in real GDP rose to 69 percent in 2001-2002 from about 66 percent in 1981-1982 and settled at about 68 percent in 1991-1992 (Table 3). It remained at that level throughout the 1990s, eventually returning to 69 percent in 2001-2002.

In light of the increasing role of knowledge-based service-oriented activities, we may expect to see the services share in the economy continue to rise and perhaps even accelerate in the future. On the other hand, looking at the relatively stable services share in the 1990s and an increase of just one percentage point in recent years, one is led to wonder whether the share of services in GDP will, in fact, continue to rise.

Even though the education, public administration, health care and social assistance sectors grew faster in the 1990s than in the 1980s, their shares in total GDP declined since their growth rates did not keep pace with other sectors. On the other hand, industries such as professional, scientific and technical services, information and cultural services, and wholesale trade increased their shares. They constituted the fastest growing services industries and their growth rates exceeded that of the manufacturing sector.

In comparison with the 1990s, in recent years the shares of business services industries rose and those of non-business services industries (such as health, education and public administration) fell. As a result, in 2001-2002, the share in the total economy accounted for by the whole business sector (both goods and services) rose to 85 percent (leaving only 15 percent for the non-business sector). This was up from 80 percent a decade earlier (Figure 2).[8] The rise in the share of services-producing industries in the business sector more than compensated for the fall in the share of goods-producing industries. In the 1990s, the business sector was 80 percent of the economy, with 32 percent of that share accounted for by goods-producing industries and 48 percent contributed by services-producing industries. By 2001-2002, the business sector constituted 85 percent of the economy and within that total, the services sector accounted for 54 percent and the goods sector made up the remaining 31 percent. In terms of the non-business part of the economy, almost all of it (98 percent) is accounted for by the services sector.

TABLE 3

DISTRIBUTION AND GROWTH OF REAL GDP FOR THE CANADIAN ECONOMY (1997 PRICES)

	SHARE			GROWTH RATE[a]	
	1981-1982	1991-1992	2001-2002	1991-1992 OVER 1981-1982	2001-2002 OVER 1991-1992
ALL INDUSTRIES	**100.0**	**100.0**	**100.0**	**2.4**	**3.2**
Goods-producing Industries	*34.2*	*32.1*	*31.0*	*1.7*	*2.9*
Manufacturing	16.3	15.7	16.9	2.0	4.0
Services-producing Industries	*65.8*	*67.9*	*69.0*	*2.7*	*3.4*
Wholesale Trade	3.4	4.8	5.9	5.9	5.3
Retail Trade	5.8	5.4	5.6	1.6	3.7
Transportation and Warehousing	4.5	4.6	4.6	2.6	3.4
Information and Cultural Industries	2.5	3.2	4.5	4.8	7.1
FIRRMC[b]	17.8	19.0	19.8	3.1	3.7
Professional, Scientific and Technical	2.6	2.9	4.7	3.6	8.3
Administrative and Support, Waste Management and Remediation	1.6	2.2	2.1	5.3	3.2
Educational Services	6.7	6.1	4.6	1.3	0.4
Health Care and Social Assistance	6.9	7.3	5.8	3.0	0.9
Arts, Entertainment and Recreation	1.1	0.9	0.9	0.7	3.6
Accommodation and Food Services	3.2	2.5	2.4	–0.4	2.9
Other Services (Except Public Administration)	2.1	2.1	2.3	2.2	4.1
Public Administration	7.3	7.1	5.7	2.0	0.9

Notes: a. Average annual compound growth rates.
b. Finance and insurance, real estate and renting and leasing and management of companies and enterprises. It includes three NAICS 2-digit industries (NAICS 52 — finance and insurance, NAICS 53 — real estate and rental and leasing and NAICS 55 — management of companies and enterprises).

Source: Statistics Canada, CANSIM Table no. 379-0017.

FIGURE 2

SHARE OF REAL GDP IN CANADA (IN PERCENT)

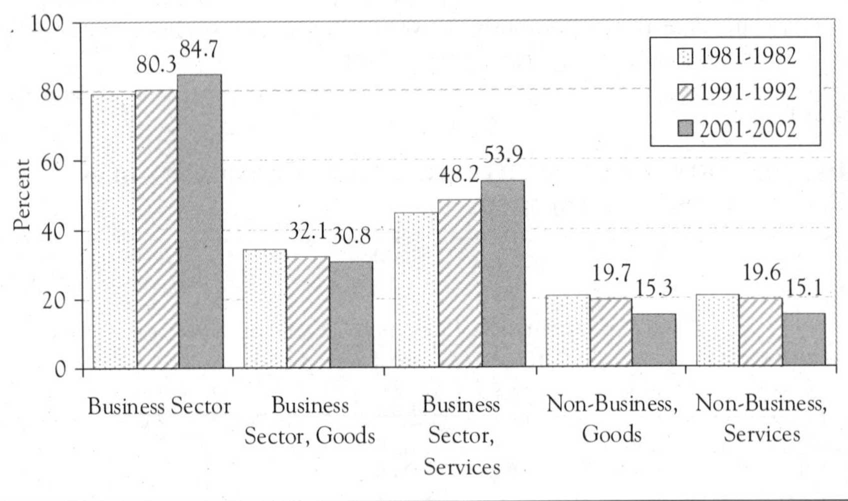

Source: Statistics Canada.

Such trends indicate that the Canadian economy is becoming more services-oriented, albeit at a slow pace. It also suggests that this is happening because of the falling shares of other non-manufacturing goods-producing industries (e.g. construction, utilities and agriculture). In contrast, the share of manufacturing in total GDP has increased by more than one percentage point (a higher percentage point increase than the services sector) in 2001-2002 compared with 1991-1992.

EMPLOYMENT IN SERVICES

IN TERMS OF EMPLOYMENT, the services sector accounted for 90 percent of total job creation in Canada between 1976 and 2002. As a result, the share of employment in the services sector rose from 66 percent in 1976-1977 to 74 percent in 2001-2002 (Table 4). This increase largely took place during the 1980s with the services shares of employment reaching 73 percent by 1991-92. The retail industry accounted for the largest share of employment in this period (12 percent of the total employment in the economy) followed by health care and social assistance at 10 percent, and then by professional, scientific and technical, educational services, and by accommodation and food services, each of which had shares of 6.5 percent. Employment growth between 1991 and 2002 was strongest for the industry called management of companies and enterprises and administration and support (MCAS). Its annual compound growth rate was

6 percent. Another industry that recorded a very high annual growth rate (5 percent) was professional, scientific and technical services, which increased its overall share in total employment by 1.8 percentage points. Employment in the information, cultural and recreation industry also grew annually by a healthy rate of 3.6 percent. The employment restructuring that occurred in the 1990s also involved a shrinkage in the employment shares for finance and insurance, real estate and leasing, and public administration.

TABLE 4

AVERAGE ANNUAL INDUSTRY SHARE OF EMPLOYMENT (PERCENT)

	TOTAL EMPLOYMENT			FULL-TIME EMPLOYMENT		PART-TIME EMPLOYMENT	
	1976-77	1991-92	2001-02	1991-92	2001-02	1991-92	2001-02
Goods-producing Sector	*33.9*	*27.0*	*25.6*	*30.5*	*29.6*	*11.6*	*8.1*
Manufacturing	18.7	14.5	15.1	17.0	17.8	3.3	3.0
Services-producing Sector	*66.1*	*73.0*	*74.4*	*69.5*	*70.4*	*88.4*	*91.9*
Wholesale Trade	NA	3.2	3.6	3.6	4.1	1.5	1.5
Retail Trade	NA	12.8	12.2	10.6	9.9	22.5	22.0
Transportation and Warehousing	5.7	4.8	5.0	5.2	5.4	3.4	3.1
Finance and Insurance	NA	4.5	4.2	4.8	4.6	3.1	2.7
Real Estate and Leasing	NA	2.0	1.6	2.0	1.5	2.2	1.9
Professional, Scientific and Technical	2.7	4.7	6.5	5.0	6.9	3.3	4.8
MCAS[a]	1.7	2.5	3.8	2.3	3.5	3.5	5.0
Educational Services	6.8	6.8	6.5	6.6	5.9	7.7	9.2
Health Care and Social Assistance	8.1	10.3	10.3	9.2	9.5	15.3	14.2
Information, Culture and Recreation[b]	3.7	3.9	4.6	3.7	4.3	4.7	6.1
Accommodation and Food Services	4.6	6.0	6.5	4.5	4.8	12.8	14.0
Other Services (Except Public Administration)	4.4	4.7	4.5	4.4	4.3	5.9	5.6
Public Administration	6.6	6.7	5.1	7.6	5.8	2.8	2.0

Notes: The data in the table include both employees and the self-employed. The share calculation is based on the number of people employed, not on the number of hours worked. The sum across industries adds up to 100.

NA: data not available.

a. Management of companies and enterprises and administration and support, waste management and remediation services. It includes 2 NAICS 2-digit industries (NAICS 55 — management of companies and enterprises and NAICS 56 — administrative and support, waste management and remediation services).

b. This includes 2 NAICS 2-digit industries (NAICS 51 — information and culture and NAICS 71 — arts entertainment and recreation).

Source: Statistics Canada, Labour Force Survey, CANSIM Table 282-0008.

The share of services employment differed substantially for full-time and part-time workers. In 2001-2002, only 70 percent of all full-time employees worked in the services sector. In contrast, 92 percent of all part-time employees worked in services. Even though the proportion of part-time employment to total employment remained the same for the economy as a whole over this period (see the discussion below), the share of part-time workers that were employed in the services sector increased from 88 percent in 1991-1992 to 92 percent in 2001-2002. At the same time, part-time employment in the goods-producing sector fell from 12 percent to 8 percent. In 2001-2002, the industries that saw increases in the share of part-time employment included: professional, scientific and technical services, MCAS, education, information, cultural and recreation services, as well as accommodation and food industries.

Moving beyond the composition of total employment, another interesting issue is how each industry's employment is distributed between part-time and full-time workers, between employees and the self-employed, and between public- and private-sector employment. This breakdown is shown in Table 5. This table reveals that the falling share of full-time employment that Canada experienced in the 1980s stabilized in the 1990s. The share of full-time employment in the economy fell from 87 percent in 1976-77 to 82 percent in 1991-92 and remained at that level through 2001-2002. In the 1980s, the falling trend of full-time workers was due entirely to changes in the services sector, where the share of full-time employment fell from 83 percent in 1976-77 to 77.6 percent in 1991-1992 and remained at that level a full decade later. This stability in the share of full-time workers in total services employment is mirrored by the fact that the share of part-time employment has also remained stable (22.4 percent in 1991-1992 and 22.8 percent in 2001-2002). The constant share of part-time workers in total services employment shown in Table 5 implies that the full-time and part-time workers are increasing at the same pace. Overall, the services sector's share of part-time workers rose (Table 4) as the numbers of part-time workers in goods-producing industries fell.

There has been little change within the services sector industries in the proportion of full-time to part-time employees. Some industries such as transportation and warehousing and educational services saw small increases in the share of full-time employment, whereas there were decreases in others, including the health care and social assistance, and information, culture and recreation industries.

Trends in self-employment moved in opposite directions in the services and goods-producing sectors between 1991-1992 and 2001-2002: self-employment as a proportion of total employment fell in the goods-producing sector but it increased in services. As Table 5 shows, however, in 2001-2002, there were still proportionately more people who were self-employed in the goods sector (16.1 percent of total goods sector employment) than in the services sector (15 percent). The share of the self-employed in total employment rose in all services

TABLE 5

AVERAGE ANNUAL SHARE OF EMPLOYMENT BY NATURE AND CLASS OF WORKERS (PERCENT)

	SHARE OF FULL-TIME EMPLOYMENT IN TOTAL EMPLOYMENT[a]			SHARE OF SELF-EMPLOYED IN TOTAL EMPLOYMENT[b]		SHARE OF PUBLIC EMPLOYEES IN TOTAL EMPLOYMENT[c]	
INDUSTRIES	1976-77	1991-92	2001-02	1991-92	2001-02	1991-92	2001-02
All Industries	**87.0**	**81.5**	**81.6**	**14.9**	**15.3**	**25.6**	**22.2**
Goods-producing Sector	*94.6*	*92.1*	*94.2*	*19.5*	*16.1*	*6.1*	*3.9*
Manufacturing	97.3	95.7	96.4	5.0	4.3	0.4	0.1
Services-producing Sector	*83.1*	*77.6*	*77.2*	*13.2*	*15.0*	*32.4*	*28.5*
Trade	77.7	72.4	72.6	14.9	12.6	1.2	1.0
Transportation and Warehousing	92.2	87.0	88.6	13.8	17.3	29.2	22.1
FIRE[d]	91.0	85.2	85.4	11.0	14.6	6.0	6.6
Professional, Scientific and Technical	90.7	86.8	86.5	31.3	32.9	1.9	1.3
MCAS[e]	81.5	74.6	75.6	21.9	25.5	2.4	1.3
Educational Services	83.2	79.2	74.0	2.4	4.7	90.0	91.8
Health Care and Social Assistance	80.5	72.7	74.8	11.2	12.0	59.9	56.1
Information, Culture and Recreation	83.6	77.5	75.8	12.4	14.3	18.1	15.6
Accommodation and Food Services	69.1	60.9	60.4	10.0	9.9	N	N
Other Services (Except Public Administration)	78.9	76.7	76.9	29.6	33.3	0.7	N
Public Administration	94.5	92.4	92.9	0.1	0.0	98.2	99.7

Notes: "N" stands for negligible amount; however, since the data were suppressed, we cannot find the exact share. Checking data for total and private employees, it turns out that the share of public employees was less than 0.1 percent in these industries.
a. The data include both employees and the self-employed, and the remaining percent is covered by part-time employment.
b. The remaining percent is covered by employees.
c. The remaining percent is covered by private employees.
d. Finance and insurance and real estate as well as rental and leasing.
e. Management of companies and enterprises and administration and support, waste management and remediation services (industries with NAICS codes 55 and 56).

Source: Statistics Canada, Labour Force Survey, CANSIM Table 282-0008.

industries except in trade and in accommodation and food services. The largest increases in the shares of the self-employed were seen in transportation and warehousing, finance and real estate, MCAS, and professional, scientific and technical services. These are all industries in which one third of all workers are self-employed. In terms of the differences between private- and public-sector employment, health care and social assistance, educational services, and public administration are sectors with a majority of public-sector employees. Not surprisingly, almost all workers in public administration are public-sector employees.

Next, we look at the distribution of employees (excluding the self-employed) by establishment size. It appears that higher proportions of services employees are working in establishments with a small number of employees compared with the situation in the goods-producing sector. Based on data for 1997-2002, only 26 percent of employees in the goods-producing sector were working in establishments with fewer than 20 employees compared to 36 percent in the services sector (Table 6). Other services such as accommodation

TABLE 6

SHARE OF EMPLOYEES BY ESTABLISHMENT SIZE, 1997-2002 (PERCENT)

INDUSTRIES	WITH FEWER THAN 20 EMPLOYEES	WITH 20 TO 99 EMPLOYEES	WITH 100 TO 500 EMPLOYEES	WITH MORE THAN 500 EMPLOYEES
All Industries	**34.0**	**32.6**	**21.2**	**12.2**
Goods-producing	*25.9*	*29.9*	*28.6*	*15.5*
Manufacturing	15.9	30.3	34.9	18.8
Services-producing	*36.7*	*33.5*	*18.7*	*11.1*
Trade	44.0	36.6	16.8	2.6
Transportation and Warehousing	27.0	32.9	25.4	14.7
Finance, Insurance, Real Estate and Leasing	38.6	33.1	16.9	11.5
Professional, Scientific and Technical	39.1	32.1	21.1	7.7
MCAS[a]	48.1	29.8	16.2	5.9
Educational Services	17.8	46.5	18.5	17.2
Health Care and Social Assistance	30.2	24.2	23.0	22.5
Information, Culture and Recreation	28.1	32.1	23.1	16.7
Accommodation and Food Services	49.1	40.6	8.7	1.7
Other Services (Except Public Administration)	72.9	19.3	6.4	1.4
Public Administration	21.5	31.0	27.6	19.9

Note: a. management of companies and enterprises and administration and support, waste management and remediation services (industries with NAICS codes 55 and 56).

Source: Statistics Canada, Labour Force Survey, CANSIM Table 282-0076.

and food, MCAS, and transportation and warehousing are characterized by a high proportion of employees working in establishments of 20 employees or less. In contrast, transport and warehousing, educational services, health care and social assistance, and information, culture and recreation were sectors with a relatively high share of workers employed in large establishments with more than 500 employees.

In terms of gender, the majority of employees in the services industries are female. They constitute as much as 84 percent of the employees in health care and social assistance (Figure 3). More than 60 percent of the employees in finance and insurance, real estate and leasing, educational services, and accommodation and food industries are female.

The share of young employees between ages 15-24 years of age is also higher in services than in manufacturing. About 18 percent of all services-sector employees fall into this age group.

To sum up, the services sector accounts for 70 percent of all full-time employment in Canada, a share comparable to its 69 percent contribution to real GDP. However, the services sector has proportionately more part-time employment than its share of GDP, and its share of part-time employment has remained stable over the past decade. The share of self-employment has been rising in the services industries. More people working in services are employed in smaller establishments: more than 70 percent of services employees work in establishments with fewer than 100 employees. In manufacturing, the comparable figure is only 46 percent. There are more women working in the services sector than in the goods sector. The proportion of young employees is also larger in services than in the goods-producing sector.

FIGURE 3

GENDER AND AGE CHARACTERISTICS OF EMPLOYEES, 1997-2002 (PERCENT)

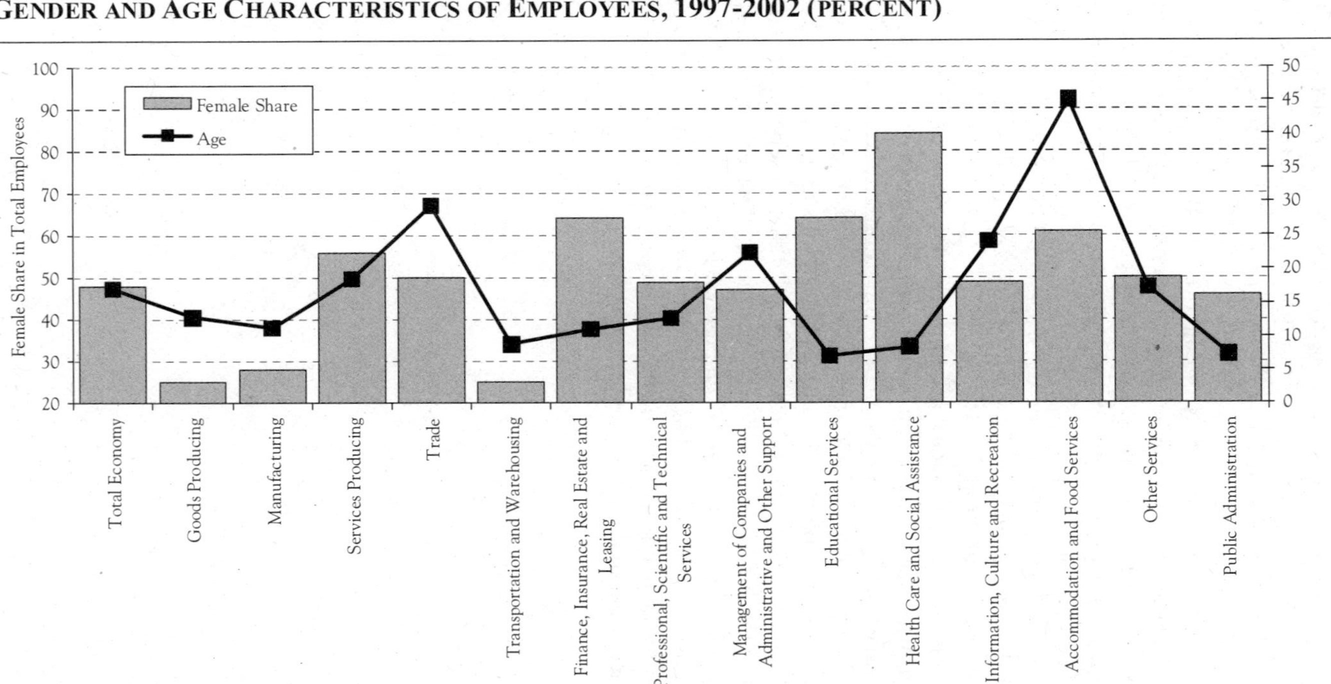

Source: Statistics Canada, Labour Force Survey. CANSIM Table 282-0076.

PRODUCTIVITY AND WAGES IN SERVICES

SO FAR, SERVICES OUTPUT AND EMPLOYMENT have been presented separately. This section brings them together to consider the role of services in the growth of labour productivity. Standard indicators of labour productivity show that the services contribution to overall productivity growth is relatively limited compared to the size of the sector. In the past two decades, half or more of the productivity growth in the business sector was attributable to manufacturing. In certain instances, however, services sector industries did make important contributions. For example, in 1990-2000 retail trade and telecommunication carriers industries achieved a higher annual productivity growth rate than that of the manufacturing sector (Figure 4).

It is observable that there is lower labour productivity growth measured for the services sector and for its components. This may, however, be due to problems with measuring output that are more acute in services than in manufacturing. As Triplett and Bosworth (2001) have argued, what would be the output of an insurance company? What is the output of a consulting firm

FIGURE 4

COMPOUND ANNUAL PRODUCTIVITY GROWTH RATE, 1980-2000 (PERCENT)

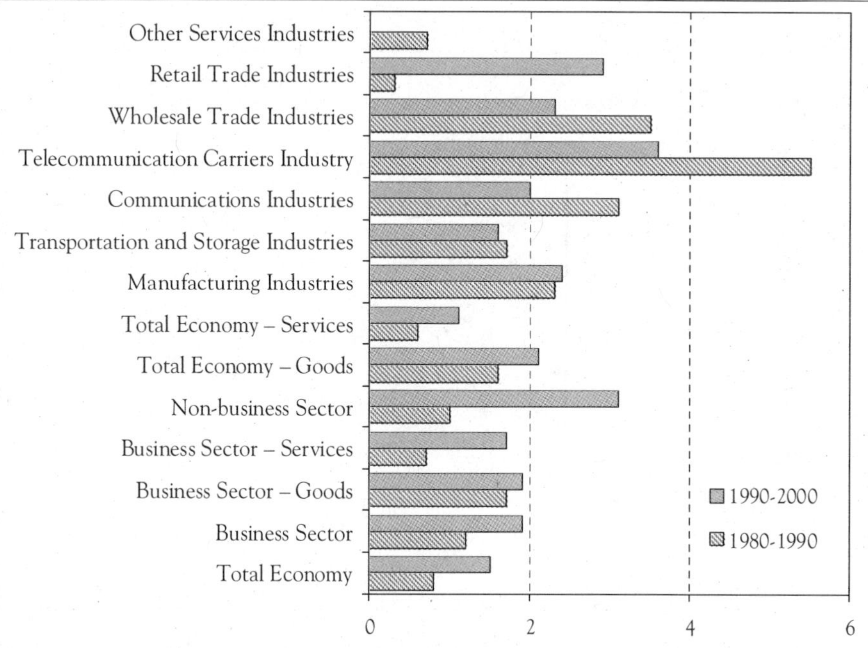

Source: Statistics Canada.

specializing in economics or statistics? In what units would those outputs be measured? When the economic concept to be measured is not clear, the output measure and price indexes are necessarily problematic. Similarly, in an effort to analyze the productivity paradox caused by measurement error, Diewert and Fox (1999) convincingly argue that the proliferation of new products and new processes could have led to a systematic underestimation of productivity growth. This measurement problem could be the reason that we see negative productivity growth in some services industries over a long period!

The productivity growth of an industry should somehow be reflected in wage rates. As industries become more productive, their hourly wage rates would be expected to rise. Hence, one could expect the hourly wage of the goods sector to be higher than that of the services sector. It is generally considered that the average services-sector job tends to be low-skilled, but services also contain some of the best-paid and most highly skilled jobs. Figure 5 plots the hourly wage rates in 84 industries (29 in goods and 55 in services). The numbers on the x-axis are the numbers corresponding to the NAICS codes given in Appendix A. To differentiate the goods and services parts of the economy, we have drawn a vertical line, keeping goods-producing industries on the left and services-producing industries on the right.

FIGURE 5

AVERAGE HOURLY WAGE, BY INDUSTRY (1998-2001)

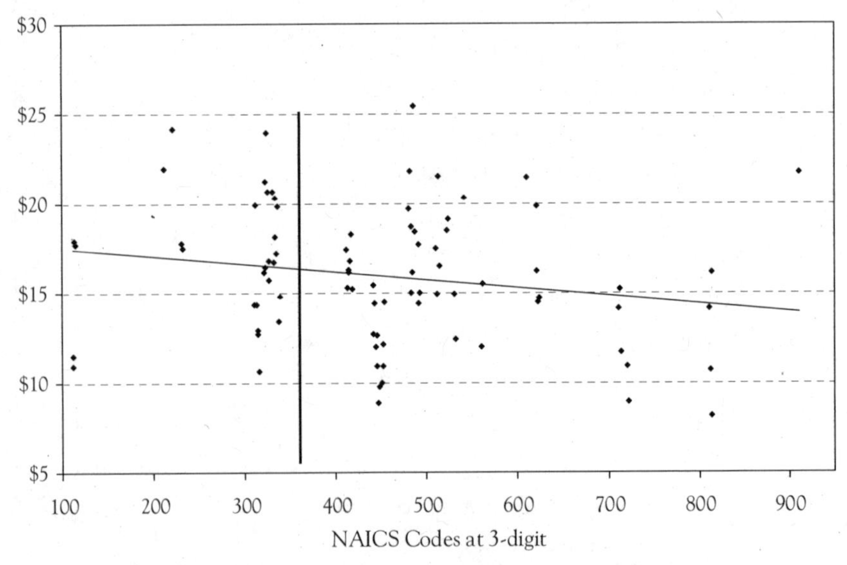

Note: Four industries with NAICS 3-digit codes of 912, 913, 914 and 915 are not included in the graph because data are not available.

Source: Statistics Canada, Labour Force Survey.

The higher average hourly wage in the goods sector compared with services is depicted by the downward sloping line in the graph. As we move to the right of the vertical line, we are dealing with services industries. For example, taking $15 an hour as a comparison point, we see that proportionately more goods-producing industries are above that level than is the case for services. However, there is not much difference between the two sectors in the dispersion of the hourly wage distribution. For example, the hourly wage rate in 19 goods-producing industries out of 29 (66 percent) and 37 services-producing industries (67 percent) falls within the range of one standard deviation from the mean.

Given that the overall average hourly wage in the goods sector is higher than the average hourly wage in the services sector, the next question is how this wage gap has changed over time for the two sectors and across workers with different levels of educational attainment (skill levels). In order to evaluate the change that is taking place in hourly wages, we compute the share of employees in the goods (services) sector who were paid less (more) than the average hourly wage in the services (goods) sector. We do that by taking data from 286 industries (some at 3-digit and some at 4-digit NAICS levels) for two time periods, 1991-1992 and 2001-2002. Table 7 shows that there are industries in the goods sector with an average hourly wage that is lower than the average hourly wage in the services sector. However, the salaried workers in these industries expressed as a share of total goods-sector employment has fallen from 34 percent in 1991-1992 to 23 percent in 2001-2002. The proportion of hourly-paid employees has remained constant at about 17 percent for this period. Thus overall, the share of goods sector employees who receive less than the average hourly wage in the services sector has declined.

Another perspective is offered by columns 3 and 4 of Table 7. They show that there are services industries which are paying more than the average hourly wage in the goods sector. Moreover, the share of employees in these industries compared to the total services sector has increased for salaried employees (from 8 to 11 percent) and decreased for hourly paid employees (from 27 to 25 percent). The share of salaried employees in the goods sector who are paid less than the services sector average has fallen, and the share of salaried employees in the services sector who are paid more than the goods sector average has risen. This implies that the dispersion in the distribution of the hourly wage is increasing in the services sector. Overall service-sector wages have not been keeping pace with goods-sector wages. Indeed, the average relative salary of salaried employees in the services sector vis-à-vis the goods sector has fallen from 88 percent in 1991-1992 to 83 percent in 2001-2002.

The industry-specific wages of hourly-paid employees are converging; the share of employees in the goods sector who receive less than the average in the services sector has remained almost constant, and the share of employees in the services sector who are paid more than in the goods sector average has fallen. The average relative hourly wage in the services sector vis-à-vis the goods sector rose to 80 percent in 2001-2002 from 78 percent in 1991-1992.

TABLE 7

SHARE OF EMPLOYMENT (PERCENT)

	In Goods-Producing Sector with Average Hourly Wage less than the Average Hourly Wage in Services-Producing Sector		In Services-Producing Sector with Average Hourly Wage more than the Average Hourly Wage in Goods-Producing Sector	
	Salaried Employees	Hourly Paid Employees	Salaried Employees	Hourly Paid Employees
1991-1992	33.9	16.9	8.1	26.5
2001-2002	23.2	17.4	11.4	24.6

Note: For this table, first we computed two average hourly wages for 1991-1992 and 2001-2002 for all industries for both salaried employees and hourly-paid employees. Second, we took the series for salaried employees and separated all industries into the *goods sector* whose average hourly wage was *lower* than the average hourly wage in the services sector in the 1991-1992 period and computed the share of employment of these industries in total employment in the goods sector. This result is given in row 1, column 1. We repeated the same process for year 2001-2002, and the result is given in row 2, column 1. Next, we took the series on hourly-paid employees and repeated the process above, with the results that are reported in row 1, column 2 and row 2, column 2. Next, we separated all industries in the *services sector* whose average hourly wage was *higher* than the average hourly wage in the goods sector for years 1991-1992 and computed the share of employment of these industries in total employment in the services sector. The result is given in row 1, column 3. The result for year 2001-2002 is given in row 2, column 3. We repeated the same process for hourly-paid employees, and the result is reported in the last column.

Source: Statistics Canada, Survey of Employment, Payrolls and Hours (SEPH), CANSIM Table 281-0024.

Another data source (Table 8) shows that between 1969 and 1997, the real hourly wage of workers in the goods sector rose annually by 1.8 percent in the goods sector and by 0.2 percent in the services sector. However, the trend was different across decades and across educational attainment groups in the services sector. In the 1970s (1969-1979), the real hourly wage of workers with post secondary and university degrees fell and that of workers with less than high school education rose, exactly compensating for the fall for more educated workers. In the 1980s (1979-1988), the real wage of all workers fell, except for university graduates whose rate rose at a pace comparable to that of their counterparts in the goods-producing sector. In the 1990s (1988-1997), the real wage of workers in all educational attainment groups rose, with a huge acceleration for university-educated workers (an annual rise of 5.3 percent). Even though the real wage for the services sector as a whole did not rise faster than in the goods sector in any of the decades examined, in the 1990s, the real wages of highly educated workers rose faster in the services sector than they did in the goods sector.

TABLE 8

ANNUAL CHANGES IN REAL HOURLY WAGES BY EDUCATIONAL ATTAINMENT (PERCENT)

GROUP OF WORKERS	1969-1979	1979-1988	1988-1997	1969-1997
Goods-producing Industries				
All	*1.3*	*2.0*	*1.9*	*1.8*
0-8 Years of Schooling	2.7	2.2	–0.2	1.6
Some or Completed High School	1.2	2.0	1.0	1.4
Post Secondary Education	0.2	1.7	2.1	1.3
University Degree or More	–4.3	2.9	4.8	1.0
Services-producing Industries				
All	*0.0*	*–1.3*	*1.8*	*0.2*
0-8 Years of Schooling	1.9	–1.0	1.2	0.8
Some or Completed High School	0.1	–1.3	1.0	–0.1
Post Secondary Education	–1.2	–1.7	1.8	–0.4
University Degree or More	–6.7	2.8	5.3	0.2

Note: This table is prepared using data on 119 industries by SIC code. To obtain this table, we deflated the total amount of wages and salaries for each group of workers for each of 119 industries by its Fisher price index of gross output (indexed 1992 = 100) for each year. This industry-wide real wage was then divided by the number of hours worked to obtain the hourly real wage for each type of labour in each industry and year. Then for each group and industry, we took the log difference of the hourly wage of the first and the last years of each period, multiplied it by 100 and divided it by the number of years in that period. Then, we obtained an annual weighted average of hourly real wage changes of different labour groups, the weight being each industry's average share of the wage bill, and the average taken from the first and last years of each period. For example, for the sub-period 1969-1979, the industry's average wage bill share for 1969 and 1979 was taken as the weight.

Source: Statistics Canada.

Table 8 shows that the pattern of no change or a falling trend in real wages for services sector employees in the 1970s and the 1980s was reversed in the 1990s. Even so, the rate of increase in real wages in services was slightly lower than in the goods sector. As a result, the gap in hourly wages between the two sectors continued to diverge over time, though at a slower pace. Also, the share of employees in the services sector who earned more than the average hourly wage in the goods sector rose. This rise came from those services industries that employed a larger proportion of university-educated workers.

INTERDEPENDENCE BETWEEN THE GOODS AND SERVICES SECTORS

THE ROLE OF SERVICES in overall economic activity is growing. This reflects higher consumer and business demand as well as outsourcing of services-related activities from manufacturing firms (Avery 1999). It is argued that a growing number of goods-producing industries are outsourcing services jobs that were previously performed in-house. As a result, interdependence between the two sectors is rising. Furthermore, as information and telecommunication technology produced by both goods and services sectors is being used by the other sector more intensively, one would expect additional interdependence over time. The objective of this section is to examine evidence for this interdependence over the past three decades using Canada's input-output tables.

Table 9 shows the distribution of $100 in costs for the production of $100 in revenue in each goods-producing industry.[9] The last column shows that in order to generate $100 of revenue in 1997-1999, the good-producing sector used 44.6 percent of its revenue as input from the goods-producing industries, 11.2 percent as input from the services-producing industries, 5.4 percent as input from fictitious industries and the non-business sector, and the remaining 38.8 percent was paid to labour and capital as value added. It is clear that the goods-producing sector became more dependent on service-producing industries as the input content of the latter rose to 11 percent in 1997-99 from only 7.6 percent in 1967-69. This trend could also be due to outsourcing and changes in production structure. The services industries with lower proportions of input attributable to goods-producing industries include wholesale trade, and professional, scientific and technical services. Note also that interdependence among the goods-producing industries has not changed, but their shares of value added in their total revenue have fallen over time since they are using more inputs from services industries.

Interestingly, the goods-producing share of input into the production of services has fallen slightly over the years (Table 10). However, services-producing industries are using more inputs produced by other services industries. In the 1997-99 period, 21 percent of the revenue of the services-producing industries was spent to buy inputs from other services-producing industries, an increase of 9 percentage point over the 12 percent recorded in 1967-69. Here too, the biggest input increases came from the professional, scientific and technical services as well as the information and cultural industries. The share of value added in the services industries has also fallen, as it has in the goods-producing sector. However, since the services-producing industries used fewer intermediate inputs, their value added share in total revenue was 63 percent compared to 39 percent for the goods-producing industries in 1997-99.

TABLE 9

COST COMPOSITION FOR GOODS-PRODUCING INDUSTRIES[a]

	1967-1969	1977-1979	1987-1989	1997-1999
Goods-producing	*42.6*	*44.0*	*43.3*	*44.6*
Services-producing	*7.6*	*8.0*	*9.4*	*11.2*
Wholesale Trade	2.4	2.5	2.7	3.0
Retail Trade	0.8	0.7	0.6	0.4
Transportation and Warehousing	1.0	0.8	0.7	0.7
Information and Cultural Industries	0.4	0.4	0.3	0.4
Finance and Insurance	0.6	0.8	1.0	1.2
Real Estate and Rental and Leasing	0.0	0.0	0.7	0.6
Professional, Scientific and Technical Services	1.2	1.2	1.8	2.7
Management of Companies and Enterprises	0.8	0.8	1.1	1.0
Administrative and Support, Waste Management	0.1	0.4	0.4	0.8
Other Services (Excluding Public Administration)	0.3	0.4	0.1	0.4
Fictitious Industries and Non-business Sector	*6.2*	*5.3*	*5.5*	*5.4*
Value Added	*43.6*	*42.6*	*41.7*	*38.8*
Total Cost (= Revenue)	***100.0***	***100.0***	***100.0***	***100.0***

Notes: The input coefficients of (1) educational services, (2) health care and social assistance, (3) arts, entertainment and recreation (4) accommodation and food services and (5) public administration for goods-producing industries were 0s to 3 decimal places. Hence, these industries are not included in the table.

a. The input-output table based on NAICS code at the Link (L) level was used for this computation. At the Link level, there are a total of 113 industries for the whole economy. Out of these 113 industries, 92 real and 7 fictitious industries are in the business sector and the remaining 14 are in the non-business sector. Out of 92 business sector industries, 65 are goods-producing and 27 are services-producing industries. Furthermore, 5 of 14 non-business industries are classified as part of the services-producing category. Therefore, the total number of services industries in the L-level input-output tables are 32 vis-à-vis 65 goods-producing industries. The remaining 16, consisting of 7 fictitious and 9 non-business industries, are not classified by NAICS number and in the above table, they are aggregated under the third row from the bottom.

Source: Statistics Canada, input-output tables for various years.

The use of output from services-producing industries in the production of both goods and services is rising. This implies an increase in the share of gross production used as intermediate input. Table 11 shows the decomposition of how industry gross output is distributed between intermediate input and final demand. Indeed, the shares of gross output from both goods-producing and services-producing industries that were used for intermediate inputs have increased over time. In 1997-1999, two-thirds of the gross output of manufacturing and 48 percent

TABLE 10
COST COMPOSITION FOR SERVICES-PRODUCING INDUSTRIES

	1967-1969	1977-1979	1987-1989	1997-1999
Goods-producing	8.9	9.1	8.4	7.2
Services-producing	*12.1*	*14.3*	*17.0*	*21.1*
Wholesale Trade	0.8	0.8	1.1	1.3
Retail Trade	0.6	0.6	0.6	0.7
Transportation and Warehousing	2.6	2.6	2.6	2.9
Information and Cultural Industries	1.5	1.8	1.9	2.3
Finance and Insurance	1.8	2.3	2.5	2.3
Real Estate and Rental and Leasing	0.0	0.0	2.3	2.9
Professional, Scientific and Technical Services	0.7	1.0	1.7	2.9
Management of Companies and Enterprises	3.0	3.4	2.3	3.5
Administrative and Support, Waste Management	0.4	1.0	1.7	1.8
Other Services	0.7	0.8	0.3	0.5
Fictitious Industries and Non-business Sector[a]	7.2	6.8	6.9	8.3
Value Added	*71.8*	69.8	67.7	63.4
Total Cost (= revenue)	***100.0***	***100.0***	***100.0***	***100.0***

Notes: The input coefficients of (1) educational services, (2) health care and social assistance, (3) arts, entertainment and recreation (4) accommodation and food services and (5) public administration were 0s at the 3 digit level throughout the periods. As a result, they are not included in the table.

a. It includes 7 fictitious industries and 9 of 14 non-business sector industries. The remaining 5 non-business sector industries are included in the services-producing category.

Source: Statistics Canada, input-output tables for various years.

of the gross output of services industries was used as intermediate input. The shares of gross output used as intermediate inputs rose for real estate, and rental and leasing, for management of companies and enterprises, for administrative and support and waste management, and for accommodation and food services. It fell for wholesale services, transportation and warehousing, information and cultural industries, and professional, scientific and technical services. The industries with the highest shares of output used as intermediate inputs are administrative and support, professional, scientific and technical services, transport and warehousing, and information and cultural industries. On the other hand, education, retail trade, and arts, entertainment and recreation all have relatively lower shares of output used as intermediate inputs. These are industries with output that is used mostly for final consumption.

Comparing the goods and services sectors, we find that the use of the goods sector's output as an intermediate input rose from 55 percent in the 1960s to 59 percent in the late 1990s (an increase of 4 percentage points), whereas the

TABLE 11

SHARE OF GROSS OUTPUT USED AS INTERMEDIATE INPUT FOR THE WHOLE ECONOMY (PERCENT)

	1967-69	1977-79	1987-89	1997-99
Goods-producing Industries	55	56	56	59
Primary, Utilities and Construction	42	46	44	46
Manufacturing	62	62	64	66
Services-producing Industries	39	43	44	48
Wholesale Trade	57	57	54	53
Retail Trade	18	17	16	16
Transportation and Warehousing	81	82	80	77
Information and Cultural Industries	71	71	70	66
Finance and Insurance	47	51	52	47
Real Estate and Rental and Leasing[a]	0	0	31	52
Professional, Scientific and Technical Services	99	97	91	87
Management of Companies and Enterprises	41	47	57	70
Administrative and Support, Waste Management	84	94	91	93
Educational Services	4	5	5	5
Health Care and Social Assistance	8	24	27	33
Arts, Entertainment and Recreation	19	12	13	19
Accommodation and Food Services	17	16	21	26
Other Services (Except Public Administration)	30	43	29	30
Public Administration	0	1	1	2
Fictitious Industries and Non-business Sector	39	43	44	48

Note: a. The jump in the share of gross output used as inputs from zero in the first 2 periods to 31 percent in the third period raises some questions in the way data are presented in the input-output tables: the gross output of this industry used as input by other industries is recorded as 0 through all years until the 1980s but it becomes positive thereafter.

Source: Statistics Canada, input-output tables for various years.

use of the services sector's output as input rose from 39 to 48 percent (an increase of 9 percentage points) over the same period. The relative demand for intermediate inputs for services output rose faster than for goods output, while relative final demand increased more for the goods sector's output.

The interdependence of Canada's goods and services sectors can be compared with that of the United States. The 1997 input-output tables for these two countries from the Organisation for Economic Co-operation and Development (OECD) database have been used to compile Table 12. It shows that Canada's goods-producing industry used $47 worth of inputs from the goods industries and inputs of $13.5 from the services producing sector to produce $100 of revenue, with the remaining percentage being the value added. In the United States, goods-producing industries used inputs worth $41.5 from the goods-producing industries and $17 from the services-producing industries.

TABLE 12

INPUT REQUIREMENTS IN CANADA AND THE UNITED STATES, 1997[a]

	CANADA		UNITED STATES	
	GOODS-PRODUCING	SERVICES-PRODUCING	GOODS-PRODUCING	SERVICES-PRODUCING
Goods-producing	*47.0*	*10.8*	*41.5*	*9.1*
Services-producing	*13.5*	*23.9*	*17.4*	*24.0*
Wholesale and Retail Trade; Repairs	3.7	2.5	6.8	2.1
Hotels and Restaurants	0.3	0.8	0.4	0.6
Transport and Storage	2.0	2.3	2.4	1.8
Post and Telecommunications	0.6	2.2	0.4	2.0
Finance, Insurance	2.3	6.9	1.2	4.4
Real Estate Activities	0.0	0.0	0.8	3.8
Renting of Machinery and Equipment	0.0	0.0	0.2	0.3
Computer and Related Activities	0.1	0.5	0.3	1.0
Research and Development	0.0	0.0	0.1	0.3
Other Business Activities	2.9	3.9	3.9	5.5
Public Administration and Defence; Compulsory Social Security	0.5	0.8	0.0	0.0
Education	0.0	0.4	0.1	0.1
Health and Social Work	0.0	1.8	0.1	0.2
Other Services[b]	1.0	1.8	0.7	1.8
Value Added	*39.5*	*65.3*	*41.1*	*66.9*

Notes: a. The input-output tables for both countries are for 1997 in national currencies at current prices. The tables are organized in 41 industries for both countries based on ISIC Revision 3 and are not directly comparable with similar industries in the NAICS codes. For the purposes of this analysis, we aggregated the input-output tables into 27 goods-producing and 14 services industries.
b. Other services include other community, social and personal services, private households with employed persons (and extra-territorial organizations and persons).

Source: OECD, input-output (IO) database.

Thus, although the intermediate input requirements of the goods-producing industries were almost the same (about $60 in Canada and about $59 in the United States), the goods-producing industries in Canada used more intermediate input from the goods-producing industries and less from the services-producing industries than in the United States. This may be due to the fact that U.S. goods-producing industries outsource more services-related work than do their Canadian counterparts. The input requirement of the services-producing industries is not much different, but here too, the value added is slightly higher in the United States than in Canada.

CAPITAL INTENSITY IN THE SERVICES INDUSTRIES

THE PRECEDING SECTIONS complete the discussion of labour and intermediate input use for the services industries. Next, we consider the use of capital (both physical and human) — by goods- and services-producing industries. On the physical side, we concentrate more on capital intensity than on the industry share composition of capital stock. We look at two types of intensities: total capital intensity and the capital intensity of M&E, defined as the ratio of the total capital stock and the M&E stock to the number of employees.[10] Capital stock is determined by investment, which itself is a composite good of several types of assets. In this section, we also look at investment in information communications technology such as (1) computers, associated hardware and word processors, (2) communication equipment, and (3) software. On the human capital side, we look at skill intensity measured as the ratio of more educated to less educated workers.

Table 13 presents the shares of total capital stock and M&E stock in the goods and services sectors and their capital- and M&E-intensities. The share of total capital stock in the services sector increased marginally to 57 percent in 2001 from 55 percent in 1991, and that increase came mostly from the non-manufacturing industries. However, the share of M&E in the services industries has risen substantially: it reached 49 percent in 2001 as compared with 41.5 percent in 1991. This increase has come from both the manufacturing and non-manufacturing industries. Even though the services sector shares of total capital and M&E capital stock have increased, these shares are still far below the services sector share of GDP. The faster growth of the M&E share compared with the share of the total capital stock in the services sector implies that the share of M&E in total capital of the services industries has been rising.[11]

Next, we compare a number of capital and M&E intensive industries and their shares of total capital and M&E for the years 1991 and 2001. The industries are at the NAICS 3-digit level. They are defined as capital- or M&E-intensive if their capital- or M&E- to-employee ratio is larger than the national capital- or M&E- to-employee ratio. Column 4 shows that in 1991 there were 10 out of 28 capital-intensive industries in the goods-producing sector, 6 out of 21 in manufacturing, and 12 out of 60 in the services sector. By 2001, both the number of capital-intensive industries and the share of capital stock in these capital-intensive industries fell in goods-producing industries. However in services, by 2001 more industries appear as capital-intensive and the share of these industries in total capital stock also increased. In terms of M&E capital, there were more M&E-intensive industries and the share of M&E capital rose over time in the services sector.

TABLE 13

SECTORAL SHARE OF CAPITAL AND RATIO OF PHYSICAL CAPITAL TO TOTAL EMPLOYMENT

	SHARE (IN PERCENT)		CAPITAL-INTENSIVE INDUSTRIES		M&E-INTENSIVE INDUSTRIES	
	IN TOTAL CAPITAL STOCK	IN M&E STOCK	NUMBER OF INDUSTRIES	SHARE IN TOTAL CAPITAL STOCK (IN PERCENT)	NUMBER OF INDUSTRIES	SHARE IN TOTAL M&E (IN PERCENT)
1991						
Goods-producing	*44.7*	*58.5*	*10*	*34.9*	*15*	*47.9*
Manufacturing	12.9	31.0	6	8.0	12	28.4
Services-producing	*55.3*	*41.5*	*12*	*38.8*	*9*	*27.4*
2001						
Goods-producing	*43.1*	*51.1*	*9*	*32.9*	*17*	*41.5*
Manufacturing	12.2	28.0	5	6.4	12	24.8
Services-producing	*56.9*	*48.9*	*14*	*41.4*	*12*	*30.8*

Notes: Capital stock and M&E stock data are fixed non-residential geometric (infinite) end-year net stock evaluated at current dollars for the whole economy. Employment is measured as the number of employees (both hourly paid and salaried workers) from the SEPH database. To prepare this table using the industries defined at the NAICS three-digit level as listed in Appendix A, we computed the number of industries that are capital-intensive and M&E- intensive. Industries that have higher than the national capital to labour employment ratio and a higher M&E capital stock to labour employment ratio are defined as capital intensive and M&E intensive industries, respectively. At the 3-digit level, there are, altogether, 99 industries, 32 of which are goods-producing (among them 21 manufacturing) and 67 are services-producing. Of these 99 industries, there were no data for four primary industries and seven services-producing industries. Therefore, the table above is based on 28 goods-producing industries and 60 services-producing industries. However from other information available, it was known that the 11 industries for which we do not have data are not capital intensive or M&E intensive.

Source: Statistics Canada.

Some services industries are becoming more capital-and M&E-intensive. However, for the majority of services industries, the capital-labour ratio has not changed much over the past decade. Figure 6 plots the change in capital intensity between 1991 and 2001 for 85 industries. It appears that there is only minimal change in capital-intensity in some goods-producing industries and in most of the services industries (the marks are close to the x-axis). Furthermore, except for a few of the industries in the services sector, the change in capital stock was below the average national change (indicated by a line parallel to the *x*-axis). Even though a small number of industries are becoming more capital-intensive, the majority of services industries are still using a lot less capital per employee than the goods-producing industries.

FIGURE 6

CHANGE IN CAPITAL INTENSITY PER EMPLOYEE IN A DECADE

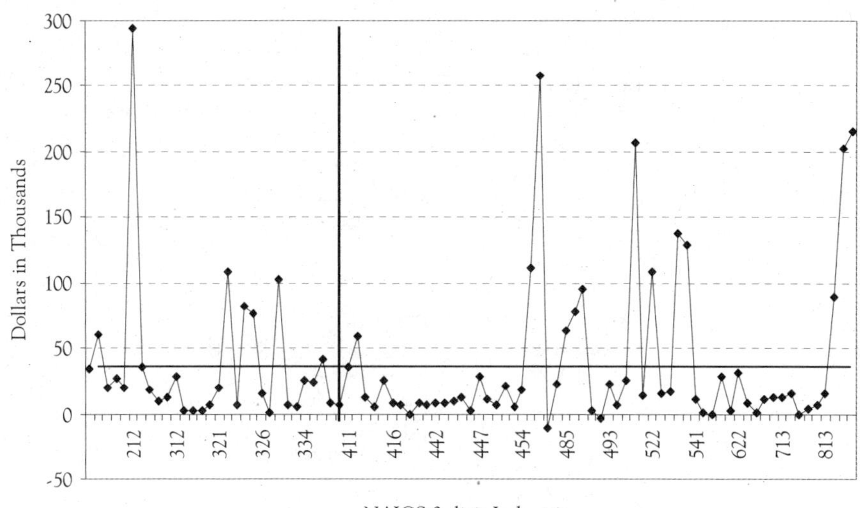

Notes: Of the 3-digit industries, industries with code numbers 111, 112, 114, 115, 521, 526, 533, 551, 814, 914 and 919 are not included as we do not have data on capital-intensity for them. Furthermore, industries 211, 221 and 486 are also excluded as outliers since their change in capital intensity was very high. For example, for NAICS 211, the "oil and gas extraction" industry, the change in per employee capital intensity was 2.8 billion; for NAICS 221, which is "utilities", it was 0.6 billion; and for NAICS 486, which is "pipeline transportation", it was 3.9 billion. Since the inclusion of these industries would make the graph more cluttered, which would make it harder for readers to see the change in capital intensity in other industries, we have not included them in the graph.

The numbers on the x-axis are the numbers corresponding to the NAICS codes, given in Appendix A. To differentiate the goods and services parts of the economy, we have drawn a vertical line at 339 on the horizontal axis, the last industry code for goods sector (just before 411); the goods-producing industries are to the left and the services-producing industries to the right.

Source: Statistics Canada.

A similar story holds for the change in M&E-intensity (though we did not plot this). The correlation coefficient between the change in capital-intensity and M&E-intensity was 0.88 indicating that there was not much difference between changes in the two series. Using Spearman rank correlation coefficients for capital-intensity and M&E-intensity, we found that the industries with relatively higher total capital- and M&E-intensity in 1991 remained so in 2001. The rank correlation coefficients of capital-intensity for 84 industries in 1991 and in 2001 was 0.96 and that for M&E-intensity for the same period was 0.91, indicating that the rank of the industries did not change significantly over the sample period. Hence, despite the increase in these two intensities, the relative ranking of the industries remained almost the same.

FIGURE 7

SHARE OF ICT INVESTMENT IN TOTAL INVESTMENT (IN PERCENT)

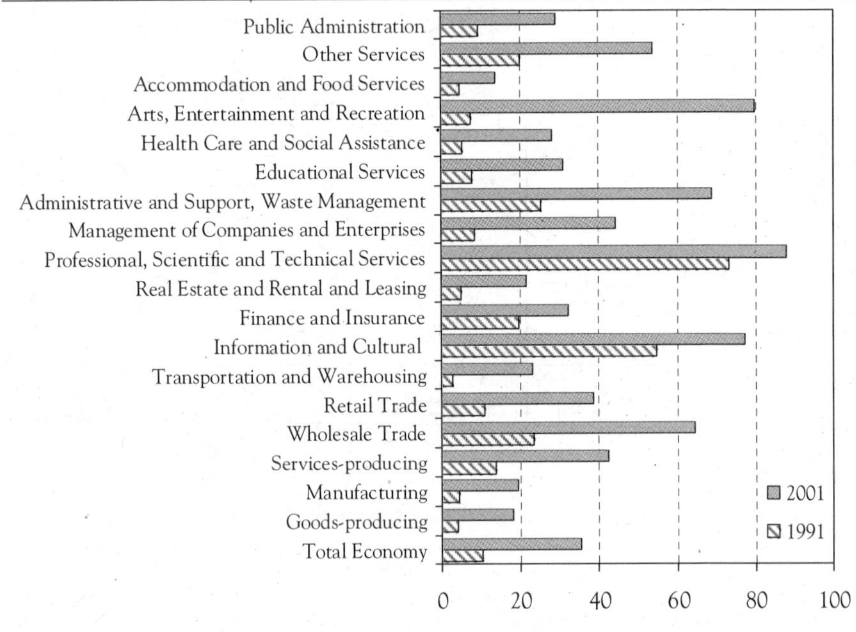

Note: The data on information and communication technologies were obtained by adding investment for 3 types of assets. These assets are: (1) computers, associated hardware and word processors (2) communication equipment and (3) software. The data were in Fisher chain index form; therefore in some cases, the sum of all components may not add up to the total value. However, the ratio of these 3 types of investment to total investment indicates the intensity of ICT in total investment.

Source: Statistics Canada.

Next, we look at investment in core ICT assets. It is clear that the services sector puts a higher proportion of its investment into ICT assets than the goods-producing industries do. For example, in 2001, ICT accounted for more than 40 percent of total investment in the services sector, whereas in manufacturing it was 20 percent (Figure 7). The services industries are proportionately heavier users of ICT. There are several services industries including wholesale trade that put more than 60 percent of their investment expenditure into ICT.

This completes our discussion on the physical capital-intensity of services industries. The other very important aspect to look at is human capital-intensity. This can be defined as the ratio of highly educated workers to less educated workers. Table 14 shows that in 1988-1997, better educated workers accounted for 54 percent of all services employment but only 42 percent in goods-producing employment. Furthermore, 14 percent of workers in the

TABLE 14

ANNUAL SHARES OF HOURS WORKED AND WAGE EARNINGS BY EDUCATIONAL ATTAINMENT (PERCENT)

	HOURS			WAGE BILLS		
	1969-77	1979-88	1988-97	1969-77	1979-88	1988-97
Goods-producing						
Less Educated Workers	76.1	64.8	57.6	76.6	60.4	49.5
More Educated Workers	23.8	35.2	42.4	23.4	39.6	50.5
(Workers with a University Degree or More)	4.0	6.4	9.0	5.5	8.2	13.8
Services-producing						
Less Educated Workers	68.5	55.9	46.5	69.7	52.2	39.6
More Educated Workers	31.5	44.1	53.5	30.3	47.8	60.4
(Workers with a University Degree or More)	6.6	10.0	14.2	10.1	13.5	21.9

Note: Less educated workers include workers with 0-8 years of schooling and some or completed high school. More educated workers include workers with post secondary education and university degrees or more.

Source: Statistics Canada.

services sector attained an educational level of university degree or better, whereas this was the case for only 9 percent of workers in the goods-producing sector. It is clear from Table 14 that there are proportionately more university and post-secondary workers in the services sector than in goods-producing industries.

INTERNATIONAL TRADE AND FOREIGN DIRECT INVESTMENT IN SERVICES

THIS SECTION GOES BEYOND the domestic economy to evaluate the performance of Canada's services industries in trade orientation and export growth. This includes a calculation of the revealed comparative advantage (RCA) of services industries in Canada vis-à-vis three G-7 countries: the United States, Japan and the United Kingdom.

It is well known that many services are not as tradable as goods outside of the local market. Some services such as retail trade, real estate, education, health care and social assistance, management of companies and enterprises, and public administration are almost non-tradable by definition outside of local markets and there is little or no resale for some of these services. Obviously there will not be as much trade occurring in these industries compared with manufacturing industries. Table 15 shows that the share of total exports in gross output of the services-producing sector was not quite 9 percent in 1997-99, which is lower than the goods-producing sector as a whole and significantly lower than the manufacturing sector. Even so, there is a growing export orientation in many of the services industries and in some industries it has become very strong. For example, in the late 1990s, industries such as wholesale, transportation and warehousing, arts, entertainment and recreation, accommodation and food services, and professional, scientific and technical services saw at least 15 percent of their production exported to foreign markets.

Services exports have grown faster than manufacturing exports in the past two decades. In some services industries, annual export growth has been recorded at the two-digit level (Table 16). As a result, the services-producing sector accounted for 16 percent of Canada's total exports in 1997-1999.[12] The largest services exporters are wholesale, transportation and warehousing, professional, scientific and technical services, accommodation and food services, finance and insurance, and information and cultural industries. Together, these five industries constitute about 85 percent of services exports. Some of these industries had very healthy growth rates as well. For some, including wholesale

TABLE 15

SHARE OF TOTAL EXPORTS IN GROSS OUTPUT (PERCENT)

	1967-69	1977-79	1987-89	1997-99
Total Economy	**10.7**	**13.2**	**14.7**	**21.5**
Goods-producing Industries	*17.9*	*22.8*	*26.0*	*40.0*
Manufacturing	23.0	29.3	36.1	56.9
Service-producing Industries	*2.5*	*3.0*	*5.3*	*8.5*
Wholesale Trade	7.6	9.7	10.5	17.8
Retail Trade	0.1	0.1	0.4	0.6
Transportation and Warehousing	5.8	6.4	10.8	17.6
Information and Cultural Industries	1.9	2.8	5.9	10.6
Finance and Insurance	3.0	4.1	6.7	8.5
Real Estate and Rental and Leasing	0.0	0.0	1.1	1.7
Professional, Scientific and Technical Services	4.0	8.8	7.8	14.5
Management of Companies and Enterprises	0.4	0.6	3.0	2.7
Administrative and Support, Waste Management	8.6	5.7	9.2	13.7
Educational Services	0.4	0.4	0.6	1.0
Health Care and Social Assistance	0.2	0.2	0.3	0.5
Arts, Entertainment and Recreation	0.2	0.3	12.6	17.0
Accommodation and Food Services	3.1	2.1	13.1	15.8
Other Services	1.5	1.5	0.6	1.9
Public Administration	0.0	0.1	0.1	0.5
Fictitious and Non-business Industries	*4.7*	*4.7*	*4.4*	*4.5*

Note: Total exports are the sum of domestic exports and re-exports. And the share of re-exports in total exports is very small, e.g., in 1999 about 95 percent of total exports were domestic exports.
Source: Statistics Canada, input-output tables for various years.

trade, the information and cultural industries, and professional, scientific and technical services, growth was faster than for the goods-producing sector.

Overall, Canada has a trade surplus in services, with an exports-to-imports ratio of 1.2 in 1997-99. Among the five largest services industries, there is a trade surplus in wholesale trade, transportation and warehousing, and professional, scientific and technical services.

Canada's performance in services trade can be compared with three other countries: the United States, Japan and the United Kingdom, using revealed

TABLE 16

GROWTH AND INDUSTRY COMPOSITION OF EXPORTS AND TRADE BALANCE

	AVERAGE ANNUAL GROWTH IN EXPORTS (PERCENT)		SHARE IN TOTAL EXPORTS (PERCENT)		EXPORTS TO IMPORTS RATIO
	1987-89 OVER 1977-79	1997-99 OVER 1987-89	1987-89	1997-99	1997-99
Total Economy	**10.5**	**9.1**	**100**	**100**	**1.1**
Goods-producing Industries	*9.8*	*9.0*	*81.8*	*81.2*	*1.0*
Manufacturing	10.8	9.5	68.5	71.0	0.9
Services-producing Industries	*16.5*	*10.5*	*13.9*	*15.9*	*1.2*
Wholesale Trade	12.0	11.3	2.9	3.5	3.4
Retail Trade	27.7	7.4	0.1	0.1	1.7
Transportation and Warehousing	14.5	10.0	3.1	3.4	1.6
Information and Cultural Industries	16.8	13.3	0.9	1.3	0.8
Finance and Insurance	16.2	8.7	1.4	1.4	0.9
Real Estate and Rental and Leasing		10.6	0.2	0.2	0.5
Professional, Scientific and Technical	13.8	16.0	1.1	2.1	1.1
Management of Companies	23.0	5.1	0.5	0.3	0.9
Administrative and Support	20.1	10.8	0.8	0.9	0.9
Educational Services	14.2	9.2	0.1	0.1	0.8
Health Care and Social Assistance	14.8	8.0	0.1	0.1	0.4
Arts, Entertainment and Recreation	60.4	12.1	0.4	0.5	0.8
Accommodation and Food Services	30.8	6.6	2.2	1.7	0.8
Other Services	–2.7	19.4	0.1	0.1	2.2
Public Administration	15.1	13.7	0.0	0.0	1.0
Fictitious and Non-business Industries	*8.9*	*5.2*	*4.2*	*3.0*	*8.2*

Note: The growth rates are annually compounded.
Source: Statistics Canada, input-output tables for various years.

comparative advantage (RCA). For the computation of RCA, we use the following formula for each industry for which we have data:

$$(1) \qquad RCA_{ij} = \frac{x_{i,Canada}}{X_{Canada}} / \frac{x_{ij}}{X_j}$$

with j = United States, Japan and United Kingdom,

where the subscript i denotes an industry and j a comparison country; x_{ij} is the value of exports of commodity i by country j, and Xj is the total value of exports of country j to the world. Similarly, $x_{i,Canada}$ is Canada's exports in industry i and X_{Canada} is Canada's total exports to the world. As a first approximation, if $RCA_{ij} > 1$ (< 1), we take this to mean that there is a revealed comparative advantage (disadvantage) for that industry or for all the exports for Canada compared to country j. The RCA results are given in Table 17.

TABLE 17

INTERNATIONAL TRADE-RELATED MEASUREMENTS FOR CANADA, UNITED STATES, UNITED KINGDOM AND JAPAN

	REVEALED COMPARATIVE ADVANTAGE			EXPORT ORIENTATION[a]			
	U.S.	U.K.	JAPAN	CANADA	U.S.	U.K.	JAPAN
Goods-producing	-	-	-	39.5	9.9	25.5	10.0
Services-producing	-	-	-	7.5	2.7	7.4	2.4
Wholesale and Retail Trade; Repairs	1.6	1.2	1.8	8.6	4.3	10.2	3.9
Hotels and Restaurants	0.1	1.2	0.6	14.6	0.3	20.1	2.1
Transport and Storage	0.8	0.5	1.2	33.3	12.0	12.4	11.2
Post and Telecommunications	0.7	0.7	0.3	5.5	1.4	4.0	0.7
Finance, Insurance	1.3	1.2	0.6	5.1	3.5	8.7	2.1
Real Estate Activities	0.0	0.0	0.0	0.0	0.1	0.4	0.0
Renting of Machinery and Equipment	0.0	0.0	0.0	0.0	2.4	3.2	1.0
Computer and Related Activities	0.7	1.2	0.4	12.6	1.5	7.3	0.7
Research and Development	0.0	0.0	0.0	0.0	2.4	32.8	0.1
Other Business Activities	1.6	1.9	0.3	13.7	5.1	14.7	1.4
Public Administration and Defence Compulsory Social Security	0.0	0.4	0.0	1.1	0.0	0.8	0.0
Education	0.3	1.4	0.0	1.0	0.5	1.6	0.0
Health and Social Work	0.3	0.4	0.0	0.6	0.1	0.1	0.0
Other Services	0.6	0.6	0.8	9.4	2.0	6.1	1.8

Notes: All the input-output tables are for 1997 in national currencies at current prices except for the United Kingdom, for which the input-output table was for 1998. The industries are based on ISIC codes.

a. This is the export-to-gross-output ratio multiplied by 100.

Source: OECD, input-output (IO) database.

Canada has a comparative advantage in wholesale and retail trade vis-à-vis the United States, Japan and the United Kingdom. There are only two other industries where Canada has a comparative advantage over the United States: finance and insurance, and other business activities. When compared with the United Kingdom, in addition to these three industries, Canada also has a comparative advantage in hotels and restaurants, computer and related activities, and education. In comparison with Japan, Canada only has a comparative advantage in distribution services, and transport and storage. Canada's industries are more export-oriented than those of the United States and Japan. However, the services sector in the United Kingdom appears to be equally outward-oriented. In terms of individual industries, among the four countries in the comparison, Canada has the highest ratio of export to gross output in transport and storage, post and telecommunication, and computer and related activities.

In terms of their export growth, export orientation and revealed comparative advantage, Canadian services industries perform well vis-à-vis their U.S., U.K. and Japanese counterparts. However, one could argue that the relative performance of the Canadian services industries vis-à-vis the Canadian goods industries is weak. For example, the goods-to-services export orientation ratio for Canada is about 5.0, whereas this ratio is 3.7 for the United States, 3.4 for United Kingdom and 4.2 for Japan.

In terms of Canadian direct investment abroad (CDIA) in 2000-2002, services accounted for a higher share (58 percent) than did goods-producing industries (42 percent). Most of the services share consisted of investment related to the finance and insurance industry. The other industries where CDIA is concentrated are communications, transportation services, and general services to business and government. In terms of foreign direct investment (FDI) flowing into Canada, the services share has risen from 26 percent in 1987-88 to 30 percent in 2001-2002 (Table 18). The largest share of this comes from the finance and insurance industry, and consumer goods and services.

TABLE 18

INDUSTRY SHARE OF STOCK OF FOREIGN DIRECT INVESTMENT (PERCENT)

	CANADIAN DIRECT INVESTMENT ABROAD		FOREIGN DIRECT INVESTMENT IN CANADA	
	1987-1988	2001-2002	1987-1988	2001-2002
Goods-producing	*56.1*	*42.2*	*74.0*	*70.5*
Services-producing	*43.9*	*57.8*	*26.0*	*29.5*
Finance and Insurance Industry	25.3	39.4	17.1	19.5
Transportation Services	4.2	3.9	0.5	1.0
General Services to Business and Government	0.4	3.9	0.9	1.3
Education, Health and Social Services	0.3	1.7	0.0	0.0
Accommodation, Restaurant and Recreation	1.6	2.9	1.3	1.5
Food Retailing	0.6	0.0	0.9	0.3
Consumer Goods and Services	4.8	0.7	4.0	4.1
Communications	6.6	5.3	1.3	1.8

Note: This table is based on Standard Industrial Classification (SIC) code, as data by NAICS code are not available yet.
Source: Statistics Canada, CANSIM Table 376-0038.

INNOVATION IN SERVICES[13]

INNOVATION IN AN INDUSTRY is generally estimated either from input use or from output indicators of innovation such as patents, or from a combination of these indicators. If one uses an output indicator such as patents, then the services industries are not found to be particularly innovative. Their activities generally do not meet the criteria for patents and are covered under other forms of intellectual property protection such as copyrights and trademarks, which are not commonly included in innovation statistics. More significantly, casual observation suggests that many businesses deliberately do not seek patents because of disclosure requirements and/or the costs involved. A patent is an imperfect indicator of innovation for the services sector and thus researchers also use information on inputs to test for innovation.

Ideally, a measure of innovation activities from the input-side should be broad-based and cover both research and development as well as non-R&D expenditures such as the share of highly educated people in the workforce, the capital-per-employee ratio, the share of ICT as a proportion of total investment and the acquisition of technology. This broad coverage is particularly important as many small- and medium-sized enterprises (SMEs) may not have distinct R&D activities and learning-by-doing occurs at all stages in their activities. As Lipsey and Carlaw (1998) mention, in most SMEs the performance of R&D and the production of knowledge using already known techniques are intermixed with no clear dividing line between them. To capture the whole spectrum of innovative activities one has to look at several indicators apart from expenditures on R&D. Taking this perspective, earlier sections have already presented the situation of services industries in terms of knowledge intensity, capital intensity and ICT investment intensity, which are three important indicators of innovation activity. In this section we focus on R&D expenditure — the other category of investment that is often described as critical to innovation.[14] We will also present information on ICT use as an indicator of technology acquisition.

Table 19 shows that Canadian business expenditure on R&D (BERD) has been growing faster in services than in the goods-producing industries. By 2002, the share of research originating in the services sector had reached about 35 percent, as compared with 18 percent in the 1980s.[15] As the last column shows, by 2002, BERD in the services sector had grown by 61 percent in comparison with the average annual amount of R&D during 1991-2001. The corresponding growth rate in manufacturing, at 31 percent, was only about half of what it was in the services sector. The services industries with the highest growth in BERD were: computer and related services, engineering and scientific services, communication, and transportation and storage.

TABLE 19

AVERAGE SHARE AND GROWTH OF TOTAL BERD

	SHARE			GROWTH
INDUSTRIES	1980-1990	1991-2001	2002	IN 2002 OVER 1991-2001
Total Economy	100.0	100.0	100.0	38.4
Goods-producing	*81.9*	*70.4*	65.5	28.9
Manufacturing	72.7	64.5	61.3	31.0
Services-producing	*18.1*	29.6	34.5	60.9
Transportation and Storage	0.7	0.3	0.5	202.4
Communication	2.6	2.3	2.4	62.0
Wholesale Trade	1.7	5.7	4.4	3.1
Retail Trade	0.3	0.4	0.1	–58.1
Finance, Insurance and Real Estate	2.4	3.0	2.2	8.4
Computer and Related Services	3.3	6.5	9.7	97.1
Engineering and Scientific Services	6.6	8.9	11.4	76.7
Management Consulting Services	0.3	0.6	0.2	–47.3
Other Services	0.9	2.0	3.6	140.7

Note: BERD denotes business expenditure on R&D.
Source: Statistics Canada.

The fact that a high (or low) share of R&D is undertaken within an industry may not mean that this is a highly innovative industry (nor does it mean the contrary). The share of R&D performed in an industry is only one indicator of innovation and by no means the only one that can be used. It is an important factor that we would like to understand better. Looking at the share of BERD in services, one could conclude that services industries are becoming more innovation-oriented. Also note that in terms of R&D expenditure, a restructuring seems to be taking place among services industries as well: industries such as distribution services and management consulting services have lost ground if judged by their shares of BERD.

Despite the phenomenal growth in share of BERD for services industries, the R&D intensity of services remains considerably below that of the goods sector, even though some services have a high technological component. For example, in 1999, the goods sector's share of BERD was 72 percent whereas the services share of BERD was only 28 percent. The BERD to GDP ratio was 2.4 percent for the goods-producing sector, but it was 4 percent in manufacturing and only 0.5 percent in services. Figure 8 shows the shares of GDP and BERD in the services industries. The industries that have higher shares of BERD than

FIGURE 8

INDUSTRIAL COMPOSITION OF VALUE ADDED AND BERD, 1999

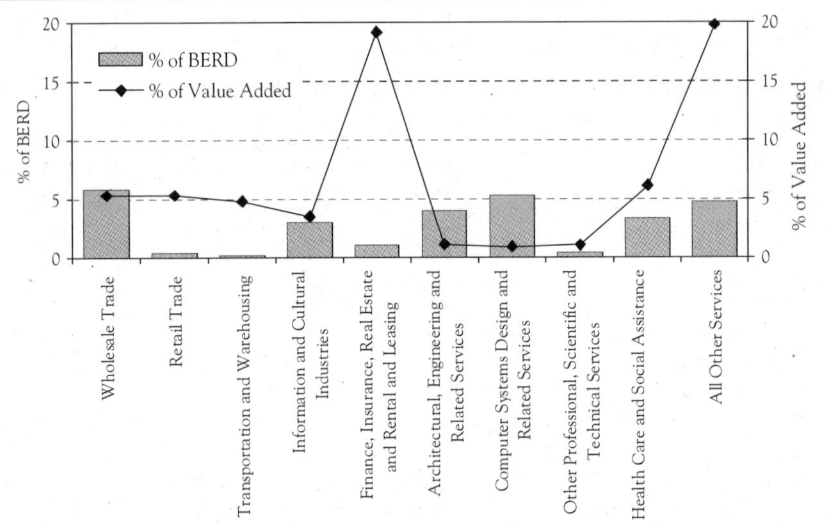

Notes: Both BERD and GDP figures are reported at current prices. We use the data for 1999 for this chart because this is the latest year for which value added data at current prices are available.

Source: Statistics Canada (2002) Industrial Research and Development, Catalogue no. 88-202-XIB and input-output table for 1999, at the working level.

their shares of GDP are viewed as being R&D-intensive and their R&D-to-GDP ratios are higher than the national average. Using this criterion, we see that the wholesale trade, architectural engineering, and computer system design industries are the most R&D-intensive industries in the services sector. Based on a survey conducted by the OECD, Young (1996) reports that in Canada, over half of the R&D in services is software-related, which is twice the proportion reported in manufacturing.

Table 20 looks at whether or not R&D intensity differs by country of control. When compared with the 1980s, R&D intensity increased in the 1990s for both Canadian-controlled and foreign-controlled firms. In the 1980s,

TABLE 20

INTRAMURAL BERD, BY COUNTRY OF CONTROL

	BERD AS A PERCENT OF PERFORMING COMPANY REVENUES[a]				TOTAL INTRAMURAL BERD OF CANADIAN CONTROLLED FIRMS AS A PERCENT OF ALL INTRAMURAL BERD	
	CANADIAN CONTROL		FOREIGN CONTROL			
	1980-1990	1991-2001	1980-1990	1991-2001	1980-1990	1991-2001
All Industries	**1.4**	**2.0**	**1.1**	**1.3**	**63**	**68**
Manufacturing	1.7	2.6	1.2	1.2	55	63
Services-producing	*1.1*	*1.6*	0.9	*3.1*	85	*76*
Transportation and Storage	0.1	0.2	6.5	0.9	100	100
Communication	0.9	0.9	0.9	3.4	NA	NA
Wholesale Trade	2.0	1.3	1.3	2.7	50	51
Retail Trade	1.7	0.8	0.1	8.2	NA	100
Finance, Insurance and Real Estate	0.7	0.5	0.2	0.7	96	91
Computer and Related Services	11.5	13.6	5.6	11.7	93	80
Engineering and Scientific Services	11.8	11.5	33.6	32.6	83	76
Management Consulting Services	17.6	9.4	0.9	15.4	100	100
Other Services	5.8	5.3	1.8	11.1	89	90

Notes: NA: data not available.
a. Performing company is defined as the organization which carried out the R&D and submitted the return. In the case of a consolidated return, the performing company could include several companies. It also may include divisions of an enterprise which sends in separate returns or organizations such as industrial non-profit organizations.

Source: Statistics Canada.

Canadian-controlled industries had higher R&D intensities in both manufacturing and services when compared with foreign-controlled industries. By the 1990s, however, Canadian-controlled manufacturing industries maintained higher R&D intensity than their foreign counterparts, but Canadian-controlled services firms had slipped behind foreign-controlled services companies. At the same time, for Canadian-controlled industries, manufacturing was more R&D-intensive than services, whereas the reverse was true for foreign-controlled industries.

When compared with the period between 1980 and 1990, the services sector in general became more R&D-intensive between 1991 and 2001. Among Canadian-controlled industries, however, only computer and related services showed an increase in R&D intensity: all other Canadian-controlled services posted a decline. By contrast, there was an increase in R&D intensity among all foreign-controlled industries with the exception of transportation and storage, and engineering and scientific services. The last two columns of Table 20 show that the share of BERD for Canadian-controlled industries in total BERD has increased in manufacturing and decreased in services. Canadian-controlled industries are spending proportionately more on research in manufacturing than in services. The lowest share of Canadian-controlled services expenditure on R&D is in wholesale, where the sector contributes only about half of the total expenditure on R&D.

Services are more likely to employ a higher share of professional researchers (Table 21). The share of professionals engaged on R&D in the services industries has increased from 24 percent in the 1980s to 39 percent in the 1990s. The industries with increasing shares of professional researchers include: wholesale trade, finance and insurance, computer and related services, and engineering and scientific services. Similarly, the share of university graduates among professional researchers has also increased in services. Interestingly, the share of workers with a master's or doctor's degree in services is lower than the share of professional researchers. This contrasts with goods-producing industries where the share of those with master's or doctor's degrees is higher than the share of professionals. This suggest that there are proportionately more holders of bachelor's degrees involved in services R&D than there are in the goods sector. There is only one industry where the share of professionals is lower than the share of graduates, and that is engineering and scientific services.

Another question for consideration is how R&D performers are distributed among Canadian-controlled and foreign-controlled industries. The number of R&D performers in Canadian-controlled industries has more than quadrupled in the 1990s when compared to the 1980s (Table 22). This increase came from both the goods and services sectors, but slightly more is attributable to the latter. In terms of foreign-controlled industries, the overall number of R&D performers remained almost the same: there were only 487 R&D performers among foreign-controlled industries in the 1990s, which represents only a marginal increase from 434 in the 1980s. Among Canadian-controlled industries, the largest number of R&D performers was in computer and engineering services.

TABLE 21

COMPOSITION OF PROFESSIONAL PERSONNEL ENGAGED IN R&D

	SHARE OF PROFESSIONALS[a]		SHARE WITH A MASTER'S OR DOCTORATE DEGREE[b]	
INDUSTRY	1980-1990	1991-2001	1980-1990	1991-2001
All Industries	100	100	100	100
Goods-producing	*75.6*	*61.5*	*78.5*	*68.5*
Manufacturing	69.5	57.8	69.1	62.4
Services-producing	*24.4*	*38.5*	*21.5*	*31.5*
Transportation and Storage	0.6	0.3	0.4	0.2
Communication	4.3	1.8	3.4	1.0
Wholesale Trade	2.4	6.2	1.7	5.1
Retail Trade	0.3	0.4	0.3	0.3
Finance, Insurance and Real Estate	1.6	2.9	1.2	1.5
Computer and Related Services	5.1	12.7	3.2	7.4
Engineering and Scientific Services	8.2	10.8	9.4	12.7
Management Consulting Services	0.5	1.0	0.3	0.7
Other Services	1.3	2.6	1.5	2.5

Notes: R&D personnel are calculated in full-time equivalent, which is the sum of the number of persons who work solely on R&D projects *plus* estimates of time spent for persons working only part of their time on R&D.

a. Except professionals, the other occupational category engaged in R&D are "technicians" and "others".

b. The other category among professionals is holders of a bachelor's degree.

Source: Statistics Canada.

TABLE 22

NUMBER OF R&D PERFORMERS, BY COUNTRY OF CONTROL

	CANADA		FOREIGN	
	1980-1990	1991-2001	1980-1990	1991-2001
All Industries	**2,201**	**8,012**	**434**	**487**
Goods-producing	*1,158*	*3,934*	*374*	*361*
Manufacturing	1,040	3,383	349	331
Services-producing	*1,043*	*4,079*	60	*127*
Transportation and Storage	19	45	1	2
Communication	14	44	2	2
Wholesale Trade	150	840	26	56
Retail Trade	23	136	1	1
Finance, Insurance and Real Estate	46	157	5	12
Computer and Related Services	248	1,180	6	25
Engineering and Scientific Services	399	1,005	14	20
Management Consulting Services	47	185	1	2
Other Services	97	486	5	6

Source: Statistics Canada.

The next issue to consider is technology acquisition, which is another indicator of innovation (Table 23). Services industries are strong users of productivity-increasing ICT. When industries use ICT, they use knowledge that is embedded in intermediate goods and technology. In each of the services industries other than accommodation and food services, the share of employees using computer terminals or workstations is higher than in manufacturing. In

TABLE 23

DIRECT ACCESS TO INFORMATION AND COMMUNICATION TECHNOLOGIES, 2002

	Percent of Employees			Percent of Enterprises	
	Personal Computers, Workstations or Terminals	E-mail (Electronic Mail)	Internet	Electronic Data Interchange	Network/ Information Security Control
Private Sector	*65*	*49*	*52*	*55*	*23*
Manufacturing	45	35	35	71	35
Wholesale Trade	70	55	57	69	29
Retail Trade	60	36	41	52	31
Transportation and Warehousing	48	33	37	43	15
Information and Cultural Industries	92	88	88	81	36
Finance and Insurance	78	69	67	74	48
Real Estate and Rental and Leasing	66	47	52	41	19
Professional, Scientific and Technical Services	94	86	87	73	27
Management of Companies and Enterprises	55	49	48	37	10
Administrative and Support, Waste Management	64	50	53	54	19
Educational Services	81	76	76	79	28
Health Care and Social Assistance	76	46	50	56	33
Arts, Entertainment and Recreation	71	64	65	62	14
Accommodation and Food Services	27	12	14	36	12
Other services (Except Public Administration)	64	44	49	43	14
Public Sector	*81*	*73*	*74*	*95*	*83*

Source: Statistics Canada, CANSIM Table 358-0007.

terms of the percentage of employees using e-mail, only transportation and storage scores lower than manufacturing. For Internet use, all services except accommodation and food service score higher than manufacturing. Only the use of electronic data interchange is higher in manufacturing than in services, with the exception of finance and insurance, and professional, scientific and technical services, which have slightly higher rates of use. The data in Table 23 suggests that the services industries are the main users of ICT, which in turn might be expected to improve their economic performance.

In terms of the conventional output indicators like numbers of patents, the services industries may not look innovative, but they certainly appear innovative and increasingly so if one uses input measures such as those presented in this study. Our research suggests that R&D-intensity, skill-intensity and ICT-intensity are all increasing in the services-producing industries.

ICT AND SERVICES

TRADITIONALLY, SERVICES INDUSTRIES were to be regarded mainly as users of technology produced by manufacturing industries. This view is no longer appropriate since the services sector also includes a number of industries which focus on supplying ICT. This section examines the relationship of ICT to services (detailed ICT industry names with NAICS codes are provided in Appendix B). As detailed in Appendix C, the ICT sector constituted 6 percent of GDP, provided about 4 percent of total employment, enjoyed 43 percent of BERD, and contributed 6 percent of exports and 12 percent of imports in 2002.[16] Most of this ICT-related contribution to GDP and employment was generated in the services sector, as shown in Table 24. In 2002, in terms of the total contribution to GDP generated by the ICT sector, services-sector ICT contributed 81 percent, leaving only 19 percent for ICT manufacturing. A similar pattern can be seen in employment. Most of the ICT industries fall under the category of "information and cultural industries" (all NAICS codes starting with 51). Some of them fall under "wholesale" (starting with NAICS codes 41) and "professional, scientific and technical services" (starting with NAICS codes 54). Interestingly, however, when it comes to R&D, it is the manufacturing sector that dominates: in 2001, 68 percent of the R&D performed in ICT-related industries was in the manufacturing sector.

TABLE 24

ICT SECTOR ACTIVITIES (SHARE IN TOTAL, PERCENT)

		GDP[a]		EMPLOYMENT[b]		R&D[c]		EXPORTS
NAICS	DESCRIPTION	1997	2002	1997	2002	1997	2002	2002
	Total ICT Manufacturing	*25.2*	*18.9*	*22.3*	*16.7*	*75.9*	*68.3*	*76.8*
	Total ICT Services	*74.8*	*81.1*	*77.7*	*83.3*	*24.1*	*31.7*	*23.2*
4173/ 41791	ICT Wholesaling	3.3	3.5	15.5	13.3	2.3	1.8	
51121	Software Publishers	4.4	7.5	35.2	46.5	6.6	5.9	
51322	Cable and Other Program Distribution	4.8	4.2	2.0	3.0	2.3	5.6	
5133	Telecommunications Services	45.1	44.2	24.9	20.5			
51419	Information Services	0.9	0.8			0.1	0.3	
51421	Data Processing Services	1.2	1.6			0.3	0.2	
54151	Computer Systems Design and Related Services	14.2	18.6			12.5	17.9	
53242	Office Machinery and Equipment Rental and Leasing	1.0	0.8					

Notes: There are no data available for ICT NAICS 81121, except for R&D expenditure, and the share of this in total BERD is a negligible 0.1 percent.
a. GDP is expressed in basic prices (in 1997 constant dollars).
b. In employment, the data on 51419 include employment in industries 51121, 514191, 51421 and 54151 (which is self-employment). As a result, ICT employment data also include the self-employed.
c. The data on NAICS 51322 also include data on NAICS 5133.

Source: Statistics Canada.

CONCLUSIONS

WHEN COMPARED WITH OTHER G-7 COUNTRIES, the relative importance of services to the Canadian economy has fallen despite the fact that the contribution of services to our GDP and employment continues to increase. The contribution to real GDP by the services sector rose faster than that by the goods sector in both the 1980s and 1990s. As a result, the services sector now accounts for 69 percent of GDP and 74 percent of total employment measured in terms of persons, and its importance continues to grow.

The services-sector share of employment differs substantially for full-time and part-time employees: it accounts for 70 percent of full-time and 92 percent of part-time employment. Moreover, the proportion of part-time employment in the services sector is rising.

Self-employment as a share of total employment is rising in the services sector while falling in the goods-producing sector. In services, about 15 percent of total employment is self-employment.

More than 70 percent of employment in the services sector is in small establishments where there are fewer than 100 employees as compared to only 46 percent for the goods sector. The majority of employees in the services sector are female.

Even though productivity growth in services industries improved in the 1990s over what it had been in the 1980s, many services industries still appear to lag behind the manufacturing sector. It is possible, however, that this is partly attributable to measurement. As currently measured, the services sector makes a relatively smaller contribution to aggregate labour productivity growth compared to its share of GDP. However, there are services industries where productivity growth is higher than in manufacturing.

The average hourly wage in the services industries is lower than in the goods-producing industries. However, there are services industries that pay a lot higher wages and salaries than the average for goods-producing industries and there are goods-producing industries that pay a lot less than the average for the services sector. The share of employees in the services sector who are earning more than the average hourly wage in the goods-producing sector is rising.

Between 1969 and 1997, the real hourly wage for workers in the services sector rose annually by 0.2 percent, compared to 1.8 percent in the goods-producing sector. However, the pace of increase in the services sector has varied considerably over time and by educational attainment. In the 1970s (1969-1979), the real hourly wage of more educated workers (post-secondary and university graduates) actually fell and that of less educated workers (less than or equal to a completed high-school education) rose. In the 1980s (1979-1988), the real wage of all workers in the services sector fell except for university graduates whose rates rose even faster than the rate in the goods-producing sector. In the 1990s (1988-1997), the real wage of all workers with all levels of educational attainment rose, with a huge acceleration for university educated workers (an annual rise of 5.3 percent). Even though for any decade studied the real wage in the services-producing sector did not rise faster than in the goods-producing sector, in the 1990s, the real wage of highly educated workers rose faster in the services-producing sector than in the goods-producing sector.

The share of the goods-producing sector as an input in the production of services has fallen slightly over the years, while the services-producing industries are using more input produced by other services industries. In addition, the goods-producing industries have become more dependent on inputs from services. This may indicate that the goods-producing sector is outsourcing some tasks to the services sector that had previously been performed in-house. In comparison with the United States, it appears that the goods-producing sector in Canada uses more input from goods-producing industries and less from the services-producing industries. If the relative price of services-to-goods was approximately the same in the two countries, the above trends imply that goods-producing industries in the United States outsource more to the services sector than do their Canadian counterparts.

The services sector shares of total capital stock and stock of M&E have increased over time. Moreover, the share of the latter is rising faster. Almost all services industries are becoming more capital- and M&E-intensive. However, the increases in capital and M&E-intensities are lower than the national average for many services industries. Only a handful of services industries have realized increases in intensities above the national average.

In terms of the share of ICT in total investment, the average performance of the services industries is better than for the goods-producing industries. In the services sector, ICT-intensity (the ratio of investment in ICT compared to total investment) is twice that of the goods-producing sector. And ICT accounts for two-fifths of total investment in services industries.

The services industries are becoming increasingly more export-oriented. The ratio of exports to gross output (export intensity) was about 9 percent in 1997-99, an increase of more than 3 percentage points over the position 10 years before.

Canadian services industries are more export oriented than their counterparts in the United States, the United Kingdom and Japan. Furthermore, Canada has a revealed comparative advantage over all three of those countries in the distribution services (wholesale and retail trade). Canada also has a RCA in finance and insurance vis-à-vis the United States.

Close to 60 percent of the stock of Canadian direct investment abroad is in the services industries, whereas only 30 percent of the stock of inward foreign direct investment is in the services sector.

Services industries are becoming more innovative in terms of capital- intensity, M&E-intensity, skill-intensity and the use of advanced technologies. They are also becoming more innovative when judged by their R&D expenditures. In the 1980s, only 18 percent of total business expenditure on R&D in Canada was in the services industries; whereas by 2002, that share had increased to 35 percent. The average growth of BERD in the services industries in 2002, compared to the annual average for 1991-2001, was almost double the growth in manufacturing. However, the BERD to GDP ratio in the services sector is still only half a percentage point, which is very low compared to 4 percent in manufacturing. There are a few industries, however, which display a BERD to GDP ratio that is higher than the national average.

R&D intensity differs by country of control. In the 1990s, among Canadian-controlled companies, R&D intensity was higher in manufacturing than in services. On the other hand, foreign-controlled companies had higher R&D intensities in services than in manufacturing.

Besides being heavy users of ICTs, services industries also have an important role to play in ICT production. The overall ICT sector which contributes 6 percent of Canada's GDP is dominated by services industries which account for 81 percent of the ICT sector's contribution to GDP, 83 percent of ICT employment, and 34 percent of R&D spending on ICT.

In short, the Canadian services sector is becoming more dynamic, innovative, outward-oriented, productive and skill-intensive when looked at overall. There is, however, a considerable degree of diversity among the services industries and the gap between the services sector and manufacturing does not seem to be narrowing.

APPENDIX A

TABLE A1

INDUSTRY DETAILS AT NAICS 2-DIGIT AND 3-DIGIT LEVELS

	NAICS	LEVEL	INDUSTRIES
A	Goods-producing		
	11	*2*	***Agriculture, Forestry, Fishing and Hunting***
	111	3	Crop Production
	112	3	Animal Production
	113	3	Forestry and Logging
	114	3	Fishing, Hunting and Trapping
	115	3	Support Activities for Agriculture and Forestry
	21	***2***	***Mining and Oil and Gas Extraction***
	211	3	Oil and Gas Extraction
	212	3	Mining (except Oil and Gas)
	213	3	Support Activities for Mining and Oil and Gas Extraction
	22	***2***	***Utilities***
	221	3	Utilities
	23	***2***	Construction
	231	3	Prime Contracting
	232	3	Trade Contracting
	31-33	***2***	***Manufacturing***
	311	3	Food Manufacturing
	312	3	Beverage and Tobacco Product Manufacturing
	313	3	Textile Mills
	314	3	Textile Product Mills
	315	3	Clothing Manufacturing
	316	3	Leather and Allied Product Manufacturing
	321	3	Wood Product Manufacturing
	322	3	Paper Manufacturing
	323	3	Printing and Related Support Activities
	324	3	Petroleum and Coal Products Manufacturing
	325	3	Chemical Manufacturing
	326	3	Plastics and Rubber Products Manufacturing
	327	3	Non-Metallic Mineral Product Manufacturing
	331	3	Primary Metal Manufacturing
	332	3	Fabricated Metal Product Manufacturing
	333	3	Machinery Manufacturing
	334	3	Computer and Electronic Product Manufacturing
	335	3	Electrical Equipment, Appliance and Component Manufacturing
	336	3	Transportation Equipment Manufacturing
	337	3	Furniture and Related Product Manufacturing
	339	3	Miscellaneous Manufacturing

TABLE A1 CONTINUED

B	**Services-producing**		
	41	2	Wholesale Trade
	411	3	Farm Product Wholesaler-Distributors
	412	3	Petroleum Product Wholesaler-Distributors
	413	3	Food, Beverage and Tobacco Wholesaler-Distributors
	414	3	Personal and Household Goods Wholesaler-Distributors
	415	3	Motor Vehicle and Parts Wholesaler-Distributors
	416	3	Building Material and Supplies Wholesaler-Distributors
	417	3	Machinery, Equipment and Supplies Wholesaler-Distributors
	418	3	Miscellaneous Wholesaler-Distributors
	419	3	Wholesale Agents and Brokers
	44-45	2	Retail Trade
	441	3	Motor Vehicle and Parts Dealers
	442	3	Furniture and Home Furnishings Stores
	443	3	Electronics and Appliance Stores
	444	3	Building Material and Garden Equipment and Supplies Dealers
	445	3	Food and Beverage Stores
	446	3	Health and Personal Care Stores
	447	3	Gasoline Stations
	448	3	Clothing and Clothing Accessories Stores
	451	3	Sporting Goods, Hobby, Book and Music Stores
	452	3	General Merchandise Stores
	453	3	Miscellaneous Store Retailers
	454	3	Non-Store Retailers
	48-49	2	Transportation and Warehousing
	481	3	Air Transportation
	482	3	Rail Transportation
	483	3	Water Transportation
	484	3	Truck Transportation
	485	3	Transit and Ground Passenger Transportation
	486	3	Pipeline Transportation
	487	3	Scenic and Sightseeing Transportation
	488	3	Support Activities for Transportation
	491	3	Postal Service
	492	3	Couriers and Messengers
	493	3	Warehousing and Storage
	51	2	Information and Cultural Industries
	511	3	Publishing Industries
	512	3	Motion Picture and Sound Recording Industries
	513	3	Broadcasting and Telecommunications
	514	3	Information Services and Data Processing Services
	52	2	Finance and Insurance
	521	3	Monetary Authorities — Central Bank
	522	3	Credit Intermediation and Related Activities
	523	3	Securities, Commodity Contracts, and Other Financial Investment and Related Activities

TABLE A1 CONTINUED

524	3	Insurance Carriers and Related Activities
526	3	Funds and Other Financial Vehicles
53	2	Real Estate and Rental and Leasing
531	3	Real Estate
532	3	Rental and Leasing Services
533	3	Lessors of Non-Financial Intangible Assets (Except Copyrighted Works)
54	2	Professional, Scientific and Technical Services
541	3	Professional, Scientific and Technical Services
55	2	Management of Companies and Enterprises
551	3	Management of Companies and Enterprises
56	2	Administrative and Support, Waste Management and Remediation Services
561	3	Administrative and Support Services
562	3	Waste Management and Remediation Services
61	2	Educational Services
611	3	Educational Services
62	2	Health Care and Social Assistance
621	3	Ambulatory Health Care Services
622	3	Hospitals
623	3	Nursing and Residential Care Facilities
624	3	Social Assistance
71	2	Arts, Entertainment and Recreation
711	3	Performing Arts, Spectator Sports and Related Industries
712	3	Heritage Institutions
713	3	Amusement, Gambling and Recreation Industries
72	2	Accommodation and Food Services
721	3	Accommodation Services
722	3	Food Services and Drinking Places
81	2	Other Services (except Public Administration)
811	3	Repair and Maintenance
812	3	Personal and Laundry Services
813	3	Religious, Grant-Making, Civic, and Professional and Similar Organizations
814	3	Private Households
91	2	Public Administration
911	3	Federal Government Public Administration
912	3	Provincial and Territorial Public Administration
913	3	Local, Municipal and Regional Public Administration
914	3	Aboriginal Public Administration
919	3	International and Other Extra-Territorial Public Administration

Source: Statistics Canada.

APPENDIX B

TABLE B1

NAICS-BASED ICT SECTOR INDUSTRIES

MANUFACTURING	
33331	Commercial and Services Industry Machinery Manufacturing
33411	Computer and Peripheral Equipment Manufacturing
33421	Telephone Apparatus Manufacturing
33422	Radio and Television Broadcasting and Wireless Communications Equipment Manufacturing
33431	Audio and Video Equipment Manufacturing
33441	Semiconductor and Other Electronic Component Manufacturing
33451	Navigational, Measuring, Medical and Control Instruments Manufacturing [includes 2 (two) 6-digit codes]
33592	Communication and Energy Wire and Cable Manufacturing
SERVICES	
41731	Computer, Computer Peripheral and Pre-Packaged Software Wholesalers-Distributors
41732	Electronic Components, Navigational and Communications Equipment and Supplies Wholesalers-Distributors
41791	Office and Store Machinery and Equipment Wholesalers-Distributors
51121	Software Publishers
51322	Cable and Other Program Distribution
5133	Telecommunications [includes 5 (five) six-digit codes in the following: 51331-51334, 51339]
51419	Other Information Services [includes 2 (two) 6-digit codes]
51421	Data Processing Services
53242	Office Machinery and Equipment Rental and Leasing
54151	Computer Systems Design and Related Services
81121	Electronic and Precision Equipment Repair and Maintenance

Source: Statistics Canada, Catalogue No. 56-504-XPE, "Beyond the Information Highway: Networked Canada," 2001.

APPENDIX C

TABLE C1

SHARE OF TOTAL ICT SECTOR AND ICT SERVICES IN GDP, EMPLOYMENT, BERD, AND TRADE

	1997	2002
Share in Total GDP		
Total ICT Sector	4.0	6.0
Total ICT Service	3.0	4.9
Share in Total Employment		
Total ICT Sector	3.2	3.8
Total ICT Service	2.5	3.1
Share in Total BERD		
Total ICT Sector	40.7	43.1
Total ICT Service	9.8	13.6
Share in Total Exports of Goods and Services		
Total ICT Sector	8.2	6.4
Total ICT Service	1.3	1.5
Share in Total Imports of Goods and Services		
Total ICT Sector	1.2	0.9
Total ICT Service	14.4	12.0

Source: Statistics Canada.

ENDNOTES

1 For measurement issues on services, see Diewert (Chapter 15 in this volume), Diewert and Nakamura (1999, 2003, forthcoming), Diewert and Fox (1999), Wolff (1999) and Triplett (1999).

2 NAICS Canada consists of 20 sectors (2-digit code) with 15 services industries and five goods-producing industries. At the 3-digit (subsector) level, in total there are 99 industries (67 services-producing and 32 goods-producing ones). At the 4-digit level (the industry group), there are a total of 321 industries, with 198 services-producing and 123 goods-producing ones. Finally, at the 5-digit (industry) level, there are 734 industries, with 457 of these in services and the remaining 277 in the goods sectors.

3 Fictitious industries are created to record a particular type of expense incurred by all industries in the economy when there is no reasonable way of distributing that expense across industries. For example, Statistics Canada has data on expenses incurred in (and revenue created by) advertising and promotion activities from the supply side but it has no way of knowing how much of that was demanded by each industry. In such situations, the total expenses on these activities are recorded under one category called "advertising and promotion" even though there is no real industry by that name. Also note that non-business comprises the non-profit and government sectors.

4 For Canada, the GDP data in constant prices are more recent by two to three years than those in current prices. This is because annual estimates of industry GDP are derived within a framework of input-output tables based on annual surveys and censuses. These data in current prices have detailed accounts of gross outputs and intermediate inputs, and hence allow calculation of industry value added. It takes generally two to three years for these data to be released after the surveys are taken. Then by deflating these data by an appropriate price index, the constant price value added is derived residually as the difference between the two.

For two full years following the issuing of the most recent input-output tables, the derivation of GDP must rely on a less comprehensive database, usually supplied by monthly surveys. But monthly survey data are useful for making projections in constant prices, not in current prices. Even though monthly surveys provide reasonable estimates of gross output, they provide only very limited information on intermediate input. As a result, we cannot compute value added. Nevertheless, with the assumptions that changes in outputs or inputs reflect changes in value added, estimates of GDP are derived using either outputs or inputs as indicators. The assumption that value added moves with output or input seems more appropriate for constant price data because technological advances which permit a different amount of output to be produced from the same amount of inputs normally occur slowly. As a result, the constant price value added data are more up-to-date than the current price ones.

5 The services segment of the economy is comprised of three major categories: business services, personal services and government services. The first two categories can broadly be called business-sector services and the last category can be called non-business sector services.

6 Again, the difference in the relative inflation rates of goods and services in the two countries could be a factor behind the widening shares of services-sector contributions to GDP. If the relative price of services to goods rises in one country faster than in the other, then the share of services will increase faster in the country with higher relative services price increases.

7 According to Figure 1, the nominal dollar share of services fell slightly in 1999. However, in real terms, the share of services increased by one percentage point. This seemingly contradictory scenario might have arisen because of the different time periods for which data are available. The current price GDP data are available only up to 1999, whereas real data are available up through 2002 (with services share growth occurring mainly in 2001 and 2002). In real terms, the share of services in 1999 was constant, as it had been through the 1990s, at 68 percent. Before we conclude that the services share is rising faster in real terms than in current prices, we need to examine the data at current prices beyond year 2000.

8 The whole business sector consists of all sectors in the economy (both goods- and services-producing industries) except government and non-profit institutions. On the other hand, as defined in Endnote 6, business sector services cover only the services part of the whole business sector but without personal services in it.

9 Note that, by construction, in the input-output table, for each and all industries revenue is equal to the cost. And the business profit is included as a payment to capital input, and hence is counted as value added.

10 It would have been desirable to use employment hours rather than number of employees as the denominator, but data limitations prevented us from doing so. Since the share of the self-employed is not very different across services industries and we are looking at change in intensity, the result we see here may not be very different from what we would have calculated if we had had data on the number of employment hours.

11 Total capital is the sum of building, engineering and M&E capital, with the first two components known as structural capital. Even though the share of M&E in services is rising, the share of M&E capital in the total capital stock in the services sector is still lower than the share in the goods sector. For example, the share of M&E in the total capital stock in the services sector was 18 percent during the 1992-2002 period, whereas for the goods-producing sector it was 31 percent and for manufacturing it was 53 percent.

12 The share of services exports in total exports of goods and services based on the balance of payments (BOP) during the same period would be about 13 percent. The main reason for this discrepancy is that under BOP, the transportation cost to the border point is counted as goods trade, whereas in the input-output data, this component is counted as services trade.

13 Due to a lack of historical NAICS data on research and development related issues, in this section the industry level data are based on SIC codes. However, at the level of aggregation for which the data are available, most of the industries are the same in both systems. Therefore for many industries, the data used in this section would also be the same had we used the NAICS codes.

14 Lipsey and Carlaw (forthcoming) shows that total factor productivity (TFP) does not measure technological change, and explains that the treatment of R&D in national accounts also is problematic. They explain that if a firm switches resources from making machines to performing R&D to design better machines, the change will be recorded as fall in output with no change in input costs, and hence, a reduction in TFP. However, in reality there was no technological regression: resources were diverted from direct production to R&D. See Nakamura, Tiessen and Diewert (2003) for specifics about the issues this type of situation raises for the accounting profession and how Canadian accounting treatment of research and development does and does not conform to practices in the United States and elsewhere.

15 An OECD study (1996), lists the following factors that account for the rise in R&D: (i) the improved statistical coverage which differentiates R&D expenditure in services from manufacturing, (ii) increased research in new product development, (iii) business outsourcing which reflects the spinning off of research activities to other firms and (iv) government outsourcing, which reflects an increasing tendency for governments to "buy" rather than "make" R&D.

16 Recall that BERD denotes business expenditure on R&D.

ACKNOWLEDGMENTS

I would like to thank Someshwar Rao and Renée St-Jacques for their comments on the earlier version of the study.

BIBLIOGRAPHY

Avery, Peter. 1999. "Business and Industry Policy Forum on the Service Economy: Background Report," DSTI/IND (99) 19. Paris: OECD.

Baldwin, John R., Guy Gellatly, Joanne Johnson, and Valerie Peters. 1988. "Innovation in Dynamic Service Industries," Catalogue No. 88-516. Ottawa: Statistics Canada.

Diewert, W. Erwin. 2006. "Services and the New Economy: Data Needs and Challenges," chapter 15 in Richard G. Lipsey and Alice O. Nakamura (eds.). *Services Industries and the Knowledge-Based Economy*. The Industry Canada Research Series. Calgary: University of Calgary Press.

Diewert, W. Erwin, and Alice O. Nakamura. 1999. "Benchmarking and the Measurement of Best Practice Efficiency: An Electricity Generation Application," *Canadian Journal of Economics*, 32 (2): 570-588.

————. 2003. "Index Number Concepts, Measures and Decompositions of Productivity Growth," *Journal of Productivity Analysis,* 19 (2/3): 127-160.

————. (forthcoming). "The Measurement of Aggregate Total Factor Productivity Growth," in J.J. Heckman and E. Leamer (eds.). *Handbook of Econometrics Methods*.

Diewert, W. Erwin, and Kevin J. Fox. 1999. "Can Measurement Error Explains the Productivity Paradox?" *Canadian Journal of Economics*, 32(2): 251-280.

Grubel, Herbert G., and Michael A. Walker. 1989. "Service Industry Growth: Causes and Effects," Vancouver, B.C.: The Fraser Institute.

Lipsey, Richard G. 2006. "Policy Challenges in the New Economy," chapter 3 in Richard G. Lipsey and Alice O. Nakamura (eds.). *Services Industries and the Knowledge-Based Economy*. The Industry Canada Research Series. Calgary: University of Calgary Press.

Lipsey, Richard G., and Kenneth I. Carlaw. 1998. "A Structuralist Assessment of Technology Policies — Taking Schumpeter Seriously on Policy," Working Paper No. 25. Ottawa: Industry Canada.

————. (forthcoming). "The Measurement of Technological Change."

Mohnen, Pierre, and Thijs ten Raa. 2000. "Productivity Trends and Employment across Industries in Canada," in Thijs ten Raa and Ronald Schettkat (eds.). *The Growth of Service Industries: The Paradox of Exploding Costs and Persistent Demand*. Cheltenham, UK: Edward Elgar Publishing, pp. 105-118.

Nakamura, Alice O., Peter Tiessen, and W. Erwin Diewert. 2003. "Information Failure as an Alternative Explanation of Under Investment in R&D," *Managerial and Decision Economics*, 24 (2-3): 231-239.

Organisation for Economic Co-operation and Development. 1996. *Science, Technology and Industry Outlook*. Paris: OECD.

Statistics Canada. 2001. "Beyond the Information Highway: Networked Canada," Catalogue no. 56-504-XPE. Ottawa: Statistics Canada.

Statistics Canada. 2002. "Industrial Research and Development," Catalogue no. 88-202-XIB. Ottawa: Statistics Canada.

Triplett, Jack E. 1999. "The Solow Productivity Paradox: What Do Computers Do to Productivity?" *Canadian Journal of Economics*, 32 (2): 309-334.

Triplett, Jack E., and Barry P. Bosworth. 2001. "Productivity in the Services Sector" in Robert N. Stern (ed.). *Services in the International Economy*. Ann Arbor, MI: The University of Michigan Press, pp. 23-52.

Wolff, Edward N. 1999. "The Productivity Paradox: Evidence from Indirect Indicators of Service Sector Productivity Growth," *Canadian Journal of Economics*, 32 (2): 281-308.

Young, Alison. 1996. "Measuring R&D in the Services," STI Working Paper. Paris: OECD.

René Morissette, Yuri Ostrovsky & Garnett Picot
Statistics Canada[*]

5

Relative Wage Patterns Among the Highly Educated in a Knowledge-Based Economy

INTRODUCTION

AN IMPORTANT DEBATE IN THE ECONOMICS LITERATURE concerns the interpretation of the changes in the relative wages of university and high-school graduates (i.e. the "university premium" or "education premium"). Does the rising education premium signal changes in the balance of supply and demand between university and high-school graduates (as most studies argue), or does it pertain to changes in institutional factors (unionization level, public-sector policies, etc.), the balance of trade and other factors? Although all these factors may contribute to changes in the relative wages of university graduates, researchers attempt to pinpoint leading determinants of the education premium. Understanding this mechanism is important by itself and may provide further insights into the role of human capital in economic growth, the problem of income inequality and other economic issues. Furthermore, policy makers may adopt different strategies toward educational subsidies if such subsidies lower relative wages by facilitating shifts in the education attainment of the work force (Murphy, Riddell, and Romer 1998).

Several studies have observed that despite many similarities between the Canadian and U.S. economies, the relative wage trends in Canada and the United States over the past 20-25 years have been quite different. Figure 1, taken from Burbidge, Magee and Robb (2002) shows how median weekly earnings of male and female university graduates aged 25-64 and employed full-time evolved relative to their counterparts with no university degree. In the United States, the university/non-university weekly earnings ratio increased from 1.3 in 1981 to

[*] This paper represents the views of the authors and does not necessarily reflect the opinions of Statistics Canada.

FIGURE 1

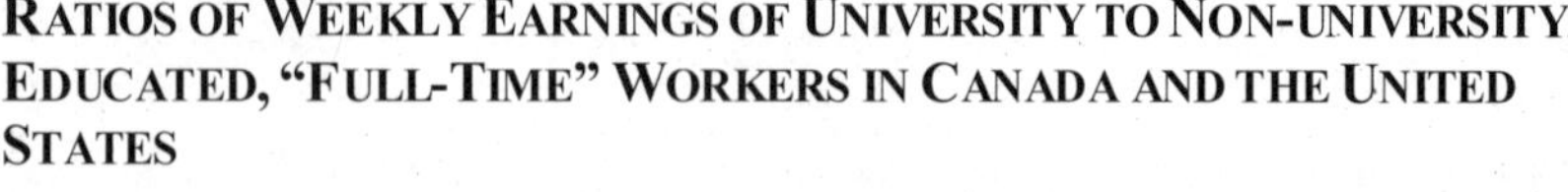

RATIOS OF WEEKLY EARNINGS OF UNIVERSITY TO NON-UNIVERSITY EDUCATED, "FULL-TIME" WORKERS IN CANADA AND THE UNITED STATES

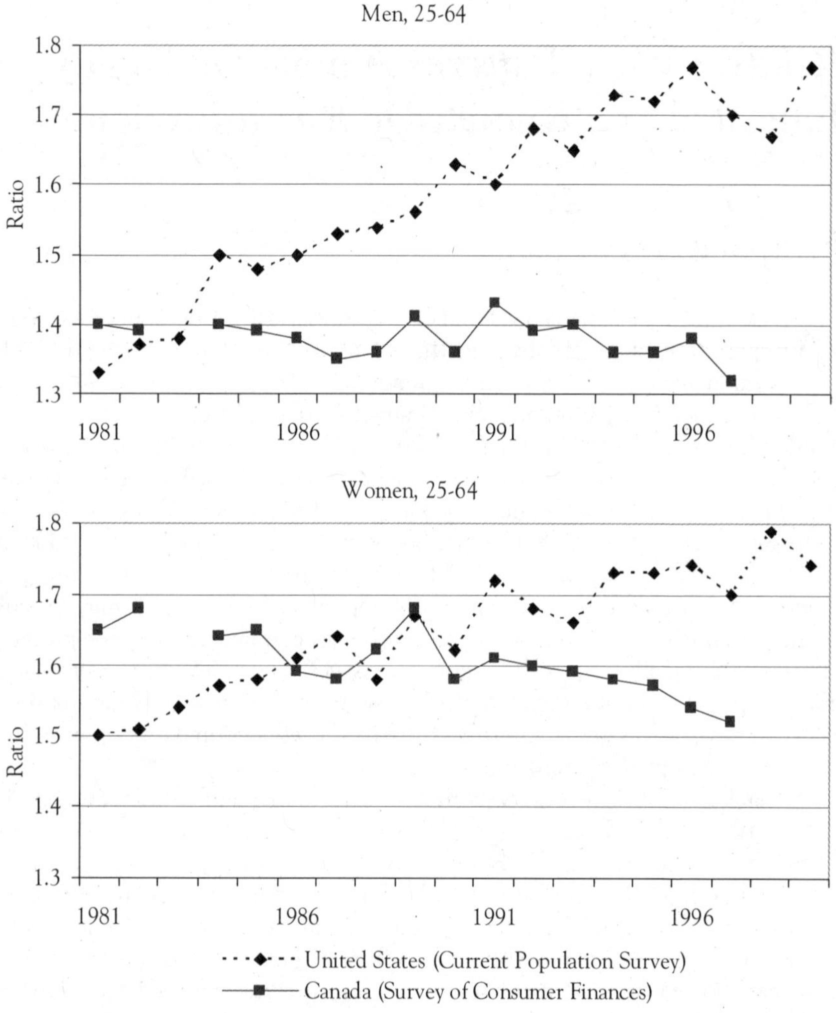

Source: Burbidge, Magee and Robb, 2002.

almost 1.8 in 1999 for men. During the 1981-2000 period, the corresponding ratio remained almost unchanged around 1.4 in Canada. Relative weekly earnings of female university graduates also increased in the United States (from 1.5 in 1981 to 1.74 in 1999) but they fell in Canada (from 1.65 to 1.5).

The differences between Canada and the United States have been used to arrive at various conclusions (Freeman and Needels 1993; Card and Lemieux 2001; Burbidge et al. 2002). As Burbidge et al. (2002) remark, "authors have located themselves on a spectrum running from demand-and-supply-explains-everything to institutional-differences-explain-everything." Most studies relate Canada-U.S. differences in the education premium to differences in the relative supply of university graduates (Freeman and Needels 1993; Murphy et al. 1998). On the other hand, Burbidge et al. argue that the relationship between the supply of university graduates and the wage premium is far from being clear-cut. They observe that while Canada-U.S. differences in skill premium can be explained by differences in the relative supply of young university graduates for the period 1988 to 1999, this relationship does not hold for the period 1981 to 1988.

Recently, more attention has been paid to disaggregating relative wage trends into gender- or age-specific trends. For instance, younger and older workers may not be perfect substitutes and if so, different relative wage patterns can emerge. Card and Lemieux (2001) show that most of the growth in relative wages of university graduates in the United States can be attributed to younger workers. They conclude that the rising premium for higher education among the younger but not older workers is related to 1) steadily increasing relative demand for more highly educated workers, 2) changes in the cohort-specific supply of highly educated workers. Notably, growth in the educational attainment of the young stopped in the 1980s and 1990s, but continued among other cohorts.

In this study we extend previous work on the evolution of the education premium in three ways. One, we include evidence from the most recent Canadian census, thereby analyzing the evolution of wage differences across education levels over the 1980-2000 period.

Two, we investigate whether the constancy of the university/high-school earnings ratio which is observed in the aggregated date actually masks offsetting trends across industries. Specifically, we assess whether the relative wages of university graduates have evolved differently in high-knowledge industries (i.e. industries with high research and development (R&D) and human capital indicators) compared to medium- and low-knowledge sectors. A common concern among policy makers is that greater demand for highly skilled workers — caused by skill-biased technological changes and/or other forces — might not be satisfied by the existing supply of highly skilled workers and might result, *at least temporarily*, in fast-growing wages among university graduates employed in expanding industries.[1] In this context, a flat aggregate education premium profile in Canada may mask differences in sector-specific trends. For example, falling relative wages in low-knowledge industries may offset rising relative wages in the high-knowledge sector. If so, policy makers may be missing important signals of changing supply/demand balance in the knowledge-based economy.

Three, we provide additional information about the changing demand for highly skilled workers by comparing relative wages of university graduates holding degrees in "applied" fields (mathematics, engineering and computer sciences) to those of other university graduates ("field" premium). An argument similar to the one above also applies here. Rising relative wages in the "applied" fields may signal higher demand for particular types of workers, while the demand for those holding other degrees may be falling. If this were the case, a relatively constant university/high-school earnings ratio would conceal important changes in the structure of labour demand.

Our main finding is that despite considerable employment growth in high-knowledge industries, changes in the education premium in these industries have been remarkably similar to those observed in other industries in the private sector. The university wage premium tends to be higher in the high-knowledge sector, but the trends are similar to those of other industrial sectors. Furthermore, while we observe accelerating employment growth among university graduates in the high-knowledge sector and among university graduates with "applied" degrees in the late 1990s, we do not detect any significant divergence in the "field" premium.

We do observe differences in trends pertaining to the university wage premium between the public sector and government, on one hand, and the commercial sectors, on the other. For example, the trends toward a rising university wage premium observed among young workers in the private sector are not evident in the public sector. It may be that relative wages respond less to changes in the supply/demand balance or the institutional structure in the public sector. Overall, our general impression is that the emergence of a knowledge-based economy has not, so far, resulted in a significant increase in the education premium in the aggregate, although a rising premium has been observed among young workers.

We proceed as follows. The first section discusses our data sample and defines our industry classification. It is followed by a section that documents employment trends by industry and field of study over the past two decades. Next, there is a comparison of the evolution of the education premium for workers in different age groups. This is followed by an exploration of the differences in education premium profiles by industry. The last section investigates the issue of a "field" premium. It is followed by a summary of our findings and conclusions.

DATA AND CONCEPTS

THE DATA ARE DRAWN FROM THE 1981, 1986, 1991, 1996 and 2001 Census files and are based on information for approximately 5 percent of the Canadian population. When we examine employment trends (as in the section immediately following) or labour supply trends, our sample consists of individuals aged 25 to 55 who are not full-time students and who are employed or active during the Census reference week (i.e. in May/June of 1981, 1986, 1991, 1996 and 2001).[2]

When we analyze the evolution of wages in subsequent sections, our sample consists of individuals aged 25 to 55 who are not full-time students and who had positive wages and salaries and positive weeks worked during the reference year (e.g. 1980 for Census 1981). In order to focus on the returns to human capital, we exclude individuals with income from self-employment. Our dependent variable is weekly wages, which is obtained by dividing annual wages and salaries by the number of weeks worked during the reference year.

We classify industries into high-, medium-, and low-knowledge industries (henceforth HKI, MKI and LKI respectively) based on R&D and human capital indicators according to Lee and Has (1996) (Table 1).[3] Educational services, health care and public administration sectors (EHPA) constitute a separate category. We follow Baldwin and Johnson (1999) in classifying industries into HKI (science-based industries in their terminology) but retain Lee and Has's grouping into MKI and LKI. Some industries have mixed high- and medium-knowledge components. These industries are included in HKI when the high-knowledge components appear to dominate.

The categories in italics in Table 1 show which services-producing industries are included in HKI, MKI and LKI. These industries are explicitly identified as services in an industry classification (for instance, *engineering and scientific services* or *services incidental to mining*) as well as industries that in our judgment do not involve production (*transportation, storage and warehousing*, etc.). We identify 24 services industries in all three sectors.

The industry classifications available in Census data vary over time. Most of the Census files used in the study provide the Standard Industry Classification (SIC) 80 sub-sector.[4] However, the 1981 Census provides only the SIC 70 classification, while the 2001 Census provides only the North American Industrial Classification System (NAICS) 97 sub-sector. While the differences between SIC 70 and SIC 80 can often be easily reconciled, the differences between NAICS 97 and SIC 80 are more problematic. The 2001 Census data files provide only four-digit NAICS 97 codes and some of our matching decisions have required judgment calls. Although more detailed codes would further improve matching, we believe that, for the most part, we are able to match NAICS 97 and SIC 80 fairly closely based on the full description of each industry code.

We group educational attainment into four categories: less than high school, completed high school (but no post-secondary education), some post-secondary education and a completed university degree (bachelor or higher). Contrary to studies combining data from the Survey of Consumer Finances, the Survey of Labour and Income Dynamics and the Labour Force Survey (e.g. Burbidge et al. 2002), our measure of educational attainment is fully consistent over time since the educational categories used in various censuses have remained constant throughout the period.[5]

We also consider two different age groups because labour market conditions for younger workers (aged 25-35) likely differ from those faced by older workers

TABLE 1

KNOWLEDGE INTENSITY CLASSIFICATION

HIGH KNOWLEDGE	MEDIUM KNOWLEDGE	LOW KNOWLEDGE
Scientific and Professional Equipment	Other Manufacturing Products	Fishing and Trapping
Communication and Other Electronic Equipment	*Management Consulting Services*	Other Electrical Products
Aircraft and Parts	*Other Business Services*	Wood
Office, Store and Business Machines	Other Transportation Equipment	Furniture and Fixtures
Architecture, Engineering, Scientific and Related Services	Primary Metals, Ferrous and Non-Ferrous	Logging and Forestry
Pharmaceutical and Medicine Products	Textiles	*Transportation*
Electric Power Systems	Paper and Allied Industries	*Storage and Warehousing*
Other Chemical Products Industries	Mining (includes quarries in 2001)	Agriculture
Machinery	Rubber	*Retail Trade*
Refined Petroleum and Coal Products	Plastics	*Personal Services*
Pipeline Transportation	Non-Metal Mineral Products	Quarries and Sand Pits
Other Telecom Industries	*Wholesale Trade*	*Accommodation, Food and Beverage Services*
Services Incidental to Agriculture	Crude Petrol and Gas	Clothing
Industrial Chemical Industries	Fabricated Metal Products	Leather
Record Player, Radio and TV Receiver Industries	Motor Vehicles and Parts	
Plastic and Synthetic Resin Industries	Food	
Electrical Industrial Equipment Industries	Beverages	
Agricultural Chemical Industries	Tobacco	
Communication and Energy Wire and Cable Industries	*Finance Insurance and Real Estate*	
*Computer and Related Services**	*Other Utilities (excluding electrical power)*	
Telecommunication Broadcasting Industries*	*Services Incidental to Mining*	
Motion Picture, Audio and Video Production and Distribution*	*Other Services*	
	Printing and Publishing	
	Construction	
	Amusement and Recreational Services (except motion picture production and distribution)	
	Postal and Courier Service	
	Membership Organizations	
	Accounting and Bookkeeping Services	
	Advertising Services	
	Offices of Lawyers and Notaries	
	Employment Agencies	
	Railroad Rolling Stock Industry	
	Boatbuilding and Repair Industry	
	Jewellery, Sporting Goods and Toys, Sign and Display Industry	
	Household Appliance Manufacturing	
	Paint and Varnish, Soap and Cleaning Compounds, and Toilet Preparations Industries	

Note: * Industries with mixed components; *italics* indicate commercial services.
Sources: Baldwin and Johnson (1999) and Lee and Has (1996).

(aged 36-55). Those in the early stages of their professional careers are less likely to have access to internal labour markets and their wages and employment status are likely to be more sensitive to changes in demand. This is also consistent with previous studies that document different education premium profiles for different age groups in Canada.

The information on total years of schooling that would allow us to determine individual experience is only available for 1985, 1990 and 1995. We construct a "potential experience" variable as a proxy for actual experience. We define "potential experience" as "age" minus "potential years of schooling" minus 6 (the usual age of entering primary school), where "potential years of schooling" are calculated as conditional means of total years of schooling for each level of education in 1985-1995 (i.e. years for which the variable "total years of schooling" is available).

EMPLOYMENT TRENDS: 1981-2001

BETWEEN 1981 AND 2001, total employment rose 49 percent in Canada (Table 2). Employment growth was spread unequally as employment in high-knowledge industries rose a solid 84 percent, more than double the rates observed in medium- and low-knowledge industries (52 percent and 32 percent, respectively). Half of the employment growth of the high-knowledge sector took place during the second half of the 1990s. Employment in this sector rose much faster among services-producing firms than among their goods-producing counterparts. In fact, employment in the former group almost tripled while it rose only 33 percent among the latter group. As a result, services-producing firms ended up accounting for about one half of all jobs in high-knowledge industries in 2001, a much larger proportion than observed in 1981 (33 percent). The faster employment growth observed in services-producing firms occurred also in low- and medium-knowledge industries, although at a more moderate pace. By 2001, high-knowledge industries accounted for roughly 10 percent of total employment, compared to 8 percent in 1981.

Between 1981 and 1996, employment of university graduates grew at a remarkably similar pace in HKI, MKI and LKI. However, the number of jobs held by university graduates rose drastically in HKI between 1996 and 2001. As a result, employment of university graduates in HKI registered an increase of 245 percent (3.45–1) between 1981 and 2001, a much faster increase than was observed in other industries (Table 3). Meanwhile, the number of employed high-school graduates rose only 31 percent in high-knowledge industries, compared to 75 percent and 92 percent in medium- and low-knowledge industries respectively. As a result, the ratio of employment of university graduates to high-school graduates grew from 1.3 to 3.4 in HKI.[6] The corresponding ratio rose only from 0.7 to 1.1 in medium-knowledge industries and from 0.3 to 0.4 in low-knowledge industries. Similar conclusions hold when we consider the ratio of employment of individuals with *at least* some post-secondary education to those with *at most* a high-school diploma.

TABLE 2

SHARES OF EMPLOYMENT AND EMPLOYMENT GROWTH BY KNOWLEDGE-BASED SECTORS (IN PERCENT)

	Shares of Employment					Employment Growth (1981=1)			
	1981	1986	1991	1996	2001	1986	1991	1996	2001
Low Knowledge	**28.8**	**29.0**	**28.0**	**27.3**	**25.5**	**1.15**	**1.27**	**1.31**	**1.32**
Services	72.2	73.8	77.2	78.4	76.8	1.17	1.35	1.43	1.40
Goods	27.8	26.2	22.8	21.6	23.2	1.08	1.04	1.02	1.11
Medium Knowledge	**38.8**	**37.5**	**37.2**	**38.5**	**39.7**	**1.10**	**1.25**	**1.38**	**1.52**
Services	46.2	50.7	53.8	58.1	58.8	1.21	1.45	1.73	1.94
Goods	53.8	49.3	46.2	41.9	41.2	1.00	1.08	1.07	1.17
High Knowledge	**7.9**	**7.8**	**8.0**	**8.2**	**9.8**	**1.12**	**1.32**	**1.43**	**1.84**
Services	33.4	34.7	41.7	43.8	52.0	1.17	1.65	1.88	2.87
Goods	66.6	65.3	58.3	56.2	48.0	1.10	1.16	1.21	1.33
Education, Health and Public Administration	**24.6**	**25.8**	**26.8**	**26.1**	**25.0**	**1.19**	**1.42**	**1.48**	**1.51**
Total	**100**	**100**	**100**	**100**	**100**	**1.14**	**1.30**	**1.39**	**1.49**
Services*	**54.8**	**58.0**	**61.3**	**64.0**	**64.0**	**1.19**	**1.41**	**1.59**	**1.73**
Goods*	**45.2**	**42.0**	**38.7**	**36.0**	**36.0**	**1.04**	**1.08**	**1.08**	**1.18**

Note: * Excluding "Education, Health and Public Administration".
Source: Data from 1981, 1986, 1991, 1996 and 2001 Canadian Census files.

TABLE 3

SHARES OF EMPLOYMENT AND EMPLOYMENT GROWTH BY KNOWLEDGE-BASED SECTORS AND LEVELS OF EDUCATIONAL ATTAINMENT (IN PERCENT)

	Shares of Employment					Employment Growth (1981=1)			
	1981	1986	1991	1996	2001	1986	1991	1996	2001
Low Knowledge									
University	4.3	5.3	6.0	7.7	8.8	1.41	1.78	2.38	2.71
Some Post-Secondary	33.3	35.9	39.0	42.9	44.1	1.24	1.48	1.70	1.75
High School	13.6	15.0	18.9	19.4	19.8	1.26	1.76	1.88	1.92
Less than High School	48.9	43.8	36.1	29.9	27.4	1.03	0.93	0.80	0.74
Medium Knowledge									
University	9.9	11.8	13.7	16.3	17.8	1.32	1.74	2.30	2.78
Some Post-Secondary	40.1	42.1	44.1	46.7	47.8	1.15	1.37	1.59	1.81
High School	14.0	14.7	17.2	16.8	16.1	1.15	1.54	1.66	1.75
Less than High School	36.2	31.5	25.0	20.4	18.4	0.96	0.86	0.78	0.77
High Knowledge									
University	17.9	21.0	24.3	29.0	33.6	1.32	1.79	2.33	3.45
Some Post-Secondary	46.9	48.0	49.7	49.6	49.2	1.15	1.40	1.52	1.93
High School	13.9	13.3	13.6	11.8	9.9	1.07	1.29	1.22	1.31
Less than High School	21.3	17.7	12.4	9.6	7.4	0.93	0.77	0.64	0.64
Education, Health and Public Administration									
University	30.1	32.7	32.5	35.7	37.5	1.30	1.54	1.75	1.89
Some Post-Secondary	42.7	43.8	45.1	45.4	46.2	1.22	1.50	1.57	1.64
High School	9.5	9.3	10.9	10.3	9.3	1.17	1.64	1.60	1.49
Less than High School	17.7	14.2	11.4	8.7	7.0	0.93	0.92	0.72	0.60
Total									
University	**13.8**	**16.0**	**17.4**	**20.1**	**22.0**	**1.32**	**1.64**	**2.01**	**2.36**
Some Post-Secondary	**39.3**	**41.2**	**43.4**	**45.5**	**46.6**	**1.19**	**1.44**	**1.60**	**1.76**
High School	**12.8**	**13.3**	**15.7**	**15.4**	**14.7**	**1.18**	**1.60**	**1.68**	**1.72**
Less than High School	**34.1**	**29.6**	**23.4**	**19.0**	**16.8**	**0.99**	**0.89**	**0.77**	**0.73**

Source: Data from 1981, 1986, 1991, 1996 and 2001 Canadian Census files.

Hence, high-knowledge industries both increased their employment levels and the average education level of their workforce much more rapidly than medium- and low-knowledge industries between 1981 and 2001. This suggests that the demand for highly skilled workers rose faster in HKI than in MKI and LKI.

EXPLORING GENDER AND AGE DIFFERENCES

WE BEGIN BY DEMONSTRATING THE IMPORTANCE of disintegrating relative weekly wage profiles of university graduates in Canada by looking at the differences in age and gender wage profiles. Figure 2 shows the ratio of median weekly earnings of university graduates to those of high-school graduates over the 1980-2000 period. The ratio is presented for all workers aged 25 to 55 (top left panel), workers aged 25-35 and those aged 36-55 (top right panel), women from both age groups (bottom left panel) and finally, men from both age groups (bottom right panel).

In the aggregate, the university premium displays no trend: relative median weekly wages of university graduates (compared to high-school graduates) have been holding steady at about 1.6 since 1980. The picture is quite different if we look separately at younger (age 25-35) and older (36-55) workers. While relative median weekly wages for older workers are higher, they have fallen from about 1.9 in 1980 to slightly above 1.7 in 2000. During the same period, relative median weekly wages for younger workers have slightly increased from about 1.45 to 1.50.

Further decomposition by gender shows a particularly large decline in the relative median weekly wages of prime-aged women (from over 2.0 in 1980 to slightly over 1.8 in 2000) and growth in the relative median weekly wages of younger women (from under 1.6 in 1980 to about 1.8 in 2000). Relative median weekly wages of men rose in both age groups. However, the growth was higher for younger men.

Having observed substantial differences in the patterns for male and female university graduates from different age groups, we now examine how changes in relative wages are related to changes in the relative supply of university graduates. To do so, we show, for each gender-age group, the fraction of labour force participants with a given education level during the Census reference week (Table 4).

Not surprisingly, we observe substantial increases in the relative supply of university graduates for both men and women of all ages. Changes among young women are particularly impressive. While in 1981 there were more young women with a high-school diploma than university graduates, in 2001 there were almost three times as many university graduates as high-school

FIGURE 2

UNIVERSITY/HIGH-SCHOOL WAGE RATIO

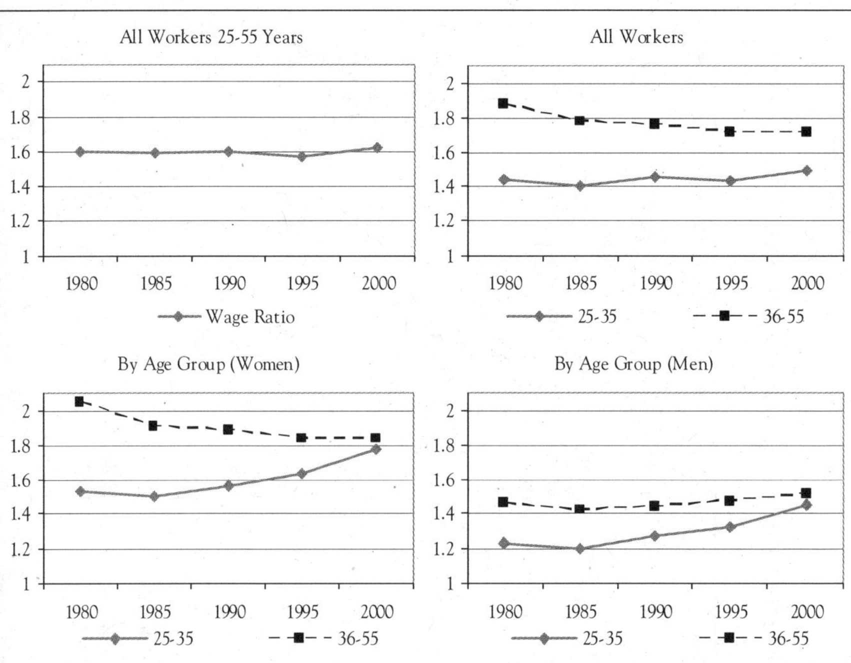

Source: Data from 1981, 1986, 1991, 1996 and 2001 Canadian Census files.

graduates. Similar trends, although on a smaller magnitude, are observed among women aged 36-55. In 1981, there were considerably fewer university graduates (with an 8 percent share of the labour force) than high-school graduates (13 percent share); however, in 2001 the situation was reversed (20 percent and 18 percent, respectively).

Changes in the relative supply of university graduates were not as dramatic among young men. While the proportion of the labour force with a high-school diploma was almost unchanged in 2000 compared to 1980 — around 14 percent — the proportion of young male labour force participants with a university degree increased from 17 percent to 22 percent. Among men 36-55, both the fraction of university graduates and high-school graduates increased between 1980 and 2000 in similar proportions. The fraction of university graduates increased from 13 percent to 21 percent, while the proportion of high-school graduates increased from 9 percent to 14 percent.

While changes in weekly hours worked by women and in the types of occupations they hold pose a challenge to interpretation of the patterns documented

TABLE 4

SHARES OF LABOUR FORCE AND EMPLOYMENT GROWTH BY GENDER, AGE GROUP AND LEVELS OF EDUCATIONAL ATTAINMENT

	SHARES OF LABOUR FORCE (IN PERCENT)					LABOUR FORCE PARTICIPATION GROWTH (1981=1)			
	1981	1986	1991	1996	2001	1986	1991	1996	2001
Women (25-35)									
University	15.4	16.3	17.1	22.7	28.1	1.30	1.52	1.85	2.11
Some Post-Secondary	41.9	44.4	47.5	50.1	50.3	1.30	1.55	1.49	1.38
High School	18.8	17.7	18.1	14.6	10.9	1.15	1.31	0.97	0.67
Less than High School	23.9	21.6	17.2	12.6	10.6	1.11	0.99	0.66	0.51
Women (36-55)									
University	8.0	12. 2	14.8	17.7	19.6	1.96	3.14	4.43	5.80
Some Post-Secondary	35.7	38.7	40.8	43.5	45.6	1.39	1.93	2.43	3.00
High School	12.9	14.0	18.4	18.7	17.9	1.39	2.40	2.89	3.26
Less than High School	43.5	35.2	25.9	20.1	16.9	1.04	1.01	0.92	0.92
Men (25-35)									
University	16.7	16.1	15.4	18.2	21.6	1.06	1.04	1.09	1.15
Some Post-Secondary	43.2	44.0	45.6	47.2	48.3	1.11	1.19	1.10	0.99
High School	13.4	13.3	15.1	14.8	13.5	1.08	1.26	1.12	0.89
Less than High School	26.8	26.6	24.0	19.8	16.6	1.08	1.01	0.74	0.55
Men (36-55)									
University	12.9	16.6	18. 7	19.8	20.5	1.43	1.89	2.23	2.60
Some Post-Secondary	35.8	38.0	40.8	43.3	44.8	1.18	1.48	1.76	2.05
High School	8.6	9.7	12.5	13.4	14.0	1.27	1.90	2.28	2.68
Less than High School	42.7	35.7	28.0	23.6	20.8	0.93	0.87	0.81	0.80

TABLE 4 CONTINUED

Total (25-35)									
University	16.1	16.2	16.2	20.3	24.7	1.15	1.23	1.39	1.52
Some Post-Secondary	42.7	44.2	46.5	48.6	49.3	1.19	1.33	1.26	1.15
High School	15.6	15.2	16.5	14.8	12.3	1.12	1.29	1.04	0.78
Less than High School	25.6	24.4	20.9	16.4	13.8	1.09	1.00	0.71	0.53
Total (36-55)									
University	**11.0**	**14.7**	**17.0**	**18.8**	**20.1**	**1.58**	**2.24**	**2.84**	**3.47**
Some Post-Secondary	**35.8**	**38.3**	**40.8**	**43.4**	**45.2**	**1.26**	**1.65**	**2.02**	**2.41**
High School	**10.2**	**11.5**	**15.1**	**15.8**	**15.8**	**1.33**	**2.14**	**2.57**	**2.96**
Less than High School	**43.0**	**35.5**	**27.1**	**22.0**	**18.9**	**0.97**	**0.91**	**0.85**	**0.84**

Source: Data from 1981, 1986, 1991, 1996 and 2001 Canadian Census files.

above for female workers, it is important to emphasize that the increase in the education premium observed among young men occurred in conjunction with an increase in the relative supply of university graduates in this group, thereby suggesting a growing *relative* demand for university graduates among new entrants into the labour market. Furthermore, the constancy of the university/high-school earnings ratio observed among prime-aged men has coincided with a constant relative supply of university graduates in this group.

Taken together, the wage patterns documented for various age-gender groups clearly indicate that the constancy of the university/high-school earnings ratio observed in the aggregate masks offsetting trends found among more narrowly-defined demographic groups. Likewise, it is conceivable that the evolution of the education premium observed within age-gender cells conceals diverging trends across industries. This may be so for at least two reasons. First, the factors underlying wage determination in the public sector likely differ from those in the private sector. Second, the pace of technological change, the rate at which firms innovate, the growth of competition within industries or from abroad and union density — four potentially important factors in the wage determination process — may evolve quite differently across private sector industries. Hence, there is no reason, *a priori*, to assume that the aforementioned patterns will hold for all sectors of the economy.

DISAGGREGATING THE DATA BY INDUSTRY

DESCRIPTIVE EVIDENCE

TO ASSESS WHETHER DIFFERENT INDUSTRIES display different patterns, we plot relative median weekly wages of university graduates for each of the four industrial groups defined above: high-knowledge industries, medium-knowledge industries, low-knowledge industries and educational services, health and public administration. We do so for each of the age-gender groups. To assess the robustness of our results, we calculate weekly earnings of university graduates relative to three different groups: individuals with some post-secondary education (excluding those with a university degree), individuals with less than high-school education as well as high-school graduates. The results are shown in a series of charts in the Appendix.

For young men and prime-aged women, the education premium — however defined — displays quite different trends in EHPA compared to the three other industrial sectors. In EHPA, the relative weekly wages of young male and prime-aged female university graduates fell between 1980 and 2000. However, they rose in all three other sectors. Thus, the declining education premium observed among prime-aged women in the aggregate clearly provides a misleading view of the evolution of educational wage differentials in private sector industries.

For all workers except prime-aged men, the education premium rose in low-, medium- as well as high-knowledge industries. Whether the increase was more pronounced in high-knowledge industries than in other industries is unclear. Relative weekly wages of female university graduates employed in HKI do not appear to have risen more than those of their counterparts employed in MKI or LKI. Only young male university graduates employed in HKI have seen their earnings relative to high-school graduates rise faster than their counterparts employed in MKI or LKI.

In contrast, prime-aged male university graduates employed in LKI have experienced a substantial deterioration in their relative earnings. There is almost no evidence that their counterparts in MKI and HKI have improved their position relative to lower-educated workers during the 1980-2000 period.

Taken together, these results indicate that, for young workers and prime-aged women, the education premium displays similar positive trends across private sector industries. To investigate whether these patterns hold for workers with comparable labour market experience, we now turn to multivariate analysis.

MULTIVARIATE ANALYSIS

OUR REGRESSION ANALYSIS OF THE EDUCATION PREMIUM is based on standard log-wage quantile regressions with dummy variables for different educational attainments entering as explanatory variables. Our control variables include potential experience, potential experience squared, a part-time/full-time dummy variable and a dummy variable for different geographic regions.[7] Separate median (or 50th quantile) regressions are run for each age-gender-industry combination and each year, thereby providing a fairly flexible specification of wage determination.

Figure 3 shows the resulting university premium trends for LKI, MKI, HKI and EHPA. The regression results confirm most of the patterns found in the raw data. First, consistent with the raw data, the inspection of the university/high-school earnings ratio shows a rising education premium in HKI, MKI and LKI for young workers and prime-aged women. Second, there is little evidence that the university wage premium increased faster in HKI than in other sectors. Third, for all age-gender groups, regression results confirm that EHPA displays quite different trends compared to HKI, MKI and LKI. Fourth, as in previous analyses, we see greater differences across age groups than across sectors of varying knowledge intensity. Specifically, in both high- and medium-knowledge industries, the education premium is much greater among young workers than among their older counterparts. Moreover, while the education premium rose in all three private-sector industries for young men, it rose only in MKI for prime-aged men.

FIGURE 3

UNIVERSITY EFFECT RELATIVE TO HIGH-SCHOOL DIPLOMA

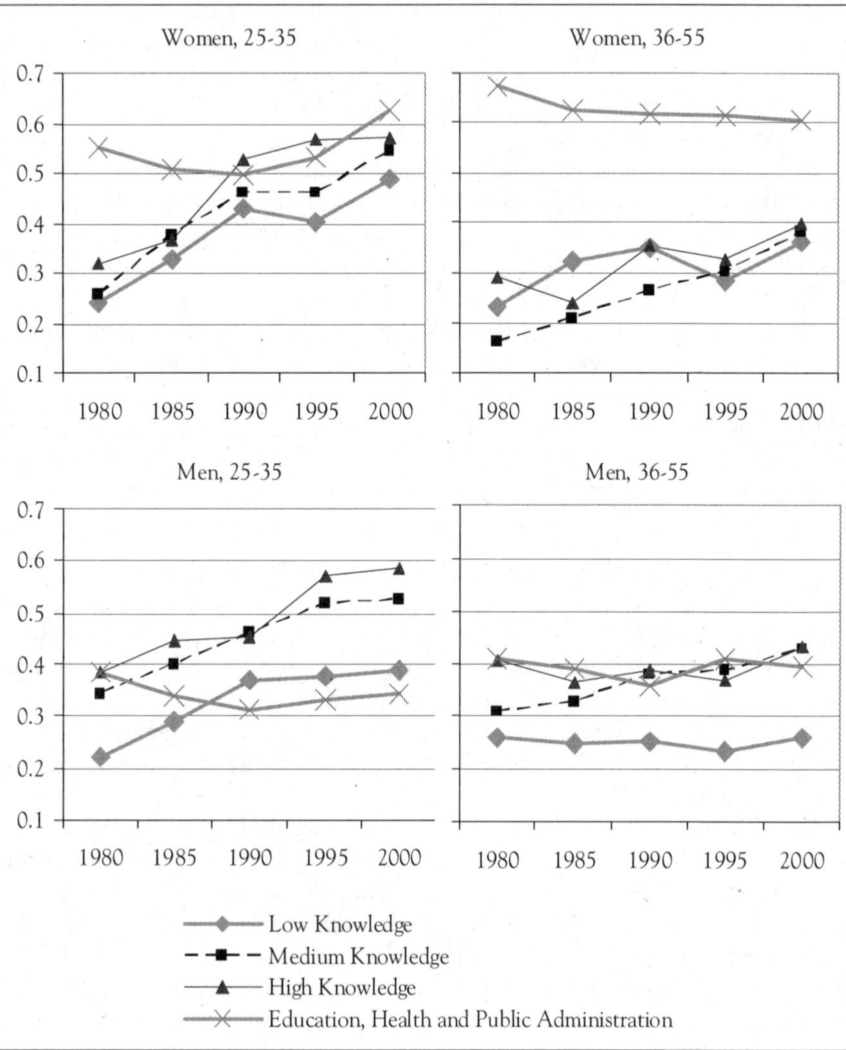

Source: Data from 1981, 1986, 1991, 1996 and 2001 Canadian Census files.

If men and women of similar ages are close substitutes, then wage patterns should also be examined in samples that combine them. We do so in Figure 4, where separate quantile regressions are run for each age-industry combination and for each year. Once again, we find little evidence that the education premium grew faster in high-knowledge industries than in other sectors.

FIGURE 4

UNIVERSITY EFFECT (RELATIVE TO HIGH-SCHOOL DIPLOMA)

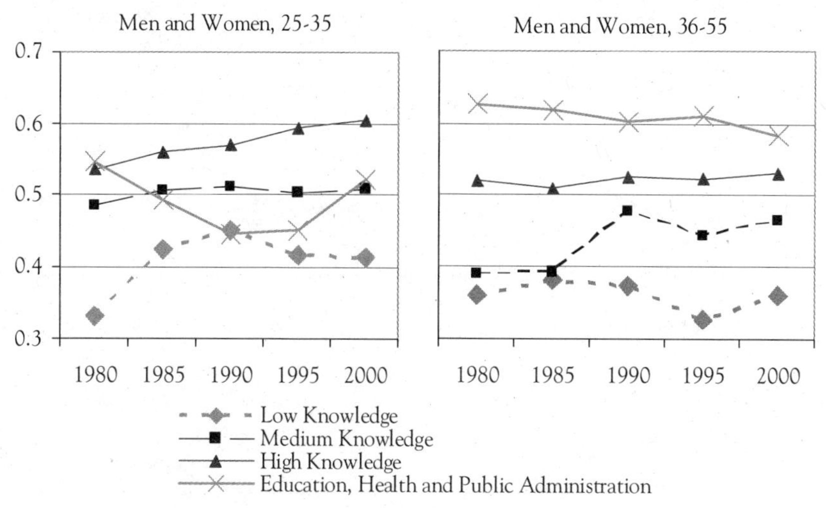

Source: Data from 1981, 1986, 1991, 1996 and 2001 Canadian Census files.

An increase in the education premium does not necessarily imply that *real* weekly wages of university graduates have increased over time. To investigate whether this is the case or not, we compute predicted median log-weekly wages of both university graduates and high-school graduates from the aforementioned quantile regressions (Figure 5). The predicted log weekly wages are in 2000 constant dollars and are set equal to 1.0 in 1980.

The results are striking. Predicted real median weekly wages of young male university graduates either fell (in LKI and EHPA) or remained fairly constant. In contrast, those of young female university graduates rose at least 20 percent in all sectors except EHPA, where they show little variation. In all three private sector industries, predicted real median weekly wages of young male high-school graduates fell almost 20 percent while those of their female counterparts either remained fairly constant (in MKI and LKI) or fell slightly (in HKI). Thus, while real weekly earnings of young men have been either falling markedly or stagnating, those of young women have been rising substantially or dropping slightly.

Prime-aged women also enjoyed greater earnings growth than their male counterparts in all sectors (Figure 6). Predicted real wages of prime-aged male university graduates and high-school graduates have shown remarkably little variation in high-knowledge industries, thereby suggesting that wages of men 36-55 employed in this sector were almost unaffected by whatever structural

FIGURE 5

PREDICTED MEDIAN REAL LOG WEEKLY WAGE (1980=1)

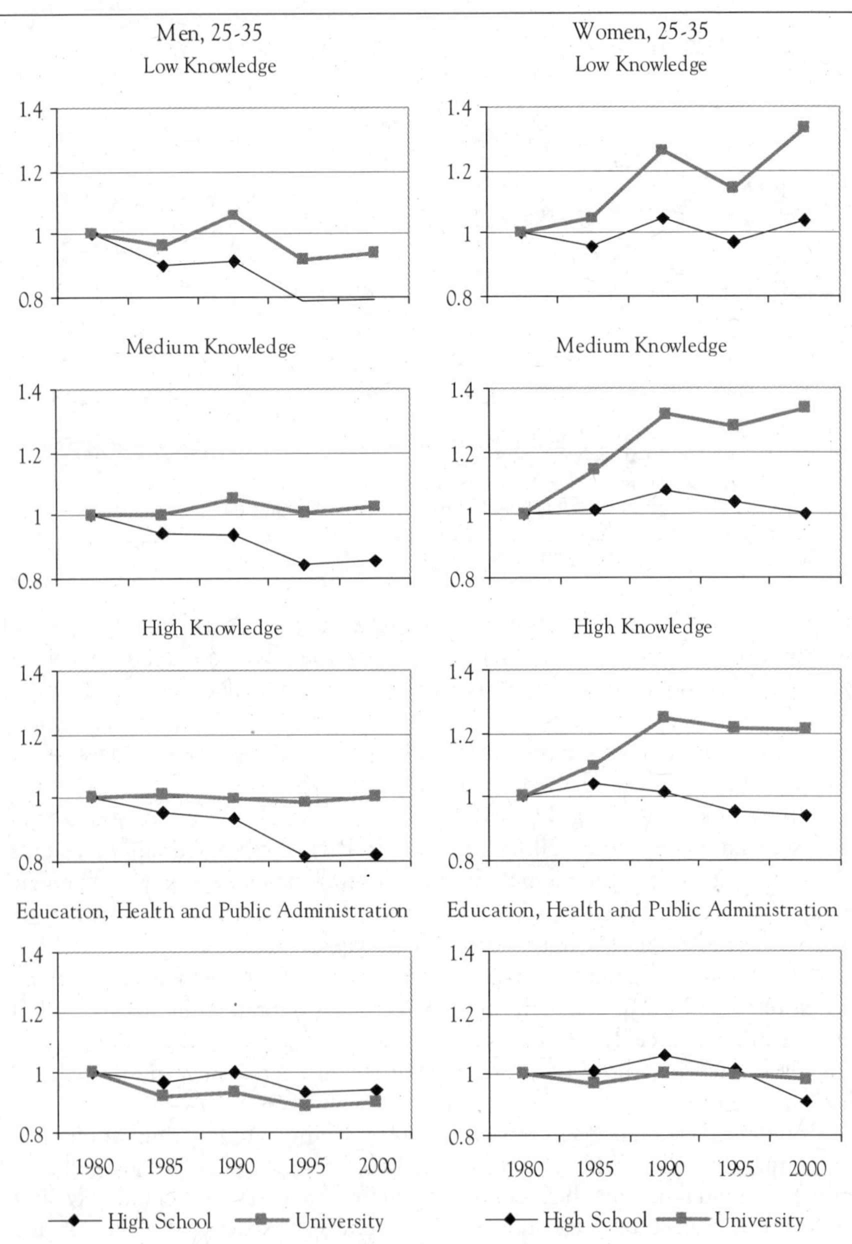

Source: Data from 1981, 1986, 1991, 1996 and 2001 Canadian Census files.

FIGURE 6

PREDICTED MEDIAN REAL LOG WEEKLY WAGE (1980=1)

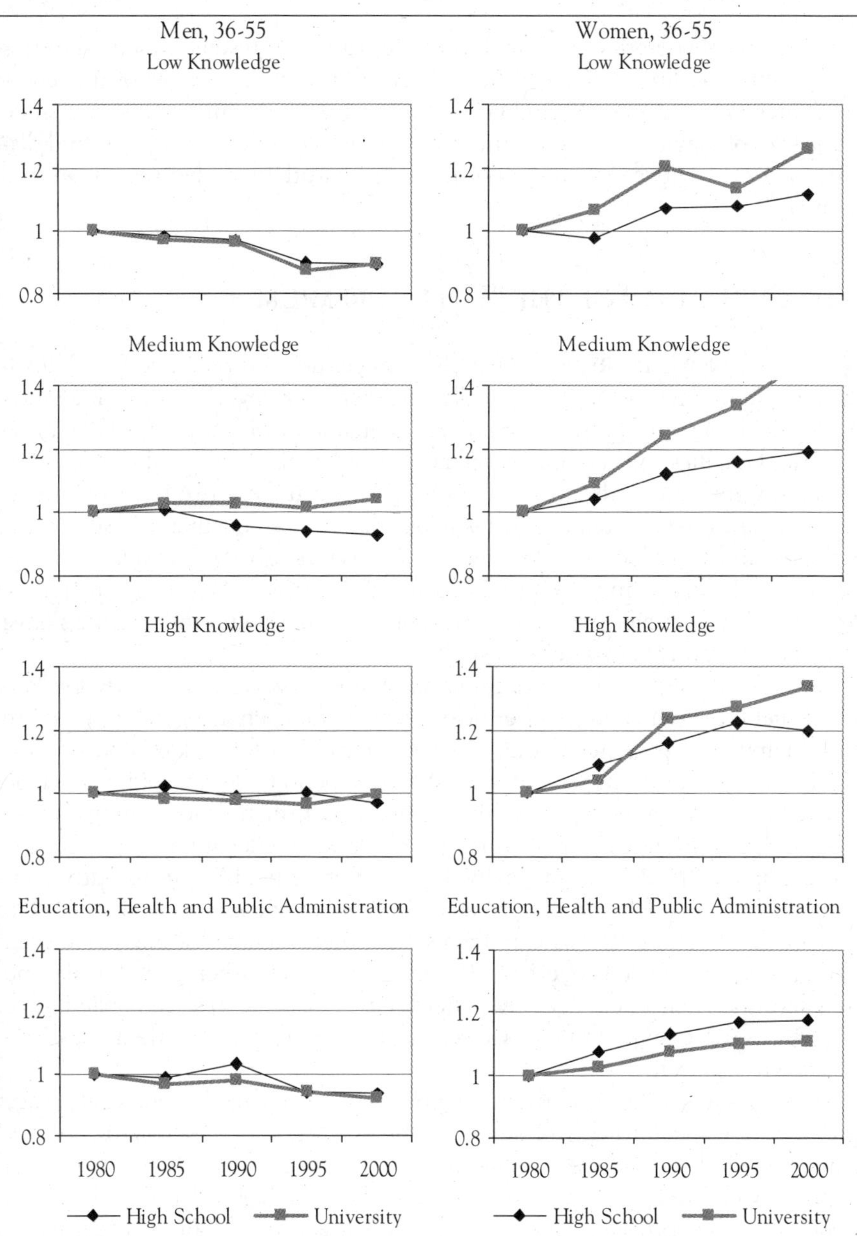

Source: Data from 1981, 1986, 1991, 1996 and 2001 Canadian Census files.

changes the Canadian economy experienced during the 1980s and 1990s. This does not appear to be the case in low-knowledge industries, where predicted wages of prime-aged male university and high-school graduates fell about 10 percent.

Overall, the descriptive analysis and the regression results presented in this section provide little evidence that relative wages or real wages of university graduates and high-school graduates have evolved differently across the three industries of varying knowledge intensity that we consider. Rather, we find distinct patterns between young and prime-aged workers or between men and women.[8]

The Evolution of the "Field" Premium

In an economy increasingly based on the use and production of knowledge, the demand for highly skilled workers may evolve quite differently across fields of study. Earnings of university graduates with degrees in engineering, mathematics and computer sciences may be higher than those of other university graduates. Also, the earnings gap between these two types of university graduates may increase as firms adopt new (often, computer-based) technologies and introduce new products and services. So far, Canadian studies (Heisz 2001; Finnie and Frenette 2003) have documented earnings differences by field of study at a given point in time, but have not found that earnings have evolved differently across fields of study.

To assess whether the education premium has evolved differently for "applied" fields as compared to other fields of study, for each age-gender group, we ran separate log-wage median regressions in each year for which we had information on field of study, i.e., for the 1985-2000 period. Our regressions include five educational categories (less than high school, high school completed — which is the omitted group — some post-secondary education, university degree in applied fields and university degree in other fields), four industry controls (HKI, MKI, LKI, and EHPA) as well as the set of control variables used in the previous section. We also ran regressions where men and women of a given age group were pooled together, the underlying notion being that male and female workers of similar ages are perfect substitutes. We defined applied fields of study as those related to engineering, applied sciences and mathematics. The results are shown in Table 5.

For all age-gender groups except prime-aged women, the university wage premium for applied fields of study was greater than for other fields. For instance, median log wages of young male university graduates with a degree in applied fields were 58 points higher than those of high-school graduates in 2000 while the corresponding difference amounted to 44 points in other fields. More important, among young men and women, the education premium for

TABLE 5

MEDIAN REGRESSION ANALYSIS: UNIVERSITY/HIGH-SCHOOL PREMIUM FOR "APPLIED" AND "NON-APPLIED" FIELDS OF STUDY (STANDARD ERRORS IN PARENTHESES)

	EDUCATION PREMIUM: UNIVERSITY/HIGH SCHOOL			
	1985	1990	1995	2000
Women (25-35)				
Applied degrees	0.547 (0.017)	0.549 (0.016)	0.562 (0.014)	0.613 (0.013)
Not applied degrees	0.436 (0.007)	0.466 (0.007)	0.481 (0.007)	0.543 (0.008)
Men (25-35)				
Applied degrees	0.469 (0.010)	0.484 (0.008)	0.524 (0.011)	0.577 (0.011)
Not applied degrees	0.351 (0.008)	0.380 (0.007)	0.414 (0.009)	0.435 (0.009)
Women (36-55)				
Applied degrees	0.487 (0.023)	0.509 (0.017)	0.497 (0.014)	0.543 (0.012)
Not applied degrees	0.528 (0.008)	0.527 (0.006)	0.528 (0.005)	0.523 (0.005)
Men (36-55)				
Applied degrees	0.426 (0.008)	0.428 (0.007)	0.427 (0.007)	0.443 (0.007)
Not applied degrees	0.355 (0.006)	0.369 (0.006)	0.383 (0.006)	0.389 (0.006)
Men and Women (25-35)				
Applied degrees	0.616 (0.009)	0.584 (0.008)	0.584 (0.009)	0.616 (0.008)
Not applied degrees	0.479 (0.006)	0.465 (0.005)	0.463 (0.006)	0.475 (0.006)
Men and Women (36-55)				
Applied degrees	0.632 (0.010)	0.631 (0.008)	0.591 (0.007)	0.591 (0.007)
Not applied degrees	0.523 (0.006)	0.538 (0.005)	0.523 (0.004)	0.506 (0.004)

Source: Data from 1981, 1986, 1991, 1996 and 2001 Canadian Census files.

applied fields did not grow more rapidly than that for other fields. In fact, when young men and women were pooled together, the education premium observed in 2000 was, for both fields, almost identical to that observed in 1985. Only among prime-aged women did the education premium for applied fields display a different pattern than that for other fields of study. Thus, along with Heisz (2001) and Finnie and Frenette (2003), we found very little evidence that relative wages of university graduates rose faster in applied fields of study than in other fields.

CONCLUSIONS

THIS STUDY DOCUMENTED THE EVOLUTION of relative wages and real wages of university graduates and high-school graduates over the 1980-2000 period. The results presented confirm that the constancy of the university/high-school earnings ratio observed in the aggregate—and documented in several previous studies—masks diverging trends across groups of workers. Our main finding is that even though employment grew much faster in high-knowledge industries than in other sectors during the past two decades, trends in relative wages and real wages of university and high-school graduates have displayed remarkably similar patterns across industries. In other words, the acceleration of employment growth in high-knowledge industries has not been accompanied by an acceleration of real and relative wages of university graduates in this sector (relative to other sectors).

We also found no evidence of an acceleration of (relative) wage growth among university graduates with a degree in applied fields of study. In contrast, we found markedly different wage patterns across age groups and also between men and women. In all private sector industries, young and prime-aged female university graduates experienced faster wage growth than their male counterparts. Meanwhile, real wages of young male university graduates were either stagnating or falling slightly while those of male high-school graduates dropped sharply.

While not inconsistent with the existence of *specific* labour shortages in narrowly-defined sectors, our examination of the wage patterns of highly educated workers has revealed little evidence that would support the notion of a *widespread* imbalance between the demand and supply of highly skilled workers in Canada.[9] Rather, it has brought back a simple idea: the possibility that the increasing supply of young women in the labour market influences the wage growth of their male counterparts. Given that young men and women in identical fields of study are very close substitutes, we should expect a negative correlation between young women's growth in labour supply in specific fields of study and young men's wage trajectories in the same fields of study. The extent to which this is true is certainly a question for further research.

APPENDIX

FIGURE A1

WEEKLY EARNINGS OF UNIVERSITY GRADUATES RELATIVE TO 'SOME POST-SECONDARY,' 'HIGH-SCHOOL' AND 'LESS THAN HIGH-SCHOOL' CATEGORIES, WOMEN (25-35)

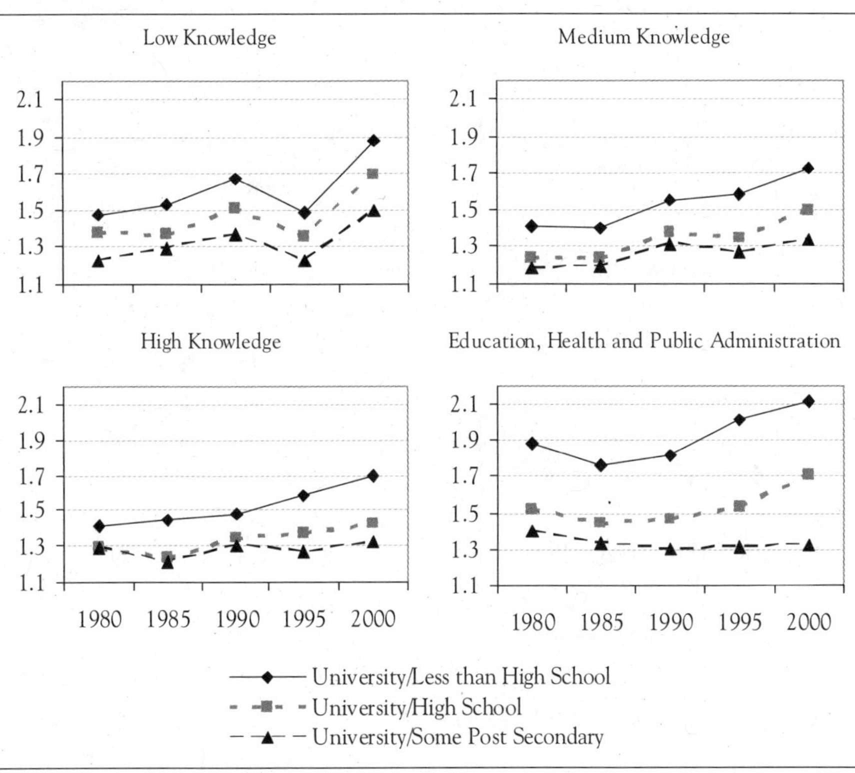

Source: Data from 1981, 1986, 1991, 1996 and 2001 Canadian Census files.

FIGURE A2

WEEKLY EARNINGS OF UNIVERSITY GRADUATES RELATIVE TO 'SOME POST-SECONDARY,' 'HIGH-SCHOOL' AND 'LESS THAN HIGH-SCHOOL' CATEGORIES, WOMEN (36-55)

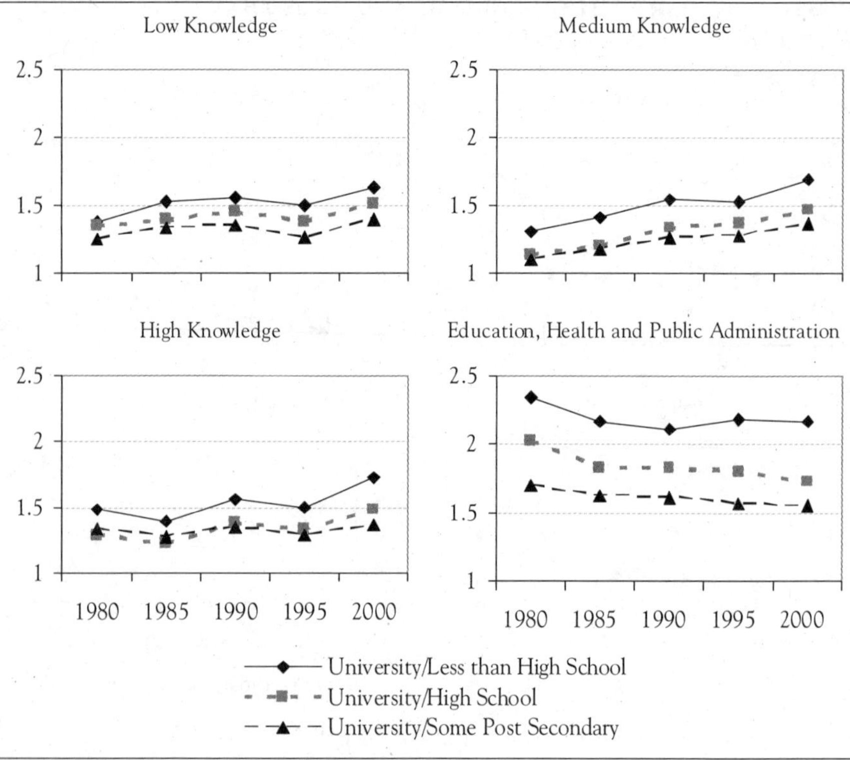

Source: Data from 1981, 1986, 1991, 1996 and 2001 Canadian Census files.

FIGURE A3

WEEKLY EARNINGS OF UNIVERSITY GRADUATES RELATIVE TO 'SOME POST-SECONDARY,' 'HIGH-SCHOOL' AND 'LESS THAN HIGH-SCHOOL' CATEGORIES, MEN (25-35)

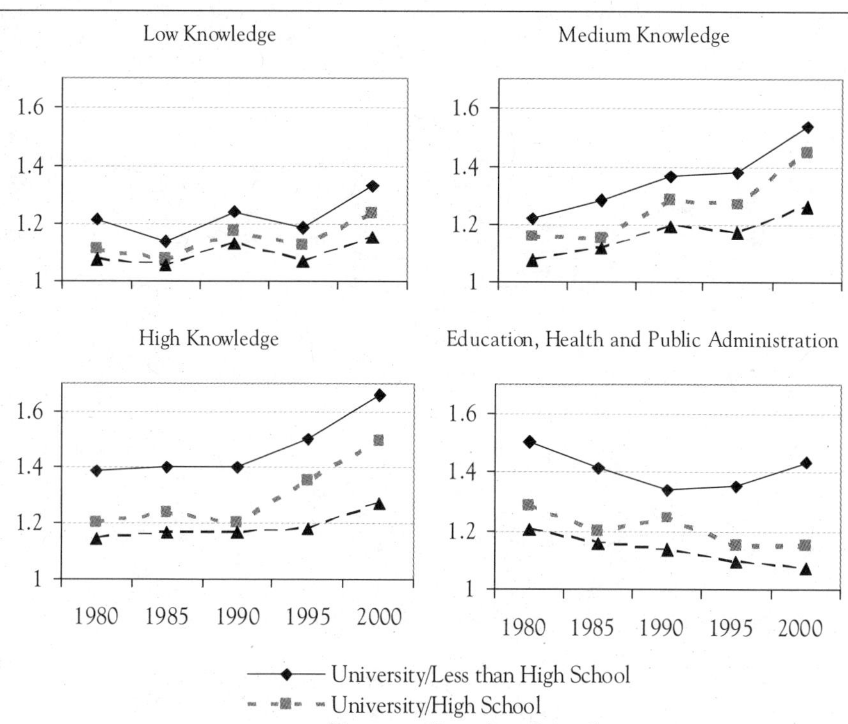

Source: Data from 1981, 1986, 1991, 1996 and 2001 Canadian Census files.

FIGURE A4

WEEKLY EARNINGS OF UNIVERSITY GRADUATES RELATIVE TO 'SOME POST-SECONDARY,' 'HIGH-SCHOOL' AND 'LESS THAN HIGH-SCHOOL' CATEGORIES, MEN (36-55)

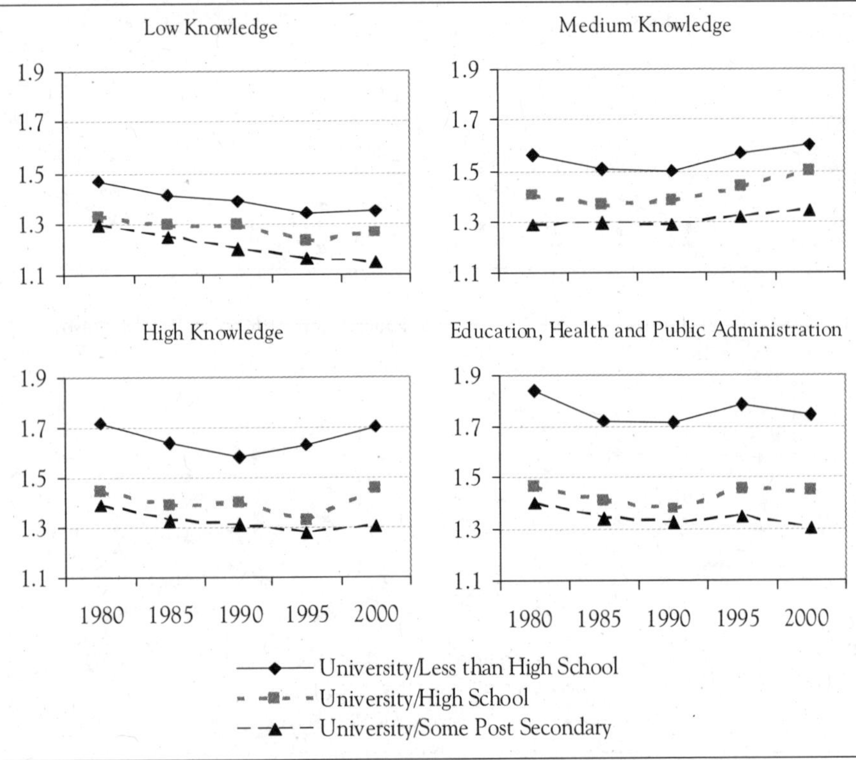

Source: Data from 1981, 1986, 1991, 1996 and 2001 Canadian Census files.

ENDNOTES

1 Efficiency wage models (e.g. Salop 1979; Shapiro and Stiglitz 1984) explain why firms are observed to pay equivalent workers different wages, even in the presence of labour mobility. They could also explain why observationally equivalent workers enjoy, over a given period, faster earnings growth than those in other industries. For instance, if the costs of training highly skilled workers rose faster in some industries than in others, firms in the former set of industries may find it profitable to raise wages of these workers in order to reduce labour turnover and restrict the growth of training costs.

2 Since student status is not reported in the 1986 Census, we exclude full-time students in all years except 1985. Freeman and Needels (1993) find that the inclusion of full-time students in 1985 has no significant effect on conclusions regarding the evolution of the education premium.

3 Lee and Has (1996) divide industries on the basis of three R&D measures: the R&D-to-sales ratios, the proportion of R&D personnel to total employment, and the proportion of professional R&D personnel to total employment; and three measures of human capital: the ratio of workers with post-secondary education to total employment, the ratio of knowledge workers (occupations in the natural sciences, engineering and mathematics, education, management and administration, social sciences, law and jurisprudence, medicine and health, and writing) to total employment, and the ratio of the number of employed scientists and engineers to total employment (Baldwin and Johnson 1999). High-knowledge industries are those that fall in the top third on the basis of two of the R&D measures *and* two of the human capital indices.

4 Both Baldwin and Johnson (1999) and Lee and Has (1996) base their classification on SIC 80.

5 In contrast, studies combining the aforementioned surveys rely on the Labour Force Survey (LFS) education question, the wording of which changed in 1989. Because of changes in the LFS education question, Burbidge et al. (2002) are constrained to compare the earnings of university graduates to those of *all other* workers, and this constitutes a fairly wide category whose educational attainment can rise over time. Our use of comparable educational categories allows us to compare earnings of university graduates to those of high-school graduates, two categories which are conceptually well defined.

6 Between 1980 and 1995, it rose from 1.3 to 2.5. It then increased further to 3.4 between 1995 and 2000.

7 To calculate the years of experience, we have to know the total number of years spent in school. Since the total number of the years of schooling is not available for all census years, we have created the "potential number of the years of schooling," a conditional mean of total years of schooling for each educational level, based on the years in which the real total number of school years is available. The total experience is then calculated as *age* minus *potential years of schooling* minus 6.

8 It is worth keeping in mind, however, that we examine log differences in medians, which may conceal distributional (interquantile) shifts in relative wages. We checked this possibility by constructing similar profiles for the 20th and 80th percentiles. We were mostly concerned that median profiles may conceal large increases in education premiums among the highest paid workers (that is highest paid university graduates relative to the highest paid high-school graduates). Our comparison of median profiles and 80th percentile profiles in all knowledge-based industries revealed little evidence of any growing divergence that would support this view.

9 Gingras and Roy (1998) come to a similar conclusion.

BIBLIOGRAPHY

Baldwin, John R., and Joanne Johnson. 1999. *The Defining Characteristics of Entrants in Science-Based Industries*. Catalogue no. 88-517-XPB. Ottawa: Statistics Canada.

Burbidge, J.B., L. Magee, and A.L. Robb. 2002. "The Education Premium in Canada and the United States," *Canadian Public Policy* 23 (2): 203-14.

Card, D., and T. Lemieux. 2001. "Can Falling Supply Explain the Rising Return to College for Young Men? A Cohort-Based Analysis," *Quarterly Journal of Economics* 116: 705-46.

Finnie, Ross, and M. Frenette. 2003. "Earning Differences by Major Field of Study: Evidence from Three Cohort of Recent Canadian Graduates," *Economics of Education Review* 22: 179-92.

Freeman, R.B., and K. Needels. 1993. "Skill Differentials in Canada in an Era of Rising Labor Market Inequality," in D. Card and R.B. Freeman (eds.), *Small Differences that Matter*. Chicago: University of Chicago Press.

Gingras, Y., and R. Roy. 1998. "Is There a Skill Gap in Canada?" Applied Research Branch, research paper R-98-9E. Ottawa: Human Resources Development Canada.

Heisz, A. 2001. "Income Prospects of British Columbia University Graduates," Analytical Studies Branch, research paper series no. 170. Ottawa: Statistics Canada.

Lee, F., and H. Has. 1996. "A Quantitative Assessment of High-Knowledge Industries Versus Low-Knowledge Industries." in Peter Howitt (ed.), *The Implications of Knowledge-Based Growth for Micro-Economic Policies*. Industry Canada Research Series. Calgary: University of Calgary Press, pp. 39-81.

Murphy, K., W.C. Riddell, and P. Romer. 1998. "Wages, Skills, and Technology in the United States and Canada," Working Paper No. 6638. Washington, D.C.: National Bureau of Economic Research.

Salop, S.C. 1979. "Model of the Natural Rate of Unemployment" *American Economic Review* 69: 117-25.

Shapiro, C., and Joseph E. Stiglitz. 1984. "Equilibrium Unemployment As a Worker Discipline Device," *American Economic Review* 74: 433-44.

Panel

Knowledge-Economy and Services: Perspectives and Issues[1]

A Policy for Services? Don't Tilt

William Watson
McGill University

I WANT TO BEGIN BY THANKING INDUSTRY CANADA for inviting me to participate in this colloquium. Every two or three years the department asks me to come and speak at one of their events. I say essentially the same thing every time, which is that the department should be shut down. (If you have capitalism, why do you need a department of industry?) And yet they keep inviting me back. Either they forget what I say or they hope I will have rehabilitated myself or moles are doing the inviting or, finally, maybe it really is true that in every Canadian soul there is a kernel of masochism. (I should mention that in abolishing the department I would, of course, spare the research section, which does much interesting work.)

WHAT ECONOMY IS NOT KNOWLEDGE-BASED?

THE TITLE OF THIS SYMPOSIUM is "Services Industries and the Knowledge-Based Economy." Let me immediately take issue with the term "knowledge-based economy." Has there ever been an economy that was *not* knowledge-based? It is a conceit of university professors and other highly credentialed commentators that knowledge is imparted mainly by formal learning. In fact, most human activities are knowledge-based. The humblest hunter-gatherer needs an exhaustive knowledge of his surroundings and prey in order to survive. Most of us "symbolic analysts," as Robert Reich once called us, would be helpless if deposited in natural surroundings without "the knowledge." (I am reminded of this every summer when my children insist I take them fishing.)

When we say "knowledge-based economy" what most of us really have in mind is "computer-based economy" or "organized-research economy" or "economy in which formal education is an important input." Though more descriptive, these phrases are also more clumsy. The most elegant phrase for our current circumstances is, of course, "the information age," even if it suggests, again wrongly, that information has not always been important. But this too will surely pass. We have had "modernism" and now "post-modernism." We have had "industrial" and now "post-industrial." Perhaps in the "post-information age" I will not receive 25 e-mails a day advising me on how I can overcome my anatomical inadequacies so as to further endear myself to my spouse.

IS "THE SERVICE SECTOR" POLICY-RELEVANT?

LEAVING ASIDE THE POSSIBILITY OF ADMINISTRATIVE INCOMPETENCE, I expect I have been invited here because of my interest in, and general scepticism about, public policy. If so, the question instantly arises: is "services" a policy-relevant aggregation? In my view it is not. Services *are* different from goods, even if many services are different from many other services (shoe shines from banking or computer upkeep, for instance). But is the difference between goods and services policy-relevant? I can't see how. There may be a need for policies in different service sectors, but surely not in services overall. As a reasonably traditional, market-oriented economist, I would look for policies whose rationale was grounded in the idea of market failure, preferably correctible market failure, but I don't see why we should expect to find more of such market failures in the services sector than elsewhere, or indeed a generic market failure in this sector. So the task of making public policy is the same in services as it is elsewhere: to hunt through the great haystack of economic activities and find those needles where market failure is severe and policy is likely to be a useful corrective.

IS MANUFACTURING PASSÉ?

BEFORE GOING ON TO DISCUSS MARKET FAILURE in slightly more detail, let me stand up for a moment for manufacturing, a sector which in some circles is thought to have a musty air about it. Before we dismiss manufacturing entirely, it is important to realize that many very progressive-seeming services use manufacturing inputs. In fact, if you buy the argument that when people talk about the "knowledge-based economy" they really do mean the "computer-based economy," then almost the entire fuss is about an output of the manufacturing sector. As is well known, the U.S. productivity miracle that has received so much attention in the last few years is centred in precisely two *manufacturing* sectors. The puzzle, until recently, was that the very rapid growth in productivity experienced in this corner of manufacturing — which has grown so rapidly it is no longer just a corner of manufacturing but has taken over a third of all manufacturing space — has not spread to services.

On the other hand, manufacturing should not be justified merely because it can be of use to services (a reversal of the argument of 20 or 30 years ago when the typical apology for services was that they often were useful inputs into manufacturing). Even in those parts of manufacturing where growth has not been hyper-charged and where there is no special symbiosis with computers or services or even knowledge, utility may still be generated and money made. It would be a mistake to organize our policies so as to slight perfectly profitable industries simply because they were thought old-fashioned.

Should Policy Tilt?

That gets me to my overall policy prescription, which is not to tilt. Tilting is as unproductive in policy as in pinball or windmills. For more than a century, from the National Policy and even beforehand all the way down to the 1980s, this country's industrial policies tilted toward manufacturing, at least officially. In fact, there was also lots of assistance, both regulatory and fiscal, to resource industries, despite our shame at hewing wood and drawing water, and perhaps from time to time to services, as well. To the extent that such policies were designed to offset the official tilt toward manufacturing, they were doubly wasteful. A tilt toward *all* economic activity — preferably in the form of lower tax rates — would have made more sense than offsetting assistance to each and every sector. The politics of offsetting assistance may well be attractive: it certainly maximizes the number of ribbon-cutting ceremonies. But I suspect that even as a sophisticated and subtle second-best stratagem, its economics are truly dismal.

We would only compound our folly if we now replaced the historic tilt toward manufacturing with a tilt toward services. The lesson we should have learned from our first century of industrial policy is to welcome economic activity of whatever kind people are interested in undertaking and, by and large, financing by themselves. To this end, it might be useful symbolically if the Department of Industry changed its name. If we do not also endow ourselves with a Department of Services — and my own view is that we already have far too many departments — we should change it to the Department of Industriousness. Or Diligence. Or maybe, Enterprise. (George W. Bush, recently enumerating the many failings of French society, is said to have complained, "You know, they don't even have a word for *entrepreneur*.") On a less frivolous note, the General Agreement on Trade in Services, which aims to bring the same liberalization to international trade in services that the General Agreement on

Tariffs and Trade brought to international trade in goods, is a very useful policy innovation. So is the GST (goods and services tax), which redresses the anomaly that, from 1922 to 1990, a country "angst-ridden" and self-conscious about its underdeveloped manufacturing sector levied a special tax on the output of that very sector. It would be wrong to replace this push toward industrial neutrality by any new attempt to favour one sector over another.

INFORMATION-BASED POLICY?

NONE OF THIS IS TO SUGGEST there will never be market failures in services; only that there is no generalized market failure having to do with services. Is it possible to say anything more general than that? In Ottawa these days much thought is given to the Canada-U.S. productivity gap — and with good reason: it has been a concern since the pioneering work of the Wonnacott brothers in the 1960s and its persistence is truly puzzling, despite the adoption of the remedy they proposed, a Canada-U.S. Free Trade Agreement. Unfortunately, a recent report from the Conference Board of Canada (2003) suggests the problem is not that we have too few explanations of the gap but too many. Thus:

- thirty per cent of the difference in the growth of output per hour in manufacturing between Canada and the United States arises from differences in the two countries' capital stocks;
- differences in industrial structure account for "more than 25 per cent" of the gap in total factor productivity in manufacturing;
- "almost all the differences" in the recent growth of labour productivity between the two countries "can be attributed to the greater growth of self-employment and the poorer income performance of this group in Canada";
- and, finally, one quarter of the "large and widening productivity gap" in manufacturing can be explained by the fact that we have more small- and medium-sized enterprises (SME) — SMEs generally having lower productivity than larger firms — while another three-quarters follows from our SMEs being less productive than U.S. SMEs.[2]

By my count that comes to something like 225 per cent of the gap explained. The country may have a productivity problem but its economists clearly do not. Having an over-abundance of explanations may be better than having no explanation at all, but it does not help much in deciding what to do.

I suppose that one grand study or even a meta-study of all the studies might reconcile these various conclusions, though I suspect not at any early date. But even if the required study eventually is done, there is still the question of how, once we do finally decide which variables are at the heart of our productivity disadvantage, we go about fixing things.

Suppose, for example, we conclude the fault really is that too many of our firms are too small. What do we do then? Do we provide tax and regulatory incentives for small firms to become larger? (How much larger?) Or do we simply outlaw firms smaller than a certain size or force them to merge? The very idea seems silly. A traditional, market-oriented economist such as myself is bound to think that firms achieve the size they do for a reason. If Canadian firms, on average, are smaller than American firms, there must be some good reason in the logic of profit-seeking that causes this difference. If that is true and if we go ahead and cause firms that want to be small to become too big, we may well reduce economic efficiency.

Of course, we might find that our abundance of small firms results from an existing small-firm policy bias. Politicians certainly like them. They are said to be great job creators. Thus, small firms face preferential corporate tax rates and are exempt from many burdensome regulations. If we do find we have an overabundance of small firms as a consequence of the existing policy bias in favour of them, then I would happily favour policies to create a level playing-field between small businesses and large. Given the customarily chummy relationships between local members of Parliament and local businessmen and women, I expect removing many of our favours for small business will be difficult politically. But of all the public policies we do need in Canada, a policy on the optimal size of firm is not one.

THE LIPSEY CRITIQUE

THE REMARKS I'VE JUST MADE ARE TYPICAL, I would argue, of how economists look at the problem of industrial policy: don't develop favourite industries; keep the playing-field level; provide framework assistance in the form of well-defined and -policed property rights, price stability, sound macroeconomic management and so on, and in addition to all that, seek out and try to correct specific market failures if you think they are large and correctible, always keeping in mind the possibility of government failure. But beyond that, keep hands-off. This is not just the preferred policy of the *National Post*, but I would argue, of mainstream economics.

At the conference on which this book is based, I was honoured to serve as foil to Richard Lipsey, one of Canada's best-ever economists. In Lipsey's version, I am representative of his many neoclassical friends and critics, whose view of industrial policy is that the state should be largely neutral except in providing generalized incentives to research and development, which may throw off external benefits. Beyond that, the market will take care of things. In fact, I am not quite so neoclassical. I'm persuaded that market failure is relatively common and that markets often do not work that well. But I am also persuaded that neither do governments work well — a proposition that perhaps does not require elaboration during the year of the great sponsorship scandal. In my view, leaving things to the market is therefore usually the lesser of two inefficiencies.

As far as Lipsey is concerned, this standard economist's view is dismally inadequate. In his truly enthralling conference presentation, which spanned 10,000 years of economic and technological history, he made a convincing case that fundamental innovation does not lend itself to conventional neoclassical analysis. The changes technology can render — and that digital technology is likely rendering — are truly fundamental. But when fundamental change is taking place across a broad range of economic activities, the unknowns involved do not lend themselves to the usual neoclassical analytics. At times of technological transformation like these, we find ourselves wandering, if you will, not down a familiar road potholed by risk but through a black night of uncertainty. Our ignorance of the way the world will look in 10 or 25 or 50 years is as vast and deep as the many new fields of knowledge currently being opened up.

I don't disagree with any of that. To quibble for a moment on the details: I'm not wholly convinced the world is changing more rapidly than it has in recent centuries. At the turn of the century, many people observed that the changes in technology and styles of living wrought between 1900 and 1950 were greater than in the 50 years that followed. The telegraph may well have marked a sharper turning point in human affairs than even our beloved Internet. But grant Lipsey his point. Perhaps it has been an age of miracle and wonder for some time. It clearly *is* an age of miracle and wonder in many fields and we simply have no idea how things will turn out. (Or rather, we have many ideas of how things will turn out but no way of deciding among them.) The world *is* changing rapidly and in ways we truly cannot fathom.

Confronted with this pervasive uncertainty, economic tools built for a world of mere risk or even worse, perfect certainty, are inadequate. (In fact, I don't think our tools for dealing with risk are all that good: I've never seen an estimate of research and development externalities, for instance, that I'd bet more than $100 on.) In an earlier contribution to this series, Lipsey and Carlaw (1996) characterized the problem of investing in projects with uncertain returns as trying to pull yellow balls (failure), blue balls (success) or red balls (knowledge that may be useful in other projects) out of an urn when you don't know how many balls of each type — if any — are in the urn or whether the urn contains other urns that must be investigated before the main search can be continued. That strikes me as a brilliant way of summarizing the Dali-esque world of deep uncertainty.

But my reaction to this game is that it's one I really don't want my governments playing. This is not strictly a result of my aversion to all government activities. In fact, I expect many high-payoff investments are available to them where risk and uncertainty are both very low. The windows at my children's public school, for instance, badly need painting and repair, and most were designed, for reasons of safety, not to open. Because the heating system works too well and apparently can't be fixed, the temperature even on the coldest of winter days is an enervating 30-plus degrees, which is conducive more to sleep than learning. This has been a problem for a number of years and we are on the waiting list for remediation but so far nothing has been done. Similar tales could be told about our local health care system. I would much prefer that my tax dollars be spent harvesting this very low-hanging fruit than on financing voyages of exploration into areas of deep technological uncertainty.

And, of course, I'm bound to think that a social institution (government) that cannot properly maintain the windows on a public school is unlikely to be much use in helping commercialize deep uncertainty. No doubt Lipsey and Carlaw (1996) would qualify this prejudice as too pessimistic. In their study, they grade 30 different examples of government attempts to foster important technological innovation, ranging from the Anglo-French Concorde, to the Airbus, to various countries' attempts to bootstrap national computer industries to Canada's own IRAP (Industrial Research Assistance Program), which they record as a success, though mainly, it seems, on the strength of a survey of IRAP users, which is a poor substitute for a comprehensive cost-benefit analysis. As good social scientists, they try to draw policy lessons from the experience they examine. Among their most frequent conclusions is that "policy needs to be flexible," a rule they thought important in at least eight of their case studies. I don't disagree, having drawn the same conclusion in a similar study some time ago (Watson 1982). But the governments I'm familiar with are not very good at being flexible. They have, in Charles Lindblom's famous phrase, "Strong thumbs, no fingers." For obvious fiduciary reasons, they have to act bureaucratically. Being at bottom political institutions, they become committed to projects and find it difficult politically to abandon them. They are also, of course, invaluable social institutions. We would not have civilization without them. But asking them to take on very difficult tasks for which they are not well suited usually is not a wise investment of their time, effort and money.

ENDNOTES

1 Panel remarks by Garnett Picot and Pierre Sauvé appear as chapters. Jayson Myers of Canadian Manufacturers & Exporters did not submit a paper. We report William Watson's panel remarks here.

2 Conference Board of Canada (2003), pp. 63-68.

BIBLIOGRAPHY

Conference Board of Canada. 2003. "Performance and Potential 2003-4." *Defining the Canadian Advantage*. Ottawa: Conference Board of Canada.

Lipsey, Richard G., and Kenneth I. Carlaw. 1996. "A Structuralist View of Innovation Policy," in Peter Howitt (ed.). *The Implications of Knowledge-Based Growth for Micro-Economic Policies*. Industry Canada Research Series. Calgary: University of Calgary Press, pp. 255-337.

Watson, William. 1982. *A Primer on the Economics of Industrial Policy*. Toronto: Ontario Economic Council.

Steven Globerman &
Western Washington University

Daniel Shapiro & Aidan Vining
Simon Fraser University

6

Location Effects, Locational Spillovers and the Performance of Canadian Information Technology Firms

INTRODUCTION

THERE IS INCREASING INTEREST IN THE ROLE played by the agglomeration of firms in specific locations (clusters), and the technological spillovers within and between clusters, specifically as these condition the performance and innovative behaviour of firms (Globerman 1979, Jaffe 1986, Audretsch and Feldman 1996, Krugman 1998, Porter 2000). Recently, researchers have investigated and reported in depth on the role of firm location and the economic determinants and impacts of industrial clusters in a wide variety of industrial and geographical contexts (e.g. Ellison and Glaeser 1997, Braunerhjelm, Carlson, Cetindamar and Johansson 2000, Cantwell and Santangelo 2002).

Notwithstanding the substantial literature that has emerged on the broad issue of clustering, relatively little research has been conducted on Canadian industries and regions. At the same time, however, the issue of industrial clustering, especially in technology-intensive industries, has become an important focus for Canadian policymakers. Specifically, concerns have been raised about the limited number of "high-tech" clusters in Canada compared to the United States, as well as the apparently weaker economic performance of high-tech firms in Canada compared to those in the United States (Globerman 2001).

A number of hypotheses have been offered for the alleged disadvantages faced by high-tech firms in Canada. These hypotheses consider the limited size of regional Canadian markets, government regulatory and tax policies that increase the costs and lower the profitability of innovative activity, lower levels of research and development in Canadian industrial firms compared to the United States, and less effective competition in domestic markets compared to competition facing U.S. producers (Globerman 2001). Indeed, many supporters of economic integration between Canada and the United States view such integration as a way of overcoming a number of the disadvantages that Canadian producers face in developing and sustaining viable industrial clusters. They argue that this is particularly the case for those disadvantages that are associated with Canadian producers competing in relatively-protected and small domestic markets (Rugman and D'Cruz 1993).

The role that economic integration with the United States might play in promoting the growth of high-tech firms in Canada is conditioned by a number of factors. They include, among other things, the degree to which industrial clusters in the United States are complements to, or substitutes for, comparable clusters in Canada. For example, to the extent that the geographical scope of high-tech clusters is relatively broad, firms located in Canada may be able to enjoy technological spillovers and other benefits associated with "membership" in an industrial cluster located in geographically-proximate regions in the United States. Conversely, if the geographical boundaries of viable high-tech clusters are fairly narrow, and the local conditions supporting the growth of those clusters are idiosyncratic, it would be extremely difficult for Canadian clusters to develop and grow in competition with already-established U.S. clusters.

The broad purpose of this study is to identify the degree to which specific locations in Canada are more or less supportive of successful high-technology companies. Our intention is not to identify why firms are geographically distributed in Canada as they are, nor is it to identify and evaluate alternative definitions of clusters. Rather, it is to identify whether specific regions in Canada have, or have not, been successful in supporting the growth of high-technology firms, in this instance, Canadian information and communication technology (ICT) firms. Consideration of this latter issue includes an assessment of the degree to which proximity to U.S. ICT clusters affects the economic performances of firms in Canada.

This study estimates the effects of location on the growth of high-tech firms in Canada, after controlling for other, firm-specific factors that might determine growth rates. It starts by creating a base model of firm growth derived from Gibrat's Law that does not include locational variables, and then augments it with variables indicating the location of the firm. The locational variables are measured at different levels of aggregation, including the province and the census metropolitan area (CMA). In addition, we use the firm's postal code to further disaggregate the measure of location to account for effects operating within CMAs. This analysis reveals that generally there are no effects at the provincial or CMA level. However, we do find evidence that, other things being equal, firms resident in the Toronto CMA, and specifically those in the M4 and M5 postal codes, experience growth advantages. Moreover, we find that the greater the distance of other firms from these postal codes, the lower are their growth rates, other things being equal. Finally, we examine whether or not proximity to U.S. ICT clusters has an effect on the growth rates of Canadian firms. We find only limited evidence that such is the case.

This study proceeds as follows. The next section offers a summary and integration of the relevant literature dealing with industrial clusters. This is followed by an overview of our sample of ICT firms including their location and performance characteristics. The discussion then moves to the measurement of performance. It also identifies the main hypotheses we examine using our sample data and specifies an econometric model to test those hypotheses. Then we report on and assess the results of our statistical estimations. A summary and set of policy conclusions are provided at the end.

REVIEW OF THE LITERATURE

IDENTIFICATION OF POTENTIAL LOCATION FACTORS that promote the economic success of firms is informed by the literature on clustering. Specifically, this literature identifies potential economies arising from agglomeration that offer productivity enhancing opportunities for firms located in a region. The broad sources of agglomeration economies have been reviewed in Krugman (1991) and elsewhere. The three main underlying sources of agglomeration economies that are associated with clusters are: (1) the pooling of specialized labour market skills; (2) the availability of non-traded inputs in relatively large variety and at relatively low cost, and (3) spillovers of information related to best-practice technology (Globerman 2001). The literature on clustering has recently focused on a number of issues related to these three main underlying sources of agglomeration economies.

SPECIALIZED VERSUS GENERAL ECONOMIC ACTIVITY

ONE BROAD ISSUE THAT THE LITERATURE ADDRESSES is whether the advantages inherent in clustering are primarily associated with increased economic action within a specific sphere of activity or whether the advantages are realized through the larger overall (diversified) size of a region. In other words, research has focused on whether agglomeration economies tend to be industry-specific or whether they increase with the overall size and scope of industrial activity in a region.[1] On the one hand, some authors suggest that "urbanization economies" are associated with spillovers generated by the spatial proximity of actors from many diverse industries (Boschma and Lambooy 1999). In contrast, others posit that agglomeration economies are generated by the physical proximity of specialized producers or by the proximity of producers that share a common scientific or technological base of knowledge (Feldman and Francis 2001, Surico 2003).

The available empirical evidence on the issue of the degree to which agglomeration economies are activity-specific is quite mixed. For example, Acs and Armington (2003) find that in U.S. regions, greater geographic specialization (or a lower level of industrial diversity) leads to slower rather than faster growth. They also find a negative and statistically-significant relationship between regional growth and the density of employment in specific industries. On the other hand, Feldman and Audretsch (1999) find that innovation activity tends to be lower in industries located in cities specialized in economic activity in that industry. However, a strong presence of complementary industries, sharing a common science base, appears to be particularly conducive to innovative activity. This latter result is similar to conclusions drawn by Swann and Prevezer (1996). In a study comparing the dynamics of industrial clustering in computing and biotechnology, they conclude that the main promoters of growth of firms in both industries are strength in own-sector employment within a cluster. Technological links between sectors do not appear to play an important role in promoting the growth of incumbent firms. It seems that incumbents are more efficient at absorbing spillovers within their own sectors. At the same time, Swann and Prevezer find that intersectoral feedback strongly encourages entry into the computing industry.

Such differences in findings are perhaps not surprising given significant differences in methodologies and industry samples. In particular, a number of studies have focused on technology spillovers that are a subset of the factors contributing to agglomeration economies, while others have focused on overall or summary measures of the performance of a cluster. One might expect technology spillovers to be related to the sharing of a common science base: that is, one might expect technology spillovers to be positively related to a concentration of firms in a given industry or in a set of closely-related industries. On the other hand, the efficiency advantages of clusters that are related to the availability of specialized inputs, business support services and the like should be more strongly associated with the overall size of the region and include those industries that are not closely related.

The interaction between the industrial composition of a region and its economic performance has obvious policy implications, some of which may be politically challenging. In particular, if a critical mass of related scientific and technical activities is required for a region to become a sustainable cluster, a relatively small country such as Canada must be prepared to allow the bulk of specific high-tech industrial activities to be concentrated in a small number of geographical locations. Similarly, if overall economic activity contributes positively to the growth of high-tech clusters, traditional government policies to promote investment in "have-not" regions of Canada face a high probability that they will fail to generate sustainable high-tech clusters in those regions.

The Role of Scientific Infrastructure

THE EXISTING LITERATURE FOCUSES SIGNIFICANT ATTENTION on a number of factors other than size and industrial composition that contribute to the emergence and growth of industrial clusters. One factor that has been particularly linked to high-tech clusters is the scientific infrastructure of the region. Scientific infrastructure attributes include: the presence in the region of universities with research and teaching capabilities in science and engineering (van den Panne and Dolfsma 2002); the extent of private and public research and development activities carried out within the region (Antonelli 1994); the number of scientists and engineers working in the region relative to other regions (Blind and Grupp 1999); and the presence of entrepreneurs together with the organizations and institutions that co-evolve to support entrepreneurship, e.g., venture capital firms (Feldman and Francis 2001).

In broad terms, the findings support the existence of significant linkages between the scientific and engineering infrastructure of a region and that region's ability to attract and sustain viable high-tech clusters. It should be noted however that the evidence suggests that infrastructure is a necessary, but not sufficient, condition for successful high-tech clustering. For example, Feldman and Francis (2001) emphasize that the history of high technology in the United States is marked by cluster failures. Specifically, there are numerous examples of clusters that were not able to adapt to economic or technological shocks: entrepreneurs and start-up firms in such clusters ceased operations or moved to other regions, when the local environment turned negative.[2]

A specific focus of the literature is the role of public-sector scientific and technological activity. This focus is of potential importance to the Canadian situation, as critics of Canadian research and development (R&D) performance have highlighted not just Canada's relatively low overall R&D intensity, but also the relatively high share of R&D that is undertaken within government research institutions or government-supported research organizations. On balance, the literature provides support for the hypothesis that the research presence and activities of government and not-for-profit research institutions promote the growth and sustainability of high-tech clusters and firms. For example, both Autant-Bernard (2001) and Blind and Grupp (1999) find evidence that the presence of public-sector research organizations in a region encourages technology transfers and technology spillovers to private-sector organizations. Similarly, Prevezer (1997) examines clustering in the biotechnology sector and concludes that biotechnology companies in a region appear to be attracted more by the presence of biological and medical research centres than by the presence of other private-sector biotechnology companies.

On the whole, therefore, the existing literature suggests that the funding and performance of innovation by both the public and private sectors in Canada are complementary in their contribution to industrial clustering, although the overall levels of funding may be inadequate to generate the emergence of prominent high-tech clusters. An important caveat is that the degree of complementarity might be specific to the activity in question. For example, Blind and Grupp (1999) argue that a region's public R&D infrastructure does not appear to be an important contributor to industrial activity in the areas of electronics or data processing. Swann and Prevezer (1996) also note that the presence of firms involved in the development and production of computer hardware exerts a stronger influence on the presence of software companies in a region than does the existence of basic scientific infrastructure.

INTRA-CLUSTER SPILLOVERS

THE CONCEPT OF DISTANCE IS CENTRAL to the idea of spatially-based clusters. If distance is not factored in, an ICT firm in Ottawa can be in the same cluster as an ICT firm in Tokyo. The geographical proximity of participants within successful clusters is now being investigated in a wide variety of contexts. Existing studies provide a substantial amount of evidence about the geographical scope of clusters. Unfortunately, the available evidence is still inconclusive. Indeed, there are conflicting theoretical positions on the issue. For example, numerous authors suggest that the benefits derived by firms from proximity to similar firms attenuate rapidly with distance. Audretsch (1998) summarizes this position succinctly in his assertion that close geographical proximity is necessary to facilitate knowledge spillovers, because knowledge is vague, difficult to codify and often only serendipitously recognized. On the other hand, Autant-Bernard (2001) posits that technological innovations in information and communication technologies are reducing the importance of geographic distance as a conditioner of technological spillovers. In other words, the marginal costs of transmitting and absorbing technological knowledge are increasingly less sensitive to physical distance. Gunderson (2001) points to anecdotal evidence highlighting the integrated technological world of North America, including the cross-border personal networks that have been established by the approximately 80,000 Canadians who reside in Silicon Valley.

Existing studies tend to focus on the extent of technological spillovers for both private and public sector innovation activities. As noted previously, the evidence is inconclusive. For example, Anselin, Varga and Acs (1997) find that spillovers of university research into innovation extend over a range of 50 miles from the innovating metropolitan statistical area (MSA), but not with respect to private R&D activities. More generally, Rosenthal and Strange (2003) find that agglomeration economies attenuate rapidly with distance: the effect on own-industry employment within the first mile is as much as 10 to 100 times larger than the effect occurring at a distance of two to five miles. Beyond five miles, attenuation is much less pronounced. On the other hand, Bernstein (1989) finds significant evidence of both inter-industrial and intra-industrial spillover effects for a sample of Canadian industries at the national level. In a broad review of the literature, Surico (2003) highlights evidence of external economies that spill over regions and cut across states and even country boundaries (see next section).

INTER-CLUSTER AND INTERNATIONAL SPILLOVERS

A CLOSELY-RELATED ISSUE IS THE QUESTION OF SPILLOVERS across clusters and, indeed, across country borders. This is really the within-cluster question writ large: if technological knowledge is a pure public good with marginal costs of consumption that are invariant with distance, then neither intra-cluster nor inter-cluster distance should matter. A relatively large number of studies have documented the significance of international technology spillovers in a wide variety of industrial and geographical settings. This literature is too extensive to review in detail. Figure 1 lists a number of relatively recent studies and summarizes their main findings.

Keller (2002) has recently provided important evidence on this question. He relates R&D spending in the United States, the United Kingdom, Japan, Germany and France to the productivity levels of nine other Organisation for Economic Co-operation and Development (OECD) countries, including Canada, using the distance between sending and recipient countries. His broad finding is that "technology is to a substantial degree local, not global… the distance at which the amount of spillovers is halved is about 1,200 kilometres."[3] Of specific relevance to this study, he finds that Canada benefits extensively from U.S. technology spillovers. He presents somewhat mixed evidence on temporal effects, such as those relating to the hypothesis that technological change is reducing communication costs and, therefore, the costs of distance. On balance, however, he finds evidence that distance is becoming somewhat less important over time. Furthermore, Keller finds that language difference is an additional barrier to knowledge spillovers (Rauch 1999). Bernstein (2000) offers findings that are supportive of Keller. Specifically, he identifies research and development spillovers from the U.S. manufacturing sector into Canada. The extensive use of communication networks and the integration with the U.S. economy create the potential for these spillovers.

Closely related, albeit more indirect, evidence on international spillovers comes from the patent literature. Jaffe, Trajtenberg and Henderson (1993) and Jaffe and Trajtenberg (1999) find evidence that U.S. patents cite other U.S. patents more than they cite foreign patents. Similarly, Eaton and Kortum (1996, 1999) find that there are stronger intra-country patenting effects. Thus, there is evidence that international spillovers occur, but the distance over which they are relevant may not be that great.

FIGURE 1

SUMMARY OF LITERATURE ON TECHNOLOGY SPILLOVERS

	AUTHOR	GEOPOLITICAL REGION	FINDINGS
1	Okabe (2002)	East Asia	R&D spillovers through trade with OECD
2	Frantzen (2002)	OECD	Intra- and inter-sectoral R&D spill-overs
3	Branstetter (2001)	Japan, United States	Knowledge spillovers are primarily international
4	Alston (2002)	International	Interstate and international R&D spill-overs
5	Hanel (2000)	Canada	International technology spillovers smaller than domestic spillover
6	Johnson and Evenson (1999)	International	R&D spillovers between countries and industries
7	Bayoumi, Coe and Helpman (1999)	International	R&D spillovers among industrial countries
8	Bernstein and Mohnen (1998)	United States, Japan	R&D spillovers from United States to Japan but not reverse
9	Engelbrecht (1997)	OECD	Significant international R&D spill-overs
10	Evenson (1997)	OECD	International spillovers increase productivity
11	Verspagen (1997)	OECD	International R&D spillovers. United States and Germany are largest contributors
12	Capron and Cincera (1998)	Worldwide	International productivity spillovers. Japan especially benefits
13	van Meijl and van Tongeren (1998)	China and Other Countries	Technology spillovers to China
14	Frantzen (2000)	OECD	Domestic and foreign R&D spillovers
15	Bissant and Fikkert (1996)	India	International and domestic R&D spill-overs
16	Coe and Helpman (1995)	International	High returns to domestic R&D and international spillovers

Source: Bissant and Fikkert (1996).

INTERNATIONAL SPILLOVERS: UNITED STATES TO CANADA

IN THIS STUDY, THE MAGNITUDE OF TECHNOLOGY SPILLOVER from the United States to Canada assumes a central importance, particularly to the extent that the ability of firms in Canada to benefit from such spillovers is a function of their geographic proximity to high-tech clusters in the United States. Both Keller (2002) and Bernstein (1998) find evidence of such spillovers.

Related to the issue of whether technology spills over from the United States to Canada is the question of the mechanism(s) by which the spillovers occur. Intra-corporate technology transfers that take place within multinational companies in Canada are one such mechanism. In particular, considerable evidence suggests that intra-corporate transfers are an especially robust mechanism for introducing newer and more commercially-important proprietary technology into Canada (Davidson and McFetridge 1985). However, there is little evidence bearing upon the issue of whether the physical distance between affiliates of multinational companies affects the degree and speed of technology transfers within a worldwide organization.

SUMMARY OF LITERATURE

IT SEEMS FAIR TO CONCLUDE that while there is a substantial literature addressing the issue of industrial clustering, there is no strong consensus on the precise characteristics of geographical regions that promote and sustain the commercial success of clusters. Nor is there agreement about limitations on the geographical expanse of clusters, or their impact on firm performance. Technology spillovers, a major contributor to clustering, have been shown by some studies to be dampened by geographical distance. However, there is also abundant evidence of inter-industrial and intra-industrial spillovers at national and international levels. Taken at face value, the latter evidence suggests that technology spillovers can take place over substantial geographical distances. The inconclusive, even contradictory, nature of much of the evidence on the geographic reach of clustering and its impact on firm performance heightens the relevance of this study.

IMPLICATIONS FOR POLICY

BOTH THE INTRA-CLUSTER AND INTER-CLUSTER GEOGRAPHICAL SCOPE of high-tech clusters is of vital interest to Canadian policymakers. In particular, the issue of whether geographical proximity to U.S. clusters affects the commercial viability of high-tech firms located in Canada has profound implications for government policies that directly or indirectly affect the locational choices of high-tech firms in Canada. For example, if border effects discourage international technology spillovers, this strengthens arguments for encouraging new investment in already established large domestic industrial clusters such as the greater Toronto region, especially if domestic technology spillovers are strongly constrained by geographical distance. But, if technology spillovers from the United States to Canada are unaffected by the border, viable industrial clustering may be feasible in relatively small Canadian urban areas, such as Halifax, that are relatively close to major U.S. high-tech clusters, i.e., the Boston area, even though they are relatively far from Canada's major urban cluster(s).

The precise nature of the clustering phenomenon is also relevant. For example, if clusters are primarily associated with overall industrial activity rather than with the extent of economic activity in specific industries or scientific disciplines, the sustainability of technology clusters in Canada is linked *de facto* to the growth of a small number of large metropolitan areas. Public policies that directly or indirectly encourage the dispersion of economic activity and human capital from the largest urban agglomerations will be at odds with policies designed to promote technology clusters of a certain critical size.[4] On the other hand, if a critical threshold of scientific and commercial activity, specialized in a particular technological discipline, characterizes successful software locations in Canada, the commercial viability of firms outside of a few major metropolitan areas is at least feasible. This is especially relevant to the extent that public infrastructure, such as research institutes and universities, is relatively well dispersed geographically when compared to the dispersion of leading Canadian corporations.

In the next section of the study, we describe our sample ICT firms. Then we go on to discuss the empirical model employed to identify the determinants of economic growth among those companies. We then provide statistical estimates of the importance of the variables included in the model and assess the implications of the statistical findings. The implications are extended to policy recommendations in the final section of the study.

SAMPLE AND DATA

BASIC DATA WERE COMPILED from the 1999-2002 editions of the Branham 300 list of high-technology companies in Canada (www.branhamgroup.com). All of the companies are, in fact, engaged in ICT activities. The data cover four years of activity (1998-2001). We employ two sample periods, one for the period 1998-2000 (referred to as period 1), and one for 1998-2001 (referred to as period 2). For period 1, there is complete data for 244 continuing firms; for period 2, which includes the high-technology crash, the sample falls to 189 firms. Branham provided the following data for each firm:

1. sales revenue over the relevant period, from which we calculated growth rates;
2. the year the company was established;
3. whether the company is publicly-traded or privately-held;
4. the address of the head office, including postal code; and
5. the business sector of the company (software, wireless software, web development, Internet service provider, applications service provider, diversified service provider).

In addition, for a smaller sample of firms, data were available indicating the percentage of foreign ownership in the firm, and the percentage of sales attributable to exports. Where data were missing, the company web site was accessed to obtain the information needed. The postal code in the address of each firm was used to classify it according to its location by province, by census metropolitan area, or by area within a city (Figure 2). The latter involved using the first three digits of the postal code, as explained below. Additional data were also collected at both the provincial and CMA levels. These included provincial gross domestic product (GDP) and GDP per capita, provincial and CMA populations, earnings per capita at the CMA level, expenditures on research at provincial and CMA levels, and educational attainment at each level. The use of these data in subsequent econometric models is described below.[5]

There are possible limitations to our data. The data reported by Branham rely upon voluntary reporting by firms to solicitations from the Branham Group. As such, there may be self-reporting biases in terms of the characteristics of firms that do and do not report. Put simply, firms that report may have significantly different characteristics than firms that do not report. Unfortunately, it is not possible to assess the validity and relevance of this potential

FIGURE 2

THE LOCATION OF SAMPLE FIRMS

concern. However, there is no obvious reason why fast-growing firms in the Toronto region would be over-represented relative to fast-growing firms elsewhere in Canada. An over-representation in our sample of fast-growing firms in Toronto relative to other locations is the potential bias of concern to this study as will become clear in the discussion of our model.

The time period over which we observe firm growth is unlikely to be representative. Our sample period encompasses the height of the high-tech boom, and its subsequent crash. However, as with the sample of firms, the potential bias of concern would be that firms in certain locations, particularly Toronto, grew relatively faster in this period than would normally be the case. We have no reason to believe that this is the case.

The geographic distribution of sample firms is summarized in Table 1. Specifically, the percentage of the sample firms located in each province is shown in the second column. The percentage of sample firms distributed by CMA is reported in the fourth column. Clearly, the geographical location of firms in our sample is highly concentrated with about 60 percent of firms headquartered in Ontario. Of the Ontario-based firms, slightly over two-thirds (about 41 percent of the total sample) are headquartered in Toronto. This concentration in Ontario and the Toronto CMA is clearly disproportionate to Ontario's size relative to other provinces, and to Toronto's size relative to other CMAs.[6] By comparison, the provincial share of sample companies located in British Columbia is quite comparable to

TABLE 1

GEOGRAPHIC DISTRIBUTION OF SAMPLE FIRMS, 1998-2000

PROVINCE	% OF FIRMS	CMA	% OF FIRMS
Newfoundland	1.2	Vancouver	10.5
Prince Edward Island	0.0	Calgary	6.5
Nova Scotia	0.5	Edmonton	2.4
New Brunswick	1.6	Winnipeg	2.8
Quebec	11.3	Montreal	8.9
Ontario	60.1	Ottawa	15.7
Manitoba	2.8	Toronto	40.7
Saskatchewan	1.2	Waterloo	2.0
Alberta	8.5	Fredericton	1.6
British Columbia	12.5	Burlington	1.6
Territories	0.5	All other	7.3

Notes: Number of observations is 244. The percentages may not add to 100 percent due to rounding. The percentages do not change much if the sample period is extended to 2001. Only data for the top 10 CMAs are reported.

that province's relative size in the national economy. Conversely, the Quebec and Alberta shares are below those predicted by the relative sizes of those provinces.

Very few CMAs in Canada can be considered high-tech clusters. Indeed, two CMAs (Toronto and Ottawa) are locations for almost 56 percent of our total sample. Three CMAs (Toronto, Ottawa, and Vancouver) account for the locations of over two-thirds of our sample. The prominent degree of clustering is not necessarily surprising. What seems evident is that the size of regions alone does not explain the pattern of clustering observed in Table 1.

Hence, there would seem to be merit in identifying the factors that encourage the emergence and growth of successful ICT firms. We do so by relating the economic performance of our sample firms to their headquarters' location. Specifically, we relate sales growth of our sample firms to attributes including their location. If firms located in specific regions grow faster than those located elsewhere, other things being constant, those regions support successful clusters.

ESTIMATION MODEL

THE CONCEPTUAL FRAMEWORK for our model specifies that the core determinants of firm growth are initial firm size and the age of the firm. The basic specification follows from Evans (1987a, 1987b), and is based on Gibrat's Law. The model of firm growth is as follows:

$$(1) \qquad Growth(i,t) = G^{\beta}\left[Size(i,t'), Age(i,t)\right] e^{[\mu(i,t)]} t' > t > 0, \left[\mu(i,t) \sim (iid)\right]$$

where $Growth(i,t)$ is the growth of $firm_i$ between period t and t' $[sales(i,t') - sales(i,t)]$; $Size(i,t)$ is the size of $firm_i$ at time t measured by sales (revenue);[7] $Age(i,t)$ is the age of $firm_i$ at time t, measured by the age from date of founding; β is a growth parameter; and $\mu(i,t)$ is $firm_i$'s draw from the common distribution of growth rates. It is further assumed that $\mu(i,t) \sim N(\alpha, \sigma^2)$, and therefore that:

$$(2) \qquad \mu(i,t) = \alpha + \xi(i,t) \text{ where } E\left[\xi(i,t)\right] = 0.$$

Taking the natural logarithm (Ln) of both sides of Equation (1) produces the following cross-sectional relationship:[8]

$$(3) \qquad \begin{aligned} &Growth = Ln\ Size(i,t' - Ln\ Size(i,t))/d = \alpha + \beta_s\ Ln\ Size(i,t) + \\ &\beta_a Ln\ Age(i,t) + \xi(i,t) \\ &\left\{\varepsilon_{(i,t)} \sim (iid), t' > t > 0, d = (t' - t)\right\}. \end{aligned}$$

The logarithmic relationship between firm growth and firm size identifies whether or not larger firms enjoy a systematic competitive advantage compared to smaller firms. Similarly, the estimated relationship between firm growth and age identifies the extent to which younger firms can leverage innovation activities to attain superior commercial performance compared to older firms. A plausible expectation is that in a technology-intensive activity such as software development, smaller and younger firms will grow faster than larger and older firms (Hamilton, Shapiro and Vining 2002).

The measurement of performance is problematic in industries or sectors that are in the embryonic or growth stages of development, as is the case with new high-tech industries. In this regard, the important role of growth has been recognized since the seminal work of Penrose (1959). Its critical importance in high-technology contexts is also well-recognized (Eisenhardt and Schoonhoven 1990). Here, reinvestment of internal cash flow may well be large for many years, or even decades. High-tech industries also have a high ratio of intangible assets that are difficult to value using traditional accounting-based performance measures (Dierickx and Cool 1989). Given these problems, probably the most common approach is to treat either survival (Audretsch and Mahmood 1995) or growth as the measure of performance. Frequently, empirical studies examining high-tech industries provide little explicit discussion of the appropriateness of growth as a dependent variable, suggesting that there is a wide consensus on its usefulness (e.g. Almus and Nerlinger 1999, Niosi 2003). In practice, the usual approach to measuring performance in embryonic and growth technology sectors is to average revenue growth over a number of years (e.g., SubbaNarisima, Ahmed and Mallya 2003, Sadler-Smith, Hampson, Chaton and Badger 2003). An advantage of the empirical framework that we employ is that models based on Gibrat's Law have proved successful in controlling for firm-specific determinants of growth.

Table 2 summarizes the basic research methodology and specifications. We begin with a base model, derived from Gibrat's Law as specified above, and then augment it with a series of location variables. At each stage, we test for the collective significance of the location terms.

TABLE 2

SUMMARY OF RESEARCH METHODOLOGY

	MODEL ESTIMATED	RESULTS
Specify and Estimate the Base Model	Firm growth, over the period 1998-2000 or 1998-2001, as a function of initial size, initial age, ownership status (public/private) and export activity	See Table 3.
Test for Business Sector Effects	Add dummy variables for business sector (software, wireless software, web development, Internet service provider, applications service provider, telecommunications service provider, diversified service provider).	None of the dummy variables together, or in various combinations are statistically significant and are therefore omitted from the base model.
Test for Provincial Effects	1) Add provincial dummy variables to the base model. 2) Add continuous province-level variables to the base model (provincial GDP, number of top 50 universities, percentage of population with university degrees, amount of research performed in the province by various groups).	1) The unrestricted model that includes the provincial dummy variables is rejected in favour of the restricted base model. Only the Ontario variable is statistically significant (positive), but only for 1998-2000. See Table 4. 2) Continuous variables were highly correlated and could not be included in the same equation. Most were positive and statistically significant when entered singly. See Table 3.
Test for CMA Effects	1) Add CMA dummy variables to the base model. 2) Add continuous CMA-level variables to the base model (earnings per capita, population, number of top 50 universities, research by top 50 universities, percentage of university graduates).	1) The unrestricted model that includes all CMA dummy variables is rejected in favour of the unrestricted base model; a model that includes only the CMA dummy variable for Toronto is not rejected. 2) The continuous variables are highly correlated and must be entered singly. Only the variable measuring research by top 50 universities is statistically significant (for 1998-2000). See Table 5.
Test for Intra-CMA Effects and National Spillover Effects	Add dummy variables for firms sharing the same first two digits of their postal code to the base model. Add a variable for distance of each firm (based on postal code) from centre of M4/M5 postal code (Toronto).	The unrestricted model is rejected indicating that in general intra-CMA effects do not exist. After eliminating areas with very few firms, the results indicate that only the Toronto area (M2, M4, M5, M9), and Waterloo (N2) had important effects, but not for all periods. Firm growth is negatively correlated with distance from M4/M5. See Table 6.
Test for International Spillover Effects	Add variables for distance from firm's postal code or city to U.S. ICT clusters. Several variables were considered.	There is weak evidence (see Table 7) that distance from a U.S. cluster negatively affects growth rates.

Estimation Results

TABLE 3 REPORTS THE ESTIMATION RESULTS for a simple regression in which the natural logarithm of sales growth is first regressed against the natural logarithm of (1998) sales revenue and (1998) age of the company. Equations (2) and (6) in Table 3 show that initial sales are negatively and significantly related to sales growth for both sample periods. Age is negatively related to growth, but the coefficient is statistically significant only in the second period.[9, 10]

Several other variables were added to this basic estimating equation. Specifically, a dummy variable was included, taking a value of unity if a company is Canadian-owned and zero if the firm has foreign ownership.[11] Another takes a value of unity if a company is publicly-traded and zero otherwise. A third variable identifies a company's export intensity measured as (exports/sales). To the extent that a Canadian affiliate of a multinational company (MNC) is advantaged by access to its parent company's technology, the coefficient for the foreign-ownership variable is expected to be positive. However, if MNC affiliates have a reduced capability to undertake indigenous innovation, the foreign ownership coefficient should be negative.

The sign of the coefficient for the publicly-traded versus private-ownership dummy variable is also uncertain. To the extent that publicly-traded firms are

TABLE 3

BASE MODEL ESTIMATES

	Period 1 (1998–2000) Dependent variable is: Ln (2000 Sales) – Ln (1998 Sales)				Period 2 (1998–2001) Dependent variable is: Ln (2001 Sales) – Ln (1998 Sales)			
Equations	(1)	(2)	(3)	(4)	(5)	(6)	(7)	(8)
Ln (1998 Sales)	–.151*** (.050)	–136** (.068)	–.163** (.080)	–.186* (.101)	–.115*** (.018)	–.070*** (.020)	–.072*** (.026)	–.056* (.032)
Ln Age (1998)		–.117 (.129)	–.104 (.131)	–.045 (.204)		–.224*** (.087)	–.221*** (.089)	–.241*** (.089)
Publicly-traded			.238* (.138)	.270 (.190)			.047 (.109)	.014 (.240)
Exports as a Percentage of Revenues				.002*** (.000)				.003*** (.001)
Constant	1.932*** (.503)	2.056*** (.644)	2.187*** (.473)	2.136*** (.560)	1.568*** (.206)	1.728*** (.232)	1.757*** (.235)	1.506*** (.232)
R^2 (Adjusted)	.217	.223	.238	.272	.151	.157	.154	.197
n	240	240	240	207	189	189	189	166

Notes: Figures in parentheses are heteroscedastic-consistent (White 1980) standard errors. *** p < .001, **p < .05, *p < .01

better able to raise capital in order to fund innovative activities, the empirical relationship between sales growth and publicly-traded firms should be positive. An alternative hypothesis is that widespread share ownership that often follows from public trading enables managers to dissipate shareholder wealth in activities that detract from promoting innovation and improved commercial performance. In fact, many of the publicly-traded firms in our sample are relatively small. Hence, shareholders are likely to be able to monitor managerial behaviour more effectively than is the case for larger firms. Therefore, on balance, we would expect sales growth to be positively related to being publicly-traded.

The relationship between firm growth and export intensity should be positive. High-tech firms that are capable of competing in foreign markets presumably enjoy firm-specific competitive advantages that also contribute to faster sales growth in their domestic market. Equations (3), (4), (7) and (8) in Table 3 report the results of adding the "publicly-traded" dummy variable, as well as the export intensity variable to the basic Gibrat equation.[12] The export intensity coefficient is, as expected, positive and statistically significant. The dummy variable for public ownership is positive but statistically significant in only one equation. In fact, there is substantial collinearity between the age and public ownership variables, especially for the second period, which might partially account for the statistical insignificance of the public-ownership dummy variable in most estimated equations. Although the export variable is consistently positive and statistically significant, data were not available for all firms resulting in a loss of observations. As a consequence, we report only results using a base model that excluded exports, unless its inclusion affects the results.

Other control variables included in the basic model were dummy variables identifying the ICT business sector in which a sample company had the majority of its sales. The sample companies were classified according to one of the following sectors: software, wireless software, web development, Internet service provider, applications service provider and diversified service provider. While these sectors share some common exogenous economic influences, market conditions may differ sufficiently across sectors to create differential growth opportunities for firms in the various sectors. Therefore, we tested for the importance of business type by including the business sector dummy variables. In fact, none of the sector dummy variables were statistically significant. Moreover, an F-test indicated that the business-type dummy variables were collectively not significantly different from zero. Therefore, we do not report the results of estimations including the sector dummy variables.

Our primary focus is on whether a firm's geographical location affects its economic performance. We first examine whether provincial location matters by including dummy variables identifying the province in which a sample firm is located. An F-test reveals that these dummy variables are collectively not statistically significant. However, there is some evidence that some provincial effects do exist. Specifically, when a dummy variable is specified in which firms located in Ontario are assigned a value of unity while other firms are assigned a zero value, the provincial dummy variable is positive and statistically significant in the first sample period [Table 4, Equation (1)]. It is positive but statistically insignificant in the second sample period [Table 4, Equation (4)].

As noted earlier, research infrastructure in a region has been found to promote scientific clusters in that region. The overall size and scope of economic activity has also been linked to the existence of commercially-successful clusters. Consequently, we included certain provincial characteristics in the basic estimating equation in place of the provincial dummy variables. These include:

1. gross domestic product (absolute and per capita);
2. number of "top 50" universities;
3. dollar amount of research expenditures by the top universities in the province;
4. percentage of the provincial population with a university degree; and
5. dollar amount spent on research performed in the province by the federal and provincial governments, private companies and educational institutions.

TABLE 4

TESTING FOR PROVINCIAL EFFECTS

	PERIOD 1 (1998–2000)			PERIOD 2 (1998–2001)		
EQUATIONS	(1)	(2)	(3)	(4)	(5)	(6)
Ln (1998 Sales)	–.167**	–167**	–.166**	–.075***	–.076***	–.076***
	(.080)	(.080)	(.081)	(.026)	(.026)	(.027)
Ln Age (1998)	–.102	–.114	–.122	–.217***	–.229***	–.225***
	(.133)	(.132)	(.131)	(.088)	(.089)	(.090)
Publicly-traded	.238*	.239*	.236*	.048	.050	.045
	(.139)	(.138)	(.138)	(.109)	(.109)	(.109)
Ontario	.160**			.095		
	(.080)			(.085)		
Number of Top 50 Universities		.019***			.010*	
		(.006)			(.006)	
Total Dollars of Research Performed (Ln)			.096***			.062*
			(.029)			(.035)
Constant	2.121***	2.012***	1.466***	1.718***	1.700***	1.298***
	(.491)	(.457)	(.428)	(.206)	(.223)	(.320)
R^2 (Adjusted)	.246	.258	.257	.155	.158	.162
n	240	240	240	189	189	189

Notes: Figures in parentheses are heteroscedastic-consistent (White 1980) standard errors.
*** p < .001, ** p < .05, *p < .01

We also included variables measuring the percentage of sample firms located in the province. This variable is meant to identify commercial benefits associated with a concentration of ICT-specific activity in a given province. Other potentially relevant variables are discussed in the literature. For example, Saxenian (1994) highlights the "openness" of industrial cultures in different regions; Almeida and Kogut (1999) emphasize inter-firm mobility; Agrawal and Cockburn (2003) stress the presence of "anchor tenants" in a region, or large firms that generate significant technological spillovers that can be capitalized upon by smaller firms. Unfortunately, it was not possible to construct measures of all potentially relevant location variables for our sample of Canadian firms. Moreover, at the detailed (e.g. postal code) levels at which some of our equations are estimated, it seems unlikely that variables such as openness and inter-firm mobility will vary much across relatively contiguous areas.

The independent variables identified in the preceding paragraph are strongly inter-correlated.[13] Thus, we report equations that include the variables providing the strongest statistical performances. Specifically, Equations (2) and (3) and Equations (5) and (6) (in Table 4) report results including the number of top 50 universities and the total dollars of research performed in the province (expressed as a natural log value). The coefficients for both variables are positive and statistically significant. Since Ontario has a relatively high concentration of top-rated universities and accounts for a relatively large share of research carried out in Canada, the positive provincial effect identified for Ontario presumably reflects, at least in part, the relatively strong scientific and technological infrastructure in the province.

We next evaluate whether location effects can be identified at finer geographic levels. From the sample firm's mailing address, we were able to assign each firm to a Canadian metropolitan area. Our sample firms are distributed over 20 CMAs. We created dummy variables for 19 of the CMAs and added them to the basic estimating equation. An F-test indicated that CMA effects were not present: the basic estimating equation was preferable to one that included the dummy variables. However, of the 20 CMAs, half had three or fewer firms in the sample. We therefore created a new set of dummy variables comprising the CMAs with the most firms, with the deleted category comprising all other firms and CMAs. These dummy variables were added to the baseline model, and F-tests again indicated that the basic estimating model was preferable to the model including these CMA dummies.

We further reduced the dummy variables to the five CMAs with the largest number of sample firms (Vancouver, Calgary, Toronto, Ottawa-Hull and Montreal), with all other CMAs forming the excluded category. Once again, an F-test ruled against the collective significance of these variables. Finally, we specified a dummy variable taking a value of unity for firms located in the Toronto CMA and zero otherwise. The estimation results when including the Toronto dummy variable in the basic estimating equation are reported in Table 5, Equations (1) and (5). The dummy variable is positively signed and statistically significant in both periods. When the Ontario dummy variable is added to these two equations, its coefficient is statistically insignificant. This result suggests that the Ontario provincial effect identified earlier likely reflects the location advantages of its largest city, Toronto.

To identify whether specific characteristics of CMAs influence growth, we specified a series of continuous variables measured at the CMA level. They included:

1. total income;
2. total population;
3. per-capita income;
4. number of top 50 universities;
5. total research expenditures of the top universities;
6. number of university graduates in the CMA; and
7. the percentage of sample firms located in the CMA.

TABLE 5

TESTING FOR CMA EFFECTS

	PERIOD 1 (1998–2000)				PERIOD 2 (1998–2001)			
EQUATIONS	(1)	(2)	(3)	(4)	(5)	(6)	(7)	(8)
Ln (1998 Sales)	–.170**	–084***	–.155**	–.162**	–.080***	–.077***	–.070***	–.074***
	(.080)	(.025)	(.071)	(.078)	(.023)	(.027)	(.026)	(.027)
Ln Age (1998)	–.106	–.248***	–.116	–.102	–.219***	–.226***	–.224***	–.226***
	(.132)	(.061)	(.118)	(.138)	(.088)	(.092)	(.089)	(.091)
Publicly-traded	.236*	.132*	.225*	.237*	.160	.060	.043	.048
	(.137)	(.070)	(.130)	(.140)	(.108)	(.109)	(.109)	(.109)
Toronto CMA	.225***				.169*			
	(.072)				(.089)			
CMA University Research (Ln Dollars)		.110***				.063		
		(.043)				(.060)		
CMA University Graduates (Percent)			–1.756				–.626	
			(2.003)				(1.060)	
CMA Number of Top 50 Universities				–.007				.021
				(.034)				(.034)
Constant	2.165***	2.056***	2.667***	2.956***	1.7538***	1.026**	1.930***	1.736***
	(.470)	(.644)	(.972)	(.498)	(.230)	(.532)	(.375)	(.229)
R^2 (Adjusted)	.257	.243	.247	.235	.164	.153	.152	.151
n	240	232	240	240	189	181	189	189

Notes: Figures in parentheses are heteroscedastic-consistent (White 1980) standard errors.
*** $p < .001$, ** $p < 0.05$, *$p < 0.01$

As shown in Table 5, only the coefficient for university research spending is statistically significant and only in the first time period. The inference one might draw is that Toronto enjoys a variety of advantages owing to its broad size and scope that are difficult to identify precisely. The large amount of research carried out in leading universities might help ICT firms to grow faster across our entire sample of CMAs. However, other specific location attributes do not seem to be related to the growth of ICT firms identified at the CMA level.

It is possible that location effects operate more narrowly than at the CMA level. We therefore used the postal codes of our sample firms to create more disaggregated measures of location. Specifically, we grouped our firms into 45 locations defined at the two-digit postal code level.[14] We specified 44 postal code dummy variables and included them in the basic estimating equation. For both periods, the postal code dummies were (collectively) statistically insignificant. When the estimation was repeated with the number of dummy variables limited to postal codes in Ontario, Quebec, Alberta and British Columbia, the dummy variables were, again, collectively insignificant.

We then focused on Ontario by estimating a model that specified dummy variables for two-digit postal code locations for Ottawa, Kanata, Markham, Mississauga, Burlington/Hamilton, North York, Waterloo, as well as three areas of Toronto. For period 1 (1998-2000), the coefficient for the three Toronto postal codes (M4, M5, M9), North York (M2) and Waterloo (N2) are all positive and statistically significant [Table 6, Equation (1)].[15] When export intensity was included in the estimating equation [Table 6, Equation (2)], only the Toronto area and North York postal code dummies remained significant.[16] For period 2 (1998-2001), the Toronto and Waterloo coefficients are statistically significant in Equation (1). However, when the export intensity variable is included (Equation (5)), they are both statistically insignificant. Furthermore, the percentage of sample firms in the two-digit postal code was never statistically significant. The latter suggests that a concentration of ICT firms at the two-digit postal code level is unrelated to firm growth.

The results to this point suggest that the two-digit postal codes comprising the city of Toronto form a unique cluster for successful ICT companies in Canada. Specifically, ICT firms located in that cluster grow faster than other ICT companies in Canada, holding other things constant. While our analysis does not precisely identify why ICT firms located in the city of Toronto appear to enjoy competitive advantages, it would not seem that the advantages derive from a concentration of ICT activity, *per se*, in Toronto. Rather, the city's large overall size and the research activities of the country's largest university are more likely to underlie the superior performance of Toronto-based ICT companies.

Having identified the city of Toronto as a unique location for successful ICT companies, we evaluate whether distance from Toronto, and especially distance from the M4/M5 postal codes, affects the growth performance of our

TABLE 6

TESTING FOR INTRA-CMA AND NATIONAL DISTANCE EFFECTS

	PERIOD 1 (1998–2000)			PERIOD 2 (1998–2001)		
EQUATIONS	(1)	(2)	(3)	(4)	(5)	(6)
Ln (1998 Sales)	–.168**	–.190*	–.154**	–.079***	–.057*	–.079***
	(.081)	(.113)	(.070)	(.028)	(.030)	(.022)
Ln Age (1998)	–.087	–.035	–.116	–.216**	–.236***	–.215***
	(.131)	(.206)	(.130)	(.088)	(.084)	(.088)
Publicly-traded	.233*	.267	.207**	.126	.011	.164
	(.137)	(.189)	(.090)	(.109)	(.122)	(.105)
Exports as a Percentage of Revenues		.003***			.003***	
		(.001)			(.001)	
Toronto (M4, M5, M9)	.350***	.219**		.199*	.031	
	(.112)	(.107)		(.115)	(.101)	
North York (M2)	.340*	.277*		.148	.163	
	(.175)	(.170)		(.233)	(.258)	
Waterloo (N2)	.351***	.220		.663***	.370	
	(.140)	(.190)		(.246)	(.248)	
Ln Distance to Centre of M4/M5 Postal Code			–.061***			–.043**
			(.016)			(.020)
Constant	2.119***	2.089***	2.450***	1.736***	1.502***	1.968***
	(.472)	(.561)	(.432)	(.225)	(.222)	(.268)
R^2 (Adjusted)	.260	.278	.256	.174	.190	.180
n	240	206	240	189	165	189

Notes: Figures in parentheses are heteroscedastic-consistent (White 1980) standard errors. *** $p < .001$, ** $p < 0.05$, *$p < 0.01$.

sample firms. We do so by specifying a variable that identifies the distance of a sample firm (based on its postal code) from the centre of the M4/M5 postal code.[17] When the distance variable (measured as the natural logarithm of kilometre distance) is included in the basic estimating equation [Table 6, Equations (3) and (6)], the estimated coefficient is negative and statistically significant in both periods. Hence, the further away from the city of Toronto a firm is located, the weaker its growth performance. Apparently, there are economic spillovers from the Toronto cluster that diminish systematically with distance. Moreover, the logarithmic specification suggests that the impact of distance is non-linear, with the most important benefits accruing to firms that are closer to Toronto. The same result is obtained when firms within the M4/M5 postal code are all coded as being zero-distant from the centre.

It might be noted in passing that the results reported in Table 6 are somewhat sensitive to the inclusion or exclusion of the variable measuring exports as a percentage of revenues. In particular, the statistical significance of the Waterloo dummy variable decreases with the inclusion of the export-intensity variable. Unfortunately, the unavailability of data on exports for a relatively large number of firms in our sample means that the sample sizes for Equations (2) and (5) are smaller than those for the other reported equations and that contributes to the observed instability of some of the coefficients. From our perspective, what is relevant is that the coefficients for the Toronto dummy variable are statistically significant in virtually all of the specifications.

In order to determine the economic importance of a Toronto location, we examined both the growth premium for Toronto firms and the growth penalty for locating outside of Toronto. In order to calculate the Toronto growth premium, we use the estimated coefficients from Table 5 [Equations (1) and (5)] and Table 6 [Equations (1) and (4)]. For each time-period, we calculated the expected growth rate of a firm of average size and age regardless of location and compared that to the growth rate of a firm of average size and age located in either the Toronto CMA or in downtown Toronto. The period 1 logarithmic growth rate for a firm of average size and age, regardless of location, was calculated as .385. Location in the Toronto CMA added to this growth by .225, an increase of almost 60 percent. A similar calculation for period 2 suggests that location in the Toronto CMA increases the logarithmic value of growth by about 35 percent over the second sample period. In period 1, a firm of average size and age located in the downtown Toronto postal code grew at almost twice the rate of firms of average age and size located anywhere in Canada. In period 2, the calculated growth rate for a downtown Toronto firm was approximately 42 percent higher than the calculated growth rate for a firm ignoring location. These numbers suggest the existence of a relatively large growth premium for locating in Toronto.

In a second exercise, we assess how the growth penalty associated with locating outside of Toronto varies with distance. We proceed by using the estimated coefficients from Equations (3) and (6) in Table 6. We first calculate the estimated growth rate for a firm of average size and age regardless of location and use the estimated coefficient for the "distance from the M4/M5 postal code" variable to calculate the logarithmic growth rate for firms located at hypothetical distances from the downtown Toronto postal code. These calculations are summarized in Figure 3 which reports the growth penalty (in terms of logarithmic growth) associated with distance from Toronto. The distances represent the sample minimum distance (1.17 km), the sample maximum (3,350 km), the sample mean (833 km) and various distances in between. Displacement from downtown Toronto by as little as 10 km has a significant growth penalty for an average firm. Specifically, firms located 10 km from downtown Toronto grow at a 10 percent slower rate than firms located one km from

FIGURE 3

GROWTH AND DISTANCE FROM TORONTO

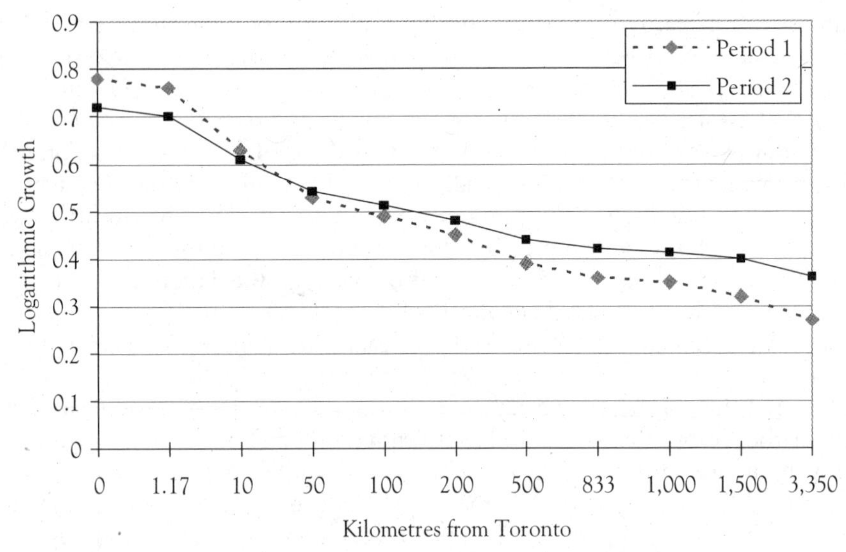

downtown Toronto in period 1. Firms located between 100 and 150 km from downtown Toronto grow at slightly less than two-thirds the rate of firms located one km from downtown. Firms located 1,500 km from the downtown core grow somewhat less than half as quickly as firms located 1 km from downtown. In short, there is a consistent and significant growth penalty associated with increased distance from downtown Toronto, but the growth penalty increases less than proportionally with distance.

The last issue we consider is whether the location of our sample firms with respect to U.S. ICT clusters influences their growth performance. This was accomplished by including in the estimating equations variables that measured the distance of the firm from U.S. clusters, as identified by the cluster-mapping project at Harvard Business School. The distance was measured either as the distance (in logarithm of kilometres) from the firm's postal code to the centre of the U.S. cluster; or from the firm's city centre to the centre of the U.S. cluster. U.S. clusters were identified as cities in which there are leading clusters of software firms.[18]

A number of distance-related measures were employed. First, we measured the distance of a firm from the largest U.S. software cluster (San José) or the nearest of the "top 2" clusters (San José or Boston). We also measured distance to the nearest "top 10" cluster (by size) in the United States, as well as the average distance of the Canadian firm from the top 10 U.S. clusters. When we included each of the measures in the basic estimating equations, our results suggested that international spillover effects may be present, but they are difficult to identify precisely (Table 7). Among other things, the distance variables are often correlated with other variables of importance, most notably distance from Toronto.[19] The variable representing distance from the largest U.S. cluster was never statistically significant, and the results including this variable are not reported. The coefficient for the variable representing the distance to the nearest of the top two clusters was negative and statistically significant in period 1 [Table 7, Equation (1)]; however, it became statistically insignificant with the inclusion of the variable representing distance from

TABLE 7

TESTING FOR INTERNATIONAL SPILLOVER EFFECTS

	PERIOD 1 (1998–2000)				PERIOD 2 (1998–2001)			
EQUATIONS	(1)	(2)	(3)	(4)	(5)	(6)	(7)	(8)
Ln (1998 Sales)	–.152**	–154***	–.152*	–.154**	–.079***	–.079***	–.078***	–.079***
	(.070)	(.022)	(.071)	(.070)	(.023)	(.022)	(.022)	(.022)
Ln Age (1998)	–.103	–.121	–.089	–.115	–.213***	–.215***	–.213**	–.216***
	(.124)	(.126)	(.128)	(.129)	(.088)	(.089)	(.089)	(.090)
Publicly-traded	.194**	.215**	.176**	.212**	.132	.166	.116	.160
	(.096)	(.095)	(.090)	(.090)	(.106)	(.105)	(.105)	(.104)
Toronto (M4, M5, M9)	.334***		.374***		.191*		.189*	
	(.112)		(.114)		(.116)		(.116)	
North York (M2)	.317*		.363**		.135		.138	
	(.173)		(.176)		(.228)		(.231)	
Waterloo (N2)	.342***		.372***		.659**		.657***	
	(.134)		(.144)		(.254)		(.248)	
Ln Distance to Centre of M4/M5 Postal Code		–.054***		–.057***		–.042**		–.036*
		(.019)		(.015)		(.020)		(.019)
Ln Distance to Nearest of Top 2 U.S. Clusters	–.159**	–.084			–.077	–.016		
	(.081)	(.104)			(.069)	(.099)		
Ln Distance to Nearest Top 10 U.S. Cluster*Ln Cluster Size			.012	.011			–.005	–.016*
			(.009)	(.007)			(.009)	(.009)
Constant	3.109***	2.976***	1.107**	1.716***	2.258***	2.075**	2.095***	2.279***
	(.944)	(.734)	(.550)	(.731)	(.730)	(.737)	(.754)	(.731)
R^2 (Adjusted)	.258	.255	.257	.259	.180	.175	.178	.176
n	240	240	240	240	189	189	189	189

Notes: Figures in parentheses are heteroscedastic-consistent (White 1980) standard errors. *** p < 0.001, ** p < 0.05, *p < 0.01

Toronto [Table 7, Equation (2)]. The average distance to the top 10 clusters was never statistically significant and the results are unreported. The distance to the nearest top 10 cluster was statistically insignificant. However, when an interaction term between the distance to the nearest top 10 cluster and the size of the cluster was included as an independent variable, the coefficient is negative and statistically significant (at the 0.10 level) in period 1, but not in period 2 [Table 6, Equations (3), (4), (7) and (8)].

It is possible that the spillover benefits from being located closer to a U.S. cluster are relevant only for firms located outside the city of Toronto. Specifically, it might be the case that location in the Toronto cluster generates essentially all of the agglomeration economies available to ICT firms given current technology. The potential to improve performance, therefore, increases as a firm is more distant from Toronto and closer to a comparable U.S. cluster. We attempted to test this hypothesis by excluding from the estimating sample all ICT companies located in Toronto. By and large, the results do not differ much from those reported in Table 7. On balance, the evidence for international spillovers increases modestly. For example, the coefficient for the distance to the nearest of the top two U.S. clusters is strongly statistically significant in both sample periods.[20]

In comparing Tables 6 and 7, the results for the other included variables are quite consistent. In particular, the coefficient for the distance to the centre of Toronto remains strongly significant. The Toronto postal codes (M4, M5, M9) and the Waterloo (N2) postal code become more consistently significant in the equations reported in Table 6.

CONCLUSIONS AND IMPLICATIONS

THE MAIN PURPOSE OF THIS STUDY is to identify whether specific regions in Canada promote the economic success of ICT companies and, if so, what are the attributes that contribute to the performance of firms in a particular region. It is fair to say that we offer more reliable conclusions about the former issue than about the latter issue. While the findings of our study are not conclusive, the evidence is fairly persuasive that there are a very limited number of economic locations in Canada that contribute to the growth of ICT firms. Indeed, the city of Toronto arguably comprises the clearest example of a successful geographic location for Canadian ICT companies. There is also some evidence, albeit less consistent, that successful locations exist in North York and Waterloo. The North York location might reflect its relatively close geographical proximity to the city of Toronto, while the success of the N2 (Waterloo) code could well reflect the proximity of the highly successful and relatively large computing department and expertise of the University of Waterloo. There is some evidence that the concentrated presence of universities in the Toronto region and the large amount of research activity associated with the universities' presence encourage the growth of Toronto-based ICT companies.

Our study also provides some clear evidence of spillovers from centres of clustering. In particular, it shows that firms located closer to Toronto grow faster than firms located further away, all other things constant.[21] Our findings also hint at the presence of international spillovers from U.S. clusters. That is, Canadian firms located closer to major U.S. clusters seem to enjoy growth benefits compared to those located further away. This seems particularly true for firms that are not located in Toronto, since the latter may already enjoy most, if not all, of the available benefits from agglomeration economies given their presence in the Toronto cluster. Spillover benefits from U.S. clusters are more difficult to identify statistically than those from the Toronto cluster, perhaps suggesting the presence of "border effects."

An obvious question that arises is why ICT firms choose to locate outside of the Toronto region when there are seemingly large and distinct commercial benefits to locating within that region. One possible answer is that our estimates are implicitly measures of the average impact of location choice and not the marginal impact. Thus, given the current geographical distribution of firms, at the margin, there may be essentially no net benefits to locating in Toronto, especially given higher costs in the Toronto area. However, it is also possible that location decisions on the part of Canadian companies have not been optimal. With less than perfect information, and with non-economic factors affecting the geographic preferences of owners, firms may be established in regions that fail to provide the benefits available in Toronto and, perhaps, in several other Ontario locations. Government policies that directly or indirectly subsidize the setting-up of companies in "have-not" regions would exacerbate any propensity toward an uneconomic geographic decentralization of Canadian companies. Presumably, uneconomic location choices will threaten the viability of Canadian companies in the long run. We intend to explore this phenomenon in future research.

One policy inference to be drawn from this study is that location matters to the performance of Canadian ICT companies. In particular, the further from Toronto a company is established, the less likely it is to enjoy superior economic performance, at least on average. This finding is a strong caution against governments in Canada directly or indirectly subsidizing the location of software firms outside of Toronto or promoting the relocation of firms from Toronto. To some extent, the disadvantages of being more remote from Toronto may be partially offset by closer proximity to large U.S. clusters. However, the largest U.S. clusters are fairly distant from many Canadian regions, and border effects may attenuate the magnitude of international commercial spillover benefits in the ICT sector. The relevance of geographic distance may be particularly prominent for the two or three largest U.S. clusters that may well be the most important potential sources of international spillovers.

A second, but much more tenuous inference, is that sub-CMA regions can partially compensate for an absence of economic activity of the scale and scope enjoyed by Toronto by leveraging the presence of leading universities and their associated research activity. Waterloo might be a model in this regard, although more study is required to determine if Waterloo's experience in software activity is idiosyncratic or whether it can be generalized to other types of activity and other regions.

On balance, our results offer more support for the notion that the Canadian economy is too small to support many geographically diversified clusters, and that policies directed at creating such diversity may be misplaced. One must be cautious in applying such a conclusion to all high-tech firms. For one thing, the coefficients of determination of our estimated models suggest that we may be ignoring important influences on high-technology firm growth that are capable of being influenced by government policy. For another, our sample excludes technology firms rooted in the physical, chemical and biological sciences. Thus, there are no pharmaceutical, biotech, fuel cell, or environmental engineering firms included. It remains to be seen whether the kind of results we find for ICT firms extend to all high-tech firms.

A concern might be raised that our sample time period, or more accurately our two sample time periods, are unrepresentative in that they incorporate the high-tech stock market bubble, as well as the aftermath of its bursting. However, since we are focusing on Canadian firms, and since the stock market bubble was much less pronounced in Canada than in the United States, this concern is mitigated. Perhaps a more important observation is that there is no particular reason to believe that a bubble in stock market prices would have affected sales revenue growth, let alone biased the growth in sales in favour of Toronto-based firms. In this regard, the limitations of using firm growth as a performance measure must be acknowledged and future research should both extend the sample period and the sophistication of the performance measures.

Our analysis also does not address questions of cluster sustainability. The ecology of dominant clusters observed over relatively short periods may indeed require the scale and scope of complementary services that only very large centres can provide, but they may also inhibit innovation and change. In the same manner that incumbent firms may ignore disruptive technologies, dominant clusters may find it difficult to support newly developed technologies.

APPENDIX 1

SOURCES OF DATA

R&D Data

Thompson, J. December 2002. *Estimates of Canadian Research and Development Expenditures (GERD), Canada, 1991 to 2002, and by Province, 1991 to 2000* (Publication No. 88F0006XIE No. 15). Ottawa, ON: Statistics Canada. Retrieved February 25, 2003 from www.statcan.ca/cgi-bin/downpub/listpub.cgi?catno=88F0006XIE2002015.

Research Infosource Inc. 2002. *Canada's Top 50 Research Institutes*. Retrieved on March 3, 2003 from www.researchinfosource.com/2002-top50.pdf.

Population Data

Statistics Canada. 2002. *Population and Dwelling Counts, for Canada, Provinces and Territories, 2001 and 1996 Censuses*. Ottawa, ON: Statistics Canada. Retrieved February 25, 2003 from www12.statcan.ca/english/census01/product/standard/popdwell/Table-PR.cfm.

Statistics Canada. 2002. *Population and Dwelling Counts, for Census Metropolitan Areas and Census Agglomerations, 2001 and 1996 Censuses*. Ottawa, ON: Statistics Canada. Retrieved February 25, 2003 from www12.statcan.ca/english/census01/ products/standard/popdwell/Table-PR.cfm.

GDP Data

Statistics Canada. 2002. *Gross Domestic Product, Expenditure-Based* (Cansim Table No. 3840002). Ottawa, ON: Statistics Canada. Retrieved February 25, 2003 from http://80-dc2.chass.utoronto.ca.proxy.lib.sfu.ca/cgi-bin/cansim2/getArray.pl?a=3840002.

Earnings Data

Statistics Canada. 2002. *Earnings Groups, Total Work Activity, for Both Sexes, for Canada, Provinces and Territories.* Ottawa, ON: Statistics Canada. Retrieved April 14, 2003 from www12.statcan.ca/english/census01/products/highlight/Earnings/Page.cfm?Lang=E&Geo=PR&View=1a&Table=1a&StartRec=1&Sort=2&B1=Both&B2=All.

Statistics Canada. 2002. *Earnings Groups, Total Work Activity, for Both Sexes, for Census Metropolitan Areas and Census Agglomerations*. Ottawa, ON: Statistics Canada. Retrieved April 14, 2003 from www12.statcan.ca/english/census01/products/highlight/Earnings/Page.cfm?Lang=E&Geo=CMA&View=1a&Table=1a&StartRec=1&Sort=2&B1=Both&B2=All.

Education Data

Statistics Canada. 2002. *Level of Educational Attainment for the Age Group 25 to 64, 2001 Counts for Both Sexes, for Canada, Provinces and Territories*. Ottawa, ON: Statistics Canada. Retrieved February 25, 2003 from www12.statcan.ca/english/census01/products/highlight/Education/Page.cfm?Lang=E&Geo=PR&View=1b&Table=1a&StartRec=1&Sort=2&B1=Counts01&B2=Both.

Statistics Canada. 2002. *Level of Educational Attainment for the Age Group 25 to 64, 2001 Counts for Both Sexes, for Census Metropolitan Areas and Census Agglomerations*. Ottawa, ON: Statistics Canada. Retrieved February 25, 2003 from www12.statcan.ca/english/census01/products/highlight/Education/Page.cfm?Lang=E&Geo=PR&View=1b&Table=1a&StartRec=1&Sort=2&B1=Counts01&B2=Both.

Statistics Canada. 2002. *Level of Educational Attainment for the Age Group 25 to 64, Percentage Distribution for Both Sexes, for Canada, Provinces and Territories*. Ottawa, ON: Statistics Canada. Retrieved February 25, 2003 from www12.statcan.ca/english/census01/products/highlight/Education/Page.cfm?Lang=E&Geo=PR&View=1b&Code=0&Table=2a&StartRec=1&Sort=2&B1=Distribution&B2=Both.

Statistics Canada. 2002. *Level of Educational Attainment for the Age Group 25 to 64, Percentage Distribution for Both Sexes, for Census Metropolitan Areas and Census Agglomerations — 20% Sample Data*. Ottawa, ON: Statistics Canada. Retrieved February 25, 2003 from www12.statcan.ca/english/census01/products/highlight/Education/Page.cfm?Lang=E&Geo=CMA&View=1b&Code=0&Table=2a&StartRec=1&Sort=2&B1=Distribution&B2=Both.

APPENDIX 2

METHODOLOGY FOR CALCULATING DISTANCES BETWEEN CITIES AND BETWEEN FIRMS

IN ORDER TO CALCULATE THE DISTANCES BETWEEN CITIES, the longitude and latitude of each Canadian city used in the study was obtained from the National Resources Canada web site at http://geonames.nrcan.gc.ca/, while the locations of the U.S. cities were obtained from www.bcca.org/misc/qiblih/latlong_us.html. Subsequently, each longitude and latitude was entered into The Great Circle Calculator (www.gb3pi.org.uk/great.html), a program that computes the distance (in miles) between two cities based on the longitude and latitude of each city. Distances were converted to kilometres for estimation purposes.

In order to ensure the accuracy of the Great Circle Calculator's computations, 15 distance calculations were randomly selected from the list. Subsequently, these distances were recalculated using a surface distance calculation program found at www.wcrl.ars.usda.gov/cec/java/lat-long.htm that also uses the longitude and latitude of a city to compute distances. There were no discrepancies found between the Great Circle Calculator's results and those of the surface distance calculator.

To calculate the distance from the centre of the M4/M5 postal code to all other relevant postal codes, we had to first determine the postal code that defined the centre of the combined M4/M5 region.

In order to do so, a forward sortation area (FSA) map provided by Canada Post was used. Specifically, this map displayed the boundaries for all FSAs in Canada. After tracing the border of the M4/M5 postal codes, several points on the perimeter were graphed. The *x,y* coordinates on the graph permitted the calculation of an approximate centre of the M4/M5 FSA boundaries using the following calculation:

$$\frac{x1+x2 \ldots xn}{n}, \qquad \frac{y1+y2 \ldots yn}{n}$$

This calculation resulted in the centre of the M4/M5 postal code boundary being located on the eastern boundary of the M4/M5 forward sortation area. Visual inspection confirmed this approximate location. To obtain an approximate centre of this area, we used Mapquest (www.mapquest.com/), a program that provides street-level detail of Canadian locations. This process resulted in determining that the centre was located in the M4K 3E5 postal code. We analyzed the sensitivity of the estimates to this calculation by moving the centre from 1-3 kilometres west (towards downtown Toronto) and found that this did not affect the results.

To obtain the longitude and latitude of every relevant postal code, a Statistics Canada database that lists the coordinates of every postal code in Canada was used. Each relevant postal code together with the required locational information was extracted from the database. Subsequently, each longitude and latitude was entered into The Great Circle Calculator (www.gb3pi.org.uk/great.html), and the distances were computed.

The method for calculating distances from every postal code to each of the top 10 U.S. clusters is exactly the same as calculating distances from cities to U.S. clusters with one exception. Instead of using the longitude and latitude of cities, the coordinates of each postal code (obtained from the Statistics Canada database) were used.

Longitude and Latitude References

Look-up Latitude and Longitude – USA. n.d. Retrieved April 11, 2003 from www.bcca.org/misc/qiblih/latlong_us.html.

Natural Resources Canada. 2003. *Canadian Geographical Names Database*. Ottawa, ON: Natural Resources Canada. Retrieved April 11, 2003 from http://geonames.nrcan.gc.ca/search/search_e.php.

Statistics Canada. September 2002. *Postal Code Conversion File*. (Publication No. 82F0086XDB). Ottawa, ON: Statistics Canada.

Canada Post. 2003. *Forward Sortation Area Maps*. Ottawa, ON: Canada Post. www.canadapost.ca/personal/tools/pg/fsamaps/pdf/Canada.pdf retrieved May 30, 2003.

ENDNOTES

1 Some authors specifically identify agglomeration economies as a concentration of firms engaged in a specific activity, while clusters are identified as the degree to which firms in related activities are co-located. This distinction corresponds, in spirit, to our distinction between economies associated with a concentration of firms engaged in the same, or similar, scientific and technological activities and economies associated with a relatively large group of diversified firms, providing a broad scope of complementary activities.

2 It might also be noted that the importance of scientific infrastructure likely declines with the maturity of the business activity in question.

3 Wolfgang Keller, "Geographic Localization of International Technology Diffusion," *American Economic Review*, 92 (1), 2002, p. 120.

4 For example, immigration programs that focus on attracting entrepreneurial and investor class immigrants to less densely-populated regions promote the location of the associated capital flows outside of the three main urban centers that attract the vast majority of immigrants to Canada, namely Toronto, Montreal and Vancouver.

5 The sources of data utilized in the study are summarized in Appendix 1.

6 By way of illustration, Ontario accounts for around 40 percent of Canada's population and GDP. The Figure 2 map provides a literal picture of the concentrated geographical location of Canadian high-technology firms.

7 Kirchoff and Norton (1994) conclude that assets, sales and employment are equivalent in terms of testing for Gibrat's Law. It should be noted that our sales growth estimates aggregate a firm's sales to its headquarters' location.

8 Anywhere log appears, it should be read as the natural logarithm (Ln).

9 The specification used for estimation regresses firm growth (measured as the difference in ln firm size) on initial firm size. Implicitly, initial size appears on both sides of the equation, leading to potential bias in the estimated coefficients. As a consequence, all equations were also estimated using alternative specifications. One specification regressed final period firm size on initial firm size (and age). In other specifications, firm growth was maintained as the dependent variable, but continuous measures of initial size were replaced by dummy variables. Two alternative sets of dummy variables were employed: one set for firms above (below) mean firm size and one for firms that were one standard deviation above or below the mean. The first alternative resulted in one dummy variable (equal one if firm size was above the mean), and the second in two dummy variables (equal one if the firm was one standard deviation above or one standard deviation below the mean). None of these alternatives produced results substantively different from those reported in the text. The only coefficient that was affected by the alternatives was the age coefficient which was more often significant in alternative specifications.

10 The sensitivity of our regression coefficients to the inclusion of extremely fast or slow-growing firms in our sample was evaluated by excluding and including firms with growth rates that were more than one standard deviation above or below the mean and then comparing the estimated results. No significant differences in the estimated coefficients were identified when excluding the extreme observations.

11 The percentage of foreign ownership among our high-tech firms is markedly bi-polar. That is, the sample is essentially divided between fully foreign-owned firms and entirely Canadian firms.

12 The foreign ownership dummy variable was consistently insignificant and was subsequently excluded from the basic estimating equation.

13 Simple pair-wise correlation coefficients generally exceed 0.8.

14 We combined the three digit postal codes (L3R and L4B) with downtown Toronto to create the two-digit Toronto intra-CMA area. This was done to reflect the geographical contiguity of the three regions.

15 An F-test indicated that the three Toronto postal codes could be grouped into one dummy variable, and we have reported results for the combined specification.

16 North York is geographically quite close to the combined Toronto postal code.

17 The distance estimate is based on average longitude and latitude differences. Details on how distances between locations are calculated are provided in Appendix 2.

18 The U.S. clusters are identified by the Institute for Strategy and Competitiveness, cluster-mapping project, Harvard Business School (www.isc.hbs.edu/econ-clusters.htm; accessed February 24, 2005). The U.S. clusters are defined at the level of metropolitan area.

19 In particular, firms close to the large Boston cluster are also close to the Toronto cluster. Alternative measures of distance might focus on travel time and costs between locations. Consideration of alternative measures of distance is a focus of future research.

20 These results are unreported. They are available from the authors upon request.

21 This finding might be somewhat at odds with that of Anselin et al. (1997) who found that localization effects are among the most pronounced for the software industry. Note that since the distance effect is specified in log-form, our results show that spillovers decrease less than proportionally with distance.

ACKNOWLEDGMENTS

THE AUTHORS WISH TO THANK Clayton Mitchell for exceptional research assistance, Mick Carney for useful discussions, and Ajay Agrawal for detailed comments and suggestions.

BIBLIOGRAPHY

Acs, Zoltan, and Catherine Armington. 2003. "Endogenous Growth and Entrepreneurial Activity in Cities," U.S. Bureau of the Census, Center for Economic Studies, Discussion Paper 03-02, mimeo.

Agrawal, Ajay, and Iain Cockburn. 2003. "The Anchor Tenant Hypothesis: Examining the Role of Large, Local R&D-Intensive Firms in University Knowledge Transfer," *International Journal of Industrial Organization*, 21(9): 1227-1253.

Almeida, Paul, and Bruce Kogut. 1999. "Localization of Knowledge and the Mobility of Engineers in Regional Networks," *Management Science*, 45 (7): 905-917.

Almus, Matthius, and Eric A. Nerlinger. 1999. "Growth of New Technology-Based Firms: Which Factors Matter?" *Small Business Economics*, 13 (2): 141-54.

Alston, Julian. 2002. "Spillovers," *Australian Journal of Agricultural and Resource Economics*, 46 (3): 315-46.

Anselin, Luc, Attila Varga, and Zoltan Acs. 1997. "Local Geographic Spillovers between University Research and High Technology Innovations," *Journal of Urban Economics*, 42 (3): 422-48.

Antonelli, Cristiano. 1994. "Technological Districts, Localized Spillovers and Productivity Growth," *International Review of Applied Economics*, 8 (1): 18-30.

Audretsch, David B. 1998. "Agglomeration and the Location of Innovative Activity," *Oxford Review of Economic Policy*, 14 (2): 18-29.

Audretsch, David B., and Maryann P. Feldman. 1996. "Knowledge Spillovers and the Geography of Innovation and Production," *American Economic Review*, 86 (3): 630-640.

Audretsch, David, and Talat Mahmood. 1995. "New Firm Survival: New Results Using a Hazard Function," *Review of Economics and Statistics*, 77 (1): 97-103.

Autant-Bernard, Corinne. 2001. "Science and Knowledge Flows — Evidence From the French Case," *Research Policy*, 30 (7): 1069-78.

Bayoumi, Tamin, David T. Coe, and Elhanan Helpman. 1999. "R&D Spillovers and Global Growth," *Journal of International Economics*, 47 (2): 399-428.

Bernstein, Jeffrey I. 1989. "The Structure of Canadian Interindustry R&D Spillovers and Rates of Return to R&D," *Journal of Industrial Economics*, 37 (3): 315-28.

————. 1998. "Factor Intensities, Rates of Return, and International R&D Spillovers: The Case of Canadian and U.S. Industries," *Annales d'économie et de statistique*, January-June (49-50): 541-64.

————. 2000. "Canadian Manufacturing, U.S. R&D Spillovers, and Communication Infrastructure," *Review of Economics and Statistics*, 82 (4): 608-15.

Bernstein, Jeffrey I., and Pierre Mohnen. 1998. "International R&D Spillovers between U.S. and Japanese R&D Intensive Sectors," *Journal of International Economics*, 44 (2): 315-38.

Bissant, Rakesh, and Brian Fikkert. 1996. "The Effects of R&D, Foreign Technology Purchase and Domestic and International Spillovers on Productivity in Indian Firms," *Review of Economics and Statistics*, 78 (2): 187-99.

Blind, Knut, and Harcolf Grupp. 1999. "Interdependencies Between the Science and Technology Infrastructure and Innovation Activities in German Regions: Empirical Findings and Policy Consequences," *Research Policy*, 28 (5): 451-68.

Boschma, Ron A., and Jan G. Lambooy. 1999. "Evolutionary Economics and Economic Geography," *Journal of Evolutionary Economics*, 9 (4): 411-429.

Branstetter, Lee. 2001. "Are Knowledge Spillovers International or International in Scope?" *Journal of International Economics*, 53 (1): 53-79.

Braunerhjelm, Pontus, Bo Carlson, Dilek Cetindamar, and Dan Johansson. 2000. "The Old and the New: The Evolution of Polymer and Biomedical Clusters in Ohio and Sweden," *Journal of Evolutionary Economics*, 10 (5): 471-488.

Cantwell, John, and Grazia Santangelo. 2002. "The New Geography of Corporate Research in Information and Communication Technology," *Journal of Evolutionary Economics*, 12 (1-2): 163-197.

Capron, Henri, and Michele Cincera. 1998. "Exploring the Spillover Impact on Productivity of World-wide Manufacturing Firms," *Annales d'économie et de statistique* January-June (49-50): 565-587.

Coe, David T., and Elhanan Helpman. 1995. "International R& D Spillovers," *European Economic Review*, 39 (5): 859-87.

Davidson, William H., and Donald G. McFetridge. 1985. "Key Characteristics in the Choice of International Technology Transfers," *Journal of International Business Studies*, 16 (2): 5-21.

Dierickx, Ingemar, and Karel Cool. 1989. "Asset Stock Accumulation and Sustainability of Competitive Advantage," *Management Science*, 35 (12): 1504-11.

Eaton, Jonathan, and Samuel Kortum. 1996. "Trade in Ideas: Patenting and Productivity in the OECD," *Journal of International Economics*, 40 (3-4): 251-78.

————. 1999. "International Technology Diffusion: Theory and Measurement," *International Economic Review*, 40 (3): 537-70.

Eisenhardt, Kathleen, and Claudia Bird Schoonhoven. 1990. "Organization Growth: Linking Founding Team, Strategy Environment and Growth Among US Semiconductor Ventures, 1978-1988," *Administrative Science Quarterly*, 35 (3): 504-29.

Ellison, Glenn, and Edward L. Glaeser. 1997. "Geographic Concentration in US Manufacturing Industries: A Dartboard Approach," *Journal of Political Economy*, 105 (5): 889-927.

Engelbrecht, Hans-Jurgen. 1997. "International R&D Spillovers, Human Capital and Productivity in OECD Economies: An Empirical Investigation," *European Economic Review*, 41 (8): 1479-88.

Evans, D. 1987a. "The Relationship Between Firm Growth, Size, and Age: Estimates for 100 Manufacturing Industries," *Journal of Industrial Economics*, 35 (4): 567-581.

————. 1987b. "Tests of Alternative Theories of Firm Growth," *Journal of Political Economy*, 95 (4): 657-675.

Evenson, Robert. 1997. "Industrial Productivity Growth Linkages Between OECD Countries, 1970-90," *Economic Systems Research*, 9 (2): 221-30.

Feldman, Maryann P., and David B. Audretsch. 1999. "Innovation in Cities: Science-Based Diversity, Specialization and Localized Competition," *European Economic Review*, 43 (2): 409-29.

Feldman, Maryann P., and Johanna Francis. 2001. "Entrepreneurs and the Formation of Industrial Clusters," Baltimore: Johns Hopkins University, mimeo.

Frantzen, Dirk. 2000. "R&D Intersectoral and International Knowledge Spillovers and Human Capital: An Empirical Investigation," *Economia Internazionale*, 53 (4): 487-505.

————. 2002. "Intersectoral and International R&D Knowledge Spillovers and Total Factor Productivity," *Scottish Journal of Political Economy*, 49 (3): 250-303.

Globerman, Steven. 1979. "Foreign Direct Investment and 'Spillover' Efficiency Benefits in Canadian Manufacturing Industries," *Canadian Journal of Economics*, 12 (1): 42-56.

————. 2001. *The Location of Higher Value-Added Activities*, Occasional Paper No. 27. Ottawa: Industry Canada.

Gunderson, Morley. 2001. "North American Economic Integration and Globalization," Toronto: University of Toronto, mimeo.

Hamilton, Oliver, Daniel Shapiro, and Aidan Vining. 2002. "The Growth Patterns of Canadian High-Tech Firms," *International Journal of Technology Management*, 24 (4): 458-472.

Hanel, Petr. 2000. "R&D, Interindustry and International Technology Spillovers and the Total Factor Productivity Growth of Manufacturing Industries in Canada 1974-1989," *Economic Systems Research*, 12 (3): 345-61.

Jaffe, Adam B. 1986. "Technological Opportunity and Spillovers of R&D: Evidence from Firm's Patents, Profits and Market Values," *American Economic Review*, 76 (5): 984-1001.

Jaffe, Adam B., and Manuel Trajtenberg. 1999. "International Knowledge Flows: evidence from Patent Citations," *Economics of Innovation and New Technology*, 8 (1-2): 105-36.

Jaffe, Adam B., Manuel Trajtenberg, and Rebecca Henderson. 1993. "Geographic Localization of Knowledge Spillovers as Evidenced by Patent Citations," *Quarterly Journal of Economics*, 108 (3): 577-98.

Johnson, Daniel, and Robert Evenson. 1999. "R&D Spillovers to Agriculture: Measurement and Application," *Contemporary Economic Policy*, 17 (4): 432-56.

Keller, Wolfgang. 2002. "Geographic Localization of International Technology Diffusion," *American Economic Review*, 92 (1): 120-42.

Kirchhoff, B., and E. Norton. 1994. "Testing Gibrat's Law: The Effects of Time Period and Measurement," Working Paper. Newark, NJ: New Jersey Institute of Technology.

Krugman, Paul. 1991. *Geography and Trade*. Cambridge, MA: MIT Press.

————. 1998. "What's New About the New Economic Geography," *Oxford Review of Economic Policy*, 14 (2): 7-17.

Niosi, Jorge. 2003. "Alliances Are Not Enough: Explaining Rapid Growth in Biotechnology Firms," *Research Policy*, 32 (5): 737-50.

Okabe, Misa. 2002. "International R&D Spillovers and Trade Expansion: Evidence from East Asian Economies," *ASEAN Economic Bulletin*, 19 (2): 141-54.

Penrose, Edith. 1959. *The Theory of the Growth of the Firm*. New York: Wiley.

Porter, Michael E. 2000. "Location, Competition, and Economic Development: Local Clusters in a Global Economy," *Economic Development Quarterly*, 14 (1): 15-34.

Prevezer, Martha. 1997. "The Dynamics of Industrial Clustering in Biotechnology," *Small Business Economics*, 9 (3): 255-71.

Rauch, James E. 1999. "Networks Versus Markets in International Trade," *Journal of International Economics*, 48 (1): 7-35.

Rosenthal, Stuart S., and William C. Strange. 2003. "Geography, Industrial Organization and Agglomeration," *Review of Economics and Statistics*, 85(2): 377-393.

Rugman, Alan, and Joseph D'Cruz. 1993. "The Double Diamond Model of International Competitiveness: The Canadian Experience," *Management International Review*, 33(2): 178-196.

Sadler-Smith, Eugene, Yve Hampson, Ian Chaton, and Beryl Badger. 2003. "Managerial Behavior, Entrepreneurial Style, and Small Business Performance," *Journal of Small Business Management*, 41(1): 47-67.

Saxenian, A. 1994. *Regional Advantage: Culture and Competition in Silicon Valley and Route 128*. Cambridge, MA: Harvard University Press.

SubbaNarisima, P., S. Ahmed, and S. Mallya. 2003. "Technological Knowledge and Firm Performance of Pharmaceutical Firms," *Journal of Intellectual Capital*, 4 (1): 20-43.

Surico, Paolo. 2003. "Geographic Concentrations and Increasing Returns," *Journal of Economic Surveys*, 17 (5): 693-709.

Swann, Peter, and Martha Prevezer. 1996. "A Comparison of the Dynamics of Industrial Clustering in Computing and Biotechnology," *Research Policy*, 25 (7): 1139-57.

van den Panne, Gerben, and Wilfred Dolfsma. 2002. "The Odd Role of Proximity in Knowledge Relations- High Tech in the Netherlands," Delft, The Netherlands: Delft University of Technology, mimeo.

van Meijl, Hans, and Frank van Tongeren. 1998. "Trade, Technology Spillovers and Food Production in China," *Weltwirtschaftliches Archiv*, 134 (3): 423-49.

Verspagen, Bart. 1997. "Estimating International Technology Spillovers Using Technology Flow Matrices," *Weltwirtschaftliches Archiv*, 133 (2): 226-48.

White, H. 1980. "A Heteroscedasticity-Consistent Covariance Matrix Estimator and a Direct Test for Heteroscedasticity," *Econometrica* (48): 817-838.

Comment

Ajay Agrawal
University of Toronto

THIS ESSAY OFFERS SOME THOUGHTS on the study "Location Effects, Locational Spillovers and the Performance of Canadian Information Technology Firms" by Steven Globerman, Daniel Shapiro and Aidan Vining. The study was prepared for the Micro-Economic Policy Analysis (MEPA) division at Industry Canada and presented at the conference "Services Industries and the Knowledge-Based Economy" in Winnipeg, in October 2003. The comments presented in this essay are based on my discussant remarks presented at that conference.

The study by Globerman et al. has much to offer; it is interesting, important and provocative. It is interesting because it addresses the topical and intellectually challenging issue of regional advantage and is one of the few empirical studies to do so using Canadian data. It is important because this topic has clear implications for Canadian productivity and economic growth, and the nature of this research lends itself directly to informing public policy. And it is provocative because it draws conclusions that suggest some reasonably radical implications for public policy: it estimates a significant performance gain that results from agglomeration and thus questions the notion of spreading government support for the founding of new information technology (IT) firms across "have" and "have not" regions. Instead, the study proposes focusing attention on just a few select "have" regions, such as Toronto. Research results that stimulate thinking and also have direct policy implications are surprisingly rare and deserve recognition.

However, it is precisely because this study offers a compelling argument in favour of some radical rethinking of public policy that it is important to examine its limitations and consider the implications of these limitations with respect to its overall findings.

It is worthwhile to begin by clarifying the research question that this study addresses. The authors state that their intention "is to identify *why* specific locations in Canada are more or less supportive of successful IT firms."[1] While the study does suggest some reasons why regions may vary in their ability to support economically successful IT firms, the empirical analysis is actually focused only on whether, in fact, regions do vary.

For example, results presented in Table 4 suggest that there is an Ontario effect but do not explain why. The study begins to examine "scientific infrastructure" but only reports two elements (number of top 50 universities and total dollars of research performed by sample firms) that are likely concentrated in Ontario. The results, however, do not control for the identified Ontario effect. Similarly, at the CMA level, the focus is on the presence of a Toronto effect, rather than on why Toronto offers IT firms a growth advantage. Again, partial support is found for CMA university research measured in dollars, but this is likely concentrated in Toronto and the results presented do not control for the identified Toronto effect. Finally, similar results are presented in Table 6 that reflect the presence of regional advantage at the two-digit postal code level. (Incidentally, it is interesting to note that these results are not robust enough to accommodate the addition of a control for export intensity. So it would be useful to include prior results at the city and provincial level that control for export intensity, given its significance at the two-digit postal code level.) Thus, it is important to clarify that while the study does offer a thoughtful literature review concerning theories that explain why some regions offer greater advantages for growth, the empirical results reported here only explore whether there actually *is* regional variation in the sales growth of IT firms in Canada. Even so, that is still a very interesting and important research question.

There are many competing theories that explain why there might be variance in regional advantage. This study builds on the theories of agglomeration and clusters. Although these terms are used interchangeably in the study, they have been employed with distinct meanings in certain other settings. Namely, agglomeration may specifically refer to the degree to which an industry is geographically concentrated above and beyond what would be expected given a random distribution of firms relative to the general distribution of economic activity as well as controlling for the discreteness of firms (Ellison and Glaeser 1994). Clusters may refer to the degree to which related organizations (interconnected companies, specialized suppliers, service providers, firms in related industries, and associated institutions such as universities, standards agencies and trade associations) are co-located (Porter 1998; Marshall 1920).

In addition to the literature referenced in the study, other studies offer alternative theories that seek to explain why some cities provide better growth environments than others. Although it is beyond the scope of this article to review that literature here, I will mention a few alternative theories to offer the reader a flavour of the other types of explanations that have been proposed. Saxenian (1994) argues that regions with particular industrial cultures (open rather than secretive, cooperative rather than self-sufficient, adventurous rather than risk-averse, decentralized rather than centralized) are more conducive to firm success. Almeida and Kogut (1999) argue that inter-firm mobility (the propensity for engineers to move from one company to another) varies across cities and that those areas with greater circulation within their regional labour networks offer locational advantages.

Additionally, Florida (2002) argues that cities with a "creative ethos" (diverse, tolerant and open to new ideas) offer a regional advantage for firm productivity. Agrawal and Cockburn (2003) argue that cities with one or more "anchor tenants" (large, local, R&D-intensive firms with related technological interests) provide a superior environment for growth. In other words, there is a growing list of explanations for regional advantage, but few studies have offered empirical evidence that supports one theory over others. This seems like an obvious direction for new studies to pursue, and the interesting work here by Globerman et al. offers evidence that regions do matter to economies, including Canada's, and so highlights the need for further research to understand why.

Next, consider the concept of performance that lies at the heart of the empirical analysis. While the dependent variable (sales growth) selected for the analysis is certainly reasonable, it does have a few drawbacks and one in particular that should be noted. The prescriptive tone of the study suggests that policy should be concerned with maximizing "success," which is measured here by growth in sales over time. However, to some extent, this measure does not reflect overall performance considering costs. As a result, particularly under conditions where firms may be temporarily focused on market share rather than profitability, such as was arguably the case in the IT industry during much of the period under investigation, sales may be a biased measure of performance.

For example, if labour costs are significantly higher in bigger cities and labour comprises a significant portion of total software development costs, then software firms in larger cities must sell more units, at the same price, than their smaller-town rivals in order to generate the *same* profits. Under this scenario, the bigger city firms would appear to be more successful, even though all firms have achieved equal performance in terms of profitability. Having noted this concern, I am sympathetic to the authors' decision to use sales growth for their dependent variable. I recognize the difficulty in collecting profit data, particularly from private companies, and so raise this point simply as a caveat for the reader.

It is also worthwhile to note the limitations to measuring "distance" in kilometres. At one point in the study, the authors estimate the degree to which spillovers from Toronto diminish systematically with distance. Given the geographic distribution of firms in the sample, which are located in a reasonably small number of cities and are unevenly distributed among them (more than 75 percent of firms are located in Toronto, Ottawa, Vancouver, Montreal or Calgary), this metric seems questionable. Is Vancouver further from Toronto than Calgary (or even Winnipeg) in any meaningful way? Similarly, some economists have argued that San Francisco is "closer" to Boston than Kansas since ideas seem to travel faster between the two coastal cities, as evidenced by citation analysis. Why do economists think that distance matters? Usually they cite reasons associated with costs, which include travel time and convenience, among other factors. Perhaps some alternative measures, such as frequency of flights between two destinations, would complement measurements in kilometres to offer a more meaningful measure of distance.

The study is rather brief in its description of its data sample. While it does note the source of the list of firms (the Branham 300 list of high-technology companies in Canada — www.branhamgroup.com), the authors are silent on how this list was originally constructed. Specifically, the reader is left without any ability to gauge the potential for sample selection bias.

However, it is possible to deduce a potential for bias. The following excerpt was taken from the Branham Group web site, which solicits entries for its list:

> As done over the past ten years, Branham is looking for your support and assistance in creating the most comprehensive intelligence on Canadian Information Technology companies. Participating in this listing is an excellent opportunity to receive ***FREE*** National exposure for your firm.[2]

The Branham Group is located in Ottawa, Ontario. Consider the following scenario. There is a cost (effort) associated with filling out the application form, especially since it requests specific financial performance information, and so not every firm does it. The Branham Group needs firms on its list and so encourages the high performance firms that it is familiar with to fill out the survey. Since the Branham Group is located in Ontario, it is likely most familiar with firms located there. This would not necessarily bias results if the Ontario firms encouraged to apply are randomly drawn. However, if the Branham Group disproportionately encourages higher performing Ontario firms to apply, it would bias results towards an Ontario performance effect. Far fetched and contrived? Perhaps, but it would be nice to have this type of sample selection concern allayed.

The study is based on data that is drawn from a unique period (1998-2001) in economic history in general and for the information technology sector in particular. The technology-laden Nasdaq Composite Index rose approximately 220 percent from 1,570 on January 1, 1998 to just over 5,000 in March 2000. As of October 2003, it stood at around 1,880, only 20 percent above the January 1998 value. Arguably, information technology was among the most volatile components of the Nasdaq during the period under investigation. For example, while the Nasdaq Index doubled in that period, Cognos, the top ranked software firm on the list in 1999, increased in price by over 500 percent. Like many firms in the industry, however, Cognos, lost more than 80 percent of that increase by late 2001.

The study briefly acknowledges that this was an unusual period and offers two sets of results: 1998-2000 and 1998-2001. However, it would be useful to provide a discussion that: 1) explains in detail why examining these two periods addresses the unusual volatility experienced in this sector over the period in question, 2) interprets the difference in results across these two periods, and 3) offers the authors' thoughts on their remaining level of concern regarding the ability to generalize their results to a more "normal" economic timeframe. While the study does focus on sales growth (not market capitalization), the unusual conditions of inflated valuations, low cost of capital, and overall "irrational exuberance" could not have left sales figures unaffected. This issue is important and demands consideration.

The study would benefit from more descriptive data. In particular, it would be useful to know the distribution of sales growth and revenue size across firms, perhaps cross-tabulated with CMAs. One conceivable scenario, for example, is that most firms had modest sales growth, with the exception of only a very few companies that grew substantially over the period under investigation. To what extent are such firms in the tail of the distribution dictating the slope of the regression line? If this is not the case, a table providing these data would allay such concerns. Either way, providing descriptive statistics would confirm that the authors have suitably addressed any particular distributional properties of the data adequately with appropriate econometric techniques.

The study could offer even more insight by providing some sense of how to interpret key coefficients in terms of their relative magnitudes. While the authors discuss the sign and statistical significance of key coefficients, they do not offer an interpretation of their magnitudes. It is worthwhile to unscramble the functional form and discuss the economic significance of the coefficients, at least at the mean. In other words, certain coefficients are statistically significant, but are they economically important? Such interpretations would help these results offer further insight for policy makers. For example, is the performance premium for locating in Toronto large enough to compensate for the higher labour costs in that city? Conversely, if the federal government continues to encourage the founding of IT companies in "have not" regions, how much is that distributional policy costing in terms of forgone sales growth?

While I fully appreciate the difficulty in doing so, this study and many like it would benefit greatly if it offered some empirical evidence of causality rather than simple correlations. This is perhaps the single greatest general weakness of studies on regional advantage. The sheer number of competing hypotheses explaining regional advantage that are able to comfortably coexist are testament to the general paucity of evidence that directly supports causality arguments. Clearly, generating such evidence is not trivial. However, any efforts made in this regard would be useful, and acknowledging that the results presented may be suggestive of a causal relationship, but are actually only correlations, would clarify the nature of the study's contribution. To reiterate though, this comment applies to the literature in general, not just this study.

Finally, since this study offers additional evidence that agglomeration enhances performance, it further inspires the need to increase our understanding of *why* it is that geographic proximity to related firms has this positive effect. As Krugman (1991) points out, agglomeration leads to thicker factor markets, greater availability of non-traded inputs and increased spillovers. Given progress in communications technologies, one might wonder why spillovers could still be mediated by geographic distance. A preliminary study suggests that technology spillovers may occur disproportionately between individuals with social relationships (Agrawal, Cockburn and McHale 2003). To the extent that social relationships are mediated by geographic proximity, spillover benefits from agglomeration are understandable.

To conclude, I enjoyed reading this study. It tackles an important question that is central to much of the thinking behind recent Canadian policy on science, technology and industry as evidenced by the increasing usage of terms such as "technology clusters" and "industry clusters" that have appeared in both federal and provincial government publications. The authors offer compelling empirical evidence that "location matters" and that while distributional policies might appear socially just, they come at the cost of reduced sales performance. The critical points offered above should not minimize the important contribution of this study, but rather highlight the challenges associated with conducting this type of research. By illustrating the importance of regional variations in economic behaviour, this study will inspire future research to further explore mechanisms at the regional level that influence firm productivity. Thus, this study and the stream of research that follows will better inform regional and federal public policy.

ENDNOTES

1 Globerman, Shapiro and Vining (2003), Chapter 6 of this volume, p. 2, emphasis mine.

2 Quotation from Branham Web site, October 5, 2003; emphasis theirs.

BIBLIOGRAPHY

Agrawal, Ajay, and Iain Cockburn. 2003. "The Anchor Tenant Hypothesis: Examining the Role of Large, Local, R&D-Intensive Firms in University Knowledge Transfer," *International Journal of Industrial Organization*, 21(9): 1227-1253.

Agrawal, Ajay, Iain Cockburn, and John McHale. 2003. "Gone But Not Forgotten: Labor Flows, Knowledge Spillovers, and Enduring Social Capital," Working Paper 9950. Cambridge, MA: National Bureau of Economic Research.

Almeida, Paul, and Bruce Kogut. 1999. "Localization of Knowledge and the Mobility of Engineers in Regional Networks," *Management Science*, 45 (7): 905-917.

Ellison, Glenn, and Edward L. Glaeser. 1994. "Geographic Concentration in US Manufacturing Industries: A Dartboard Approach," Working Paper 4840. Cambridge, MA: National Bureau of Economic Research.

Florida, R. 2002. *The Rise of the Creative Class*. New York: Basic Books.

Krugman, Paul. 1991. *Geography and Trade*. Cambridge, MA: MIT Press.

Marshall, A. 1920. *Principles of Economics*. (8th edition). New York: Macmillan and Co., Ltd. (First edition published 1890.)

Porter, Michael E. 1998. "Clusters and Competition: New Agendas for Companies, Governments, and Institutions," *On Competition*. Cambridge, MA: Harvard Business School Press.

Saxenian, A. 1994. *Regional Advantage: Culture and Competition in Silicon Valley and Route 128*. Cambridge, MA: Harvard University Press.

John Whalley
University of Western Ontario

7

Liberalization in China's Key Services Sectors Following Accession to the World Trade Organization: Some Scenarios and Issues of Measurement

OVERVIEW

AS PART OF ITS ACCESSION to the World Trade Organization (WTO), China has made commitments in the services area that are simultaneously extraordinarily deep and wide ranging. The adjective "breathtaking" has frequently been used to describe them. Its undertakings seem to suggest that over a five-year period from 2002 to 2007, China will open all of its markets to full international competition from foreign service providers in a series of key areas: distribution, telecommunications, financial services, professional business and computer services, motion pictures, environmental services, accounting, law, architecture, construction, and travel and tourism. China will remove all barriers to entry in the form of discriminatory licences to operate and all conduct-related barriers in the form of differential regulations for domestic and foreign entries. This study focuses on the possible implications of implementing these commitments over the next five years.

The study documents and assesses the significance of Chinese policy changes that WTO accession implies in three key service categories: banking, insurance and telecommunications. It considers whether it is likely that they will be implemented in their entirety, as undertaken at China's signature of the Treaty of Accession in 2002. Taken at face value, it would seem that China will have extraordinarily open markets for these services by 2007 and for banking, it will have perhaps the most open market in the world. The starting point for these policy changes, however, seems so highly restricted that doubts have been raised about the feasibility of implementing them over such a short time, even if threats of eventual retaliation from WTO partners accelerate the process. WTO members are monitoring the implementation of China's WTO commitments and should it falter, they may turn to dispute resolution mechanisms or retaliation thereafter. This study discusses what scenarios such liberalization might follow, and asks whether these commitments can really be implemented as undertaken. Other issues touched upon include how large the potential market for these services might be, and how much foreign penetration one could realistically expect in this area.

To evaluate possible impacts, this study discusses the limited amount of literature on trade liberalization that recognizes the individual characteristics of key services areas and contrasts it to the larger body of literature that treats all services as analytically equivalent to goods and that discusses services liberalization in a conventional trade policy framework.[1] The study then outlines a general theoretical framework for both discussing and measuring the impacts of liberalization in these areas and discusses its applicability to China. Most analytical literature on trade policy still discusses barriers to services trade as if tariff equivalents were involved, but the barriers at issue are quite dissimilar to tariffs since there is no customs clearance for services. For instance, China is planning to use progressive expansion of allowable foreign ownership and geographical coverage of licences as the instruments of liberalization. Granting of licences is discrete and modelling their removal using an *ad valorem* tariff equivalent can be misleading. How should we think about negotiated liberalization in these areas as it applies to the Chinese case, and how does it compare to using an alternative continuous protective instrument like a tariff for which rates can be varied? And what of gradually easing geographical limitations on licences by extending them to more cities: how does such continuous liberalization behave relative to conventional tariff-based liberalization?

Finally, the study discusses what liberalization might involve quantitatively. Are the gains likely to be as large as some have claimed[2] and who might benefit? How might such liberalization affect overall economic performance in China and what are the relevant scenarios? How large a share of world service markets could be involved, and what of new competition and new opportunities abroad? Will activity in liberalized areas in China continue to be via domestic-foreign joint ventures as at present, or will that change? And what might be the implications for liberalization elsewhere in other countries?

Trade Liberalization in Key Services Categories

Before embarking on a more concrete discussion of the impacts of China's WTO accession in the key services areas of banking, insurance and telecoms, it may first be useful to discuss the broader literature on services liberalization in general. Most of this is descriptive, relatively little is analytical and most of it does not distinguish between different services categories on the basis of their characteristics.[3]

The presumption underlying most discussions of the interest countries may have in the liberalization of trade in services is that countries gain from more open services trade in ways that are similar to the liberalization of trade in goods. This reflects the idea that countries have differing comparative advantages in the production of both goods and services, and that more open trade will allow comparative advantage to be more fully exploited in all countries. Put simply, the thinking is that propositions regarding the gains from freer trade apply equally to both goods and services. There are, however, many complications with this line of argument even though it is instinctively where most academic economists seem to finish in their thinking.

Services constitute a majority of activity in the economies of most members of the Organisation for Economic Co-operation and Development (OECD) as measured by employment and by gross domestic product (GDP): they represent a smaller but still large portion of activity for developing countries. So-called "core" services can best be thought of (Melvin 1989) as relating to intermediation through time (banking, insurance) or space (telecoms, transportation, retailing, wholesaling), with a wide range of additional service items, making up the balance of what most people refer to as services (tourism, consulting services, government services, utilities). This diverse range of activities is typically treated in both quantitative and theoretical work as a single homogenous entity, frequently labelled as services for the sake of convenience, though its heterogeneity seems clearly to call for a different treatment of each area.

Whether goods and services differ in important ways raises the issue of whether they need to be approached differently in evaluating the impacts of liberalization for each. Much, if not most, of the existing literature treats services as analytically similar to goods. The approach is to define a single product, commonly called producer services, which is an input into production and against which trade protection operates through a tariff-like instrument. Liberalization is then a reduction in or elimination of the tariff equivalent. Not surprisingly, the results of models that use this approach are similar to those analyzing trade liberalization in goods. In numerical models of goods liberalization, small positive gains accrue to most countries if no factor mobility effects are captured (Whalley 2003).

In reality, since services facilitate transactions, they typically provide the economic function of intermediation either through time or space. This idea is reflective of a heterogeneous group of activities spanning banking, insurance, transportation, telecoms, consulting services, retail and wholesale trade, and several others. Explicitly modelled in this way, this can produce implications for trade liberalization that differ from conventional goods analysis.

Ryan (1990, 1992) shows, for instance, that if banking is explicitly modelled as intermediation services so that banks themselves do not directly provide utility but instead facilitate intermediation between borrowers and lenders, then liberalization of trade in banking services can reduce GDP, and even welfare. Based on this approach, Chia and Whalley (1997) have produced a numerical example of trade liberalization in banking services that worsens welfare. The results derived from such examples reflect the use of specific analytical structures, parameter values and functional forms and are thus not general results. These results do, however, suggest a further weakening in the general presumption that gains will result in countries where liberalization of services trade occurs. Bhattarai and Whalley (1998) provide a related analysis of the implications of liberalization in network services (effectively telecoms) where the same theme emerges that recognition of the special features of individual services changes the analysis of the impacts of services liberalization. They show how, with network externalities present, the division of the gains from liberalization in service networks differs from the case of goods. More generally, there is no reason to think that trade liberalization in goods and services are independent of each other: for instance, liberalization in services when tariffs still apply to goods can easily be welfare worsening.

Even if trade in goods and services are treated as analytically similar, then how countries benefit from services trade liberalization is subject to all of the nuances set out in the literature on policy for the liberalization of trade in goods. While most academic economists seem to believe that there are benefits for all countries from freer trade in goods, over the years they have nevertheless devoted a considerable portion of their intellectual energy to producing arguments as to why the contrary may be true. These include arguments for an optimal tariff (an improvement in terms of trade arising from protection), for the protection of infant industries, for tariffs that transfer rents (rent shifting), and tariffs that offset other domestic distortions.

There are also qualifying arguments about protection of trade in goods that relate in one way or another primarily to developing countries and these also come into play in discussing the impacts of liberalization in services. One example is offered by a Lewis trade model with traditional practices in agriculture (average rather than marginal product pricing of labour). In this case, the protection of the traded-goods sectors is called for to pull labour into modern sectors that compete with imports. In a Harris-Todaro model with an urban sector characterized by downwardly rigid real wages and unemployment, an import subsidy can be beneficial.

The liberalization of trade in services differs from goods liberalization in another respect: to achieve meaningful trade liberalization in services, modifications on restrictions to factor mobility may be required, something that may not be needed for goods liberalization. This is recognized in modes 3 and 4 of the General Agreement on Trade in Services (GATS) that relate to the mobility of both capital (foreign direct investment) and labour (service providers). With restricted or segmented factor markets (and especially labour markets), large effects can come if services liberalization becomes an indirect mechanism for liberalizing domestic factor markets. This is a central issue for countries that have long pushed for liberalization of immigration controls in OECD countries, since global services liberalization may be a vehicle for them to achieve this end

(Hamilton and Whalley 1984, Winters 2002 and Winters, Walmsley, Wang and Grunberg 2002).

A further issue in discussing trade liberalization in services and its impacts on individual countries is that the types and forms of liberalization need to be fully and carefully specified. For goods trade, most discussion of liberalization focuses on tariffs and rather less on other instruments, since barriers to the flow of goods typically arise as customs and other physical restraints on trade are administered at national borders.

Barriers to the provision of services may operate through entry barriers to local markets (rights to establish, or to provide services), rules on conduct (regulation), restrictions on the number and size of competitors in a market (competition rules), or in a number of other ways. As a result, more barriers come into play with services trade than with goods trade. The barriers are more complex, and their effects are more numerous. Market structure, conduct and performance are all key and all need to be evaluated when discussing the quantitative impacts of liberalization of services trade on individual countries.

Also, since services generally have no tangible form and cannot be physically restrained at the border, foreign service providers typically need access to the national market either for the service itself or for themselves or their agents. The entity that provides the service (or the service providers themselves) may be restricted in terms of mobility, and it is effectively here that many restraints on services trade operate. Within the services trade community, and in the policy literature in general, there is an understanding that the outcomes of services liberalization will depend heavily on the regulatory environment.

All these considerations and more need to be borne in mind when approaching the liberalization of services trade in China as a result of that country's accession to the WTO. The specific characteristics of the Chinese economy also need to be taken into account. These characteristics include extensive activity by state-owned enterprises (SOE), losses by many (or most) state-owned enterprises, extensive non-performing loans, powerful provincial governments and interprovincial competition, limited property rights and seemingly weak legal enforcement. Analyzing the impacts arising from the terms of China's WTO accession involves all the difficulties and limitations on the mechanical application of the literature on trade liberalization as posed above, since services are involved, and must also confront the many formidable challenges that Western style neo-classical economics faces in making sense of economic phenomena observed in contemporary China.

CHINA'S BANKING, INSURANCE AND TELECOMS SECTORS AND THE IMPLICATIONS OF CHINA'S WTO ACCESSION

OVERVIEW

THE CHANGES THAT ARE SCHEDULED for China's key services sectors as part of WTO accession are extremely far reaching. In the banking area, through participation in the WTO Financial Services Agreement within the framework of the GATS, China has committed itself to full market access for foreign banks within five years. The current regime restricts foreign banks. They are not allowed to conduct local currency (*Remnimbi*) business with foreign businesses or individuals. There are also geographical restrictions on the establishment of foreign banks. These types of restriction will be lifted: China will allow internal branch banking and provide national treatment for all the activities permitted to foreign entities. Two years after WTO accession, activities using local currency will be allowed and five years after accession, dealings with Chinese individuals will be permitted.

Few foreign insurers operate in the Chinese market: prior to WTO accession, China limited foreign insurance operations by city and terminated existing rights on grounds that might seem arbitrary. In its WTO commitments, China agreed to limit licences only on prudential grounds with no limits on the number of licences issued. China will progressively eliminate geographical restrictions on licences within three years, and will also allow internal brokerage.

In telecoms, China's Ministry of Information Industry has agreed to new rules for basic and value-added services in telecoms. It is committed to allowing for more foreign ownership and less geographical restriction of licences. This will limit the ability of dominant local carriers to keep rates high and depress demand for telecommunications services and electronic commerce. China has also agreed in its accession protocol to submit to a special trade policy review mechanism under which the WTO's 16 subsidiary bodies and committees will review the country's progress on implementation each year for the next eight years. If fully implemented, all these commitments amount to a major new opening of access to the Chinese market for foreign suppliers of core intermediation services.

BANKING[4]

FOREIGN FINANCIAL INSTITUTIONS are being permitted to provide foreign currency services in China immediately following Chinese accession to the WTO and without any restrictions as to clients or location. The *Remnimbi* (or foreign exchange certificate), which serves as the local currency, will remain nonconvertible for now. However, local currency business will be opened up in a step-by-step fashion over a five-year period ending in 2007. Within four years of accession, China will also open up the provision of banking services in local currency to foreign banks in 20 cities arranged in five groups. Within five years of accession, foreign financial institutions will be allowed to provide retail banking services in local currency everywhere and to all Chinese clients. Foreign institutions will also be allowed to provide intermediary and advisory services freely, including deposit services, financial lending services, as well as advice on mergers and acquisitions, and investment in securities.

A number of foreign or joint venture banks have already received licences as part of the implementation of China's WTO commitments. These include the Bank of East Asia, Citibank, Hang Seng, HSBC and Standard Chartered. Rights to offer *Remnimbi* lending to foreign companies and individuals have been extended beyond regional pilot programmes. When China's WTO commitments are fully implemented, the entire Chinese banking sector will be completely open to foreign competition.

It does not seem that there is any other economy of any significant size anywhere in the world that currently comes close to this degree of openness in the regulatory framework applied to financial institutions. The only exceptions are smaller countries that are tax havens such as the Cayman Islands or the Bahamas. What is more, the starting point for these reforms is very far removed from the planned end point, in part because the past role of the Chinese banking sector differed sharply from that in an OECD economy. As a result, there have inevitably been doubts expressed as to China's ability to fully implement these commitments.

The extensive changes that the Chinese banking system will have to undergo to implement the provisions of WTO accession reflect the history of China since 1949, as a centrally-directed economy with a unique political order. Prior to the economic reforms of the 1990s, China had a planned economy in which the development of heavy industry was the key economic priority.[5] The financial system was a central and integral part of this planning structure, much as in the former Soviet Union (Holtzman 1951). Regular financial market activities were banned, and the People's Bank of China (PBOC) was the single financial institution in the country. It acted both as a central bank and as a provider of banking services via deposits and loans, but loans were made almost exclusively to state-owned enterprises.

Today, the Chinese banking system exhibits greater variety in its financial institutions and the PBOC now acts solely as a central bank. Even so, the functions of the banking system are still largely as they were before. State-owned enterprises remain the largest borrower from the banking system,[6] and four large state-owned banks conduct most of this business. Relatively few individuals have bank accounts. When personal assets such as houses or automobiles are acquired, they are usually paid for in full. Any financing for such transactions usually reflects informal credit such as loans from family or friends.

State-owned enterprises typically lose money: consequently state-owned banks have major difficulties with non-performing loans. Official estimates put these as high as 25 percent of all outstanding loans, but unofficial estimates are as high as 50-60 percent (Zhang 1999, Yuan 2000 and Bonin and Huang 2002). The Central Bank continually recapitalizes the state banks that in turn lend money to loss-making state-owned enterprises. It is still believed in China that this structure can persist as long as growth continues at high levels, and indeed it has persisted over the past 15 years, or so. If growth significantly slows, however, trouble may follow for the banking system and with it the industrial sector and the real side of the economy.[7]

The top tier of the Chinese banking system (the largest part of the system) consists of four large state banks; China Industry and Commerce Bank, China Agriculture Bank, Bank of China, and China Construction Bank. These account for the majority of non-performing loans made to state-owned enterprises. They are under no explicit mandate to lend heavily to state entities, but do so on the grounds that such loans are safe because they are state-to-state loans. This is despite the fact that recipient enterprises lose money and cannot directly service their debt. The expectation is that the state (via the banking system) will bail out loss making enterprises and the loans involved will eventually be repaid.

The second tier involves locally owned banks, such as the Shanghai Bank and the Shenzhen Development Bank. These operate in ways that are similar to the state-owned banks, but are under different political control (typically provincial or municipal). The third tier consists of three major policy-based regional shareholder commercial banks: the Construction Agricultural Development Bank, the Import/Export Bank and the Bank of China (foreign currency bank). A fourth tier involves mixed individual enterprise-owned banks. Ownership here includes state-owned enterprises, local enterprises and local governments.

Few of these banks issue securities that are traded on stock markets. Currently there are only four banks for whom trading takes place and this is in class A shares (which are only allowed to be held by Chinese residents).

Direct participation by foreign financial institutions in this banking system is extremely limited, but it is beginning. According to Lin (2001), by early 2000, foreign banks and financial institutions had already established 191 representative offices and subsidiaries in 23 city locations in China, with total assets of U.S.$36 billion.[8] Many foreign banks have also recently been allowed to upgrade their representative offices to branches and to conduct local currency business in Pudong and Shenzhen. Even more recently, foreign financial institutions have acquired minority share-ownership in smaller mixed-ownership banks. For instance, Newbridge Financial acquired a 15 percent interest in Shenzhen Development Bank, and Citicorp took a 5 percent interest in Pudong Development Bank.

But to complete the implementation of China's WTO accession commitments by 2007, major additional changes will have to occur. If enacted, these would substantially change the structure of the Chinese economy (also Lin 2000). For instance, foreign entry into banking services could provide strong competition for local banks that are not only believed to be inefficient but also saddled with large non-performing loans. Some believe that the local banking industry could be strongly affected by such changes and thus that these changes cannot easily be accommodated. Others argue that an incentive will remain for China to keep the *Remnimbi* non-convertible so that foreign banks will have little initial access to *Remnimbi* deposits and hence will be unable to make local currency loans. Another argument sometimes heard is that only the local Chinese banks fully understand how business is done in China, and hence local banks will keep most of their market share, especially in more remote rural areas.

It should be recalled, however, that subsidies to state-owned entities are also to be terminated as part of the WTO accession process. Thus loan activities based on an expectation that subsidies will continue must also undergo change. China's WTO commitments as they affect banking services thus need to be seen in their totality, both as they relate directly to the banking sector and also to other sectors in the economy. Given the scope of all China's commitments, it seems that the banking system must change from a structure that *de facto* continually recapitalizes loss-making state-owned enterprises to something resembling a more conventional commercial banking system, offering genuine intermediation. For this to happen, the whole real side of the economy must also undergo substantial change along with the banking sector, which is what WTO accession implicitly foresees. OECD country negotiators in the WTO assume that Chinese negotiators were aware of this reality, even though it was not formally acknowledged.

INSURANCE

THE PRESENT SITUATION OF INSURANCE in China differs considerably from that of banking, and implementation of WTO commitments in this area will likely be easier to achieve. Most insurance activity in China is business-related. There is relatively little personal life or house insurance, although the car insurance market is growing rapidly with the growth in automobile ownership.

The tiering of insurance companies differs from that in the banking sector since there is no insurance analogue to the central bank. The top tier consists of wholly state-owned insurance companies which are non-profit and account for approximately 70 percent of Chinese insurance business: the largest of these companies is Peoples Insurance and Life. Next are joint-share insurance companies, owned by state-owned enterprises of which the largest is Pacific. Then come joint-venture insurance companies of various forms, followed by wholly foreign-owned companies offering insurance services directly, largely to Chinese companies. The latter tier typically consists of branches of foreign insurance providers.

Unlike banking, foreign entry into China's insurance market is already permitted through licensing. Even though they are building from a small base, foreign insurance providers already have an entry point. Licences for life insurance operations in certain cities have been granted to American International and Sun Life. Indeed, the main barriers to foreign activity in insurance seem to be less policy-related and more market-driven.[9] Foreigners see the Chinese market as complicated because of organizational forms that are unusual to foreign companies, legal and other arrangements, differing business customs, and the need for Chinese language skills to conduct business. Foreign insurance companies seem to find it hard to do business in China and their entry into that market has been difficult. As a result, foreigners do not always accept licences to operate there, even when they are offered. According to Chinese insurance providers, many opportunities for joint ventures have not been taken up even though there are no formal barriers to prevent them from being pursued.

Thus, in insurance, foreign entry into the Chinese market is already possible and permitted, though foreigners do not seem to be quick to take up new opportunities. As a result, the terms of WTO accession in insurance appear to pose fewer problems for China than in banking since the market seems *de facto* to be open to foreigners, even if legally it appears to be closed. As a result, WTO accession in insurance may pose fewer adjustment pressures for China than it does in banking.

TELECOMS[10]

SEVEN TELECOM OPERATORS are currently licensed in China, reflecting a regulatory structure inherited from reforms in 1999. The most significant entity in the sector is China Telecom (CT), originally part of the Ministry of Posts and Telecommunications and established as a separate entity in 2000. CT controls 99 percent of China's main fixed-line phone capacity. Next comes China Unicom, the major mobile phone operator, established in 1994. It is followed by a series of enterprises with regulatory approval to operate in various telecom markets. These include a satellite operator, ChinaSat, a broadband IP network developer, China Netcom, as well as China Telecommunications Broadcast Satellite Corporation, Jitong and China Railways Communications.

At present, two large state-owned providers (China Unicom and Telecom China) dominate the market. There is regulation of both rates and market entry. This structure applies to both basic telecom services (hardwire and mobile) and to peripheral add-on services. Rates are set above international levels and the profits of these utilities are a significant source of revenue for both national and provincial governments.

The main commitments in telecommunications stemming from China's WTO accession involve the partial removal of limits on market access (especially the right to establish) and the removal of limits on national treatment. Foreign investment will be allowed in the sector, but initially with geographical restrictions and with limits placed on the level of ownership. Geographical restrictions are to be removed and the foreign ownership limit is to be raised to

49 percent at once for most basic services, within two years for so-called value-added services, within five years for mobile telephones, and six years for international services.

As part of WTO accession, China has also signed the WTO *Telecommunications Agreement* that requires foreign service providers to be given free entry into this market by 2007. This would place China on a par with recent practices in the larger OECD economies, where foreign providers frequently and freely accessed domestic markets and large rate reductions resulted.

Telecoms raise issues around liberalization that differ from banking and insurance. One involves the revenue implications for national and provincial governments after foreign telecoms enter, since both levels of government benefit from the revenues generated by regulated utilities that are either directly or indirectly under their management. Other barriers to new entrants arise from the fact that existing providers benefit from prior joint participation in existing network structures and that consumers incur costs in switching to a new provider after entry occurs. The analytical basis for assessing the welfare consequences of telecom liberalization in light of these features seems little studied generally, even before the special features of the Chinese situation are factored in.

SCENARIOS FOR IMPLEMENTATION OF WTO COMMITMENTS

AS ALREADY NOTED ABOVE, China's commitments in key service areas seem so extensive that they inevitably lead to some questions about both the feasibility and the likelihood of full implementation. The commitments demanded of China for WTO accession were agreed to as part of China's latest drive towards modernization. Once in place, they become WTO commitments subject to dispute settlement and enforcement through retaliation. The key issue is whether China can retain enough autonomy to keep the unique economic structure it now has and whether political opposition will ensue and in some way limit full implementation of these commitments.

In arguing against the feasibility of China's commitment, concerns usually focus on the possible disappearance of much of domestic industry in the service categories under WTO implementation,[11] the potential unacceptability of this were it to happen, the political impact of the resulting labour market dislocation, as well as the perceived strategic need for domestic service industries (as argued by Brazil for its own banking sector in the WTO, for instance). Believers in such liberalization would stress the benefits to China from the gains from trade, but such benefits, even if achieved, will likely not remove opposition to change. A conjecture that has been advanced is that Chinese negotiators either were not really fully aware of what they were committing to or they believed there was some form of escape still available through other unconstrained regulatory instruments such as new types of licences. Those taking this line often argue that all these pressures will likely force some kind of *de facto* renegotiation of accession terms or a slowing of implementation, even though other WTO members would likely respond that renegotiation is impossible since the commitments involved are all set out in firm contractual form.

Those arguing in favour of the feasibility of China's WTO commitments suggest that services liberalization, to be implemented in China, fits into a wider developmental strategy for the containment of state-owned enterprises, the achievement of efficiency gains and improvements in resource allocation. The claim is that domestic service industries can compete in an internationally-freer environment. One possible supporting mechanism sometimes suggested involves other policy elements in the equation that will shield Chinese industry from adjustment (such as an inconvertible *Remnimbi* in the case of banking). Since implicit threats to pursue WTO dispute settlement and retaliation (if necessary) characterize the position of the United States and other OECD countries in their WTO negotiations (in public at least), the argument is that China will have no choice but to implement its commitments in these key service areas.

A further possibility is whether some renegotiation of Chinese accession terms in services could be part of an agreed package of global trade policy changes following the termination of the Multi Fibre Arrangements (MFA) in 2004. This is based on the assumption that global free trade in textiles and apparel (a dominant Chinese interest) will not follow the termination of the MFA, and that some new globally-managed trade regime in textiles and apparel will emerge from negotiations. To achieve this, OECD members may have to pay a price elsewhere and part of this could be to agree to slow down or change the implementation process for China's WTO accession. If this were to occur (which is highly conjectural at this point), the form both of a new textile order and a slowing down of Chinese WTO commitments could follow any of several paths.

Many question marks thus remain regarding China's objectives in negotiating WTO services liberalization, its ability to implement it and the resolve of foreigners to push it through. The discussion that follows assumes full implementation and evaluates potential impacts on this basis, but readers should keep in mind that many questions remain about what will really happen as the process unfolds.

Analytic Structures for Evaluating Chinese WTO Commitments in Services

The key elements of services liberalization implied by China's WTO commitments are in areas where intermediation services dominate, namely banking, insurance and telecoms. The services at issue primarily involve various types of intermediation through time (as in banking), space (telecoms) or across risk categories (insurance): transportation is largely excluded. To evaluate the possible impacts of liberalization in these areas in China, some analytical structure is needed. It should be noted that current analytical literature on liberalization in key services sectors is limited and in many ways not particularly helpful, not just for China but for any economy.

A first observation to make is that when tariffs apply to trade in goods, services liberalization need not be welfare improving, even in simple trade models, if goods and services interact in some way. Also the analytical basis for the desirability of free trade in these services categories is more fragile than many realize since existing literature on services liberalization generally does not take into account the individual characteristics of particular service items. Thus it may be misdirected to undertake a general discussion of the desirability of free trade in all services as if they were all analytically similar.

As Ryan (1990, 1992) points out, services based on intermediation do not themselves typically directly enter preferences. In the case of banking, for instance, it is only commodities purchased with the financing obtained that directly affect any individual's welfare. Individuals with identical consumption of other goods get the same utility from a car, for example, whether it is debt financed or whether it is purchased with cash. The use of intermediation services to arrange the financing of a car does not, in and of itself, directly provide utility. Financial intermediation services bring together borrowers and lenders and this facilitates intertemporal trade, but intermediation requires real resources. The two theorems of welfare economics will typically not hold in such a world since real resources are used to facilitate trade. It is also not obvious that, from a global efficiency point of view, free international trade in banking services will be preferred to autarky.[12]

Trade liberalization in banking services will affect resource allocation and welfare in ways that can differ from effects obtained using more conventional models with no transaction costs. The outcome is ambiguous because gains from trade coexist with increased resource use in intermediation activities that directly generate no welfare. The outcome depends on the configuration of initial endowments, consumption patterns and the volumes of desired transactions, with resource use in transaction costs depending on the pattern of transactions between agents.

Chia and Whalley (1997) use a transactions cost framework to construct numerical examples which show how free international trade in banking services can be either globally welfare-worsening or welfare-improving. Their examples use a model with constant elasticity of substitution (CES) preferences, two countries [Home (*H*) and Foreign (*F*) and two time-dated consumption goods (c_1 and c_2)]. Intermediation cost margins are assumed for the two countries *H* and *F* respectively. They follow the same approach as in the applied general equilibrium literature of calibration of a model to an initial micro-consistent equilibrium data set, followed by an equilibrium solution for a counterfactual equilibrium. In their examples, the initial equilibrium involves autarky in banking services, while the counterfactual equilibria each involve free international trade in banking services.

To construct an example which shows welfare-worsening liberalization for all individuals in all countries, they fix the consumption patterns in each region in an assumed microconsistent equilibrium data set which they use in calibration, and then they vary the endowment patterns and elasticities in their model parameterization until they find a counterfactual equilibrium with the desired property that services liberalization is welfare worsening. Each manipulation they make changes the volume of trade effects under liberalization and they are able to relatively quickly produce a welfare-worsening example. In one example, they report all consumers in both countries are made worse off by liberalization in banking services by the same proportion of income through accompanying transfers between consumers.

Ryan (1990) provides a theoretical explanation for these results. He shows that it is possible for freer trade to cause total world output to fall (as resources required by services rise) while welfare as a whole rises. The paradox arises because intermediation services do not enter the utility function directly, even though they enter via the mix of goods consumed. Thus, when free trade permits access to more efficient intermediation services, world output of final goods may fall (or, as is the case in this paper, more resources may be paid to servicers) but each agent consumes a better mix of goods than was available in autarky. If agents consume a better mix of goods under free trade, they are also consuming more intermediation services. If services are not considered as part of welfare, then simply calculating post free-trade aggregate bundles using pre-trade prices can seemingly lead to the result that free trade is welfare worsening.

Ryan further shows that the result depends upon the elasticity of intertemporal substitution, since this affects the demand for intermediation services as barriers to their trade are removed. He shows that for CES utility functions, a necessary (though not sufficient) condition for world output to fall is that the elasticity of substitution is strictly greater than one. The numerical results of Chia and Whalley are consistent with the theoretical explanation offered by Ryan. Both taken together suggest some caution in accepting the proposition that liberalization of trade in intermediation-type services will necessarily lead to welfare gains in a country.

In more recent work, Ng and Whalley (2003) explore a further characteristic of Chinese liberalization in services as it might apply to goods trade, namely the progressive geographical expansion in coverage of licences to include more and more of the country over time. They highlight two central features of Chinese services liberalization that are present in all the three areas of banking, insurance and telecoms, namely the use of geographical expansion in licences and the progressive raising of allowed ownership levels for foreign investors as liberalization vehicles. They discuss how, in the absence of tariffs for protective purposes (typically not possible for intermediation services), available protective measures such as licences are discrete instruments. Foreign firms either have a license to operate or they do not, and no continuity exists in the use of the instrument.

Ng and Whalley evaluate the implications of progressive geographical expansion of licences and argue that this provides a continuous (and negotiable) instrument in the case where licensing is the only feasible instrument of protection. They consider an economy with, in the case of trade in goods, administratively-feasible internal borders which are shiftable and for which zones can be constructed. In one zone, trade takes place at world prices; in the other, it takes place behind the protective effect of a tariff.

They then consider parameterizations for these two economies for which there is observationally equivalent trade liberalization. They analyze liberalizations across the two with identical trade flow impacts, but which yield sharply differing welfare impacts. One such liberalization is in a traditional goods trade model of a single, integrated market economy with a tariff. The other is in an economy with a shiftable border for a protected zone, as described above. In the first, liberalization of goods trade occurs by reducing the tariff. In the other, liberalization of goods trade occurs by moving the location of the free trade zone, leaving the tariff rate unchanged. They consider cases of both pure exchange economies and economies with production.

In the numerical examples they provide, even with similar preferences and production structures, welfare gains from liberalization that yield equivalent trade impacts are larger by factors of up to four for zone liberalization. These results suggest that conventional trade policy formulations of services liberalization might perform poorly as predictors of welfare impacts arising from liberalization of the type characterizing key Chinese service sectors upon WTO accession.

Liberalization in service networks is discussed in a recent piece by Bhattarai and Whalley (forthcoming). They model economies with networks linking consumers, who both exchange messages and trade goods. They first consider disjoint networks in which consumers have interdependent preferences with utility increases as a consequence of the number of message contacts with other consumers, but consider networks to be initially country-specific. Liberalization across countries in telecoms is the joining together of two disjoint networks. In this case, if a small and large country integrate, then consumers in the small country receive large per capita benefits since they receive large increases in call frequency due to access to a larger message market. The reverse is true for the larger country. The net effect is that gains from liberalization are typically of roughly equal absolute size across countries independent of relative country size. This differs from the case of trade in goods where small countries typically gain proportionately more.

The analytical literature relevant for assessing the impacts of Chinese services liberalization may be limited, but it clearly does suggest that a mechanical application of insights from conventional trade policy literature for goods market liberalization to Chinese WTO accession in services may well be misleading. There is relatively little literature on the welfare impacts of services liberalization that explicitly incorporates the unique economic characteristics of each type of service. The implications of existing work seem to be first, that gains to China need not occur and second, that conventional tariff-based analyses of impacts (as in Dee and Hanslow 2000) may be misleading and that division by country of gains from services liberalization may differ from what is typical for trade in goods.

QUANTIFYING THE EFFECTS OF SERVICES LIBERALIZATION IN CHINA

QUANTIFYING THE IMPACTS OF SERVICES LIBERALIZATION and especially of banking liberalization in China is extremely difficult, and this is so for a number of reasons. In addition to the fact that there is little analytically-based literature currently available on banking liberalization for any country, several special features of the Chinese environment and situation need to be taken into account. These include the role of the banking sector as a mechanism for recapitalizing state-owned enterprises, the degree of non-performing loans and the need for additional reforms to accompany banking liberalization. At this point, information on the situation with non-performing loans in the banking system is only available on a fragmentary basis and is unreliable (Lu, Thanyavelu and Hu 2001, and Bonin and Huang 2002).

As a result, there are strongly competing schools of thought as to what might happen upon full implementation of WTO accession terms but these are not necessarily reflective of evaluation using analytical structures. Some see inefficient Chinese banks[13] as being swept aside after the implementation of WTO commitments, replaced by competitive and more efficient foreign banks unencumbered by bad debts. Others see domestic banks with superior knowledge of local markets continuing to thrive in a more open-market environment. Those advocating the second view emphasize the importance of the local banks' knowledge of local market conditions, the complex legal environment and differing customs of practice, and the role of an inconvertible *Remnimbi* in protecting local banks. Bonin and Huang (2002) evaluate both of these two scenarios as possible outcomes of liberalization, without being able to decide easily which is more likely.

Major difficulties in evaluating data on barriers to services trade are a further problem, not only for China but also more broadly. Much of the available data on services trade barriers is frequency data: it follows earlier work by Hoekman (1995) and was subsequently refined by Dee and Hanslow (2000) and others.[14] These estimates are aimed at yielding tariff-like equivalents of barriers to flows of banking services, but are unsatisfactory in practice since they do not necessarily represent binding restrictions on trade, such as licences. Using barrier estimates of this form, the gains or losses to China from banking liberalization have been given some rudimentary quantification, for example by Dee and Hanslow (2000). Such estimates show large effects in the region of 18 percent of GDP for banking and telecom reforms combined. Using the global trade analysis project (GTAP) modeling framework and database, they evaluate trade and welfare effects of removing barriers in a traditional model structure. The model is similar to that used to analyze liberalization in goods except that factor mobility (capital flows) is included in the analysis.

Dee and Hanslow report global gains of approximately US $130 billion arising from global services trade liberalization under a Doha Round WTO scenario. About US $100 billion of this total would accrue just from liberalization in China. The results of their model for global services trade liberalization seem to imply that the effects of giving foreigners access to the Chinese banking market will dominate all other aspects of global services trade liberalization over the next few years. Whether such gains will occur in practice remains to be seen.

Dee and Hanslow offer no explanation for their result other than to say that large barriers to services flows are involved in the Chinese case. Their barrier estimates are indeed large — a little over 250 percent as tax equivalent barriers to foreign affiliate capital accessing the Chinese market. These estimates reflect the strong assumption that trade barriers to all services in China can be represented as tax equivalents (mark ups of price over cost) and this applies equally to banking, telecoms and other services. They use a study by Kalirajan, McGuire, Nguyen-Hong and Schuele (2001) which measures the effects of foreign access restrictions on the net interest margins of banks and suggests that this is a direct measure of bank mark-up of price over cost. They also use Warren's (2001) measure of the effects of trade restrictions on the quantity of telecommunications services delivered, converting these to price impacts, using estimates of price elasticities of demand for telecommunication services. Dee and Hanslow's results thus follow directly from their large barrier estimates for China when used in a conventional trade model.

One can also ask if these barrier measures are satisfactory. In China, four large state-owned banks provide most of the financing for the large state-owned enterprise sector, and these suffer from major non-performing loans and experience losses. Rate spreads at the margin are high, but foreign entrants to market lending under similar conditions would also require large spreads. Smaller private banks that lend only to the commercial sector have smaller spreads. At the margin, therefore, to assume a 250 percent barrier to foreign capital trying to enter Chinese service markets may make little sense.

An alternative way to estimate the potential effects of services liberalization in China is to look at the outcome under present regulation and then to assess this relative to a free market equilibrium in a structure which explicitly models the characteristics of the services involved. In banking, for instance, one can argue that the net effect of the present structure is to effectively exclude the private sector from access to credit, while credit is over-extended to the typical state-owned enterprise. The net effect is that there is too much capital in the

SOE sector and too little capital in the private sector. This situation is reflected in Figure 1, where the free market outcome is what is implied by liberalization and the hatched area represents the area of potential gain from liberalization.

Using assumptions that the SOE sector is four times the size of the private sector in China's non-agricultural economy, that the differential rate of return on capital is 25 percent across the two sectors, and that the production function exponent parameter on the variable capital input in both sectors is 0.5, the gain to China from financial market liberalization is of the order of 25 percent of GDP. Such estimates are discussed in Ng (2003), where a range of sensitivity calculations for such estimates is also reported. While such estimates are conjectural at best, they do suggest large potential benefits to China from banking liberalization under these scenarios.

If, however, liberalization of banking were to occur with no change in the soft budget constraint arrangement for the SOE sector, if its losses continued to be covered by the state and if the banking sector continued to be used to recapitalize loss-making state-owned enterprises, then liberalization would only lead to further expansion in the SOE sector and an efficiency loss for the Chinese economy. Under this view of the world, current restrictions on banking are needed to limit the loan activity of state-owned enterprises which believe that

FIGURE 1

GAINS FROM LIBERALIZATION AFFECTING THE ALLOCATION OF CAPITAL BETWEEN PRIVATE AND STATE-OWNED ENTERPRISE SECTORS IN CHINA

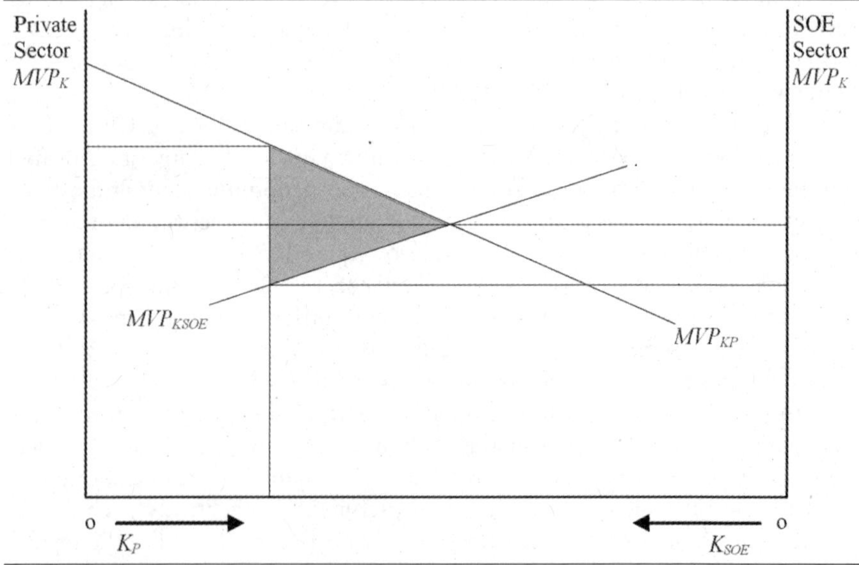

government bail-outs of all losses will occur should they borrow more funds. Thus, while seemingly large potential gains might ensue for China from WTO liberalization of financial services (and also potentially of insurance and telecoms), the reference point used in evaluation makes a major difference. In such calculations, how the real side of the economy is modelled also makes a large difference.

Other ways of viewing the interaction between China's banks and its state-owned enterprises also affect the way in which welfare gains or losses might result from liberalization. If one views Chinese state-owned enterprises as captured jointly by management and workers, and if managers use the enterprise to extract loans from the state for enterprises they form while workers shirk, then the result is a joint outcome that is Pareto inferior. Loans to the state-owned enterprise sector then already go indirectly to the private sector (via management of state-owned enterprises and their private sector activity), and the net effect of liberalization in banking may largely be to reduce transaction costs. This would be reflected in reduced consumption of restaurant meals in China and other transaction activities. If this were accompanied by reduced labour shirking, this could be the biggest effect of banking liberalization in China. Quantifying the effects of liberalization accompanying the implementation of WTO commitments is thus difficult for China's key services sectors. It seems likely that large effects might ensue, but the reference point for their evaluation makes it difficult both to quantify these effects and to determine in which direction they will occur.

CONCLUDING REMARKS

IT IS BEYOND DOUBT that China has made wide-ranging commitments in the areas of banking, insurance and telecoms as part of the terms of its accession to the WTO. This paper has examined whether or not China will be able to fully implement these commitments over the implementation period from 2002 to 2007, and with what effect. Few changes in the global economy over the next few years match the scale of changes implied in Chinese services arrangements. Literature is ambiguous as to whether effects will be beneficial or harmful for China, whether they will be large or small, or who may be affected and in what way.

This study has highlighted the many gaps in both our knowledge of, and approach to, an evaluation of the likely impacts of one of the most important sets of changes that the global economy will experience in the next five years. Models of services liberalization in general are unsatisfactory in accounting for many economic phenomena. Data is sparse in China. Different reference points for evaluation offer different perspectives as to the direction, let alone the size, of the impact.

The research that does exist suggests that large positive gains will occur both for China and the global economy. At the same time, however, large changes in both China's financial structure and its real-side economy have to take place. Much of China's intermediation services activity (banking for instance) underpins the current structure of the economy, which is still dominated by state-owned enterprises. State-owned banks are, in effect, a vehicle for recapitalizing loss-making state-owned enterprises rather than a means of intermediating private sector borrowers and lenders as they are in OECD economies. The scope of change that WTO accession mandates in China is vast and poorly understood. Whether this is feasible in the five years from 2002–2007, only time will tell. The more negative scenario, however, is that implementation is not feasible and that China (and the world) are on a collision course toward retaliation sanctioned by the WTO after 2007.

ENDNOTES

1 See Copeland (2002) and Whalley (2003).

2 In a recent modelling exercise using the GTAP database and modelling framework, Dee and Hanslow (2000) project gains of 18 percent of GDP for China from banking reforms alone. This reflects a large initial spread in borrowing and lending rates, which is assumed to be greatly narrowed by liberalization. See also the quantification of Chinese WTO accession in Walmsley and Hertel (2001).

3 Much of this is reviewed in Whalley (2003).

4 See also the detailed discussion of China's banking sector and the implications of WTO accession in Bhattasali (2002).

5 See Lin, Cai and Li (1998) for a discussion of this evolution.

6 See the description in Broadman (2001).

7 See the repeated expression of concerns on this score by Western economists such as Lardy (1998).

8 Bhattasali (2002) reports the same data.

9 This may be more the perception on the Chinese side than that of OECD trade negotiators, but is as communicated to me on a recent visit in China.

10 See the extensive discussion of the telecoms situation in Pangestu and Mrongowius (2002).

11 Bhattasali (2002) discusses the likelihood of this in the banking sector.

12 General equilibrium models incorporating transaction costs were developed some years ago by Foley and others (Foley 1970). They differ from the standard Arrow-Debreu model, which underlies conventional Heckscher-Ohlin trade theory and standard analysis of the gains from trade, in that in the presence of transaction costs, the effective resource endowment of the economy (i.e. net of resource use in transactions) is affected by the volume of trade.

13 See the discussion in Xu and Lu (2001) and Cull and Xu (2000).

14 See the discussion in Whalley (2003).

ACKNOWLEDGMENTS

I am grateful to my discussant John McHale, participants in the Industry Canada Conference on Services Industries and the Knowledge-Based Economy, Winnipeg, October 16–18, 2003, and to David Wang of Unicentury, Shanghai, and Justin Lin of CEPR, Peking University for extremely helpful discussions and comments. Shunming Zhang [Tsinghua and University of Western Ontario (UWO)] and Terry Sicular (UWO) have also provided helpful comments. Eric Ng has provided helpful research assistance and comments.

BIBLIOGRAPHY

Bhattarai, Keshab, and John Whalley. 1998. "The Division and Size of Gains from Liberalization of Services Networks," Washington, D.C.: National Bureau of Economic Research Working Paper No. 6712, August; forthcoming in *Review of International Economics*.

Bhattasali, D. 2002. "Accelerating Financial Market Restructuring in China," (mimeo). Washington, D.C.: World Bank.

Bonin, J.P., and Y. Huang. 2002. "Foreign Entry into Chinese Banking: Does WTO Membership Threaten Domestic Banks?" *The World Economy*, 25 (August): 1077-1094.

Broadman, H.E. 2001. "The Business(es) of the Chinese State," *The World Economy*, 24 (July): 849-876.

Chia, Ngee Choon, and J. Whalley. 1997. "A Numerical Example Showing Globally Welfare-Worsening Liberalization of International Trade in Banking Services," *Journal of Policy Modelling*, 19(2) (April): 119-27.

Copeland, Brian. 2002. "Benefits and Costs of Trade and Investment Liberalization in Services: Implications from Trade Theory," in J.M. Curtis and D.C. Ciuriak (eds.) *Trade Policy Research 2002*. Ottawa: Department of Foreign Affairs and International Trade.

Cull, Robert, and Lixin Colin Xu. 2000. "Bureaucrats, State Banks, and the Efficiency of Credit Allocation: The Experience of Chinese State-owned Enterprises," *Journal of Comparative Economics*, 28, 1-31.

Dee, P., and K. Hanslow. 2000. "Multilateral Liberalisation of Services Trade," Canberra: Productivity Commission Staff Research Paper, Ausinfo.

Foley, Duncan. 1970. "Equilibrium with Costly Marketing," *Journal of Economic Theory*, 2 (3) (September): 276-91.

Hamilton, B., and John Whalley. 1984. "Efficiency and Distributional Implications of Global Restrictions on Labour Mobility: Calculations and Policy Implications;" *Journal of Development Economics*, 14(1-2) (January-February): 61-75.

Hoekman, B. 1995. "Assessing the General Agreement on Trade in Services," in W. Martin and L. Alan Winters (eds.) *The Uruguay Round and the Developing Economies.* Discussion Paper No. 307. Washington, D.C.: World Bank, pp. 327-64.

Holtzman, F. 1951. *Banking in the Soviet Union*. New York: Columbia University Press.

Kalirajan, K., G. McGuire, D. Nguyen-Hong, and M. Schuele. 2001. "The Price Impact of Restrictions on Banking Services," in Christopher Findlay and Tony Warren (eds.) *Impediments to Trade in Services: Measurement and Policy Implications*. New York: Rutledge.

Lardy, N.R. 1998. "China and the Asia Financial Contagion," *Foreign Affairs* (July/August).

Lin, J.Y. 2000. "What is the Director of China's Financial Reform?" in Went Cai and Feng Lu (eds.) *China Economic Transition and Economic Policy*. Beijing: Peking University Press, pp. 296-301.

————. 2001. "WTO Accession and Financial Reform in China," *The Cato Journal*, 21 (Spring/Summer): 13-19.

Lin, J.Y., Fang Cai, and Zhou Li. 1998. *The China Miracle: Development Strategy and Economic Reform*. Hong Kong: Chinese University Press.

Lu, D., S.M. Thanyavelu, and Q. Hu. 2001. "Biased Leading and Non Performing Loans in China's Banking Sector," (mimeo). Singapore: National University of Singapore.

Melvin, James R. 1989. "Trade in Producer Services: A Heckscher-Ohlin Approach," *Journal of Political Economy*, 97(5) (October): 1180-96.

Ng, Eric 2003. "Assessing the Impacts of Banking Liberalization in China," (mimeo). London, Ontario: University of Western Ontario.

Ng, Eric, and John Whalley. 2003. "Geographical Expansion as Trade Liberalization," (mimeo). London, Ontario: University of Western Ontario.

Pangestu, M., and D. Mrongowius. 2002. "Telecommunications in China: Facing the Challenges of WTO Accession," (mimeo). Washington, D.C.: World Bank.

Ryan, Cillian. 1990. "Trade Liberalization and Financial Services," *The World Economy*, 13, (3) (September): 349-366.

————. 1992. "The Integration of Financial Services and Economic Welfare," in L. Alan Winters (ed.) *Trade Flows and Trade Policy After 1992*. Cambridge: Cambridge University Press, pp. 92-118.

Walmsley, T.L., and T.W. Hertel. 2001. "China's Accession to the WTO: Timing is Everything," *The World Economy*, 28 (August): 1019-1050.

Warren, Tony. 2001. "The Impact on Output of Impediments to Trade and Investment in Telecommunications Services," in Christopher Findlay and Tony Warren (eds.). *Impediments to Trade in Services: Measurement and Policy Implications*. New York: Rutledge.

Whalley, John. 2003. "Assessing the Benefits to Developing Countries of Liberalization in Services Trade," Draft Report prepared for OECD Trade Directorate.

Winters, L. Alan. 2002. "The Economic Implications of Liberalizing Mode 4 Trade," Joint WTO-World Bank Symposium on 'The Movement of Natural Persons (mode 4) under the GATS'. Geneva: WTO, April 11-12.

Winters, L. Alan, T.L. Walmsley, Z.H. Wang, and R. Grunberg. 2002. "Negotiating the Liberalization of the Temporary Movement of Natural Persons," Discussion Paper 87. Sussex U.K.: University of Sussex, October.

Xu, Guoping, and Lei Lu. 2001. "Incomplete contracts and moral hazard: China's financial reform 1990's," *Journal of Financial Research* (Tin Rong Yan Jiu), 2: 28-41.

Yuan, Gangming. 2000. "An Empirical Analysis of Non-performing Loans in China's SOEs," *Economic Research Journal* (Tan Ji Yan Jiu), 5: 12-20.

Zhang, Jie. 1999. "Non performing Loans of State Owned Banks in Transition Economy," *Journal of Financial Research* (May).

Comment

John McHale
Queen's University

IN A FASCINATING AND WIDE-RANGING REVIEW of China's liberalization commitments in the services sector, John Whalley has provided us with a valuable "state of play" description of one of this decade's most important international economic developments. Professor Whalley illustrates China's commitments by focusing on banking, insurance and telecommunications; he evaluates the plausibility of those commitments, and he reviews both theory and evidence on the desirability of services free trade for the economy in general and for China in particular. On the whole, I think it is fair to describe his views on the credibility and desirability of the commitments as being one of nuanced skepticism. He is skeptical that China is truly willing and able to meet its far-reaching commitments. He is sceptical that rich countries will be willing to use the legal mechanisms at their disposal, both within the WTO framework and outside it, to enforce compliance. He is also skeptical about the widespread assumption that services sector liberalization *must* be welfare enhancing, pointing, in particular, to the wide range of results that exist in the theoretical literature. At the risk of exaggerating his skepticism, he clearly allows for the probability that following through on China's commitments will not be strongly welfare enhancing.

I will use the remainder of this comment to play the devil's advocate and note some reasons to be more optimistic about both the credibility of the commitments and the gains that are likely to be realized from following through on them.

What reasons do I have for believing that China will allow internationally unparalleled access to foreign services sector firms, particularly in the financial area? My most important reason is that it goes with the grain of Chinese government efforts to continue market-based institutional reforms and to impose financial discipline on the state-owned enterprise sector. Over the past decade, China has used its high savings rate to support very fast growth despite a massive misallocation of capital to the SOE sector through the state-dominated banking system. Reformers in the government realize that, once the relatively easy early catch-up phase has passed, sustaining high growth rates requires a shift to allocating capital on market principles. With bad loans conservatively estimated at one-quarter of total loans, domestic financial reform will be difficult. Foreign investment in the banking system could allow for the recapitalization of existing banks, together with the emergence of a well-capitalized non-state dominated banking sector, operating on market principles. Furthermore, policymakers have undoubtedly learned from the Asian Crisis of 1997-98, which showed the dangers inherent in capital account liberalization, when it is combined with a weak domestic financial system. China largely avoided contagion from its crisis-afflicted neighbours because of the inconvertibility of its capital account. As China develops, however, international experience shows that it will become harder to sustain capital account restrictions. Thus Chinese policy makers — together with policy makers throughout Asia — know that they must preemptively strengthen their financial systems. Removing investment restrictions on rich-country financial institutions offers a short-cut to a more market-based system.

One of the reasons that observers are pessimistic about China's commitments is that the liberalization implied will be disruptive to incumbent firms and their employees. Outside of joint ventures, the threat to incumbents is real. But it is easy to exaggerate the threat to workers. First, the type of liberalization at issue falls mainly under mode 3 of the General Agreement on Trade in Services. This mode relates to allowing foreign services firms to have a domestic presence. Following their investments, foreign firms will have to rely on Chinese workers to staff their operations. Thus mode 3 liberalization will tend to cause less overall labour market disruption than traditional import trade liberalization. Second, any trade liberalization is easier when the domestic economy is booming and domestic labour markets are tight — which is certainly the case in the Chinese economy at present.

What about the credibility of rich-country enforcement of Chinese commitments? If we focus on the United States, there is no shortage of signs that politicians and the public are ready to hold China to account. Although economists tend to play down the importance of bilateral trade deficits, the trade deficit that the United States has recently been running with China, amounting to approximately U.S.$11 billion a month, has a great deal of political visibility. Suspicions are raised further by the belief that China is getting an "unfair advantage" by keeping its currency artificially weak. The relatively jobless recovery in the United States is also fueling a backlash against the China-bound outsourcing of manufacturing jobs. The backlash would surely intensify if China were seen as reneging on commitments to liberalize sectors where politically-influential U.S. firms are seen as having a competitive advantage. The recent imposition of punitive tariffs on a short list of textile products demonstrates a willingness of the government to act when powerful U.S. interests are threatened.

I turn now to reasons for being optimistic about significant welfare gains to China from services sector liberalization. In fairness, Professor Whalley notes that the gains may be large — but the current state of the literature makes it hard to say so definitively. While his point about the range of results in the literature is well taken, I think that the case for expecting large welfare gains is stronger than he allows, and services industries are less peculiar from the point of view of economic analysis than he contends. The first reason for being optimistic about large welfare gains is simply China's obvious comparative advantage in manufacturing. Given current institutional arrangements, the opportunity cost of tying up resources in the provision of inefficient services must be high. This is especially true given that the economy is showing clear signs of overheating as its manufacturing exports soar. The second reason for optimism is that services sector liberalization will increase the range of consumer and business services that are available — which theory shows can lead to large welfare gains. To take the example of insurance, the Chinese population does not have access to anything that is close to the range of insurance products that are commonplace in richer countries. While this is partly due to China's stage of development, the weakness of the domestic insurance industry is also to blame. To the extent that liberalization increases the range (and reduces the cost) of insurance products, the welfare gains from risk reduction could be enormous. The third reason for optimism is the aforementioned hardening of SOE budget constraints that would come with a more market-based financial system. Such budget constraints could help reduce the misallocation of savings that is the biggest threat to continued fast growth, a point emphasized by Whalley. A final reason for optimism is that, although China may lack comparative advantage in internationally-traded services at present, the country's productivity growth record in manufacturing shows a national ability to learn international best practice quickly when faced with competitive markets and appropriate incentives. The presence of internationally-leading foreign firms would lead to technological and knowledge transfer that could shift the balance of comparative advantage in the future. Forward looking policy makers should see services sector liberalization as part of a broader modernization process, and not as the surrender of an important part of the economy to foreign firms.

In closing, Professor Whalley's paper is a timely reminder of the stunning scope and importance of China's services sector liberalization commitments, and a reminder not to be complacent about those commitments. His warning and doubts are well taken. However, I take the basic thrust of this comment to be that China has simply too much to lose for it to accept too much backsliding on those commitments.

Walid Hejazi[1]
University of Toronto

8

Canada's Experience with Foreign Direct Investment: How Different Are Services?

INTRODUCTION

SUCCESS IN ELIMINATING THE FEDERAL DEFICIT over the 1990s allowed Canada greater flexibility in its economic choices. As a result, it could become a "'northern tiger' — a preferred destination for knowledge workers, trade and investment, and a centre of excellence in innovation, science, research and education." (John Manley 2002). The beginning of the 21st century therefore saw the federal government increase its focus on Canada's ability to attract key "internationally mobile factors": foreign direct investment, research and development (R&D) and human capital (Head and Ries 2004). This change in focus is not surprising given that Canada's attractiveness for at least two of these three factors had previously been disappointing.[2]

In 1970, Canada's stock of inward FDI stock was four times its stock of outward FDI. Today, however, outward FDI exceeds inward.[3] As a result, although Canada has been able to maintain its share of the world's rapidly growing stocks of outward FDI, its share of the world's stock of inward FDI has been falling (Figure 1). These patterns are of concern, especially given that the U.S. economy has been maintaining its share of inward world FDI and decreasing its outward share. Another way of expressing this is to say that the *propensity (relative to global trends)* for U.S. multinational enterprises (MNEs) to locate abroad has fallen whereas that for Canadian MNEs to locate abroad has not. On the other side, the propensity for foreign firms to locate in Canada has fallen, whereas the propensity for foreign MNEs to locate in the United States has not.

Canada's R&D performance has been weak, with Canada ranking far behind many of our trading partners (Figure 2). This poor R&D performance has been linked to both Canada's productivity gap with the U.S. economy and the depreciating value of the Canadian dollar.

The relevant question, however, is why should policy makers be concerned about the trends in Canadian FDI noted above? There is a rich discussion of the costs and benefits of both inward and outward FDI to home and host countries.

FIGURE 1

CANADA'S CHANGING FDI SHARES

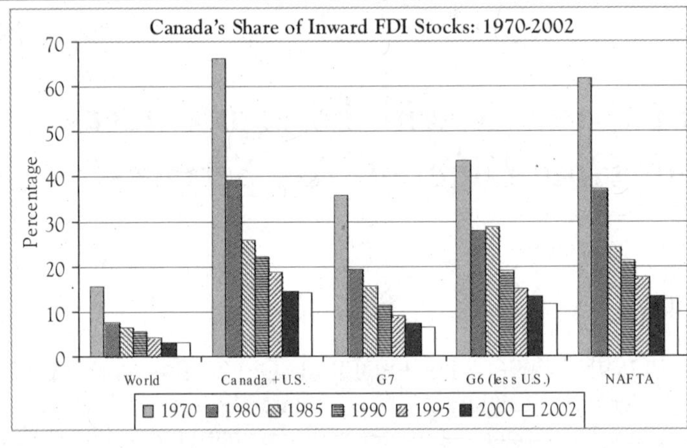

Although the Canadian share is falling on the inward side

Canada is maintaining its outward share

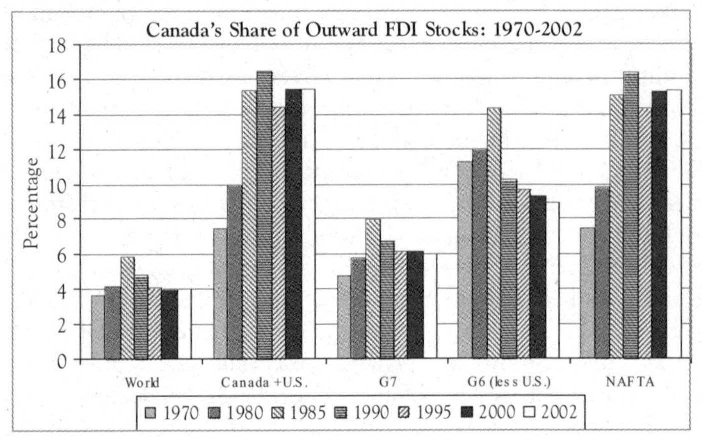

Source: Data retrieved from the World Investment Report, 2003.

First, inward FDI is an important source of R&D diffusion (Hejazi 2001; Hejazi and Safarian 1999a; van Pottelsberghe and Lichtenberg 2001). Second, foreign firms have both higher levels of productivity and propensity to trade than do Canadian firms (Baldwin and Sabourin 2001; Trefler 1999; Tang and Rao 2001). Third, inward FDI contributes to domestic capital formation. On the outward side, using data for G-7 countries, Rao, Legault and Ahmad (1994) find that there is either a positive or no relationship between trends in the stock of Canadian outward FDI and capital formation. Hejazi and Pauly (2002, 2003) extend this analysis to establish that the impact of FDI on domestic capital formation at

FIGURE 2

EXPENDITURE ON R&D

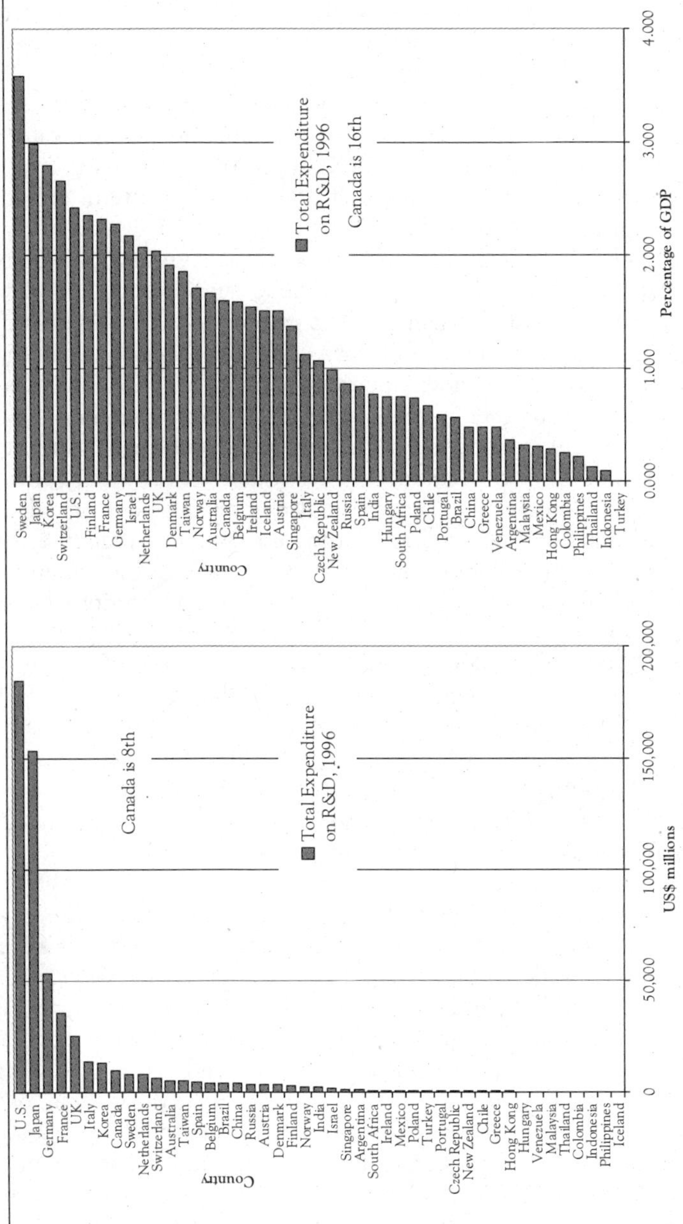

Source: Data retrieved from World Competitiveness Report, 2000.

the industry level is very much a function of its underlying motivation. Finally, many studies have found a complementarity between international trade and FDI (Brainard 1997; Graham 1993; Hejazi and Safarian 1999b, 2001, 2004; Lipsey and Weiss 1981, 1984; Ahmad, Rao and Barnes 1996; and Safarian and Hejazi 2001). In short, FDI has been shown to be important in many ways to both home and host economies and thus trends in Canada's inward and outward FDI must be of concern to Canadian policy makers as well as to the private sector.

Given that we believe changing patterns of FDI can have a significant impact on our economy, we need a formal analysis to identify the factors underlying such changes. These factors must be measured at the aggregate, bilateral and industry levels. With a better understanding of the factors and with a clear assessment of whether the net effects of changing FDI patterns are positive or negative, identified trends can be reinforced or discouraged accordingly.

There has been relatively little discussion of the costs and benefits of FDI at the industry level. Two recent papers by Hejazi and Pauly (2002, 2003) have assessed the impact of these changing FDI patterns on capital formation. Their findings indicate that the impact of inward FDI on Canadian domestic capital formation depends on the underlying motivation for the FDI, and this effect is tied to the trading partner as well as to the intra-firm trading strategies of MNEs. They conclude that inward FDI complements Canadian capital formation regardless of the source country. These results for the inward side stand in contrast to their finding that outward FDI can complement or reduce Canadian capital formation, depending on the destination of that FDI. There remains, however, a large void in the literature in terms of considering other effects of industry-level FDI, such as the impact on productivity vis-à-vis R&D spillovers, or the impact on trade, to name just two issues.

The purpose of this study is threefold. First, Canada's FDI position is put into a global context. It is relatively well-known that Canada has seen its share of inward FDI fall over the past three decades, at the same time as there has been a surge in the level of Canada's outward FDI. These trends will be presented on a regional and a global basis. Canada's performance will also be benchmarked against other major economies. The data description shows that Canada has been transformed from what was primarily a host economy for FDI in the 1970s to an important home country for outward FDI. Furthermore, the ratio of Canada's outward to inward FDI continued to increase through 2002.

Second, and more importantly, this study decomposes Canada's FDI by industry. Relatively little is known about the sectoral composition of Canadian inward and outward FDI, and hence this paper fills an important gap. The data presented here indicate that the surge in Canada's outward FDI is in large part attributable to a surge in investment in services and this is true whether we consider Canadian FDI in the United States, the United Kingdom, or the rest of the world. On the inward side, the surge in FDI flowing into Canada in the last half of the 1990s was attributable to investment in Canada's manufacturing sector. In contrast to outward FDI, there is no observed increasing trend toward foreign investment in Canadian services on the inward side.

The third purpose of this study is to identify the factors that help explain these changing patterns of FDI. Using industry-level data on inward and outward FDI for Canada, we estimate a model of FDI determinants to explain these changing trends. What is most important about these results is that the model estimated for services differs from the model for non-services in a statistically-significant way. These differences are especially strong in considering Canada's inward FDI from the United States, the United Kingdom and the rest of the world, but not from Japan. On the outward side, the differences are much weaker, with most of the differences here being driven by the impact of the North American Free Trade Agreement (NAFTA).

The format of this study is as follows. The next section puts Canada's FDI position within a global context. Then the study focuses on the changing distribution of Canada's inward and outward FDI at the industry level. This is followed by a section that derives our estimating equation. Then the study gives empirical estimates and finally offers some conclusions.

CANADA'S FDI POSITION IN A GLOBAL PERSPECTIVE

IN 1970, CANADIAN INWARD FDI relative to gross domestic product (GDP) was 30 percent, whereas the ratio of outward FDI to GDP was only 7 percent. That is, Canada had four times more inward than outward FDI (Figure 3). Over the 1970s, Canada's inward ratio fell steadily to 20 percent where it remained relatively stable until 1996 when it began to increase. On the other side, the outward ratio increased steadily over the entire sample period, overtaking the inward ratio in 1997. By 2002, outward FDI was more than 20 percent higher than inward FDI. Canada has moved from being predominantly a host economy for FDI to one that is an important home economy.[4,5]

An important question that arises is how Canada's FDI experience has compared with that of other countries. Table 1 compares the growth in outward FDI over the 1980 to 2002 period relative to the growth of inward FDI. This is done for the largest 21 developed economies, as well as for Mexico and all developing countries combined. The column headed (B/A) tells us whether the outward or inward ratio has grown more quickly. If the ratio in that column is greater than 1, this indicates that outward has grown more rapidly than inward. On the other hand, if this number is less than 1, then inward has grown more rapidly. The results indicate that only 6 of the countries listed have ratios that are below 1 (indicating that inward has grown faster than outward). On the other hand, 16 countries have ratios greater than 1. That is, most countries have experienced a faster growth in their outward FDI stocks than inward. Canada is included in this group. What is interesting is that Canada ranks fifth. That is, Canada's experience over the 1980s and 1990s with respect to changes in outward and inward FDI is not unique: similar phenomena are occurring in many other countries. Furthermore, Canada is by no means an outlier vis-à-vis its FDI experience.

FIGURE 3

CANADA'S OPENNESS TO FDI

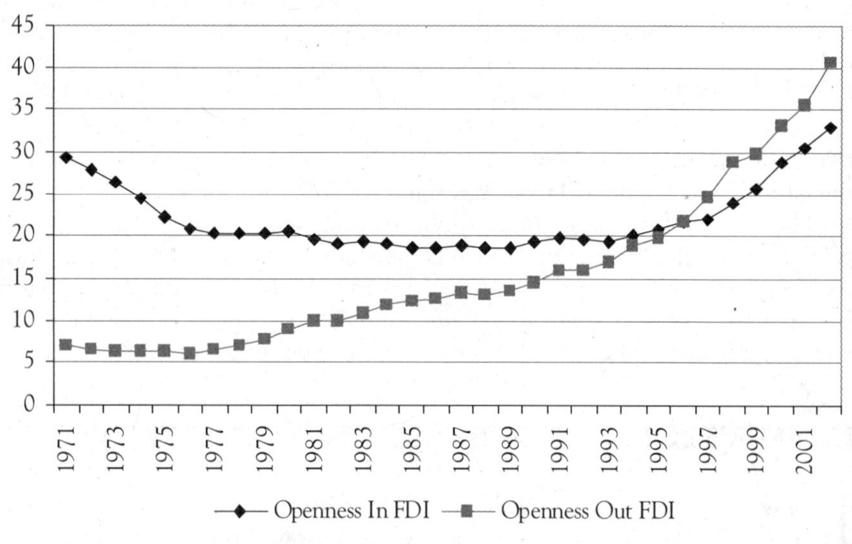

Source: Data retrieved from Statistics Canada's online data through the University of Toronto's Chass Data Centre.

Canada has also seen significant changes in its bilateral FDI patterns over the past 30 years. Figure 4 plots the pattern of Canada's outward and inward FDI vis-à-vis the United States, South and Central America (S&CA), Europe, Africa, the Pacific Rim (PAC RIM), and the rest of the world (ROW). There are several immediately obvious trends that stand out. First, both Canada's outward and inward FDI have exploded over the past 15 years. Second, Canada's FDI is increasingly diversifying away from the United States. Third, Europe's share of Canada's outward FDI has remained relatively constant whereas its share of Canada's inward FDI has increased. Finally, both the Pacific Rim and the rest of the world have increased their share of Canada's outward FDI.

TABLE 1

GROWTH IN OUTWARD FDI TO GDP RELATIVE TO INWARD FDI TO GDP, OECD COUNTRIES, 1980 TO 2002

	OPENNESS TO INWARD FDI						A	OPENNESS TO OUTWARD FDI						B		
	1980	1985	1990	1995	2000	2002	2002/ 1980	1980	1985	1990	1995	2000	2002	2002/ 1980	B/A	RANK
World	6.7	8.4	9.3	10.3	19.6	22.3	3.33	5.8	6.6	8.6	10.0	19.3	21.6	3.72	1.12	
Developed Countries	4.9	6.2	8.2	8.9	16.5	18.7	3.82	6.2	7.3	9.6	11.3	21.4	24.4	3.94	1.03	
Australia	7.9	14.5	23.7	27.9	28.9	32.2	4.08	1.4	3.8	9.8	14.2	22.0	22.9	16.36	4.01	4
Austria	4.0	5.6	6.1	7.5	16.1	20.6	5.15	0.7	2.0	2.6	5.0	13.2	19.5	27.86	5.41	2
Belgium and Luxembourg	5.8	21.2	27.8	38.3	79.1	81.8	14.10	4.8	11.0	19.4	27.4	72.8	72.9	15.19	1.08	14
Canada	20.4	18.4	19.6	21.1	29.0	30.4	1.49	8.9	12.3	14.7	20.3	33.3	37.6	4.22	2.84	5
Denmark	6.1	6.0	6.9	13.2	42.0	41.7	6.84	3.0	3.0	5.5	13.7	41.6	43.4	14.47	2.12	7
Finland	1.0	2.5	3.8	6.5	20.2	27.0	27.00	1.4	3.4	8.2	11.6	43.4	52.8	37.71	1.40	10
France	3.8	6.9	7.1	12.3	19.9	28.2	7.42	3.6	7.1	9.1	13.2	34.1	45.8	12.72	1.71	9
Germany	3.9	5.1	7.1	7.8	25.2	22.7	5.82	4.6	8.4	8.8	10.5	25.9	29.0	6.30	1.08	13
Greece	9.3	20.2	6.7	9.3	11.2	9.0	0.97	6.0	7.1	3.5	2.6	5.2	5.3	0.88	0.91	18
Ireland	155.6	163.5	72.3	60.7	124.4	129.1	0.83		43.4	24.5	20.2	29.3	29.9	0.69	0.83	19
Italy	2.0	4.5	5.3	5.8	10.5	10.6	5.30	1.6	3.9	5.2	8.8	16.8	16.4	10.25	1.93	8
Japan	0.3	0.3	0.3	0.6	1.1	1.5	5.00	1.8	3.2	6.6	4.5	5.8	8.3	4.61	0.92	17
Netherlands	10.8	18.8	23.3	28.0	66.7	74.9	6.94	23.7	36.1	36.3	41.6	83.3	84.7	3.57	0.52	20

Table 1 Continued

	Openness to Inward FDI						A	Openness to Outward FDI						B		
	1980	1985	1990	1995	2000	2002	2002/1980	1980	1985	1990	1995	2000	2002	2002/1980	B/A	Rank
New Zealand	10.3	8.9	18.2	42.1	47.0	50.3	4.88	2.3	6.6	14.7	12.5	13.2	12.9	5.61	1.15	12
Norway	10.4	11.7	10.7	12.8	18.6	17.4	1.67	0.9	1.7	9.4	15.4	20.7	20.0	22.22	13.28	1
Portugal	12.3	18.7	14.8	17.1	26.9	36.0	2.93	1.7	2.4	1.3	3.0	16.2	26.2	15.41	5.27	3
Spain	2.3	5.2	12.8	18.7	25.8	33.2	14.43	0.9	2.6	3.0	6.2	29.4	33.0	36.67	2.54	6
Sweden	2.2	4.2	5.3	12.9	41.0	46.0	20.91	2.8	10.4	21.3	30.5	53.8	60.5	21.61	1.03	15
Switzerland	7.9	10.4	15.0	18.6	36.3	44.2	5.59	20.0	26.0	28.9	46.4	97.5	111.3	5.57	0.99	16
United Kingdom	11.8	14.1	20.6	17.6	30.5	40.8	3.46	15.0	22.0	23.2	26.9	63.1	66.1	4.41	1.27	11
United States	3.0	4.4	6.9	7.3	12.4	12.9	4.30	7.8	5.7	7.5	9.5	13.2	14.4	1.85	0.43	21
Developing Countries	12.6	16.4	14.8	16.6	31.1	36.0	2.86	3.8	3.8	3.9	5.8	12.9	13.5	3.55	1.24	
Mexico	3.6	10.2	8.5	14.4	16.8	24	6.67	1.6	2.1	1.8	2.1	1.9	1.9	1.19	0.18	

Notes: For Ireland, the growth runs from 1985 to 2002 as the 1980 numbers are missing.
For Belgium-Luxembourg, the growth runs from 1980 to 2001 as the 2002 numbers are missing.

Source: World Investment Report, 2003.

FIGURE 4

CANADA'S FDI STOCK PATTERNS: 1970-2000

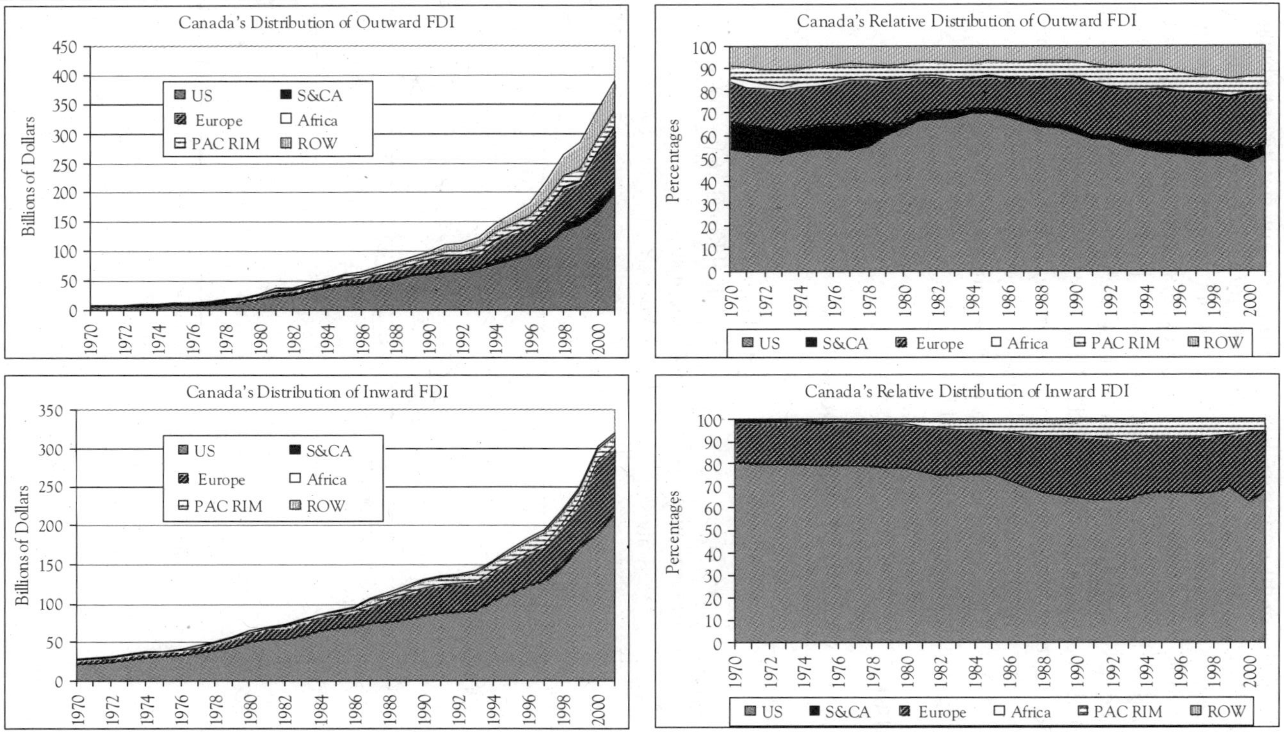

Canada's Distribution of Outward FDI

Billions of Dollars
450
400
350
300
250
200
150
100
50
0
1970 1972 1974 1976 1978 1980 1982 1984 1986 1988 1990 1992 1994 1996 1998 2000
US
S&CA
Europe
Africa
PAC RIM
ROW

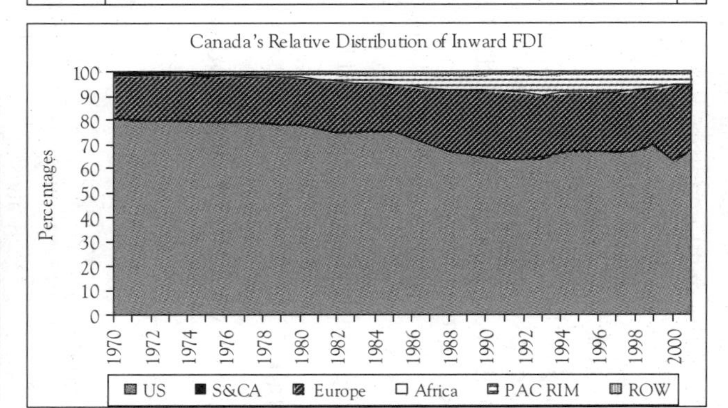

Canada's Distribution of Inward FDI

Billions of Dollars
350
300
250
200
150
100
50
0
1970 1972 1974 1976 1978 1980 1982 1984 1986 1988 1990 1992 1994 1996 1998 2000
US
S&CA
Europe
Africa
PAC RIM
ROW

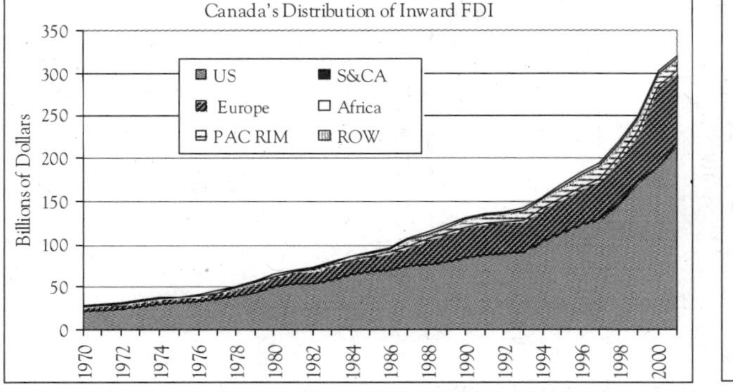

Source: Data retrieved from Statistics Canada's online data through the University of Toronto's Chass Data Centre.

Finally, Figure 5 provides the balance of FDI, defined as outward FDI stocks less inward, for the G-7 countries, plus Mexico. Over the 1970 to 1985 period, seven of the eight countries listed did not see any significant changes in their FDI balance. The only exception is the United States, which saw its FDI balance surge over the 1970s and fall by a larger amount over the first five years of the 1980s. The 1985 to 2002 period experienced significantly more changes than did the previous period. Specifically, Japan, the United Kingdom and France have seen their FDI balances increase significantly, whereas Mexico has seen its balance fall significantly. Canada, Italy, Germany and the United States have all seen their FDI balances increase but not to the same extent as Japan, the United Kingdom and France. Once again, these data indicate that Canada's FDI experience is in no way an outlier. Other countries are experiencing similar changes in their FDI positions.

FIGURE 5

BALANCE ON FDI: MAJOR COUNTRIES

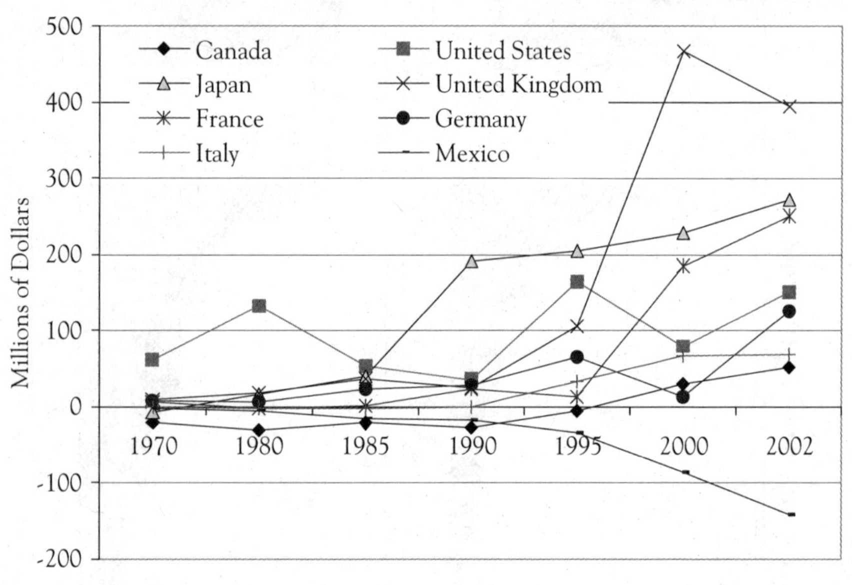

Source: Data retrieved from World Investment Report, 2003.

CHANGES IN CANADA'S INDUSTRY LEVEL FDI

BROAD DISAGGREGATION: NATURAL RESOURCES, MANUFACTURING, AND SERVICES

BURIED BENEATH CANADA'S CHANGING FDI TRENDS at the aggregate level are significant changes at the industry level, especially on a bilateral basis.[6] Consider the data provided in Table 2. Panels A and B show the distribution of Canada's outward and inward FDI by industry for 1983 and 2001, respectively. Panel C provides the *change* in the distribution by investment partner. We will focus our discussion here on Panel C. Over the period 1983 to

TABLE 2

CHANGES IN CANADA'S INDUSTRY LEVEL FDI

PANEL A. DISTRIBUTION OF CANADA'S FDI, BY INDUSTRY, 1983

	Outward			Inward		
	Natural Resources	Manu-facturing	Services	Natural Resources	Manu-facturing	Services
United States	29.1	32.3	38.6	33.4	40.8	25.8
United Kingdom	23.3	44.9	31.0	25.9	28.6	45.6
Rest of World	33.7	30.8	35.8	35.2	18.8	46.0
Total	29.8	32.8	37.4	33.1	36.4	30.5

PANEL B. DISTRIBUTION OF CANADA'S FDI, BY INDUSTRY, 2001

	Outward			Inward		
	Natural Resources	Manu-facturing	Services	Natural Resources	Manu-facturing	Services
United States	16.0	22.1	61.9	25.2	45.3	29.4
United Kingdom	5.5	27.5	42.5	9.4	58.9	31.4
Rest of World	18.8	29.4	58.0	24.1	55.1	20.8
Total	16.1	25.5	58.4	23.6	48.9	27.5

PANEL C. CHANGE IN DISTRIBUTION, 1983 TO 2001

	Outward			Inward		
	Natural Resources	Manu-facturing	Services	Natural Resources	Manu-facturing	Services
United States	–13.1	–10.1	23.3	–8.2	4.6	3.6
United Kingdom	–17.9	–17.5	11.5	–16.5	30.3	–14.2
Rest of World	–14.8	–1.4	22.2	–11.1	36.3	–25.2
Total	–13.7	–7.3	21.1	–9.5	12.5	–3.0

Note: The sum of the outward changes to the United Kingdom is not zero because of data limitations, resulting in our ability to classify only 75% of the Canadian FDI into the United Kingdom.

Source: Data provided through special runs from Statistics Canada.

2001, the *share* of Canada's outward FDI in the United States for services increased by 23.3 percent, whereas the shares in natural resources and manufacturing fell by 13.1 percent and 10.1 percent, respectively. On the inward side, the share of inward FDI from the United States going to natural resources fell by 8.2 percent, whereas the shares going to manufacturing and services increased by 4.6 percent and 3.6 percent, respectively.

What is surprising about the data on the outward side is the similarity across trading partners. That is, although the quantitative changes over the period differ when considering the United States, the United Kingdom, or the rest of the world, qualitatively, the changes are the same: a reduction in the importance of natural resources and manufacturing, and an increase in services. This is not the case on the inward side. Although the importance of services increased for U.S. FDI into Canada (though only slightly), services have become significantly less important as regards FDI from the United Kingdom and the rest of the world. Also, whereas manufacturing increased slightly in importance as regards FDI from the United States, manufacturing has become very much more important for FDI from the United Kingdom and the rest of the world.

In summing up across all trading partners, natural resources are less important for both outward and inward FDI. On the other hand, both services FDI and manufacturing FDI have been affected asymmetrically. Although services are significantly more important in Canada's outward FDI, they are marginally less important for inward FDI. In contrast, manufacturing has become more important on the inward side but less important on the outward side. The changes are plotted in Figure 6.

The changing composition in Canada's FDI can be seen by considering the data in Figure 6 from a different perspective. Figure 7 shows that in 1982, the share of Canada's inward and outward FDI in natural resources, manufacturing and services were roughly equal, each accounting for about a third of Canada's total FDI. Over the period of 1982 to 2001, Canada's share of inward FDI in manufacturing has increased steadily, accounting for about half of Canada's inward FDI stock in 2002. Although in 1999 services were more important than natural resources on the inward side, in the years 2000 and 2001 the importance of natural resources increased and that for manufacturing fell. In short, the manufacturing sector is the most important attractor of FDI into Canada. On the outward side, the picture is different. There, the services share of Canada's FDI has continued to trend upward, accounting for about 60 percent of Canada's outward FDI in 2002. On the other hand, both manufacturing and natural resources have seen their shares of outward FDI fall, with natural resources falling significantly more than manufacturing.

FIGURE 6

CHANGES IN THE SECTORAL DISTRIBUTION OF CANADIAN FDI

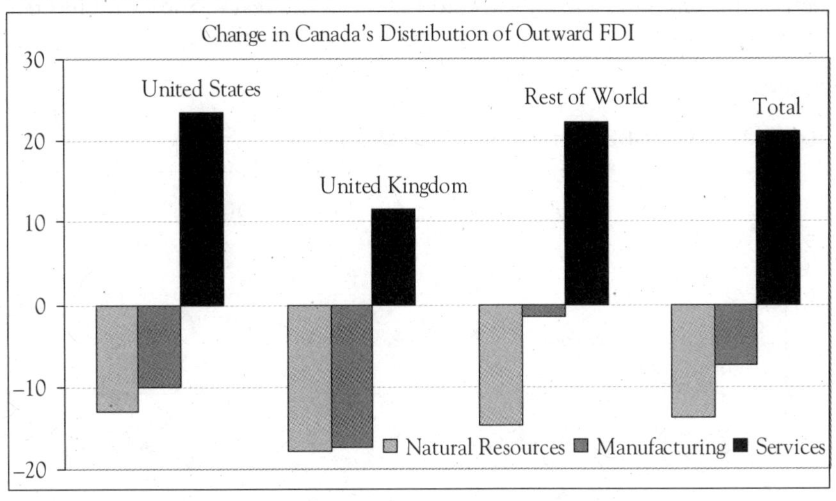

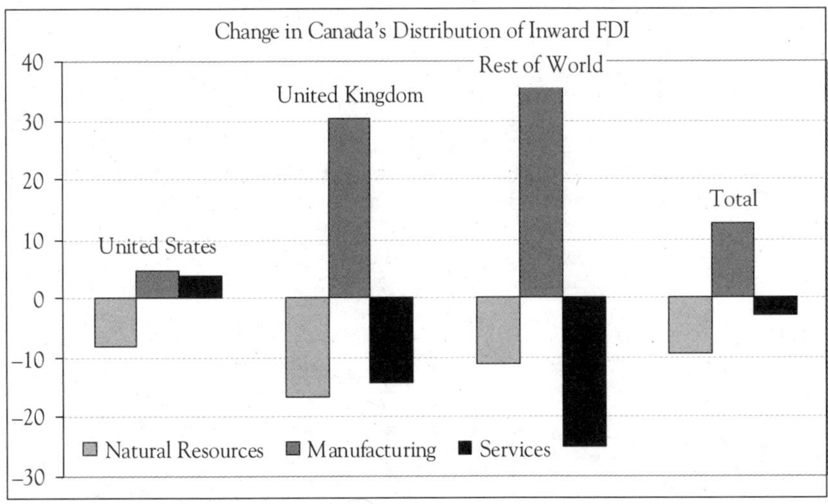

Source: Data provided through special runs from Statistics Canada.

Breaking these data down into Canada's FDI with the United States and the rest of the world (Figure 8), we see a strikingly similar pattern on the outward side, but a much different one on the inward side. Specifically, a majority of Canada's outward FDI to the United States and the rest of the world is in services, followed by manufacturing, with natural resources being the least important. On the other hand, for inward FDI from the United States, manufacturing remains the most important industry followed by services — and this has been the case for much of the sample. In contrast, this pattern has only recently emerged for FDI from the rest of the world. That is, since 1997, much of the surge in Canada's inward FDI from the rest of the world has been in manufacturing.

FIGURE 7

INDUSTRY DISTRIBUTION OF CANADIAN FDI

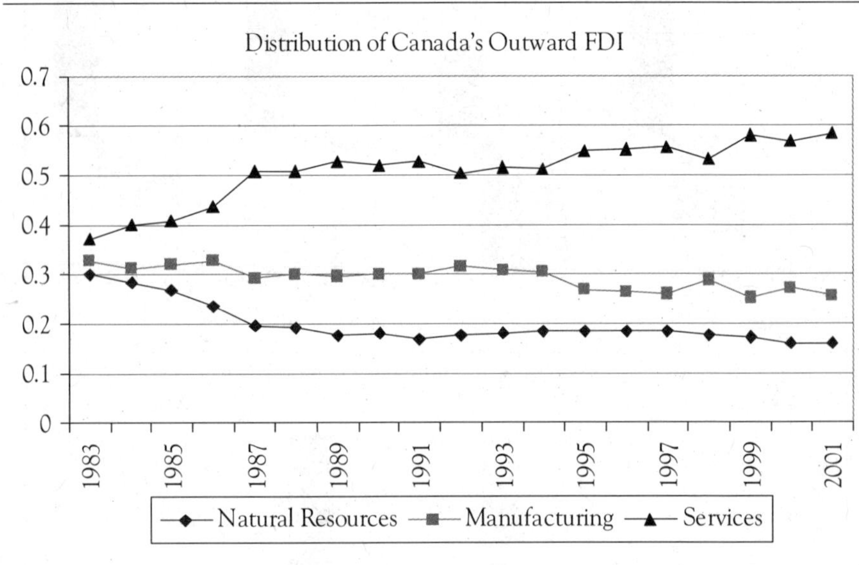

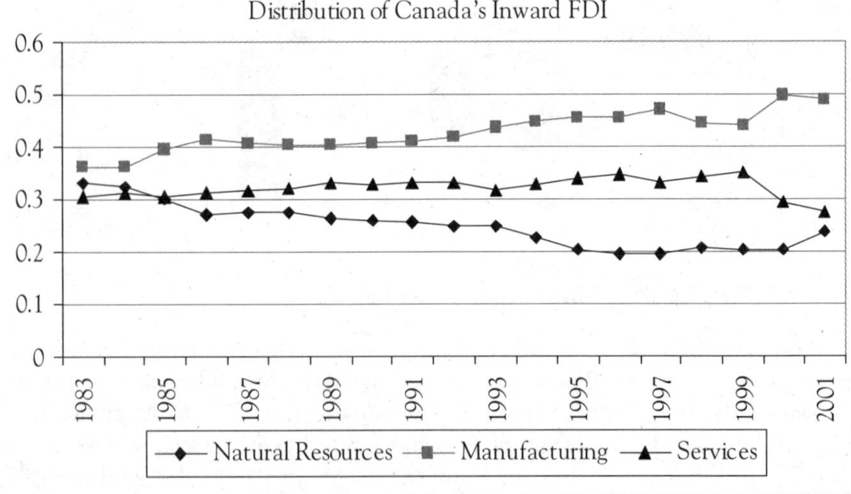

Source: Data provided through special runs from Statistics Canada.

FIGURE 8

INDUSTRIAL DISTRIBUTION OF CANADIAN FDI IN THE UNITED STATES AND THE REST OF THE WORLD

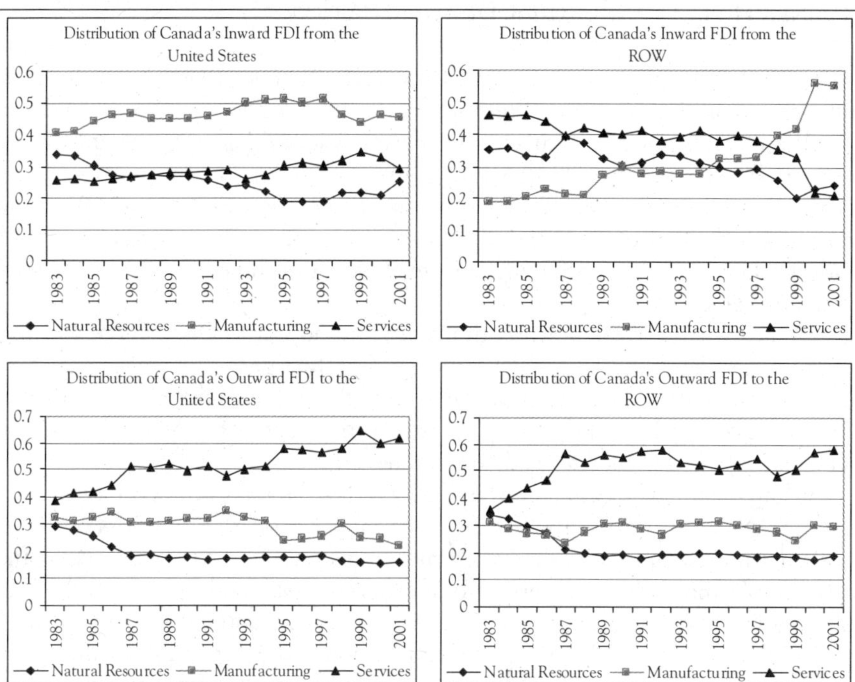

Source: Data provided through special runs from Statistics Canada.

FDI moving into Canada is motivated by market access (in terms of both services and non-services), by access to natural resources, and *perhaps* by factor price differences given the weak performance of the Canadian dollar over the period in question. It is clearly the case from these data that natural resources are playing a decreasing role in attracting FDI into Canada. Given free trade between Canada and the United States, market access is becoming less important as a driver for FDI moving from the United States into Canada, except for non-tradeables (services), but even this has not grown rapidly over the 1983-2001 period. In contrast, market access should play a major role in non-U.S. FDI flowing into Canada, although non-North American MNEs can also locate in the United States and export to Canada from there. As indicated in the discussion above, the share of FDI from all destinations moving into Canadian manufacturing has increased, whereas the share flowing into services is up only slightly. This *may* indicate that foreign MNEs are increasingly locating in Canada to produce manufactured goods, which in turn are used to supply both the Canadian and U.S. markets.[7] As indicated in Cameron (1998), over the period 1990-1992, foreign-controlled firms in Canada had an export orientation that was twice as high as that of domestic firms. In addition, foreign-controlled firms have higher productivity levels than domestic firms (Trefler 1999).

A FINER LEVEL OF INDUSTRIAL DISAGGREGATION

THE DATA PRESENTED IN THE PREVIOUS SECTION used a very broad level of disaggregation, namely natural resources, manufacturing and services. The discussion clearly indicates that on the inward side, manufacturing remains an important sector attracting FDI into Canada, whereas on the outward side, services are the most important motivator of Canadian FDI abroad. We now turn to a finer level of industrial disaggregation based on the system of standard industrial classification (SIC) at the C level. A list of these 15 industries is provided in Table 3.

Figures 9 to 11 break down both inward and outward FDI, into the 15 SIC-C industries. Each figure has three panels. The first gives the share of FDI in each sector in 1983 and the second in 2001. The bars in each panel sum to 100 percent. The third panel gives the change in the share of FDI in each industry. The bars in panel C therefore add up to zero.

What is immediately apparent in Figure 9A is the relative importance of industries A to H in 2001 (below the horizontal line in the figure). These are both natural resource and manufacturing industries. We do not see these industries playing such an important role on the outward side (Figure 9B). This observation points to a sharp difference between Canadian inward and outward FDI in 2001. Canada's inward FDI is much more concentrated in manufacturing and natural resources than is its outward FDI.

TABLE 3

LIST OF INDUSTRIES (SIC-C 1980)

1	A	Food, Beverage, and Tobacco
2	B	Wood and Paper
3	C	Energy
4	D	Chemicals, Chemical Products and Textiles
5	E	Metallic Minerals and Metal Products
6	F	Machinery and Equipment (Except Electrical Machinery)
7	G	Transportation Equipment
8	H	Electrical and Electronic Products
9	I	Construction and Related Activities
10	J	Transportation Services
11	K	Communications
12	L	Finance and Insurance
13	MNO	General Services to Business, Government Services, Education, Health and Social Services
14	PQ	Accommodations, Restaurants, Recreation Services and Food Retailing
15	R	Consumer Goods and Services

FIGURE 9A

DISTRIBUTION OF INWARD FDI FROM THE WORLD, BY SECTOR

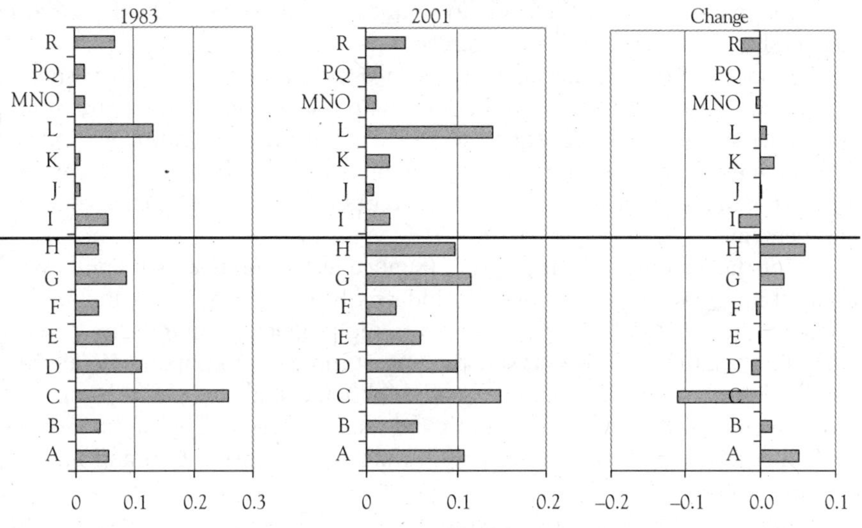

Source: Data provided through special runs from Statistics Canada.

FIGURE 9B

DISTRIBUTION OF OUTWARD FDI TO THE WORLD, BY SECTOR

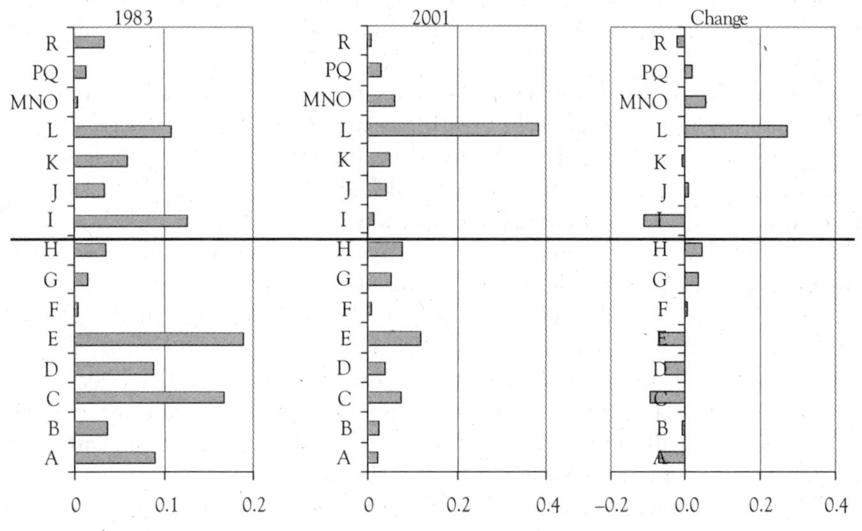

Source: Data provided through special runs from Statistics Canada.

As for the service industries (above the horizontal line in the figure), the big industry for both outward and inward FDI is L (finance and insurance). This industry plays a far larger role on the outward side — in 2001, almost 40 percent of Canada's outward FDI was in finance and insurance. On the inward side, its share only amounted to 13 percent.

In terms of Canada's inward FDI, the two industries that saw their shares increase most are H (electrical and electronic products) and A (food, beverage and tobacco). Industry C (energy) saw its share fall the most. Although industries G (transportation equipment), K (communications), B (wood and paper), and L (finance and insurance) saw their shares increase, these increases were relatively small.

As for the outward side, industry L (finance and insurance) is far and away the most important sector, followed by industry E (metallic minerals and metals products), industry H (electrical and electronic products) and industry C (energy). The industry groups that saw the largest increases in importance are industries L (finance and insurance) and MNO (general services to business, government services, education, health and social services). The two industries that saw their shares fall the most were industry I (construction and related activities) followed by industry C (energy).

Figures 10A and 10B show the industrial distribution for Canada's inward and outward FDI *vis-à-vis* the United States, and Figures 11A and 11B show it for the rest of the world. There are two dramatic similarities in the change in the distribution of FDI to the United States and the rest of the world. Specifically, the share of Canadian inward FDI into industry C (energy) from both the United States and the rest of the world fell dramatically. Another similarity occurs on the outward side, where industry L (finance and insurance) saw its share increase both for Canadian FDI locating in the United States and in the rest of the world.

The change in the distribution of Canadian FDI vis-à-vis the United States differs sharply from Canadian FDI with the rest of the world. Specifically, on the inward side, the United States saw its share in industry A (food, beverage and tobacco) fall, whereas the share of FDI from the rest of the world locating in Canada's industry A increased dramatically. Also, the share of U.S. FDI in Canada into industries G and H increased sharply, whereas there were much smaller increases for these industries from the rest of the world.

On the outward side, the share of Canada's FDI locating in the United States in industry C (energy) fell more dramatically than was the case for the rest of the world. In contrast, industry I (construction and related activities) saw its share of outward FDI fall far more dramatically for the rest of the world than for the United States. There are many other differences as well, with only the most significant ones highlighted in this discussion.

These data indicate that the stock of Canada's outward FDI is dominated by services, followed by manufacturing, with natural resources playing a relatively

FIGURE 10A

DISTRIBUTION OF INWARD FDI FROM THE UNITED STATES, BY SECTOR

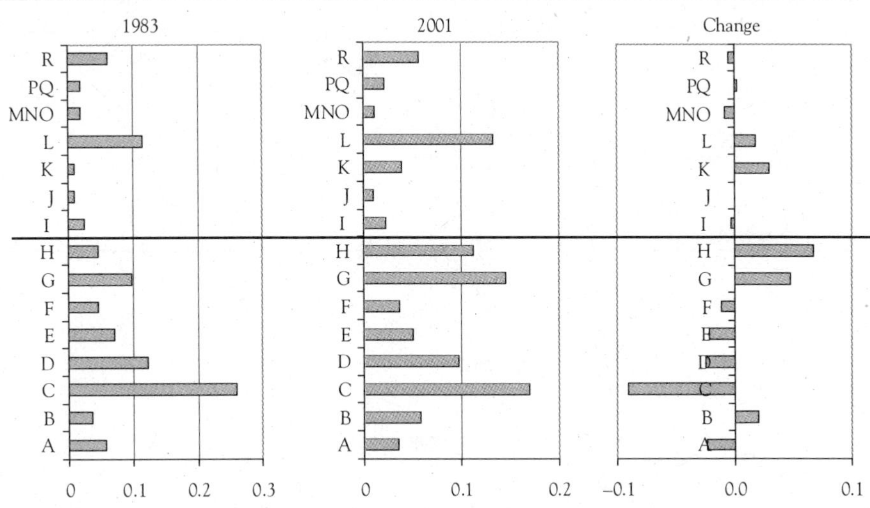

Source: Data provided through special runs from Statistics Canada.

FIGURE 10B

DISTRIBUTION OF OUTWARD FDI TO THE UNITED STATES, BY SECTOR

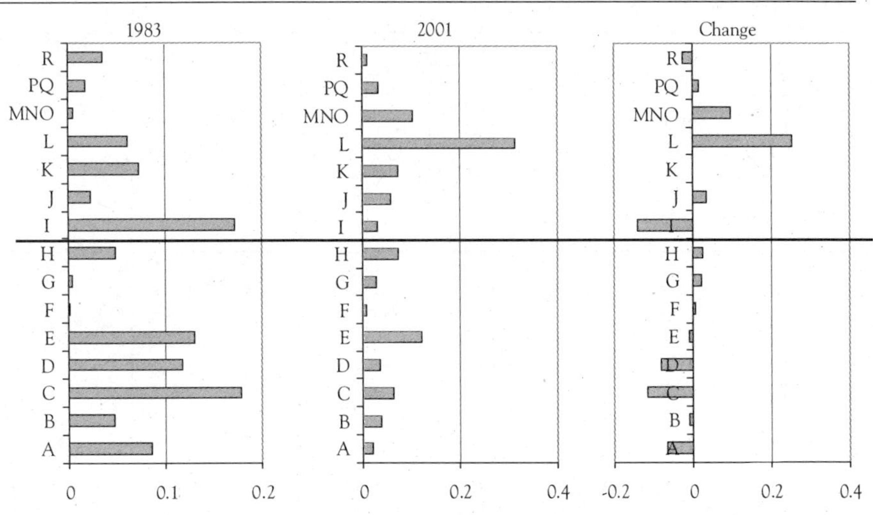

Source: Data provided through special runs from Statistics Canada.

FIGURE 11A

DISTRIBUTION OF INWARD FDI FROM THE REST OF THE WORLD, BY SECTOR

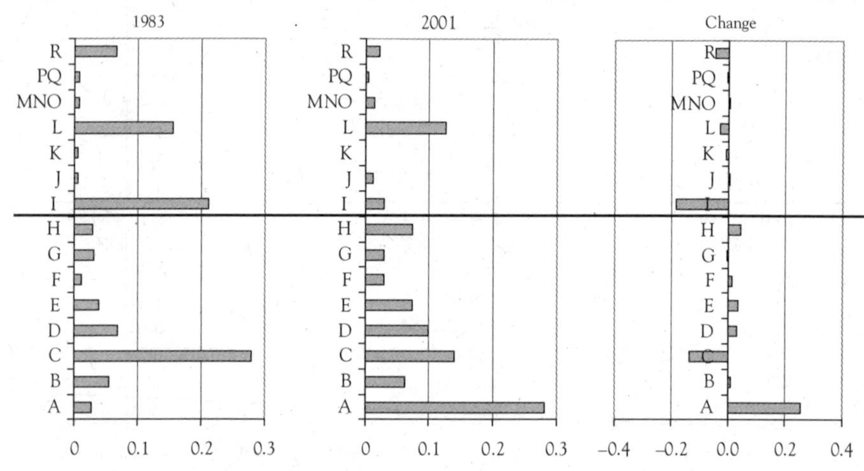

Source: Data provided through special runs from Statistics Canada.

FIGURE 11B

DISTRIBUTION OF OUTWARD FDI TO THE REST OF THE WORLD, BY SECTOR

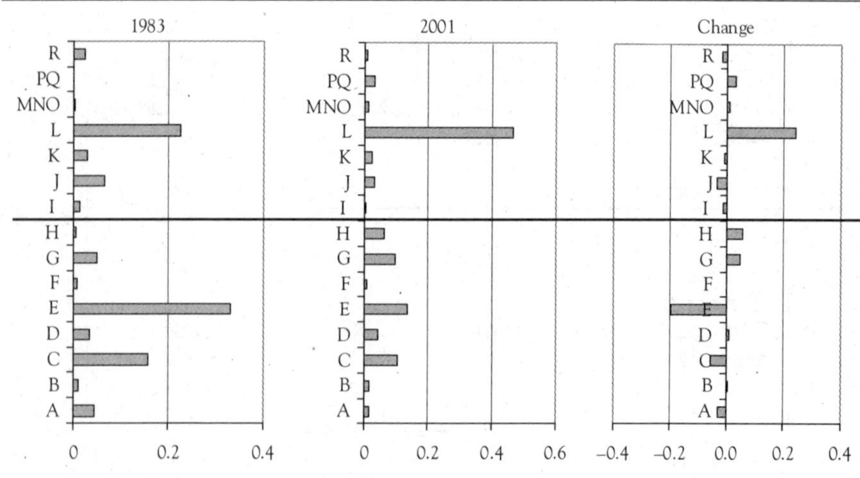

Source: Data provided through special runs from Statistics Canada.

small role. In contrast, on the inward side, manufacturing is the most important sector, followed by services and then natural resources. In addition, although this trend is similar for the United States and the rest of the world on the outward side, this is not the case on the inward side. A majority of Canada's inward FDI from the United States remains in manufacturing, whereas this has only recently been the case for inward FDI from the rest of the world.

THE ESTIMATING EQUATION

THE PREVIOUS DISCUSSION OF TRENDS in Canada's FDI is clearly important in helping to understand the changing importance of various industries. The next step is to consider the factors that explain these changes. There is a separate issue of whether or not these changing industry-level patterns are *good* for the Canadian economy but the welfare implications of these changing FDI trends lie outside the scope of this analysis, suggesting an important area for future research.

The following analysis measures the factors that underlie these changing trends in FDI. The methodology used is very much a function of the available data. As indicated above, data on Canada's inward and outward FDI at the SIC-C industry level have been obtained over the period from 1983 to 2001. These data include Canada's total inward and outward FDI for each of the 15 SIC-C industries, as well as bilateral data for these industries vis-à-vis the United States, the United Kingdom, and the rest of the world.[8]

In thinking about the factors that are likely to influence Canada's FDI at the sectoral level, I have identified the following important production function factors: corporate profitability and corporate taxes, R&D expenditures, price indexes for intermediate inputs and hours worked, capital stocks and depreciation rates, export and import propensities, import duties and interest rates. I assemble these data for use in estimating their importance as drivers of Canada's changing FDI patterns. The data on production functions are for different industrial classifications and are expressed in different units than the FDI data. I therefore carefully transformed all of the data to make it compatible with the SIC-C 1980 classification. This represented an enormous job that is obviously subject to some criticism. Convertibility tables were available to transform the SIC-E trade data classification into the SIC-C FDI classification, though this task was relatively straightforward. In contrast, there are no convertibility tables available to help transform data from the other classifications into the SIC-C FDI classification. I therefore was forced to transform this data using detailed industry descriptions for each data set. Gera, Gu and Lee (1999) carried out a similar exercise. I use Table 1 in Gera, Gu and Lee as a guide to ensure that the distribution of our data by industry is similar to theirs. A similar data set was used in Hejazi and Pauly (2003). These data will be used here to identify the relevant economic factors that explain Canada's changing patterns of FDI.

The estimating equation can be written as follows:

$$(1)\qquad FDI_{j,t} = \beta_0 + \beta_1 GCCA_{j,t} + \beta_2 NST_{j,t} + \beta_3 RD_{j,t} + \beta_4 TAXPD_{j,t} + \beta_5 TIF_{j,t} + \beta_6 HWF_{j,t} + \beta_7 IMPTOT_{j,t} + \beta_8 EXPTOT_{j,t} + \beta_9 IMPTOTD_{j,t} + \beta_{10} TBILL_t + \beta_{11} NAFTA_t + \beta_{12} CUSFTA_t + \gamma NATRES_j + e_{jt}$$

for $j = 1\ldots15$ industries and $t = 1983$ to 1998. We therefore have 240 observations. This is done for both outward and inward FDI. The variables are defined as follows:

GCCA measures capital consumption allowances allowed for tax purposes
NST measures capital stocks
TAXPD measures corporate taxes paid
TIF is a price index for intermediate inputs
HWF is a price index for labour inputs
IMPTOT captures how open that sector is to imports
EXPTOT captures how open that sector is to exports
RD measures R&D spending
IMPTOTD measures duties paid on imports
TBILL is an interest rate variable
NAFTA is a dummy variable for the NAFTA
CUSFTA is a dummy variable for the Canada-U.S. FTA
NATRES is a dummy variable for natural resource industries

With the exception of *TBILL, NAFTA* and *CUSFTA*, all the variables in the model are measured at the industry level and are measured relative to gross output by industry. Equation (1) is estimated for total Canadian inward and outward FDI as well as on a bilateral basis with the United States, the United Kingdom, and the rest of the world. Furthermore, the model is estimated in logarithms.

In order to test whether services are different, we interact each of the factors in the model with a services dummy. Therefore, define SERV as a dummy variable equal to 1 for the services industries, and zero otherwise. The model is estimated in the following form:

$$\begin{aligned}(2)\qquad FDI_{j,t} = {} & \beta_0 + \\ & \beta_1 GCCA_{j,t} + \beta_2 NST_{j,t} + \beta_3 RD_{j,t} + \beta_4 TAXPD_{j,t} + \beta_5 TIF_{j,t} + \\ & \beta_6 HWF_{j,t} + \beta_7 IMPTOT_{j,t} + \beta_8 EXPTOT_{j,t} + \beta_9 IMPTOTD_{j,t} + \\ & \beta_{10} TBILL_t + \beta_{11} NAFTA_t + \beta_{12} CUSFTA_t + \gamma NATRES_j + \\ & \delta_0 SERV + \\ & \delta_1 SERV \times GCCA_{j,t} + \delta_2 SERV \times NST_{j,t} + \delta_3 SERV \times RD_{j,t} + \\ & \delta_4 SERV \times TAXPD_{j,t} + \delta_5 SERV \times TIF_{j,t} + \delta_6 SERV \times HWF_{j,t} + \\ & \delta_7 SERV \times IMPTOT_{j,t} + \delta_8 SERV \times EXPTOT_{j,t} + \\ & \delta_9 SERV \times IMPTOTD_{j,t} + \delta_{10} SERV \times TBILL_{jt} + \\ & \delta_{11} SERV \times NAFTA_t + \delta_{12} SERV \times CUSFTA_t + e_{jt.}\end{aligned}$$

The impact of any factor for non-services is simply captured by the βs. On the other hand, the estimated impact for services will be the sum of the β and the δ for each factor. If services are not different, then the estimated values for the δs will be zero. To the extent that the importance of each of the factors that drive services FDI differs from that for non-services, this will be captured by the statistical significance of the δ parameters. An F test is also provided to determine if all of the δs are jointly zero. That is, the F test is a joint test that will determine whether services are different. The F statistic tests the hypothesis that $\delta_1 = \ldots = \delta_{12} = 0$. If it is small, we accept the hypothesis that the model that explains manufacturing also explains services. On the other hand, if the F statistic is large, we reject the hypothesis and this indicates that the models are different.

EMPIRICAL ESTIMATES

THE ESTIMATION RESULTS for the inward and outward FDI model presented in the previous section are provided in Tables 4 and 5, respectively. The major results are summarized below.

As Canadian capital consumption allowances for tax purposes (GCCA) become more generous, Canadian outward FDI declines while inward FDI rises. The only exception to this pattern is Canadian inward FDI from the rest of the world (ROW). Also, these results are generally the same for both services and non-services: the only exception is inward FDI from the United States, where inward FDI in services is not very sensitive to capital consumption allowances.[9]

The capital intensity of industries (*NST*) is measured by capital stock relative to gross output. As this variable (*NST*) rises, outward FDI increases but inward FDI falls. This pattern holds for all but Canada's inward FDI from the United Kingdom and the ROW. There is no measured difference in the impact between services and non-services industries, as all the services dummy interaction terms are statistically insignificant.

R&D intensity is related in a strongly positive way to Canada's outward FDI to all locations. This is in sharp contrast to the inward side where R&D is statistically insignificant. Furthermore, these results are similar for both the services and non-services industries.

Corporate taxes paid are related in a strongly positive way to Canada's outward FDI to all locations included in the analysis except the United Kingdom. The results for inward FDI are mixed: inward FDI from the United Kingdom and the ROW are negatively related to taxes paid in Canada, whereas inward FDI from the United States and Japan are both positively related to corporate taxes paid in Canada.

We next consider the impact of the cost of intermediate inputs (*TIF*). Although the coefficient estimates for *TIF* are strongly significant, they are estimated to be small. As the costs of intermediate inputs in Canada increase, total inward FDI into Canada increases, as do sub-totals from the United States, the

United Kingdom and Japan, but the total from the ROW declines. The opposite is true for outward FDI: as *TIF* increases in Canada, there is less outward FDI to all locations. These relationships differ from what one might expect, but the coefficient estimates are very small. A possible explanation is that the quality of the inputs is also higher, thus explaining higher costs. If quality measures were included, these signs would likely reverse. There is no measured difference between services and non-services industries.

A price index for labour inputs (*HWF*) is negatively related to inward FDI from the United States and the ROW, and related in a strongly positive way to outward FDI to all locations. There is no statistically-significant difference in this estimate for services and non-services industries.

The next several variables measure the links between Canada's FDI and trade-related attributes. These include export and import intensities by industry, as well as a measure of duties paid, and finally, the effect of the two free trade agreements within North America, namely the Canada-U.S. Free Trade Agreement (FTA) and the NAFTA.

The larger the import intensity of each industry, the more inward FDI there is in total as well as from the United States and the United Kingdom, but not from Japan or the ROW. Outward FDI is unrelated to the import intensity, with the exception of the ROW, where the larger the import intensity the lower the inward FDI. These results are estimated to be the same for both services and non-services.

Export intensities are considered next. As the export intensities of each industry rise, Canada's total inward FDI as well as its total FDI from the United States and the United Kingdom falls, but inward FDI from Japan and the ROW rises. As for outward FDI, as export intensity rises, Canada's total outward FDI as well as FDI to the United States and the United Kingdom fall, but it rises to the ROW. These results are estimated to be the same for both services and non-services.

Import duty rates are considered next. The reduction in Canada's import duty rates over the period is associated with a fall in Canada's total inward FDI, as well as a reduction in Canada's inward FDI from the United States and the ROW. Inward FDI from Japan increased as Canadian import duties fell. Canada's outward FDI seems to have been unaffected by changes in Canada's duty rates. These effects are the same for both services and non-services.

The results above relating to trade intensities and duty rates have to be qualified by the overall impacts of the Canada-U.S. FTA and the NAFTA on Canadian FDI. The NAFTA is estimated to have reduced Canada's inward FDI in total, as well as from the United States, the United Kingdom and Japan, but not the ROW. On the outward side, the NAFTA is estimated to have increased Canada's total outward FDI as well as Canada's outward FDI to the United Kingdom and the ROW, but not to the United States. The Canada-U.S. FTA, on the other hand, is estimated to have increased Canada's inward and outward FDI with the United States, but not any other country for which this is measured.

TABLE 4

ESTIMATING THE MODEL FOR INWARD FDI

	INFDITO		INFDIUS		INFDIUK		INFDIJP		INFDIROW	
	COEF	T-STAT	COEF	T-STAT	COEF	T-STAT	COEF	T-STAT	COEF	T-STAT
C	–0.914	–4.37	–0.790	–3.91	–0.192	–3.20	–0.002	–0.06	0.068	0.78
SC	0.952	2.84	0.732	2.26	0.212	2.20	0.008	0.17	0.009	0.06
GCCA	3.181	10.31	3.661	12.31	0.114	1.29	0.269	5.94	–0.595	–4.61
NST	–0.283	–6.88	–0.406	–10.24	–0.003	–0.23	–0.037	–6.19	0.126	7.33
RD	–1.482	–1.09	–1.279	–0.97	0.094	0.24	–0.401	–2.00	–0.297	–0.52
TAXPD	0.252	0.30	2.310	2.86	–0.822	–3.42	0.862	7.01	–1.236	–3.53
TBILL	–0.003	–0.41	–0.007	–1.14	0.001	0.30	–0.001	–1.20	0.004	1.43
TIF	0.002	4.50	0.002	5.38	0.000	3.32	0.000	0.13	–0.001	–3.93
HWF	0.000	–0.56	0.000	–2.14	0.000	1.48	0.000	–0.95	0.000	2.57
IMPTOT	0.940	8.08	0.746	6.65	0.177	5.30	0.008	0.48	0.017	0.34
EXPTOT	–0.241	–2.12	–0.301	–2.74	–0.184	–5.63	0.031	1.88	0.243	5.11
IMPTOTD	1.888	3.93	4.881	1.83	0.268	0.34	–1.184	–2.91	5.738	4.96
NAFTA	–0.142	–3.19	–0.129	–2.99	–0.044	–3.43	–0.022	–3.31	0.030	1.62
CUSFTA	0.095	2.01	0.098	2.17	0.011	0.81	0.011	1.58	–0.015	–0.75
TIME	–0.007	–0.67	–0.020	–2.13	–0.004	–1.41	0.001	0.65	0.018	4.29
NAT	0.082	1.99	0.034	0.85	0.056	4.73	–0.003	–0.57	–0.008	–0.46
SGCCA	–2.606	–1.40	–3.519	–1.96	–0.122	–0.23	–0.218	–0.80	1.035	1.33
SNST	0.190	0.59	0.292	0.94	0.001	0.02	0.041	0.87	–0.103	–0.77
SRD	–1.156	–0.32	2.111	0.04	–2.118	–0.15	0.252	0.03	–1.149	–0.76
STAXPD	1.154	0.12	–4.530	–0.50	0.824	0.30	–1.007	–0.73	4.860	1.23
STBILL	0.007	0.58	0.007	0.62	0.000	0.04	0.001	0.87	0.000	–0.06

Table 4 Continued

	INFDITO		INFDIUS		INFDIUK		INFDIJP		INFDIROW	
	COEF	T-STAT	COEF	T-STAT	COEF	T-STAT	COEF	T-STAT	COEF	T-STAT
STIF	–0.002	–3.22	–0.002	–2.44	–0.001	–2.71	0.000	–0.69	0.000	–0.22
SHWF	0.001	1.58	0.001	1.59	0.000	0.93	0.000	0.56	0.000	–0.51
SIMPTOT	–1.294	–0.99	–3.001	–0.30	–2.055	–0.69	–0.521	–0.34	–1.238	–1.21
SEXPTOT	1.333	0.45	–1.293	–0.18	2.548	0.30	1.915	0.44	1.078	1.29
SIMPTOTD	–0.978	–0.08	–0.182	–0.36	5.559	0.04	9.545	0.14	1.646	0.59
SNAFTA	0.162	2.43	0.171	2.67	0.051	2.64	0.021	2.20	–0.060	–2.16
SCUSFTA	–0.101	–1.41	–0.076	–1.09	–0.004	–0.20	–0.012	–1.13	–0.021	–0.71
AdjR^2		0.995		0.989		0.916		0.818		0.986
F statistic Ho: $\delta_1 = ... = \delta_{12} = 0$		8.921		6.893		3.414		1.243		5.120
Are Services Different?		Yes		Yes		Yes		No		Yes

TABLE 5

ESTIMATING THE MODEL FOR OUTWARD FDI

	OUTFDITO		OUTFDIUS		OUTFDIUK		OUTFDIROW	
	COEF	T-STAT	COEF	T-STAT	COEF	T-STAT	COEF	T-STAT
C	0.086	0.39	–0.165	–1.45	0.064	1.00	0.190	1.68
SC	–0.588	–1.66	–0.247	–1.35	–0.137	–1.33	–0.200	–1.15
GCCA	–2.174	–6.66	–0.607	–3.62	–0.403	–4.25	–1.160	–7.11
NST	0.348	7.98	0.113	5.03	0.062	4.91	0.170	7.92
RD	18.118	12.56	11.620	15.68	3.087	7.36	3.410	4.72
TAXPD	4.663	5.26	3.020	6.63	–0.271	–1.05	1.910	4.30
TBILL	0.002	0.32	0.002	0.49	0.002	0.92	0.000	–0.40
TIF	–0.001	–3.71	0.000	–1.51	0.000	–2.51	0.000	–4.39
HWF	0.001	7.38	0.001	7.69	0.000	2.12	0.000	5.61
IMPTOT	–0.069	–0.56	–0.015	–0.24	0.058	1.61	–0.110	–1.81
EXPTOT	–0.298	–2.47	–0.354	–5.73	–0.048	–1.38	0.100	1.74
IMPTOTD	0.045	0.02	0.915	0.61	–0.927	–1.09	0.060	0.04
NAFTA	0.118	2.49	–0.003	–0.11	0.029	2.09	0.090	3.87
CUSFTA	0.040	0.81	0.052	2.02	–0.003	–0.20	–0.010	–0.34
TIME	0.005	0.45	–0.006	–1.17	0.004	1.19	0.010	1.40
NAT	–0.099	–2.27	–0.050	–2.22	0.037	2.88	–0.090	–3.92
SGCCA	0.737	0.37	–0.311	–0.31	–0.002	0.00	1.050	1.07
SNST	–0.035	–0.10	0.018	0.10	–0.004	–0.04	–0.050	–0.29
SRD	3.987	0.07	6.656	0.60	3.499	0.22	–1.170	–0.60
STAXPD	9.130	0.91	3.976	0.77	2.781	0.96	2.370	0.47
STBILL	0.009	0.78	0.004	0.66	0.002	0.43	0.000	0.62

TABLE 5 CONTINUED

	OUTFDITO		OUTFDIUS		OUTFDIUK		OUTFDIROW	
	COEF	T-STAT	COEF	T-STAT	COEF	T-STAT	COEF	T-STAT
STIF	0.000	0.30	0.000	0.58	0.000	0.35	0.000	–0.20
SHWF	0.000	0.02	0.000	–0.11	0.000	0.34	0.000	–0.04
SIMPTOT	–1.420	–0.95	–7.952	–1.41	0.805	0.25	–3.270	–0.60
SEXPTOT	1.601	0.91	15.601	0.96	7.570	0.83	5.430	0.34
SIMPTOTD	–1.037	–0.23	–2.245	–0.33	–1.941	–1.26	1.150	0.60
SNAFTA	0.111	1.78	0.825	1.70	0.044	1.14	0.090	2.62
SCUSFTA	–0.101	–1.33	–0.076	–1.94	–0.009	–0.41	–0.020	–0.42
AdjR^2		0.961		0.972		0.787		0.900
F statistic Ho: $\delta_1 = ... = \delta_{12} = 0$		1.879		1.863		1.256		2.329
Are Services Different?		Yes		Yes		No		Yes

We now consider the differential impact of these trade agreements on services and non-services industries. Specifically, the NAFTA had a negative impact on inward FDI into Canadian manufacturing and natural resources, but a marginally-positive impact on Canadian FDI into services. The impact of the Canada-U.S. FTA was no different whether one considers total Canadian inward FDI into services or manufacturing FDI. On the outward side, the NAFTA is associated with an increase in Canada's FDI to the United States and the rest of the world, but not to the United Kingdom.

The final tests presented in Tables 4 and 5 relate to whether, in an overall sense, there is anything different about services. An F statistic is calculated to test whether all the services interaction terms are jointly zero ($\delta_1=\delta_2=\ldots=\delta_{12}=0$). The last row of each table indicates whether or not the services variables, when combined with the other factors in the model, add enough information to justify their inclusion in the estimation. The evidence indicates that, overall, services are different than non-services industries. That is, the effects of our factors, in a statistical sense, do vary by the services or non-services nature of industries. The two exceptions occur for inward FDI from Japan and outward FDI to the United Kingdom, where the models for services and non-services are the same.

POLICY IMPLICATIONS AND CONCLUSIONS

CANADA HAS BEEN TRANSFORMED from what was primarily a host economy for FDI in the 1970s to what became an important home country: by 1997, Canada had more outward FDI than inward. Furthermore, the ratio of Canada's outward to inward FDI continued to increase through 2002. The data presented here indicate that the surge on the outward side is in large part attributable to the surge in services FDI — and this is true whether we consider Canada's FDI in the United States, the United Kingdom, or the rest of the world. On the inward side, the surge in Canada's inward FDI in the last half of the 1990s is driven by FDI into Canada's manufacturing sector. In contrast to the outward side, we do not see an increasing trend in services FDI on the inward side. This asymmetry in Canada's inward and outward FDI is an important development for the Canadian economy that has not been observed in studies that only focus on aggregate measures of FDI.

This study estimates a model where FDI is linked to several production function variables. The most important result, of course, is that the relative importance of factors that explain FDI in services industries is indeed different from those in non-service industries. These differences are stronger for inward than for outward FDI.

One important result relates to the link between FDI and corporate taxes paid as well as capital consumption allowances. Specifically, the estimation results show that corporate taxes paid in Canada are an important factor in explaining the surge in Canada's outward FDI. Offsetting this is the generosity of capital consumption allowances which was not only related to less outward FDI but was also an important factor in attracting FDI into Canada. These results imply therefore that reducing taxes may reverse the trends we have described to some degree.

Another important result relates to the significance of R&D intensity as a predictor of outward FDI. This is entirely consistent with international business theory: firms develop firm-specific advantages through FDI and then move abroad to exploit these advantages.

But herein lies a difficult policy dilemma. A careful assessment would be needed to identify whether reversal of the observed trends is in the public interest. To the extent that Canadian FDI is moving abroad to exploit firm-specific advantages, perhaps such investments should be encouraged. On the other hand, if firms are moving abroad because of relatively high taxes or a lack of skilled labour, then such investments are likely bad for Canada. It is likely that both of these factors are in play and hence it is difficult to see whether a policy intervention is wise. Second, it is unclear whether any benefits that would flow from such a policy could justify the reduction in government tax revenue. These are two important issues that render policy making very difficult in this context.

The analysis presented here has filled an important gap in terms of understanding changes in Canada's industrial distribution of FDI and the economic factors that have contributed to these trends. More work is needed, however, in order to identify whether these changing patterns of FDI at the industry level are a positive or a negative development for the Canadian economy. As we know, there is a large literature that indicates that FDI brings many benefits and has a net positive effect on an economy. There is less of a consensus vis-à-vis the benefits of outward FDI on the home country. In any case, most studies have been undertaken at the aggregate level and thus there is a need for more work to be done at the industry level. The ongoing importance of manufacturing for Canada's inward FDI and the growing importance of services for Canada's outward FDI must be assessed in terms of their likely impact on the Canadian economy before policy can be formed to address these changes.

To draw policy implications from an analysis of such trends, we must first understand what impact these changing FDI patterns have had on the Canadian economy. If increased Canadian investment abroad has positive effects on the Canadian economy, then such investments should be encouraged. On the other hand, if the effects of such investments are negative, the underlying *cause* of the increased outward FDI must be understood in order to direct policy formulation. Consider the following examples. If Canadian MNEs are increasingly locating abroad for efficiency reasons such as access to unskilled labour, then such investments should be seen as beneficial to the Canadian economy in the long run: domestic resources will move to higher value-added industries as these low value-added activities move abroad. On the other hand, if Canadian

MNEs are being driven to locate abroad by factors such as a lack of skilled labour, high taxes, or a poor R&D environment in Canada, then policy changes may be needed to remedy the deficiencies driving such investment.

ENDNOTES

1 Correspondence to Walid Hejazi, Rotman School of Management, University of Toronto, 105 St. George Street, Toronto, Ontario, Canada, M5S 3E6, or hejazi@rotman.utoronto.ca.

2 This study focuses on FDI. For a discussion of Canada's R&D performance in a global perspective, see Le and Tang (2004). For a discussion about the issue of Canada's brain drain or brain gain, see Finnie (2001) and Zhao and Drew (2000).

3 Over the period 1970-2002, Canada's outward FDI stock has grown at a compound rate of 15.9 percent whereas the inward stock has grown at 9.3 percent. These data are reported at historical costs. The growth rates for real exports and real imports over the same period were 6.6 percent and 7.2 percent, respectively (Hejazi and Safarian 2004).

4 It must be pointed out that the data used here are reported on a historical cost basis. The ratios would likely differ if market value data were used. Unfortunately, market value data are not available.

5 As can be seen in Figure 3, the inward ratio began to rebound in the second half of the 1990s. This is likely related to evidence indicating that Canadian productivity rebounded in the post 1995 period (Rao, Sharpe and Tang, Chapter 14 of this volume). This productivity rebound may have contributed to the increase in Canadian FDI relative to GDP in the second half of the 1990s, or it may have been the result of the rebound.

6 Industry detail on the FDI for other countries is not reviewed in this paper.

7 A significant productivity gap has emerged between Canada and the United States. This gap can be attributed to two "product innovating" industries: computers and machinery. In contrast, Canada has done well in "process-innovating" low-end manufacturing industries. That is, Canadian industries have been able to cut costs more effectively than U.S. manufacturing industries. Furthermore, these are exactly the industries that experienced the largest tariff reductions in the Canada-U.S. Free Trade Agreement (Trefler 1999).

8 We have some of these data for Mexico and Japan, but they are not used, given the large number of missing data observations (due to confidentiality issues).

9 This result can be seen by looking at the GCCA coefficient for inward FDI in Table 5, which is estimated at 3.661, and subtracting from this the statistically significant services interaction term below, estimated at –3.519. That is, the net impact of GCCA on services FDI from the United States into Canada is very small, and certainly much smaller than it is for manufacturing and natural resources FDI into Canada.

BIBLIOGRAPHY

Ahmad, Ashfaq, Someshwar Rao, and Colleen Barnes. 1996. *Foreign Direct Investment and APEC Economic Integration*. Working Paper No. 8. Ottawa: Industry Canada.

Baldwin, John R., and David Sabourin. 2001. "Impact of the Adoption of Advanced Information and Communication Technologies on Firm Performance in the Canadian Manufacturing Sector," Statistics Canada Working Paper. Ottawa: Statistics Canada.

Brainard, S. Lael. 1997. "An Empirical Assessment of the Proximity-Concentration Trade-off Between Multinational Sales and Trade," *American Economic Review*, 87 (4): 520-544.

Cameron, Richard A. 1998. *Intra-firm Trade of Canadian-Based Transnational Companies*. Working Paper No. 26. Ottawa: Industry Canada.

Finnie, Ross. 2001. "The Brain Drain: Myth or Reality, *Choices* (Institute for Research in Public Policy), 7 (6).

Gera, Surendra, Wulong Gu, and Frank C. Lee. 1999. *Foreign Direct Investment and Productivity Growth: The Canadian Host-Country Experience*. Working Paper No. 30. Ottawa: Industry Canada.

Graham, Edward. 1993. "U.S. Outward Direct Investment and United States Exports: Substitutes or Complements — With Implications for U.S. — Japan Policy," Washington, D.C.: Institute for International Economics.

Head, Keith, and John Ries. 2004. "Making Canada the Destination of Choice for Internationally Mobile Resources," Discussion Paper No. 14. Ottawa: Industry Canada.

Hejazi, Walid. 2001. "Access to Foreign R&D Does Not Undermine Domestic R&D Efforts," *Policy Options*, October, 2001: 43-48.

Hejazi, Walid, and Peter Pauly. 2002. *Foreign Direct Investment and Domestic Capital Formation*. Working Paper No. 36. Ottawa: Industry Canada.

————. 2003. "Motivations for FDI and Domestic Capital Formation," *Journal of International Business Studies*, 34: 282-9.

Hejazi, Walid, and A.E. Safarian. 1999a. "Trade, Foreign Direct Investment, and R&D Spillovers," *Journal of International Business Studies*, 30 (3), third quarter: 491-511.

————. 1999b. "Modeling Links Between Canadian Trade and Foreign Direct Investment." *Perspectives on North American Free Trade Series*. Ottawa: Industry Canada.

————. 2001. "The Complementarity Between U.S. FDI Stock and Trade," *Atlantic Economic Journal*, 29 (4).

————. 2004. "Determinants of FDI Location: A Comprehensive Test," University of Toronto Working Paper. Toronto: University of Toronto.

Le, Can D., and Jianmin Tang. 2004. "Why Does Canada Spend Less on R&D than its Key Trade Competitors?" unpublished Industry Canada working paper.

Lipsey, Robert E., and Merle Yahr Weiss. 1981. "Foreign Production and Exports in Manufacturing Industries," *Review of Economics and Statistics*, November: 488-494.

————. 1984. "Foreign Production and Exports of Individual Firms," *The Review of Economics and Statistics*, pp. 304-8.

Manley, John. 2002. Speech given to the Canadian Club, February 11, 2002.

Rao, Someshwar, Marc Legault, and Ashfaq Ahmad. 1994. "Canadian-Based Multinationals: An Analysis of Activities and Performance," in Steven Globerman (ed.). *Canadian Based Multinationals*. The Industry Canada Research Series. Calgary: University of Calgary Press, pp. 63-123.

Rao, Someshwar, Andrew Sharpe, and Jianmin Tang. 2006. "Productivity Growth in Services Industries: A Canadian Success Story," chapter 14 in Richard G. Lipsey and Alice O. Nakamura (eds.). *Services Industries and the Knowledge-Based Economy*. The Industry Canada Research Series. Calgary: University of Calgary Press.

Safarian, A.E., and Walid Hejazi. 2001. *Canada and Foreign Direct Investment: A Study of Determinants*. Toronto: University of Toronto Centre for Public Management.

Tang, Jianmin, and Someshwar Rao. 2001. *R&D Propensity and Productivity Performance of Foreign-Controlled Firms in Canada*. Working Paper No. 33. Ottawa: Industry Canada.

Trefler, Daniel. 1999. "Does Canada Need A Productivity Budget?" *Policy Options*, July-August: 66-71.

van Pottelsberghe De La Potterie, Bruno, and Frank Lichtenberg. 2001. "Does Foreign Direct Investment Transfer Technology Across Borders?" *Review of Economics and Statistics* 83 (3): 490-497.

Zhao, John, and Doug Drew. 2000. "Brain Drain and Brain Gain: The Migration of Knowledge Workers from and to Canada, *Education Quarterly Review*, 6 (3).

Comment

John Ries
University of British Columbia

DESPITE THE KEY ROLE played by foreign direct investment in international services transactions and the potential effects of FDI on national welfare, there is little systematic knowledge of the determinants of services FDI. The globalization of services and FDI are intimately intertwined, as foreign affiliates are the primary means for delivering services to consumers located overseas. The

World Trade Organization (WTO) estimates that the cross-border supply of services (excluding tourism) is worth roughly $1 trillion whereas $2 trillion was delivered through a commercial presence (foreign affiliates).[1] Services FDI may also have impacts on welfare: A firm's decision on where to locate its services activities will affect employment, incomes and possibly knowledge creation.

Walid Hejazi's study addresses this neglected area of investigation. His analysis can be grouped into three complementary exercises, each addressing a specific question:

- Benchmarking: How does Canadian services FDI compare to a reasonable benchmark?
- Explaining: What explains deviations of services FDI from this benchmark?
- Advising: What policies may be used to influence services FDI?

Benchmarking is a useful starting point for evaluating services FDI. Canada's FDI levels are different from those of the United States and other countries and have trended differentially over time. To understand whether Canada's FDI experience is "unusual", it is important to develop a "benchmark" indicating what we might expect for Canada in terms of FDI levels and growth. Hejazi compares Canada's FDI performance to other countries to provide an international perspective. I would like to augment his discussion of Canada's FDI by examining the FDI of OECD countries relative to a theoretical benchmark.

The earlier version of Hejazi's study used a "gravity model" specification of FDI. More commonly applied to trade flows, this model posits that the flows of an activity from country *i* to country *j* should be proportional to the "mass" of economic activity in each country and inversely proportionally to the distance between the countries. In the "frictionless" FDI gravity model where the distance effect is non-existent, the specification is:

(3) $$FDI_{ij} = (GNI_i/GNI_w) \times GNI_j$$

where *GNI* represents gross national income and subscripts *i* and *j* pertain to the source and destination countries, respectively.

The basic idea of this specification is that the FDI flowing from country *i* to country *j* should be proportional to country *j*'s *GNI*. What should this proportion be? The gravity model specifies it as country *i*'s share of world economic output.[2]

This relationship can be manipulated to provide a prediction of a country's share of world FDI. Summing over all destination countries to generate total FDI for country *i* (FDI_i) yields:

(4) $$FDI_i = GNI_i \times (1-s_i) \quad \text{where } s_i = GNI_i / GNI_w.$$

World FDI is obtained by summing this expression over all countries:

(5) $FDI_w = GNI_w \times (1–H)$ where $H=\sum s_i^2$.

These equations yield an expression for country *i*'s share of world FDI:

(6) $FDI_i/FDI_w = GNI_i/GNI_w \times [(1–s_i)/(1–H)]$.

Equation (6) reveals that FDI shares are related to GNI shares and an adjustment for country size ($s_i=GNI_i /GNI_w$) and the concentration of world economic output (*H*). Larger countries (those with high s_i values) will have FDI shares that fall short of their GNI shares. A simple example demonstrates the logic of this specification. Consider a two-country world with one country twice as large as the other. Suppose the large country makes twice as many investments because it has twice the number of firms (say 120 versus 60). Now think of each firm as choosing an investment location by throwing darts at a map of the (two-country) world. Because the large country is twice the size of the small country, it will have twice the "target area" on the map. Two-thirds of the large country's investments will land internally and thus not be recorded as *foreign* investments whereas the remaining one-third (40 investments) will be foreign investments. On the other hand, two-thirds of the small country's investments (40 in total) will be in the large country and recorded as foreign investment. The large country's share of world FDI (one-half) is below its GNI share whereas the small country's FDI share is greater than its GNI share. Essentially, being large implies less cross-border activities because the large internal market provides opportunities within the border. Country size needs to be taken into account when creating a benchmark for FDI.

Figures 1 and 2 compare inward and outward FDI shares of various OECD countries to the country's benchmark. Each point corresponds to an OECD country using 2002 data.[3] The points are labelled with each country's two-digit isocode. The vertical axis represents a country's share of OECD FDI and the horizontal axis the country's benchmark as expressed by the right-hand-side of Equation (6). The figure does not show countries with FDI shares less than 0.001 (Iceland in Figure 1 and Czech Republic, Hungary, Iceland, Poland, Slovakia, and Turkey in Figure 2). If the benchmark predicts actual FDI shares perfectly, all observations should be on the 45-degree line.

The figures reveal that most countries' FDI corresponds to the benchmark as the majority of the points are near to the 45-degree line. On the inward side (Figure 1), Ireland (ie) is a positive outlier and Japan (jp) a negative outlier. For outward investment, New Zealand (nz), Greece (gr) and Mexico (mx) have much less outward investment than what is predicted by the benchmark. Canada (ca) is slightly higher but very close to its benchmark for both inward and outward FDI for 2002.

Figures 3 and 4 show plots of the ratio of actual FDI shares to the benchmark for four countries — Canada, Finland, Great Britain and the United

FIGURE 1

INWARD FDI SHARES RELATIVE TO BENCHMARK

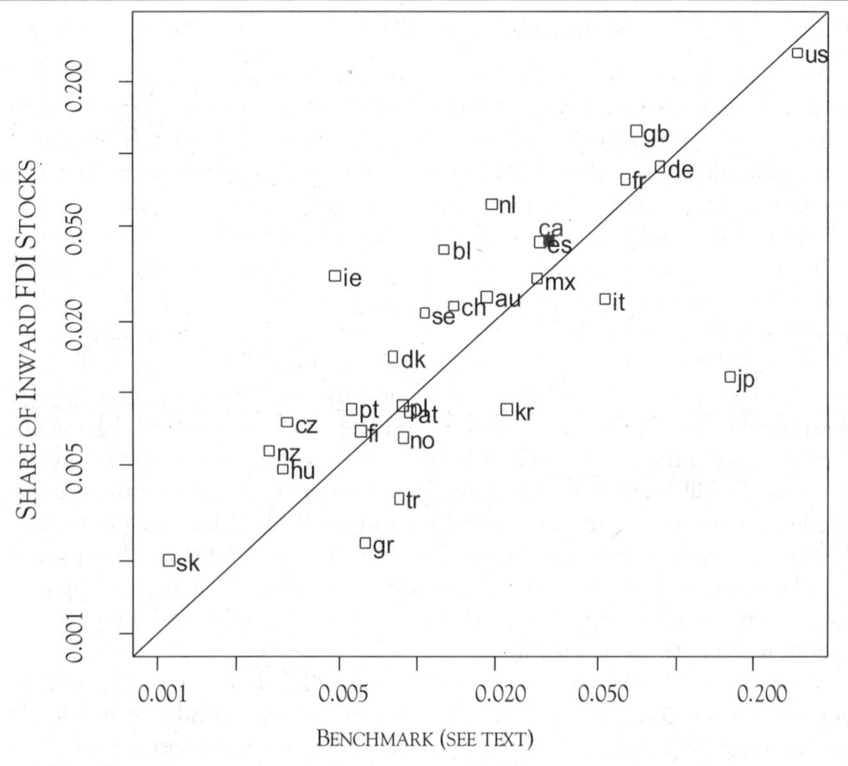

States — for the years 1980-2002. When the ratio exceeds 1, FDI shares exceed their predicted levels. Hejazi's Table 1 shows that, for most OECD countries, the ratio of outward FDI to GDP is growing relative to the ratio of inward FDI to GDP. Figures 3 and 4 will indicate whether these trends are moving countries towards or away from the benchmark.

Figure 3 reveals that over time, shares of inward FDI are converging towards the theoretical benchmark derived from the frictionless gravity equation. This indicates that, whatever frictions were present that made FDI diverge from predicted levels, these have declined over time. Portraying outward FDI, Figure 4 shows us a slightly different story. Convergence seems to have been occurring through about 1997 and then Great Britain and Finland moved away from the benchmark and ended up with higher than predicted inward FDI shares.

What should we take away from this benchmarking exercise? First, it is important to account for the economic mass of countries when modeling the determinants of FDI. Hejazi does this by controlling either for GDP or capital

FIGURE 2

OUTWARD FDI SHARES RELATIVE TO BENCHMARK

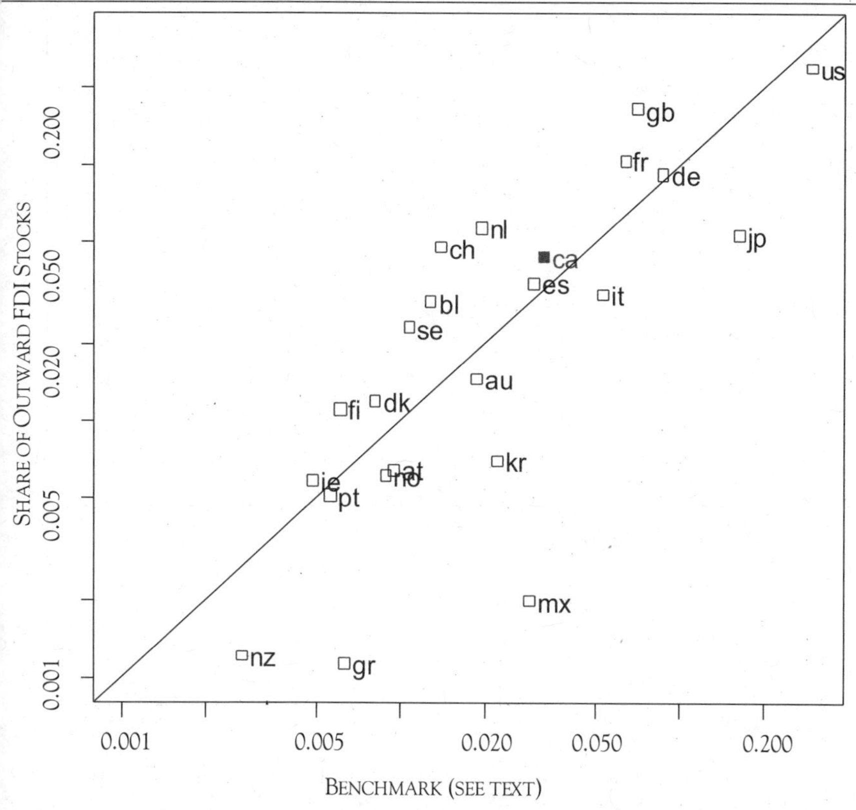

stocks. Second, while frictions seem to have been reduced over time they are still important, especially for outward FDI. Third, either different frictions apply to inward and outward FDI or frictions have asymmetric effects in inward and outward FDI. Analysis needs to *explain* why FDI deviates from the benchmark. Most of Hejazi's study is devoted to the task of explaining the sources of variation in FDI by using regression analysis. In his analysis, variables such as distance, openness, language and taxes capture frictions that cause FDI to deviate from what may be expected based on the economic size of the home and host countries. A final note concerns services data availability. The diagrams in this discussion show aggregate FDI because data on services FDI for a large sample of countries are not available. While the data for aggregate FDI shows Canada to be near its benchmark, an analysis of services FDI may generate a different story.

FIGURE 3

TRENDS IN INWARD FDI SHARES RELATIVE TO BENCHMARK

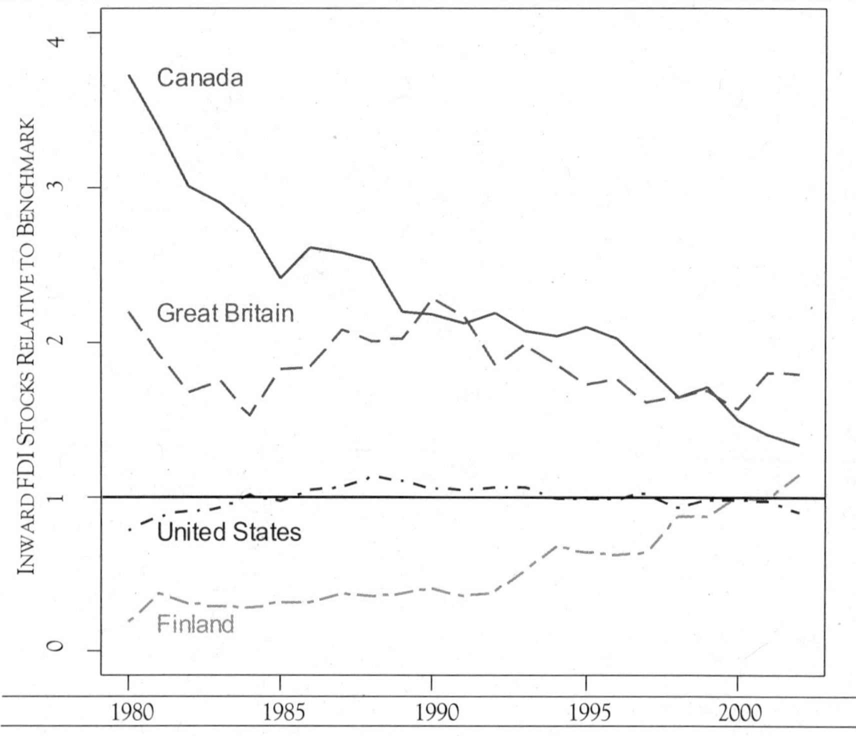

Beyond the academic exercise of explaining FDI, the analysis has potential relevance to policy. Namely, it can suggest policies that can be used by Canada to influence inward and outward FDI in ways that increase welfare in Canada. Two questions must be answered in order to make policy recommendations:

- What are the welfare effects of inward and outward FDI?
- What cost-effective policies may be employed to influence FDI?

Hejazi's discussion suggests that the overall welfare effects of FDI are positive. While this may be true, the effects may not be large in magnitude. Moreover, policies that may influence FDI may be quite costly. For example, even if foreign investors respond to lower taxes, Canada may not want to change the nation's tax system simply to bring in a few more investors.

Hejazi's study is a useful first step in putting Canada's FDI into context and understanding what factors influence its location. With improvements in data collection and development of theoretical models of services, Hejazi and empirical researchers like him will continue to develop knowledge about the impacts and determinants of services FDI that will serve as a guide for public policy.

FIGURE 4

TRENDS IN OUTWARD FDI SHARES RELATIVE TO BENCHMARK

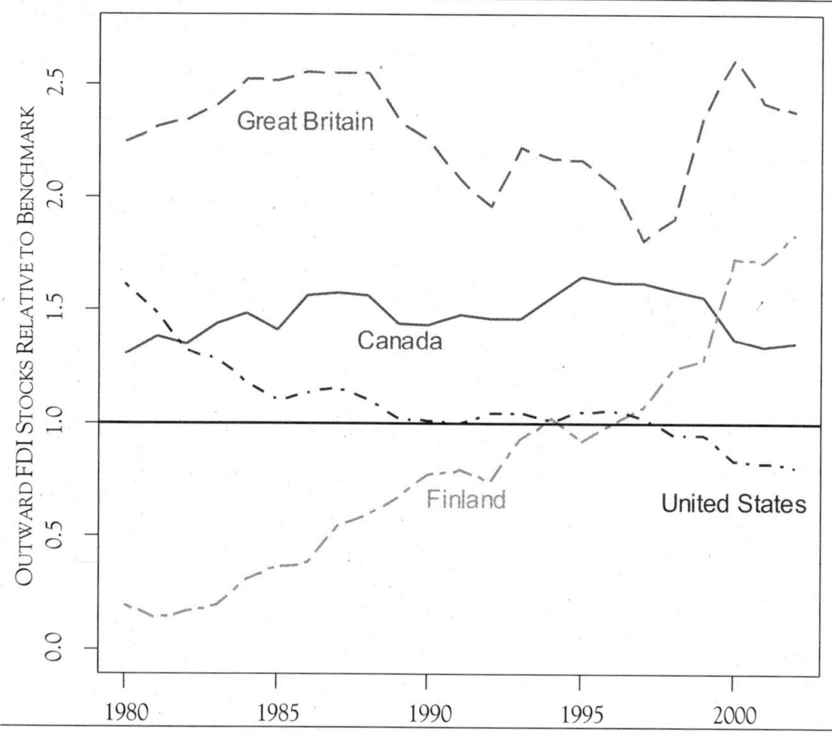

ENDNOTES

1 "Trends in Services Trade under GATS Recent Developments," Symposium on Assessment of Trade in Services, World Trade Organization, March 14-15, 2002.

2 The micro-foundations of the gravity model have been established for trade but not for FDI. Thus, it is better to view this specification for FDI as a "hypothesized" relationship rather than one that can be derived from theory.

3 Keith Head helped me derive the benchmark and produce the figures. We obtained data on inward and outward stocks of FDI from the United Nations Conference on Trade and Development's Foreign Direct Investment database. GNI figures come from the World Bank's World Development Indicators.

BIBLIOGRAPHY

World Trade Organization. 2002. "Trends in Services Trade under GATS Recent Developments," Symposium on Assessment of Trade in Services, World Trade Organization, March 14-15.

Anita Wölfl[*]
Organisation for Economic Co-operation and Development

9

Productivity Growth in the Services Industries: Patterns, Issues and the Role of Measurement

INTRODUCTION

RECENT YEARS HAVE BEEN MARKED by growing policy interest in the services economy. This relates to two facts. First, the services sector accounts for between 60 and 80 percent of aggregate production and employment in the Organisation for Economic Co-operation and Development (OECD) economies and it continues to grow. Second, productivity growth has not accelerated in many of the services industries in many countries despite evidence of the increased use of efficiency-enhancing tools such as information and communication technologies (ICT). Taken together, these two facts may raise concerns about the future performance of OECD economies.

The poor performance of the services sector has typically been attributed to certain characteristics of the sector. For instance, services are perceived to be less intensive in their use of physical capital; they typically show a lower degree of innovation and knowledge accumulation; they are characterized by smaller firm-size; and they typically focus on domestic or regional markets, which implies that they do not confront international competition to the same degree as the manufacturing sector.

These perceptions should be revisited, however. Some services industries in some OECD countries have experienced strong productivity growth recently. Moreover, certain services, such as financial and business services, are relatively knowledge intensive and focus on customers in international markets, implying that they are faced with intense competition. Small firm size may not necessarily be a negative factor in productivity growth: it may also reflect a competitive business environment in which new entrants force incumbents to increase productivity. Much also depends on whether services

* Anita Wölfl now works for the Centre d'études prospectives et d'informations internationales (CEPII) in Paris, France.

industries address final or intermediate demand. Finally, measurement may play a part. Zero or negative productivity growth in services industries might reflect underestimation because of biases in the measurement of the output and productivity growth of specific services industries.

This study examines the empirical evidence of services sector performance across OECD countries. First, it analyzes recent patterns of productivity growth and resource allocation across and within the services and the manufacturing sectors. Next, it analyzes the determinants of productivity growth and their impact on productivity performance in different services industries. Finally, it assesses the role of measurement of productivity growth both for the services sector and for the economy as a whole.

THE ROLE OF THE SERVICES SECTOR IN THE ECONOMY

THE SERVICES SECTOR VERSUS THE MANUFACTURING SECTOR

IN QUANTITATIVE TERMS, the services sector had become the single most important sector in almost all OECD economies by 1970 (Figure 1). The services share of the economy grew strongly thereafter. By 2000, it amounted to between 60 and 80 percent of total value added in most OECD economies.

Generally, this trend reflects a growing demand for services as incomes rose in most OECD countries over the 1980s and 1990s.[1] Some differences can be distinguished, however. A first group of countries, which includes the United States, Denmark, Belgium, France, the Netherlands, and the United Kingdom, has had a relatively high share of services-sector value added since the 1970s or has experienced strong increases in the services-sector share of value added from what were initially low levels: in this group the services sector share of value added rose above 70 percent by 2000. In a second group of countries, which included Austria, Germany, Italy, Sweden and Spain, the services sector accounted for between 65 percent and 70 percent of total value added in 2000: in these countries the services sector shares have increased continuously since the 1970s. Finally, there is a third group of countries where the services-sector share of value-added shares was around or below 65 percent in 2000. In these countries, the value-added share of the services sector remains low, as in Korea, or shows only slight increases over the period, as in Canada and Norway.

FIGURE 1

SHARES OF THE SERVICES SECTOR IN VALUE ADDED OVER TIME (IN PERCENT)

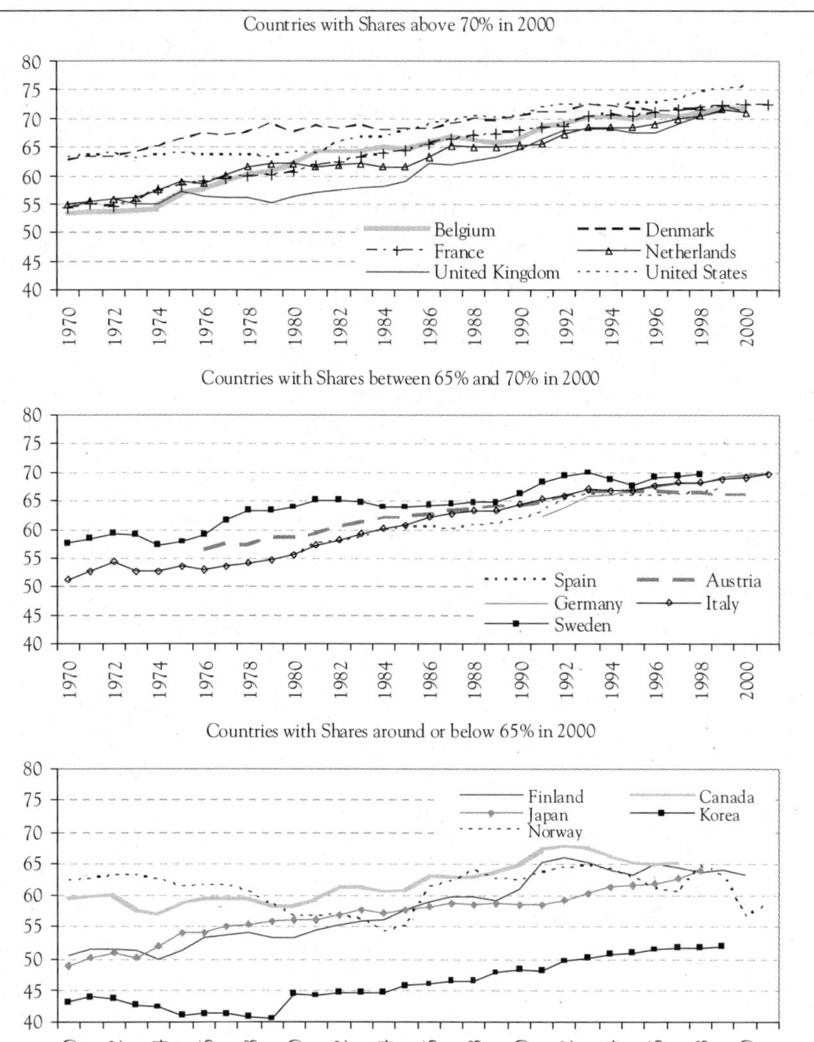

Notes: Shares in total value added at current prices. The services sector covers International Standard Industrial Classification (ISIC) classes 50-99. For the detailed list of industries, see the OECD Internet page on the STAN Database. (www.oecd.org/document/15/0,2340,en_2649_34445_1895503_1_1_1_1,00.html). Accessed February 10, 2005.

Source: OECD STructural ANalysis (STAN) Database 2002.

Figure 2 points to an imbalance in the growth of the manufacturing and the services sectors in OECD economies. It demonstrates the difference between relatively strong productivity growth in the manufacturing sector and low productivity growth in the services sector. This is illustrated by the position of country points around the grey line in the graph. Equal productivity growth in the manufacturing and services sectors would result in all country points being on or close to that line. Most countries are located to the right of the line, however. Productivity growth is thus much higher in manufacturing than in services in (almost) all OECD countries – albeit productivity growth has been increasing in the services sector relative to the manufacturing sector (Wölfl 2003). In most countries, services productivity growth is only about one half of manufacturing productivity growth. In the United States, Sweden and Finland, it is less than one-third.

FIGURE 2

GROWTH IN VALUE ADDED PER PERSON EMPLOYED IN MANUFACTURING AND SERVICES, 1990-2000 (ANNUAL COMPOUND GROWTH RATES, IN PERCENT)

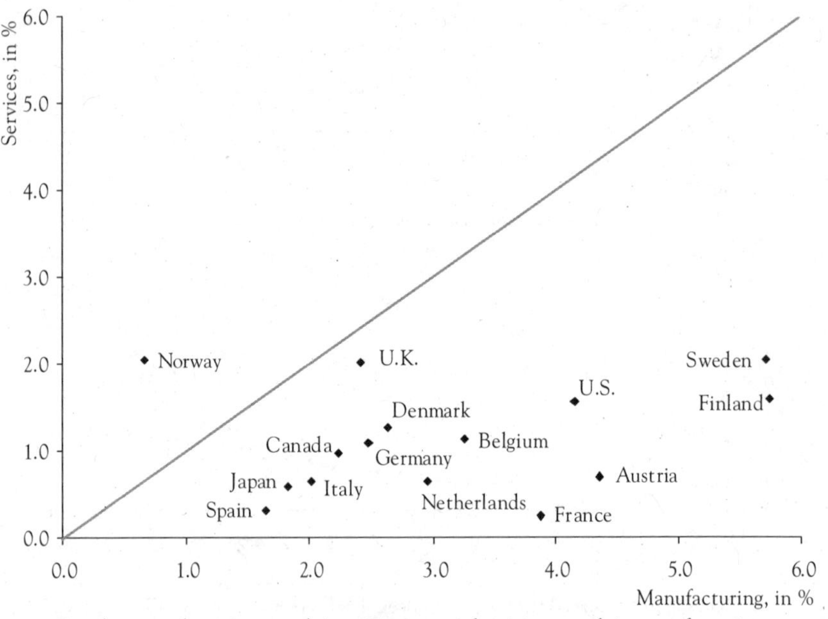

Grey line: productivity growth in services = productivity growth in manufacturing

Notes: Figures are for the indicated years or for the most recent year available. The services sector covers ISIC classes 50–99 (see note for Figure 1).

Source: OECD STAN Database 2002.

THE IMPLICATIONS OF UNBALANCED GROWTH

THIS PATTERN OF UNBALANCED GROWTH may have adverse affects on overall economic growth. In a seminal paper, Baumol (1967) stressed the possible long-term consequences of an imbalance in the growth of a productive manufacturing sector and an unproductive or stagnant services sector (see Box 1). Indeed, productivity developments in OECD economies in the 1960s showed that increasingly unbalanced growth across sectors induces resource reallocation towards the sector that is characterized by slow or zero growth, and this could eventually slow down aggregate growth. During the persistent decline of productivity growth rates in several countries over the 1970s and 1980s, several authors re-examined this issue, searching for ways to "cure" the disease.

In recent years, Baumol's theory has been challenged by the observation that several services industries display relatively high productivity growth rates, sometimes over a long period. One possible reason is the presence of increasing returns to scale in some services industries, such as those related to ICT, or the strong uptake of productivity-enhancing ICT-equipment during the 1980s and 1990s.[2] Moreover, services industries not only produce for final demand but also for intermediate demand, which implies that they are indirectly contributing to aggregate productivity growth.

This study examines the current relevance of Baumol's theory. It uses the OECD STtructural ANnalysis (STAN) Database as well as the OECD input-output tables to provide empirical evidence on the role of services in the economy as well as the performance of different industries within the services sector. The study focuses on growth of labour productivity, as measured by value added per person employed. It provides comparable and reliable cross-country and cross-industry empirical evidence on productivity growth performance on a highly disaggregated level. Data on capital input per industry to compute multifactor productivity growth are not available for the level of disaggregation required and for a sufficiently large number of countries. Finally, value added as an output indicator is less sensitive to changes in the allocation of inputs between labour and intermediate goods, partly, for example, because of outsourcing. This is notably relevant in the analysis of productivity growth in services that is the main interest of this study.[3]

Box 1
Cost Disease and the Services Sector: Baumol's Theory

The main idea behind Baumol's Cost Disease is that the tendency for unbalanced growth across sectors induces resource reallocation towards the slowly growing or stagnant sector, eventually slowing down aggregate growth. Baumol's views derive from the empirically-based assumption that the economy consists of two distinct sectors. The first is a growing (manufacturing) sector, characterized by technological progress, capital accumulation and economies of scale. The second one is a relatively stagnant (services) sector, consisting of services such as education, performing arts, public administration, health and social work. Due to the nature of this second sector, the potential for technological progress would only be temporary. These services might thus be characterized by an eventual increase in the costs that would have to be incurred in providing them.

The crucial point for differentiation between the two sectors lies in the role of labour. In the first sector, labour is mainly an input in the production of some final good. In the second sector, labour is rather an end in itself. In order to stress the point, Baumol (1967) assumes that labour is the only input into production, with the total supply of labour being constant. Furthermore, wages in the two sectors are assumed to change in parallel to money wages, and thus to income in the economy, rising as rapidly as output per person hour in the growing sector. As a consequence, costs (i.e. wage costs) would steadily increase in the stagnant sector, while costs could be held constant within the growing sector, due to the productivity growth that can be achieved there.

This leads to two possible scenarios of inter-sectoral resource allocation and aggregate economic performance. In the first scenario, there is a tendency for the output of the stagnant sector to disappear. This would mainly be the case if demand for services is not highly price or income inelastic. In the second scenario, however, the relative supply of both sectors' goods is assumed to be constant. Either the demand for the stagnant sectors' goods is highly price inelastic, as is the case for social and health services, or production of these sectors is subsidized, as is the case in cultural services. In this second scenario, an increasing share of labour would have to be transferred to the stagnant industry, while the share of labour allocated to the growing industry would eventually approach zero.

In the long term, the second scenario would lead to declining aggregate productivity growth, as the weighted average of the two sectors with the weights being the relative employment shares of each contributing sector. However, whether growth of gross domestic product per capita also declines, and thus the long-term ability of countries to create wealth, cannot be said *a priori*. It depends on the relative growth of productivity and labour utilization per sector.

Despite the intuitive appeal of Baumol's argument and its foundation in empirical evidence, two factors argue against declining aggregate productivity growth. First, not all services industries are stagnant; ICT use, for instance, has improved productivity growth in several countries. Second, declining aggregate productivity growth might only occur if these services industries produce final goods, not if they produce intermediate inputs (Oulton 1999).

PRODUCTIVITY PERFORMANCE IN SERVICES INDUSTRIES

FIGURE 3A SHOWS that some industries within the services sector are characterized by strong productivity growth. These include business-related services such as financial intermediation, as well as post and telecommunication services.

Average annual productivity growth rates amount to about 4.5 percent in financial intermediation and about 10 percent in post and telecommunications. These growth rates are comparable to high-growth industries within manufacturing such as machinery and equipment, where productivity growth has been averaging 5 percent since the 1980s. Moreover, business-related services are also industries that show a strong increase in value-added shares. In particular, finance and insurance services now account for about 20 to 30 percent of value added in the total economy, while their respective shares were between 10 and 20 percent in 1980 (Wölfl 2003).

Relatively strong productivity growth can also be found, albeit to a lesser degree, in wholesale and retail trade and in transport and storage services. Productivity growth rates in these services are on average about 2.5 percent, which is equivalent to productivity growth in the economy as a whole. Positive growth rates in these services are sometimes attributed to the introduction of cost-reducing technologies such as ICT, which have helped to enhance logistics in wholesale trade and in transport services, and enhance inventory control in retail trade. Triplett and Bosworth (2002), for instance, examined U.S. productivity growth over the 1995-2000 period, and found that ICT equipment contributed between 30 and 37 percent of labour productivity growth in business services, wholesale trade and transportation services. In wholesale and retail trade, competitive pressures, notably related to the expansion strategies of large incumbents such as Wal-Mart, are perceived to be a main driver for productivity growth (Baily 2003). Low productivity growth rates are typically found in social and personal services. These industries are relatively labour-intensive and the potential for growth in labour productivity is relatively small.

Figures 3A and 3B show also large disparities in productivity growth rates across countries for most services industries. To some degree, this reflects differences in aggregate economic performance. For example, Japan shows lower and declining productivity growth in several services industries as compared with other countries. In contrast, Australia and the United States show relatively high and increasing productivity growth rates for most services industries. Industry-specific factors also affect the differences in productivity growth. Some countries, such as Denmark, Finland, Sweden, the United Kingdom and the United States, show relatively high productivity growth in those services in which they are specialized (Wölfl 2003).

FIGURE 3A

LABOUR PRODUCTIVITY GROWTH IN SERVICES — INDUSTRIES WITH RELATIVELY STRONG GROWTH (AVERAGE ANNUAL GROWTH RATES, IN PERCENT)

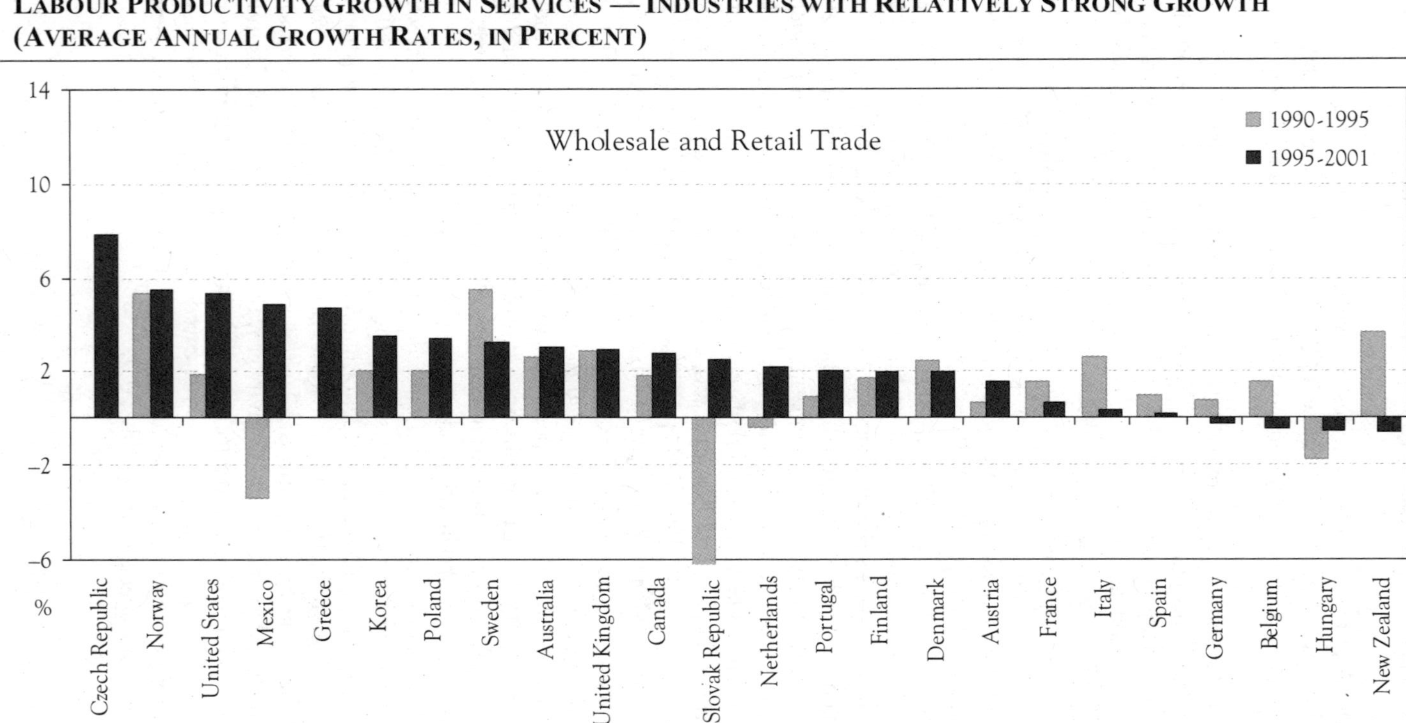

FIGURE 3A CONTINUED

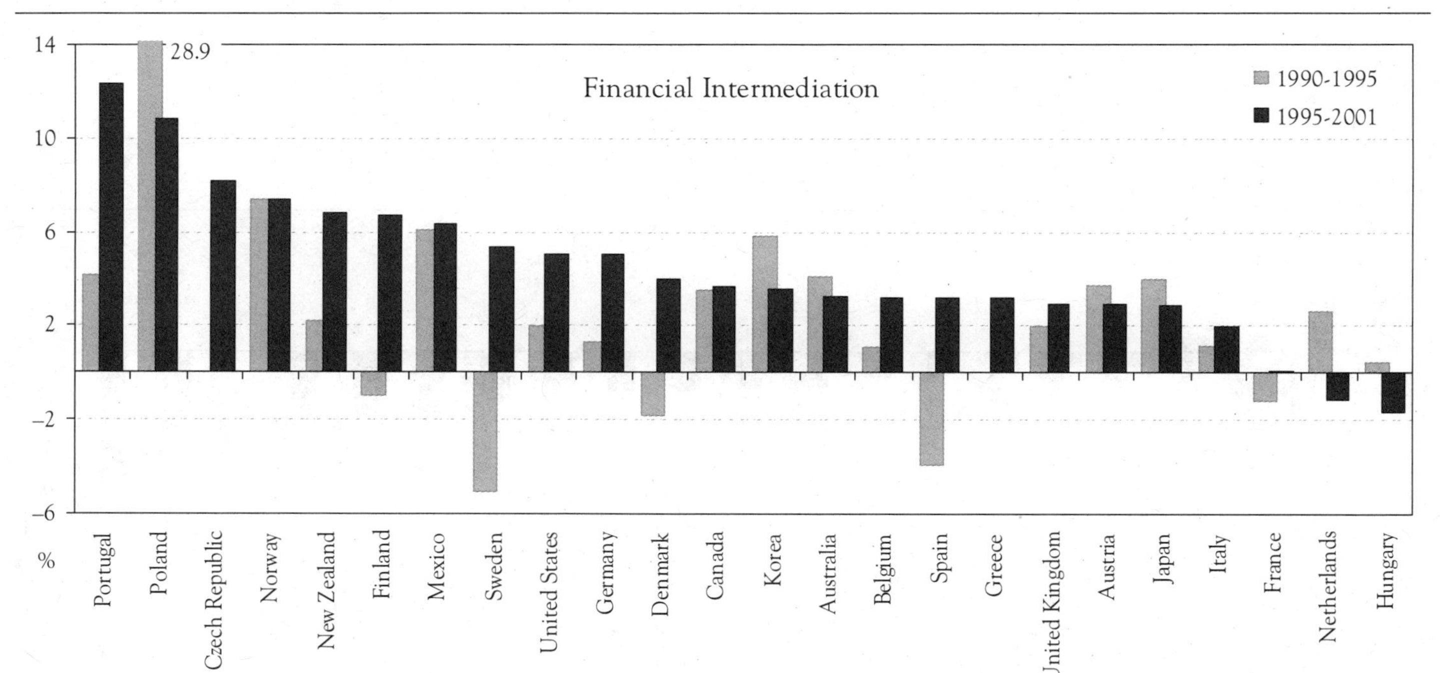

FIGURE 3A CONTINUED

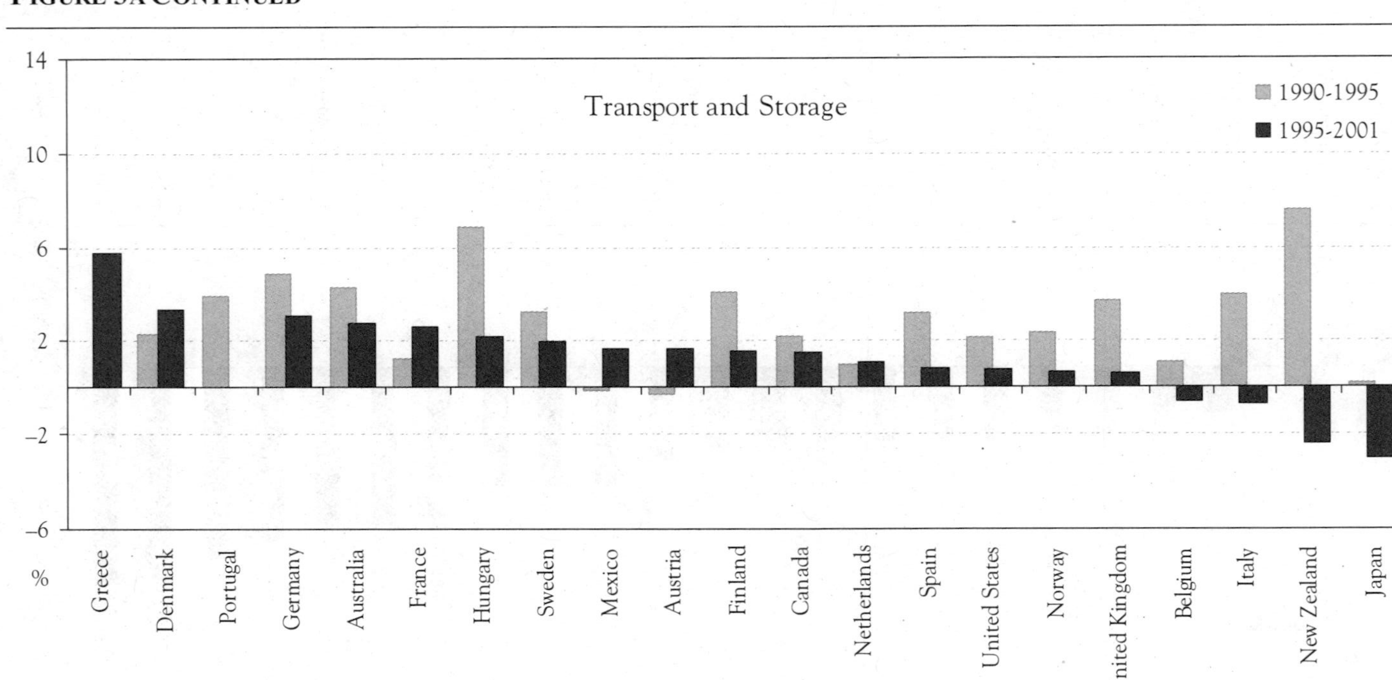

FIGURE 3A CONCLUDED

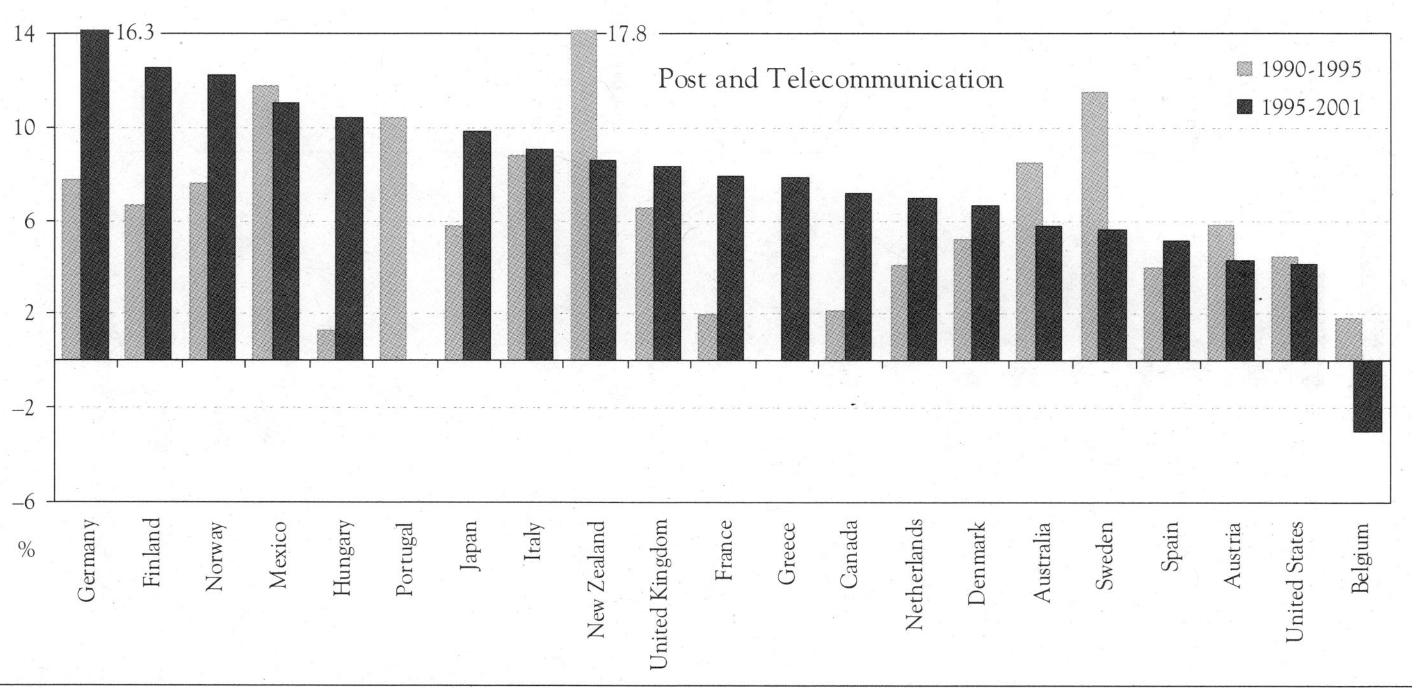

Source: OECD STAN Database 2003.

FIGURE 3B

LABOUR PRODUCTIVITY GROWTH IN SERVICES — INDUSTRIES WITH RELATIVELY WEAK GROWTH (ANNUAL AVERAGE GROWTH RATES, IN PERCENT)

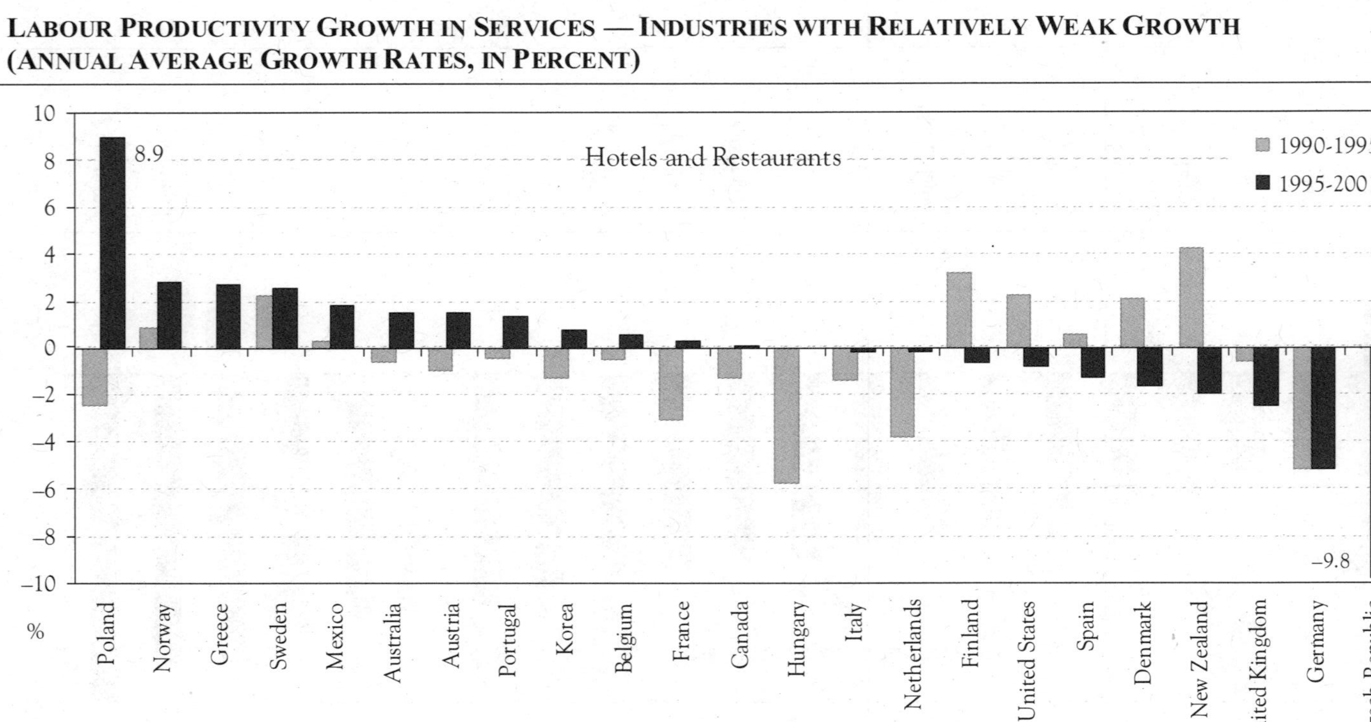

FIGURE 3B CONTINUED

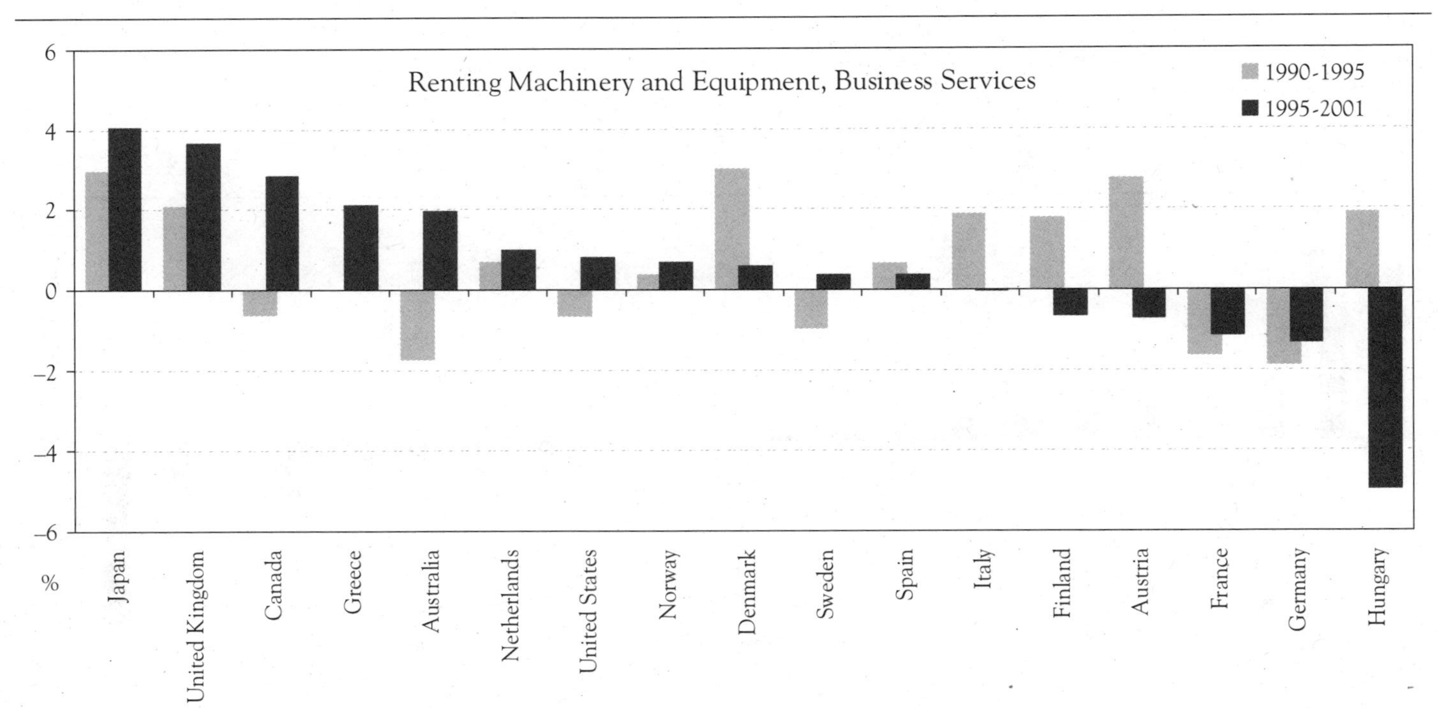

FIGURE 3B CONTINUED

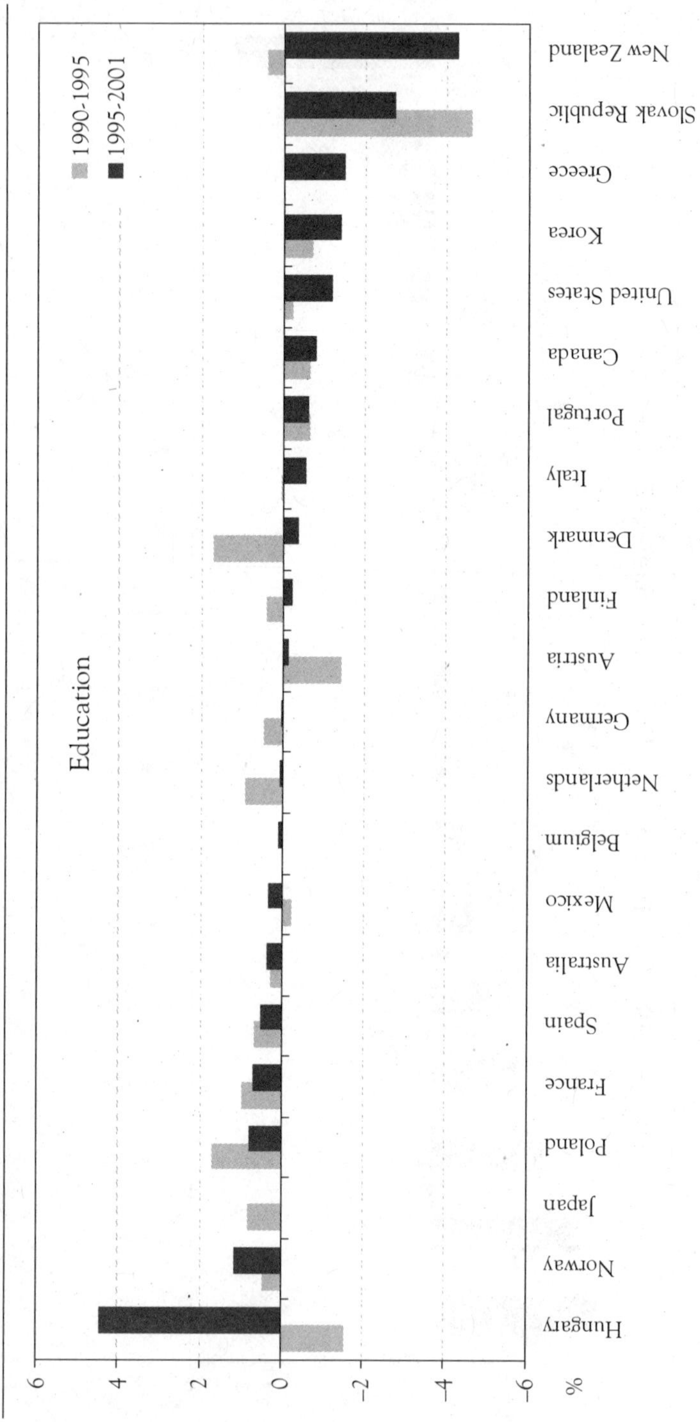

FIGURE 3B CONCLUDED

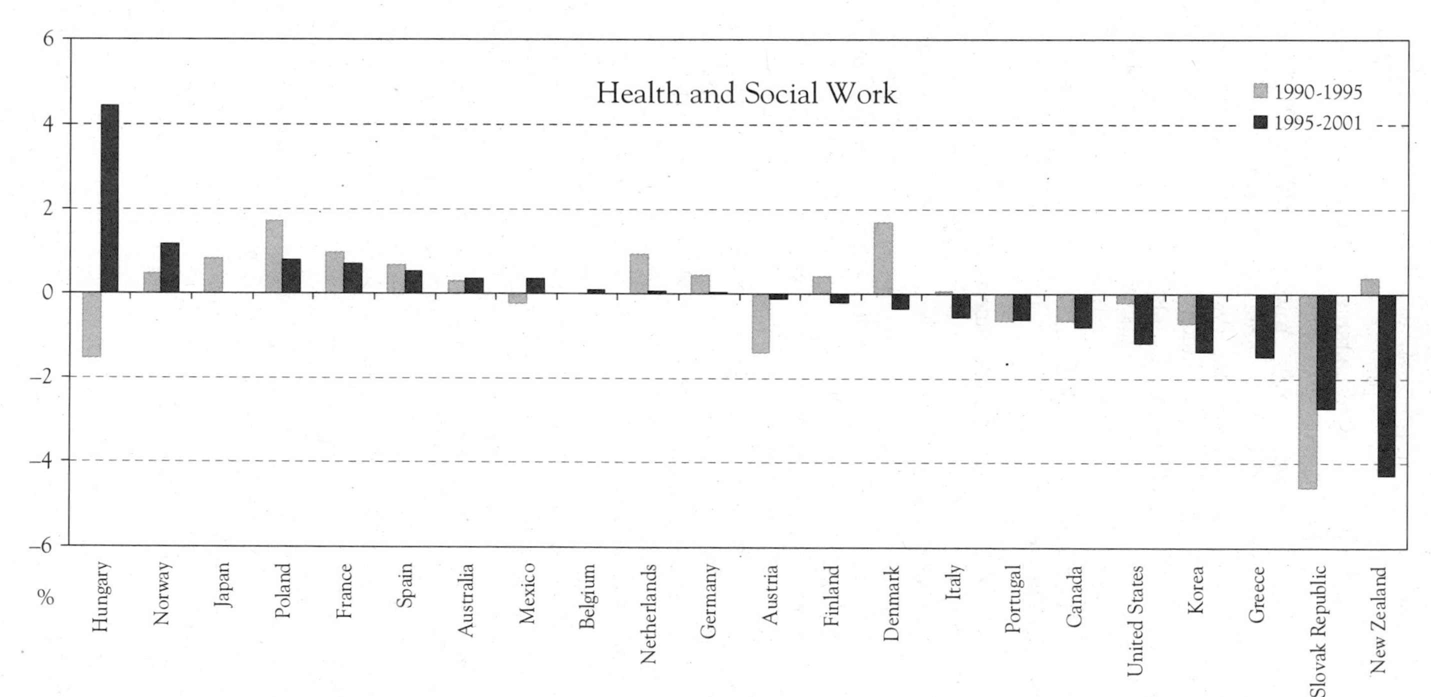

Source: OECD STAN Database 2003.

Finally, several services industries show a large variation in productivity growth over time.[4] This is especially the case for wholesale and retail trade, and in some countries, for hotels and restaurants. For instance, Japan and France showed relatively high productivity growth in the 1980s in wholesale and retail trade but only relatively low productivity growth rates in the 1990s. In contrast, countries such as Norway and the United States had low productivity growth in the 1980s but improved strongly over the 1990s. Moreover, Figure 3 shows that several industries have had negative productivity growth over long periods. This is especially the case for hotels and restaurants, renting of machinery and equipment and business services, as well as for education, health and social work.

THE CONTRIBUTION OF SERVICES INDUSTRIES TO AGGREGATE PRODUCTIVITY GROWTH

WHILE SOME SERVICES INDUSTRIES have experienced high productivity growth, this does not imply that these high-growth industries have also contributed strongly to aggregate productivity growth. Figure 4 shows that in many OECD countries, the manufacturing sector — and not services — still accounted for the bulk of aggregate productivity growth between 1995 and 2001. This is also because in many cases, high productivity growth in certain services is offset by low or negative productivity growth in other services industries, such as social services or hotels and restaurants, which in some countries make up a relatively high share of value added (Wölfl 2003). This has particularly been the case in Korea, Norway and Austria, and to a lesser degree in Finland. In Belgium and Canada, and to some degree also in the Netherlands, the contributions of high growth services industries, such as finance and business services or transport, storage and communications were almost fully balanced by the negative contributions of social and personal services, and of trade, hotels and restaurants.

In some OECD countries, however, the contribution of the services sector to overall productivity growth has increased during the past 10 years. This is true for the United States, Australia, Finland, Germany, the United Kingdom and Japan, and the contribution may increase even more in the future.

In these cases, aggregate productivity growth can be attributed to high-growth services industries such as finance, insurance and business services, as well as transport, storage and communications. A detailed examination of the data summarized in Figure 4 shows that these high-growth services contributed about 1 to 2 percentage points, i.e., about one-third, to aggregate productivity growth between 1995 and 2000 in several OECD countries, and their relative contributions increased in the late 1990s (Wölfl 2003).

In addition, as shown above, the share of services in total value added increased continuously since the 1970s in almost all OECD countries and amounted to about 60 to 80 percent in 2000. Thus by aggregation, an increase in productivity growth in services by about 1.1 percentage points would be sufficient to achieve a 1 percentage point increase in aggregate productivity growth. To achieve an equivalent increase in aggregate productivity growth, the manufacturing sector would have to realize productivity growth of about 4.7 percentage points.[5]

FIGURE 4

CONTRIBUTIONS TO AGGREGATE LABOUR PRODUCTIVITY GROWTH, 1995-2002* (IN PERCENTAGE POINTS)

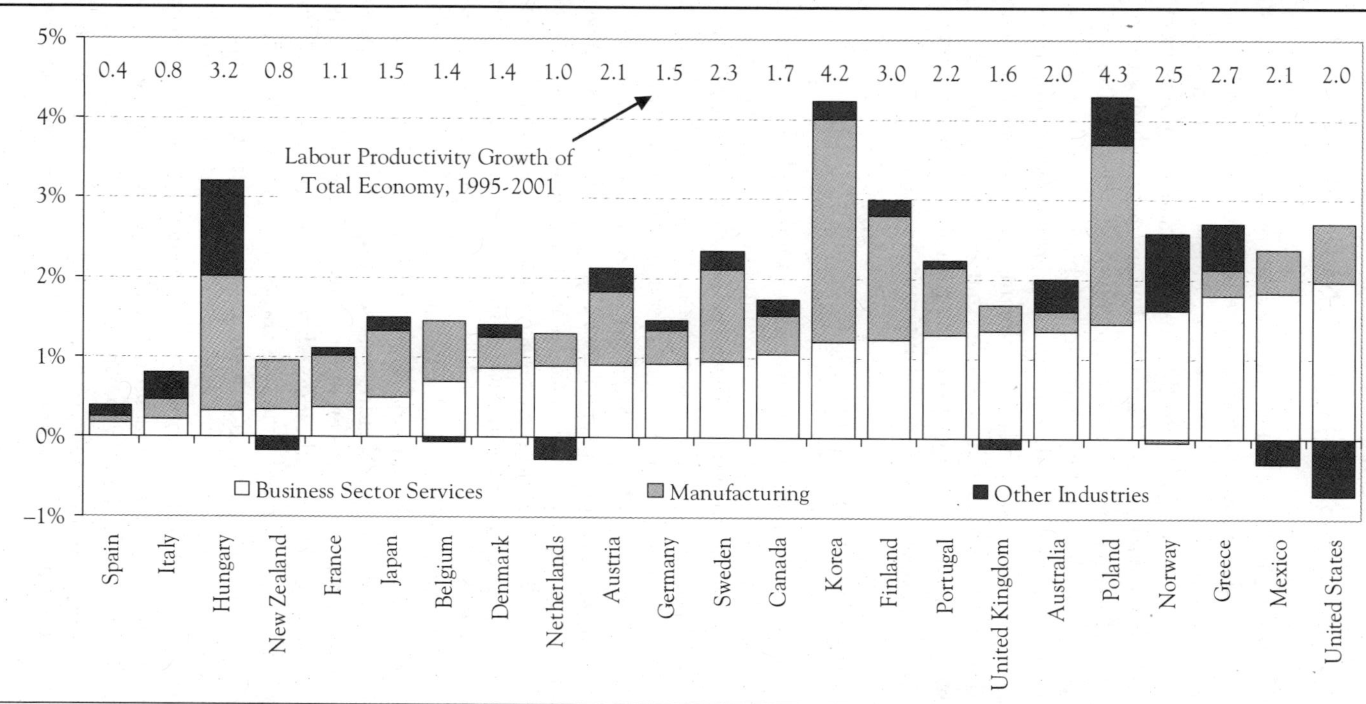

Note: * or nearest year available.
Source: OECD STAN Database 2003, Scoreboard 2003.

Productivity Growth and the Specific Characteristics of Services Industries

FROM A POLICY POINT OF VIEW, the key question is how cross-industry differences in productivity growth rates arise and how they can be addressed in order to achieve higher growth in aggregate productivity. An important issue in this context is whether the relatively poor performance of the services sector is due to specific characteristics of services that are not conducive to productivity growth. Services are, for instance, often perceived to be less intensive in their use of physical or human capital and to be characterized by the prevalence of small firms. They are also thought to be more protected from international competition than are many manufacturing industries. By contrast, growth theory and empirical evidence have shown that economic growth is driven precisely by these factors, i.e., investment in physical and human capital, technology and innovation, competition and enterprise creation.

The Role of Physical Capital

FIGURE 5 SHOWS the ratio of capital stock to total employment in selected services industries relative to the respective ratio in the overall economy.

It suggests that the intensity with which an industry uses physical capital in its operations has some impact on cross-industry differences in productivity growth. Transport, storage and communications services, for instance, have a very high capital-to-labour ratio relative to the overall economy for most of the OECD countries for which data on capital stock are available. These industries also show strong productivity growth rates. In addition, Figure 5 shows an increase in the capital to labour ratio in most services industries, especially in financial services which is one of the industries where there are strong increases in productivity growth over time. The capital-to-labour ratio is, however, not the sole determinant for productivity growth. In the case of wholesale and retail trade, for instance, the capital-to-labour ratio is only one fourth of the level of the economy as a whole, and it is much higher in social services than in trade services. In both, trade and social services, however, productivity performance is relatively low.

A different picture prevails, if one differentiates among assets. Figure 6 uses the example of the United States to show that services industries use ICT-related capital to a larger degree than do manufacturing industries. In 2001, ICT capital in services industries amounted to an average of about 15 percent of total capital, while it amounted to an average of about 5 percent across manufacturing industries. In addition, the share of ICT capital in services had increased significantly since 1995, whereas in manufacturing, the rise was less steep. A particularly strong use of ICT capital relative to total capital can be observed for business, education and financial services, as well as wholesale and retail trade.[6]

FIGURE 5

RATIO OF PHYSICAL CAPITAL TO TOTAL EMPLOYMENT OF BROAD SERVICES INDUSTRIES

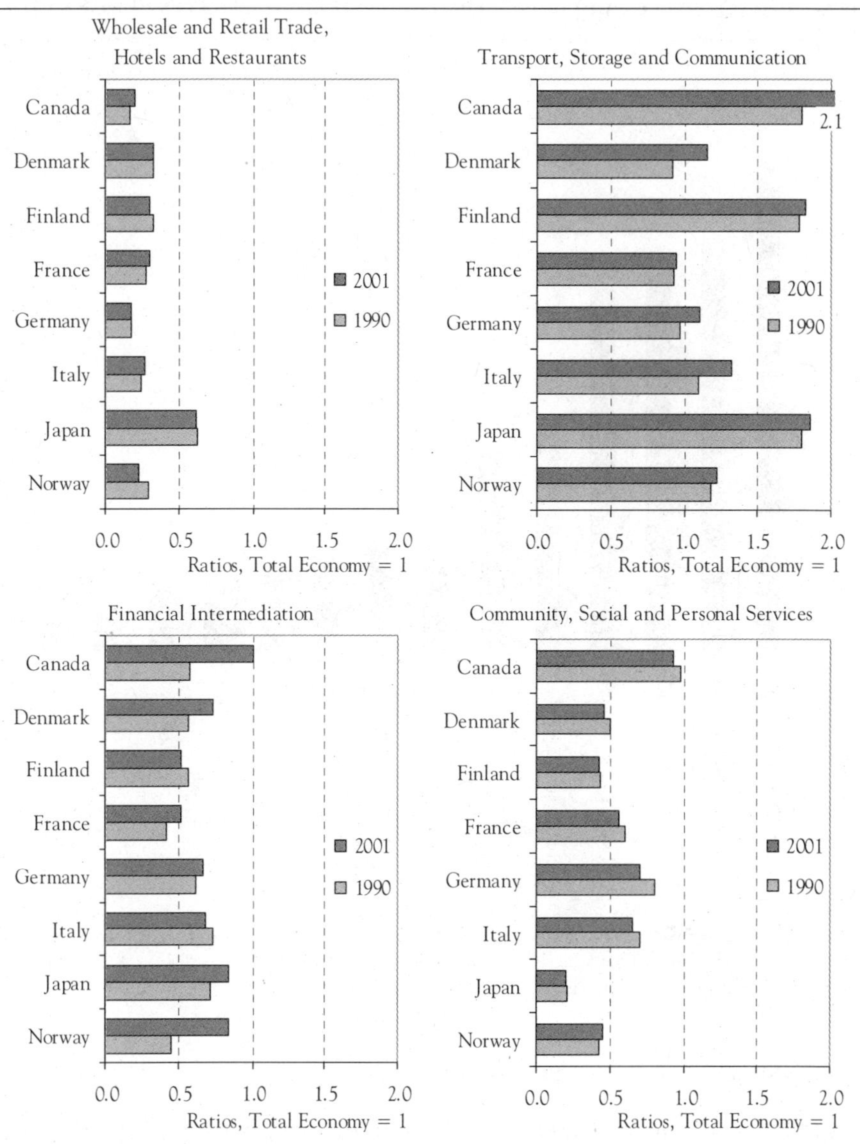

Note: Capital stock in constant-prices per total employment, relative to the total economy.
Source: OECD STAN Database 2003, selecting countries for which data on capital stock were available.

FIGURE 6

ICT CAPITAL STOCK AS A PERCENTAGE OF TOTAL STOCK OF MACHINERY AND EQUIPMENT FOR THE UNITED STATES (IN PERCENT)

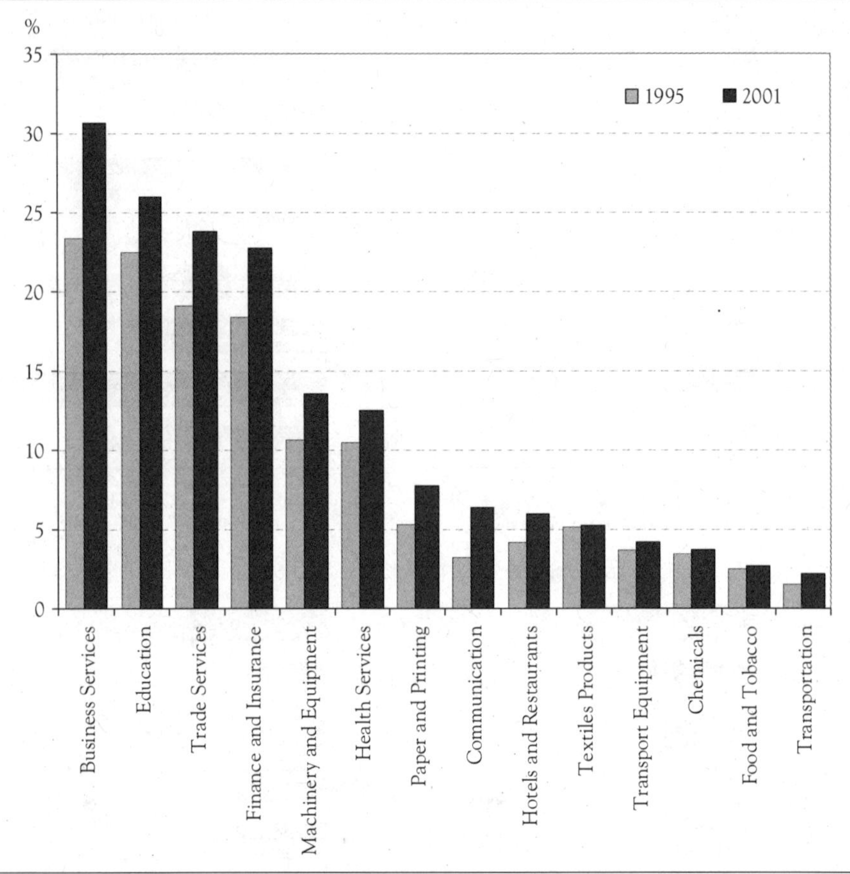

Note: The graph shows estimates by the U.S. Bureau of Economic Analysis of the net stock of ICT capital related to the total stock of machinery and equipment.

Source: U.S. Bureau of Economic Analysis, 2002.

THE KNOWLEDGE-INTENSITY OF SERVICES

FIGURES 7 TO 9 SHOW that services are not necessarily low-technology industries. In some OECD countries, according to Figure 7, services industries account for between 20 to 30 percent of overall business research and development (R&D); and in several countries this share has increased strongly since 1991. An especially prominent share of services in business R&D can be observed in Norway,

Australia, Spain, Denmark and the United States, while services account for only about 10 percent of overall business R&D in countries such as Japan, Germany, France and Sweden. While the high share of services industries in total R&D in some countries may partly reflect improvements in measurement, services do indeed increasingly perform R&D — albeit with cross-industry differences in the extent and the process of innovation. For instance, consultant, communication and financial services are more innovative than services such as social and personal services or hotels and restaurants; a similar difference could be observed with regards to productivity performance. In addition, the shift from R&D performed by manufacturing toward R&D performed by services may reflect increased outsourcing of R&D from manufacturing companies to firms that specialize in providing R&D services.

Undertaking a high share of R&D within an industry does not necessarily make it a high-technology industry. Innovations depend also on the competencies that are available within a firm or economy. Figure 8 shows that the share of highly skilled persons in total employment is higher in the services than in the manufacturing sector for all European countries for which data were available.

FIGURE 7

SHARE OF SERVICES INDUSTRIES IN BUSINESS R&D (IN PERCENT)

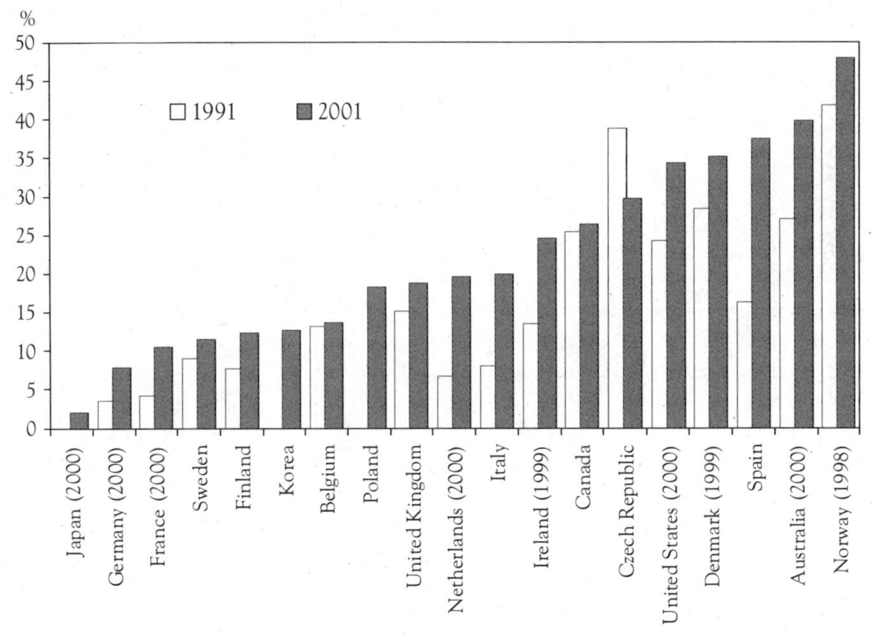

Note: The services sector covers ISIC classes 50-99 (see note for Figure 1).
Source: OECD, Analytical Business Enterprise Research and Development (ANBERD) database 2003.

Especially high shares of skilled persons can be found in financial intermediation, as well as in renting of machinery and equipment and other business services, and to a lower but still substantial degree in some social services, notably education and health services. These cross-industry differences in skill-intensity are also reflected in earnings differentials across industries (OECD 2001b); earnings are relatively high in some producer services and some social services as compared with manufacturing industries.

In addition, productivity growth in some services industries may result primarily from the use of knowledge that is embodied in intermediate goods or technologies. For example, services industries are strong users of ICT that increases productivity ICT (OECD 2003b). A notable example is Australia, which does not have a strong ICT-producing sector: it is the services sector in Australia that uses ICT technologies to achieve strong aggregate productivity growth. To take another example, as a means of making sales and purchases, the Internet has a stronger role in some services industries than it does in the manufacturing sector, and this is in line with empirical evidence from firm-level studies (OECD 2003a). The Internet is especially important for the wholesale

FIGURE 8

SHARE OF HIGHLY SKILLED EMPLOYMENT IN TOTAL EMPLOYMENT PER SECTOR, 2002 (IN PERCENT)

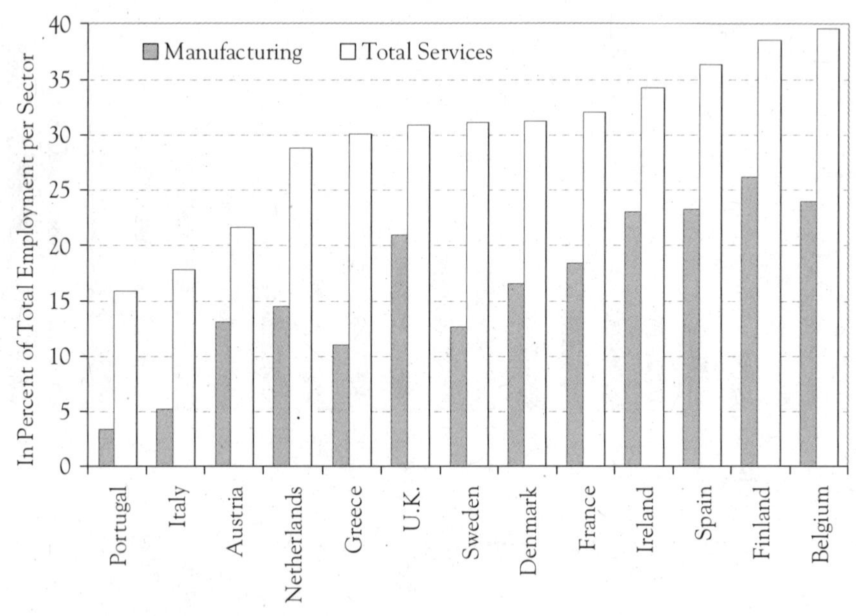

Note: The services sector covers ISIC classes 50-99 (see note for Figure 1).
Source: OECD, Labour Force Survey 2003.

and retail trade sector where it is used for sales and purchases by an average of about 50 percent of firms across all OECD countries for which data are available (OECD 2003b).

THE SIZE OF SERVICES FIRMS

THERE IS NO CLEAR ANSWER to the question of how the size of services firms can be used to explain low productivity growth in services industries. Figure 9 shows that the distribution of firm size is more skewed towards small firms in the services sector than it is in manufacturing. This is the case for all countries for which data are available. In comparison with manufacturing firms, a smaller

FIGURE 9

FIRM SIZE STRUCTURE OF THE SERVICES AND THE MANUFACTURING SECTORS (SHARE OF FIRMS PER SIZE GROUP AS A PERCENTAGE OF ALL FIRMS PER COUNTRY, AVERAGE 1997-2000)

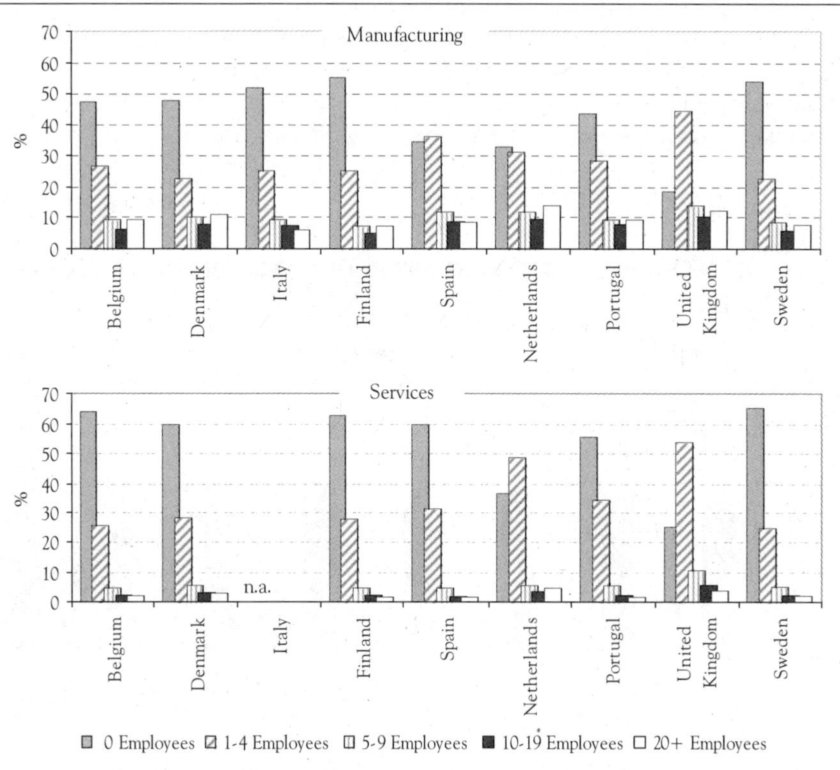

Notes: n.a. = not available. The services sector covers ISIC classes 50-99 (see note for Figure 1).
Source: OECD, Eurostat 2003, Brandt (2004).

percentage of services firms have more than five employees. Differences between manufacturing and services are especially large for single-person firms.

The observed distribution of firm sizes can have two possible and opposite effects on productivity growth. On the one hand, the small size of services firms may reflect markets that are open to entry and exit. Ease of entry may impose a (potential) threat to all firms and may thus indirectly induce productivity increasing activities by incumbent firms.[7] For example, the rate of firm entry is significantly higher in services industries than it is in manufacturing industries. On the other hand, strong productivity growth may not emerge if small firm size weakens the potential for firm growth over the long term. For instance, firm-level evidence shows that several services firms stay small over a long time period while manufacturing firms grow. One factor constraining growth might be that there are few opportunities to exploit economies of scale. This would be the case if the market were not big enough to support expansion. Such a situation may be more likely for services industries, notably those focused on domestic or regional, rather than international, markets.

SERVICES AS USERS AND PROVIDERS OF INTERMEDIATE INPUTS

FIGURES 10 TO 12 illustrate the potential increase in the importance of the services sector for aggregate productivity growth, both because of its weight in total value added and because of the interdependencies between services and manufacturing industries. Figure 10 shows that if total final demand for services

FIGURE 10

CHANGE IN OUTPUT WITH INCREASE IN DEMAND FOR SERVICES, 1997 (IN PERCENT)

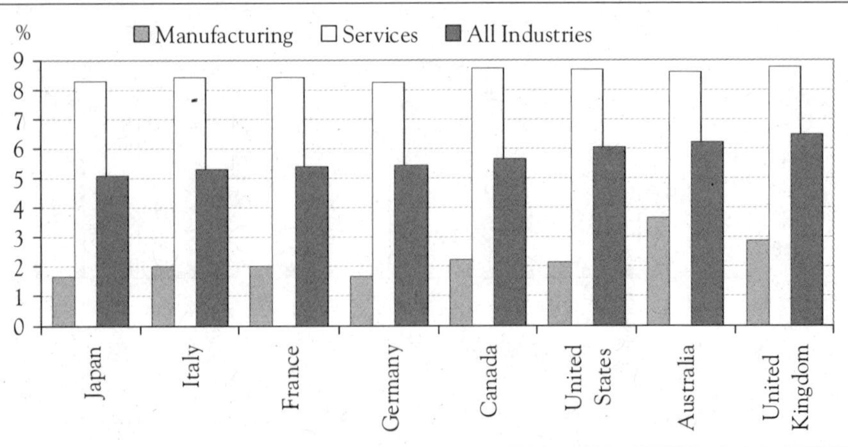

Notes: Italy: 1992; Australia, Germany, France, United Kingdom: 1995.
Source: OECD input-output tables.

increased by 10 percent while total final demand for manufacturing goods stayed constant, total output would increase by an average of about 5.5 percent across the sample countries. In contrast, if total final demand for manufacturing increased by about 10 percent leaving services demand constant, total output would only increase by an average of about 3 percent (Figure 11). This result may largely relate to the size of the services sector which accounts for an average of about 60 to 70 percent of total output across these countries. Due to aggregation effects, an increase in the output of the services sector raises total output more than an equivalent increase in manufacturing output.[8]

Figures 10 and 11 reveal that the effects of demand increases also depend on the interdependencies between the manufacturing and services industries. An increase in total demand for manufacturing by 10 percent, leaving demand for services unchanged, would increase total output of services by about 1 percent on average across the sample countries (Figure 11). It would raise the output of other industries within the manufacturing sector but would leave output in the services industries relatively unchanged. The opposite is true in the case of services (Figure 10). An increase in services demand by 10 percent, leaving demand for manufacturing unchanged, would raise manufacturing output by an average of about 2 percent across the sample countries. This may reflect the fact that services are strong users of intermediate inputs and technologies such as ICT. An increase in demand for services would have a strong effect on the output of manufacturing industries, especially for medical and precision instruments as well as for office and accounting machinery manufacturing in several countries.

FIGURE 11

CHANGE IN OUTPUT WITH INCREASE IN DEMAND FOR MANUFACTURING, 1997 (IN PERCENT)

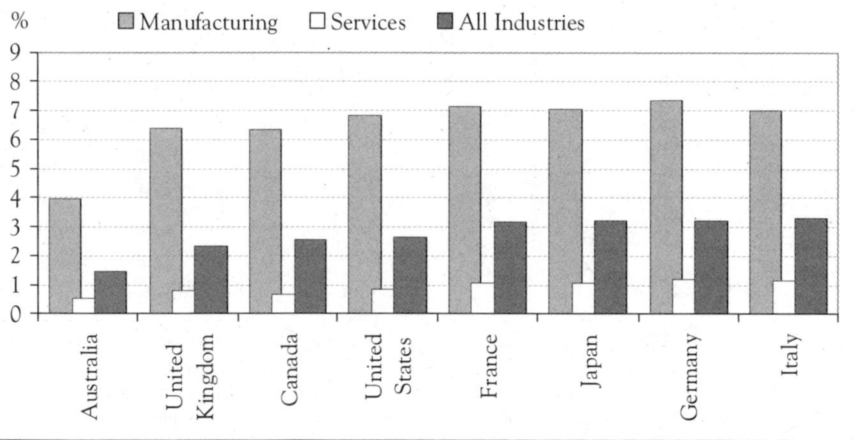

Notes: Italy: 1992; Australia, Germany, France, United Kingdom: 1995.
Source: OECD input-output tables.

Figure 12 illustrates the interdependencies between manufacturing and services industries on an industry-level, using Japan as an example. It shows the effect of a 10 percent increase in final demand for motor vehicle manufacturing, wholesale and retail trade and health and social work on the output of selected industries. Figure 12 suggests that the effect of an increase in demand for services on the output of other industries may be ascribed to certain specific industries. In the case of Japan, these are wholesale and retail trade, hotels and restaurants, transport and storage, and health and social work. For instance, an increase in demand for both wholesale and retail trade as well as health and social work would strongly increase the output of several manufacturing industries, especially industrial chemicals, rubber products, medical and precision instruments and motor vehicles manufacturing.

FIGURE 12

CHANGE IN OUTPUT WITH INCREASING DEMAND — INDUSTRY-LEVEL EVIDENCE FOR JAPAN, 1997 (IN PERCENT)

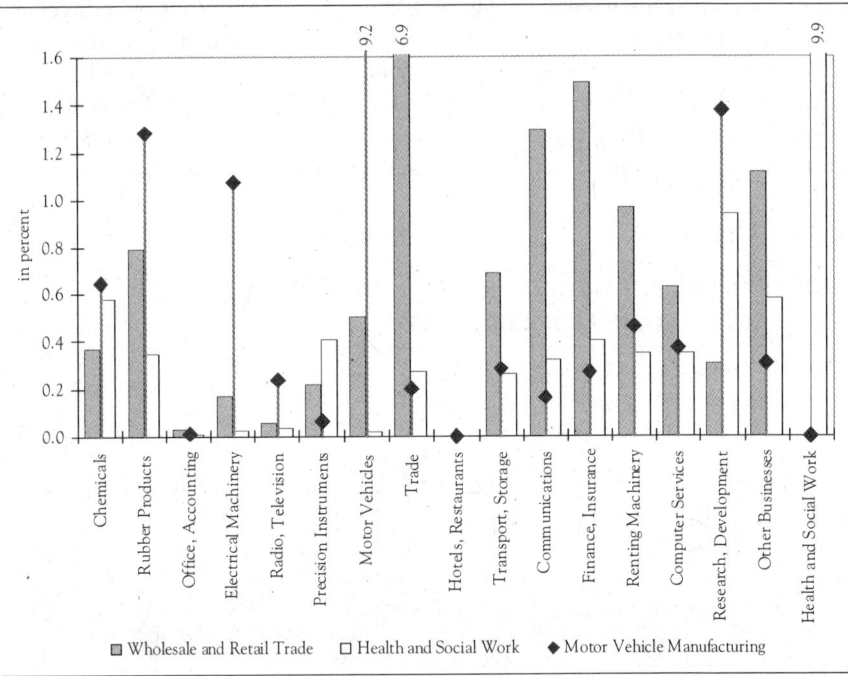

Note: Change in output of selected industries resulting from a 10 percent increase in total final demand for wholesale and retail trade, health and social work, or motor vehicles manufacturing. For example, if total final demand for motor vehicles manufacturing increased by 10 percent, output in R&D services would increase by 1.4 percent.

Source: OECD input-output tables for Japan, 1997.

Figure 12 suggests also that services industries increasingly contribute indirectly to aggregate productivity growth through the provision of intermediate inputs. This may either happen via the outsourcing of specific services from manufacturing to specialized business-related services firms, such as those providing R&D services, or by using specific services to improve the management of manufacturing production, for example through the use of just-in-time delivery or modular production. An increase in total final demand for motor vehicle manufacturing, for instance, would increase output in other manufacturing industries especially rubber products and electrical machinery manufacturing. It would, however, also increase output in services such as renting of machinery and equipment and computer-related services. A particularly strong effect would be observable for the output of research and development services: an increase of 10 percent in total final demand for motor vehicles manufacturing would increase the output of R&D services by about 1.4 percent.

Figure 13 shows that services are also not always focused on domestic markets for final demand. The services sector consists of relatively heterogeneous industries with regards to the relative importance of intermediate and final goods production.

The traditional view of services is still shaped by community, social and personal services where about 80 percent of all output is aimed at final consumption most of which is accounted for by government consumption.[9] Only about 10 percent of such services are for intermediate demand. Transportation, storage and communication services present a different picture. The demand structure for this services industry group is similar to manufacturing industries, as is its pattern of productivity growth. On average, more than half of transport and communications services are used as intermediate inputs while the share of services in final demand is relatively low, accounting for about 20 percent. Finance, insurance, real estate and business services are also characterized by a very high share of intermediate goods production as part of total gross output. The increasing exposure to international markets also has to be taken into account. In smaller countries such as the Netherlands, Denmark or Norway, exports account for about 30 to 40 percent of total production. One reason may be the increasing number and quality of modes by which services can be traded. This includes cross-border supply, consumption from abroad as in the case of tourist services, or establishing a commercial presence through affiliates or the presence of natural persons.

FIGURE 13

SHARE OF INTERMEDIATE AND FINAL DEMAND IN GROSS OUTPUT OF BROAD SERVICES INDUSTRIES (IN PERCENT)

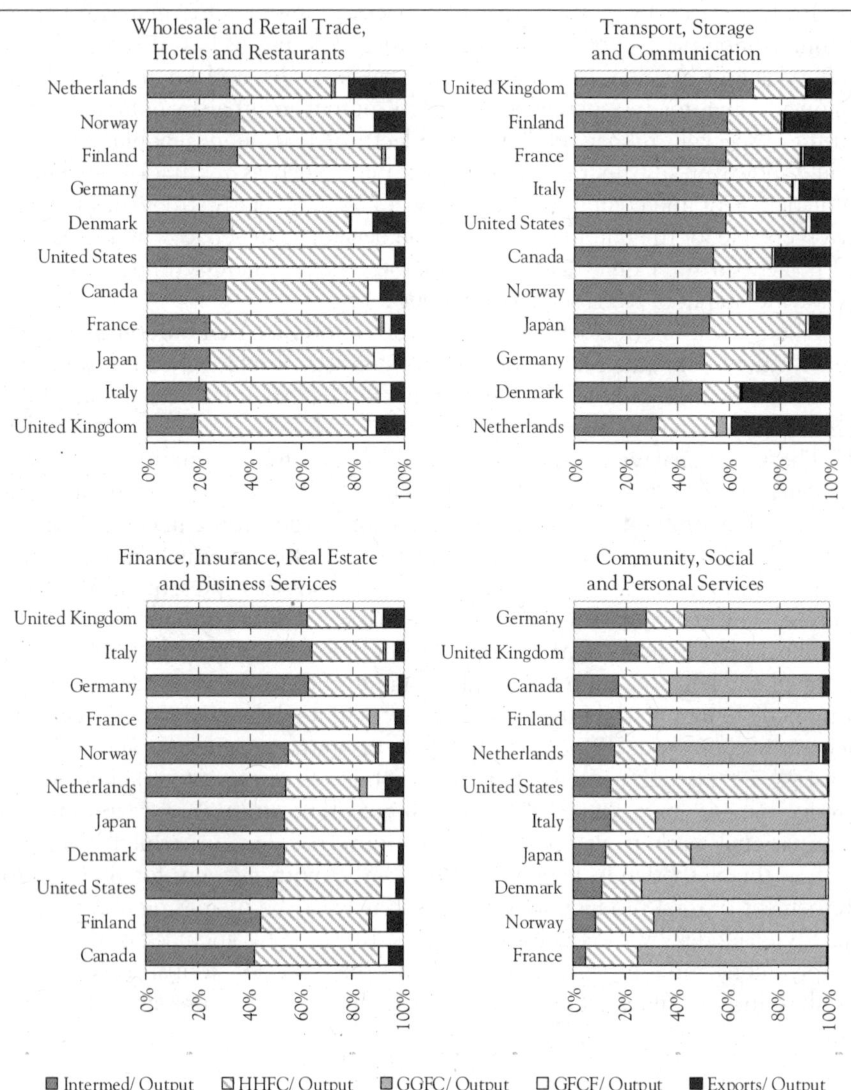

Notes: The services sector covers ISIC classes 50-99. Total output is composed of intermediate goods, household goods (HHFC), government goods (GGFC), capital formation (GFCF) and exports.

Source: OECD input-output tables, 1995, 1997.

THE ROLE OF MEASUREMENT

THE EMPIRICAL EVIDENCE presented above points to low or negative productivity growth rates over long periods for several services industries, despite other evidence, such as rapid technological change and increased competitive pressures that might argue for an opposite trend. The evidence may, however, be linked to underestimation of services productivity growth. Moreover, inadequate measurement of output or prices of services that are used as intermediate goods might lead to underestimation of aggregate productivity growth. The effect of different measurement biases on the measurement of aggregate productivity would depend on the importance of the mis-measured services industries to other industries and to overall production. This section analyzes how measurement bias might influence industry and aggregate productivity growth. It considers what is meant by 'bias in measuring services labour productivity growth', whether there is evidence for underestimation of services productivity growth due to measurement bias, and the possible impact of a measurement bias in services industries on aggregate productivity growth.

MEASUREMENT BIAS – SOME PRIOR CONSIDERATIONS

AS DEPICTED IN FIGURE 14, there are three areas where measurement biases may arise. These relate to the choice of inputs, the choice of outputs at current and constant prices, and to the method of aggregation across industries. These channels result from breaking down labour productivity growth, based on value added, into its main components. For present purposes, labour productivity growth based on value added is defined as the rate of change of value added at constant prices per unit of labour input. And growth in value added is defined as the weighted difference between growth in constant-price gross output and intermediate inputs, with the current price shares of value added and intermediate inputs in gross output as weights.[10]

The first component of measurement bias relates to the choice of inputs. In the case of labour productivity growth, this means measuring the primary input, labour, in terms of the total number employed or total hours worked. One main potential source of measurement bias in the labour input, especially in cross-country comparisons, arises from differences in definitions or in data collection or in other methodological aspects of how estimates are arrived at for employment and hours worked. These problems may differ across industries, especially for the measurement of hours worked, if it involves issues such as the treatment of part-time labour. Some empirical illustrations are presented below.

Another issue arising from the choice of inputs is the relationship between labour input and intermediate input. This is particularly relevant because of the increasing tendency of firms toward outsourcing. Measurement problems might, in particular, arise indirectly via the input-output flow of goods and services. As will be shown below, measurement bias influences the productivity growth of industries through the share of difficult-to-measure intermediates such as financial services, through total intermediates, and through the way the constant-price value added of these services industries is estimated.

The second measurement component relates to the choice of output at current and constant prices. This component of measurement bias has elicited the most discussion in the context of services productivity growth. The most relevant issue is the computation of constant-price value added. It is, for instance, difficult for several services to isolate the price effects that are due to changes in the quality or mix of services arising from pure price changes, and to adjust for such quality changes in the price index. Several manufacturing industries also present challenges in estimating an appropriate price index but there are reasons for assuming that measurement problems may be more serious in the services sector than in manufacturing. One such area is how to define the output of specific services industries. Empirical evidence and common practice in statistical offices also suggest that there is a lack of information from which to

FIGURE 14

BREAKDOWN OF LABOUR PRODUCTIVITY GROWTH INTO ITS MEASUREMENT COMPONENTS

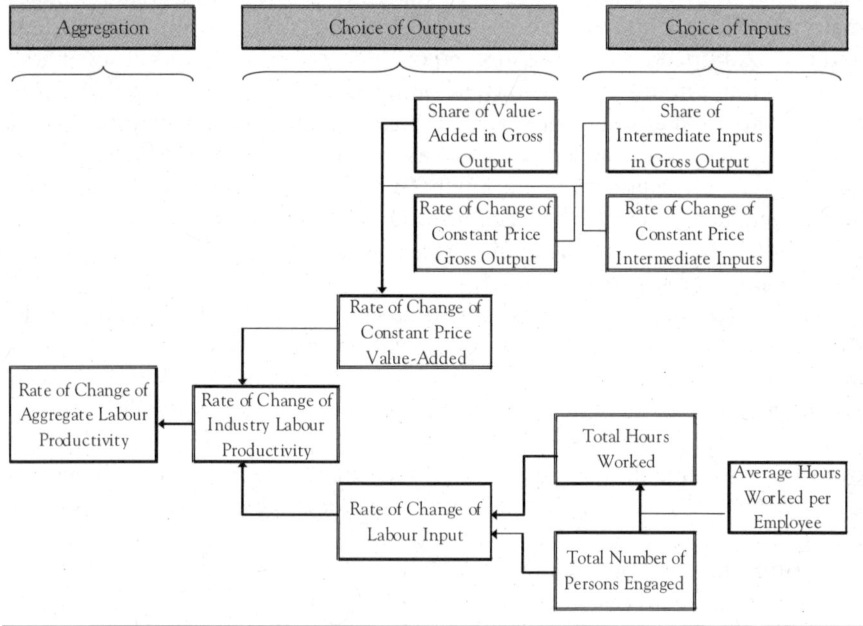

Note: For a more formal analysis or labour productivity growth and its measurement components, see OECD (2001a).

Source: OECD.

estimate price indexes in services such as health care, telecommunications, computer-related services and personal services.

As a result, different OECD countries use different measures for the computation of constant-price value added (Wölfl 2003). In general, there are three methods. One, constant-price value added can be estimated by deflating current-price value added with a price or wage index. Alternatively, base-year value added can be extrapolated using a volume index. Two, either deflation or extrapolation may be based on a single- or a double-indicator method. In that respect, the recommended procedure is the use of double deflation (or double extrapolation), where output and intermediate input are each deflated by the most appropriate index. Three, deflation or extrapolation may be based on output or input variables such as a gross output price or volume index as compared to an index of wage rates or employment. Some empirical evidence will be presented below.

The third component of potential measurement bias relates to the estimation of aggregate productivity growth. There are two main channels through which a measurement bias in services might work through to the aggregate level. The first channel is via aggregation and is related to the relative weight that is attributed to the mis-measured services in total value added and employment for the economy. The second channel concerns the role of specific services as intermediate inputs for other industries. This has implications for the question of whether productivity growth is under-estimated for services as compared to manufacturing or, alternatively, productivity growth is overestimated for manufacturing as compared to the services industries.

The following sections present results from an empirical analysis of the extent and the impact of measurement bias for labour productivity growth. This follows the breakdown into the three main components of measurement bias described above. The discussion looks at those issues that can be addressed through cross-country or sectoral analysis, notably the measurement of labour input and computation of constant price value added, as well as the possible impacts of these measurements on aggregate measures of productivity growth. This quantitative analysis will provide, to the extent possible, a tool to diagnose key areas of measurement problems in services themselves, and the channels through which sectoral measurement problems influence aggregate productivity growth.

EMPLOYMENT OR HOURS WORKED

FIGURE 15 PRESENTS the results of cross-country comparisons of labour productivity growth between 1990 and 2000 whereby labour productivity is measured either as value added per person employed or value added per hour worked. Figure 15 compares the effect of different measures of labour input on the estimation of labour productivity growth for manufacturing and services.[11] For several countries, there are relatively small differences between labour productivity growth per person employed and per hour worked across countries and sectors. Differences range between 0.1 percent and 0.3 percent for both manufacturing and services. In general across all countries, the absolute difference between productivity growth in manufacturing and services is larger if productivity growth is measured per person employed than if it is measured per hour worked. For Canada, for instance, Maclean (1997) shows that the differences between manufacturing and services productivity growth were particularly high between 1962 and 1971 if productivity growth was measured per hour worked as opposed to per person employed. The period was one in which hours worked declined rapidly in the services sector.

Measurement has an important impact on these findings. Adjustment for hours worked is thus of considerable importance in measuring and comparing productivity growth at the sectoral level, although data constraints currently do not allow this for many countries. For the countries and industries for which data have been available, working hours are in general lower and declining in the services sector while they are relatively high and, in some countries, increasing in

FIGURE 15

LABOUR PRODUCTIVITY GROWTH PER PERSON EMPLOYED AND PER HOUR WORKED IN MANUFACTURING AND SERVICES, 1990-2000 (COMPOUND ANNUAL GROWTH RATES)

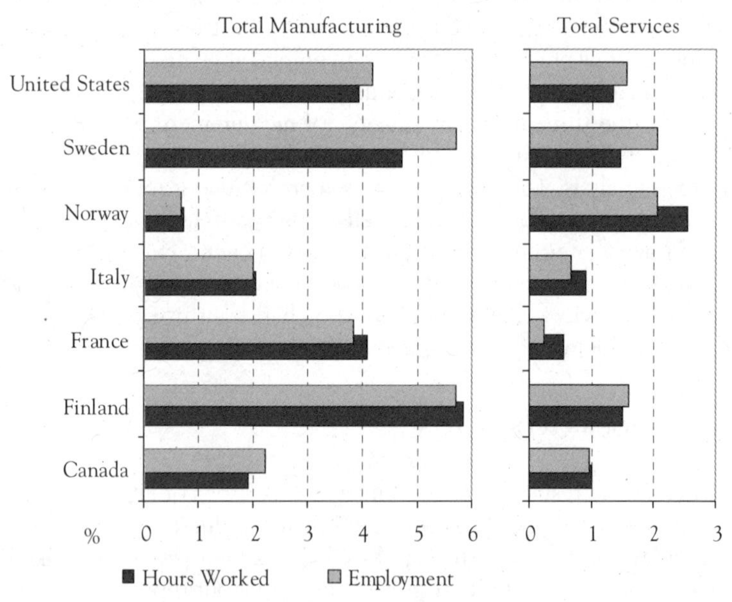

Note: The services sector covers ISIC classes 50-99.
Source: OECD STAN Database 2002.

the manufacturing sector (Wölfl 2003). Average working hours per employed person range between 1,300 and 1,700 hours per year in the services sector and between 1,500 and 2,000 hours per year in manufacturing.[12] Average hours worked are lowest in personal and social services and highest in transport and communications services, and financial and business services.

Adjustment for hours worked is particularly important because of cross-industry and cross-country differences in shares of self-employed persons and part-time work. Since such workers do not have regular working hours, measuring them is difficult and may not be comparable across industries and countries. OECD (2001b), for instance, showed that the incidence of part-time jobs was much higher in services than in manufacturing. Part-time jobs constitute a particularly high share of all jobs in personal and social services and in retail trade. Figure 16 shows that even though it is decreasing, self-employment is a much higher share of total employment in services than in manufacturing industries. It shows also that the level and development of self-employment as a share of total employment differs across countries.

The source of data for hours worked also affects comparability of estimates of hours worked. For example, the labour force surveys that are the main source of information on hours worked may overestimate hours worked by self-employed workers. Differences in the share of self-employed workers and other possible differences across sectors in the measurement of hours worked may, therefore, affect the comparison of productivity growth across sectors. This may also lead to greater uncertainty in estimates of productivity growth in the services sector than in the manufacturing sector.

FIGURE 16

SHARE OF SELF-EMPLOYED PERSONS AS A PERCENTAGE OF TOTAL EMPLOYMENT (IN PERCENT)

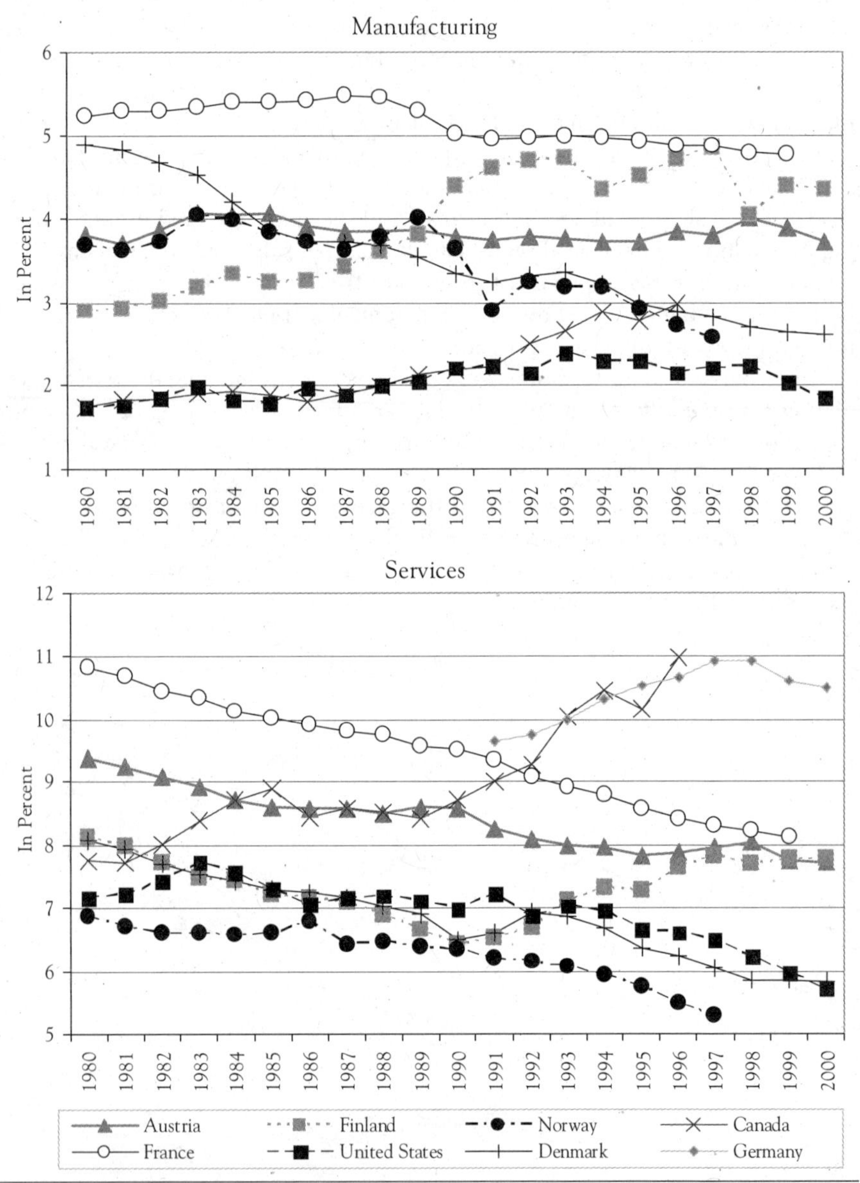

Note: The services sector covers ISIC classes 50-99.
Source: OECD STAN Database 2002.

THE COMPUTATION OF CONSTANT PRICE VALUE ADDED AND PRODUCTIVITY GROWTH IN SERVICES

AS DISCUSSED ABOVE, it is more difficult for services than for manufacturing to identify output clearly and to divide current-price time series into volume and price components. One indication of this difficulty is in the large variety of implicit deflators for identical industries across countries, notably in wholesale and retail trade, transport and storage services, post and telecommunications, and in financial services (Figures 17 and 18). Country-specific factors, such as the pattern of overall economic development, regulatory reform and the role of competition may all affect this diversity. However, it is also likely to reflect the broad variety of methods that are used by different OECD countries in services where there is no standard measure of constant-price value added (Wölfl 2003).

Problems in measuring constant-price value added directly influence the rate of productivity growth derived using those measurements. In health services, for instance, most OECD countries use information on labour input as the only available indicator to derive constant-price value added. However, such input-based methods cannot grasp changes in the quantity and quality of

FIGURE 17

IMPLICIT DEFLATORS OF VALUE ADDED FOR WHOLESALE AND RETAIL TRADE SERVICES (INDEX, TOTAL ECONOMY = 100)

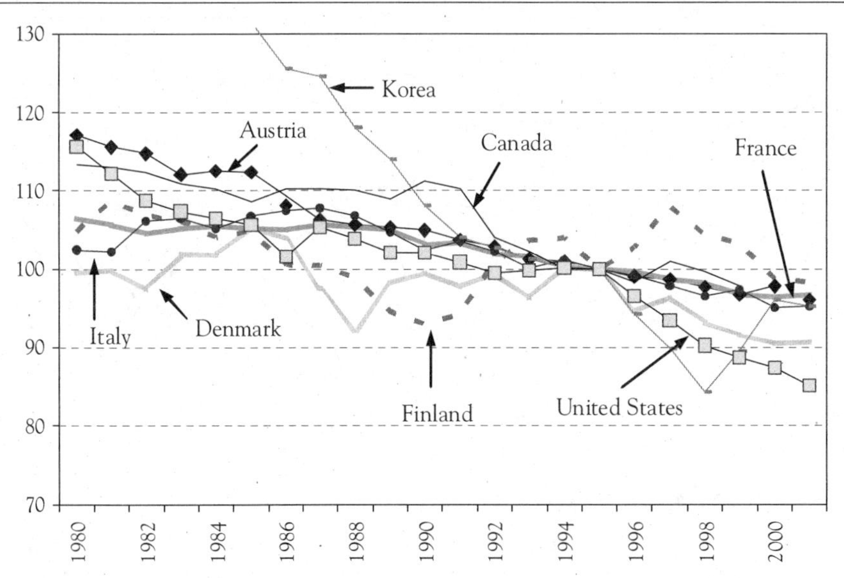

Note: Base year: 1995, index of constant-price value added rebased to 1995 for Finland and Canada.
Source: OECD STAN Database 2003.

output, and typically presume zero productivity growth. In wholesale and retail trade (Figure 17), statistical practice usually assumes a direct relationship between the services provided and the volume of sales. Constant-price value added is computed by deflating retail margins, using the volume of sales or the sales price index as a reference (Ahmad, Lequiller, Marianna, Pilat, Schreyer, and Wölfl 2003). Such a treatment, however, ignores changes in the quality of distribution services that are not associated with the volume of sales. Such changes might include enhanced convenience or the tailoring of services to specific needs. Moreover, the volume measure of distribution as computed in current practice would change in line with the sales price, which serves as a proxy for volume measures of distribution services. This would also be the case if the sales price of the good sold changes due to a change in the quality of the good sold. However, this direct link between the volume of distribution services and the price or the quality of the good sold does not necessarily exist.

Measurement problems also reduce the comparability across countries of productivity growth estimates. Large cross-country differences in the price index can be found, for instance, in post and telecommunications services. This

FIGURE 18

IMPLICIT DEFLATORS OF VALUE ADDED FOR FINANCIAL INTERMEDIATION SERVICES (INDEX, TOTAL ECONOMY = 100)

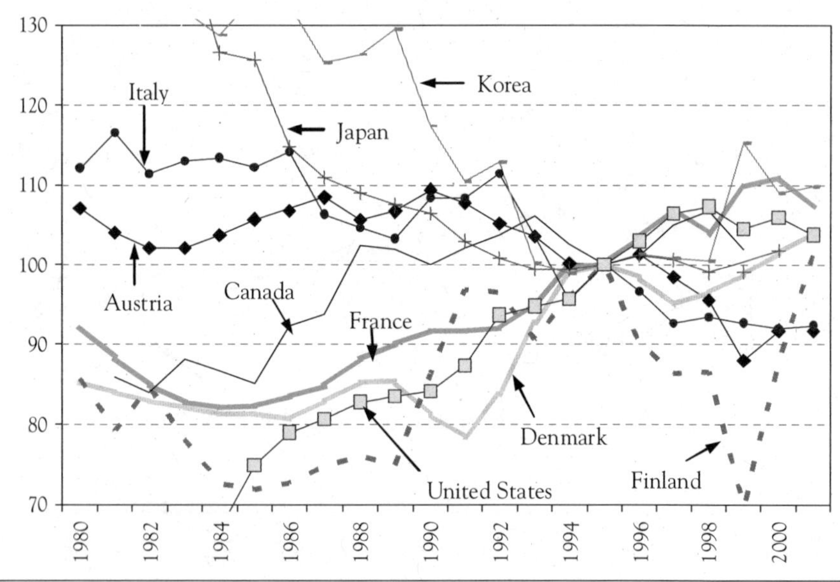

Note: Base year: 1995, index of constant-price value added rebased to 1995 for Finland and Canada.

Source: OECD STAN Database 2003.

is primarily due to the difficulty of finding an appropriate quality-adjusted price index.[13] Another example is financial services (Figure 18). Although the basic approach to measuring the production of financial services is similar across OECD countries, there are, for instance, differences in the degree to which financial services are considered intermediate purchases by other industries or final purchases by consumers (Ahmad et al. 2003). In addition, in countries where no adequate indicator of volume exists, the value of financial services is deflated by applying base-period interest margins to the inflation-adjusted stock of assets and liabilities. This approach does not take account of quality changes and may not sufficiently track the volume of transactions.

Figure 19 illustrates that the method used to compute constant-price value added directly affects the development of value added and, therefore, productivity growth per industry. The influence of measurement is examined by calculating how the time series of value added would develop if various alternative methods to compute constant-price value added were used. The example provided is taken from Denmark since time-series data are available for a whole range of input and output variables, allowing for the calculation of several different price and volume indices.[14]

FIGURE 19

SCENARIOS OF VALUE-ADDED INDICES USING ALTERNATIVE METHODS TO COMPUTE CONSTANT-PRICE VALUE ADDED — DENMARK

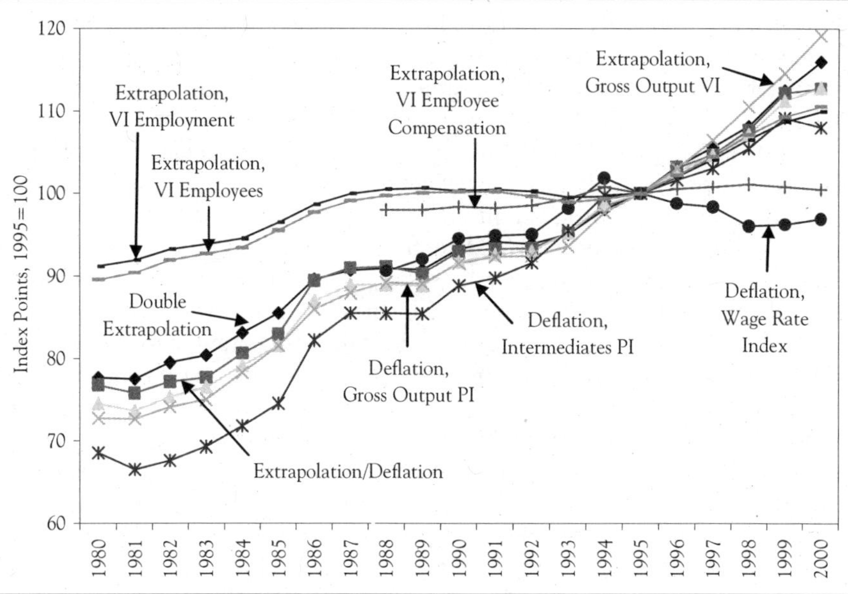

Note: VI denotes volume index, PI price index.
Source: OECD STAN Database 2002.

MEASUREMENT BIAS IN SERVICES AND ITS IMPACT ON AGGREGATE PRODUCTIVITY GROWTH

THE PRECEDING ANALYSIS HAS SHOWN that measurement bias in services industries might lead to underestimation of productivity growth in some services industries. What follows will consider whether this sort of underestimation of productivity growth in services industries might lead to estimates of slower aggregate productivity growth. The effect of measurement bias in services on aggregate productivity growth is analyzed using a Slifman-Corrado type of thought experiment.[15] This examines what would happen if negative productivity growth rates were not negative but set to zero. Such a thought experiment is primarily intended to show the potential size of the problem. It does not suggest that negative productivity growth necessarily implies mis-measurement, nor does it suggest that the size of the adjustment made in the present study is the correct one.[16] However, such a thought experiment does provide an initial picture of the extent of potential underestimation of productivity growth in industries with services inputs. It can be regarded as a diagnostic tool to examine key areas for measurement problems.

There are two possible indirect effects of mis-measurement on the productivity growth reported for the whole economy. As long as the services industry under consideration produces mainly for final demand, the increase in real output due to a correction for measurement bias would lead to an increase in the productivity growth reported for this industry.[17] Through aggregation across industries, this adjustment would eventually raise aggregate productivity growth. However, if the services industry for which real output is underestimated mainly produces for intermediate production, the increased output leads to higher growth in the value of intermediate inputs that are used by other industries. All other things equal, productivity growth in these industries would be lower, which might limit the effect of an increase in productivity growth in the services producing industry for which output has been adjusted. The total effect depends thus on the extent and type of measurement bias, on the share of production of the mis-measured services industry destined for intermediate demand, and on the weight as well as the productivity growth achieved in industries that produce services and in industries that use services.

Figures 20 and 21 illustrate the simulated impact of potential underestimation of services productivity growth. This simulation or "what-if experiment" is divided into three steps.[18] The first step consists of calculating the percentage change in the measure of gross output that would have been required to achieve a zero measure of productivity growth in industries where the current measure of productivity growth is negative. The second step consists of using input-output tables to estimate the effect that this percentage change in the measure of gross output would have on the growth rate of intermediate inputs of the other industries. The final step is to calculate the adjusted measures of growth in value added and, thus, productivity growth rates by industry and for the whole economy.

FIGURE 20

EFFECT ON INDUSTRY AND AGGREGATE PRODUCTIVITY GROWTH WHEN NEGATIVE SERVICES PRODUCTIVITY GROWTH RATES ARE SET TO ZERO — GERMANY AND FRANCE (IN PERCENT)

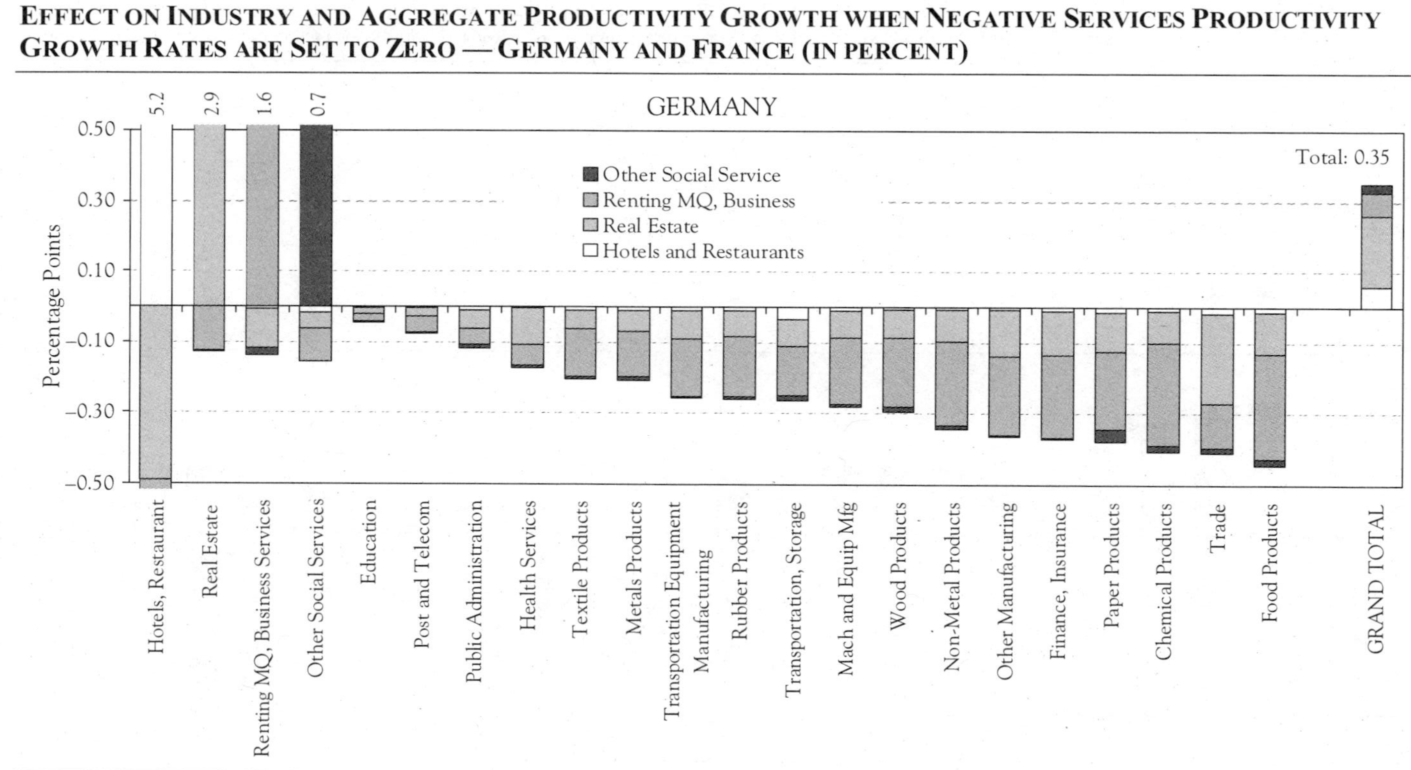

FIGURE 20 CONCLUDED

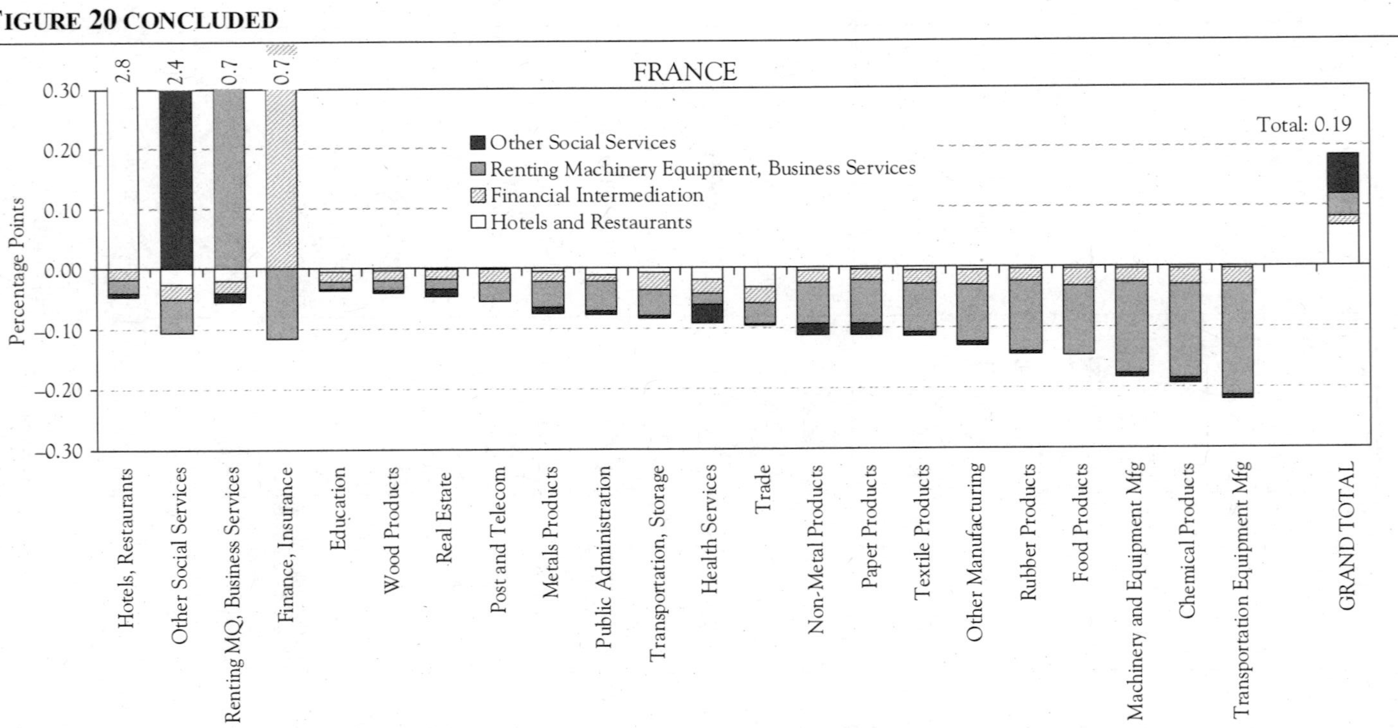

Note: The industries are ranked according to the total effect, if all negative services productivity growth rates are set to zero.

Source: OECD STAN Database 2002, input-output tables 1995, 1997.

FIGURE 21

EFFECT ON INDUSTRY AND AGGREGATE PRODUCTIVITY GROWTH WHEN NEGATIVE SERVICES PRODUCTIVITY GROWTH RATES ARE SET TO ZERO — THE UNITED STATES (IN PERCENT)

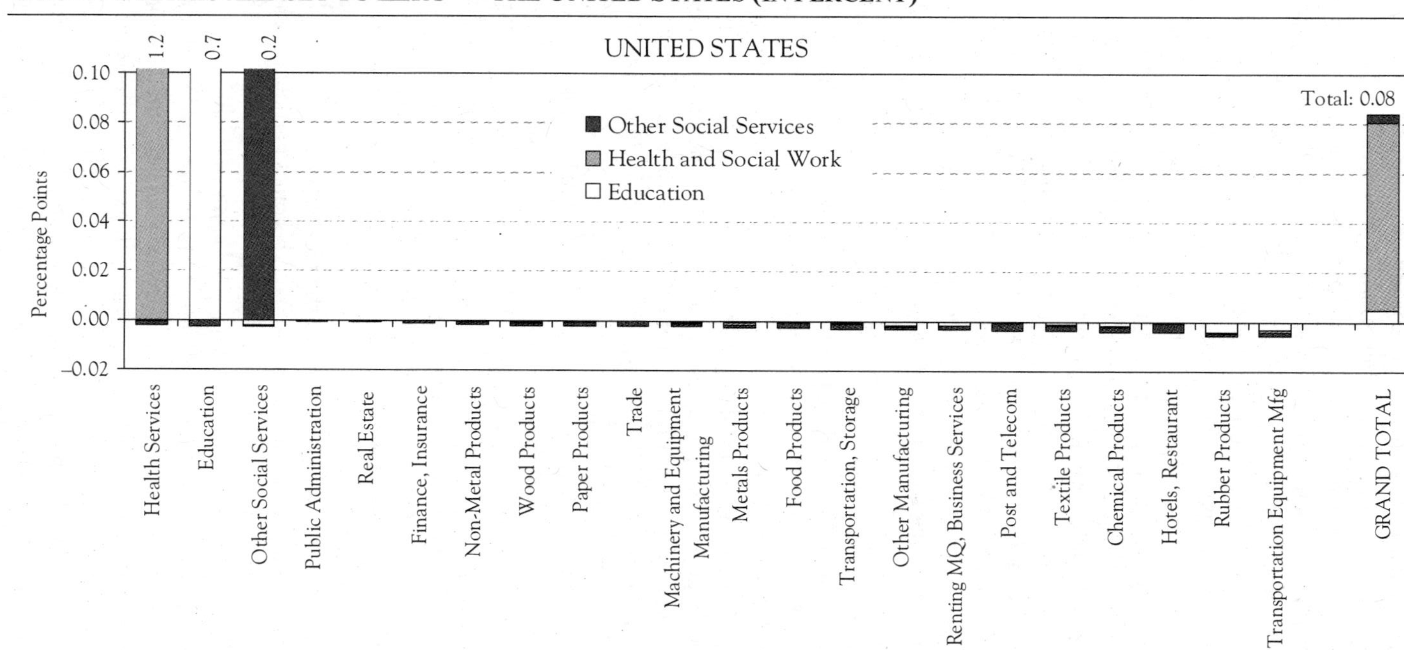

Note: The industries are ranked according to the overall effect, if all negative services productivity growth rates are set to zero.
Source: OECD STAN Database 2002, input-output tables 1995, 1997.

Because of data constraints, the analysis can only be applied to selected countries and has to be based on appropriate assumptions about the relationship between the growth rate of gross output and value added as well as intermediate input flows. The countries for which the simulation exercise is undertaken are France, Germany and the United States (Figures 20 and 21). France experienced negative productivity growth over the 1990-2000 period in hotels and restaurants, finance and insurance, renting of machinery and equipment, as well as other social services. In the United States, services with negative productivity growth rates are education, health and social work and other social services. In Germany, hotels and restaurants, real estate services, renting of machinery and equipment, as well as other social services experienced negative productivity growth over the 1990-2000 period. Since these services industries have a considerable weight in the economy and differ in the degree to which they produce for final or intermediate demand, the simulation for these three countries can provide a broad set of conclusions concerning the direct and indirect impacts of mis-measurement in services industries on aggregate productivity growth.

Two main results arise from this analysis. First, the effect on industry and aggregate productivity growth depends on the extent of the measurement bias. In the case of Germany, output growth had to be adjusted more than in France in almost all industries with negative productivity growth. Aggregate productivity growth would increase by about 0.35 percentage points in Germany as compared to 0.19 percentage points in France. Second, the effect depends on the share of production of each mis-measured services industry that is destined for intermediate demand. There seems to be almost no effect on the measured productivity growth of other industries arising from a correction for hotels and restaurants, a services industry that produces primarily for final demand. In contrast, a correction for services such as renting of machinery and equipment, financial intermediation or real estate, would ripple across all industries, since these services industries mainly produce for intermediate demand. For instance, a correction in renting of machinery and equipment in Germany would reduce measured productivity growth in other industries by about 0.1 to 0.2 percentage points, since intermediate inputs would grow more rapidly than initially measured and output growth would thus be lower.

The relevance of both the extent of the measurement bias and the degree of production destined for intermediate demand becomes particularly clear in comparing the results for France and Germany with those for the United States (Figure 21). First, the upward revision of the productivity growth rate for all services under consideration is lower in the United States than in France or Germany. Also, as a result, the change in the productivity growth rate of all industries is lower. Second, the services where the United States showed negative productivity growth rates at this level of aggregation are education, health and social work as well as other social services. As mentioned above, these industries produce mainly for final demand and only to a small extent for intermediate production.

Both factors together might explain the relatively small impact of a correction for measurement bias on productivity growth in other industries and in aggregate for the United States as compared to France or Germany.

Overall, the thought experiment presented here suggests that the principal impact of possible mis-measurement might be a shift in the attribution of productivity growth to specific sectors of the economy. This could imply a greater contribution to total productivity growth of services sector industries characterized by mis-measurement, and a smaller contribution of other sectors, including manufacturing. The impact on aggregate productivity growth is not clear, *a priori*, but the results for Germany, France and the United States suggest that strong positive effects on services industries might be reduced by negative indirect effects on aggregate productivity growth exerted by the industries that are using the adjusted services as intermediate inputs. Therefore, the final effect on aggregate productivity growth might be relatively small.

CONCLUSIONS

THERE IS NO UNAMBIGUOUS ANSWER to the question of whether productivity performance in services industries may slow down aggregate growth. On an aggregate level, patterns of productivity growth suggest a large differential between a progressive manufacturing sector on the one hand and a rather stagnant services sector on the other. There are also some signs of weak productivity performance within the services sector. Productivity growth is low or negative in services industries such as social and personal services. It is even low in some business services despite the use of cost-reducing technologies. In addition, most services are still characterized by relatively low capital-intensity in comparison with other industries. Several services, notably social services as well as hotels and restaurants, are focused on domestic markets and on the satisfaction of final demand. As a result, they do not face intensive international competition. Finally, the small size of many services firms may imply that there is low potential for such small firms to grow.

Not all of the evidence is quite so compelling, however. Several services industries show productivity patterns that are typical of high-growth manufacturing industries. These include transport and communications services, financial intermediation, and, to a lesser degree, wholesale and retail trade. Some services are also characterized by a relatively high capital-to-labour ratio, they are important contributors to overall business R&D, or they use new, productivity-enhancing technologies such as ICT. In addition, the small firm size of services may reflect the easy entry and exit of firms, and this may spur productivity increasing activities by all market participants. Finally, services sectors such as financial intermediation and communication services are also strongly engaged in international competition.

There is substantial evidence that low or negative productivity growth rates in services are partly linked to problems with the measurement of services productivity growth. First, different definitions and data sources used for employment and hours worked might bias international comparisons of labour productivity growth. Second, the way constant-price value added of services is computed strongly influences the development of output or value added over time and, consequently, productivity growth by industry. Finally, there is evidence that a potential underestimation of services productivity growth could lead to an underestimation of aggregate productivity growth via the flows of intermediate inputs. The significance of this effect would depend on the type and extent of the measurement bias and the role played by the underestimated services in other industries and in the whole economy.

The empirical evidence shown in this study can give only a preliminary and rather descriptive picture of the role of the services economy and its productivity performance. There is considerable scope for additional research.

First, work could be done to include more countries in order to support a better cross-country assessment of the factors determining cross-industry differences in productivity growth as well as the interdependencies between industries and their effects on productivity growth. For example, because data is lacking, factors such as innovation, firm size and skill-intensity could not be analyzed for all countries and industries. The role of other factors, such as the intensity of competition, trade and the degree of regulation, has not been analyzed in detail. In addition, this study only barely touched on the role of changing interdependencies between manufacturing and services industries or the role of outsourcing for productivity growth.

Second, more work could be done on the measurement of productivity growth in services industries. Some countries have recently taken steps to improve the measurement of output and the OECD is working with its member countries to enhance measurements in several areas including financial services, insurance and software. Further progress would improve measures of productivity growth and enhance our understanding of the cross-country differences in productivity growth performance. This may also include work on comparing different measures of productivity growth, something that was not possible in this study because of limitations in the data.

ENDNOTES

1 OECD countries are characterized by growing incomes and ageing societies: these changes make it likely that the demand for many services will increase further in the future.

2 For more in this respect, see Baily and Gordon (1988), Fixler and Siegel (1999), Triplett and Bosworth (2002), and OECD (2003a).

3 See OECD (2001a) for a detailed description of how to measure productivity growth.
4 Strong variation over time can be observed, especially if productivity developments in OECD economies in the 1980s are also taken into account (Wölfl 2003).
5 These calculations assume an aggregate productivity growth rate of 2 percent and growth rates of 3 percent in manufacturing and 1 percent in services, and a share of 70 percent of services in total value added.
6 See OECD (2002) and OECD (2003a, b) for further indicators regarding the use of ICT by services industries.
7 See Brandt (2004) for an extensive empirical analysis of firm entry and survival.
8 These calculations are based on total-use input-output tables. The increase in total output may thus also imply an increase in imports to some degree.
9 The strong role of government consumption shows that several of these services are public goods, particularly in those countries that are characterized by strong welfare states.
10 Consistent with the whole study, the role of measurement is analyzed for labour productivity growth as measured by growth in value added per labour input. The *OECD Productivity Manual* provides an extensive description of measurement issues (OECD 2001a). For a short discussion of measurement of services output and productivity, see Kendrick (1985). See Wölfl (2003) for an overview of previous empirical studies.
11 The countries examined are those for which data on employment and hours worked are available in STAN. In the case of Italy, productivity growth per hour worked has been calculated as value added per full-time equivalent employment due to lack of data on hours worked.
12 The numbers refer to total hours worked per person employed per year. If one assumes five weeks of annual leave and holidays, 1,700 hours per year would be equivalent to about 36 hours per week.
13 The impact of the introduction of hedonic prices for ICT-related goods on output and productivity growth has been analyzed in several studies, for example Schreyer (2001).
14 For a detailed description of the methods used, see Wölfl (2003) and OECD (1996).
15 See Slifman and Corrado (1996), Gullickson and Harper (1999, 2002), Sharpe, Rao and Tang (2002) and Vijselaar (2003).
16 While setting negative productivity growth rates to zero may overstate the size of the measurement problem, it is also possible that it understates the size of the problem. Actual or correctly-measured productivity growth rates might be substantially above zero.
17 As was indicated above, the effect on the growth rate of productivity depends on the extent of the measurement bias over time. For instance, the measurement bias might be directly proportional to the output itself and might thus increase output in such a manner that productivity growth in this industry would be the same as in the case where there is no correction.
18 See Wölfl (2003) for details on the assumptions and the procedure applied.

ACKNOWLEDGMENTS

This study benefited from comments during the Industry Canada Conference on "Services Industries and the Knowledge-Based Economy," Winnipeg, October 2003, notably Alice Nakamura. The views expressed in this study are those of the author and do not necessarily reflect those of the OECD or any of its member countries.

BIBLIOGRAPHY

Ahmad, N., F. Lequiller, P. Marianna, D. Pilat, P. Schreyer, and Anita Wölfl. 2003. "Comparing Labour Productivity Growth in the OECD Area: the Role of Measurement," STI/STD/ELS Working Paper 2003/14. Paris: OECD.

Baily, M.N. 2003. "Information technology and productivity: recent findings," presentation at the American Economic Association Meetings, January 3.

Baily, M.N., and R.J. Gordon. 1988. "The Productivity Slowdown, Measurement Issues, and the Explosion of Computer Power," *Brookings Papers on Economic Activity*, (2): 347-420.

Baumol, Wiliam J. 1967. "Macroeconomics of Unbalanced Growth: the Anatomy of Urban Crisis," *American Economic Review*, 57 (3): 415-426.

Brandt, N. 2004. "Business Dynamics in Europe," DSTI-Working Paper. Paris: OECD.

Fixler, D.J., and D. Siegel. 1999. "Outsourcing and Productivity Growth in Services," *Structural Change and Economic Dynamics* (10): 177-194.

Gullickson, W., and M.J. Harper. 1999. "Possible Measurement Bias in Aggregate Productivity Growth," *Monthly Labor Review*, February.

———. 2002. "Bias in Aggregate Productivity Trends Revisited," *Monthly Labor Review*, March.

Kendrick, J.W. 1985. "Measurement of Output and Productivity in the Service Sector," in R.P. Inman (ed.) *Managing the Service Economy, Prospects and Problems*. Cambridge: Cambridge University Press, pp. 111-133.

Maclean, D. 1997. "Lagging Productivity Growth in the Service Sector: Mismeasurement, Mismanagement or Misinformation," Working Paper 97-6. Ottawa: Bank of Canada, March.

OECD. 1996. *Measuring Value-Added in Services*. Paris: OECD.

———. 2001a. *Measuring Productivity – OECD Manual, Measurement of Aggregate and Industry-Level Productivity Growth*. Paris: OECD.

———. 2001b. "The Characteristics and Quality of Service Sector Jobs," in OECD *Employment Outlook*, pp. 89-128.

———. 2002. *Measuring the Information Economy*. Paris: OECD.

———. 2003a. "ICT and Economic Growth – Evidence from OECD Countries, Industries and Firms." Paris: OECD.

———. 2003b. "STI-Scoreboard 2003." Paris: OECD.

Oulton, N. 1999. "Must the Growth Rate Decline? – Baumol's Unbalanced Growth Revisited," London: Bank of England.

Schreyer, P. 2001. "Computer Price Indices and International Growth and Productivity Comparisons," Statistics Working Papers STD/DOC (2001)1. Paris: OECD, April.

Sharpe, Andrew, Someshwar Rao, and Jianmin Tang. 2002. "Perspectives on Negative Productivity Growth in Service Sector Industries in Canada and the United States," paper presented at Workshop on Service Sector Productivity, May 17th, Brookings Institution, Washington, D.C.

Slifman, L., and C. Corrado. 1996. "Decomposition of Productivity and Unit Costs," *Occasional Staff Studies*, OSS-1. Washington, D.C.: Federal Reserve Board.

Triplett, Jack E., and Barry P. Bosworth. 2002. "'Baumol's Disease' Has Been Cured: IT and Multifactor Productivity in U.S. Services Industries," paper prepared for a Workshop on Services Industry Productivity, September, Brookings Institution, Washington, D.C.

Vijselaar, F.W. 2003. "ICT and Productivity Growth in the Euro Area: Sectoral and Aggregate Perspectives," in the proceedings of the IVIE Workshop on "Growth, Capital Stock and New Technologies", by the BBVA Foundation.

Wölfl, Anita. 2003. "Productivity Growth in Service Industries – An Assessment of Recent Patterns and the Role of Measurement," STI-Working Paper 2003-07. Paris: OECD.

Comment

Alice O. Nakamura
University of Alberta

THIS IS A COMMENTARY on the carefully researched and thought provoking 2003 OECD study titled "The Services Economy in OECD Countries — Trends and Issues" by Anita Wölfl. The first section of my comments provides a selective overview of the study. In the second section, I raise issues concerning some of the conclusions and recommendations. The final section concludes.

In the empirical part of her study, Wölfl compares labour productivity growth estimates for the services sector and manufacturing industries in different OECD countries. Wölfl makes the following points. She uses her own empirical findings and results generated by others to argue that on average, services sector industries had lower productivity growth than goods producing manufacturing industries in all OECD countries. She outlines the basic features of Baumol's Cost Disease. She then raises questions about the validity of the premises underlying Baumol's Cost Disease and about whether the stated consequences of this disease are a cause for concern among OECD countries.

Wölfl notes that conventional wisdom attributes the relatively low services sector productivity growth that has been measured to four main factors:

1. Services industries tend to be less intensive in their use of physical capital.
2. Services industries tend to engage in less knowledge accumulation.
3. Services sector firms tend to be smaller in size.
4. Services firms tend to be more focused on domestic or regional markets.

As regards the last of these points, Wölfl notes that others have inferred from this observation that services firms are exposed to less international competition as compared to the manufacturing sector firms, and thus have less need to try to improve their productivity.

Wölfl goes on to observe that concerns about low productivity growth in the services sector extend beyond just the provision of these services. There is also worry that the services sector might increasingly siphon off resources from the rest of the economy, thereby undermining the national standard of living. Wölfl explains that these worries were given formal expression and scientific credibility with the publication of a paper by William Baumol in the *American Economic Review* in 1967. That paper was the main impetus for concerns about Baumol's Cost Disease that Wölfl partially debunks: a 'disease' that has come to be viewed by many as an inherent feature of services sector industries. In Wölfl's words:

> The main idea behind Baumol's Cost Disease is that the tendency of unbalanced growth across sectors induces resource reallocation towards a slowly growing or stagnant sector, eventually slowing down aggregate growth. Baumol's views derive from the empirically-based assumption that the economy consists of two distinct sectors. The first is a growing (manufacturing) sector, characterized by technological progress, capital accumulation and economies of scale. The second one is a relatively stagnant (services) sector, consisting of services such as education, performing arts, public administration, health and social work. (See Box 1).

She then presents reasons for questioning the validity of the Baumol Cost Disease interpretation.

Wölfl notes that, in fact, not all services industries have had low productivity growth. She notes that the financial intermediation and telecommunications industries are among the exceptions to the low growth stereotype.

Wölfl also points out that there has been a great deal of investment in capital equipment in some services industries as well as a great deal of innovation and knowledge accumulation. She notes that many of these industries are characterized by the growing and significant use of knowledge embodied in intermediate inputs and in the new technologies adopted. Moreover, despite the widespread perception that services industries generally do not conduct as much formal R&D as do manufacturing industries, Wölfl notes that there is evidence that some services industries do perform a considerable amount of R&D. Indeed, the services industries as a whole account for between 20 and 30 percent of overall business R&D in OECD countries and this share has increased strongly since 1991.

Wölfl also acknowledges that the share of what is formally classified as R&D performed is not the only plausible indicator of innovativeness. She sees the share of highly skilled persons in total employment as another indication. This share is higher in the services sector than in manufacturing in all European countries for which data are available. She notes, for example, that there is a high level of skills in the social services, health services and education sectors.

On the firm size issue, Wölfl affirms that services industries do tend to be characterized by smaller firm size. She notes, however, that this need not drag down services sector productivity. She acknowledges that the smaller size of the firms in most services sector industries could mean there are few barriers to entry. The resulting higher incidence of entry and exit of firms in these industries could mean that only the most productive survive.

Wölfl's conclusions can be summarized as follows. She finds that some services industries have had relatively good productivity growth. She downplays the alleged consequences of Baumol's Cost Disease. Yet she nevertheless reports that some services industries, especially social services and education, have had very low rates of productivity growth and that these are significantly lower than those in the manufacturing industries. Alleged low productivity in some of the services sector industries has been seized on by some in the public policy arena as a basis for recommendations such as more privatization for services that are mostly delivered through the public sector, and hence where competitive forces are allegedly weak.

MEASUREMENT PROBLEMS

WÖLFL'S DISCUSSION of the conditions influencing Baumol's Cost Disease is compelling. Less persuasive is the evidence upon which she bases her conclusions about low productivity growth in services such as education. Some of these industries are ones where measurement problems are especially serious. Wrong facts can lead policy makers to adopt the wrong remedies. It may not always be better to report and consider the implications of empirical findings when the data are not adequate to support the analysis.

Wölfl herself calls attention to two specific measurement issues that are relevant.[1]

One of these is that this study and the others that it draws from rely on measures of labour productivity. Yet the measures of labour used tend to differ from one study to another. Wölfl's study focuses on growth of labour productivity as measured by value added per person employed. Differences in the distribution of hours of work for different industries and different nations are not fully controlled for. More importantly, the use of other input factors apart from labour is also not controlled for.

Many researchers have used and drawn conclusions from labour productivity measures. For example, Edwin Dean and Kent Kunze (1992a) of the U.S. Bureau of Labor Statistics (BLS) give comparative productivity results that also are based on labour productivity measures. There has also been criticism of this approach. For instance, Erwin Diewert (1992) writes:

> My first criticism is that these productivity measures are labor productivity measures and hence that they may be very imperfect indicators of changes in the industry's total factor productivity. Total factor productivity measures are much more useful than labor productivity measures....

Dean and Kunze (1992b) rebut Diewert's criticism. They note that the BLS has had an aggressive multifactor productivity measurement program. They go on to claim that: "In fact, as the bureau increases its multifactor coverage, productivity measures often reflect the trends and changes in the industry multifactor measures." They note that: "Furthermore, the labor productivity measures ... can be prepared with fewer resources and less developmental time."

However, labour productivity measures are fatally flawed for making productivity comparisons between services and manufacturing industries, or indeed between any industries where there are large differences in the use of labour as a proportion of total input and where there are differences in the growth rates for different types of input quantities. The reliance on a labour productivity measure is partly responsible for the results arrived at by Wölfl and others who have adopted similar approaches.

If we had measures of both total and labour input for all of the industries compared in the Wölfl study, then we could compute the labour share of total input for each industry and rank the industries from largest to smallest according to that labour share. Services industries such as education would surely occupy the top of that list. Such an ordered list of industries could be divided into two equal groups, the one being the industries in which labour is a higher share of total input (the top half of the list), and the other being the industries where its share is lower (the bottom half). The services industries that Wölfl reports as having lower labour productivity growth would end up in the group for which labour is a higher proportion of total input, and manufacturing industries would mostly end up in the other group.

Labour productivity growth will tend to be greater than total factor productivity growth for any industry where other input factors are important and where the quantity of those other inputs has been growing faster than the quantity of labour. Wölfl reports that the manufacturing industries have tended to invest more in capital equipment and also that employment has been growing less rapidly in those industries. These observations suggest that labour productivity will tend to overestimate total factor productivity growth to a greater degree for manufacturing than for most of the services industries.

Wölfl also mentions that manufacturing firms are increasingly outsourcing services functions. This outsourcing includes many functions that are relatively labour-intensive. If a manufacturing firm goes from carrying out a services function in-house to outsourcing it, some of the labour inputs that had been associated with this function may be transformed into non-labour inputs that will be ignored by the labour productivity measure used in this study. Thus, the trend toward outsourcing in the manufacturing industries may also have contributed to the pattern of results presented in the Wölfl study.

A second measurement issue, acknowledged by Wölfl, has to do with how output is measured for some of the social services. Productivity is usually measured as the ratio of output quantity to input quantity, or as a ratio of output quantity to the quantity of some input component such as labour in the Wölfl study.

Output is hard to measure for some services industries, such as social services and education. Sometimes measures of input are used as proxies for the level of output. But while input usage may be an indicator of output, this sort of proxy causes the measured output to move together with the measured input, so the measured productivity growth will be essentially zero, by construction.

Despite these serious measurement problems, Wölfl reports results and others may be tempted to draw policy recommendations based on them.

POLICY FORMATION GIVEN INADEQUATE DATA

GOVERNMENT, BUSINESS AND OTHER ANALYSTS face many situations where choices must be made, but the data needed to make choices informed by sound statistical evidence are not at hand. This situation introduces an auxiliary, but important, additional choice that will be considered first: whether to push for improved data. Data improvements have costs. We must ask what the best possible data would be, and what could be done with this information if we had it. We should then ask how much it would cost to get that data.

However, suppose that for now at least, the information needed to properly measure something on which important decisions hinge is simply not available. The trouble with using statistical analyses based on poor data in situations like this is that policy makers have no sensible rules of thumb for how to incorporate that information. Indeed, the qualifications stated in research reports such as those noting that the empirical conclusions are based on inadequate data, typically become detached from those conclusions once they enter the policy formation process, and the reported conclusions tend to take on lives of their own as legitimate empirical facts.

ENDNOTE

1 Other data problems plaguing services sector industry productivity estimation are discussed and documented in Griliches (1992).

BIBLIOGRAPHY

Baumol, William J. 1967. "Macroeconomics of Unbalanced Growth: the Anatomy of Urban Crisis," *American Economic Review*, 57 (3): 415-426.

Dean, Edwin R., and Kent Kunze. 1992a. "Productivity Measurement in Service Industries," in Zvi Griliches, *Output Measurement in the Service Sectors*. National Bureau of Economic Research, Studies in Income and Wealth, Volume 56. Chicago: University of Chicago Press, pp. 73-101.

———. 1992b. "Reply," in Zvi Griliches, *Output Measurement in the Service Sectors*. National Bureau of Economic Research, Studies in Income and Wealth, Volume 56. Chicago: University of Chicago Press, pp. 104-106.

Diewert, W. Erwin. 1992. "Comment," in Zvi Griliches, *Output Measurement in the Service Sectors*. National Bureau of Economic Research, Studies in Income and Wealth, Volume 56. Chicago: University of Chicago Press, pp. 101-103.

Griliches, Zvi. 1992. *Output Measurement in the Service Sectors*. National Bureau of Economic Research, Studies in Income and Wealth, Volume 56. Chicago: University of Chicago Press.

Petr Hanel
University of Sherbrooke and
Centre interuniversitaire de la recherche sur la science et la technologie

10

Innovation in the Canadian Services Sector

INTRODUCTION

SERVICES DOMINATE THE CANADIAN ECONOMY. They contribute 68 percent of gross domestic product (GDP) and employ 75 percent of total labour. Several services industries have recorded significantly faster growth rates than the manufacturing sector. The most dynamic services industries are using and benefiting from new information and communication technologies (ICT) to a greater degree than the rest of the economy. Several services industries also recorded significantly faster growth in labour productivity than business as a whole.[1]

Innovation in services is beginning to be recognized as an important source of the recent productivity surge in the U.S. economy. Services industries have played an essential role in the rapid diffusion of ICT that is bringing productivity gains not only to manufacturing industries but increasingly to essential non-production activities (Feldstein 2003).

In spite of the economic importance of the services sector, innovation and technological change in services have attracted less attention than they have in manufacturing. This is partly because of the traditional view of services as being a residual activity that is supplier-driven and lagging in innovation. The great heterogeneity of services industries does not help in changing this perception. On the one hand, there are very important differences between rapid innovation in the manufacturing sector and in the more traditional services. On the other hand, there is a growing convergence of the fast growing ICT-based services industries with high-growth manufacturing industries.

A brief history of ideas about innovation in services industries would start with a period of benign neglect of the topic altogether. This would be followed by a reluctant recognition that some technologically-progressive services industries are using selected product innovations supplied by a few high-tech manufacturing industries. Only in the last couple of years has a body of theoretical and empirical research begun to emerge that is grappling with innovation in services not as a subservient sub-specie of manufacturing innovation, but as an object of inquiry with its own distinctive features. It is still too early to predict whether this will result in a more coherent, comprehensive and universally applicable understanding of innovation, as the proponents of convergence argue, or a conceptual framework specific to services innovation that is adapted to the uncomfortable heterogeneity of this vast and important sector.

The objective of this study is to review the empirical information on the extent of innovation activities in Canadian services industries and to assess how Canada's innovation in services compares with that of its competitors.

Since innovation in services was a non-issue for a long time, and the sector is composed of very different industries, it is necessary first to introduce and discuss the concepts and measures used in assessing innovation in services.[2] The section immediately following presents an overview of concepts and measurements used to analyze research and development (R&D) and innovation in services industries together with a discussion of their limitations and problems. Next, there is an overview of innovation in the Canadian services sector. This is followed by a comparison of Canadian R&D in services with our main competitors in the United States and the European Union. The study ends with some general concluding remarks.

INNOVATION IN SERVICES — CONCEPTS, MEASURES AND STATISTICS

IN HIS INTRODUCTION TO THE COLLECTION of essays on output measurement in services, Zvi Griliches (Griliches 1992) notes that owing to their heterogeneity, the concept of services covers many activities that have little in common. In many services activities, it is not exactly clear what is being transacted, what is the nature of the output and what services correspond to the payments made to their providers. The prices are not always related to what was delivered and received by the user of the services. The outcome or output of many services not only depends on the services provider but also on the user or the consumer of the services. This is characteristic of many services that consist of exchanging or delivering information and/or applying knowledge, as is the case in technical business services.

When the output of a services industry cannot be clearly defined, how should we treat changes in this output? Because of their underlying heterogeneity, it is difficult and often impossible to make output comparisons over space and over time for some services. In many services the boundary between manufacturing activity and services activity is unclear and shifting.[3] All these questions and problems arise when we want to measure services innovations.

The emerging empirical research on innovation in services suggests that the conceptual framework based on innovation in manufacturing is missing several key distinctive characteristics when applied to services innovations:

- Much innovation in services has not been well captured by the traditional indicators of innovative inputs (R&D activities) and outputs (patents).

- R&D in services industries is often oriented to addressing specific problems or projects rather than being organized in a permanent separate R&D department.

- Many services organizations are typically small or even very small. They face problems common to any small firm as well as obstacles specific to services firms. Their innovation activities are likely not captured by the statistical procedures developed for large-scale industrial innovation. Insofar as government innovation policies are geared to larger industrial firms, small services innovators may not qualify for such benefits.

- Some services are among the leading users of new technologies. ICT use, in particular, is spreading rapidly, transforming even many traditional services.

- Like other industries, services are users of ICT hardware. In addition, however, several services industries are also creators of software indispensable to ICT hardware. It is thus misleading to think of services as passive users of ICT technologies.

- Many services innovate by introducing new ways of delivering existing or new services. Some innovate by changing the way the services are 'produced,' i.e., process innovations. Important innovations can also consist of changing organizational structures. Increasingly, innovations in services are also based on technological opportunities provided by the rapid evolution of ICT, or by addressing the challenges created by them.

- As in manufacturing where highly innovative, R&D-intensive industries co-exist with industries that are less inclined to innovate, high-tech services co-exist with traditional and much less innovative services. The gap between the two is probably even larger in services than in manufacturing. Unfortunately, little is known about innovation in the more traditional services.

- Innovation in many services is an interactive process. Unlike many industrial innovations, the success of innovations in many services depends on both the services provider and the user. In some services such as business services, inputs from the client are crucial for the creation of new or improved services products. This aspect is not well captured by the predominantly 'industrial' focus of innovation studies in the services sector.

- The growing involvement of customers in the use or consumption of some services, such as electronic commerce, requires a fair amount of knowledge and involvement on their part. The end "product" is a sort of self-service, but it is crucially dependent on the services provider.
- The interactive character of most services and the fact that many services cannot be separated from the competence of the persons who provide them underlines the importance of the personal contact, training and tacit knowledge of services providers.
- Intellectual property (IP) created by services innovations is less frequently protected by intellectual property rights (IPRs) than are manufactured goods. Many services innovations are difficult to protect against imitation. Because of their unique character, services display a different approach to using IPRs. However, as the evolution of U.S. patent legislation and practice shows, protection of IPRs in the technologically most advanced services is converging with the approaches typical in manufacturing.
- The immaterial character of services and the importance of interaction with customers create several challenges not encountered in innovations in goods-producing industries. Thus in some respects, the innovation system in services industries is complex and different from the innovation system typical of manufacturing. In other respects, however, there is a growing convergence between innovation in services and in manufacturing.
- The difference between goods-producing industries and services is becoming increasingly blurred. Some services resemble manufacturing industries more than they do traditional services.[4] As manufacturing becomes more flexible, industrial products may be increasingly customized and presented as services satisfying a specific combination of needs (Gallouj and Weinstein 1997).
- There is a trend toward standardization of some services that parallels the increasing particularization (customization) of others (Hipp, Tether and Miles 2000).

INNOVATION MEASUREMENT IN SERVICES INDUSTRIES

UNTIL FAIRLY RECENTLY, innovation studies were primarily the domain of economic and business historians. From the early 1960s, the OECD started to collect and publish R&D statistics based on common methodological guidelines *(Frascati Manual)*. These R&D statistics included selected services industries but the coverage varied from country to country and the statistics on R&D in services industries left a lot to be desired (Young 1996).

Students of innovation and technological change were increasingly aware that R&D activities are but one input to innovation, albeit a very important one. It was not until the early 1990s, however, that major industrial countries started to conduct representative statistical surveys of manufacturing firms aimed at capturing this complex phenomenon in its entirety.[5]

The conceptual framework underlying innovation surveys in manufacturing was built on a long tradition of research going back to Schumpeter (1934). In order to get internationally comparable statistics on innovation, the OECD experts elaborated international guidelines for innovation surveys as stated in the *Oslo Manual* (OECD 1992). The first version of the *Oslo Manual* was focused on technological innovation in industrial sectors only and services industries were not included.

The first revision of the OECD *Oslo Manual* (OECD/Eurostat 1996) provides guidelines for surveys of innovation in services industries. The methodology proposed for surveys of services innovations is heavily influenced by the industrial and technological perspective adopted from manufacturing surveys. The definition of innovation proposed by the *Oslo Manual* (OECD/Eurostat 1996) is as follows:

> A technological product innovation is the implementation/ commercialisation of a product with improved performance characteristics such as to deliver objectively new or improved services to the consumer. A technological process innovation is the implementation/adoption of new or significantly improved production or delivery methods. It may involve changes in equipment, human resources, working methods or a combination of these.[6]

Since the interpretation of the definition in some services activities is less than straightforward, the *Oslo Manual* provides a series of examples for what constitutes an innovation in various services industries (see Appendix 1 at the end of this study).

Until recently, information on innovation activities in the Canadian services sector was limited to R&D statistics that cover most services industries. The first survey of innovation that specifically included a subset of 'dynamic services industries' was conducted by Statistics Canada in 1996. Some related statistical information on specific aspects of innovation and/or technological change in services is also available from other Statistics Canada surveys. Before reviewing the principal conclusions and questions suggested by these surveys it may be useful to consider some limitations and problems involved in measuring R&D and innovation in services industries.

Limitations and Problems of R&D Surveys in Services Activities

Relatively good, internationally comparable and consistent statistics are available on the industrial R&D in manufacturing industries and utilities conducted in OECD countries [see the Analytical Business Enterprises Research and Development (ANBERD) database]. By contrast, information on R&D in services for most countries other than Canada is sketchy, difficult to compare and mostly unavailable. In the conclusion to an assessment of the state-of-the-art in measuring R&D in services, Young (1996) wrote: "…it may be several years before a full set of comparable data for services R&D is available and the quality of existing data for a number of member countries is still not satisfactorily documented at the OECD." There has not been much improvement since then. It should be stressed, however, that in spite of some problems discussed below, Canadian statistics on R&D have included services in a more consistent and detailed manner than those of most other OECD countries.

Some of the unresolved issues are as follows:

- coverage of R&D in the services industries;
- the content of R&D is often different in services; and
- organization of R&D and the system of innovation is different in services than in manufacturing.

Coverage of R&D in the services industries

The current definition of R&D used by Statistics Canada is still entirely focused on natural and engineering sciences.[7] Even though the survey of industrial R&D includes several services industries which are likely to conduct a significant proportion of their R&D in the social sciences and humanities (SSH), nevertheless, research and development in SSH is not recognized and not included. As social sciences are more likely to be part of R&D performed in services industries than in other parts of the business sector, the existing surveys of R&D in Canada are probably underestimating the extent and value of R&D done in services (Gault 1995).

The narrow definition of R&D used in Canada and other industrialized countries is surprising since the internationally recommended definition of R&D activity in the *Frascati Manual* is broader and includes research in social sciences.[8] A comparison of the Frascati definition and its illustrative examples with the definition of R&D in the questionnaire for the Statistics Canada Industrial R&D survey reveals that the Canadian definition is too restrictive. The Canadian situation, however, is not unique.[9] In his overview of surveys of R&D in services, Akerblom (2002) writes that the micro-information on R&D in innovation surveys is generally not consistent with R&D statistics.[10]

The content of R&D is often different in services

The concepts and measurements appropriate to R&D in manufacturing industries are applied — often with little or no adjustment — to the measurement of innovation in services industries. This '*manufacturing-based paradigm*' (criticized by Gallouj and Weinstein 1997 and Howells 2000 among others) is characterized by indicators and metrics that measure technological innovation in manufacturing industry. It does not easily fit the practical reality of services. Unlike goods, services do not have an autonomous existence defined by their technical specifications (Djellal and Gallouj 1999). As noted by Akerblom (2002), operational definitions and measures from industrial surveys may seem abstract and difficult to apply to certain services, especially to financial or personal services. There are clearly problems of interpretation and misinterpretation of what fits and does not fit the definition of R&D. The *Frascati Manual* and the Canadian R&D survey questionnaire cite examples of what should and what should not be included in R&D. The problem is that some of these examples are prone to changing interpretations over time since yesterday's discovery becomes today's routine.

Organization of R&D and the System of Innovation is Different in Services Than in Manufacturing

The organization of R&D in services differs markedly from the typical R&D departments found in manufacturing firms. There are some exceptions, as in the case of certain knowledge intensive business services (see Hipp et al. 2000) where firms operate R&D departments in the same way as do R&D-intensive manufacturing companies. In many other services industries, however, innovation is achieved with little or no activity that corresponds to 'technological R&D' as defined in the manufacturing-based paradigm. National reports on innovations surveys conducted in Europe (Sundbo and Galouj 1999) show that many innovation activities in services are organized in formalized "ad hoc groups" and that many firms create task teams instead of functional departments.

INFORMATION ON INNOVATION IN SERVICES

The Concept and Definition of Innovation in Services

The guidelines for definitions used in *innovation surveys* have changed over time. Even though the revised version of the *Oslo Manual* (OECD/Eurostat 1997) expanded the definition of the term 'product' to cover both goods and services, the manual does not take into account the specificities of innovations in services. The definition of innovation (introduced above) maintains the qualification of 'technological'-product innovation and 'technological'-process innovation. This may influence the rate of innovation identified, as suggested by the report on the Dutch and German surveys where the innovation question did not include the adjective 'technological' (Hipp et al. 2000).

Product-Process Innovations

Industrial innovations are usually classified as either a product or a process innovation. However, as shown in Baldwin and Hanel (2003), even manufacturing innovations do not conform neatly to this clear-cut classification. A more comprehensive classification allowing respondents to select a combination of the two characteristics was often selected in surveys. These 'complex' innovations were in many respects more significant than the simpler ones fitting one of the two innovation types. As Djellal and Gallouj (1999) argue, product and process are 'nebulous' concepts in services innovation, where it is often problematic to locate the boundaries between the two.[11] The problem is compounded by the fact that services are generally intangible. The services may be embodied not in technologies but in the competencies of individuals or organizations. Thus, when dealing with services, organizational innovation should be included in addition to product and process innovations.

Organizational and Disembodied Innovation Activities

Surveys from Europe (Licht and Moch 1999, Sundbo and Galouj 1999 and Howells 2000 to name only a few) as well as Canada (Baldwin, Gellaltly, Johnson and Peteers 1998, Earl 2002a, b) offer a growing body of evidence suggesting that some innovative activity in services is typically organizational and disembodied in nature and therefore very difficult to capture with traditional, industry-based innovation metrics. Typically, activities other than formal R&D account for larger shares of total innovation cost in services than they do in manufacturing. The innovation process in services has become more collective, i.e., the whole organization is geared to participate in it.

Interaction Between Services Providers and Their Clients

When the students of innovation abandoned the old linear model in favour of a more realistic interactive one (Kline and Rosenberg 1986), they started paying more attention to the inter-relationships among innovators, their market partners and other external sources of innovation. One of the important and distinctive features of services innovation, especially in knowledge-intensive business services, is their interactive character. The communication between the services provider and user is an important aspect of service provision and so is the technical competence of the client. Both may influence the final outcome of the services transaction. The intensity, means and quality of interaction involved in services innovations deserve more attention than the simple enumeration of sources of innovation included in existing surveys of innovation.

Asymmetry of Information

Many services such as business services provide knowledge and, as in all markets for information, information asymmetry becomes an issue. Clients are often asked to pay a price for information without being able to assess its value. The difficulty is even greater when these services are new (Djellal and Gallouj 1999).

The Size of Services Firms

In some of the most dynamic services industries, such as technical business and R&D services, firms are very small, typically employing fewer than 20 persons.[12] Unless sampling is adjusted to take this reality into account, their activities, contribution and needs may be underestimated. Insofar as information gathered in innovation surveys serves to guide public policies toward innovation, the specific circumstances of the smallest firms may not be properly addressed.

Is There a 'Services Innovation System'?

As Tether and Metcalfe (2003) argue, in contrast to innovations in manufacturing where interactions and interdependencies between innovators, their suppliers, clients, competitors and institutions of technological and scientific infrastructure form multiple *sectoral* systems of innovation, services innovations are more likely to be structured according to functions or *problems and/or opportunities* rather than by sectors. Since problems and opportunities change over time, the boundaries of systems of innovation in services are not fixed but tend to be dynamic and evolving.

In conclusion, our information about R&D and innovation in services industries is still very rudimentary and subject to many challenges in conceptualization and measurement. Empirical evidence that illustrates this state of affairs is the fact that two large-scale innovation surveys in the same country — Germany — produced findings that are contradictory in many respects (Djellal and Gallouj 1999).[13]

CANADA'S INNOVATION IN SERVICES — AN OVERVIEW[14]

INCIDENCE OF INNOVATION

THE GREATEST AMOUNT OF INFORMATION on innovation in Canadian services industries is available for the three "dynamic" services industry groups: the communications, finance, and technical services industries included in the Statistics Canada Survey of Innovation, 1996.[15] The services activities included in the Survey represent almost two thirds of the value added created by all services industries: in 2000, they represented close to one third of Canada's total GDP. Coverage of the services sector is limited to most, but not all, of the fastest-growing services industries.[16]

Survey respondents were asked to indicate whether they had introduced new or improved products, new or improved processes or significant improvements in organizational structures or internal business routines. An example of a product innovation is the offering of a new service such as life insurance in the financial sector. An example of a process innovation is the introduction of new analytical techniques and associated computer software. An example of an organizational innovation is increased computerization.[17]

Over the course of the 1994-1996 period, respondents in financial services were typically the most likely to have reported the introduction of a new or improved product, process or form of organization (62 percent of respondents), followed by communications (45 percent of respondents), and technical business services (43 percent of respondents). See Table 1 for a slightly more detailed breakdown of innovation incidence by major services sectors.

It is worthwhile noting that these innovation rates exceed the innovation rate observed in Canadian manufacturing, where 36 percent of firms either introduced or were in the process of introducing an innovation in the 1989–1991 period. They are, however, in the same range as the more innovative manufacturing industries —electrical and electronic products, pharmaceuticals, chemicals and machinery (Baldwin and Hanel 2003 and also Baldwin and Da Pont 1996).[18]

The incidence of innovation in all three services industry groups is strongly associated with the size of the firm, especially in financial and technical

TABLE 1

RATE OF INNOVATION IN SERVICES SECTORS, 1994-1996

SERVICES SECTOR	RATE OF INNOVATION (% OF ALL FIRMS)
Communications	**45.0**
Telecommunications	85.0
Television and Radio Broadcasting	41.0
Financial Services	**61.8**
Banks and Other Financial Institutions	54.2
Life Insurance	75.5
Other Insurance	56.1
Technical Business Services	**42.6**
Computer Services	55.8
Engineering Services	40.7
Other Technical Business Services	35.3

Source: Baldwin et al. (1998) and Hamdani (2001).

business services. Only about 20 percent to 40 percent of the smallest firms, employing less than 20 persons, reported an innovation, while the incidence of innovation ranged from 60 percent to 100 percent in firms employing more than 500 persons. New or improved services (products) were reported more frequently than process innovations. Organizational innovations were reported even less frequently.

However, the classification of innovation into product, process and organizational innovation is not very satisfactory. As in manufacturing (Baldwin and Hanel 2003), many innovators in services engage in multiple types of innovation, with product innovation often being the core activity. Three types of innovators dominate:

- product-only innovators;
- comprehensive innovators (innovators engaged simultaneously in product, process and organizational innovation); and
- product and process innovators (Figure 1).

In technical and communication services, product-only innovation was the most common. Conversely, comprehensive innovation — involving all types of innovation — was most common in large firms in communications and in financial services (Baldwin et al. 1998).

FIGURE 1

DISTRIBUTION OF INNOVATION TYPES

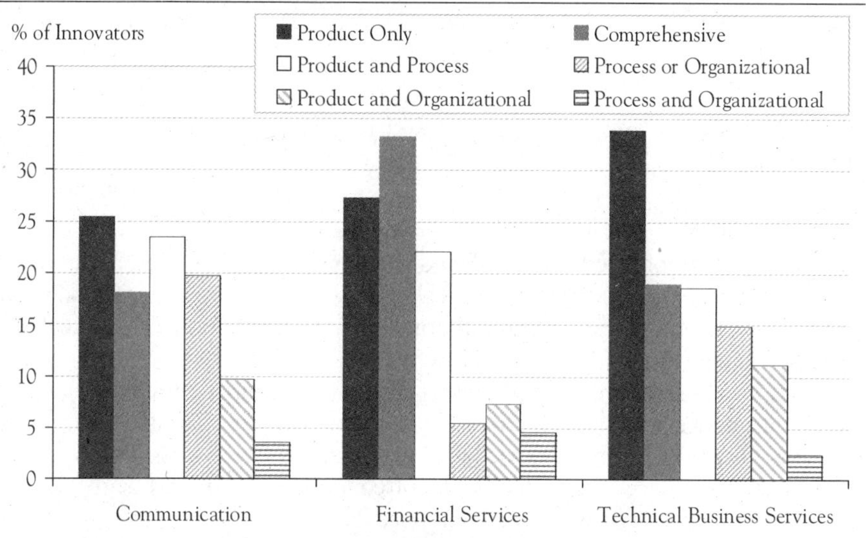

Source: Baldwin et al., 1998, based on Statistics Canada Survey of Innovation, 1996.

More than one third of innovators in communications and financial services and almost one half in technical services reported product innovations. On the other hand, process innovation is far less frequent. It was reported by only 7 percent of innovators in financial services, 12 percent in technical services and 16 percent in communications[19]. Not only is pure process innovation much rarer than product innovation or combined process-product innovation, but respondents find it difficult to distinguish among them.[20] Approximately the same percentage of respondents in each sector that reported process innovations also indicated that they had difficulties in distinguishing product from process innovation (Rosa 2003).[21]

The analytical division into product and process innovations adopted from manufacturing innovation surveys and the distinction between organizational change and process innovation is debatable when applied to services (Miles 2001). Because of the heterogeneity of services industries, innovations take various forms. Product and process innovations do respond to different factors across the three services sectors and the data support an analytical distinction between them (Rosa 2003). Surveys of Italian (Sirilli and Evangelista 1998) and German (Hipp et al. 2000) services industries came to similar conclusions. However, the concept of process innovation in services seems to be too narrowly defined, as Rosa (2003) admits. The distinction between process and organizational change innovations seems particularly unsatisfactory when applied to various modes of delivering services or to the interaction between the services-provider and clients. This is shown by the difference in the frequency with which customized and standardized services are delivered, a difference that is correlated with firm size. The proportion of standardized services increases with the size of firms (Hipp et al. 2000, also cited and discussed by Miles 2001). These aspects are especially important in knowledge-intensive services.

ORGANIZATIONAL AND TECHNOLOGICAL CHANGE IN SERVICES INDUSTRIES

THE 1996 SURVEY OF INNOVATION did not cover the whole spectrum of services industries. The more recent survey-based study by Earl (2002a) presents an overview of organizational and technological change in all sectors of the Canadian economy.[22] It provides interesting information on organizational[23] and technological[24] change in services.

The results show that the proportion of services firms that adopted organizational change was slightly lower (38 percent) than of manufacturing firms (50 percent) but higher than in the primary sector. On average, firms in the goods-related services innovate about as frequently (37 percent) as those providing intangible services (38 percent) (see Table 2). The averages, however, hide significant differences within those two types of services (Table 3).[25]

TABLE 2

ADOPTION RATES FOR ORGANIZATIONAL AND TECHNOLOGICAL CHANGE (PERCENT)

	ORGANIZATIONAL CHANGE ADOPTION RATE	TECHNOLOGICAL CHANGE ADOPTION RATE
Total Private Sector	38.3 B	43.6 B
Total Goods Producing Sector	44.2 B	45.6 B
Total Services Producing Sector	37.6 B	43.4 B
Goods Related Services	37.0 B	38.7 B
Intangible Services	37.9 B	45.5 B

Note: The letters in this table and the following one indicate data quality rating A: Excellent, B: Very good, C: Good, D: Acceptable, E: Use with caution, F: Unpublishable.
Source: Adapted from Earl (2002a, Table 1). Based on Statistics Canada, The Survey of Electronic Commerce and Technology 2000 (SECT). Reprinted with author's permission.

As shown in the earlier report (Baldwin et al. 1998) for innovations in dynamic services, there is a striking difference between smaller firms with fewer than 100 employees and larger firms in terms of the rate of adoption of organizational and technological change (Earl 2002a). In all sectors, the rate of adoption of both organizational and technological change is more than twice as high in larger firms than in smaller ones.

Since the coverage of the services sector in Earl's study is broader than in the Innovation Survey (1996), the results of the two surveys are not directly comparable. They suggest, tentatively, that the rates of adoption of organizational change over the 1998-2000 period was generally higher than was found in the 1996 survey.

The information on adoption of new technology also provides interesting insights into changes affecting services industries. First, the rate of introduction of technological change in the services producing sector (43.4 percent) was lower than in the manufacturing sector (50.6 percent) but by a smaller margin than observed for organizational change. Again, the rate of adoption of technological change increases sharply with the size of the firm.[26] The highest adoption rates for technological change were observed in information and cultural industries (63 percent) and in finance and insurance (60 percent). The lowest rates were reported in accommodation and food services. In goods-related services, the wholesale sector led the three other sectors (retail, transport and storage) with 45 percent of wholesalers introducing new or improved technology between 1998 and 2000.

Surprisingly, public organizations introduced both organizational and technological change twice as often as private firms. However, this is mostly because of the large size of public organizations. When private firms and public organizations of the same size are compared, the difference between the two is found to be negligible (Earl 2002b).

Both measures — the rates of adoption of organizational change and technological change — are conceptually closely related to the operational definition of innovation in services. To the best of my knowledge, unfortunately, because of the lack of comparable data for the services industries, no attempt has been made to examine this relationship more thoroughly. We are thus left

TABLE 3

ORGANIZATIONAL AND TECHNOLOGICAL CHANGE BY SECTOR

	ORGANIZATIONAL CHANGE %	TECHNOLOGICAL CHANGE %
Total Private Sector	**38.3 B**	**43.6 B**
Goods Producing Sector	***44.2 B***	***45.6 B***
Forestry, Fishing and Hunting	22.6 C	27.3 C
Mining and Oil and Gas Extraction	30.2 D	31.5 D
Utilities	46.4 D	64.0 D
Manufacturing	50.2 B	50.6 B
Services Producing Sector	**37.6 B**	**43.4 B**
Goods Related Services	*37.0 B*	*38.7 B*
Wholesale Trade	45.6 C	45.4 C
Retail Trade	35.9 B	37.6 B
Transportation and Warehousing	28.1 C	32.6 C
Intangible Services	*37.9 B*	45.5 B
Information and Cultural Industries	51.8 D	62.9 C
Finance and Insurance	45.6 C	59.7 C
Real Estate and Rental and Leasing	31.0 B	37.1 B
Professional, Scientific and Technical Services	39.8 B	58.6 B
Management of Companies and Enterprises	21.1C	30.9 C
Administrative and Support, Waste Management and Remediation Services	48.2 C	53.5 C
Educational Services (excluding public administration)	52.1 D	54.4 D
Health Care and Social Assistance (excluding public administration)	50.2 C	49.5 C
Arts, Entertainment and Recreation	39.4 C	42.3 C
Accommodation and Food Services	29.0 C	29.3 C
Other Services (excluding public administration)	33.4 B	38.3 B

Source: Adapted from Earl (2002a, Table 2). Based on Statistics Canada: The Survey of Electronic Commerce and Technology 2001 (SECT). Reprinted with author's permission.

with impressionistic information suggesting that on average, services have rates of introducing organizational and technological change, and presumably other types of innovation, that are only slightly below levels reported for manufacturing industries. Indeed, the adoption rate in the most dynamic services exceeds the average rate in manufacturing.

Introduction of organizational and technological change requires training and retraining of employees. Earl's (2002a) study shows that about 70 percent of the smallest firms and almost all of the largest accompanied organizational and technological changes with training. Overall, the percentage of services firms with training activities was similar to that in manufacturing.

Many firms use technologies purchased off the shelf (standard ICT equipment, software, etc.) or license them. Others have to customize or modify existing technologies and some firms develop new technologies for their exclusive use. Again, the purchasing practices of services sector firms were mostly similar to those reported by manufacturing companies.

SOURCES OF INNOVATION IN SERVICES

THE INNOVATION PROCESS CAN BE VIEWED as a learning process through which the firm generates new knowledge by acquiring, adapting, processing and generating ideas and information. Some ideas come from scientific and technological advances; others are market opportunities generated by the management and/or sales and marketing people inside the firm and by the firm's market partners. As in manufacturing, innovative ideas in services industries come from various sources, some inside the firm, others from outside. The competencies available in the firm are crucial but not sufficient to create and commercially introduce new or improved services (products), improved or new ways of performing a service or the organizational change needed to improve its delivery. As in manufacturing, firms rely to varying degrees on inputs from external market partners, competitors and various public sources grouped under the general heading of 'technological infrastructure' (Baldwin et al. 1998).

One of the characteristics of services innovation, especially in knowledge-intensive industries, is the high degree of interaction between the services providers and their clients. The services relationship — i.e., the interaction between the two — is sometimes called "servuction," a neologism that refers to producing and sustaining the services relationship (Miles 2001). This association varies enormously across the broad spectrum of services. Information on innovative ideas originating from clients reflects, very imperfectly, only one aspect of this relationship.[27]

The information on sources of innovative ideas in Canada is available only for the "dynamic" services, which were included in the 1996 Statistics Canada Survey of Innovation in services industries (Baldwin et al. 1998). Management is the most important internal source of innovative ideas in two out of the three services sectors, ranging from about 50 percent in technical business services to about 60 percent in communications and financial services.[28] In small firms where cost considerations preclude setting up separate R&D, marketing or other specialized divisions, management is naturally the central source of innovation ideas. Sales and marketing come second, ranging from about 46 percent in communications and technical business services to 54 percent in financial services. In-house R&D is most important in technical business services (57 percent), less in financial services (38 percent) and least in communications (22 percent) as illustrated in Figure 2.[29]

The crucial innovation inputs in all three services industries are, however, based on ICT. The widespread use of computers connected, by internal and external high-speed communication networks, constitutes the technology underlying most of the innovations in services (Table 4).

Innovation is often introduced in reaction to, or following suggestions by, clients, who are the most important source of innovation ideas and information. Emulation of competitors, interaction with suppliers and technology acquisition are all related to the market transactions of innovating firms. Another important category of external inputs to innovation comes from the technological infrastructure. This includes participation at conferences, trade fairs and exhibitions, accessing government information services or engaging consultants (Figures 3 and 4).

FIGURE 2

INTERNAL SOURCES OF INNOVATIVE IDEAS IN DYNAMIC SERVICES INDUSTRIES

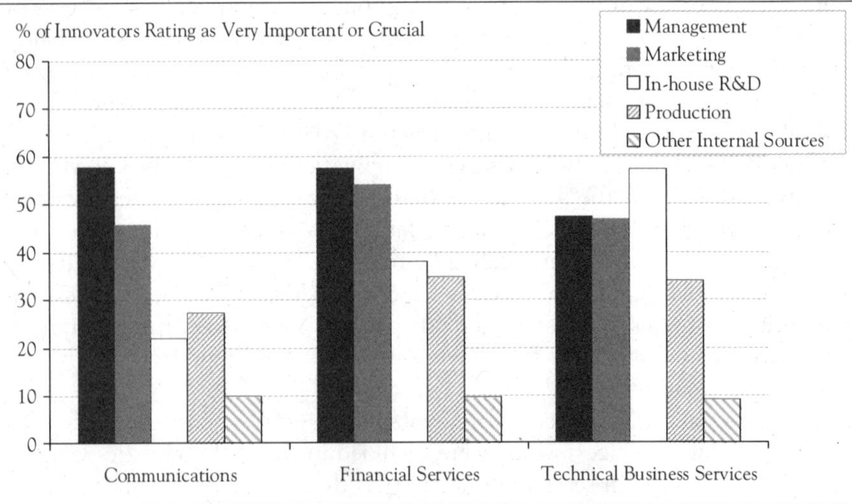

Source: Baldwin et al. (1998) based on Statistics Canada Survey of Innovation, 1996.

TABLE 4
PROPORTION OF FIRMS USING INFORMATION TECHNOLOGY BY SECTOR — CANADA, 2000 (PERCENT)

	USE OF COMPUTER	USE OF INTERNET	USE OF E-MAIL	USE OF A WEB SITE	USE OF INTERNET FOR SALE OF GOODS OR SERVICES	USE OF INTERNET TO BUY GOODS OR SERVICES
Wholesale	90	75	74	34	14	23
Retail Trade	76	53	48	23	9	13
Transport and Storage	76	57	51	13	2	15
Finance and Insurance	84	76	76	34	7	20
Real Estate and Renting	71	51	50	22	5	9
Professional, Technical and Scientific Services	95	84	85	30	7	36
Information and Cultural Industries	94	93	91	54	19	53
Management Consulting Companies	63	53	49	17	1	8
Administrative and Support Services	87	75	70	33	6	22
Educational Services	95	89	84	70	16	41
Health Care and Social Assistance	90	62	59	16	1	14
Arts, Spectacles and Leisure	87	69	62	36	5	16
Lodging and Food Services	66	44	40	18	5	10
Other Services	76	52	48	22	3	10
Manufacturing Sector	89	78	75	38	8	21
Private Sector Total	81	63	60	26	6	18

Note: According to the North American Industries Classification System (NAICS).
Source: Statistics Canada, Survey of Electronic Commerce and Technology, 2001.

FIGURE 3

IMPORTANCE OF EXTERNAL SOURCES OF INFORMATION ABOUT INNOVATION

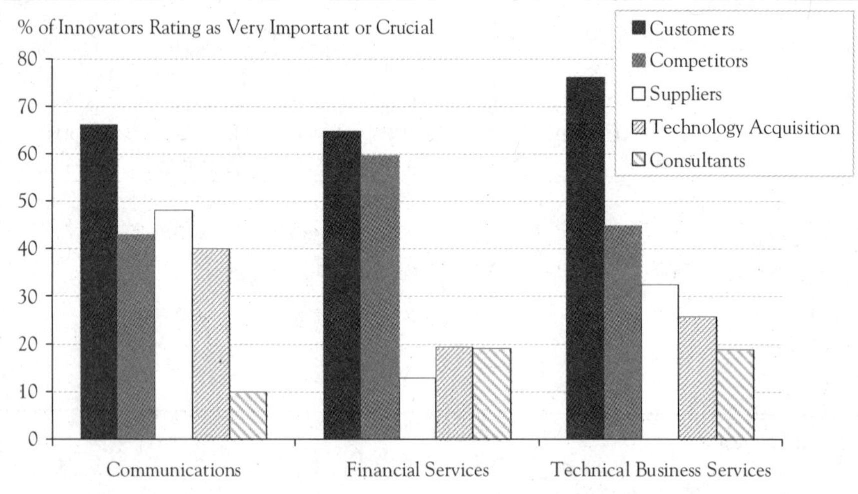

Source: Baldwin et al. (1998), based on Statistics Canada Survey of Innovation, 1996.

FIGURE 4

IMPORTANCE OF TECHNOLOGICAL INFRASTRUCTURE FOR INFORMATION ABOUT INNOVATION

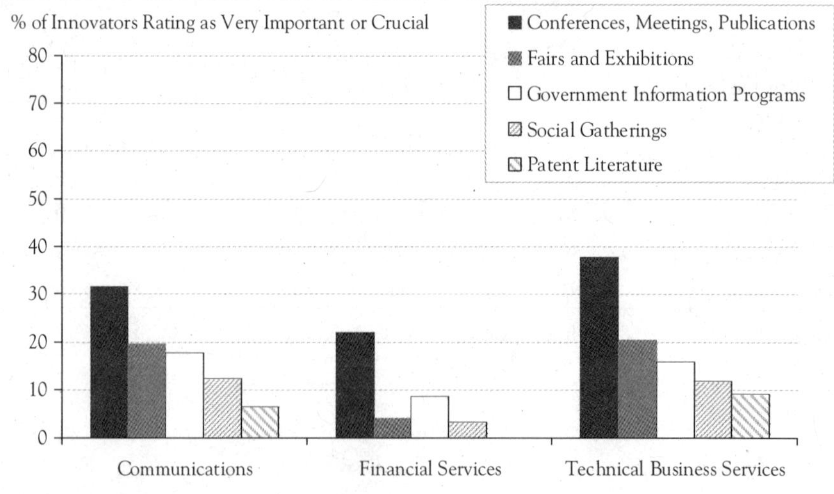

Source: Baldwin et al. (1998), based on Statistics Canada Survey of Innovation, 1996.

The absolute and relative importance of various internal and external sources of ideas and information that services firms use to create and introduce their innovations is remarkably similar to the sources of innovations in manufacturing (Baldwin and Hanel 2003).[30] The only notable difference is that in-house R&D is somewhat less important for services innovations. The importance of R&D as an internal source of innovation varies in services industries, from low in communications (22 percent) and medium (34 percent) in financial services to relatively high (60 percent) in technical services. In technical business services, R&D is about as important as in the manufacturing sector.[31] In contrast to manufacturing firms and in agreement with their interactive nature, almost half of services providers that innovate, especially in communications and financial services, are engaged in R&D partnerships and alliances.

A comparison of the most important sources of information on innovation reported by Canadian dynamic services firms with those reported by services firms in several European countries suggests that Canadian firms draw more information from their customers and suppliers than do European firms. They also seem to rely more on external sources of technical information from private and public research institutes (Table 5).

Objectives and Impacts of Innovation in Services

In keeping with their emphasis on product innovation, services sector innovators focus more on market and product-related objectives than on production-oriented goals. Maintaining or increasing market share, improving the quality, variety and flexibility of their services, adjusting to user needs and finding new foreign markets are the most frequently declared objectives of innovation activity in the three services sectors surveyed in 1996. As befits their larger scale, innovators in financial services focus on reducing costs more often than do innovators in the two other sectors. Innovating firms in the technical business services typically strive for production flexibility (Baldwin et al. 1998). Between one third and one half of firms that emphasized market-related objectives reported that innovation helped them to increase their market share (Rosa 2003, Table A7).

Aside from having an important impact on quality, reliability, user-friendliness, speed of delivery and flexibility of services, innovations also have a decisive impact on enhancing employee motivation and productivity. The highest incidence of an influence on internal productivity (reported by 25-30 percent of innovating firms) is found in financial services, followed by technical business services. For the sake of comparison, 40 percent of the innovations introduced by firms in technical business services improved the productivity of their clients.

TABLE 5

SOURCES OF INFORMATION CONSIDERED AS VERY IMPORTANT FOR INNOVATION IN THE SERVICES SECTOR* (PERCENT)

	GERMANY	BELGIUM	FRANCE	UNITED KINGDOM	IRELAND	SWEDEN	EEC	CANADA COMMU-NICATION	CANADA FINANCIAL SERVICES	CANADA TECHNICAL SERVICES FOR BUSINESS
Customers	28	48	27	65	56	57	38	66	65	76
Competitors	24	14	9	20	21	15	19	44	60	45
Suppliers	16	22	23	27	28	22	19	48	13	33
Fairs and Exhibitions	20	9	5	17	19	6	17	20	4	20
Conference, Meetings	22	14	8	8	11	4	15	32	22	38
Consultants	13	11	6	10	14	8	11	10	19	19
Higher Education Institutions	6	2	2	4	6	5	4	10	4	24
Internet or Data Base**	13	11	8	9	20	10	11	17.9	8.6	16
Private Research Institutes	n.a.	n.a.	n.a.	n.a.	n.a.	n.a.	n.a.	11	10	13
Government R&D Institutes	n.a.	n.a.	n.a.	n.a.	n.a.	n.a.	n.a.	7	negligible	11
R&D Institutes***	3	3	2	7	2	n.a.	3	9	10	12

Notes: *Proportion of the companies indicating that the source of information is very important.
** For Canada the source is: "Government information programs".
*** For Canada average of the private and Government R&D institutes.
n.a. = not available.

Source: Baldwin et al. (1998), *Innovation in Dynamic Service* and Eurostat: The Community investigation into the innovation (CIS2 1997-98) as reproduced in: Conseil de la Science et de la Technologie, *L'innovation dans les services, Pour une stratégie de l'immatériel*, Quebec, 2003.

Technical change fuelled by an accelerating rate of innovation is often accused of creating unemployment. According to information from the innovation survey, the reality is less alarming. Most innovations had no effect on employment or on worker skill requirements. As for those innovations that did have this type of effect, the percentage of firms reporting increased employment is significantly higher than the percentage of those that cut jobs. Similarly, the number of firms reporting that innovation increases the skills of workers is significantly larger than for those reporting decreases in skill requirements (Baldwin et al. 1998).

Overall, innovations in technical business services seem to have larger impacts than those in communications and financial services. Their positive impact on various aspects of quality, availability and flexibility not only improves the productivity of a sizeable proportion of their downstream clients, but it is also an essential input to the innovation activity of their clients both in services and other economic sectors.[32] The trend of manufacturing firms toward outsourcing — i.e., replacing in-house technical business services by using specialized external professional services — is blurring the distinction between manufacturing and services. It also partly explains the fast growth of technical business services and underscores their contribution to manufacturing.[33]

Intellectual Property Protection in Services Industries

In the face of fierce competition, services firms focus on retaining customers who could otherwise easily switch to competitors. Even though they do not rely on intellectual property rights (IPRs) in a legal sense as often as manufacturing firms, they do use intellectual property in other ways. They often use trademarks in combination with copyrights and patents to develop brand loyalty. Copyrights and patents are increasingly being used to protect and trade IPRs involved in computer software, business methods, communication and multimedia technologies. Firms in R&D-intensive technical business services use patents more often than those in communications and financial services. The small technical services firms rely frequently on trade secrets which are often more effective and less costly than patent protection.

The growing importance of knowledge in all spheres of economic activity led some countries, notably the United States, to reforms that extended IPRs into new fields. Some of them are directly related to innovation in certain services industries, especially the ICT-intensive ones. At the same time, court decisions involving IPRs became more "friendly" toward the owners of IPRs than to those infringing on them.

Protection of IP in the Software Industry

Until the early 1970s, the U.S. Patent Office was refusing patents on software and mathematical algorithms *per se*. In other words, it was refusing to grant patents on software and mathematical algorithms independently of any device using the software or algorithms. The protection of software was initially ensured by copyrights[34] rather than by patents. [35] This practice seems to be continuing in Canada (Vaver 2001).[36]

The arrival of personal computers was associated with an explosive growth of the software industry as well as the beginning of software patenting in the United States. More recently, the development of Internet and e-trading led to the patenting of business methods and multimedia in the United States.

The early history of the software industry and the use of IPRs to protect software and business methods (both through copyrights and patents) are documented by Graham and Mowery (2001). The authors argue that the changing judicial climate for copyright, along with other decisions affirming the strength of software patents, may have contributed to an increased reliance on patents by U.S. software firms.

As ICTs developed software, electronic data transmission and encryption methods have been accounting for a growing share of U.S. patents over the 1984-2002 period. Graham and Mowery (2001) show how this share evolved through 1997. Extending the observations period to 2002 confirms that the share of software patents continued to increase until 2000 when the trend reversed at about the time that the technology bubble burst on the stock market (Figure 5).

One way to examine Canadian innovation performance in the field of software and related ICT technologies is to look at the share of U.S. patents assigned to Canadian corporations in software-related classes. This is illustrated by the two curves in the lower section of Figure 5. The first curve (Canada's percent) shows that the share of software-related patents assigned to Canadian corporations remained very low, rarely exceeding one percent until the mid-1990s. Since then, it has increased notably. An examination of the patent assignees shows that Nortel recently accounted for an important portion of the Canadian share of U.S. patents in these classes. To assess the evolution of patents assigned to computer services and related activities, I deducted the patents awarded to Nortel. The second curve (the Canada less Nortel percentage) clearly increases over the period for which results are shown (Figure 5). The growth in the Canadian share of all U.S. patents in the software and e-commerce related classes suggests that in the second half of the 1990s, Canada improved its position in this field in terms of world patent rankings. However, at a level of one to two percent, the share is still very low for a country that is among the leading users of ICT, the Internet and e-commerce.

Business methods and e-commerce: In a 1998 decision, the U.S. Court of Appeals for the Federal Circuit, in the case of *State Street Bank vs. the Signature Financial Group*, validated a controversial software patent on "transformation of data, representing discrete dollar amounts, by a machine through a series of mathematical calculations into a final share price…". Since the State Street decision, the number of applications for patents of business methods expanded from 1,275 in fiscal 1998 to 2,600 in fiscal 1999 (Graham and Mowery 2001).

To take one example, these include patents in e-commerce for functions such as the ordering of books and other goods using the "one click" method at Amazon.com. These developments show that patent protection is becoming increasingly relevant for financial services, business services and trade. Yet, as of 2001, business methods were not patentable in Canada (Vaver 2001).

FIGURE 5

SHARES OF U.S. SOFTWARE PATENTS

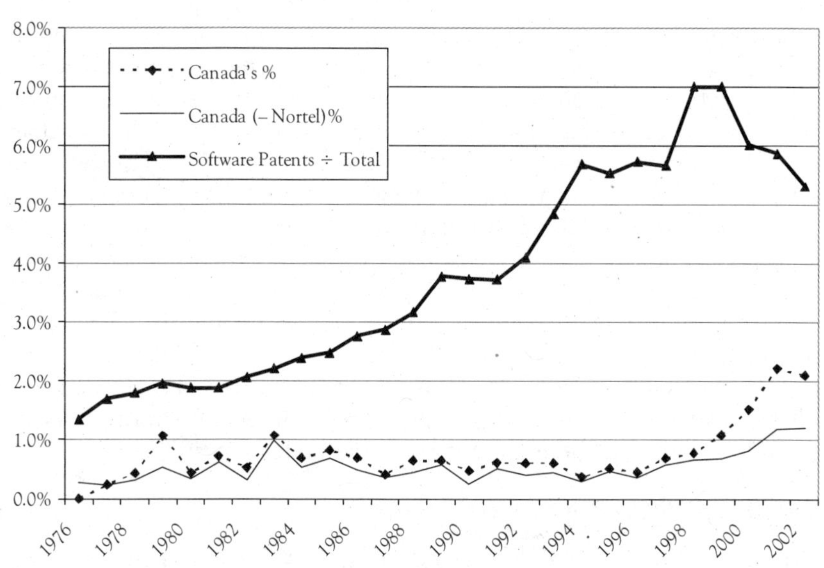

Note: The number of U.S. patents issued in international patent classes (IPC)identified below by the IPC section, classes, subclasses and groups:

G06F Electrical digital processing
3/ Input arrangements for transferring data …
5/ Methods or arrangements for data conversion …
7/ Methods of arrangements for processing data by operating upon the order …
9/ Arrangements for programme control …
11/ Error detection, correction monitoring …
12/ Accessing, addressing or allocating within memory …
13/ Interconnection of, or transfer of information or other signals …
15/ digital computers in general …

G06K Recognition of data:
Presentation of data; Record carriers; handling record carriers
9/ Methods or arrangements for reading …
15/ Arrangements for producing a permanent visual presentation …

H04L Electric Communication Technique
9/ Arrangement for secret or secure communication

Source: Special tabulation kindly provided by François Vallière, Observatoire de science et technologie-Centre interuniversitaire de la recherche sur la science et la technologie (CIRST), October 3, 2003.

Multimedia: The increasingly important field of multimedia is also protected by patents in the United States. This began in 1993 with the awarding of a patent to Compton Encyclopaedias (Graham and Mowery 2001).

Databases: The latest additions of intellectual property subject matter are databases receiving *sui generis* protection, which is a specific right to protect them against copying conferred by the European Union in 1998. In Canada, as in the United States, databases are protected by copyright and/or by business methods (Scotchmer and Maurer 2001).

IPRs and the Internet

The Internet offers an excellent illustration of the fundamental dilemma that the digital revolution created for the protection of intellectual property. On the one hand, progress in digital technology enables low-cost reproduction and the World Wide Web enables publication on a global basis. On the one hand, there are the protective provisions of intellectual property law. This led to two opposite attitudes to IP. Some innovating firms realized the potential of patents to secure and defend profitable positions in the e-commerce economy and they have been patenting intensively.[37] By contrast, the Internet is also the medium that saw the emergence of the Open Source Initiative — a loose group of volunteer programmers who collaborate to develop free software.[38] The current situation leads to various examples of IP infringement such as the use and misuse of the trademark law to protect Internet site names (cyber squatting).[39] It is likely that at some point there will be public policy intervention with respect to IPRs and the Internet, but at present, the situation remains in flux.[40]

Use of IPRs in Canadian Services Industries

Information on the use and effectiveness of IPRs in Canada comes from Baldwin et al. (1998). In the early 1990s, fewer than half of the innovators in the three "dynamic" services industries covered by their study reported using any form of property rights.

Firms were most likely to use copyrights and trademarks. Patents were used less frequently. This pattern contrasts with manufacturing where firms rarely use copyrights and rely much more on patents and trade secrets. It is likely that as in the United States (Graham and Mowery 2001), the use of patents may have increased since the time of the study.

As in manufacturing, services industries also manifest significant inter-industry differences in the use of IPRs. Firms in communications services use intellectual property rights less frequently. Innovators in financial services focus on trademarks. The greater diversity of technical business services is reflected in their tendency to use several IP instruments (Figure 6).

As in manufacturing, even those innovators that rely on the protection of IPRs do not necessarily consider these rights very effective.[41] Use of various

FIGURE 6

USE OF INTELLECTUAL PROTECTION RIGHTS

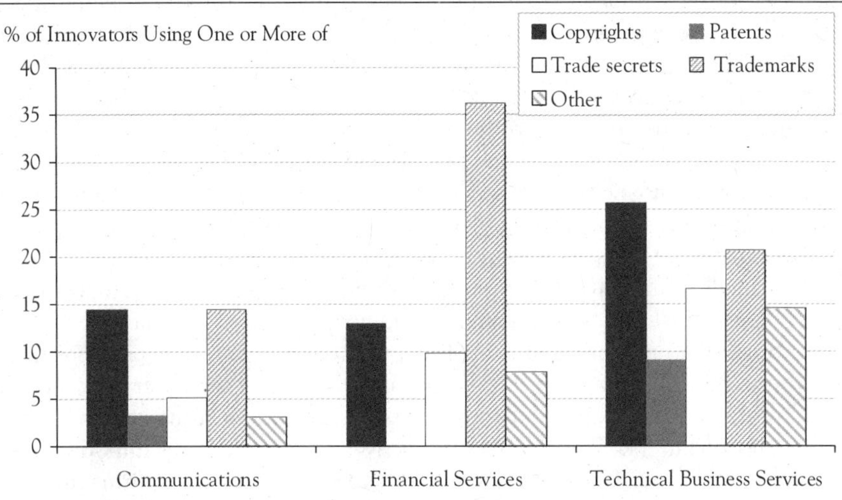

Source: Baldwin et al. (1998), based on Statistics Canada Survey of Innovation, 1996.

business strategies such as being first in the market and protecting against imitation by complexity of design are thought by many to be more effective than statutory IPRs for protection against imitation and loss of customers. Why then are firms using statutory protection at all? Increasingly, especially in the case of firms using complex information and communication technologies, statutory rights such as patents and copyrights are used for strategic purposes such as trade with their allies and competitors (Hall and Ham-Ziedonis 2001, Hanel 2003a).

OBSTACLES TO INNOVATION IN SERVICES INDUSTRIES

RESPONDENTS TO THE 1996 CANADIAN Survey of Innovation were asked to identify impediments they encountered in their innovation activity. Perception of obstacles depends on the type of services industry, the size of firm and the competitive environment.

The high cost of innovation is the most important obstacle in all three industries. Apart from high cost, innovation in the communications industry is affected by government laws and regulations to a greater degree than in the two other industries. For technical services, the lack of qualified personnel constitutes a major obstacle. Overall, financial services experiences obstacles to innovation less frequently than do the other two industries. This is likely explained by larger firm size in financial services.

The smallest firms (employing fewer than 20 persons) report obstacles in their innovation process more frequently than do the larger ones. The difference is staggering: the percentage of the smallest firms reporting an impediment is 4 to 10 times the percentage of the largest ones (with more than 500 employees). However, the relative importance of different obstacles does not vary much with firm size. The high cost of innovation is first on the list for firms of all sizes. Large firms are more concerned than smaller ones with risks related to the feasibility and success of innovation.[42] On the other hand, small firms are more concerned than the larger ones with the lack of qualified personnel and difficulties in obtaining external financing and specialized equipment. Since almost half of all innovating services firms employ fewer than 20 persons, impediments reported for this category of firms are worthy of particular attention.

The smallest firms in all sectors have difficulties obtaining external financing. These firms have little to offer as tangible collateral to financial institutions. Small manufacturing up-start firms may obtain venture capital based on the strength of their patent portfolio but innovations in many services are less easily protected by intellectual property rights and these firms can rarely use patents as collateral. This problem is likely to be particularly important, for example, in technical business services where 95 percent of all firms are very small, employing fewer than 20 persons (Gellaltly 1999).

Innovation in services is less dependent on R&D than it is in manufacturing and, if conducted, R&D is often organized less formally. It is therefore likely that innovators in services industries qualify less frequently for Canada's main public programs to support innovation, the experimental R&D tax credits and various grant programs subsidizing R&D expenditures.

The eligibility and performance criteria for access to private and public funding for innovation has so far been mainly geared to the manufacturing sector. According to these criteria, innovators in services industries compare unfavourably with their manufacturing counterparts.[43]

There are important differences between firms that conduct R&D and those that do not. The performers of R&D introduce innovations that are more complex and original and thus constitute a greater technological and administrative challenge. They face obstacles more frequently than the technically less-sophisticated firms that innovate without recourse to R&D. A similar pattern was found in manufacturing. A study by Baldwin and Hanel (2003) shows that firms introducing more original innovations that were first in the world or first in Canada relied more on R&D and encountered various obstacles more frequently than their less original counterparts. Using data on advanced technology adoption from the same survey, Baldwin and Lin (2002) examined the factors related to obstacles firms face when adopting advanced technology.[44] They also conclude that the more innovative firms face greater obstacles.

Unlike non-innovators, small, R&D-intensive innovative firms develop an overall strategy stressing financial management, quality management, improvement of market position, foreign market penetration, improvement and motivation of human resources and protection of intellectual property.[45] Since, by definition, innovating firms are agents of change, they face various obstacles more often than non-innovating counterparts that pursue routine activities.

A larger proportion of innovating firms than non-innovating firms face risks related to market acceptance and imitation of their products. Another problem more acutely perceived by innovators is lack of skilled labour. Both these difficulties are perceived more often by firms in computer services than in computer repair and in engineering.[46]

In contrast, non-innovators were more likely than innovators to report a lack of technical equipment, long administrative approval, high cost and lack of equity capital. However, the difference between the two groups with respect to high cost and lack of equity capital is not statistically significant.

Impediments to innovation are also related to the degree of competition faced by the innovating firms. Mohnen and Rosa (1999: 24) found that:

> Firms which faced less competition had a tendency to consider questions related to impediments not relevant or the impediments themselves insignificant, whereas firms facing more competition had a tendency to consider obstacles more significant.

Introducing new and improved services, along with the way they are produced and delivered, is in an example of Schumpeterian "creative destruction" that is risky, costly and difficult. In spite of experiencing various obstacles, innovating firms succeeded in developing competencies needed to overcome impediments, which shows that they were not insurmountable. The proportion of firms that encountered impediments in their innovation activities is presented in Table 6.

TABLE 6

DISTRIBUTION OF PERCEIVED BARRIERS TO INNOVATION BY INTENSITY AND BY SERVICES SECTOR (PERCENT)

	NOT RELE-VANT	CRITICAL	VERY SIGNIFI-CANT	MODER-ATELY SIGNIFI-CANT	SLIGHTLY INSIGNIFI-CANT	INSIGNIFI-CANT
	(6)	(5)	(4)	(3)	(2)	(1)
Communications	31	8	18	19	11	14
Financial Services	25	3	19	24	18	11
Technical Services	19	8	23	22	14	14
All Three Sectors	25	6	20	22	14	13

Source: Mohnen and Rosa (1999).

CANADIAN R&D IN SERVICES

CANADA'S OVERALL R&D effort does not compare advantageously with that of other developed industrialized countries. The Canadian business sector's expenditures on R&D in 2000 were only about one percent of GDP, a level that was about one third of Sweden's R&D intensity and half the R&D intensity for Canada's principal economic partner and competitor, the United States. Between 1997 and 2000, a comparison of the rate of growth of total business sector expenditures on R&D in Canada (5.6 percent/year) and in the United States (10.5 percent/year) shows that gap is increasing. This raises the question of whether or not the situation in the services sector is any different.

As discussed earlier and in more detail by Gault (1997), the R&D statistics offer an incomplete and deformed picture of the R&D activities conducted in various services industries.[47] With that caveat in mind, the available statistics on business sector R&D in services suggest several interesting findings.[48]

The R&D intensity — i.e. the ratio of expenditures on R&D to revenues — in the services sector in Canada is about as high as in manufacturing (1.8 percent and 1.9 percent respectively in 1999). It is noteworthy that several "high tech" services industries (scientific R&D, health care, management, scientific and technical consulting, computer services, and engineering and scientific services) have an R&D intensity as high or higher than most R&D-intensive manufacturing industries (see Figure 7 based on figures for R&D/revenue summarized in Table 7).

A comparison of R&D intensity in services industries between Canada and the United States shows that, as in manufacturing, U.S. firms in the services industries are significantly more R&D-oriented than their Canadian counterparts (see Table 8). According to the latest available data from both countries and bearing in mind the differences in coverage (Jankowski 2001), the U.S. lead appears particularly significant in trade, scientific R&D services, finance and insurance, and in other professional, scientific and technical services. On the other hand, Canada seems to be spending more on R&D relative to sales in management consulting and in private health-care services.[49] Differences in data availability make other comparisons impossible or too risky.

Except for a pause and dip in the mid 1990s, expenditures on R&D in the Canadian services sector were increasing over the past decade. There were, however, significant inter-industry differences. The most dynamic growth was displayed by R&D services, wholesale and retail trade and by computer and related activities. On the other hand, R&D by firms in the financial sector, in post and telecommunications and in other business activities declined (Figure 8).

Owing to statistical difficulties, an international comparison is at best risky. According to available international (OECD, ANBERD 2002, July) statistics on R&D, the services sector's share of the total business sector R&D in Canada and the United States is higher than the average for the European Union. It is, however, impossible to say to what extent the difference is due to differences in statistical coverage. There are some OECD countries whose services share of total business sector R&D is higher than Canada's (Norway, New Zealand, Denmark and Australia as noted in [OECD, ANBERD 2002, July)].

Research and development in the private sector services industries represents about 28.5 percent of total R&D performed in the Canadian business sector. While the share of services R&D in total business R&D expenditures was higher in Canada than in the United States and was increasing up to the mid-1990s, it declined thereafter. In contrast, the services share of business R&D in the United States shot up significantly in the late 1990s and was, as of 2000, superior to Canada's share by five percentage points. The evolution of R&D expenditures in services as a percentage of total business sector R&D expenditures in Canada and United States is illustrated in Figure 9.

FIGURE 7

INTENSITY OF R&D AS A PERCENTAGE OF REVENUE

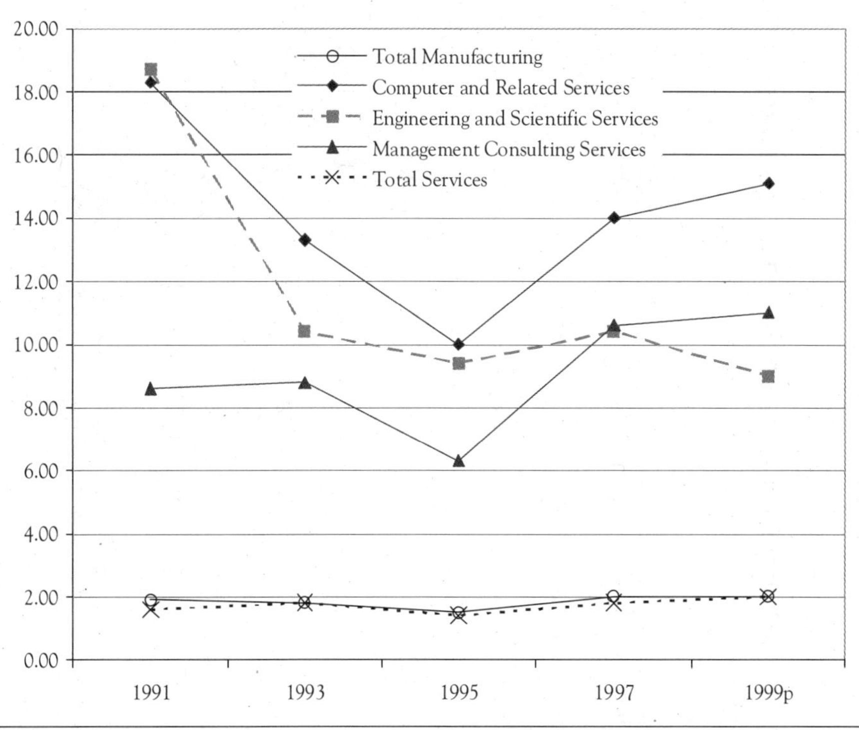

Note: p=preliminary.
Source: Author's computation from Statistics Canada, *Industrial Research and Development*. Cat. No. 88–202-XPB, Appendix.

TABLE 7

CURRENT R&D EXPENDITURES AS A PERCENT OF PERFORMING COMPANY'S REVENUES

								Control	
								Canada	Foreign
Services	1991	1993	1995	1997	1999p	1999r	2000p	2000p	2000p
Transportation and Storage	0.20	0.40	0.30	0.10	0.20	0.10	0.20	0.20	0.10
Communication	1.00	1.50	1.00	0.50	0.40				
Information and Cultural Industries						1.50*	1.60	1.40	13.20
Wholesale Trade	1.00	1.20	1.00	1.30	1.90	1.70	2.50	1.70	4.20
Retail Trade	0.70	0.40	0.90	2.60	1.90	0.80	0.40	0.40	7.80
Finance, Insurance & Real Estate	0.80	0.90	0.40	0.40	0.30	0.20	0.40	0.40	4.60
Computer and Related Services	18.30	13.30	10.00	14.00	15.10	13.00	10.80	11.50	8.80
Engineering & Scientific Services	18.70	10.40	9.40	10.40	9.00	15.20	10.00	8.70	12.20
Management Consulting Services	8.60	8.80	6.30	10.60	11.00	11.00	13.90	14.10	5.90
Scientific R&D						34.70*	39.10	40.10	30.90
Other Services	5.10	5.70	3.60	3.70	5.40	1.50*	1.30	1.00	16.50
Total Services	1.60	1.80	1.40	1.80	2.00	1.80	2.30	1.90	4.60
Total Manufacturing	1.90	1.80	1.50	2.00	2.00	1.90	2.20	3.80	1.10
Construction	1.30	3.50	0.70	0.90	1.20	1.60	5.00	5.30	3.50
Utilities	1.00	0.80	0.60	0.60	0.80	0.80	0.80	0.80	0.00

Notes: Data for 1999 are classified according to NAICS and are not strictly comparable for those industries marked by *. Figures are r=revised; p=preliminary.
Source: Statistics Canada Cat. No. 88-202-XPB, Industrial Research and Development, Intentions 2002, Appendix.

TABLE 8

COMPARISON OF U.S. AND CANADA R&D EXPENDITURES AS A PERCENT OF PERFORMING COMPANY REVENUES

YEAR	U.S. % 2000	CANADA % 1999
Manufacturing	3.6	1.9
Utilities	n.a.	0.8
Construction*	5.8	1.6
Trade	5.4	1.9
Transportation and Warehousing	n.a.	0.2
Information	4.1	1.5*
Publishing	16.3	n.a.
Newspaper, Periodical, Book and Database	2.0	n.a.
Software	20.5	n.a.
Other Information	5.1	n.a.
Finance, Insurance, and Real Estate	1.2	0.2
Professional, Scientific and Technical Services	18.3	n.a.
Architectural, Engineering and Related Services	10.8	15.2
Computer Systems Design and Related Services	12.3	13.0
Scientific R&D Services	42.9	34.7*
Other Professional, Scientific and Technical Services	6.6	1.5*
Management of Companies and Enterprises	4.4	11.0
Health Care Services	3.2	35.4
Other Non-Manufacturing	1.1	1.3

Notes: The figures for the United States are total R&D funds/domestic sales; n.a. =not available. The figures for Canada are current intramural R&D expenditures as a percent of performing company revenues.
* Construction US =R&D1999/sales 2000.

Source: Author's computations from: Statistics Canada, *Industrial Research and Development*, Intentions 2002, Cat.No. 88–202-XPB, Appendix and National Science Foundation/Division of Science Resources Statistics, *Survey of Industrial Research and Development*, 2000, tables A1 and A4.

Government and manufacturing firms have been contracting out R&D to private firms. There is some evidence that government R&D was contracted more to services industry firms than to manufacturing (Dalpé and Anderson 1997, cited by Gault 1997). There is also some evidence that services firms dominate when it comes to contract R&D (Rose 1995). It is however not clear what proportion of the growth of R&D in services can be attributed to contracting out of R&D by industrial firms.

FIGURE 8

R&D EXPENDITURES BY SERVICES INDUSTRIES IN CANADA

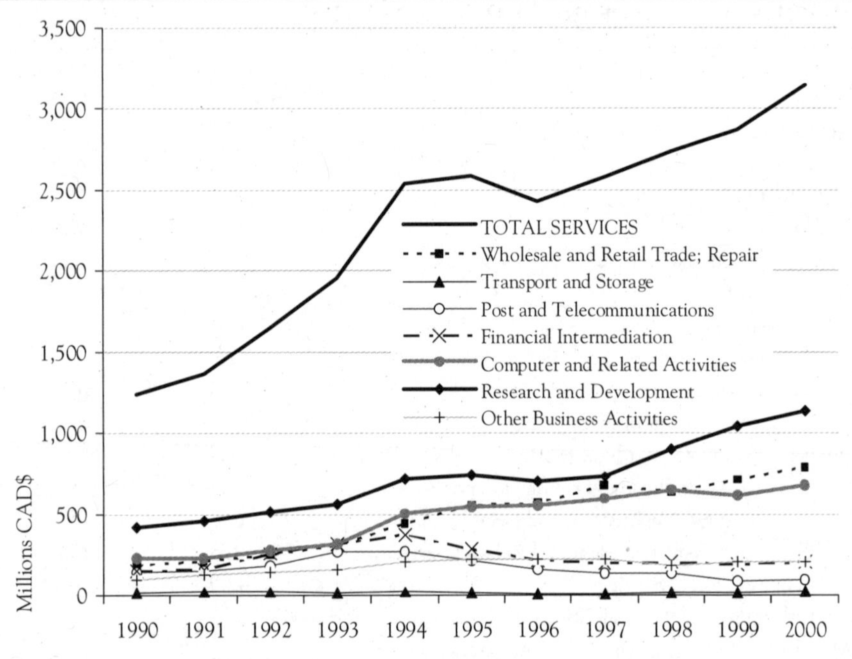

Source: Author's computation from Statistics Canada: *Industrial Research and Development*, Cat. No. 88–202-XPB, Appendix.

Services firms are very active in R&D networking. They performed about two-thirds of all R&D resulting from an agreement between firms or research institutes (Gault 1997, Rose 1995).

FIGURE 9

R&D IN SERVICES AS A PERCENT OF TOTAL BUSINESS SECTOR R&D

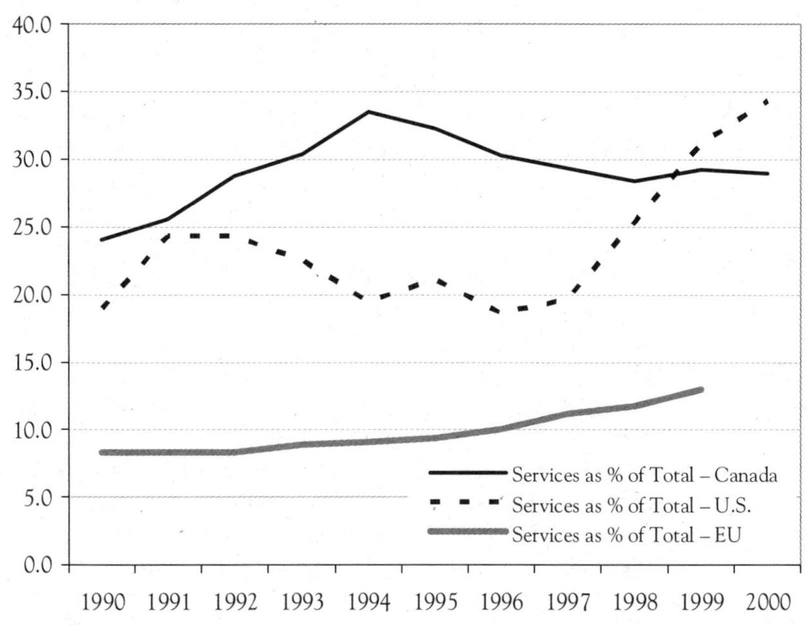

Source: Author's computation from the internationally comparable R&D database, OECD (ANBERD).

CONCLUDING REMARKS

AFTER MANY YEARS OF NEGLECT, innovation activities in services are being increasingly recognized as an important part of the national innovation system. The concept, the definitions and the measurement of innovation in services industries are more problematic than in manufacturing industries. So far, the information on innovation activities in the services industries is less complete and less reliable than the information on innovation in manufacturing industries.

Judging from the studies that analyzed the results of the innovation survey for dynamic services, an important proportion of firms belonging to the three services industries — communications, financial services and technical business services — innovate quite extensively. Organizational and technological change, mostly related to introduction of ICT, is almost as widespread in services as in manufacturing industries. The limited information on patenting in the software and e-business related fields shows that Canadian firms have recently been increasing their share of U.S. patents.

Unfortunately, there is little information on innovation in other dynamic services sectors such as wholesale and retail sales, which are believed to be among the principal sources of increasing productivity in the United States. It is unfortunate that the new Statistics Canada Survey of Innovation in Services does not include wholesale and retail trade.

The material reviewed in this study has consistently demonstrated that there are huge differences between smaller and larger services firms as regards innovation performance, behaviour, sources and impediments. Many services industries are dominated by very small firms. In view of this fact, it is hard to understand that the latest Statistics Canada innovation survey does not cover firms employing fewer than 15 employees. The survey results are unlikely to be representative of those segments of services industries dominated by the smallest firms such as some business services.

The information on Canadian R&D in services is among the most complete and consistent of any of the OECD countries. It shows that R&D in services was growing more rapidly than R&D for the business sector as a whole. On the basis of the available information, it is possible to assert that the innovation effort in the Canadian services sector is far from negligible and plays a significant role not only in the development of services but also in other sectors.

Broad international comparisons of R&D expenditures in the services sector are still risky and make little sense. The data only enable a meaningful comparison of R&D performance in Canada and the United States. Even though until the mid-1990s, Canadian services industries accounted for a larger share of total R&D expenditures than their U.S. counterparts, the situation has recently been reversed.[50] In any case, as in manufacturing, U.S. services industries spend a larger proportion of their revenue on R&D than do Canadian services firms. The recent increase of R&D performed in the U.S. services sector will further increase their competitive lead over Canadian services industries.

APPENDIX

EXAMPLES OF TECHNOLOGICAL PRODUCT AND PROCESS INNOVATIONS IN SELECTED SERVICES INDUSTRIES

WHOLESALING OF MACHINERY, EQUIPMENT AND SUPPLIES

- Creation of Web sites on the Internet, where new services such as product information and various support functions can be offered to clients free of charge.
- Publication of a new customer catalogue on CD (compact disc). The pictures can be digitally scanned and recorded directly on the CD where they can be edited and linked to an administrative system giving product information and prices.
- New data processing systems.

ROAD TRANSPORT COMPANIES

- Use of cellular phones to reroute drivers throughout the day. Allows clients greater flexibility over delivery destinations.
- A new computer mapping system, used by drivers to work out the fastest delivery route (i.e. from one destination to another). This makes it possible to offer clients faster deliveries.
- The introduction of trailers with eight globe-shaped containers instead of the usual four.

POST AND TELECOMMUNICATIONS COMPANIES

- Introduction of digital transmission systems.
- Simplification of the telecommunications net. The number of layers in the net has been reduced by using fewer but more highly automated switching centres.

BANKS

- The introduction of smart cards and multipurpose plastic cards.

- A new bank office without any personnel where clients conduct "business as usual" through the computer terminals at hand.
- Telephone banking which allows clients to conduct many of their banking transactions over the phone from the comfort of their own homes.
- Switching from image scanning to OCRs (optical character readers) in the handling of forms/documents.
- The "paperless" back-office (all documents are scanned for entry into computers).

SOFTWARE CONSULTANCY AND SUPPLY COMPANIES

- The development of a whole range of different customer packages in which clients are offered varying degrees of assistance/support.
- The introduction of new multimedia software applications that can be used for educational purposes and thus eliminate the need for a real life human instructor.
- Making use of object-oriented programming techniques in automatic data processing systems development.
- The development of new project management methods.
- Developing software applications through computer-aided design (CAD).

TECHNICAL CONSULTANCY COMPANIES

- A new method of purifying water abstracted from lakes for use as household drinking water.
- Offering customers a new "supply control system" which allows clients to check that deliveries from contractors meet specifications.
- The development of a standard for construction work carried out in already densely built-up areas (where care has to be taken not to inflict damage on any of the surrounding buildings).

ADVERTISING AND MARKETING COMPANIES

- Delivering lists of potential customers on diskette together with a list filing system (software) that allows the client firms themselves to analyse and draw samples from the list.

- Being able to assist clients in direct marketing campaigns by offering to distribute pre-labelled advertising leaflets, etc., addressed to selected households.
- Initiating a control process to check by phone with random households that they are actually receiving the adverts/leaflets they are supposed to.
- Delivering the software applications needed for clients themselves to be able to analyse data along with statistical databases.

Source: *Oslo Manual* 1996, p.33.

ENDNOTES

1 According to an OECD study (Pilat 2001) growth in labour productivity was faster in: communications, wholesale and retail sales, transportation and storage and finance than the average for business as a whole.
2 See also the review of recent studies by the *Conseil de la science et de la technologie,* Quebec, 2003. It provides a good starting point for a timely overview of the literature on innovation in services within a Canadian context.
3 To take one example, until the early 1970s, IBM (Canada) was considered a manufacturing firm producing goods. Since then it has became a provider of services.
4 The increasing popularity of leasing cars, computers and other durable goods instead of buying them is a good example of this trend. The client is in fact consuming and paying for a combination of financial, maintenance and transport services (or in the case of computers, information processing services).
5 Innovation surveys of varying scope and coverage were undertaken by individual researchers and various economic and industrial institutions in many industrial countries well before the national statistical agencies became involved in surveys of innovation based on the guidelines of the *Oslo Manual.* See De Melto, McMullen and Wills 1980.
6 *Oslo Manual.* Paris: OECD/Eurostat, 1996, p. 9.
7 R&D is systematic investigation carried out in *the natural and engineering sciences by means of experiment or analysis* to achieve a scientific or commercial advance. The reason for exclusion of social sciences is administrative. The information on R&D is collected in part from corporate tax returns to the Canada Revenue Agency (formerly the Canadian Customs and Revenue Agency). Since the R&D in social sciences is not eligible for the Scientific Research and Experimental Development tax credits, the information on R&D in social sciences is not collected. As Gault (1995) remarks, 'As social sciences R&D is more likely to be performed in services industries than in other parts of the business sector, the present surveys are expected to underestimate the value of R&D done in service industries.
8 The definition of R&D in the *Frascati Manual* is as follows:
"Research and experimental development (R&D) comprise creative work undertaken on a systematic basis in order to increase the stock of knowledge, *including the knowledge of man, culture and society* (italics by the author), and the use of this stock of knowledge to devise new applications."
9 According to Young (1996), R&D in social sciences and humanities was not included in Canada, Greece, Turkey, the United Kingdom, and the United States. And Germany, Japan, Netherlands and Norway were dissatisfied with the way the SSH were treated in their national surveys.

10 Djellal and Gallouj (1999) present a useful review of national and international surveys of innovation indicators in services and discuss some of these issues at more length.

11 However, empirical evidence (Baldwin et al. 1998) suggests that survey respondents do not have that much difficulty distinguishing between the two types of innovation.

12 For example, according to Rosa (2003), most of the Canadian firms in technical services are very small: 78 percent have fewer than 20 employees. This is even more pronounced in computer services, where the proportion rises to 86 percent.

13 As cited in Djellal and Gallouj (1999) in the ZEW survey, the hierarchy of frequency of innovations is: process innovation (53 percent); product innovations (34 percent) and organizational innovations (13 percent). In DIW which focused on Berlin, the hierarchy is completely reversed: organizational innovations (40 percent); product innovations (38 percent) and process innovations (22 percent). Their article also cites notable discrepancies in the results from various national surveys based on the more restrictive definition of innovation.

14 Unless stated otherwise, this paper examines the innovation in the private service sector, leaving aside public services.

15 The 'communications' industries include telecommunication carriers, radio broadcasters, television broadcasters, cable companies, combined radio and television broadcasters, and other telecommunication industries. The 'financial services' industries contain chartered banks, trust companies and life insurers. Finally, 'technical business services' includes four of the industries from the business service industries category: computer services, related computer services, the offices of engineers and other scientific and technical service industries. Business services considered 'non-technical' such as employment agencies, advertising, architects, lawyers and management consultants are not included. Neither are personal and government services.

16 Wholesale, the fastest growing service industry in the 1980s and 1990s (Industry Canada, March 2001), is not included in the Survey of Innovation, 1996.

17 Note that this is a more comprehensive, and in my view better, definition than the one suggested in the *Oslo II Manual*. It explicitly includes organizational innovation, which is absent in *Oslo II* (OECD/Eurostat 1997).

18 Note that a more recent survey conducted by Statistics Canada (Innovation Survey 1999) covered a sample of larger firms (firms included in the *Business Register* and employing more than 20 persons) and a more recent period (1996-1999). The survey found that about 80 percent of these larger manufacturing firms innovated. Since a very important share of firms in services are in the smallest size category, employing less than 20 persons, a more meaningful comparison is with the Innovation and Advanced Technology Survey of 1993 that also included the smallest firms employing less than 20 persons.

Several other methodological differences make a comparison of the Statistics Canada, Survey of Innovation and Advanced Technology, 1993 and the Statistics Canada innovation surveys (1999) difficult. The 1996 Survey of Innovation in service industries is methodologically closer to the former than to the latter of the two surveys of innovation manufacturing.

19 An example of heterogeneity of services innovation is provided by an analysis of innovation in engineering services (Hamdani 2001, Table 1) which shows that in this sub-sector, product innovations were far less frequent than organizational and process innovations (3.6 percent versus 15.6 percent and 23.2 percent respectively). This compared with technical services, where the results were 36 percent, 23.9 and 16.4 percent, respectively.

20 After indicating the type of innovation (product-process or organizational change) respondents were asked whether they had difficulties distinguishing between the product, process and organizational change innovation.

21 The information on the percent of innovators that had difficulties identifying organizational innovation is apparently available but was not published (Rosa 2003).

22 Statistics Canada, The Survey of Electronic Commerce and Technology 2000 (SECT) contains two questions on organizational and technological improvements. These two questions provide the first cross-economy data on this issue, covering both firms in the private sector and organizations in the public sector.

23 Organizational change is defined by a positive response to this question from SECT (2000):
"During the last three years, 1998 to 2000, did your organization introduce significantly improved organizational structures or implement improved management techniques?" An additional question on training due to organizational change was asked.

24 The following two questions determined if firms were involved in technological change and, if so, how were they involved:
"During the last three years, 1998 to 2000, did your organization introduce significantly improved technologies?"
"If yes, how did you introduce significantly improved technologies?
(*Check all that apply*):
- by purchasing off-the-shelf technologies?
- by licensing new technologies?
- by customising or significantly modifying existing technologies?
- by developing new technologies? (either alone or in conjunction with others)"

25 As Earl (2002a, p.10) writes "Within the services producing sector both the highest and lowest rates of adoption of organizational change fell within intangible services (see Table 2). For intangible services, the adoption rates for organizational change ranged from a low of 21 percent for firms in management of companies and enterprises to 52 percent for educational services and

information and cultural industries. In fact, the two private sector industries with public sector counterparts — educational services and health care and social assistance — were amongst the top three industries that underwent organizational change between 1998 and 2000. Within the goods related services, the adoption rate for organizational change ranged from 28 percent for transportation and warehousing to 46 percent for wholesale trade with retail trade (36 percent) in the middle."

26 There are, however, important differences between intangible and goods-related services. Firms employing fewer than 100 persons and providing intangible services introduced technological change more frequently than firms providing goods-related services. The relationship for larger firms employing more than 100 persons was reversed; the goods producing firms introduced technological change more frequently than firms providing intangible services. According to Earl (2002a), the adoption of technological change reported in the study probably reflected steps taken by firms to ensure that installed technology would continue to function when the date changed to the year 2000.

27 Questionnaires used in surveys of services innovations inspired by the *Oslo Manual* dominated by the technological (industrial) perspective, ignore this specific trait of services.

28 The percentage indicates the percentage of firms that rated the item crucial (5) or very important (4) on a scale ranging from (1) negligible to (5) crucial.

29 These percentages are very similar to the percentage of firms conducting R&D in each of these service industries.

30 Since the design of the questionnaire used in the Statistics Canada Survey of Innovation, 1996 (service industries) resembles more the questionnaire of the Statistics Canada Survey of Innovation and Advanced Technology, 1993 (manufacturing) than the more recent Statistics Canada Survey of Innovation, 1999 (manufacturing), we compare results of the 1996 survey in services with those of the 1993 survey of manufacturing firms.

31 It is worth noting that technical services are more dependent on universities and higher education for information about innovation than are the other two sectors — 25 percent versus 5 to 8 percent for the other two industries (communications and financial services) (Rosa 2003).

32 Consultants and private R&D institutions were considered important or crucial sources of innovation by about 20 percent of innovators both in manufacturing and service industries. In addition, some technical services are also likely to be included in the external source of innovation information under the heading "suppliers", which represented one of the two most important external inputs to innovation in manufacturing firms (Baldwin and Hanel 2003) and the third most frequent in service innovations (Baldwin et al. 1998).

33 See Tomlinson (2000) who examined the contribution of knowledge-intensive services to manufacturing in the United Kingdom.

34 Computer programs were specifically included in the *U.S. Copyright Act* in 1980.

35 There were several celebrated cases of litigation over the infringement of software copyrights. After a U.S. court decision strengthened the rights of the copyright holder in *Apple Computer vs. Franklin Computer*, the tendency was reversed by a more liberal decision regarding spreadsheet software in *Lotus vs. Borland* (Graham and Mowery 2001).

36 Vaver (2001) provides a very timely comparison of Canadian and U.S. intellectual property protection.

37 The number of U.S. Internet patents jumped by 300 percent from 1997 to 1998 with 2,193 patents issued in the latter year according to Rivette and Kline (2000).

38 The clash between these two attitudes and resulting Internet patent wars are well described in Rivette and Kline (2000).

39 Further examples of, and references to, cases of IP infringement can be found in Hanel (2003a).

40 The report by the Committee on Intellectual Property Rights and the Emerging Information Infrastructure of the National Research Council, *The Digital Dilemma — Intellectual Property in the Information Age*, (2000) recognized that given the multitude of IP business models, legal mechanisms and technical protection services that are possible, crafting a one-size-fits-all solution to the dilemma would be too rigid. The Committee recommended that: "Legislators should not contemplate any overhaul of intellectual property laws and public policy at this time, to permit the evolutionary process (described above) to play out."

41 Baldwin et al. (1998) report that over 40 percent of innovators in communications who use IP protection find copyrights to be effective and over 50 percent find trademarks to be effective. In financial services, close to 60 percent report that trademarks are an effective means of protecting their IP. In technical business services, trademarks and trade secrets are considered to be effective, copyrights less so.

42 Among impediments specific to largest firms, Mohnen et Rosa (1999) also include internal resistance to change. However, internal resistance to change is reported by only 0.54 percent of largest firms, while about 5 percent of the largest firms complain about the high cost of innovation.

43 See Preissel (2000) for a more detailed discussion of these kinds of obstacles based on interviews conducted in Germany. Except for the lack of qualified personnel, which is not an important impediment to service innovation in Germany, the importance of other obstacles is similar in both countries and therefore we can expect that the German findings are likely to apply to the Canadian situation as well.

44 Statistics Canada Survey of Innovation and Advanced Technology, 1993.

45 More than half (57 percent) of innovators in technical business services carry out R&D activities compared to 10 percent of non-innovators.

46 See Hamdani (2001), the study of innovation in Canadian engineering services, which is also based on the Statistics Canada Survey of Innovation, 1996.

47 For instance, R&D statistics for the services sector do not include research and development activities in social sciences and humanities which are particularly important in many service activities. The recent (1997) fundamental revision in industrial classification from the Standard Industrial Classification (SIC) to the NAICS may make it difficult to compare R&D in services over time. The replacement of Statistics Canada surveys of R&D in smaller firms by information from tax returns collected by the Canada Revenue Agency (Gault 1997) may lead to underestimation of R&D in many smaller firms which perform R&D but often do not claim R&D tax credits because their R&D activities are not organized and accounted according to the dominant manufacturing industry model. Based on Statistics Canada's 1993 Survey of Innovation and Advanced Technology in Manufacturing, which also included small firms employing fewer than 20 employees, Baldwin and Hanel (2003) show that of the 65 percent of manufacturing firms that conducted some R&D, only 16 percent applied for the tax credit for R&D between 1989 and 1991. According to the Statistics Canada Survey of Innovation, 1999 which included only manufacturing firms employing more than 20 persons, only about 53 percent of firms of all size that conducted R&D claimed tax credits. However, in low technology sectors, only 37 percent of smaller firms (employing 20 to 49 persons) did so (Hanel 2003b).

48 These findings cover only R&D performed by business enterprises. R&D performed by the federal and provincial governments, universities and colleges and non-profit organizations is not included.

49 This sector's R&D/sales is 35.4 percent, probably the highest of all industries in Canada. This may be a statistical fluke. By way of comparison, in the United States the ratio is only 3.5 percent.

50 Statistics Canada is about to launch a new Survey of Innovation in services that will fill some gaps in our knowledge of innovation in services.

ACKNOWLEDGMENTS

MY THANKS to Fred Gault, Louise Earl and Julio Rosa from Statistics Canada who shared with me important sources of information and helped me to understand some statistical issues. Helpful comments by Steven Globerman, Pierre Sauvé and John Jankowski are also gratefully acknowledged. Ely Hounzangbe provided able assistantship. I alone am responsible for the opinions and remaining errors.

BIBLIOGRAPHY

Akerblom, M. 2002. *R&D and Innovation Surveys in Service Sectors; Current Experience, Conceptual and Practical Problems and Future Prospects*. Paris: OECD, September.

Baldwin, John, and M. Da Pont. 1996. "Innovation in Canadian Manufacturing Enterprises", Cat. No. 88-514-XPB. Ottawa: Statistics Canada.

Baldwin, John R., and Petr Hanel. 2003. *Innovation and Knowledge Creation in an Open Economy*. Cambridge: Cambridge University Press.

Baldwin, John R., and Z. Lin. 2002. "Impediments to the Adoption of Advanced Technology in Canadian Manufacturing Industries," *Research Policy, 31* (1): 1-18.

Baldwin, John R., Guy Gellaltly, Joanne Johnson, and Valerie Peteers. 1998. "Innovation in Dynamic Service Industries," Cat. No. 88-516-XIE. Ottawa: Statistics Canada. Centre interuniversitaire de la recherche sur la science et la technologie (CIRST). *Selected tabulations*. Sherbrooke, Quebec: University of Sherbrooke.

Committee on Intellectual Property Rights and the Emerging Information Infrastructure. 2000. *The Digital Dilemma — Intellectual Property in the Information Age*. Washington, D.C.: National Academy Press.

Conseil de la science et de la technologie. 2003. *L'innovation dans les services*. Quebec City: Conseil de la science et de la technologie, June.

Dalpé, Robert, and Frances Anderson. 1997. "Contracting Out of Science and Technology Services," *Administration and Society*, 28 (4) February, 489-510.

De Melto, Dennis P., Kathryn E. McMullen, and Russel M. Wills. 1980. *Preliminary Report: Innovation and Technological Change in Five Canadian Industries*. Discussion Paper No. 176. Ottawa: Economic Council of Canada..

Djellal, F., and Faïz Gallouj. 1999. "Services and the Search for Relevant Innovation Indicators; a Review of National and International Surveys," *Science and Public Policy*, 26 (4): 218-232.

Earl, Louise. 2002a. *An Overview of Organizational and Technological Change in the Private Sector, 1998-2000*. Cat. No. 88F0006XIE2002009. Ottawa: Statistics Canada.

Earl, Louise. 2002b. *Innovation and Change in the Public Sector: A Seeming Oxymoron*. Cat. No. 88F0006XIE2001. Ottawa: Statistics Canada.

Feldstein, M. 2003. *Why is Productivity Growing Faster?* Presentation at the American Economic Association Annual Meeting session on The New Economy and Growth in the United States, (January 3-5), Washington, D.C.

Frascati Manual. 2002. *Proposed Standard Practice for Surveys on Research and Experimental Development*. Paris: OECD.

Gallouj, Faïz, and Olivier Weinstein. 1997. "Innovation in Services," *Research Policy*, 26, 537-556.

Gault, Fred. 1995. *R&D in a Service Economy*. Ottawa: Statistics Canada, Services, Science and Technology Division, mimeo.

———. 1997. *Research and Development in a Service Economy*. Ottawa: Statistics Canada, Services, Science and Technology Division, paper presented at the NATO Advanced Workshop, Quantitative Studies for S&T Policy in Transition Economies, (October 23-26), Moscow.

Gellaltly, Guy. 1999. *Differences between Innovators and Non-innovator Profiles: Small Establishments in Business Services*. Analytical Studies Branch, No. 143, Cat. No. 11F009MPE. Ottawa: Statistics Canada.

Graham, Stuart, and David Mowery. 2001. "Intellectual Property in the U.S. Software Industry," *Intellectual Property and Innovation in the Knowledge-Based Economy*. Industry Canada Conference, (May 23-24), Toronto, Ontario.

Griliches, Zvi. 1992. "Introduction" in Zvi Griliches and A. Griliches (ed.). *Output Measurement in the Service Sectors*. Chicago: University of Chicago Press, pp. 1-22.

Hall, B., and R. Ham-Ziedonis. 2001. "The Patent Paradox Revisited: An Empirical Study of Patenting in the U.S. Semiconductor Industry, 1979-1995," *RAND Journal of Economics, 32*, 101-128.

Hamdani, D. 2001. *Capacity to Innovate, Innovation and Impact: The Canadian Engineering Services Industry*. Science, Innovation and Electronic Information Division, Research paper No. 11, Cat. No. 88F0017MIE. Ottawa: Statistics Canada.

Hanel, Petr. 2003a. IPR *Business Management Practices: A Survey of Literature*. Report to Canadian Intellectual Property Office.

———. 2003b. *Impact of Government Support Programs on Innovation*. Report to Industry Canada, Innovation Market Place Division.

Hipp, C., B.S. Tether, and Ian Miles. 2000. "The Incidence and Effects of Innovation in Services: Evidence from Germany," *International Journal of Innovation Management, 4* (4): 417-453.

Howells, J. 2000. "Services and System of Innovation," in Birgitte Andersen, J. Howells, R. Hull, and Ian Miles. (eds.). *Knowledge and Innovation in the New Service Economy*. PREST/CRIC Studies in Science, Technology and Innovation. Cheltenham, UK and Northampton, MA: Edward Elgar, pp. 215-228.

Industry Canada. 2001. *Survol de l'économie des services*. Ottawa: Industry Canada, March.

Jankowski, John E. 2001. "Measurement and Growth of R&D within the Service Economy," *Journal of Technology Transfer, 26*, 323-336.

Kline, Stephen J., and Nathan Rosenberg. 1986. "An Overview of Innovation" in Ralph Landau and Nathan Rosenberg (eds.). *The Positive Sum Strategy: Harnessing Technology For Economic Growth*. Washington, D.C.: National Academy Press, pp. 275-305.

Licht, G., and D. Moch. 1999. "Innovation and Information Technology in Services," *Canadian Journal of Economics*, 32, (2) April, 363-83.

Miles, Ian. 2001. *Services Innovation: A Reconfiguration of Innovation Studies*. Discussion Paper Series. Manchester: University of Manchester, PREST.

Mohnen, Pierre, and Julio Rosa. 1999. *Barriers to Innovation in Services Industries in Canada*. Science, Innovation and Electronic Information Division, Research paper No. 7, Cat. No. 88F0017MIE No. 11. Ottawa: Statistics Canada.

OECD. 1992. *Proposed Guidelines for Collecting and Interpreting Technological Innovation Data — Oslo Manual*. Paris: OECD.

OECD/Eurostat. 1996. *Proposed Guidelines for Collecting and Interpreting Technological Innovation Data — Oslo Manual (first revision)*. Paris: OECD.

————. 1997. *Proposed Guidelines for Collecting and Interpreting Technological Innovation Data — Oslo Manual II*. Paris: OECD.

Pilat, D. 2001. "Innovation and Productivity in Services: The State of the Art," chapter 2 in *Innovation and Productivity in Services*. Paris: OECD.

Preissel, B. 2000. "Service Innovation: What Makes it Different?" empirical evidence from Germany in *Innovation Systems in the Service Economy*. Boston: Kluwer Academic Publisher.

Rivette, K., and D. Kline. 2000. Rembrandts in the Attic: Unlocking the Hidden Value of Patents. Cambridge, MA: Harvard Business School Press.

Rosa, Julio. 2003. Determinants of Product and Process Innovation in Canada's Dynamic Service Industries. Cat. No. 88F0006XIE2002017. Ottawa: Statistics Canada.

Rose, A. 1995. *Strategic R&D Alliances*. Catalogue No. 63F0002XIB1995004, no. 4. Ottawa: Statistics Canada.

Schumpeter, Joseph. 1934. *The Theory of Economic Development*.Cambridge, MA: Harvard University Press. First published in German, 1912.

Scotchmer, Suzanne, and Stephen M. Maurer. 2001. "Across Two Worlds: Database Protection in the U.S. and Europe," *Intellectual Property and Innovation in the Knowledge-Based Economy*. Industry Canada Conference, (May 23-24), Toronto, Ontario.

Sirilli, G., and R. Evangelista. 1998. "Technological Innovation in Services and Manufacturing: Results from Italian Surveys," *Research Policy*, 28, 881-899.

Statistics Canada. 1993. *Survey of Innovation and Advanced Technology*. Ottawa: Statistics Canada.

————. 1996. *Innovation Survey*. Ottawa: Statistics Canada.

————. 1999. *Innovation Survey*. Ottawa: Statistics Canada.

————. 2001. *Survey of Electronic Commerce and Technology*. Ottawa: Statistics Canada.

Sundbo, J., and Faïz Gallouj. 1999. *Innovation in Services in Seven European Countries*. Synthesis Report for the European Commission, Report No. 99-01, Roskilde University and University of Science and Technology Lille, Center for Service Studies.

Tether, B., and Stan Metcalfe. 2003. *Service and Systems of Innovation*. Centre for Research on Innovation and Competition, Discussion Paper No. 58. Manchester: University of Manchester.

Tomlinson, M. 2000. "The Contribution of Knowledge-Intensive Services to the Manufacturing Industry," in Birgitte Andersen, J. Howells, R. Hull, and Ian Miles. (eds.). *Knowledge and Innovation in the New Service Economy*. PREST/CRIC Studies in Science, Technology and Innovation. Cheltenham, UK and Northampton, MA: Edward Elgar.

Vaver, David. 2001. "Canada's Intellectual Property Framework: A Comparative Overview," *Intellectual Property and Innovation in the Knowledge-Based Economy*. Industry Canada Conference, (May 23-24), Toronto, Ontario.

Young, Alison. 1996. "Measuring R&D in the Services," STI Working Paper. Paris: OECD.

Comment

Steven Globerman
Western Washington University

PETR HANEL PROVIDES a broad and comprehensive overview of innovation in the Canadian services sector and — where possible — compares Canadian performance to the services sector performances of the United States and Western Europe. Hanel makes a number of fundamental points. One is that the innovation process in the services industries has been less well studied than the innovation process in manufacturing industries. Perhaps the main reason is the difficulty in defining and measuring output. Since a substantial share of innovation takes the form of product differentiation, measuring innovation will naturally be more difficult for activities where output takes an intangible form. Another reason is that innovation frequently takes the form of organizational change or other changes that typically accompany product or process innovations. Yet another reason related to Hanel's first point is that traditional input measures of innovation activity, such as research and development and patents, are less relevant to services businesses than to manufacturers.

Hanel's second fundamental point is that innovation in the services industries emphasizes interaction between the services provider and user. This is particularly the case for businesses that are intensive users of information communications and technology (ICT). In fact, innovation in the manufacturing sector is also characterized by extensive information exchange and cooperation between innovators and their industrial customers. What would seem to be distinctive about the services industries is that their customers are much larger in number and more heterogeneous. Hence, coordination of the innovation process between suppliers and customers is more difficult and costly in the case of services industries.

A third point made by Hanel is that size matters. Specifically, large services firms are much more likely to be innovators than are smaller firms. This, too, is a characteristic of innovation processes in the manufacturing sector. The finding that small services firms are at a disadvantage in the innovation process compared to large firms is not universally reported. For example, a Finnish study of innovation finds a clear association between company size and innovation for manufacturing industries but no corresponding difference is identified for services industries.[1] Hanel identifies lack of financing as a major barrier to innovation in the services industries, as well as a lack of qualified personnel. The lack of financing, in turn, might reflect the fact that services firms frequently do not qualify for the R&D financing for which manufacturing firms qualify. It would be interesting if largely publicly funded industries such as health care and education were also discouraged from innovating by a lack of financing. In fact, Hanel does not identify differences in the innovative behaviour of public- or private-sector services providers. The conventional assumption is that the absence of a profit motive discourages innovation; however, a more complicated analysis maintains that there are likely to be profound differences in the nature of innovation when comparing public- and private-sector organizations. For example, publicly funded hospitals in the United States tend to do more "advanced" research and experimental procedures in comparison with their privately-funded counterparts.

Hanel highlights several other findings. Services innovations are more likely to take the form of organizational changes than is the case for innovation in the manufacturing sector. However, combined product and organizational changes are the most common type of services sector innovation. Innovation rates in "dynamic" Canadian services industry groups exceed the innovation rates in Canadian manufacturing industries. Research and development is not as important to innovation in the services industries as it is in manufacturing, and intellectual property protection, at least until now, is correspondingly less important in the services industries.

The general conclusion one can draw from the literature reviewed by Hanel is that services firms introduce innovations at rates that are comparable to manufacturing firms. This is a surprising result on the surface given the traditional reports of lagging productivity performance for services industries compared to manufacturing industries. It may be the case that Baumol's Cost Disease applies only to non-dynamic services industries, and further, that the emergence of ICT-based innovations have expanded the potential for technological change across a wide range of services industries. It is also possible, however, that simple counts for innovation do not give an accurate picture of the overall economic significance of the innovation process in services firms compared to manufacturing firms. In this regard, some findings of Broersma and Brouwer (2001) are suggestive. Specifically, for a sample of Dutch services firms, they identify a negative relationship between indicators of innovativeness and productivity. They offer the hypothesis that ICT adoption by services firms takes a relatively long time to translate into productivity improvements and their time series might be too short to allow for observation of productivity growth.[2]

While the Broersma and Brouwer (2001) hypothesis might be correct, it is also possible that services firms are simply less able than manufacturing firms to take advantage of the productivity benefits of new technologies including ICT.[3] An even more problematic assessment has been made for innovations in the health care sector. Specifically, it has been suggested that the benefits of many medical innovations do not justify their costs. It is well known that specific market structures can result in "excessive" innovation; i.e., innovations that reduce social surplus. The phenomenon is driven by the incentive of firms to take economic rent from other firms. The health care sector — at least in the United States — might well be an example of "excessive" innovation. In any case, the health care experience underscores the relevance of qualifying measures of innovation by their economic impact. Apparently the data available simply do not allow for this type of analysis.

Hanel's findings suggest that easier financing and greater availability of skilled labour could promote innovation in the services industries. In specific and important industries — most notably health care, education and broadcasting — the role of government and public sector labour unions would seem to be critically important to the innovation process. In particular, the resistance of government bureaucrats and labour unions to any experimentation with new organizational forms for the delivery of health care and education would seem to be highly relevant to an understanding of the rates of technological change in those sectors.

In this regard, factors promoting innovation and technological change in the services industries might be fairly idiosyncratic to the specific industry. Getting at an understanding of such factors might require detailed case study analysis. Such case studies are obviously complements to the type of broad statistical surveys discussed in Hanel's valuable paper.

ENDNOTES

1 See Statistics Finland 2000.

2 See Broersma and Brouwer 2001.

3 While it is not the only relevant technology in services innovation, ICT is pervasive and intrinsic to almost all economic activities, and, as such, is perceived as the "great enabler" of services innovation. See den Hertog and Bilderbeek 1999.

BIBLIOGRAPHY

Broersma, L., and E. Brouwer. 2001. "Innovation in ICT Services: Explorations with Micro Data for the Netherlands," mimeo. Groningen: University of Groningen.

den Hertog, P., and R. Bilderbeek. 1999. "Conceptualizing Service Innovation and Service Innovation Patterns," Utrecht, The Netherlands: DIALOGIC.
Statistics Finland. 2002. *Innovation Activities of Enterprises*. Helsinki: Statistics Finland.

Edwin H. Neave
Queen's University

11

Technology and the Financial Services Industry

TRENDS IN FINANCIAL SERVICES

THE FINANCIAL SERVICES INDUSTRY has long been a major contributor to economic growth and development. The industry continues to gain in importance as advances in information and telecommunications technologies contribute to its increasing size and sophistication. In response to changing technologies, financial institutions around the world have massively restructured their organizations in the past two decades. The industry is increasingly a globalized activity, and the firms constituting it continue to increase both the diversity of their lines of business and their absolute size. Most of these changes result from mergers, both domestic and international. These mergers are not only taking place within the banking sector. Combinations of banking and insurance are becoming increasingly frequent, and combinations of banking and investment banking have been commonplace for some time.

Today's financial services providers (FSPs) are innovative product and service developers. Innovation has improved both their institutional operating efficiency and the effectiveness with which clients can search for products and product prices. Transaction charges for some financial services have been reduced. Consumers benefit from new and lower-priced products and services, while small businesses benefit from improved access to loans provided through credit scoring techniques. Large businesses benefit from increased availability of syndicated loans and market forms of financing. Both large businesses and the institutions that serve them benefit from improvements in risk management. Investors benefit from faster execution of securities trades, better and easier price comparisons, and thinner trading margins. However, the benefits of change do not come without some costs. As the latter part of this study shows, there are various types of costs and problems that offset but do not erase the benefits just cited.

GLOBALIZATION

GLOBALIZATION HAS STIMULATED FINANCIAL INTEGRATION, in most cases by providing incentives for mergers and acquisitions within and across national borders. Throughout the world, financial systems are witnessing increasing convergence and asset concentration. In the United States, more than 8,000 commercial and savings banks were taken over between 1987 and 1997, leaving fewer than 9,000 remaining. Between 1985 and 1997, the number of credit institutions in the European Union decreased from 12,250 to 9,285 (Schenk 2001). Globally, the value of mergers and acquisitions in financial services rose from $85 billion in 1991 to $534 billion in 1998. Cross-border capital flows have also increased dramatically since the 1980s. However, not every type of business is increasing commensurately. For example, the foreign assets of Canadian banks have not shown much or any comparable growth over the 1980s and 1990. Though the general picture is not one of uniform growth, the world's financial system is generally becoming more international and more integrated.

Increasing internationalization has been accompanied by more permissive regulation. Constraints on the ability of foreign institutions to enter previously closed domestic markets have been relaxed in many countries. The result is that some of the world's largest financial institutions now face lower barriers to entry than they used to. At the same time, other institutions face higher entry barriers as financial businesses become more technology-intensive and the costs of setting up new establishments rise.

THE NEW WORLD OF FINANCIAL SERVICES

THE FINANCIAL SERVICES INDUSTRY EXHIBITS nearly continuous technological advance. Over the past two decades, financial institutions have spent heavily on technology to automate data processing, to develop internationally connected networks of automated banking machines, to expand their Internet accessibility, and to implement various forms of wireless access that have been developed by utilities and communications companies. Non-financial companies have also entered the financial business directly as service providers. All of these changes enhance the ability of both retail and wholesale clients to conduct transactions easily from many different locations using a variety of access technologies.

Financial services are changing as well. At the wholesale level, banks are much more active in providing risk management services to their business clients. They are also more active in trading risk instruments and securities both for their clients and their own accounts. Loan sales and the advent of credit derivatives mean that banks no longer assume lending risks to the same degree that they once did. At the level of small business, credit is becoming more widely available through the services of aggregators and because of the advent of credit scoring. At the retail level, banks are combining with insurance companies to offer a spectrum of "bancassurance" products and a variety of wealth management services. Finally, many of the services traditionally offered by banks are now being provided by both financial and non-financial entities, especially over the Internet.

Technological change is having an important effect on access to the financial system. By 2005 or so, a retail client should be able to go to almost any communications device in the world, insert a card and retrieve personal financial information. The device may be an airport kiosk, a smart phone, a personal digital assistant, an automated banking machine (ABM), an Internet wireless hotspot, or possibly even a wristwatch. As late as 2000, that customer had to go to an ABM, use a land-line phone, or visit a branch to effect the same transaction. Financial institutions will know more about their customers and consequently will be able to service them better by developing a corporate memory. As information systems become increasingly better integrated, each transaction will be available to all the personnel of the institution and clients will experience much more informed levels of service.

Financial markets are also experiencing rapid and profound change. As communication costs become independent of distance and as computer systems lower trading costs, activity is moving toward electronic trading facilities that are not tied to any location. New electronic exchanges are offering a variety of Internet-based trading services that present serious competition for traditional exchanges. However colourful they were, open outcry trading pits will soon be a vestige of the past. Trading systems for equities, fixed income securities and foreign exchange are all consolidating into global operations. As securities and derivatives exchanges become more international, they are merging with exchanges in other parts of the world and are also making much heavier use of computer-based trading. In addition, remote access to trading facilities and relevant trading information is becoming increasingly widespread, particularly through the Internet. Greater information interchange and cheaper access to information is generally improving price determination, although some issues of fragmentation are also arising and require management, as discussed further below.

IMPACTS OF TRENDS

INTERNET AND WIRELESS COMMUNICATION TECHNOLOGIES are not just new distribution channels. Instead, they offer new and different ways of providing financial services. New technologies permit financial products to be commoditized and at the same time tailored to the needs of consumers.[1] There is a proliferation of access devices, including automated banking machines, personal computers, personal digital assistants, televisions with Internet access, and cellular phones, all of which are becoming the consumer's first point of contact with financial services. Enabling companies support the technology of traditional FSPs but also set up their own virtual banks.

Advances in information and communication technology support the delivery of a broad array of financial services through single providers. New providers include online banks and brokerages, as well as aggregators and portals — companies that allow consumers to compare such financial services as mortgage loans and insurance policies. Indeed in areas such as the United States, Latin America and Korea, portals are becoming a critical link between access devices and FSPs. Portal operators personalize information in their attempts to attract and retain consumers, then earn revenue by referring their customers to appropriate FSPs. Aggregators complement portals, allowing consumers to compare mortgage, insurance or lending products offered by suppliers of financial services.

E-finance embodies opportunities to broaden access, lower costs and improve the quality of financial services to both retail and commercial clients. In retail finance, the greatest change is occurring in consumer, small- and medium-sized lending, as well as rural finance. In small business, e-finance has the potential to improve the quality and scope of lending, particularly through the use of credit scoring software. For larger businesses, e-finance commoditizes securities issues and provides significantly greater opportunities for defining and trading risk instruments. Vertically-integrated financial services companies are growing rapidly and creating synergies by combining brand names, distribution networks and financial services production. Telecommunication and other non-financial companies are now providing payment and other services.

The acquisition of Ameritrade by the TD Financial Group offers one case in point. This combination represents a merger of an e-finance company with a traditional bank. The new entity offers a wider range of financial services than either of the individual companies did prior to the merger. It also represents possible new economies of scope for both banks and financial services companies. At the same time, it poses a challenge to traditional banking structures, as well as to financial regulators. It combines banking and service to financial markets in ways that present at least a potential for some conflicts of interest.

Entry has been particularly strong into financial services that offered attractive initial margins, especially if those margins could be realized through unbundling and commoditization. Such services include brokerage, trading systems, some retail banking products, bill presentment and payment gateways for business-to-business (B2B) commerce. From there, the new entrants have moved toward more highly regulated services. For example E-trade, a company offering securities trading facilities, has recently acquired a bank to provide a full range of financial services to its customers and now offers web access to its clients.

Barriers between markets have been reduced as commercial paper and corporate bonds have been substituted for bank loans to larger and better-known corporations. Similarly, on the retail level, mutual funds and other forms of jointly-owned securities portfolios have been substituted for bank deposits. These forces for disintermediation stimulate banks to expand other financial services as compensation. Banks and insurance companies are consolidating around recognized brand names to position themselves in the new environment of increased commoditization and electronic delivery. To some extent, regulatory and industry barriers have slowed the commoditization of deposit-taking and payment services, although these developments are now being accelerated by setting up online banks and by various forms of credit and debit cards, including smart cards.

There has been far less entry into markets characterized by sunk costs and low potential for commoditization potential. These include corporate advisory services, underwriting and the facilitation of mergers and acquisitions. These areas still require relationship capital, a certain size and a brand name to compete effectively. Nevertheless, these kinds of businesses are increasingly subject to global competition aimed at reaping the advantages of reputation, and brand name, and at realizing economies of scale and of scope. For sufficiently large markets, global competition will likely lead to market contestability, even if only a few providers are actually present in the market.

The Internet and other technological advances have reduced economies of scale in the production of financial services so that they can easily be unbundled and commoditized. This has happened with payment and brokerage services, mortgage loans, insurance and some forms of trade finance. Lower scale economies have reduced barriers to entry and consequently increased competition among providers of those kinds of financial services. The main financial service that still exhibits increasing returns to scale is the medium-size loan market because large databases of credit history are required to build a credit-scoring model for medium-size clients. For most other forms of credit, economies of scale have become small, as the fixed costs of screening small borrowers (under $100,000) have dropped significantly.

On the other hand, the Internet has also created new barriers to entry, especially through first-mover advantages. For example, competing with an established and well-recognized portal can be difficult and expensive. Similarly, declining economies of scale and greater competition will not always offset network externalities. For example, the value of electronic payments services largely depends on the degree to which users adopt a common standard. Trading systems, exchanges, financial portals and (possibly to a lesser extent) e-enablers all exhibit similar common standard characteristics.

BENEFITS FOR CONSUMERS AND CORPORATIONS

WIDELY AVAILABLE REAL-TIME MARKET INFORMATION lowers the cost of financial services by mitigating uncertainty, by reducing informational asymmetries[2] and by reducing the transaction costs associated with paper processing and human error. Consumers' search costs have fallen as new distribution channels have opened up and as new financial service providers emerge. For example, by using credit scoring and other techniques, FSPs can create and tailor products over the Internet without much human input and at very low marginal cost. Internet competitors do not have to rely on bricks and mortar to distinguish themselves as financial service providers. A typical customer transaction through a branch or phone call costs about $1.00, but the same transaction performed online costs only about $0.02. At the same time, sunk costs are becoming less important. These can include branch networks, knowledge of local borrowers, access to payment systems, large upfront advertising expenditures, perceptions of size and safety, long-lasting customer relationships, and substantial up-front investments in technology. Their significance is diminishing largely because electronic delivery modes do not rely on a branch network.

Financial services providers' clients often find it easy and cheap to use such services and as long as savings are passed on, these developments can deliver important benefits to clients at both the retail and the commercial levels. Companies supporting comparison shopping and portals allow Internet users to combine services from different providers cheaply and easily. For example, new aggregators such as Lending Tree allow consumers to compare the prices of financial services. The new technologies have brought substantially lower charges in securities trading. Brokerage commissions fell from an average of $52.89 a trade in early 1996 to $15.67 in mid-1998. By mid-2000, some brokerages had reduced their commissions to zero. Commissions charged by electronic communications networks (ECNs) are now at $0.05 per share and falling.

Commercial borrowers using B2B transactions and treasury operations benefit from lower transaction and search costs and from greater access to financial services. New online companies such as garage.com and techpacific.com provide a full array of services to start-up companies, including legal services, web design, accounting services, branding and advertisement, and investor relations. Venture capital firms and other investors can use these companies to screen potential start-up ideas. The use of the Internet for data mining in lending may enhance financial services outreach to the point where it eventually touches very small companies.

Web-based financial services substantially improve the financial infrastructure. They unify the Internet as a communication standard by combining a Web browser, a display standard, and by using a Web server as the access point into back-end operational systems. With these facilities, cross-selling products becomes easier, and subject to greater economies of scope. From the client's point of view, an integrated system is much more convenient than a combination of separate systems for ABMs, call centres and kiosk transactions.

E-FINANCE IN THE FINANCIAL SERVICES INDUSTRY

THIS SECTION EXAMINES some of the ways that FSPs have adopted e-finance technologies, and then discusses how those technologies have altered the role and the structure of the financial services industry.

E-FINANCE BY ADOPTATION OF FINANCIAL SERVICES FIRMS

BY THE YEAR 2000, e-finance had affected every aspect of financial intermediation, including lending to large business. Since the 1980s, credit-scoring techniques have been used to make both mortgage lending and credit card decisions. Both credit and debit cards have become important media for making payments. More recently, smart cards have also seen increasing usage. Debit card usage has become especially popular in Canada, as discussed further on.

Credit-scoring techniques have become important for lending to small businesses as well as to consumers. Although large banks were the first to adopt widespread use of credit-scoring techniques, in the United States, smaller banks have also been able to do so by purchasing services from third-party providers. With respect to large business loans, e-technology is used mainly to analyze financial statements, to make cash flow projections, and to design appropriate ways of providing credit. Securitization and risk management also benefit from the uses of e-technology.

After establishing their branch networks in the period between the 1940s and the 1970s, banks began using ABMs and telephone links as the first alternative channels for distributing products and services to retail clients. More recently, depository institutions have invested heavily in Internet distribution channels. Internet facilities have not yet replaced branch and ABM networks and it is unlikely that they will ever wholly do so. However Internet distribution is becoming increasingly more widespread. Large banks have been especially aggressive in offering these newer channels, principally because only very large institutions have been able to finance the massive technological investments that are required to set up such services. One result of greater Internet use is that branch networks are slowly shrinking. Positive-balance credit card services and inter-card payment facilities are already appearing on the scene, and appear likely to become more popular in the future.

Insurance firms have been much slower than banks in adopting e-technologies. For example, online sales of insurance products are only just beginning to appear. On the other hand, e-finance has become increasingly important in calculating policy premiums, in predicting cash flows, in investment portfolio management and in securities trading. So far, insurance firms do not appear to have offered payment services through credit cards.

Securities firms have changed substantially as a result of e-technologies. Discount brokers rely heavily on technology in carrying out their trading operations. In addition, e-finance is playing an increasing role in primary securities distribution by replacing personal contacts with online auction methods. This is happening even though it has not yet been firmly established that securities offered through open auction can be sold at smaller discounts than can offerings based on familiar, relationship-based arrangements.

EFFECTS OF E-FINANCE ON THE FINANCIAL SERVICES SECTOR

TRADITIONALLY, FINANCIAL INTERMEDIARIES have transformed illiquid securities into liquid liabilities. This role is becoming somewhat less important as the liquidity of financial assets held by intermediaries increases with the advent of e-technology. Certain kinds of transactions are being disintermediated. In some of these transactions, banks no longer act as principals: instead, they serve as agents who find counterparties. Securitization illustrates both the traditional and the innovative aspects of this picture. Banks act as principals in holding and collecting the original loans, but then issue new securities against the security of the original loan portfolio. The bank's original loans do not become more liquid when assets are securitized but the newly-issued securities are more liquid than the original loans backing them. Securitization does not usually lead to the transfer of default risk: in most cases absorbing any default risk largely remains with the bank.[3]

Changing technology means that the governance of loans can be accomplished at arm's length to a greater degree than previously. In particular, the administration of loan repayments is less costly when it is automated. Selling securities backed by the original and illiquid assets is easier if those original assets have been subjected to credit scoring. In that case, loan portfolio parameters can be more clearly defined. In these instances, additional information serves to quantify the nature of default risks somewhat more sharply than has previously been possible.

Banks are increasingly selling loans outright and in such cases they usually transfer the default risk to the purchasers. Some observers of this practice have questioned whether e-finance may reduce the banks' reliance on relationship lending and increase their reliance on credit scoring and arm's-length lending. To the extent that e-finance increases the competitiveness of the financial sector, it is possible that relationship-based lending will suffer in relation to short-term market-based decisions. On the other hand, if banking costs are reduced by increased competition, the situation of relationship-based clients could be improved.

Theory describes differences between tradeable and non-tradeable securities.[4] To the extent that relationship loans represent non-tradeable securities, transactions in tradeable securities will not directly affect the ways in which the bank governs loans represented by non-tradeable securities. Increased loan trading could work to reduce relationship lending if the relationship were found not to yield any benefit to either party. This is because with the emergence of trading as a common practice, there is a possibility that banks will define more clearly which kinds of business are best treated as relationship lending and which kinds are not. Changes of this type represent more discriminating resource allocation and actually work to improve rather than to impair the effectiveness and efficiency of the financial system.

Liquidity depends on the ability of buyers and sellers to agree on the value of financial assets and agreement regarding value is usually enhanced when informational asymmetries are reduced. To the extent that e-technology reduces informational asymmetries by lowering the costs of computation and communication, it improves liquidity and makes it easier to trade assets in the market rather than to acquire and to hold them.

Depository institutions are losing market share to mutual funds and pension funds. Although these changes are sometimes attributed to the increasing liquidity of financial assets (Allen, McAndrews and Strahan 2002), the increasing market share of savings captured by mutual funds is also partially attributable to the higher rates of return they managed to achieve up to the end of 2001. This observation is strengthened by the subsequent withdrawal of monies from mutual funds. Similarly, pension funds have captured increased market shares of household savings for a number of reasons that are not necessarily associated with increasing liquidity. Indeed these assets are not at all liquid in cases where they cannot be withdrawn until the beneficiary retires.

Since many aspects of e-finance are characterized by scale economies, the adoption of e-finance technology can lead to concentration of assets. In U.S. banking, the largest 10 organizations accounted for 27 percent of all operating income in 1990, and 45 percent in 1999 (Allen et al. 2002). As one example, electronic payments technologies require large fixed investments and very often use networks that exhibit increasing returns to scale. But what is true for one part of the financial industry is not always true for other parts: the revenues shares going to the small number of the largest companies in the insurance and securities businesses are decreasing. In part, the difference between banking and insurance may be due to the greater importance of e-finance in the asset transformation functions of the former, but the question is an open one that can only be answered definitively following additional research.

New types of FSPs, including online banks, brokerages and aggregators, are entering both domestic and international markets. Non-financial entities, including telecommunication and utility companies, are also beginning to offer payment and other services through their distribution networks. In response to these competitive challenges, banks and insurance companies are joining in the delivery of financial services either through online, in-house activities or through new ventures such as virtual banks. Major financial institutions are also acquiring ownership in promising Internet start-ups. At the same time, major telecommunications companies and companies that have developed portals are entering strategic relationships with, or acquiring an ownership position in, major financial services companies.

Even traditional forms of financial business are affected. Deposit taking can be costly for banks, especially if deposits are in small denominations. In countries where the majority of the population is lower- or low-income, technology can be used to make volume banking profitable, as has been shown in Africa. The proliferation of ABMs and the arrival of Internet-banking in Canada have allowed banks to lower the cost of providing payment and deposit services to clients. Financial institutions could use similar technology in Latin America to attract a large segment of the population not currently being serviced because of the high costs of operating branch outlets.

Risk management has changed substantially in banks and other major financial institutions. For example, banks now follow relatively aggressive policies of managing risks on their own books and they also trade risks, particularly default risks, with others. One standard assumption is that more sophisticated risk management models, better data and more computational power combine to support more effective risk management. However, the statement needs additional qualification. For example, value-at-risk techniques help characterize risks during normal operations but are much less informative about the nature of events occurring during periods of stress in financial markets. To some, the use of value-at-risk and related models provides a false degree of comfort regarding the effectiveness of managing either market or credit risk. Finally, value-at-risk models are currently better suited to managing market risk than default risk.

Banks offload some default risk through securitization but their principal methods of dealing with default risk are reselling loans and purchasing credit derivatives. The advent of credit derivatives means that default risk can be separated from the principal amounts represented by illiquid assets. Default risks are priced as well as traded when credit derivatives are exchanged among institutions, even if the exchanges are negotiated rather than carried out at arm's length in active markets. As the credit derivatives market expands and matures, debates have arisen around issues such as appropriate pricing, the nature of a default event, and the liability of the institution writing the credit derivative.

E-TECHNOLOGIES IN PAYMENT SERVICES

IN THE UNITED STATES, inter-bank payments have been carried out electronically since at least 1918, when the Fedwire payment system was established with leased telegraph wires to link accounts held at the 12 U.S. Federal Reserve banks. Today, the inter-bank payment systems in most industrialized countries use dedicated telephone networks and mainframe computers to process high volumes and large total amounts of transactions. The U.S. automated clearinghouse system, set up in the 1970s, is widely used for recurring payments as well as for the settlement of cheques. European Giro systems and credit-card associations use electronic formats to reduce paper processing. Large value transfer systems (LVTSs) have been devised to reduce the intra-day risk of bank failure before clearings have been settled.

Automated banking machines and network facilities function mainly as complements to bank branches, allowing customers remote access to their bank accounts. The number of ABMs in the United States rose from 18,500 in 1980 to 324,000 in 2000 (Allen et al. 2002). In Canada, national networks of ABM, debit cards networks and bank branches provided more than 150 banking access points per 10,000 Canadians in 2001, more than double the access points in 1996 (Canadian Bankers Association 2002). Canadians make greater per capita use of ABMs than individuals in any other leading country. The annual number of ABM transactions per capita is now: Canada 54.3, United States 39.9, Sweden 35, Netherlands 33.4 and United Kingdom 33.1 (Canadian Bankers Association 2002).

While bank clients still use relatively large numbers of cheques, credit-card and debit-card payments now account for about 25 percent of non-cash payments in the United States (Allen and Gale 2000). Canadians now use debit- or credit card-based payments almost twice as frequently as cash or cheques (Canadian Bankers Association 2002). Recurring payments such as utility bills are commonly charged to bank accounts in Canada without the need for clients to write cheques. Canadians make higher annual use per capita of debit cards than any other leading country: Canada 54.3, Netherlands 44.2, France 41.3, Belgium 38.6, United States 27.5 (Canadian Bankers Association 2002). Further development of electronic payment methods in other countries can be expected.

Personal online payment is a growing form of Internet payment in which a credit card payment from a purchaser is transferred to the seller's credit card. New wireless technology means that Canadians can now use Interac's direct payment service in taxicabs and at their front door for pizza or grocery deliveries. Some U.S. banks use a type of credit card to effect low-cost money transfers from branches in the United States to branches in Latin America. Enormous amounts of money are currently being transferred from Latinos working in the United States to their families in Latin America, but until the advent of these new arrangements, money transfers were costly. Cheap money transfer services also attract new customers, who bring their deposits and demands for other financial products such as mortgages and retirement planning.

Some grocery chains with a presence in Latin America use the Internet to allow Latinos living in the United States to purchase groceries for their family members living in Latin America. In Canada, a resident of Toronto could buy the groceries and make payment via a Loblaws Web site. The order could be transmitted electronically to a Loblaws store in Guadalajara, Mexico, where a family member could pick up the goods. Transaction costs are lower than with wire transfers and the Toronto resident is sure that the money is being used as desired. Such developments would appear to be natural outgrowths of current arrangements. Canadian banks and grocery stores already have experience with innovative partnerships: President's Choice (PC) banking represents a relationship between CIBC and Loblaws; Canadian banks such as Scotiabank are increasing their market share in countries such as Mexico and Chile.

Another development that can be expected to have a major impact on e-commerce is electronic bill presentment (EBP). Canada is on the leading edge in developing this and other similar technologies. Ultimately, FSPs will provide customers with the ability to see all their bills on the Web — including any they now receive through the mail — and to pay them online. Electronic bill presentment will lead to considerable economies for companies doing the billing, since it will cut out the costs of preparing paper statements and mailing them. Moreover, the billing companies can also provide marketing information to clients using the same channels.

E-FINANCE AND FINANCIAL MARKETS

STOCK EXCHANGES USED TO OPERATE in physical locations using face-to-face communication. Today, most of the world's stock exchanges and trading networks such as the NASDAQ use electronic trading. Foreign exchange and bond markets traditionally took the form of dealer markets that operated over the telephone rather than in any physical location. Today's foreign exchange markets have become almost fully electronic, though bond markets in most countries are still largely telephone-based.

CHANGES IN TRADING SYSTEMS

ELECTRONIC COMPUTING AND COMMUNICATION SYSTEMS have lowered the costs of trading and allowed for better price determination. In particular, electronic execution and matching imply less chance of market manipulation. Electronic trading also facilitates cross-border and inter-market transactions. Instinet, which originated as an inter-dealer trading facility, now has automatic routings to stock exchanges. Electronic communications networks (ECNs) started by feeding trades into existing markets but have increasingly become alternative trading outlets.

STOCK MARKETS

MOST OF THE WORLD'S STOCK MARKETS are now electronic. NASDAQ established the original electronic trading network in 1971, but now faces competition from a number of newly organized ECNs. Electronic communications networks have brought tighter bid-ask spreads, greater depth and less market concentration, thus improving NASDAQ liquidity (Weston 2002). Recently, E-trade has experienced a resurgence of activity in online retail trading and it is offering enhanced services to attract additional customers. Most traditional exchanges are moving from floor trading to electronic trading. Upstairs markets for block trades usually avoid exchanges altogether: they trade large blocks of stock without posting limit orders with exchange floor specialists or with automated systems. However, all these different types of markets are required by the Securities and Exchange Commission (SEC) to cross their orders on an exchange floor so as to create a central record of their transactions.

BOND MARKETS

VARIOUS COMPANIES PROVIDE ELECTRONIC and other access to current bond offerings, to trading services, and to research information in the global bond market, which transacts business worth about $250 billion a day. In most developed countries, new issues of government bonds are sold mainly at auctions by a small number of firms known as primary dealers. Secondary market trading is conducted both by the primary market dealers and by others. In the United States, Cantor Fitzgerald Securities and eSpeed, its electronic trading arm, are among the most prominent of these dealers. Electronic trading through eSpeed accounts for something in excess of $75 billion daily in dealer-to-dealer transactions. Garban Intercapital (ICAP) connects the operations of two key clearing houses: the Government Securities Clearing House and the Depository Trust Company. Garban's facilities cover a range of corporate bonds, interest-rate swaps and options, foreign exchange, mortgages (on a wholesale basis through the use of collateralized mortgage obligations), treasury bills and bonds, repurchase agreements and equities. TradeWeb is a customer-to-dealer system used by buy-side institutions and sell-side dealers with principal offices in New York and in London. Bond Book is an anonymous matching system used by buy-side institutions and sell-side broker-dealers.

FOREIGN EXCHANGE MARKETS

FOREIGN EXCHANGE MARKETS have traditionally consisted of multiple dealers. By 2001, about 90 percent of trading in foreign exchange was done electronically though trades between large corporations, and foreign exchange dealers are still largely concluded by telephone. CLS Bank was set up in late 2002 to provide continuous linked settlement of foreign-exchange transactions among the world's 50 or 60 largest banks. CLS Bank nets all transactions among banks and makes payments during the business day, thereby eliminating a form of settlement risk. The development of CLS Bank has been under discussion since the failure of Bank Herstatt in 1974 during the North American business day.

Operating Issues

In some ways, technology has given rise to new types of operating issues. One example is offered by program trading, which involves simultaneous institutional trading of many different types of shares and which often deals in high volumes. This type of trading aims to eliminate emerging arbitrage opportunities and works well during normal business conditions. However, during market crises, programmed trades cannot always be executed quickly and at market prices. As a result, program trading can serve to generate additional volume in times of crises and to exaggerate swings in market prices. For example, some types of program trading will trigger massive additional selling at times when stock prices are declining, thereby emphasizing a decline in stock price. An additional factor is that such trading creates the possibility of informational cascades in which selling by one institution may be taken as a signal for other institutions to sell.

Implications for Public Policy

Recent changes in providing financial services raise questions about the adequacy of the current approach to financial sector regulation, whether traditional reasons for regulation and supervision remain valid, and what areas of policy (e.g. competition policy, consumer protection) deserve increased emphasis. Some observers believe that recent changes may make it feasible to reduce emphasis on prudential regulation and supervision and thus to lower some kinds of safety net provisions. The principal issues, of course, are to determine where externalities have changed. In particular, some negative externalities appear to have been reduced by changing technology. At the same time, new externalities have been created, some positive and some negative. In some cases, the greater availability of information has reduced the externalities that could accompany the cessation or interruption of commercial banking operations, but changes on the retail side appear to be less important. In addition, growth in risk trading may have increased the kinds of negative externalities that might be suffered from interruption or cessation of this kind of business, as noted in the preceding discussion of operating issues.

Safety and Soundness

The need for a financial sector safety net arises from a perceived need to treat deposit-taking institutions differently from other economic agents. The main reasons for doing so are both because the costs of failure can be increased through a loss of confidence and because the costs of failure can be widespread.

As a result, most countries have provided deposit insurance since the 1930s, though some set up lender-of-last-resort facilities prior to the 1930s.

The recent emergence of both substitutes for bank deposits and alternative payment mechanisms raises the question of whether current developments in technology and deregulation are eroding the nature of what made banks special over the past 70 years. Answers to the question depend on the kinds of financial products or services being contemplated. For example, since non-financial institutions now offer deposit-taking facilities and payment facilities of various sorts, banks are no longer unique providers of these products. On the other hand, non-market types of loan transactions require the kind of specialized governance that has traditionally been provided mainly by banks and some other lending institutions. As already pointed out, the need for close governance of some loan types is changing with technology, but the need for close governance of other loan types remains. These non-marketable types of loans continue to require the attention of relationship bankers or other lenders with similar capabilities.

In most countries, banks make up the core of the payments system, largely because payment services were originally linked with the extension of credit. Now many mutual funds and most brokerage houses permit individuals to deposit their pay cheques in cash management accounts, make routine payments automatically from these accounts, and make irregular payments with 24 hours' notice. Money market accounts can be linked to a credit card, and cash withdrawals can be made from the card at ABMs. New non-bank providers of payment services use e-mail transfers, stored value cards and smart cards. Balances on stored value cards can typically be transferred without involving a depository institution.

All of these developments raise questions about how various payment systems should be regulated and what kinds of institutions should have access to those systems. Should the regulation be prudential (covered by a safety net) or should it be oriented primarily toward consumer protection? Would either prudential or consumer protection goals be furthered by requiring the payments services of non-financial corporations to be provided through bank subsidiaries? Answers to these questions depend on the likely costs of different kinds of operating problems and on the incidence of those costs.

E-finance allows deposit-taking institutions and capital markets to reach far greater numbers of clients, because transaction costs are lower and information is more widely available. Advances in information technology are reducing asymmetric information and thus the uniqueness of the proprietary information banks have about borrowers. The importance of banks as lending institutions is waning, particularly for larger corporations that rely increasingly on the securities markets for financing. At the same time, non-bank sources of financing are becoming increasingly important. As one result, the fact that corporations find it increasingly easy to access alternative forms of financing means that one danger typically associated with bank failures — disruption of business through restricted credit availability — may be decreasing somewhat.

As the financial system continues its integration with communications and computing infrastructures, FSPs will likely see a decline in the value of their franchises. More financial transactions will be commoditized and new types of FSPs will emerge. International competition will erode franchise values further. Nevertheless, established institutions with sophisticated Internet technology might be able to tap into new markets at low marginal costs and thus gain significant first-mover advantages. In addition, institutions may embody less risky portfolio structures as they increasingly diversify across products and markets.

In the future, the special nature of banks may depend on whether the overall financial safety net shrinks if the specific role of banks continues to diminish. Moreover, unless the foregoing issues are analyzed carefully, the safety net may be extended by default. Because a wider array of financial services are increasingly being provided by institutions with increasingly stronger links to non-financial companies, regulatory oversight will become more difficult. In particular, deposit insurance might get extended inadvertently to non-traditional forms of deposits. Moreover, the problems of moral hazard associated with deposit insurance can become harder to supervise in an increasingly complex financial system.

Some of these regulatory questions are actually variants of perennial challenges in the industry. For example, how do central banks prevent liquidity support from becoming solvency support as financial services providers become more complex organizations? Other questions have a novel aspect. For example, are portals appropriate organizations for giving investment advice? Should they be regulated in the same way as investment advisers? Should aggregators be licensed, regulated or supervised? How should consolidated supervision be defined? Still other questions continue to take traditional forms. For example, how can prudential regulation and supervision be better coordinated with competition policy? Finally, new thinking only partly related to changing technology is also in evidence. For example, regulation and supervision apply to activities that affect specific public policy goals, irrespective of product definition on sector and intermediary boundaries. Is regulation defined by the objectives of public policy a likely form of evolution?

Competition Policy

Competition policy aims at ensuring access, efficient production and fair pricing. Recent changes in the financial industry are making financial services more like other goods and services, and making financial markets more like non-financial markets. Financial innovation is increasingly becoming a function of the degree to which the entry of both financial and non-financial companies is permitted. In addition to raising issues with respect to the extension of the safety net as discussed earlier, the mixing of financial and non-financial activity also makes competition policy more important.

Key questions facing competition policy include: what market definitions to use, what constitutes market power, what barriers to entry exist, and what are allowable vertical and horizontal ownership structures within an industry. Are all providers of a financial service to be subject to the same competition policy? Although competition tests require a definition of a product and a market, the task is becoming more difficult as traditional financial services take on the characteristics of financial contracts and as new instruments such as weather and power derivatives blur the distinction between financial and non-financial arrangements. The continuum from cash through stored-value cards to point programs such as AirMiles makes it difficult to define payment services or deposits with precision. It is equally awkward to define barriers to entry when services cannot be well defined. Moreover the sizes and delivery modes of markets are both changing as markets increasingly become globally, rather than locally, defined.

In global markets, economic barriers to entry can have an important effect on the provision of financial services. Scale and scope economies can create barriers unless markets are contestable. On the other hand, global markets can be large enough that scale or scope economies do not create significant forms of market dominance. Nevertheless network externalities can create entry barriers once critical mass is reached, as in payment services and trading systems. Since the organizations that own the networks have natural incentives to limit access, regulators need to monitor operations to ensure that anticompetitive practices do not emerge.

Entry by non-financial entities has increased competition, particularly in services traditionally provided by banks. Aggregators have increased competition and access in mortgage markets. Similarly, new payment services bypass banks, lowering service costs and increasing quality. New entities in the brokerage business have sharply lowered commissions in many countries. At the same time, complex ownership and alliance structures are emerging so that vertical integration could eventually undermine competition. Ownership links may be used to exploit reputation and sunk costs can create barriers that limit new competition from entering markets. In other situations, the lack of competition may not result in higher prices but can still reduce product and process innovation.

Given the increasingly difficult task of defining financial markets, it becomes important to consider how best to provide financial regulation. In particular, should Canada consider having a single financial services regulator, as the United Kingdom does? Should the jurisdiction of our regulators extend to financial conglomerates?

CONSUMER PROTECTION

CONSUMER PROTECTION ISSUES INCLUDE security, privacy, transparency and investor protection. It gives rise to topics such as setting standards of protection, evaluating their impact on market development, and selecting the authorities best equipped to develop and enforce standards. The rapid proliferation of delivery channels and institutions has allowed easier comparison of prices and financial products, especially for traded securities. On the other hand, a proliferation of products and the emergence of portals can reduce transparency. New markets for securities trading present special challenges in addressing fragmentation and the difficulties in making comparisons that this creates. Regulatory solutions will have to balance the objectives of increased competition with access and fairness.

The Internet has greatly simplified the collection and sharing of credit and other data on individuals and businesses, and technology has lowered the cost of processing and using the information for financial services. At the same time, it raises privacy concerns about practices such as the inappropriate sharing of information within a financial conglomerate. Internet transactions currently present a combination of security risks and the presence of audit trails that make it relatively easy to detect infringement. Cryptographic techniques are developing rapidly, and will soon be able to deal with most security concerns arising from normal operations. However, growth in Internet services may still be slowed if it takes time to overcome the public's security concerns.

Investor protection issues have become more complex with the advent of the Internet, especially since increases in the volume of cross-border transactions raise the question of identifying the appropriate regulatory or legislative body. Many jurisdictions are not clear on what authority is entitled to regulate a particular type of transaction. The establishment of standards for e-finance transactions may also run into the issue of public goods since too many standards or too little competition might emerge if proprietary considerations dominate.

Some observers believe that increasing use of technology is likely to restrict access for the poor and the elderly. On the other hand, technology has extended the reach of the financial system in countries like South Africa, making it more accessible to poor and illiterate clients with relatively small amounts of financial business. In countries like Canada, the financial system probably has the same capacity for extension that is has demonstrated in South Africa. If management recognizes the profitability of operating small accounts, it is likely that improved forms of ABMs and debit cards will be developed to make access easier rather than more difficult.

GLOBAL PUBLIC POLICY

INCREASING GLOBALIZATION and the advent of Internet finance mean that harmonizing standards across borders is a major concern in the formulation of global public policy. At present, many countries limit the cross-border provision of financial services, but as these constraints are relaxed, there will be a greater need for harmonization. Enforcement and legal recourse across borders can be complicated. For example, one issue respecting cross-border transactions involves determining which country's standards and jurisdiction are applicable. Systemic risks can emerge from changing forms of financial activity, as shown by the Long Term Capital Management crisis of 1998. Adequate forms of risk management will entail more information sharing among regulators and self-regulatory organizations.

The extent of financial crises and the damage they can cause will likely be increased by globalization unless regulatory cooperation evolves in a way that enhances preventive measures equally among participants. Depending on how these issues are approached, the frequency and costs of crises could either become more or less serious. Regulatory cooperation appears to be expanding rapidly on many fronts, and regulators are becoming more aware of new dangers. For example, South Asian regulators are currently wrestling with the issue of how best to control the hedge-fund business in India. Indian regulators are especially concerned that a burgeoning hedge-fund business will increase the volume of short-term money flowing into and out of India, with the possibility of a negative impact on the rupee. More generally, Internet trading has a potential for increasing market volatility and large flows of short-term capital make capital account restrictions harder to enforce. On the other hand, institutions such as the CLS Bank reduce certain types of clearing risks.

CONCLUSIONS

THIS STUDY EXAMINED THE IMPORTANCE of technology and innovation to Canada's financial system. It considered the implications of new technologies for managing individual financial institutions, for operating financial markets and for the conduct of regulatory policy. The developments identified include automated banking machine networks, Internet banking, the emergence of portals and aggregators, and greater use of credit scoring. On the commercial side, institutions have moved toward making greater use of securitization, and have become heavily engaged in risk management.

Adopting new technologies has improved the operating efficiency of institutions, industry competitiveness, and search processes used by clients of the financial system. Consumers benefit from new and lower-priced products and services, and small businesses benefit from improved access to loans provided through credit scoring techniques. Large businesses benefit from increased availability of syndicated loans as well as from risk management and investment banking services. Investors benefit from faster execution of securities trades, better and easier price comparisons, and thinner trading margins.

Technological change is having an important impact on access to the financial system. The new technologies permit financial products to be commoditized and at the same time tailored to the needs of consumers. Advances in information and communication technology facilitate the delivery of a broad array of financial services through aggregators and portals. Financial markets are changing equally rapidly and profoundly: trading systems for equities, fixed income securities and foreign exchange are all consolidating and becoming global operations. However, markets characterized by sunk costs and low commoditization potential, such as corporate advisory services, underwriting and facilitating mergers and acquisitions, have seen fewer new entrants.

Members of the securities industry have been instrumental in setting up electronic exchanges, and most current trading is conducted electronically. New trading systems have improved the markets for stocks, bonds, derivatives and foreign exchange.

On the payments side, institutions have developed systems that include networks such as Interac in Canada, and Cirrus and Plus in the United States. In addition, there are a variety of clearing systems for settling inter-bank payments, securities and derivatives transactions.

Related non-financial businesses have developed non-bank forms of payment, including credit cards and electronic payment arrangements.

The changing financial landscape poses new regulatory questions: Are banks likely to remain special in the way they have been for the last 70 years? Will safety and soundness questions remain as pressing in the future as they have been in the past? How is competition policy likely to be affected by the electronic environment? How can financial and non-financial corporations in the same business be appropriately regulated? How are consumer protection issues changing? How does globalization affect the formation of public policy?

ENDNOTES

1 Examples of commoditization and tailoring familiar to many readers are electronic systems for booking airline tickets, hotel accommodation and entertainment. One might expect that these ways of temporarily leasing space (on an airplane, in an hotel, in a theatre or arena) will become more closely integrated with payment facilities than is now the case.

2 By uncertainty, we mean an environment in which it is not helpful to model a decision problem with the aid of state probabilities, either because the states cannot be defined or because the probabilities with which states might occur

are specified too diffusely to be practically relevant. By risk, we mean an environment in which states and probabilities can usefully be employed. Uncertainty is only capable of being usefully described qualitatively, but risk can be described quantitatively.

3 From the point of view of the financial institution, purchasing the new securities, valuing them could be an exercise under risk because of the kinds of data and payment guarantees available for the new securities. At the same time, the purchaser of the new securities would know little about the value of the individual loans in the bank portfolio and could well approach the problem of valuing those individual loans as a problem of valuation under uncertainty.

4 Neave (1998) identifies size of loan, liquidity of underlying assets, bank familiarity with the business, availability of collateral and frequency of transaction type as major factors determining whether individual loan instruments are or are not tradeable.

BIBLIOGRAPHY

Allen, Franklin D., and Douglas Gale. 2000. *Comparing Financial Systems*. Cambridge, MA: MIT Press.

Allen, Franklin D., James McAndrews, and Philip Strahan. 2002. "E-Finance: An Introduction," *Journal of Financial Services Research* 22, 5-27.

Canadian Bankers Association. 2002. "Technology and Banking," Toronto: Canadian Bankers Association.

Neave, Edwin H. 1998. *Financial Systems: Principles and Organisation*. New York and London: Routledge Press.

Schenk, H. 2001. "Mergers and the Economy: Theory and Policy Implications", Presentation for the Workshop on "European Integration, Financial Systems and Corporate Performance", Maastricht, February 17.

Weston, James P. 2002. "Electronic Communication Networks and Liquidity on the NASDAQ," *Journal of Financial Services Research* 22, 125-139.

Comment

Eric Santor
Bank of Canada

THE MOTIVATION FOR NEAVE'S STUDY can be summarized by the following headline: "Ameritrade seen as most likely TD partner," (*Globe and Mail*, 10 October 2003). The potential merger of an e-finance company, and a more traditional "bricks and mortar" bank, represents the possible synergies that can be attained from the integration of banks with other types of financial services companies. Neave argues that these types of mergers have become possible because of the considerable degree of innovation that has occurred within the financial industry. Consequently, it is important to assess the impacts of financial innovation and technology on the provision of financial services, and its consequences for the existing structure of the financial system. In particular, the blurring of distinctions between banking and financial markets, and the challenges it creates for regulation and supervision, need to be addressed.[1]

The contribution of this study occurs in four key areas, and each will be considered in turn. First, Neave assesses the impact of technological innovation on financial services. In this regard, the study provides a thorough summary of the many technological innovations occurring within the financial system together with concurrent developments in financial markets. Second, the study highlights the importance of e-finance and financial services. The use of information technology by banks to create new financial products and new delivery networks is changing the financial landscape dramatically. The provision of similar financial products and services by non-bank entities is also noted. Third, e-finance and financial markets are examined. Neave clearly points out how electronic trading networks are lowering the costs of trades and have led to the rise of numerous new financial markets. Lastly, Neave examines the important public policy issues at stake. In particular, he addresses how to define markets and what does contestability imply when there are first mover advantages attributable to technological innovation and investments. Perhaps most importantly, he considers the problem of how to regulate non-bank firms when they provide bank services. Overall, Neave has provided a thorough summary of the impact of information technology on the financial system. There are, however, several concerns I wish to raise.

The first is the initial assertion that because of technological and financial innovation, banks are increasingly global in nature. This raises the simple empirical question: are banks becoming more globalized? Figure 1 depicts the foreign asset exposures of Canadian banks from 1988 to 2002. At a first glance, it would appear that the absolute level of foreign exposure has increased dramatically throughout the 1990s. However, when taken as a ratio of total bank assets, the picture is less clear. Figure 2 shows that the ratio of foreign assets to total assets has remained stable. When one removes holdings of U.S. securities (see Figure 3), one observes that the ratio of foreign asset exposure to total assets is actually falling over time.[2] This is, interestingly, consistent with evidence from the U.S. banking sector, which shows little change in the ratio of foreign asset exposure to total assets (Goldberg 2001).

The second concern is the notion that the use of sophisticated risk models, in conjunction with better data and increased computational power, has allowed banks to better manage risk. For example, Value-at-Risk (VaR) models are widely used by banks to assess the riskiness of portfolios. However, Danielsson (2002) shows that most of the assumptions underlying VaR models are violated in the data, and thus banks often have misleading information regarding the risk embodied in their portfolios. Similarly, Neave argues that financial innovation has led to the development of markets for sophisticated credit derivatives in order to better hedge risk. But again, the effectiveness of credit derivatives in mitigating risk is largely unknown, since there is no information about the correlation of returns on such instruments with bank portfolios. In fact, credit derivatives could exacerbate the negative consequences of crisis events. Likewise, the execution of credit derivatives often depends on the solvency and liquidity position of counterparties, which cannot be guaranteed. For instance, many U.S. banks could not execute credit derivatives during the Russian default crisis since many of the Russian banks that were their counterparties were insolvent.

FIGURE 1

FOREIGN ASSET EXPOSURE, CANADIAN BANKS, 1988-2002 (TOTAL CLAIMS, ALL BANKS)

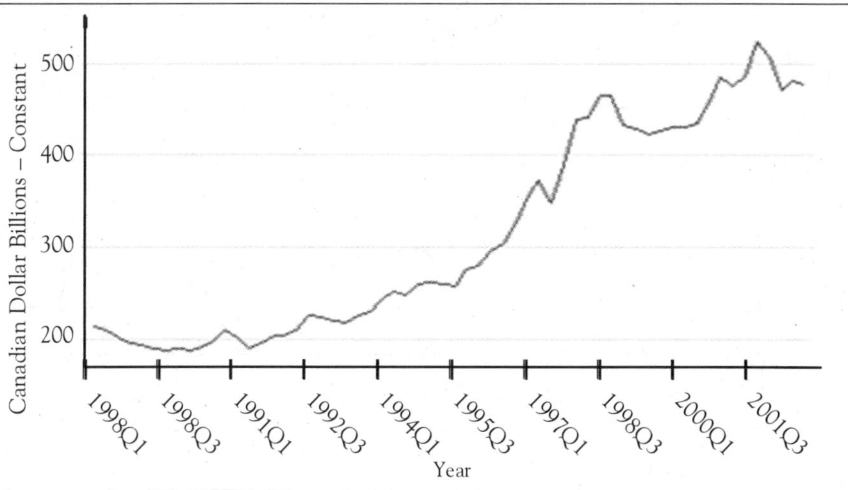

Source: Bank of Canada.

FIGURE 2

FOREIGN ASSET EXPOSURE, CANADIAN BANKS, 1988-2002 (TOTAL CLAIMS/ASSETS, ALL BANKS)

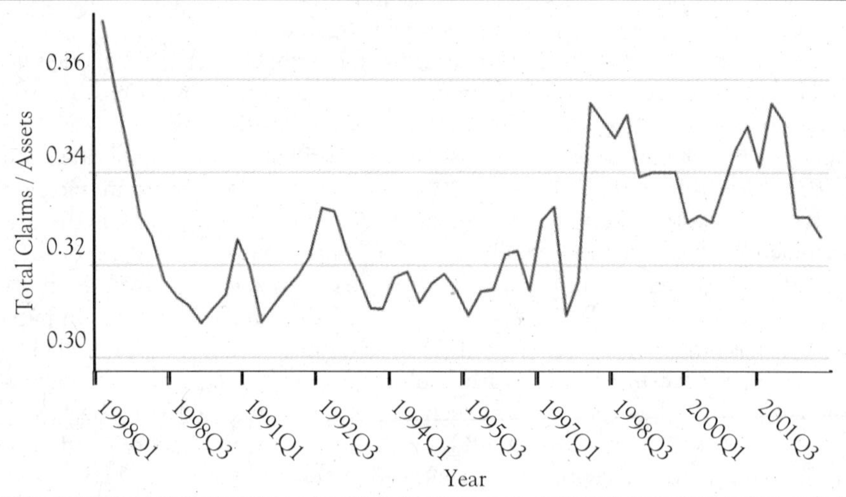

Source: Bank of Canada.

FIGURE 3

FOREIGN ASSET EXPOSURE, CANADIAN BANKS, 1988-2002 [TOTAL CLAIMS /ASSETS (U.S. EXCLUDED), ALL BANKS]

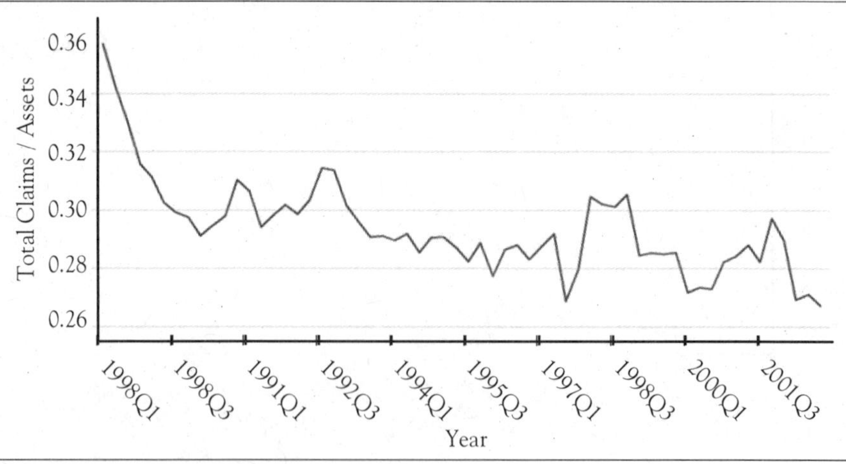

Source: Bank of Canada.

Third, Neave highlights how information technology and its application has greatly reduced problems of asymmetric information. In this respect, gains have been made, as witnessed by the successful use of credit scoring models by banks. This type of innovation has subsequently reduced the importance of the bank-borrower relationship, as more information is readily available to more financial market participants. While this is seen as an improvement, there could be negative consequences. Recent theoretical work by Gehrig and Stenbecka (2001) shows that when information can be shared by banks, collusion may occur, leading to sub-optimal welfare outcomes. Furthermore, the curtailment of relationship lending may not be welfare improving. Petersen and Rajan (1995) show that when banks have some monopoly power in the lending relationship, they are more likely to fund start-ups, which can be growth enhancing. While recognizing the benefits of financial innovation, we must also acknowledge its potential costs.

Fourth, as mentioned earlier in this comment, Neave notes the large benefits that have come from electronic trading: lower trading costs, new exchanges and more sophisticated trading have led to deeper, more liquid markets. However, the puzzle remains as to why, given their efficiency, some exchanges choose to "shut-off" their computers in periods of excessive declines. This suggests that electronic networks can have perverse consequences in the presence of crisis events. For example, the occurrence of information cascades can lead to contagion in financial markets when electronic trading systems implement program trading.

Lastly, the study raises many important public policy issues, but many remain. For instance, given the blurring of the line between what constitutes a bank and what does not, should supervision be consolidated? And how should non-bank entities be supervised, and will existing safety nets be expanded to meet this challenge? Lastly, will public policy makers be ready to ensure that all consumers will be able to take advantage of the innovation that is occurring? Poor or elderly consumers tend not to have access to computers and do not know how to use them. Will they benefit from the new products and services that are now available?

Overall, Neave provides an excellent summary of how technological and financial innovation is leading to new financial products and services, and more efficient and numerous financial markets. He also highlights many of the important policy issues raised by these innovations, and the challenge facing policy makers. It is clear, as Neave points out, that the future of financial markets will continue to evolve in ways that will challenge policy makers and regulators alike.

ENDNOTES

1 The views expressed in this paper are those of the author. No responsibility for them should be attributed to the Bank of Canada.

2 It would be difficult to argue that claims consisting of U.S. T-bills represents an increase in foreign exposure, given the risk-free nature of the asset. Also, holding of such securities may be for reasons other than simple diversification — U.S. securities are held as instruments for other activities, such as credit derivatives and securities markets.

BIBLIOGRAPHY

———. 2003. "Ameritrade Seen as Most Likely TD Partner," (*Globe and Mail*, 10 October).

Danielsson, J. 2002. "The Emperor Has No Clothes: Limits to Risk Modeling," *Journal of Banking and Finance* 26: 1273-1296.

Gehrig, T., and R. Stenbecka. 2001. "Information Sharing in Banking: a Collusive Device?" CEPR Discussion Papers, No. 2911.

Goldberg, L. 2001. "When is U.S. Bank Lending to Emerging Markets Volatile?" New York: Federal Reserve Bank of New York, mimeo.

Petersen, M., and R. Rajan. 1995. "The Effect of Credit Market Competition on Lending Relationships," *Quarterly Journal of Economics* (110): 407-43.

Zhiqi Chen
Carleton University

12

Liberalization of Trade and Investment in Telecommunication Services: A Canadian Perspective

INTRODUCTION

THE 1990S WITNESSED TREMENDOUS CHANGES in the telecommunications services industry. On the one hand, advances in technology led to a substantial reduction in the costs of communication services and the widespread adoption of new channels such as wireless communication and the Internet. On the other hand, the reform of telecommunications policy in many countries allowed for the entry of new service providers, giving consumers unprecedented choice. Globally, the World Trade Organization (WTO) agreement on basic telecommunication services came into force in 1998, committing member countries to the liberalization of trade and investment in this industry.

The objective of this paper is to conduct a study of the telecommunications services industry during the 1990s, with a focus on Canada. It starts with an overview of the state of Canada's telecommunications services industry during this period. In particular, the growth in size, infrastructure and productivity of the telecommunications industry in Canada is compared with the situation in other Organisation for Economic Co-operation and Development (OECD) countries. In the next section, data from 20 OECD countries are used to quantify the contributions of telecommunication services to economic growth. The fourth section presents an econometric model of fixed and mobile telecommunication services, which is constructed to estimate the effects of barriers to trade and investment on telecommunications infrastructure. Estimates from the above two models are then used to calculate the impact of trade liberalization. The last part of the study offers some general conclusions.

The idea that a modern telecommunications system is essential to economic growth is not new. In the literature, numerous studies have been conducted to quantify the contribution of telecommunications services to economic growth. They include Hardy (1980), Norton (1992), and Roller and Waverman (2001). All of them found evidence that telecommunications infrastructure has made a significant contribution to either the level (Hardy 1980, Roller and Waverman 2001) or the growth rate (Norton 1992) of per capita income.

The econometric analysis contained in this study goes beyond the existing studies in at least two aspects. First, this analysis takes into consideration both cellular mobile services as well as fixed network services. A significant development in telecommunications services during the 1990s was the rapid penetration of mobile services throughout the world. Indeed, in many OECD countries, the penetration rate of mobile services has exceeded that of fixed-line services. It is, therefore, essential to include cellular mobile services in any study of the effects of telecommunications services on growth. Second, this analysis measures the spillover effects of telecommunications services across countries. It has been speculated that the regional (or even worldwide) marginal product of telecommunications infrastructure can be quite high (Aschauer 1996). So far, however, there has been no empirical study that tests the existence of such cross-country spillover effects of telecommunications infrastructure.

The effects of liberalizing telecommunications services have been studied by various researchers using two different approaches. The first approach, taken by Verikio and Zhang (2001), is to use a computable general equilibrium (CGE) model. The second approach is to use econometric analysis, as has been done by Mattoo, Rathindran and Subramanian (2001) and Warren (2001). This study uses the second approach and estimates the likely effects of trade liberalization using two related econometric models. The estimation equations used in this study, however, are derived from micro models of telecommunications and economic growth rather than based on *ad hoc* relationships. They explicitly specify the linkages through which barriers to trade and investment affect telecommunications infrastructure and economic growth. Therefore, compared with those in Mattoo et al. (2001) and Warren (2001), the models used in this study are built on stronger micro foundations.

AN OVERVIEW OF CANADA'S TELECOMMUNICATIONS SERVICES INDUSTRY DURING THE 1990S

THE PURPOSE OF THIS SECTION IS TO UNDERSTAND how the state of Canada's telecommunications services industry during the 1990s compares with other OECD countries. To do so, statistics on various aspects of telecommunications services in the 29 OECD countries have been compiled and analyzed. A series of observations can be made on the basis of these statistics.

The size, infrastructure and labour productivity of Canada's telecommunications services industry grew rapidly during the 1990s. The size of the telecommunications services industry can be measured by both the magnitude of its revenue and its weight in a country's gross domestic product (GDP). As can be seen from Table 1, telecommunications services revenue in Canada grew at an average annual rate of 6.35 percent between 1991 and 2000, rising from US$11,982 million to $20,845 million. The rapid growth in telecommunications services revenue also raised its weight in Canada's GDP from 2.03 percent in 1991 to 2.94 percent in 2000. Measured in per capita terms, Canada's telecommunications services revenue grew from US$438 to US$700 during this period (Table 2).

TABLE 1

TELECOMMUNICATIONS SERVICES REVENUE

COUNTRIES	TELECOMMUNICATIONS SERVICES REVENUE (MILLIONS OF US$) 1991	2000	AVERAGE ANNUAL GROWTH RATE (%)	AS PERCENTAGE OF GDP (%) 1991	2000
Australia	8,528	14,656	6.20	2.86	3.85
Austria	3,045	5,462	6.71	1.83	2.89
Belgium	2,820	5,628	7.98	1.39	2.49
Canada	**11,982**	**20,845**	**6.35**	**2.03**	**2.94**
Czech Republic	355	2,556	24.51	1.46	5.04
Denmark	2,424	4,177	6.24	1.81	2.57
Finland	2,155	4,004	7.13	1.75	3.31
France	20,666	27,729	3.32	1.69	2.17
Germany	28,430	50,754	6.65	1.65	2.72
Greece	1,345	4,586	14.60	1.51	4.16
Hungary	466	3,210	23.92	1.39	7.04
Iceland	89	207	9.81	1.32	2.43
Ireland	1,179	2,633	9.33	2.60	2.77
Italy	18,131	33,854	7.18	1.56	3.16
Japan	49,152	122,051	10.63	1.41	2.56
Korea	6,118	17,675	12.51	2.08	3.83
Luxembourg	203	283	3.76	1.78	1.50
Mexico	4,993	12,235	10.47	1.59	2.13
Netherlands	5,532	14,215	11.06	1.91	3.87
New Zealand	1,487	2,503	5.95	3.55	4.98
Norway	2,202	4,562	8.43	1.87	2.86
Poland	1,163	7,069	22.20	1.52	4.49
Portugal	1,680	4,981	12.83	2.15	4.76
Spain	9,701	16,314	5.95	1.84	2.93
Sweden	5,140	7,300	3.97	2.15	3.21
Switzerland	5,157	8,338	5.49	2.22	3.46
Turkey	2,744	5,356	7.71	1.79	2.64
United Kingdom	23,605	53,030	9.41	2.28	3.74
United States	137,643	292,762	8.75	2.30	2.97
OECD Average			**9.62**	**1.91**	**3.36**

Source: International Telecommunications Union (ITU).

TABLE 2

TELECOMMUNICATIONS SERVICES REVENUE PER CAPITA

COUNTRIES	1991 U.S. $	2000 U.S. $	GROWTH RATE (%)
Australia	493.43	765.04	4.99
Austria	390.55	672.61	6.23
Belgium	282.59	553.84	7.76
Canada	**438.95**	**700.19**	**5.33**
Czech Republic	34.50	248.31	24.52
Denmark	470.91	783.67	5.82
Finland	428.52	773.59	6.78
France	362.70	470.84	2.94
Germany	371.47	617.00	5.80
Greece	131.10	434.06	14.23
Hungary	45.01	320.88	24.39
Iceland	343.19	735.69	8.84
Ireland	334.54	695.20	8.47
Italy	319.50	590.84	7.07
Japan	396.39	961.64	10.35
Korea	140.84	373.67	11.45
Luxembourg	521.34	642.18	2.34
Mexico	56.84	123.74	9.03
Netherlands	367.09	889.14	10.33
New Zealand	433.01	653.44	4.68
Norway	515.32	1,017.26	7.85
Poland	30.41	182.92	22.06
Portugal	170.31	496.96	12.64
Spain	249.56	406.61	5.57
Sweden	594.67	822.06	3.66
Switzerland	753.59	1,157.47	4.88
Turkey	47.89	82.03	6.16
United Kingdom	408.30	887.30	9.01
United States	546.64	1,040.30	7.41
OECD Average	**333.76**	**624.08**	**8.99**

Source: International Telecommunications Union (ITU).

An important measure of telecommunications infrastructure is the penetration rate, which represents the number of fixed and/or mobile access channels per 100 inhabitants. As can be seen from Table 3, between 1991 and 2000, the fixed network penetration rate grew at a respectable annual rate of 2.10 percent, but the penetration rate of cellular mobile services rose at a remarkable annual rate of nearly 30 percent. The penetration rate of telecommunications access channels (fixed network and cellular mobile services combined) grew from 61 to 99 per 100 inhabitants, generating a growth rate of 5.60 percent (Table 4).

TABLE 3

GROWTH IN FIXED AND MOBILE SERVICES PENETRATION RATES

	FIXED PENETRATION RATES			MOBILE PENETRATION RATES		
COUNTRIES	1991	2000	ANNUAL GROWTH (%)	1991	2000	ANNUAL GROWTH (%)
Australia	46.55	52.46	1.34	1.69	44.69	43.93
Austria	42.90	47.20	1.07	1.48	77.00	55.12
Belgium	41.05	52.18	2.70	0.52	55.40	68.16
Canada	**57.94**	**69.88**	**2.10**	**2.84**	**29.40**	**29.64**
Czech Republic	16.57	37.61	9.53	0.01	42.21	147.63
Denmark	57.34	71.78	2.53	3.42	63.11	38.26
Finland	54.04	55.02	0.20	6.35	72.04	30.99
France	51.07	57.71	1.37	0.66	49.33	61.55
Germany	43.85	61.05	3.75	0.70	58.60	63.67
Greece	40.84	53.57	3.06	0.00	56.15	98.65[a]
Hungary	10.89	37.96	14.88	0.08	30.75	93.23
Iceland	52.22	68.28	3.02	4.97	76.69	35.55
Ireland	29.72	41.99	3.91	0.91	65.75	60.94
Italy	40.65	47.39	1.72	1.00	73.73	61.24
Japan	45.37	58.58	2.88	1.11	52.62	53.51
Korea	33.55	46.37	3.66	0.38	56.69	74.27
Luxembourg	49.19	75.00	4.80	0.29	68.72	83.44
Mexico	6.86	12.47	6.87	0.18	14.24	62.20
Netherlands	47.61	61.86	2.95	0.76	67.27	64.49
New Zealand	43.46	47.64	1.02	2.10	56.33	44.08
Norway	51.43	73.62	4.07	5.48	75.09	33.74
Poland	9.32	28.32	13.14	0.00	17.46	138.31[a]
Portugal	27.31	43.03	5.18	0.13	66.49	100.37
Spain	34.12	42.62	2.50	0.28	61.65	82.17
Sweden	68.91	74.56	0.88	6.57	71.72	30.41
Switzerland	59.63	72.67	2.22	2.55	64.39	43.15
Turkey	14.23	28.17	7.89	0.08	24.71	88.19
United Kingdom	44.82	58.86	3.07	2.18	72.70	47.65
United States	55.37	66.45	2.05	3.00	38.90	32.93
OECD Average	**40.58**	**53.25**	**4.05**	**1.71**	**55.30**	**64.40**

Note: a. Annual growth rates between 1993 and 2000.
Source: International Telecommunications Union (ITU).

TABLE 4

GROWTH IN TELECOMMUNICATIONS PENETRATION RATE

COUNTRIES	1991	2000	AVERAGE ANNUAL GROWTH RATE (%)
Australia	48.24	97.16	8.09
Austria	44.38	124.19	12.11
Belgium	41.56	107.58	11.15
Canada	**60.78**	**99.27**	**5.60**
Czech Republic	16.59	79.82	19.08
Denmark	60.75	134.89	9.27
Finland	60.38	127.06	8.62
France	51.73	107.04	8.42
Germany	44.54	119.65	11.60
Greece	40.84	109.71	11.61
Hungary	10.98	68.71	22.60
Iceland	57.19	144.98	10.89
Ireland	30.63	107.74	15.00
Italy	41.65	121.12	12.59
Japan	46.48	111.19	10.18
Korea	33.93	103.06	13.14
Luxembourg	49.49	143.73	12.58
Mexico	7.04	26.71	15.97
Netherlands	48.37	129.13	11.53
New Zealand	45.57	103.97	9.60
Norway	56.92	148.71	11.26
Poland	9.32	45.78	19.34
Portugal	27.44	109.53	16.63
Spain	34.40	104.28	13.11
Sweden	75.49	146.28	7.63
Switzerland	62.19	137.06	9.18
Turkey	14.31	52.88	15.63
United Kingdom	47.00	131.56	12.12
United States	58.37	105.35	6.78
OECD Average	**42.29**	**108.56**	**12.11**

Note: Telecommunications penetration rate is the sum of penetration rates of both fixed network services and cellular mobile service.

Source: International Telecommunications Union (ITU).

Even more striking is the growth of labour productivity in telecommunications services, as measured by revenues and access channels per telecommunications employee. Telecommunication revenues per employee almost doubled from US$125,160 in 1991 to US$239,510 in 2000, representing an annual growth rate of 7.48 percent (Table 5). Access channels per employee grew at a slightly higher rate (7.76 percent) from 173 to 340 (Table 6).

TABLE 5

TELECOMMUNICATIONS REVENUE PER EMPLOYEE

COUNTRIES	1991 (THOUSANDS OF U.S. $)	2000 (THOUSANDS OF U.S. $)	GROWTH RATE (%)
Australia	105.15	247.42	9.97
Austria	166.33	294.30	6.55
Belgium	105.19	235.09	9.35
Canada	**125.16**	**239.51**	**7.48**
Czech Republic	12.31	108.51	27.35
Denmark	135.78	195.83	4.15
Finland	112.76	165.53	4.36
France	132.38	165.58[a]	2.84[b]
Germany	123.61	210.86	6.11
Greece	48.75	233.93	19.04
Hungary	21.32	154.00	24.57
Iceland	90.44	149.91	5.78
Ireland	87.86	150.87	6.19
Italy	150.72	446.59	12.83
Japan	184.75	758.08	16.98
Korea	105.59	254.44	10.27
Luxembourg	240.50	319.14	3.19
Mexico	100.89	125.97	2.50
Netherlands	179.50	242.99	3.42
New Zealand	109.67	467.62	17.48
Norway	145.21	198.38	3.53
Poland	17.48	102.43	21.71
Portugal	72.84	270.71	15.70
Spain	128.49	396.03	13.32
Sweden	121.24	254.17	8.57
Switzerland	249.05	336.23	3.39
Turkey	30.23	73.96	10.45
United Kingdom	107.79	256.19	10.10
United States	151.39	258.19	6.11
OECD Average	**115.94**	**252.15**	**10.11**

Notes: a. value for 1999;
b. the growth rate between 1991 and 1999.

Source: International Telecommunications Union (ITU).

TABLE 6

ACCESS CHANNELS (FIXED AND MOBILE COMBINED) PER EMPLOYEE

COUNTRIES	1991	2000	ANNUAL GROWTH (%)
Australia	102.80	314.21	13.22
Austria	189.00	543.41	12.45
Belgium	154.71	456.63	12.78
Canada	**173.31**	**339.57**	**7.76**
Czech Republic	59.18	348.80	21.79
Denmark	175.18	337.06	7.54
Finland	158.89	271.87	6.15
France	188.81	324.47[a]	7.00[b]
Germany	148.23	408.90	11.94
Greece	151.85	591.27	16.30
Hungary	51.99	329.76	22.78
Iceland	150.71	295.42	7.76
Ireland	80.45	233.81	12.59
Italy	196.50	915.49	18.65
Japan	216.64	876.57	16.80
Korea	254.37	701.76	11.94
Luxembourg	228.28	714.26	13.51
Mexico	124.99	271.92	9.02
Netherlands	236.54	352.89	4.55
New Zealand	115.42	744.07	23.01
Norway	160.38	290.01	6.80
Poland	53.57	256.37	19.00
Portugal	117.34	596.63	19.80
Spain	177.13	1,015.65	21.42
Sweden	153.90	452.27	12.72
Switzerland	205.52	398.13	7.62
Turkey	90.32	476.84	20.31
United Kingdom	124.07	379.85	13.24
United States	161.65	261.47	5.49
OECD Average	**151.78**	**465.49**	**13.24**

Notes: a. Value for 1999;
b. Growth rate between 1991 and 1999.

Source: International Telecommunications Union (ITU).

The growth in Canada's telecommunications services industry, however, is significantly below the average of OECD countries. Despite an impressive growth rate of 6.35 percent, Canada's telecommunication revenue growth is substantially below the average growth rate of 9.62 percent for all OECD countries (Table 1). In fact, Canada's growth rate was ranked 21st among the 29 OECD countries. Growth in the penetration rates for fixed and mobile services are both at about half of the OECD average (Table 3).

Labour productivity growth is also below the OECD average. The growth rates of revenue per employee and access channels per employee in Canada are both substantially below the OECD averages of 10.11 percent (Table 5) and 13.24 percent (Table 6).

Employment in Canada's telecommunications services industry fell in both absolute and relative terms. Between 1991 and 2000 total staff in the industry fell from 109,384 to 81,728, and telecommunications employment as a percentage of national employment fell from 0.83 to 0.56 (Table 7). While 14 of the 29 OECD countries experienced declines in telecommunications employment, Canada's decline is among the five steepest.

Declining employment itself is not necessarily a cause for concern if it is the result of improved productivity. In Canada's case, however, the drop in employment was substantially steeper than the OECD average while the growth in labour productivity was significantly below the OECD average. That trend is worrisome as it suggests that Canada is falling behind relative to other OECD countries in terms of both employment and labour productivity.

Canada maintained its lead in fixed network services, but fell far behind in cellular mobile services. This can be seen in three different areas: penetration rates, digitalization rates and the weight of mobile services in the telecommunications industry. In 1991, Canada had the third highest fixed network penetration rate among the 29 countries. In 2000, while Canada's rank fell three places to number 6, the gap in penetration rates between Canada and the number 1 country was in fact narrowed from 11 to 5 lines per 100 inhabitants (Table 3). Canada remained a country with one of the highest fixed network penetration rates. However, the same cannot be said about Canada's mobile penetration rate. In 1991, Canada was ahead of most other OECD countries with a rank of 7th place, but fell to the 4th place from the bottom in 2000 (Table 3).

In the case of fixed network services, the digitalization rate is measured by the percentage of mainlines connected to digital switches. In the case of mobile services, it is measured by the percentage of users subscribing to digital services. In 2000, Canada's digitalization rate for fixed network services was nearly 100 percent. But the rate for cellular mobile services was only 52.97 percent, which meant that Canada ranked last among the 27 countries for which the ITU published the statistic for that year (Table 8).

Table 9 shows the share held by mobile services within the telecommunications services industry for the OECD countries in 1999. In Canada, mobile services accounted for 14.29 percent of telecommunications employment, 16.20 percent of telecommunications revenue and 25.63 percent of the access channels. This contrasts with the OECD averages of 13.21 percent, 27.42 percent and 41.37 percent, respectively. While Canada is slightly above average in terms of employment, it is substantially below average in terms of revenue and access channels.

TABLE 7

TELECOMMUNICATIONS STAFF

COUNTRIES	TOTAL STAFF IN TELECOM SERVICES			AS PERCENTAGE OF NATIONAL EMPLOYMENT (%)	
	1990	1999	AVERAGE ANNUAL GROWTH RATE (%)	1990	1999
Australia	87,018	60,470	–3.96	1.11	0.69
Austria	18,415	22,986	2.49	0.54	0.62
Belgium	26,031	24,213	–0.80	0.70	0.64
Canada	**108,384**	**81,728**	**–3.09**	**0.83**	**0.56**
Czech Republic	25,112	23,685	–0.65	0.50	0.50
Denmark	17,700	18,864	0.71	0.67	0.71
Finland	20,067	21,601	0.82	0.80	0.94
France	156,615	165,446	0.61	0.71	0.73
Germany	212,000	223,000	0.56	0.74	0.62
Greece	28,026	23,652	–1.87	0.75	0.60
Hungary	22,052	17,409	–2.59	—	0.46
Iceland	959	1,458	4.76	0.76	0.95
Ireland	13,472	15,000	1.20	1.17	0.95
Italy	103,558	99,869	–0.40	0.49	0.49
Japan	272,283	245,329	–1.15	0.44	0.38
Korea	57,769	87,025	4.66	0.32	0.43
Luxembourg	703	948	3.38	0.37	0.38
Mexico	50,620	74,361	4.37	0.22	0.20
Netherlands	31,770	47,500	4.57	0.51	0.62
New Zealand	17,131	7,047	–9.40	1.16	0.40
Norway	18,794	23,727	2.62	0.94	1.06
Poland	65,000	77,187	1.93	0.40	0.52
Portugal	23,563	18,883	–2.43	0.51	0.39
Spain	78,518	52,046	–4.47	0.62	0.38
Sweden	36,500	27,878	–2.95	0.82	0.69
Switzerland	20,170	24,561	2.21	0.53	0.63
Turkey	90,085	76,769	–1.76	0.49	0.36
United Kingdom	240,236	173,300	–3.56	0.90	0.63
United States	913,000	1,047,400	1.54	0.77	0.78
OECD Average			**–0.09**	**0.67**	**0.60**

Source: OECD.

TABLE 8

DIGITALIZATION OF FIXED AND MOBILE SERVICES, 2000

COUNTRIES	FIXED LINES	MOBILE	COUNTRIES	FIXED LINES	MOBILE
Australia	100.00	98.93	Korea	79.70	100.00
Austria	100.00	97.38	Luxembourg	100.00	100.00
Belgium	100.00	94.79	Mexico	99.98	—
Canada	**99.70**	**52.97**	Netherlands	—	100.00
Czech Republic	85.72	98.52	New Zealand	100.00	70.90
Denmark	100.00	98.35	Norway	100.00	96.04
Finland	100.00	98.50	Poland	77.60	98.22
France	100.00	100.00	Portugal	100.00	100.00
Germany	100.00	99.86	Spain	86.60	98.68
Greece	93.36	100.00	Sweden	100.00	97.16
Hungary	85.80	97.65	Switzerland	100.00	100.00
Iceland	100.00	98.38	Turkey	87.31	99.43
Ireland	100.00	98.39	United Kingdom	100.00	99.76
Italy	99.70	94.21	United States	95.44	—
Japan	100.00	100.00	**OECD Average**	**96.10**	**95.86**

Source: International Telecommunications Union (ITU).

The standing of Canada's telecommunications services industry declined from a position above the OECD average to one below average. During the 1990s, the relative size, infrastructure and labour productivity of Canada's telecommunications services industry went from above the OECD average to below. The indicators that exhibit this pattern are telecommunications revenue as a percentage of GDP (Table 1), telecommunications staff as a percentage of national employment (Table 7), the penetration rate of telecommunications access channels (Table 4), telecommunications revenue per employee (Table 5) and access channels per employee (Table 6). The most dramatic fall in Canada's standing was in the penetration rate. In 1991, Canada was number 2 in terms of the number of access channels per 100 inhabitants. By 2000, Canada's ranking had fallen to 23rd place.

The general picture that emerges from the above analysis is that the performance of Canada's telecommunication services industry during the 1990s was respectable in absolute terms, but it had fallen behind relative to the OECD average in a number of areas. This is a cause for concern because, as shown by the econometric analysis in the following sections, telecommunications infrastructure is a significant factor in driving economic growth.

TABLE 9

MOBILE SERVICES, 1999 (AS PERCENTAGE OF TELECOMMUNICATIONS SERVICES)

COUNTRIES	REVENUE (%)	EMPLOYMENT (%)	ACCESS CHANNEL (%)
Australia	23.10	—	39.28
Austria	43.18	19.98	52.39
Belgium	31.11	16.43	38.26
Canada	**16.20**	**14.29**	**25.63**
Czech Republic	41.76	11.21	33.81
Denmark	20.26	20.01	41.95
Finland	39.30	11.97	53.45
France	21.32	7.26	38.74
Germany	27.55	12.69	32.72
Greece	35.22	11.07	41.03
Hungary	44.47	13.91	30.41
Iceland	24.74	14.40	47.76
Ireland	28.22	6.67	48.32
Italy	27.59	17.81	53.34
Japan	40.44	10.09	44.63
Korea	53.83	11.45	53.33
Luxembourg	14.28	6.12	40.22
Mexico	15.36	14.32	41.44
Netherlands	25.71	16.84	41.24
New Zealand	25.40	14.53	43.21
Norway	24.01	10.36	46.36
Poland	23.28	5.08	28.00
Portugal	32.60	18.31	52.48
Spain	36.50	17.20	42.74
Sweden	22.16	15.06	44.21
Switzerland	19.13	18.53	37.64
Turkey	3.46	4.93	31.03
United Kingdom	16.90	13.91	44.29
United States	18.06	15.41	31.92
OECD Average	**27.42**	**13.21**	**41.37**

Sources: Revenue and access channels are calculated using ITU data.
Employment is calculated using OECD data.

QUANTIFYING THE RELATIONSHIP BETWEEN TELECOMMUNICATIONS SERVICES AND ECONOMIC GROWTH

TO ESTIMATE THE ECONOMIC EFFECTS of liberalizing trade and investment in telecommunications services, it is necessary to quantify the relationship between telecommunications services and economic growth. Roller and Waverman (2001) prepared the most recent econometric study of the relationship between telecommunications services and economic growth.[1] Their study covered the period from 1970 to 1990. By contrast, the analysis in this study covers the more recent period from 1985 to 1998, a time of tremendous innovation and growth for the telecommunications services industry. Furthermore, this analysis goes beyond the existing studies in two areas:

1. This study covers both fixed network and cellular mobile services. Roller and Waverman (2001) only focused on the penetration rate of fixed network services. During the 1990s, however, the penetration rates of mobile services grew by leaps and bounds. As can be seen from Table 3, in countries such as Austria, Finland and Italy, the mobile penetration rate has already risen above that of fixed network services. Indeed, for the OECD as a whole, the penetration rate of mobile services surpassed that of fixed network services in 2000.

2. The analysis in this study considers the spillover effects of improvements in the telecommunications infrastructure of foreign countries. It has been shown in the literature that international trade can have significant effects on economic growth. International trade today relies heavily on modern telecommunication services. It would be extremely costly to conduct business with a foreign country if all communications had to be done through postal services and face-to-face meetings. Therefore, it is expected that improvements in telecommunications infrastructure in a foreign country can have a positive effect on domestic GDP through the trade linkage.

MODELLING THE CONTRIBUTION OF TELECOMMUNICATIONS SERVICES

THE ECONOMETRIC MODEL USED HERE is an extension of the influential model by Mankiw, Romer and Weil (1992). In a nutshell, two additional variables have been included in the production function used in Mankiw et al. These variables are domestic telecommunications capital and foreign telecommunications capital. To be more precise, I assume that the production function of an economy takes the following form:

$$(1) \qquad Y = K^{\alpha} H^{\beta} (AL)^{\gamma} T^{\theta} T^{*\delta},$$

where T and T^* represent domestic and foreign telecommunications capital, respectively. Other variables in Equation (1) have the standard interpretations: K is the capital stock (minus the stock of telecommunications capital), H is human capital stock, L is the size of the labour force and A is the level of technology. The variables L and A grow exogenously at rates n and g:

$$(2) \qquad L(t) = L(0)e^{nt};\ A(t) = A(0)e^{gt}.$$

It is assumed that $\alpha + \beta + \gamma = 1$; i.e., the production technology exhibits constant returns to scale in K, H and AL. In per capita terms, Equation (1) can be rewritten as:

$$(3) \qquad \frac{Y}{L} = \left(\frac{K}{L}\right)^{\alpha}\left(\frac{H}{L}\right)^{\beta} A^{\gamma}T^{\theta}T^{*\delta}.$$

Define a set of new variables: $y = Y/AL$, $k = K/AL$, $h = H/AL$. Let s be the fraction of output invested in non-telecommunications capital, and d the depreciation rate of the capital. The transition equation of the non-telecommunications capital stock is:

$$(4) \qquad \dot{k} = sy - (n+g+d)k.$$

In the steady state we have $k = sy/(n + g + d)$, which implies:

$$(5) \qquad \left(\frac{K}{L}\right) = \frac{s(Y/L)}{n+g+d}.$$

Substituting Equation (5) into Equation (3) and taking the log, we obtain an equation for the steady state level of output per capita:

$$(6) \qquad \begin{aligned} \ln\left(\frac{Y}{L}\right) &= -\frac{\alpha}{1-\alpha}\ln(n+g+d) + \frac{\alpha}{1-\alpha}\ln s + \\ &\frac{\beta}{1-\alpha}\ln\left(\frac{H}{L}\right) + \frac{\gamma}{1-\alpha}\ln A + \frac{\theta}{1-\alpha}\ln T + \frac{\delta}{1-\alpha}\ln T^* \end{aligned}$$

Taking the first difference of Equation (6) and replacing A by Equation (2), we obtain the following relationship between the steady state growth rate of per capita income and the growth rates of telecommunications infrastructure and other variables:

$$\Delta \ln\left(\frac{Y}{L}\right) = -\frac{\alpha}{1-\alpha}\Delta \ln(n+g+d) + \frac{\alpha}{1-\alpha}\Delta \ln s \tag{7}$$
$$+\frac{\beta}{1-\alpha}\Delta \ln\left(\frac{H}{L}\right) + \frac{\gamma}{1-\alpha}g$$
$$+\frac{\theta}{1-\alpha}\Delta \ln T + \frac{\delta}{1-\alpha}\Delta \ln T^*$$

where Δ denotes the time difference of a variable. It shows that the steady growth rate of output per capita is negatively related to population growth but is positively related to the growth rates of (non-telecommunications) savings, human capital and of greater interest to us in this study, telecommunications capital at home and abroad.

EMPIRICAL ESTIMATION

THE EMPIRICAL IMPLEMENTATION of Equation (7) involves estimating the following equation:

$$\Delta LOGY_{i,t} = \alpha_i + \beta_1 \Delta LOGS_{i.t} + \beta_2 \Delta LOGH_{i,t} + \beta_3 \Delta LOGLG_{i,t} \tag{8}$$
$$+\beta_4 \Delta LOGT_{i,t} + \beta_5 \Delta LOGT^*_{i,t} + \beta_6 t + \beta_7 LOGS_{i.t}$$
$$+\beta_8 LOGH_{i,t} + \beta_9 LOGLG_{i,t} + \beta_{10} LOGT_{i,t}$$
$$+\beta_{11} LOGT^*_{i,t} + \varepsilon_{i,t}$$

where *LOGY* is the log of GDP per working-age person, *LOGS* is the log of the savings rate for non-telecommunications capital, *LOGH* is the log of human capital, *LOGLG* is the growth rate of the working-age population, *LOGT* the log of telecommunications capital in a country, and *LOGT** is the log of telecommunications capital in foreign countries. Note that Equation (7) describes the determinants of the steady state growth rate. Both the growth rates (represented by the log differences) and the levels of the above variables are included in Equation (8) in order to incorporate transitional dynamics. Note also that the constant term α_i is country-specific, and a time trend *t* is included in Equation (8).

Table 10 presents the summary statistics for the data used in the estimation. They are for the OECD countries over the period from 1985 to 1998. Due to data limitations, only 20 countries are included in the estimation.[2] The data on GDP, working age population and human capital are from Bassanini and Scarpetta (2002). To be more specific, GDP per working age person is equal to real GDP (in 1993 purchasing power parity) divided by the population aged 15 to 64 years. The growth rate of the working age population is approximated by the log difference of population aged 15-64. The proxy for the stock of human capital is the average years of schooling of a country's population in the same age group.

TABLE 10

ECONOMIC GROWTH AND TELECOMMUNICATIONS CAPITAL: SUMMARY STATISTICS

	MEAN	STANDARD DEVIATION	MINIMUM	MAXIMUM
Y	26,774	5,618	13,398	45,089
T	53.6	18.1	14.5	118.6
*T**	54.3	12.2	38.5	89.9
H	10.7	1.6	6.8	12.9
LG	0.006	0.005	–0.003	0.021
S	0.2	0.03	0.13	0.31

The remaining data used in the estimation are from the ITU's telecommunications database. Following Roller and Waverman (2001), I use the penetration rate as a proxy for the stock of telecommunications capital. Given the increasing importance of mobile cellular services, I include the mobile penetrate rate in the telecommunications capital. To be more specific, I use the penetration rate of telecommunications access channels (i.e. the sum of the fixed network penetration rate and the cellular mobile penetrate rate) as the proxy for the stock of telecommunications capital. The foreign stock of telecommunications capital is measured by the weighted average of penetration rates in other countries, with the weights being the foreign countries' shares in total international trade of a country averaged over the sample period.

Table 11 presents the estimation results of the fixed effects Equation (8). Two versions of the equation were estimated, one with the foreign telecommunication variable *LOGT** and the other without it. As can be seen from the table, all five growth variables, $\Delta LOGS$, $\Delta LOGH$, $\Delta LOGLG$, $\Delta LOGT$ and $\Delta LOGT^*$, have the expected signs. Four of those are statistically significant. Of particular interest is that the coefficients of both domestic and foreign telecommunications capital are positive and significant. The domestic telecommunications capital is significant at the one percent level, but the foreign telecommunications capital is significant at only the 10 percent level. The magnitude of the estimated coefficient of foreign telecommunications capital is slightly larger than that of the domestic telecommunications capital. This lends support to the conjecture by Aschauer (1996) that the regional (or even worldwide) marginal product of telecommunications infrastructure may well be higher than its domestic marginal product.[3]

The results in Table 11 also show that the coefficients of most level variables are negative, and two of them are statistically significant (version 1). This suggests that the positive effects of telecommunications capital may be attenuated somewhat as a country accumulates more of the capital. A comparison of version 1 and version 2 in Table 11 shows that the removal of the foreign telecommunications variable has only a marginal effect on the size and significance of the estimated coefficients of the remaining variables.

TABLE 11

ECONOMIC GROWTH AND TELECOMMUNICATIONS CAPITAL: THE FIXED EFFECTS MODEL (DEPENDENT VARIABLE: Δ*LOGY*)

	VERSION 1	VERSION 2
Δ*LOGS*	0.183***	0.185***
	(10.677)	(11.018)
Δ*LOGH*	0.246	0.247
	(0.580)	(0.590)
Δ*LOGLG*	–0.703*	–0.695
	(–1.648)	(–1.625)
Δ*LOGT*	0.171***	0.183***
	(3.699)	(4.270)
Δ*LOGT**	0.193*	—
	(1.693)	
Time Trend	0.003*	0.001
	(1.881)	(0.989)
LOGS	–0.955	–0.011
	(–0.875)	(–1.051)
LOGH	–0.115*	–0.098
	(–1.851)	(–1.591)
LOGLG	0.106	–0.144
	(0.302)	(0.412)
LOGT	–0.017	–0.024*
	(–1.127)	(–1.721)
*LOGT**	–0.065*	—
	(–1.740)	
Number of Observations Included: 260		
R^2:	0.556	0.55
Adjusted R^2:	0.498	0.495

Notes: * significant at 10% level;
*** significant at 1% level.

For the purposes of comparison, Tables 12 and 13 present the estimation results achieved by using two alternative methods, the random effects method and the plain ordinary least squares (OLS) method. They show that the size and statistical significance of the estimated coefficient of domestic telecommunications capital is fairly consistent across all three methods. The statistical significance of foreign telecommunications capital, however, disappears when the two alternative methods are used.

Using the estimates from Table 11, we can calculate a point estimate of the contribution of a country's telecommunications infrastructure to that country's

TABLE 12

ECONOMIC GROWTH AND TELECOMMUNICATIONS CAPITAL: THE RANDOM EFFECTS MODEL (DEPENDENT VARIABLE: Δ*LOGY*)

	VERSION 1	VERSION 2
Δ*LOGS*	0.186***	0.187***
	(11.234)	(11.555)
Δ*LOGH*	–0.153	–0.151
	(–0.536)	(–0.542)
Δ*LOGLG*	–0.607	–0.590
	(–1.474)	(–1.436)
Δ*LOGT*	0.172***	0.173***
	(4.326)	(5.037)
Δ*LOGT**	0.027	—
	(0.303)	
Time Trend	–0.000	–0.000
	(–0.132)	(–0.852)
LOGS	–0.018**	–0.018**
	(–2.306)	(–2.459)
LOGH	0.017	0.017
	(1.122)	(1.122)
LOGLG	0.065	0.044
	(0.239)	(0.165)
LOGT	–0.017**	–0.018**
	(–2.190)	(–2.474)
*LOGT**	–0.010	—
	(–0.415)	
Number of Observations Included: 260		
R^2:	0.471	0.472
Adjusted R^2:	0.448	0.453

Notes: * significant at 10% level;
** significant at 5% level;
*** significant at 1% level.

economic growth during the sample period. As can be seen from Table 14, the growth in Canada's telecommunications infrastructure is estimated to have contributed 0.74 percent to the growth rate of real GDP. This is slightly lower than Roller and Waverman's (2001) estimates for the 1971-1990 period, which is 0.95 percent.

It should be noted that the estimates in Table 14 are from a single-equation model. It has been argued that a single-equation model tends to over-estimate the effects of telecommunications infrastructure on economic growth as it does not take into consideration the feedback from economic growth to

TABLE 13

ECONOMIC GROWTH AND TELECOMMUNICATIONS CAPITAL: THE ORDINARY LEAST SQUARES MODEL (DEPENDENT VARIABLE: Δ*LOGY*)

	VERSION 1	VERSION 2
Δ*LOGS*	0.187***	0.186***
	(10.928)	(11.258)
Δ*LOGH*	–0.147	–0.141
	(–0.592)	(–0.572)
Δ*LOGLG*	–0.522	–0.520
	(–1.236)	(–1.240)
Δ*LOGT*	0.193***	0.190***
	(4.916)	(5.619)
Δ*LOGT**	–0.022	—
	(–0.264)	
Time Trend	–0.001	–0.001
	(–0.671)	(–1.182)
LOGS	–0.020***	–0.020***
	(–3.221)	(–3.233)
LOGH	0.020	0.021*
	(1.613)	(1.715)
LOGLG	–0.045	–0.043
	(–0.185)	(–0.180)
LOGT	–0.019**	–0.019**
	(–2.911)	(–3.126)
*LOGT**	0.002	—
	(0.125)	
Number of observations included: 260		
R^2:	0.474	0.473
Adjusted R^2:	0.45	0.454

Notes: * significant at 10% level;
** significant at 5% level;
*** significant at 1% level.

telecommunications investment (see Roller and Waverman 2001). In practice, however, a simultaneous-equation model that incorporates such feedback can still yield unrealistically large estimates for the effects of telecommunications capital (see Model 1 in Roller and Waverman 2001). Indeed, Roller and Waverman obtained more reasonable estimates only after they introduced fixed effects into their model. In Table 14, our single-equation model, on the other hand, generates estimates that are generally compatible with the more reasonable estimates from Roller and Waverman. This suggests that a single-equation model may not be the main culprit for the unreasonably large estimates that have existed in the literature.

TABLE 14

CONTRIBUTION OF TELECOMMUNICATIONS INFRASTRUCTURE TO ECONOMIC GROWTH, 1995 AND 1998

COUNTRY	REAL GDP PER WORKING AGE PERSON 1985	1998	CAGR* (%)	TELECOM PENETRATION RATE 1985	1998	CAGR* (%)	CONTRIBUTION OF TELECOM TO GDP GROWTH RATE: ESTIMATES (%) THIS MODEL	ROLLER AND WAVERMAN[c]
Australia	24,730	32,083	2.02	39.19	77.19	5.35	0.90	0.73
Austria	24,879	31,701	1.88	36.24	77.27	6.00	1.00	0.99
Belgium	25,240	33,648	2.24	30.76	67.18	6.19	1.03	0.78
Canada	**28,136**	**33,339**	**1.31**	**48.16**	**84.15**	**4.39**	**0.74**	**0.95**
Denmark	27,083	34,209	1.81	50.63	102.41	5.57	0.93	1.19
Finland	23,033	29,477	1.92	46.05	110.22	6.94	1.15	1.35
France	25,484	31,614	1.67	41.66	77.59	4.90	0.82	2.70
Greece [a]	15,683	17,290	0.89	31.38	71.53	6.54	1.09	1.04
Ireland	18,084	32,053	4.50	19.87	68.72	10.02	1.65	0.84
Italy	22,928	28,643	1.73	30.46	81.03	7.82	1.30	0.93
Japan [b]	23,696	32,298	2.61	37.47	90.83	7.05	1.17	0.99
Netherlands	23,332	31,068	2.23	40.22	80.51	5.48	0.92	0.94
Norway	25,852	31,658	1.57	43.84	113.40	7.58	1.26	1.11
New Zealand	20,265	21,088	0.31	39.58	68.53	4.31	0.72	0.28
Portugal [b]	13,398	19,090	2.99	14.53	72.06	13.11	2.13	0.83
Spain [b]	17,922	23,467	2.27	23.22	59.28	7.48	1.24	0.92
Sweden	26,464	30,832	1.18	63.66	118.56	4.90	0.82	3.32
Switzerland	32,499	35,534	0.69	50.16	92.41	4.81	0.81	—
United Kingdom	22,676	30,208	2.23	37.49	80.54	6.06	1.01	0.94
United States	33,919	45,089	2.21	48.78	90.71	4.89	0.82	0.21

Notes: * CAGR denotes compound annual growth rate.
a. For Greece, 1996 GDP is used in place of 1998 GDP.
b. For Japan, Portugal and Spain, 1997 GDP is used in place of 1998 GDP.
c. These estimates are presented in the last column of Table 1 in Roller and Waverman (2001). They were obtained for the sample period 1971-1990.

LIBERALIZATION OF TRADE AND INVESTMENT IN TELECOMMUNICATIONS SERVICES

MEASUREMENT OF BARRIERS TO TRADE AND INVESTMENT

IN ORDER TO QUANTIFY THE EFFECTS OF LIBERALIZATION, we need a measure of barriers to trade and investment. Because telecommunications are services (as opposed to goods), the barriers to trade and investment mostly take the form of non-tariff barriers such as regulations. This makes it difficult to quantify the height of these qualitative barriers with any precision. Nevertheless, efforts have been made to construct quantitative measures of barriers to trade and investment in services such as telecommunications. The most common approach is to quantify the barriers using indices. For telecommunication services, three sets of "trade restrictiveness indices" have been constructed. The first set was constructed by Warren (2001) using information from a survey conducted by the International Telecommunications Union (ITU). The survey, entitled "Telecommunication Reform 1998," contains information on government policies toward the telecommunication industry in 136 countries (Warren 2001).[4] Using this information, Warren has constructed five separate indices, three of which are designed to capture restrictions on all potential entrants (market access), and two of which are designed to capture restrictions on potential foreign entrants (national treatment). Within each of these two groups, Warren has calculated separate indices for ongoing operations and establishment.[5] In addition, OECD (1997) and Marko (1998) have each produced their own indices of trade restrictiveness using information from the commitment schedules in the WTO Agreement on Basic Telecommunication Services.

The econometric analysis in this section is performed using Warren's indices of trade restrictiveness. There are two reasons for choosing this set of indices over the OECD's and Marko's. First, Warren's indices are a more accurate measure of the barriers that existed in these countries during the 1990s because they are based on government policies in place rather than on WTO commitments. Second, Warren constructed five separate indices rather than just one overall index. This allows for a more detailed analysis of the effects of liberalization.

In Table 15, Warren's trade restrictiveness indices are shown as modified by the Australia Productivity Commission.[6] As can be seen from the table, Canada's barriers to market access were lower than the OECD average. Relative to the OECD average, all firms in Canada faced lower barriers to establishment but higher barriers to ongoing operations. What is striking is the large difference between the foreign and domestic index in Canada (last column), which measures the degree of discrimination against foreign firms. At 0.30, it is substantially higher than the OECD average of 0.11. This suggests that Canada erected substantially higher barriers to foreign firms than to domestic firms in the area of both establishment and ongoing operations.[7]

TABLE 15

TRADE RESTRICTIVENESS INDEX, 1998

	Restrictions on All Firms (Market Access)			Restrictions on Foreign Firms (National Treatment)			
Countries	Establishment	Ongoing Operation	Domestic Total	Establishment	Ongoing Operation	Foreign Total	Discrimination Against Foreign Firms
Australia	0.0445	0.0000	0.0445	0.0445	0.0000	0.0445	0.0000
Austria	0.1333	0.0000	0.1333	0.1333	0.0000	0.1333	0.0000
Belgium	0.0334	0.0667	0.1001	0.1334	0.0667	0.2001	0.1000
Canada	**0.0400**	**0.1000**	**0.1400**	**0.1420**	**0.3000**	**0.4420**	**0.3020**
Czech Republic	0.1340	0.1333	0.2673	0.1340	0.3333	0.4673	0.2000
Denmark	0.0333	0.0000	0.0333	0.0333	0.0000	0.0333	0.0000
Finland	0.0000	0.0000	0.0000	0.0000	0.0000	0.0000	0.0000
France	0.0500	0.0000	0.0500	0.2100	0.0000	0.2100	0.1600
Germany	0.0493	0.0000	0.0493	0.0493	0.0000	0.0493	0.0000
Greece	0.1609	0.1000	0.2609	0.1609	0.3000	0.4609	0.2000
Hungary	0.1107	0.1667	0.2773	0.1607	0.3667	0.5273	0.2500
Iceland	0.2333	0.0667	0.3000	0.2333	0.2667	0.5000	0.2000
Ireland	0.1933	0.0000	0.1933	0.3533	0.0000	0.3533	0.1600
Italy	0.1369	0.0000	0.1369	0.1369	0.0000	0.1369	0.0000
Japan	0.0436	0.0000	0.0436	0.0436	0.0000	0.0436	0.0000
Korea	0.1480	0.2000	0.3480	0.2820	0.4000	0.6820	0.3340
Luxembourg	0.1667	0.0000	0.1667	0.1667	0.0000	0.1667	0.0000

TABLE 15 CONTINUED

	Restrictions on All Firms (Market Access)			Restrictions on Foreign Firms (National Treatment)			
Countries	Establishment	Ongoing Operation	Domestic Total	Establishment	Ongoing Operation	Foreign Total	Discrimination Against Foreign Firms
Mexico	0.0299	0.2000	0.2299	0.1319	0.4000	0.5319	0.3020
Netherlands	0.0300	0.0000	0.0300	0.0300	0.0000	0.0300	0.0000
New Zealand	0.0333	0.0000	0.0333	0.0333	0.0000	0.0333	0.0000
Norway	0.1667	0.0000	0.1667	0.1667	0.0000	0.1667	0.0000
Poland	0.1600	0.2000	0.3600	0.2620	0.4000	0.6620	0.3020
Portugal	0.1100	0.2000	0.3100	0.1100	0.4000	0.5100	0.2000
Spain	0.1793	0.0333	0.2127	0.1793	0.2333	0.4127	0.2000
Sweden	0.1000	0.0000	0.1000	0.1000	0.0000	0.1000	0.0000
Switzerland	0.2000	0.0000	0.2000	0.2000	0.0000	0.2000	0.0000
Turkey	0.2667	0.2000	0.4667	0.3987	0.4000	0.7987	0.3320
United Kingdom	0.0000	0.0000	0.0000	0.0000	0.0000	0.0000	0.0000
United States	0.0000	0.0333	0.0333	0.0000	0.0333	0.0333	0.0000
OECD Average	**0.1030**	**0.0586**	**0.1616**	**0.1389**	**0.1345**	**0.2734**	**0.1118**

Note: See also Warren (2001).
Source: The Web site of Australian Productivity Commission (www.pc.gov.au). (Accessed January 19, 2005).

MODELING TELECOMMUNICATION INFRASTRUCTURE

TO ESTIMATE THE EFFECTS OF LIBERALIZING trade and investment in telecommunications services, the micro model of telecommunications investment in Roller and Waverman (2001) was extended in two ways. First, both fixed network and cellular mobile services were factored into the analysis. Second, trade restrictiveness indices are included on the supply side of the model to capture the effects of barriers to trade and investment. To be more specific, the analysis seeks to define the following variables:

T_f: infrastructure of fixed network services;
T_m: infrastructure of cellular mobile services;
R: barriers to establishment and ongoing operations in telecommunication services;
P_f: price of fixed network services;
P_m: price of cellular mobile services;
I_f: investment in fixed network services;
I_m: investment in cellular mobile services;
N: number of payphones;
Y: per capita income of a country;
A: geographic area of a country.

The demand functions for fixed network and cellular mobile telecommunications infrastructure can be written as:

$$(9) \qquad T_f^d = g_f(Y, P_f, P_m),$$

$$(10) \qquad T_m^d = g_m(Y, P_f, P_m, N).$$

Demand for each type of services is assumed to depend on income level and prices of both fixed network and mobile services. In addition, demand for mobile services is expected to depend on the availability of payphones because easy access to payphones reduces the need for having a mobile phone.

On the supply side, there are two sets of equations. First, the supplies of fixed network and mobile infrastructure are functions of investment, the geographic area of a country, and the telecommunications infrastructure in the previous period:

$$(11) \qquad T_f^s(t) = h_f\big(I_f, A, T_f(t-1)\big),$$

$$(12) \qquad T_m^s(t) = h_m\big(I_m, A, T_m(t-1)\big).$$

The investments in fixed network and mobile infrastructure, in turn, are determined by the following functions:[8]

$$(13) \qquad I_f = I_f(P_f, R, A); \quad I_m = I_m(P_m, R, A).$$

Note that R, the measure of barriers to establishment and ongoing operations, enters Equation (13). Substituting Equation (13) into Equation (11) and Equation (12) we obtain:

$$(14) \qquad T_f^s(t) = \widetilde{h}_f\left(P_f, R, A, T_f(t-1)\right),$$

$$(15) \qquad T_m^s(t) = \widetilde{h}_m\left(P_m, R, A, T_m(t-1)\right).$$

From Equation (9) and Equation (14), we solve for the equilibrium price of fixed network services:

$$(16) \qquad P_f^* = P_f\left(Y, P_m, R, A, T_f(t-1)\right).$$

From Equation (10) and Equation (15), we solve for the equilibrium price of mobile services:

$$(17) \qquad P_m^* = P_m\left(Y, P_f, R, A, N, T_m(t-1)\right).$$

Substituting Equation (16) into Equation (9) and Equation (17) into Equation (10), we obtain the following reduced form solution to equilibrium values of T_f and T_m as functions of exogenous variables:

$$(18) \qquad T_f = \widetilde{g}_f\left(Y, P_m, R, A, T_f(t-1)\right),$$

$$(19) \qquad T_m = \widetilde{g}_m\left(Y, P_f, R, A, N, T_m(t-1)\right).$$

Following Roller and Waverman (2001), fixed network and cellular mobile penetration rates, denoted by TF and TM, are used as proxies for telecommunications infrastructure. Revenue per mainline (respectively per mobile subscriber) is used as the proxy for the price of fixed network (respectively mobile) services. As discussed earlier, Warren's restrictiveness indices are used as measures of barriers to establishment and ongoing operations R. Variable Y is measured by GDP per capita in U.S. dollars. Since the mobile penetration rate grew by leaps and bounds during the 1990s, a non-linear relationship between the penetration rates and income (and prices) is assumed. The estimation equations, therefore, take the following form:

$$(20) \qquad \begin{aligned} LOGTF_{i,t} = {} & \beta_1 R_i + \beta_2 LOGY_{i,t} + \beta_3 \left(LOGY_{i,t}\right)^2 \\ & + \beta_4 LOGPM_{i,t} + \beta_5 \left(LOGPM_{i,t}\right)^2 \\ & + \beta_6 LOGA_i + \beta_7 t + \varepsilon_{i,t} \end{aligned},$$

$$(21) \qquad \begin{aligned} LOGTM_{i,t} = {} & \gamma_1 R_i + \gamma_2 LOGY_{i,t} + \gamma_3 \left(LOGY_{i,t}\right)^2 + \gamma_4 LOGPF_{i,t} \\ & + \gamma_5 \left(LOGPF_{i,t}\right)^2 + \gamma_6 LOGA_i + \gamma_7 LOGN + \gamma_8 t + \varepsilon_{i,t} \end{aligned}.$$

With the exception of Warren's trade restrictiveness indices, all data used in the estimation were computed from the ITU database. They cover the period from 1992 to 2000 for 20 OECD countries.[9] Table 16 contains the summary statistics.

Before the estimation results are presented, it is instructive to take a look at the correlation coefficients between *TF* (*TM*) and the dependent variables (Table 17). Two trade restrictiveness indices are included in the table. The first one, *R*, is the total foreign index, which measures the height of barriers facing a foreign firm. The second one, *R**, is the difference between total foreign index and total domestic index. It captures the degree of discrimination faced by a foreign firm. Both fixed and mobile penetration rates are negatively correlated with these indices, indicating a possible negative relationship between penetration rates and the height of barriers to trade and investment. The signs of the other correlation coefficients in Table 17 are not surprising. The fixed (mobile) penetration rate is positively correlated with per capita income but negatively correlated with its own price. The mobile penetration rate is negatively correlated with the availability of payphones.

In the estimation equations, the error terms are modeled as an AR(1) process to correct for the problem of serial correlation. The estimation results are presented in Tables 18 and 19. In the basic model, barriers to trade and investment are measured by *R*, the total foreign index. In addition, three variations of the model are estimated by using *R**, a measure of the discrimination faced by a foreign firm. In variation 1, *R** is the only measure of barriers in the estimation equations, while in variations 2 and 3, *R** is included along with a measure of the barriers faced by a domestic supplier of fixed (mobile) services. Specifically, *RF* and *RM* are indices that measure the barriers to establishment faced by domestic

TABLE 16

TELECOMMUNICATIONS INFRASTRUCTURE AND BARRIERS TO TRADE: SUMMARY STATISTICS

VARIABLE	MEAN	STANDARD DEVIATION	MINIMUM	MAXIMUM
TF	51.89	9.04	30.51	73.62
TM	19.95	20.32	0	77
Y	23,079	7,802	8,464	43,524
PF	647.05	197.27	304.61	1,234.01
PM	829.87	533.86	239.23	3,486.8
N	203	395	4	1,910
A	1,485	3,042	30	9,221
R	0.175	0.167	0	0.51
*R**	0.066	0.096	0	0.302

Note: The units for A are thousands of square kilometres.

TABLE 17

TELECOMMUNICATIONS INFRASTRUCTURE AND BARRIERS TO TRADE: CORRELATION COEFFICIENTS

	TF	TM
Y	0.661	0.174
PF	–0.145	–0.221
PM	–0.364	–0.566
A	0.325	–0.06
N	—	–0.032
R	–0.331	–0.122
*R**	–0.242	–0.154

suppliers of fixed and mobile services. Index *RFT* (respectively *RMT*) is equal to the sum of *RF* (respectively *RM*) and the restrictiveness index of ongoing operations.[10] It is a measure of the restrictions on both establishment and ongoing operation in fixed (mobile) services faced by domestic firms.

Table 18 contains the estimation results for fixed services. It turns out that none of the trade restrictiveness indices is statistically significant, suggesting that barriers to trade and investment do not appear to have any significant effect on the penetration rate in fixed services. The variables that are statistically significant across all four models are *LOGY*, $(LOGY)^2$ and $(LOGPM)^2$. The estimated coefficients from the basic model imply that the penetration rate of fixed services increases with per capita income for countries with per capita income below US$24,408, but decreases with per capita income for countries with higher per capita income. This last result will make more sense after we review the results for the mobile services.

From Table 19 we see that the estimated coefficients of *R* and *R** are statistically significant in three out of four instances. Along with the results from the fixed service models, this suggests that the negative effect of barriers to trade and investment are mainly felt in mobile services. The significant coefficients of the per capita income variable imply that the mobile penetration rate increases with per capita income for countries with per capita income above US$15,694. Therefore, the effects of per capita income on telecommunications differ according to the level of per capita incomes. For countries with per capita incomes in the range between US$15,694 and $24,408, higher income leads to higher penetration rates of both fixed and mobile services. For countries with lower incomes, improvements in telecommunications infrastructure associated with income growth are manifested in fixed-link services. For countries with higher incomes, mobile services expand as incomes grow. Given that high income countries already have well-developed fixed-link infrastructure, it is not surprising that in these countries mobile services are the main beneficiaries of income growth.

TABLE 18

FIXED NETWORK SERVICES AND BARRIERS TO TRADE AND INVESTMENT (DEPENDENT VARIABLE: LOGTF)

VARIABLE	BASIC MODEL	VARIATION 1	VARIATION 2	VARIATION 3
T	0.022***	0.022***	0.022***	0.022***
	(6.744)	(6.747)	(6.742)	(6.737)
R	0.070	—	—	—
	(0.321)			
*R**	—	0.030	–0.023	0.114
		(0.081)	(–0.044)	(0.287)
RFT	—	—	0.091	—
			(0.146)	
RF	—	—	—	–0.438
				(–0.552)
LOGY	2.377***	2.384***	2.383***	2.391***
	(42.258)	(44.461)	(43.707)	(43.963)
$(LOGY)^2$	–0.372***	–0.374***	–0.373***	–0.375***
	(–31.162)	(–32.083)	(–31.685)	(–31.889)
LOGPM	0.058	0.059	0.059	0.059
	(1.318)	(1.330)	(1.324)	(1.340)
$(LOGPM)^2$	–0.018*	–0.018*	–0.018*	–0.018*
	(–1.726)	(–1.735)	(–1.731)	(–1.748)
LOGA	0.001	0.001	0.002	–0.003
	(0.054)	(0.039)	(0.090)	(–0.157)
Included Observations:	180	180	180	180
R^2:	0.883	0.885	0.885	0.89
Adjusted R^2:	0.878	0.881	0.879	0.885

Notes: * significant at 10% level;
*** significant at 1% level.

The results from Table 19 also confirm the conjecture that the number of payphones in a country tends to have a negative effect on the mobile penetration rate. In two out of the four models, the negative coefficient of *LOGN* is statistically significant at the 10 percent level.

The performance of Canada's telecommunications services industry during the 1990s can be better understood in light of the above estimation results. In the overview of the telecommunications services industry at the beginning of this study, it was noted that during this period Canada maintained the lead in terms of the fixed network penetration rate but fell far behind in terms of the mobile penetration rate. The net result was that Canada's combined penetration rate for the two access channels fell from 2nd to 23rd place among the 29 OECD countries. The econometric analysis in this study points to two factors that are likely responsible for this fall:

TABLE 19

CELLULAR MOBILE SERVICES AND BARRIERS TO TRADE AND INVESTMENT (DEPENDENT VARIABLE: LOGTM)

VARIABLE	BASIC MODEL	VARIATION 1	VARIATION 2	VARIATION 3
T	0.543*** (9.199)	0.535*** (9.095)	0.537*** (9.095)	0.535*** (9.128)
R	–2.914** (–2.212)	—	—	—
*R**	—	–4.513** (–2.005)	–3.541 (–1.145)	–4.375* (–1.878)
RMT	—	—	–2.503 (–0.449)	—
RM	—	—	—	1.777 (0.210)
LOGY	–4.576* (–1.805)	–4.325* (–1.690)	–4.591* (–1.749)	–4.365* (–1.705)
$(LOGY)^2$	0.831* (1.844)	0.814* (1.788)	0.853* (1.840)	0.826* (1.804)
LOGPF	7.299* (1.789)	6.787* (1.661)	7.272* (1.722)	6.836* (1.673)
$(LOGPF)^2$	–1.778 (–1.595)	–1.691 (–1.514)	–1.813 (–1.578)	–1.696 (–1.521)
LOGA	0.220* (1.659)	0.278** (2.105)	0.261* (1.894)	0.274** (2.072)
LOGN	–0.217 (–1.498)	–0.232* (1.608)	–0.227 (–1.566)	–0.239* (–1.623)
Included Observations:	180	180	180	180
R^2:	0.543	0.537	0.538	0.538
Adjusted R^2:	0.521	0.516	0.514	0.514

Notes: * significant at 10% level;
** significant at 5% level;
*** significant at 1% level.

1. Canada's relatively high barriers to trade and investment appear to have hindered the growth of mobile services. Using the estimated coefficients in the basic model, we calculate that if Canada's trade restrictiveness index on foreign firms were lowered to the average level for OECD countries, Canada's cellular mobile penetration rate would rise by 63.44 percent.[11] This means that if Canada's barriers against foreign firms were at the average height of the OECD, our mobile penetration rate in 2000 would have been 48.05, which would substantially close the gap between Canada and the OECD average in the area of mobile services. The

combined penetration rate of both access channels would have been 117.93, which would have put Canada at or above the OECD average.

2. Canada's highly developed fixed network services and, in particular, a well-developed payphone system, reduced the need for cellular mobile services and thus slowed down its adoption.

The above discussion suggests that government policy was partially responsible for the fall in the relative standing of Canada's telecommunication services industry among OECD countries.

ESTIMATING THE EFFECTS OF TRADE LIBERALIZATION

TO QUANTIFY THE EFFECTS OF TRADE LIBERALIZATION, we consider a hypothetical situation where all discriminatory policies against foreign firms are to be removed. Quantitatively this implies that the values of the foreign restrictiveness indices would be reduced to those of the domestic indices. Using the estimated coefficients from the above econometric models, we can calculate the counterfactual penetration rate associated with this hypothetical situation. The difference between the counterfactual penetrate rate and the actual one represents the effects of trade liberalization on telecommunications infrastructure. Furthermore, using the estimated coefficients from the growth model presented in the previous section, the effects of liberalization on economic growth can also be quantified. When doing so, we assume that the effects of trade liberalization are realized over a 10-year period.

Note that a substantial liberalization of telecommunication services has already taken place since the ITU survey in 1998. Canada, for example, has liberalized the facilities-based international telecommunications market (Findlay and McGuire 2003). Hence, the trade restrictiveness indices in Table 15 are no longer a good measure of the barriers to trade and investment that may be in existence today. Table 20 provides updates of the trade restrictiveness indices for selected OECD countries in 2001. We see that the only positive index value for Canada is in the area of the establishment of foreign firms, implying that the restrictions on foreign ownership are the only major barrier to trade and investment in Canada.

TABLE 20

TRADE RESTRICTIVENESS INDEX, 2001

	Restrictions on All Firms (Market Access)			Restrictions on Foreign Firms (National Treatment)			
Countries	Establishment	Ongoing Operation	Domestic Total	Establishment	Ongoing Operation	Foreign Total	Discrimination Against Foreign Firms
Australia	0.04	0.00	0.04	0.04	0.00	0.04	0.00
Canada	0.00	0.00	0.00	0.10	0.00	0.10	0.10
Japan	0.04	0.00	0.04	0.04	0.00	0.04	0.00
Korea	0.06	0.00	0.06	0.16	0.20	0.36	0.30
New Zealand	0.00	0.00	0.00	0.00	0.00	0.00	0.00
United States	0.00	0.00	0.00	0.00	0.00	0.00	0.00

Source: Findlay and McGuire (2003).

Further liberalization by Canada, therefore, will have to involve the reduction or removal of restrictions on foreign ownership. Using the method described above, I estimate that the complete removal of discriminatory barriers in the area of direct investment will increase the mobile penetration rate by 10.17 points. Given the assumption that the effects of liberalization are realized over a 10-year period, this estimate implies that liberalization will boost Canada's annual growth rate of real GDP per working-age person by 0.17 percent during the 10-year period. In other words, if Canada removes all restrictions on foreign investment, Canada's GDP per working-age person will increase by a total of about 1.7 percent over the entire 10-year period.

It is interesting to note that the magnitude of my estimate is much smaller than that obtained by Mattoo et al. (2001). They estimate that full liberalization of the telecommunications services industry would add between 1.0 to 1.3 percent to the annual growth rate of per capita GNP. Since Mattoo et al. use a different model and a different measure of barriers to trade, it is not surprising that their estimates are of different magnitudes. Pinpointing the reasons that have caused the large difference, however, is difficult.

This brings up a number of caveats about these estimates. First, the estimated coefficients used in these calculations were derived from a particular set of econometric models. As such they are sensitive to changes in the specifications of these models. Second, the barriers to trade and investment are measured by a particular set of indices. Since the construction of these indices involved the use of various assumptions about the significance of different trade restrictions, the quality of the estimates is affected by the reasonableness of these assumptions as well as by the quality of the ITU survey data from which the indices were calculated. Third and finally, no attempt has been made to quantify the statistical confidence of the estimated effects of liberalization. These numbers, therefore, can only be treated as crude estimates of the potential effects of trade liberalization.

CONCLUSIONS

DESPITE ITS RAPID GROWTH, Canada's telecommunications services industry fell behind the average for the OECD countries during the 1990s, with telecommunications infrastructure declining from 2nd to 23rd place among the 29 OECD countries. The econometric analysis conducted in this study suggests two important factors that contributed to this decline in relative standing. First, Canada's highly developed fixed network services, and in particular, a well-developed payphone system, reduced the need for cellular mobile services and thus slowed down the adoption of mobile services. Second, relatively high barriers to ongoing operations and direct investment hindered the growth of cellular mobile services. If these barriers were reduced to the average height for

OECD countries, Canada's telecommunications penetration rate would have been above the OECD average.

The econometric analysis in this study shows that telecommunications infrastructure is a significant driving force for economic growth. This implies that the decline of Canada's standing in this area should be a cause for concern as it can affect Canada's economic growth vis-à-vis other OECD countries. Estimates from this analysis show that Canada's GDP per working-age person will be increased by about 1.7 percent over a 10-year period if Canada removes all barriers to foreign direct investment in telecommunication services.

ENDNOTES

1 Other studies of the same issue were conducted by Hardy (1980), Norton (1992) and Greenstein and Spiller (1996).

2 These countries are: Australia, Austria, Belgium, Canada, Denmark, Finland, France, Greece, Ireland, Italy, Japan, the Netherlands, New Zealand, Norway, Portugal, Spain, Sweden, Switzerland, the United Kingdom and the United States.

3 In the words of Aschauer (1996, p. 389), "It may well be the case that the marginal product of telecommunications capital within a country is rather small ... and yet the regional (or even worldwide) marginal product of telecommunications infrastructure is quite high."

4 Warren (2001), p. 76.

5 To be more specific, the three indices in the area of market access measure the heights of: (1) the barriers to investment in fixed network services; (2) the barriers to investment in mobile services; and (3) the barriers to international trade. The two indices in the area of national treatment measure the heights of the barriers to investment and trade respectively.

6 The Australian Productivity Commission has streamlined and re-scaled Warren's original indices in such a way that the maximum height of barriers has an index value of one.

7 A close examination of Warren's methodology shows that Canada's high score in this area was mainly caused by the restrictions on foreign ownership and call-back services.

8 In Roller and Waverman's model (2001), the government deficit is also included as a variable in the investment equation. The analysis here covers the period from 1992 to 2000 when reforms of telecommunications policies took place in many countries and investments in telecommunications were increasingly made by private investors rather than by governments. For this reason, the government deficit is dropped from the investment equations in this model.

9 The list of 20 countries is the same as in the growth model (see endnote 2) except that Sweden had to be excluded because of missing data on the number of payphones in this country. In its place, Germany is added.

10 Warren (2001) did not construct separate indices for fixed and mobile services in the area of ongoing operations.

11 From Table 15, the gap in the total foreign index between Canada and the OECD average is, 0.4420–0.2734 = 0.1686. Using the estimated coefficient of –2.914, we see that *LOGTM* would increase by 0.4913. The growth rate for the mobile penetration rate is then [exp(0.4913)–1], or 63.44 percent.

ACKNOWLEDGMENTS

FOR COMMENTS I WOULD LIKE TO THANK Steven Globerman, Prakash Sharma, Mohammed Rafiquzzaman, Someshwar Rao, Jianmin Tang, and participants at the Services Industries and the Knowledge-Based Economy conference organized by Industry Canada in October 2003. I would also like to thank Andrea Bassanini and Stefano Scarpetta for providing part of the data used in this analysis, and E.K. Lim for research assistance.

BIBLIOGRAPHY

Aschauer, D.A. 1996. "Comment on 'The Impact of Telecommunications Infrastructure on Economic Development'," in Peter Howitt (ed.). *The Implications of Knowledge-Based Growth for Micro-Economic Policies.* Industry Canada Research Series. Calgary: University of Calgary Press, pp. 387-390.

Bassanini, Andrea, and Stephano Scarpetta. 2002. "Does Human Capital Matter for Growth in OECD Countries? A Pooled Mean-Group Approach," *Economics Letters,* 74: 399-405.

Findlay, Christopher, and G. McGuire. 2003. "Restrictions on Trade in Services for APEC-Member Economies," Report prepared for distribution by the Pacific Economic Cooperation Council.

Greenstein, S., and P.T. Spiller. 1996. "Estimating the Welfare Effects of Digital Infrastructure," Working Paper No. 5770. Washington, D.C.: National Bureau of Economic Research.

Hardy, A. 1980. "The Role of the Telephone in Economic Development," *Telecommunications Policy*, 4: 278-286.

Mankiw, N.G., D. Romer, and D.N. Weil. 1992. "A Contribution to the Empirics of Economic Growth," *Quarterly Journal of Economics*, 107 (May): 407-437.

Marko, M. 1998. "An Evaluation of the Basic Telecommunications Service Agreement," Policy Discussion Paper No. 98/09. Adelaide, Australia: Centre for International Economics Studies, University of Adelaide.

Mattoo, A., R. Rathindran, and A. Subramanian. 2001. "Measuring Services Trade Liberalization and its Impact on Economic Growth: An Illustration," Working Paper (August). Washington, D.C.: World Bank.

Norton, S.W. 1992. "Transaction Costs, Telecommunications, and the Microeconomics of Macroeconomic Growth," *Economic Development and Cultural Change*, 41 (October): 175-196.

OECD. 1997. "Assessing Barriers to Trade in Services: Pilot Study Applications to the Accountancy and Telecommunication Sectors," Paris: OECD.

Roller, Lars-Hendrik, and Leonard Waverman. 2001. "Telecommunications Infrastructure and Economic Development: A Simultaneous Approach," *American Economic Review*, 91 (3): 909-923.

Verikio, G., and X–G. Zhang. 2001. *Global Gains from Liberalising Trade in Telecommunications and Financial Services*, Productivity Commission Staff Research Paper, AusInfo, Canberra, October.

Warren, Tony 2001. "The Identification of Impediments to Trade and Investment in Telecommunications Services," in Christopher Findlay and Tony Warren (eds.). *Impediments to Trade in Services: Measurement and Policy Implications*. New York: Routledge.

Comment

Sumit K. Kundu
Florida International University

THE SERVICES SECTOR HAS GROWN into the single most important component of the gross domestic product of the developed countries — the G-7 and the members of the OECD. Within this sector, certain industries such as banking and finance, construction, insurance, retailing, software and telecommunications have played a crucial role in fostering economic growth and national development. A majority of the industries in the services sector can be classified as 'knowledge-intensive' as they rely on the technological skills of a country's workforce, especially its engineers, scientists and other technical support staff. It is to be noted that several industrialized countries have embarked upon liberalization, deregulation and privatization to enhance industrial productivity and national competitiveness in their respective services industries.

In this context, Dr. Zhiqi Chen's study on "Liberalization of Trade and Investment in Telecommunication Services: A Canadian Perspective," sheds new light on Canada's telecommunication services industry during the 1990s. Let me begin by highlighting the main contributions made by Chen in his study. These are:

1. The study documents the importance of the telecommunications industry in the economic development of OECD nations with a focus on Canada — growth, size, infrastructure and productivity.

2. Effects of barriers to trade and investment in telecommunications infrastructure are investigated.

3. The author's econometric analysis includes both cellular mobile services and fixed network services.

4. The analysis in this study measures the spillover effects of telecommunication services across countries. The author claims this to be the first study to investigate certain aspects of these effects.

5. The study estimates the effects of trade liberalization on telecommunication services based on micro models of telecommunications and economic growth. It offers an improvement on the studies of Mattoo, Rathindran and Subramanian (2001) and Warren (2001).

The study builds upon an article by Lars-Hendrik Roller and Leonard Waverman (2001) in the *American Economic Review*, investigating the relationship between telecommunications services and economic growth (1970-1990).

In the overview of Canada's telecommunications services industry during the 1990s, the following observations are made by the author:

- The size, infrastructure and labour productivity of Canada's telecommunication services industry grew rapidly during the 1990s.
- The growth in Canada's telecommunication services industry is significantly below the average for the OECD countries as a whole.

Tables are presented for the growth of telecommunications services revenue as a percentage of GDP, the growth of telecommunications services revenue per capita, the growth in the fixed and mobile services penetration rate, the annual growth rate for the telecommunications penetration rate, the growth rate for telecommunications revenue per employee, and the annual growth in access channels (fixed and mobile combined) per employee. In all the above cases, Canada's growth rate is lower than the OECD average. But is it appropriate to use the OECD figure as a point of comparison? Should the standard of comparison perhaps be an average for some subset of the services providers for the OECD?

One of the problems with using the OECD database is the wide variation in the growth of firms in the telecommunications industry operating in the member countries. This is due in part to differences in government policies towards growth, productivity and competitiveness of the telecommunications firms in the respective countries. It seems more meaningful to have clusters of countries that are comparable in terms of market size, policies towards foreign competition, and the extent of liberalization.

We observe that employment in Canada's telecommunication industry fell in both absolute and relative terms, as shown in Tables 7-9 in the study. I would like to know what percentage of the tertiary sector is accounted for by telecommunications as evidenced by jobs, export revenues, and other economic activities.

It seems that Canada has maintained its lead in fixed network services even though it has fallen far behind in cellular mobile services. If this is so, several questions still remain unanswered in Chen's study of Canada's telecommunications industry.

The first of these revolves around what was and/or is the government policy on mobile services in relation to fixed network services. When was this policy initiated? Chen finds that the standing of Canada's telecommunication services industry declined from above the OECD average to below the average. Michael Porter's (1990) classic work on "The Competitive Advantage of Nations" argues that countries which have world-class industries are the ones that will contribute the most toward economic growth. I urge the author to examine the "Competitive Advantage of Canada in Telecommunications" and compare it to the countries that have a world-class telecommunication industry.

Are the Canadian firms competitive vis-à-vis the firms of other OECD countries? What can we say concerning the market structure in various OECD nations? Where is this similar to Canada's telecommunication industry? Do certain types of market structure support enhanced competitiveness, and what is the role of the government? The changing role of government can be observed in that several industrialized countries have pursued deregulation and liberalization simultaneously.

The author conducts an econometric study for the period 1985-1998. It is not clear how this time period was chosen, and whether there was rapid growth across all the OECD countries. It would be helpful if the author could also compare the changes in the structure of Canada's telecommunication industry with the situation in other OECD nations.

This also brings us to the issue of trends in mobile services. Were government policies the same or different for mobile versus fixed network services?

The author addresses the issue of "spillover effects" with respect to improvement in the telecommunication infrastructure of foreign countries. Is the spillover more from the development of fixed network or mobile services? Also the extent of spillover from the United States to Canada needs to be looked into, as the former country has some of the world's largest telecommunication multinationals. Specifically it would be helpful to know more about the following issues:

- With respect to foreign versus domestic investment in the OECD countries, who are the major players?

- What is the extent of intra-firm trade and technology transfer in the telecommunications industry?
- What sort of restrictions on investment and trade exist for the telecommunication services?
- What has been the role of the North American Free Trade Agreement (NAFTA) in facilitating growth/competitiveness for Canadian telecommunication firms?

Chen comments that in countries such as Austria, Finland and Italy, the mobile penetration rate has exceeded that of fixed network services. Why? Is this a better growth model for some countries? Does country size matter in pursuing one type of industry policy and business strategy over another?

The Chen study seeks to measure barriers to trade and investment. The data in Table 15 on the "Trade Restrictiveness Index" for 1998 reveals that Canadian discrimination against foreign firms has been nearly three times the OECD average. Why is that? The neighbouring United States has a value of 0.0000 for this index. What should the Canadian government do to allay the fears of multinational corporations seeking to enter the Canadian market place?

Based on the results stated in Table 18, barriers to trade and investment do not appear to have any significant effect on penetration rates in fixed services. Why would this be? Is it this business segment where the Canadian telecommunication providers are competitive?

This study presents results that bear on the effects of trade liberalization. But many questions are left unanswered. Why does the Canadian government have restrictions on foreign ownership and barriers to trade and investment? This is a classic international business/international trade question with which public policy makers have struggled for years. The representatives of industries and nations seek simultaneously to enhance their competitiveness and market their production facilities or locations as attractive for foreign direct investment by multinational enterprises. From a policy-making standpoint, every government is concerned with productivity growth and enhanced competitiveness. The question that needs to be addressed is how does liberalization contribute directly to the growth of productivity and competitiveness in the telecommunication industry, and indirectly towards economic development/growth in a given nation such as Canada? I have provided a schematic framework in Figure 1 to illustrate the relationship between liberalization, productivity, competitiveness and economic growth.

FIGURE 1

RELATIONSHIP BETWEEN LIBERALIZATION, PRODUCTIVITY, COMPETITIVENESS AND ECONOMIC GROWTH

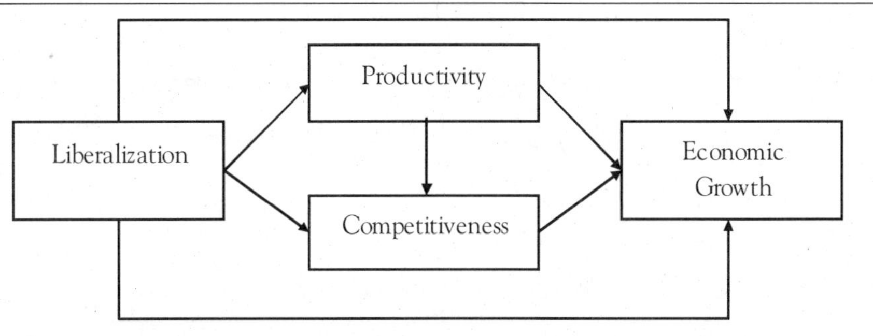

In conclusion, this study is a good starting point for understanding the impact of the liberalization of trade and investment on Canada's telecommunication services industry. The next step is to examine the determinants of industry productivity and national competitiveness. It is apparent that developed countries are looking to knowledge-based services industries such as telecommunications to create value and wealth for their respective nations, and continuously striving to find ways to pursue both increased growth of industry productivity and national competitiveness.

BIBLIOGRAPHY

Mattoo, A., R. Rathindran, and A. Subramanian. 2001. "Measuring Services Trade Liberalization and its Impact on Economic Growth: An Illustration," Working Paper (August). Washington, D.C.: World Bank.

Porter, Michael E. 1990. *The Competitive Advantage of Nations*. New York: The Free Press.

Roller, Lars-Hendrik, and Leonard Waverman. 2001. "Telecommunications Infrastructure and Economic Development: A Simultaneous Approach," *American Economic Review*, 91 (3): 909-923.

Warren, Tony 2001. "The Identification of Impediments to Trade and Investment in Telecommunication Services," in Christopher Findlay and Tony Warren (eds.). *Impediments to Trade in Services: Measurement and Policy Implications*. New York: Routledge.

C. Michael Wernerheim & Christopher A. Sharpe
Memorial University of Newfoundland

13

The Rural/Urban Location Pattern of Advanced Services Firms in an International Perspective

INTRODUCTION

GROWTH IN EMPLOYMENT within Canada's professional, scientific and technical (PST) services over the past decade has outrun all but the most optimistic expectations. This has been especially true in rural areas where total employment growth has averaged almost 10 percent annually. This is more than twice the employment growth rate for the PST economy as a whole. Undoubtedly, this is partly related to the rapid rise of investment in information and communication technologies (ICT) and its attendant increase in total factor productivity, which recent research shows helped boost economic growth in Canada and the other G-7 countries in the second half of the 1990s (Jorgenson 2001 and 2003). Since ICT is an important component of business transactions on both the input and output side of advanced services activity, productivity improvements in ICT can be expected to be a major driver of growth in both productivity and employment in a services sector that is an intense user of both human capital and ICT. Jorgenson (2003) argues convincingly that differences in methodology and data aside, the remarkable behaviour of ICT prices provide a key to productivity findings. Additional factors help explain observed differences in productivity growth between Canada, the United States and Europe. They include differential rates of generating productivity improvements from innovations and the greater rigidity of European services markets.

What are the implications of this development for the location of establishments and employment across space? By extension, how does it affect the common belief that advanced producer services[1] are capable of assuming a leading role in regional development? It is well-known that Canadian employment in advanced producer services is highly concentrated in metropolitan areas. Our survey of the international evidence suggests that metropolitan concentration is also the rule in the other G-7 countries. Various aspects of this pattern have been amply demonstrated in numerous studies over the past 10 to 15 years. This research, however, begs the question: do externalities associated with the urban core of metropolitan areas exert an attraction on PST firms outside that core, causing such firms to huddle on its fringes? Alternatively, are these firms more widely dispersed for other reasons? These issues matter as they bear on the likelihood of regional policy succeeding in influencing the locational decisions of private sector firms.

Although significant progress has been made in understanding locational issues, they remain vexing to researchers and policy makers alike. Even so, the services sector is increasingly viewed as holding new promise for remote or stagnating regions (Bailly 1995). The main idea underpinning policies imbued with this view is that advanced producer services are independent of traditional agglomeration economies, geographical advantages conferred by nature and physical proximity to a manufacturing sector. These services have often been said to act as their own growth-poles because they can attract and absorb migrating human capital. They can also extend the limits of the market since one of their chief characteristics is that they are exportable beyond regional and national boundaries. In this study we show that this claim may be overstated in reference to areas outside the metropolitan core.

While the specific questions we raise have not received much research attention, the debate about the issues underlying it has a long history. In particular, there are at least two parallel debates that bear on regional development problems. The first is whether or not the development of ICT is one of a series of positive, drastic, but temporary shocks (Malecki 2002). If not, does ICT stimulate fundamental innovation complementarities like writing, printing and electricity, which lead to permanent improvements in growth prospects (Jorgenson 2003). A second related debate is whether in an electronically-interconnected world, metropolitan areas will lose their 'spatial glue' as propinquity, concentration, place-based relations and transportation flows are gradually replaced by the ultimate 'information superhighway' (Graham 1998). Simply put, is the Internet the great geographical equalizer of employment and prosperity? Much current thinking about regional policy in Canada and elsewhere seems to be predicated on the notion that it is.

It has been observed that in Canada this is perhaps more part of a political agenda than an academic debate. Though Canada currently has no official coordinated regional development policy, a number of federal and provincial agencies and initiatives use various means to support regional (local and provincial) development efforts, some of which involve the services sector among others.[2] More important than the nature of the debate, however, is how to improve the extent to which academic research informs the political process.

It is clear from existing research that the greatest concentration of advanced services is to be found in certain metropolitan areas. In this study, we investigate locational patterns outside the metropolitan core, that is, in rural areas inside and outside the boundaries of metropolitan areas. We examine if there may also be concentrations of PST establishments in the areas outside the metropolitan core. We refer to the aggregate of all such areas as the 'non-core.' Such a concentration could occur if the spatial extent of the market is not binding on the remotely located firm. Put differently, spatial concentration could occur if the 'pull' of the metropolitan core (through agglomeration economies and need for proximity to clients) is sufficiently strong. To test our conjecture that there is no such concentration, we follow the approach by Ellison and Glaeser (1997) who formulate a statistical testing procedure based on a stochastic version of the conditional logit model. We begin by deriving unique data sets for PST establishments in the core and the non-core. We map this spatial data, and apply it to the model in order to test the so-called 'dartboard theory' of plant location. The result is a new perspective on the spatial pattern of PST activity in Canada.

In order to address these issues we begin with a review of the pertinent literature. The remainder of the study is organized as follows. The third section contains a descriptive analysis of data on employment and establishments. It is followed by a statistical test of our hypothesis about the locational decisions of services firms outside the urban core. We then review the international evidence from three countries with which Canada has important economic, historic, cultural, linguistic and political connections. The final section concludes with some policy implications and suggestions for future research.

PREVIOUS STUDIES

TO DATE, MOST RESEARCH has involved manufacturing industries and has focused on inter- and intra-urban location (Coffey and Polèse 1987). While some of this research has involved metropolitan areas in 'peripheral' regions (Perry 1991), scant attention has been paid to the determinants of location and the employment created by the entry of establishments outside metropolitan areas. Thus we know little about whether advanced services activity in rural areas differs from that in urban and metropolitan areas and if so, how. Exceptions with at least some rural or non-metropolitan orientation include Kirn (1987); Coffey and Polèse (1989); Coffey (1993); O'Farrell, Moffatt and Hitchens (1993); Glasmeier and Howland (1994); Beyers and Lindahl (1996); Eberts and Randall (1998); Gatrell (1999); Polèse and Shearmur (2002); as well as a series of studies and monographs published by the Canadian Rural Revitalization Foundation (CRRF), and the Canadian Institute for Research on Regional Development (CIRRD) since the early 1990s.[3]

We agree with Gatrell (1999) who observes that our knowledge of producer services activity in rural areas is slight, and not likely to improve given a predilection for focusing research on metropolitan areas. Such a focus ignores, for example, the importance of producer services in agricultural and other resource industries. It also ignores the fact that not all firms within a particular category of the official industrial classification necessarily perform identical functions. Firms in the same industry but located in different parts of the regional system can pursue quite different activities. Services firms in metropolitan areas may, for example, focus on or support research and development (R&D) activities. In rural areas, however, they are likely to be engaged in routine, low value-added activities (Glasmeier and Howland 1994). Research for other countries indicates that the rural services sector employs the majority of rural workers and that it has grown faster there than in urban areas (Kirn 1987; Beyers and Lindahl 1996; and Gatrell 1999). This agrees with the findings for Canada reported later in this study. What are the policy implications of this? Some authors have concluded that a peripheral region can indeed develop a vibrant services economy. However, the extent to which PST firms act as drivers of economic growth is debatable, especially in peripheral areas. A recent Canadian study indicates that the cause-and-effect relationship between services employment growth and regional gross domestic product (GDP) varies remarkably across space, casting doubt on the popular hypothesis that employment growth in services industries spurs economic growth (Wernerheim 2004).

The relatively small size of the advanced services economy in non-core areas is no doubt a key element of the explanation for this state of affairs. Our data suggest that services employment is growing faster in rural areas than in urban areas but it does so from a base that is too small to have much economic significance. However, the small size of the rural services sector also masks interesting 'intra-rural' growth patterns that may help explain observed experience. In Canada, less than 10 percent of PST employment is located outside metropolitan areas. Nonetheless, this employment can be very important to the survival of rural communities, many of which are going through extensive restructuring as a result of declines in the natural resource base (fish, forests and ores) that have traditionally sustained much of Canada's rural fabric. This circumstance undoubtedly contributes to recent policy interest in promoting the establishment of new advanced services firms in regions that lie beyond the urban shadow as a means of economic revitalization. At the same time, it is self-evident that the promotion or subsidization of advanced services in peripheral areas is a contentious policy issue since such initiatives necessarily divert public funds from competing uses in attempts to spur growth by 'correcting' location patterns generated by market forces.

There can be little doubt that in making locational choices, new firms and branch plants respond to incentives, all else being equal. This raises the question of the best way of attracting employment to a region. If advanced services firms are sufficiently footloose to locate, relocate, or branch out from metropolitan areas into rural areas, as some would argue, do the factors that determine such locational decisions vary across space? That is, are firms that locate in non-metropolitan areas less dependent on proximity to manufacturing industries and other factors that have traditionally conferred locational advantage? Moreover, does government intervention (in the form of subsidies and tax incentives) that targets advanced services firms have any sustained, as opposed to transitory, positive effect on local economic growth and rural welfare? Illeris (1991, 1996) argues that these issues are best understood by focusing on local interdependencies, rather than on the export orientation of services firms, which has attracted so much recent attention in services research. This view is consistent with the approach taken here.

LOCALIZATION IN THEORY AND PRACTICE

ALFRED MARSHALL FIRST ADVANCED the idea of agglomeration as a spatial externality in the 1890s. An extensive literature has since emerged that draws on this concept to explain why firms locate where they do and therefore why growth, productivity and investment typically differ so much across physical space. This is evident in the 'new' theories of regional growth developed over the past 25 years that focus on increasing returns, externalities and other agglomeration aspects. In the empirical literature, Krugman (1991) and others[4] have suggested that geographic agglomeration of firms in individual manufacturing industries may be more common than generally believed. Even casual observation, however, suggests that firms and employment in services industries also tend to cluster in certain regions. Not surprisingly, several recent studies have shown that advanced services industries in Canada, the United States and the European Union do indeed cluster in certain metropolitan areas.[5] Although it has been argued forcefully that the local provision of advanced producer services in a region is an important element of economic development (Perry 1990), the opportunity to study agglomeration and location decisions in services industries appears to be relatively unexploited.

In neoclassical theory, the minimization of transportation costs is key to company locational decisions. However, when space is introduced, a broader concept of agglomeration benefits is justified. For example, economies of scale induce firms to concentrate production in a small number of plants. This is reinforced by external economies that create interdependences among firm locational choices. Received wisdom holds that external economies come in two forms: localization economies that are related to own-industry scale and thus internal to the industry (Marshall 1890); and urbanization economies related to urban scale and therefore common to all firms (Hoover 1936).

Both of these intra-, and inter-industry spillovers are dynamic and serve to strengthen ties among firms, but they have different implications for the organization of space. When localization economies dominate, specialized industrial centres emerge. When urbanization economies dominate, industrial specialization also emerges but it does so in highly-diversified industrial areas (Henderson 1983; Glaeser, Kallal, Scheinkman and Schleifer 1992; and

Windrum and Tomlinson 1999). While proximity to professional services is generally preferred by newly-locating firms (Illeris 1991), the utility of the 'local' presence of advanced services is increasingly contingent upon such services meeting national or international standards. Conversely, when such standards are met, global firms often gain access to 'local' expertise through subcontracting (Wood, 1998). All else being equal, this gives advanced services firms an additional degree of freedom in making locational choices.

Rivera-Batiz (1988), and a series of studies by J. R. Markusen and J. R. Melvin in the late 1980s provided the theoretical basis for understanding the role of producer services, and how agglomeration factors and returns to scale operate in services industries.[6] Some of the earlier empirical work on how spatial externalites underpin localization and urbanization economies used aggregate data and flexible production-function approaches (Henderson 1983, 1986; Nakamura 1985; and Feser 2001), or labour-demand functions (Moomaw 1988). However, most of the recent literature has used geographically-disaggregated micro-level data and has made use of the multinomial conditional logit model developed by McFadden (1974). Since Carlton (1979, 1983) first applied this discrete-choice framework to studies of industrial location, a considerable number of studies have used it in a variety of settings involving manufacturing industries. As far as we know, to date there has been no attempt to model agglomeration and location in services industries using the conditional logit framework (Wernerheim 2003).

However, some of the findings from manufacturing-related research are likely to apply to producer services as well. One example of this is that the efficacy of business incentives (e.g. tax-credits and exemptions, loan guarantees, and wage subsidies) in attracting investment remains unclear. The empirical literature examining such impacts on firm location is fairly extensive. It has been reviewed by Carlton (1979), Wasylenko (1991), and most recently by Buss (2001). Some studies have found that tax differentials matter (Bartik 1985; and Papke 1991). Other studies have found that taxes matter only in some cases (Luger and Shetty 1985; Coughlin, Terza and Arromdee 1991; Friedman, Gerlowski and Silberman 1992; Woodward 1992; Finney 1994; and Gius and Frese 2002). Carlton (1979, 1983), for example, finds no effect when controlling for taxes and the local business climate generally. Other studies have reported similar findings.[7] Generally, there is little compelling evidence of a tax effect. Nonetheless, tax policy and other business incentives are widely used and remain a popular political tool of local governments. They will likely remain so as long as policy makers view regional development as a zero-sum game, notwithstanding mixed empirical findings (Buss 2001) and contrary to theoretical findings (Owens and Sarte 2002).

DESCRIPTIVE ANALYSIS

THE DATA

THE PROFESSIONAL, SCIENTIFIC AND TECHNICAL SERVICES SECTOR (North American Industrial Classification System [(NAICS)-C 54] with which we are concerned is a heterogeneous collection of advanced services used primarily as intermediate inputs. They are thus demanded and supplied mostly by producers of goods and services. Some providers serve only local markets and are independent of linkages with adjacent manufacturing industries (e.g. some legal and accounting services). Others export a fair share of their output or co-locate with principal demanders (e.g. some engineering and scientific services). However, they all tend to share the characteristics that matter for the present study: a high human capital content, high relative ICT-intensity, and exportability. These characteristics keep PST services in the focus of much of the contemporary regional policy debate. The starting point for this debate is the role these services play at the local level.

This study employs two principal types of annual data on PST services activity published by Statistics Canada: the first is employment and the second is the distribution by number and size of firms (or establishments).[8] The former data set derives from the Canadian Labour Force Survey (LFS) and is disseminated using a five-part taxonomy of geographical areas: urban core, urban fringe, rural fringe, small towns, and rural areas. The latter set comes from the Canadian Business Patterns (CBP) 2001 database. Data on establishments are available by census division (CD). The following is a brief review of the process by which we bring these data together and derive the spatial data set used in this study.[9]

The 288 CDs into which Canada is divided form an exhaustive and mutually-exclusive set of areas that are delineated to help in regional planning. They vary considerably in size but are generally smaller than the comparable U.S. 'economic areas' and therefore provide more detailed spatial coverage. The smallest CDs are in the most densely populated and economically important areas of the country. This makes CDs very useful for detecting spatial patterns in economic activity.

The 'urban core' of Canada is located in 27 census metropolitan areas (CMAs) and 113 census agglomerations (CAs), which also incorporate a considerable amount of non-urban territory. The CBP database allows us to determine the number of establishments in the core and non-core areas of each of the 288 CDs.[10] The distribution of establishments can then be related to the five-part LFS taxonomy referred to above (see Figure 1). In order to align the set of CDs with the set of metropolitan places, we categorize the CDs that contain all or part of a CMA or CA as 'metropolitan' (N=148), and those that do not as 'non-metropolitan' (N=140).

FIGURE 1

THE GEOGRAPHICAL TAXONOMY

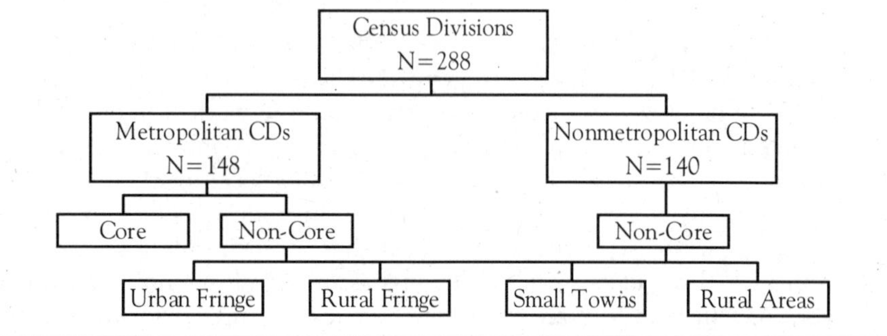

Source: Canadian Business Patterns 2001, Statistics Canada, authors' compilation.

At the heart of every CMA and CA is an 'urban core' that comprises one or more 'urban areas'. Areas inside a CMA/CA boundary but outside the core are classified as 'urban fringe' or 'rural fringe' by Statistics Canada. Any remaining area inside what we call a metropolitan CD, but beyond the boundary of the CMA or CA, is classified as 'small town' or 'rural area'. We maintain this distinction in our discussion of the employment (LFS) data as this is how these data are published. Data on establishments (CBP) are reported by CD and we have partitioned these data into 'core', 'non-core', and 'non-metropolitan' areas. The core incorporates all the contiguous urban areas that form the urban cores of the CMAs and CAs. Everything outside this core (the urban- and rural fringes, small towns and rural areas) are 'non-core'. Thus a 'metropolitan' CD will contain both a core and a non-core area. CDs classified as 'non-metropolitan', will contain only non-core areas. The CDs thus classified were geo-coded and their respective establishment counts recorded and mapped. The result is a new perspective on locational choices and the consequent penetration of advanced producer services firms into the non-core areas of Canada. It identifies the well-known concentrations in a small number of major urban sites but more interestingly, it shows how establishments are dispersed among smaller urban locations and rural areas across the country. This unique data set permits statistical testing of our hypothesis regarding firm location in the 'non-core.'

ESTABLISHMENT LOCATION

NINE CDS STAND OUT as having exceptionally large numbers of core or non-core establishments. They can be classified into three groups, two of which represent urban concentrations — the so-called 'corridors' — well-known from previous studies of other industry categories.[11] Briefly, the four CDs in the first group are located in Ontario (Ottawa, Toronto, Peel Regional Municipality and York Regional Municipality). Of these four, all but Ottawa form part of the Toronto CMA (Peel is adjacent to the western boundary of the City of Toronto, and runs northward from Lake Ontario; and the York Regional Municipality is contiguous with the northern boundary of Toronto.) None of these four CDs have any non-core firms as the urban core fills the entire CD. The second group of four 'outlier' CDs includes Calgary, Edmonton, Montreal and Vancouver. These differ from the CDs in the first group in that they do have non-core areas, although they all are strongly core-oriented, with ratios of non-core establishments to core establishments of 0.11, 0.22, 0.03 and 0.01 respectively. The very low ratio in Vancouver is an artifact of the very large size of the CD in which it is located. Its boundaries have been drawn so broadly that they encompass not only the entire Vancouver CMA, but all the urban areas of the Lower Mainland as well, leaving a relatively small non-core area.[12] The important point here is that while these ratios are to some degree artifacts of municipal boundaries, they still reflect the outcomes of locational decisions. In other words, they reflect the extent to which establishments have decided to locate outside of the urban core.

The ninth 'outlier,' Red Deer, Alberta, is perhaps the most interesting in the present context. It differs from the others in at least three important ways. One, with a population of 70,000, it is considerably smaller and thus is classified as a CA and not a CMA. Two, it has an unusually large number of establishments located outside the boundaries of the core of the CA. Only Edmonton and Calgary, the two cities that are equidistant from it to the north and south, have more firms located in the non-core portion of their CDs. Three, it would appear that Red Deer's role as a thriving service centre for the agricultural, petroleum and natural gas industries of the region may be attributable to its fortunate location on the main road between Edmonton and Calgary, and perhaps also to its abolition of business tax. It also has its own rapidly growing manufacturing sector that includes a number of important petro-chemical industries. It boasts of being the only city on the Canadian prairies that has access to a potential market of more than two million people within a 160 km radius. Red Deer is a classic example of the importance of location: the city's position and size permit it to act as a kind of intervening opportunity between two larger, highly-interconnected cities.

Given the nature of the services we are examining in this study, the dominance of this group of nine cities is hardly surprising. All have a large population, a well-educated workforce with a sizeable proportion of professional and managerial professionals, and solid industrial and social infrastructures that include transportation networks, schools, leading hospitals, proximity to universities and research institutions and attractive recreational amenities. Moreover, this group of CDs includes all or almost all of the most populous urban areas in Canada; the national capital (Ottawa), two provincial capital cities (Edmonton and Toronto) and the primary cities of two other provinces

(Montreal and Vancouver). Seven have at least one university. The only CD that does not is York, which is contiguous to the city of Toronto. Five are located in the traditional economic and cultural heartland of the country, the Great Lakes-St. Lawrence Lowland.

The geography of PST establishment locations is summarized in Table 1. Of these establishments, 93 percent are located in the 148 metropolitan CDs and 89.5 percent in the urban cores. There are approximately 92,000 core-located establishments, which comprise almost 84 percent of all PST establishments in Canada. Nearly 10 percent are located in the non-core portions of these CDs, that is to say in the urban and rural fringes, small towns and rural areas of CDs that contain all or part of a CMA or CA. This leaves only 7,238 establishments or 6.6 percent in the non-metropolitan CDs. The average number of establishments in the metropolitan CDs and in the non-metro CDs are 694 and 52 respectively. In the group of nine outliers the average is 6,894. This latter group accounts for 56.4 percent of the total number of establishments, 64.1 percent of core establishments and 25.2 percent of non-core establishments. This demonstrates the remarkable concentration of PST establishments in the metropolitan regions of Canada, which is so dramatically evident in a three-dimensional east-west aspect of Canada (Figure 2).

Thus, it is also clear that among the CDs that have non-core establishments, (most but not all do) there is surprisingly little variation in the number of establishments. Moreover, the establishments outside the urban core appear very dispersed. Clearly outlined is the corridor in the East; the so-called 'golden triangle' which takes shape at the U.S. border and runs up the Ottawa Valley, linking Toronto, Ottawa, Montreal and Quebec. The corridor in the West consists of the Vancouver-Edmonton-Calgary axis, with Red Deer clearly visible between the latter two cities.

TABLE 1

PROFESSIONAL, SCIENTIFIC AND TECHNICAL SERVICES, CANADA TOTAL EMPLOYMENT, 2002 AND THE NUMBER OF ESTABLISHMENTS, 2001

GEOGRAPHICAL AREA	EMPLOYMENT (000)	%	ESTABLISHMENTS (000)	%
Canada	993.3	100.0	109.9	100.0
Metropolitan	**905.6**	**91.2**	**102.6**	**93.4**
Urban Core	794.3	80.0	91.9	83.6
Urban Fringe	11.6	1.2	10.8	9.8
Rural Fringe	99.7	10.0		
Non-metropolitan	**87.7**	**8.8**	**7.2**	**6.6**
Small Towns	31.2	3.1	n/a	n/a
Rural Areas	56.5	5.7	n/a	n/a

Source: Labour Force Survey Estimates, CANSIM II; and Canadian Business Patterns 2001, Statistics Canada, authors' compilation.

FIGURE 2

**THE CANADIAN PST ESTABLISHMENT LANDSCAPE, 2001
TOTAL ESTABLISHMENT COUNTS BY CENSUS DIVISION — EAST TO WEST**

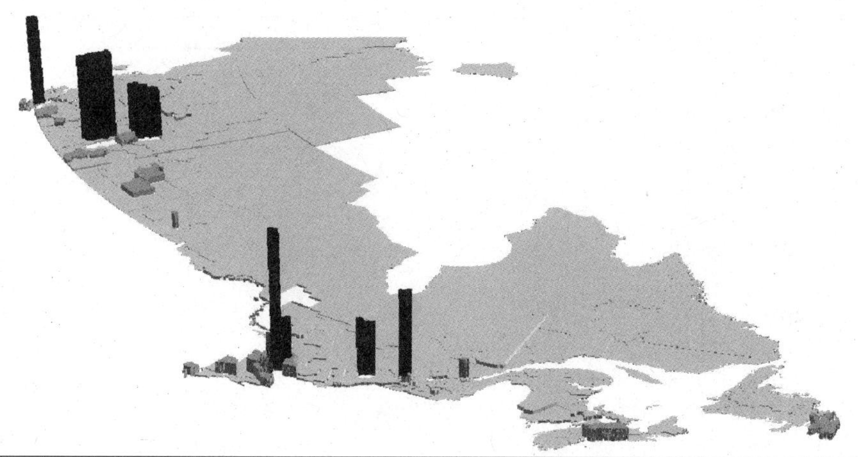

Source: Canadian Business Patterns 2001, Statistics Canada.

Another outstanding feature of the PST sector is the distribution of establishments by size. The frequency distribution (Figure 3) for each geographical aggregation is sharply skewed toward small establishments. That is, PST establishments are predominately small regardless of location. Seventy percent of all establishments employ fewer than five people. Firms with fewer than 10, and fewer than 20 employees account for 83 percent and 91 percent respectively of the total number of establishments. In *non-metro* CDs, which are by definition more rural than non-core CDs, 92 percent of establishments employ fewer than 10 people and none have more than 50. Furthermore, it is remarkable that the relative frequency (i.e. the number of establishments in each size class) in non-core areas mirrors that for core areas (not shown).

The preponderance of small establishments is also evident at the provincial level (Table 2). Quebec, one of the principal PST locations in the country, has at once the greatest concentration of very small establishments and one of the lowest concentrations of large firms. Curiously, Newfoundland, a province that is both economically and geographically peripheral, has a distribution that closely coincides with the Canadian average.

FIGURE 3

PROFESSIONAL, SCIENTIFIC AND PROFESSIONAL SERVICES, CANADA, 2001
ESTABLISHMENT SIZE DISTRIBUTION BY GEOGRAPHICAL AGGREGATION

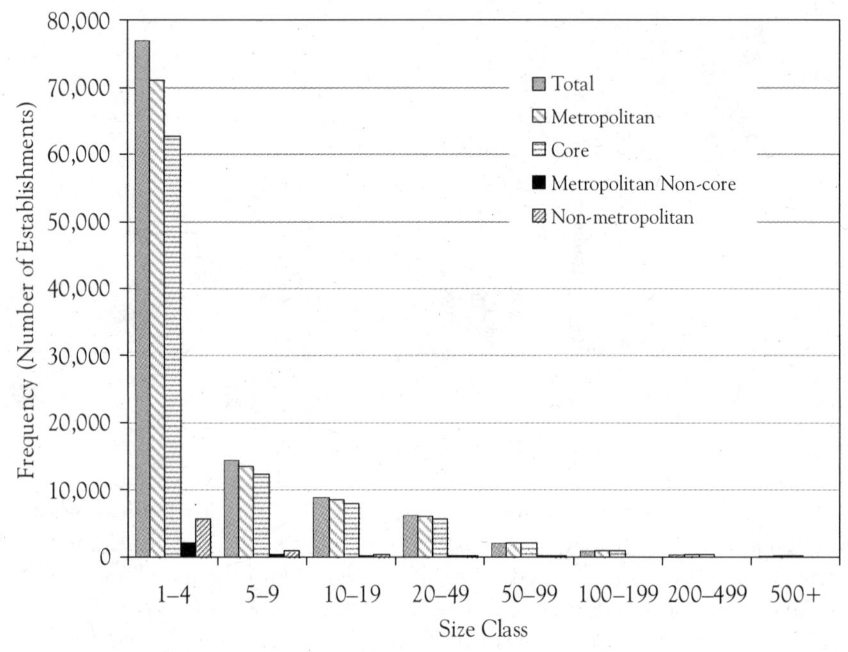

Source: Canadian Business Patterns 2001, Statistics Canada, authors' compilation.

When the non-core/core ratios by CD are aggregated at the provincial level (Table 3), Quebec and Newfoundland again stand out. That Quebec has the lowest ratio is not surprising. It is more noteworthy that only Newfoundland has a non-core concentration, while other provinces also located well away from the geographical centres of economic activity have a preponderance of firms clustered in their local urban cores. Taken together, these descriptive statistics are strongly suggestive of the low level of industrial concentration (and consequent high level of competition) that is confirmed below.

TABLE 2

PROFESSIONAL, SCIENTIFIC AND TECHNOLOGICAL SERVICES, 2001 PROPORTION OF ESTABLISHMENTS BY SIZE CLASS AND PROVINCE

	1-4 EMPLOYEES	5-9 EMPLOYEES	> 10 EMPLOYEES
Canada	**0.7**	**0.13**	**0.18**
Newfoundland and Labrador	0.7	0.13	0.17
Nova Scotia	0.66	0.15	0.19
New Brunswick	0.73	0.12	0.14
Prince Edward Island	0.66	0.18	0.17
Quebec	0.75	0.11	0.14
Ontario	0.67	0.14	0.19
Manitoba	0.67	0.14	0.19
Saskatchewan	0.69	0.14	0.17
Alberta	0.72	0.13	0.15
British Columbia	0.7	0.14	0.16

Source: Canadian Business Patterns 2001, Statistics Canada, authors' compilation.

TABLE 3

THE NON-CORE/CORE RATIO OF ESTABLISHMENT COUNTS IN METROPOLITAN CDs BY PROVINCE, 2001

PROVINCE	RATIO
Newfoundland and Labrador	1.04
Nova Scotia	0.76
New Brunswick	0.31
Prince Edward Island	0.79
Quebec	0.19
Ontario	0.44
Manitoba	0.39
Saskatchewan	1.00
Alberta	0.59
British Columbia	0.68
Canada	**0.04**

Source: Canadian Business Patterns 2001, Statistics Canada, authors' compilation.

EMPLOYMENT

TURNING TO THE LFS DATA ON EMPLOYMENT (see Table 1), we find that only 8.8 percent of total employment is in non-metropolitan areas. The number of employees and the number of self-employed (which together equal total employment) in the urban core are distributed across the provinces (Figure 4) in a manner consistent with what has been reported elsewhere in studies of the urban system (Coffey and Shearmur 1997). Suffice it to say that the same four provinces (Ontario, Quebec, Alberta and British Columbia) account for the bulk of urban core employment regardless of employment status. Given that most firms are small and concentrated in the urban core, it is not odd to find high levels of self-employment in the urban core as well. Nor does it come as a surprise that those working for others are employed almost exclusively in the private sector. Over the past several years, the public sector has accounted for a vanishing portion of PST employment — less than one percent on average (Table 4). However, this is a segment of PST activity to watch as para-public partnerships are becoming increasingly more frequent in Canada and elsewhere.

FIGURE 4

URBAN CORE EMPLOYMENT FOR PROFESSIONAL, SCIENTIFIC AND TECHNICAL SERVICES, 2002
AVERAGE ANNUAL GROWTH RATE, 1996-2002
BY PROVINCE AND EMPLOYMENT CATEGORY

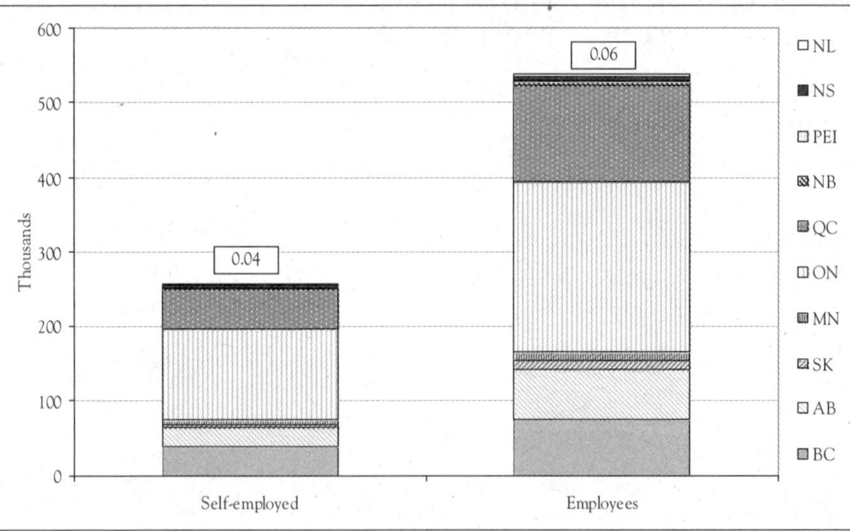

Source: Labour Force Survey Estimates, CANSIM II, Statistics Canada.

TABLE 4

PROFESSIONAL, SCIENTIFIC AND TECHNICAL SERVICES, CANADA, 1998-2002
TOTAL EMPLOYEES BY SECTOR (000S)

SECTOR	1998	1999	2000	2001	2002
Private	228.8	200.9	231.4	196.0	206.6
Public	0.0	2.0	1.5	3.1	0.0
Total:	**228.0**	**202.9**	**232.9**	**199.1**	**206.6**
Public (%)	0.0	1.0	0.6	1.6	0.0

Source: Labour Force Survey Estimates, CANSIM II, Statistics Canada.

In light of the fact that the distribution by establishment size in non-core areas mirrors that in core areas (albeit at a lower level), one expects that the four provinces just mentioned also dominate the non-core employment pattern. This is the case generally, but there are some curious exceptions. On the urban fringe, Quebec lacks a measurable presence of both employees and self-employed (Figures 5 and 6). In addition, neither Quebec nor British Columbia have many self-employed PST workers in small towns. It is also evident that PST employment in either category is extremely small in the other six provinces. This is noteworthy as these six provinces are also the most peripheral, at least in an economic sense.

The low employment levels in the non-core sector have undoubtedly helped make possible the strong annual growth rates that have been observed (see Figures 5 and 6). Outside the urban core, it is in rural areas that most of the employment growth is found. The most rapid employment growth is occurring on the rural fringe and in the most rural parts of the country; not in small towns or the urban fringe where such advanced firms may seem more likely to locate. In fact, the only segment of the non-core system that has under-performed compared with the urban core in terms of employment growth is self-employment in small towns.

Another indicator of the relatively strong performance of the economically, more peripheral provinces is the PST unemployment rate. In general, provinces with the largest economies and where most of the PST employment is found also have experienced the highest unemployment rates. Since 1996, PST unemployment rates in Alberta, British Columbia and Ontario has generally trended above the Canadian average but it has been lower in Quebec (Figure 7). However, the variances in the below-average unemployment rates for more peripheral provinces are higher. The reasons for this are difficult to untangle here as they extend beyond the PST economy proper, and thus beyond the scope of this study.[13] Nevertheless, it is safe to say that the observed pattern relates to differences in the general economic conditions between provinces as perceived by new firms making locational decisions.

FIGURE 5

NON-CORE SELF-EMPLOYMENT IN PROFESSIONAL, SCIENTIFIC AND TECHNICAL SERVICES, 2002
AVERAGE ANNUAL GROWTH RATE, 1996-2002
BY PROVINCE AND GEOGRAPHICAL AGGREGATION

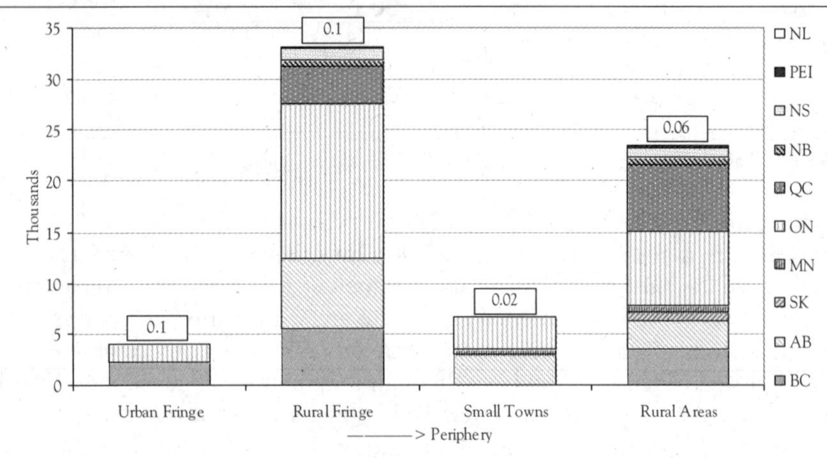

Source: Labour Force Survey Estimates, CANSIM II, Statistics Canada.

FIGURE 6

NON-CORE EMPLOYEES FOR PROFESSIONAL, SCIENTIFIC AND TECHNICAL SERVICES, 2002
AVERAGE ANNUAL GROWTH RATE, 1996-2002
BY PROVINCE AND GEOGRAPHICAL AGGREGATION

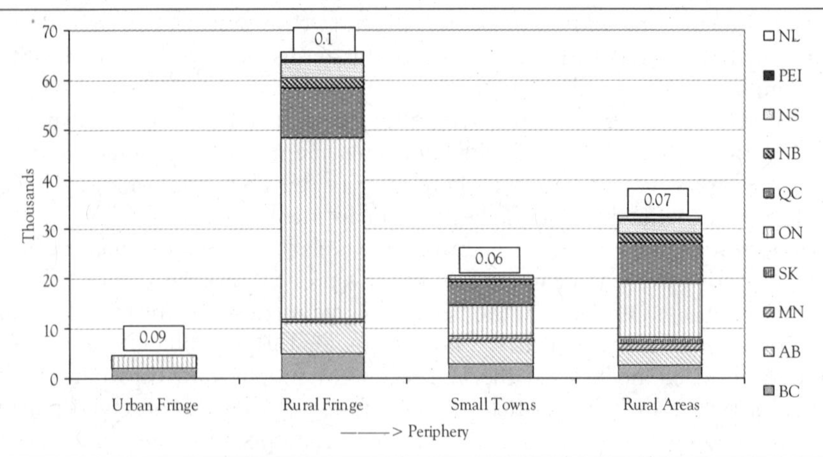

Source: Labour Force Survey Estimates, CANSIM II, Statistics Canada.

FIGURE 7

PROFESSIONAL, SCIENTIFIC AND TECHNICAL SERVICES, 1996-2002 ANNUAL UNEMPLOYMENT RATES BY PROVINCE

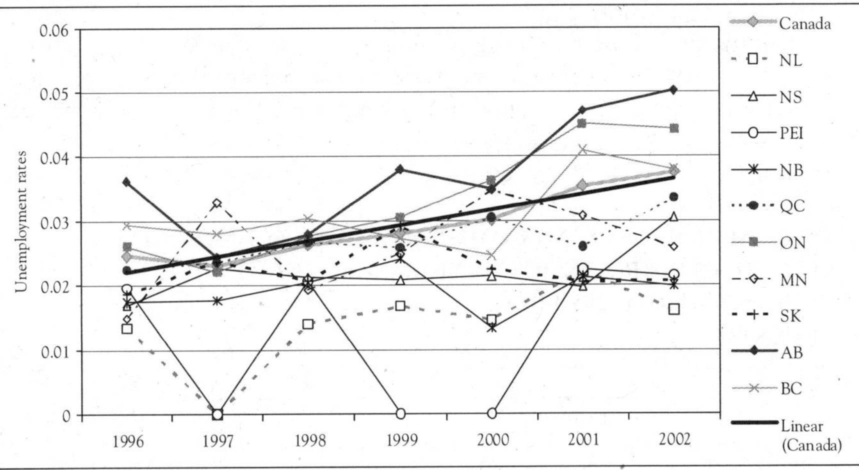

Source: Labour Force Survey Estimates, CANSIM II, Statistics Canada.

ICT AND LOCATION

AS PREVIOUSLY NOTED, much of the regional policy interest in advanced services centres on their high human capital content, and their supposed independence from agglomerative and locational constraints. It has been argued that these are features which characterize firms and industries in the so-called 'new economy.' Since Internet usage is thought to be a key factor in relaxing traditional locational constraints, it is of interest to explore briefly the extent of Internet penetration in PST industries. Recent information is available from sector-wide surveys conducted by Statistics Canada. Features of Internet usage on the supply and demand sides are mostly intuitive. But they do also reveal some trends that are perplexing and that on the surface at least, appear to run counter to some early findings on the exportability of PST services reported elsewhere in the literature (Polèse and Verreault 1989).

In particular, the use of ICT by PST service suppliers (Table 5) is increasing, *except* in the areas of business-to-business and business-to-consumer sales, both domestically and internationally. At the same time, the proportion of users (i.e. both intermediate and final demand) who do *not* use ICT is declining. The only exception is users who do not sell using ICT because customers are not ready (Table 6). However, this could simply reflect differential rates at which ICT is adapted, in which case faster adaptation on the supply side can be expected since this is arguably where most of the related innovation is taking place. These findings are interesting in light of the recent growth in PST services exports (Wernerheim and Sharpe 2003). A possible explanation is that much of the exports of these industries may not involve an online product/service deliverable even though ICT may have played a role in intermediate production stages.

The intricacies of Internet usage patterns aside, it is clear that ICT is a major component of advanced services production and delivery. For example, ICT increases the geographical extent of the market and the tradeability of services. It

TABLE 5

USE OF INFORMATION AND COMMUNICATION TECHNOLOGIES[a] ENTERPRISES IN PROFESSIONAL, SCIENTIFIC AND TECHNICAL SERVICES, CANADA, 2000-02 (PERCENT)

ENTERPRISES	2000	2001	2002
That are Presently Using the Internet	84.0	90.7	92.4
With Employees with Direct Access to the Internet	75.4	83.3	86.8
Using Electronic Data Interchange (EDI)	n/a	15.6	16.4
Using Electronic Data Exchange not on the Internet	10.3	8.9	10.9
Selling over the Internet	7.2	5.8	7.8
With Internet Sales to Consumers (B2C)	14.4	20.5	11.5
With Internet Sales to Customers outside Canada (B2B and B2C)	56.4	35.1	29.2
Buying Goods/Services over the Internet	35.8	42.1	50.6

Note: a. Internet except where indicated.
Source: Survey of Electronic Commerce and Technology, CANSIM II, Statistics Canada.

TABLE 6

INTERNET USERS IN PROFESSIONAL, SCIENTIFIC AND TECHNICAL SERVICES, CANADA, 2000-02 (PERCENT)

USERS OF THE INTERNET WHO DO	2000	2001	2002
Not Sell; Goods do not Lend Themselves to Medium	69.6	59.9	57.5
Not Buy; Goods do not Lend Themselves to Medium	68.7	67.3	55.6
Not Sell; Customers are not Ready	7.3	5.3	8.3
Not Buy; Customers are not Ready	9.9	7.1	6.3
Not Sell; Cost of Development and Maintenance Too High	5.0	6.2	12.0
Not Buy; Cost of Development and Maintenance Too High	5.6	9.0	6.9
Not Sell; Medium Available Too Slow	2.4	3.1	1.7
Not Buy; Medium Available Too Slow	7.3	5.3	8.3
Not Use Electronic Commerce; Lack of Skilled Employees	3.5	5.5	8.1
Not Use Electronic Commerce; Prefer Current Business Model	25.8	33.0	32.4

Source: Survey of Electronic Commerce and Technology, CANSIM II, Statistics Canada.

also helps push services into a new industrialized phase and so contributes to economy-wide growth in total factor productivity. What is less clear is how it has or will influence the locational decisions of PST providers. A common view is that PST services and other knowledge-intensive industries are 'footloose' and that this critical characteristic can be exploited by public policy to help ameliorate the economic problems of rural areas. The reasoning here is that the spatial structure of the world has recently been permanently altered in a direct and obvious way by ICT, thereby making possible dramatic changes in locational patterns.

There are three difficulties with this argument. One, it requires a belief in the ease with which existing patterns of location can be modified and as a corollary, that face-to-face interaction is now less important. Two, it requires a belief that the development of ICT has reduced the importance of geography by offering "instant, limitless access to some entirely separate and disembodied online world" characterized as "intrinsically equitable, decentralized and democratic" (Graham, 2002). Three, it requires a belief that ICT can compensate for the damage caused by long periods of economic downturn and disinvestment in social infrastructure in regions such as Atlantic Canada (Canadian Press 2003). Simply providing technological infrastructure cannot be expected to change this reality. It is useful to recall Foucault's reminder that it is practice, and not belief, that shapes our lives (Kitchin 1998). One of the most important practical lessons from the ongoing debate is that far from changing the nature of the metropolitan-dominated system of economic activity, ICT is reinforcing it (Graham 2001). Rather than acting as the great geographical equalizer, the Internet is reinforcing the existing urban hierarchy as e-business service firms continue to show a distinct preference for large metropolitan areas: in particular their downtown and central business district areas (Moriset 2003). Thus, cyberspace is a predominantly metropolitan phenomenon in terms of infrastructure investment, demand for services, and rates of innovation, all of which reinforce the dominance of what is already dominant (Graham 1998). Why does this happen?

One of the principal reasons is that cyberspace depends on "real-world spatial fixity", that is to say, ICT depends on the capabilities of location-specific backbone networks (Kitchin 1998). Many of these networks are 'private roads,' the origins of which are found in the history of the private telecommunications companies that set up national telephone networks in the 1870s (Malecki 2002). In its use of leased, privately-owned fibre-optic lines by global firms, the Internet tracks the past. This is because fibre-optic networks are embedded in real space. To minimize construction costs, they are often laid along highways, canals or railway lines. This in turn creates a need to overcome the high marginal cost of network extension, the so-called 'last mile connectivity problem,' which can add considerably to the cost of doing business with centrally located firms (Graham 2001). The upshot is that these factors only reinforce the topology of the old, centralized transport network, which itself usually has a metropolitan focus (Moriset 2003).

Centripetal forces dominate the locational decisions of advanced producer services suppliers to a greater extent than many other types of economic activity because so much of their success depends on face-to-face communication, handshakes and the tacit exchanges of knowledge and trust that often accompany them (Illeris 1991, 1996). Much has been made of the fact that routinized, 'back-office' functions can be hived off to remote locations perhaps continents away. However, most of the non-routine, face-to-face activity that occurs in the constructed spaces of the city, and the transportation networks which support it, has proven to be extremely resistant to simple substitution (Graham 1998). Digital delivery may be feasible, but in the final analysis it is the trust and high degree of customization of advanced services that necessitate face-to-face contact. Does this leave non-metropolitan areas outside the ambit of possibility for PST services, as the Canadian data seem to suggest?

While the jury is still out on the contribution of small- and medium-sized enterprises (SMEs) to regional growth, it is beyond dispute that SMEs depend on networks to grow. Yet, there is some anecdotal evidence that even small PST establishments contribute to the economic vitality of localized areas, although they almost exclusively serve local demand. In national terms, such firms are unlikely to add much to the export earnings derived from international PST sales. However, as firms shift their focus from local to international clients, the higher share of their revenue generated from 'traded' services may translate into higher growth rates. Given an appropriate network of linkages to manufacturing and other service industries, the value added captured by SMEs in the PST sector may contribute to sustainable regional growth. However, as Daniels and Bryson (2003) remark, this shift may not always be advantageous as it increases the complexity and cost of doing business with clients. "... thinking locally and acting locally for many of these firms may be as competitive a business strategy as thinking globally and acting locally."

Moreover, in the many 'off-line spaces' that make up so much of Canada's geography, time and space remain profoundly real (Thrift 1996). Non-metropolitan areas are often on the wrong side of the 'digital divide' that separates users and non-users of the Internet, particularly as regards broadband. Rural or peripheral areas in particular are at a distinct disadvantage in attracting and supporting new ICT-intensive service firms because of the high costs of the required accompanying infrastructure and the low priority assigned to the needs of rural areas (Gatrell 1999). Quite simply, "the phone line is too small" to make a real difference (Graham 2002). Instead it is the central business district and its tower-dwelling services firms that attract most of the investment since it is this investment that can exploit the so-called backbone networks between cities. On the one hand, this effectively reverses decades of unrelenting suburbanization, on the other hand, it deepens the digital (and urban-rural social) divide (Graham 1999).

Set against these circumstances is the particular quality of life in non-metropolitan areas with which metropolitan areas cannot compete. This includes the natural environment and lifestyle as well as inexpensive office rents. This has long been an important locational consideration, especially among the executives who make decisions about relocation or start-up. However, it is hard to escape the conclusion that non-metropolitan areas make unlikely homes to PST activities, even if the difficulties of ICT penetration into such areas are eventually overcome.

LOCATION AND AGGLOMERATION: A STOCHASTIC APPROACH

EXCLUDING THE NINE 'OUTLIER' CDs discussed above, it appears that establishments elsewhere are dispersed but the ratios of non-core to core establishments are remarkably 'clustered.' If it is indeed the case that the core exerts an irresistible attraction proportional to the number of establishments in the services sector in question, then a plot of non-core versus core PST establishments in the 288 CDs (Figure 8) would show a positive relationship. This appears to be the case as the fitted trend line has a slope coefficient

FIGURE 8

PROFESSIONAL, SCIENTIFIC AND TECHNICAL SERVICES, CANADA, 2001 CLUSTERS OF ESTABLISHMENTS (NUMBERS) IN URBAN CORE AND NON-CORE AREAS (N=288)

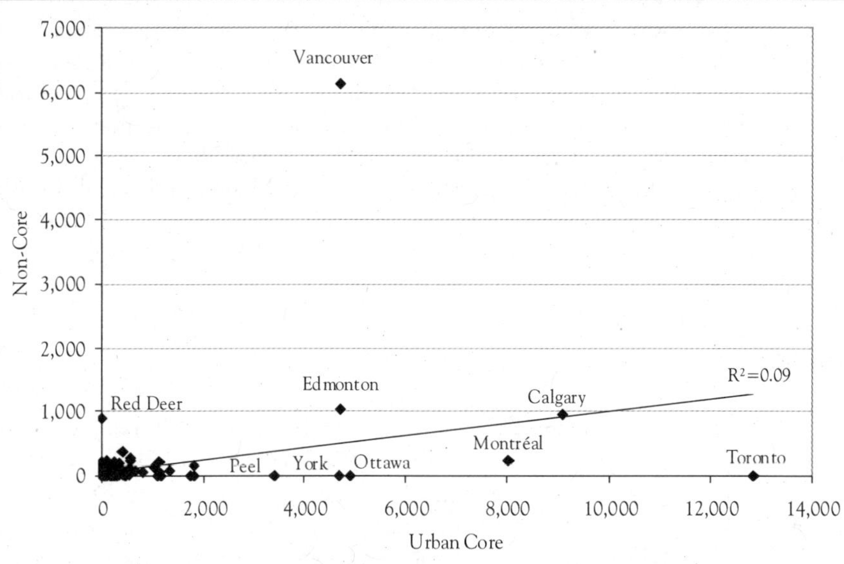

Sources: Canadian Business Patterns 2001, Statistics Canada, authors' compilation.

significant at the 1-percent level. This conclusion does not change if the nine outliers are dropped from the population of CDs. Yet, Figures 2 and 8 admit of the possibility that the location pattern outside the urban core is random. To examine this hypothesis we employ an especially compelling index of spatial concentration.

Four of the most frequently used measures of spatial concentration include the location quotient, the Gini index, the index of dissimilarity, and the entropy index. Ellison and Glaeser (1997) have added a novel index of their own to this list. They developed a stochastic model of firm location in which industry-specific spillovers, natural advantage and pure random chance contribute to geographic agglomeration. In particular, they developed a test for the dartboard theory of plant location. This is, in other words, a test for whether observed levels of concentration are higher than would be expected if plants choose locations at random, for example by throwing darts on a map. Unlike other concentration indices, the Ellison and Glaeser index controls for the size distribution of firms by incorporating the Herfindahl index. It also allows for differences in the size of the geographic areas for which data area are available. This is its chief merit: an industry will not appear localized solely because employment is concentrated in a few plants. Nor does geographic concentration by itself imply the existence of knowledge spillovers since natural advantages have the same effect in their model. Knowledge (or technological) spillovers arise from sharing labour markets, intrafirm trade, capitalizing on local knowledge and other factors that increase profits derived from locating near firms in the same industry or sector. The Ellison and Glaeser (1997) and Maurel and Sédillot (1999) indices are both scaled to take the value of zero if plant concentration is what would be expected if the location was chosen randomly. This is the expected outcome when the sum total of agglomerative forces is zero. This subsection presents the Ellison and Glaeser index, and the modifications proposed by Maurel and Sédillot. We then apply Canadian data to both models to test whether the dartboard theory explains PST services location in non-core areas. Ellison and Glaeser and Maurel and Sédillot both consider manufacturing industries. The only other application of the Ellison and Glaeser model of which we are aware is Head, Ries and Swenson (1995) who studied foreign direct investments in Asia.

THE MODEL

TO SEE HOW the Ellison and Glaeser and Maurel and Sédillot indices are derived, consider the profit maximization problem faced by an investor seeking a location for a new plant or branch plant. The consensus of the literature discussed in the second section of this study is that this locational decision is best cast in a conditional logit framework. Suppose that there are N establishments in the PST sector, and M geographic sub-areas of the country (CDs) in which they can locate. The decision by the kth plant to locate in v_i is profit-maximizing if the profit received by a typical plant from locating in area i, π_{ki}, is higher than elsewhere. The probability that CD i is chosen by establishment k can then be written:

$$(1) \qquad P_{ki} = prob(\pi_{ki} > \pi_{kl}) \quad \forall l, l \neq i\,.$$

Thus, $i >_k l$ if and only if:

$$(2) \qquad \pi_{ki} = \max\{\pi_{kl}; \forall l, l \neq i\}\,.$$

Following Ellison and Glaeser, write profits accruing to the kth establishment from locating in area i as:

$$(3) \qquad \log \pi_{ki} = \log \overline{\pi}_i + g_i(v_1, \ldots, v_{k-1}) + \varepsilon_{ki}\,,$$

where $\overline{\pi}_i$ is a random variable of observed and unobserved area characteristics capturing natural (geographic) advantages. The effects of positive industry-specific spillovers from establishments that have already chosen locations are denoted $g_i(v_1, \ldots, v_{j-1})$, and ε_{ki} is a stochastic term specific to the kth plant. If the $\{\varepsilon_{ki}\}$ are independent, have a Weibull distribution with an extreme-type-value 1 and there are no spillovers,[14] then the locational choices are conditionally independent random variables and the problem takes a conditional logit form. Ellison and Glaeser impose certain parametric restrictions[15] on the $\{\pi_i\}$ and write the problem thus:

$$(4) \qquad prob\{v_k = i | \overline{\pi}_1, \ldots, \overline{\pi}_M\} = \frac{\overline{\pi}_i}{\sum_j \overline{\pi}_j}$$

where the expectation $\overline{\pi}_i$ reflects average profitability of locating in area i. According to Ellison and Glaeser, the expected value of the term on the right-hand side of the equation can then be thought of as the share of area i in aggregate employment (in all services sectors), denoted as x_i. This provides the crucial link to the spatial concentration estimator. To see this, note that the index of raw geographic concentration proposed by Ellison and Glaeser is expressed as:

$$(5) \qquad G_{EG} \equiv \sum_i (s_i - x_i)^2\,.$$

It is constructed by writing s_i for the share of PST employment only in area i, and x_i as above.[16] Ellison and Glaeser prove that if the N establishments locate sequentially to maximize profit functions (Equation 3) then

$$(6) \qquad E(G_{GE}) = \left(1 - \sum x_i^2\right)[H + \gamma(1 - H)]\,.$$

On the right-hand side of the equation, H is the Herfindahl index of the industry's plant size distribution, and γ captures the agglomeration benefits of two (here observationally equivalent) types; those arising from 'natural advantage' conferred by geography (e.g. access to natural resource endowments, and associated traditional transport cost savings), and those associated with 'intellectual spillovers' such as common access to a highly educated workforce, face-to-face contact with suppliers and clients, and a sophisticated socio-economic infrastructure. The principal result is the proof that $E(G_{GE})$ is related to the spillovers, the plant size distribution, and the size of areas for which employment data are available. Solving for γ in Equation (6) yields the Ellison and Glaeser index of geographic-industrial agglomeration as

(7) $$\gamma_{EG} = \frac{G_{EG} - H}{1 - H}.$$

This measure can be used empirically to test hypotheses about agglomerative plant behaviour such as the dartboard theory of plant location. Ellison and Glaeser describe the testing procedure, and provide appropriate trigger values for the estimator γ_{EG}.

An alternative index of geographic concentration is proposed by Maurel and Sédillot for use in the Ellison and Glaeser modelling framework. The Maurel and Sédillot index is written

(8) $$G_{MS} \equiv \left(\sum_i s_i^2 - \sum_i x_i^2\right) \Big/ \left(1 - \sum_i x_i^2\right).$$

Accordingly the estimator is expressed as

(9) $$\gamma_{MS} = \frac{G_{MS} - H}{1 - H}.$$

In both cases γ measures the correlation between the locational decisions of two plants in the same industry. Maurel and Sédillot show that an industry with a random distribution of plants (when plant location choices are independent) will have $E(\gamma) = 0$, regardless of the value of H. Thus, $\gamma = 0$ does not imply that plants are spread uniformly across space, but that plants are only as concentrated as would be expected if location choices were independent (there were no spillovers), and random across regions (there were no natural advantages). The equation $\gamma > 0$ implies that agglomeration forces dominate dispersion forces, causing the industry to be localized. Consequently, if $\gamma < 0$, then dispersion forces dominate clustering forces, causing plants to be as scattered as possible.[17]

DATA AND RESULTS

THE DATA USED IN THIS STUDY cover the CDs comprising the 'non-core' part of the 109,960 PST establishments obtained from CBP 2001 as described above. That is, we used the establishments located in the non-core of metropolitan CDs plus those in non-metropolitan CDs. The data are applied to both the Ellison and Glaeser, and Maurel and Sédillot agglomeration models. As explained above, the models share the Herfindahl index of industrial concentration. The low value of this index (Table 7) indicates that the industry is also highly competitive in its rural setting.[18] The raw geographic concentration is what distinguishes the Maurel and Sédillot model from the original Ellison and Glaeser model. The measure of primary interest is the geographic-industrial concentration index γ, which takes both industrial concentration and geographic concentration into consideration. Interestingly, both models calculate a negative value for γ, indicating scattering behaviour on the part of establishments.

Ellison and Glaeser find that almost every U.S. manufacturing industry in their sample displays excessive concentration. Maurel and Sédillot report a similar pattern of localization of manufacturing for France. To test for statistical significance, we use the equation for the variance of the estimator provided by Maurel and Sédillot. The result shows that our estimate is significant at the 1 percent level. We thus reject the dartboard theory and conclude that dispersion forces dominate agglomeration forces as PST firms in rural areas appear to have dispersed deliberately. We take this to mean that in an industry that is inherently highly competitive, new small individual establishments in rural areas primarily expect to serve a very small local market. Even if some services export activity is possible, it may make sense for such establishments to locate well away from rural competitors.

Ellison and Glaeser, and Maurel and Sédillot both propose additional means of testing for co-agglomeration between establishments in different industries. This is in order to take into account both intra- and inter-industry concentration. These indices relax the assumption that firms belong to the same industry

TABLE 7

PROFESSIONAL, SCIENTIFIC AND TECHNICAL SERVICES, 2001 MEASURES OF CONCENTRATION, NON-CORE CANADA

SOURCE OF INDEX:	INDUSTRIAL	RAW GEOGRAPHIC	GEOGRAPHIC-INDUSTRIAL
Herfindahl	0.0086	–	–
Ellison and Glaeser	–	0.0005	–0.0082
Maurel and Sédillot	–	0.0008	–0.0078

and thus allow for the benefits that may arise from proximity to plants that buy and sell each other's inputs and outputs. (In a future extension of this work, we intend to include urban areas as well as industries that are principal buyers of PST services inputs.)

The International Evidence on Services Location

A REVIEW OF THE INTERNATIONAL EVIDENCE shows that geographical and data-related differences notwithstanding, the regional distributions of advanced services in Canada, the United States, the United Kingdom and France are remarkably similar. The most obvious commonality is the urban bias in firm location. Since this is also a characteristic of manufacturing firms, it is tempting to hypothesize that both types of industries co-locate in urban areas. It is possible that services industries follow in the wake of traditional manufacturing as it undergoes technical change and structural adjustments. Such adjustments include the externalization of services, a process that opens up new markets for a wide range of entrepreneurial firms providing advanced services.

Data measurement problems can make international comparisons difficult. In addition, researching non-core services activity raises its own data problems. Glasmeier and Howland (1994) argue that most methods of data collection have been developed for non-rural contexts, which can distort the measurement of rural service activity. For example, urban and rural firms may produce vastly different value added, but classification systems such as the NAICS place them in the same industry. This can distort the relative contribution of rural and urban firms. Data for disaggregated geographic areas are often subject to confidentiality restrictions that can dramatically increase the cost of compiling such data and thus limit public access to it.

Comparing countries in terms of the spatial patterns of firm location and employment adds another dimension to the problem. Researcher-defined aggregations of heterogeneous services activities give rise to taxonomic problems associated with comparability that are well-known and extensively discussed in the literature (for example, Allen 1992; and Wernerheim and Sharpe 1999, 2003). Problems in interpreting data can arise even in the analysis of one country if NAICS industries are (re-)aggregated arbitrarily or ad hoc. In cross-country comparisons, these problems are compounded if different industry classification systems are involved. Even when identical systems are introduced in different countries, as has recently happened in Canada, the United States and Mexico, comparability remains a problem, both domestically and internationally. Finally, Polèse and Sheamur (2002) emphasize problems around the definition of 'rural' and its application in an international context. More specifically, they look at the connotations carried by the term. We venture that in Canada and the United States, 'rural' in the context of regional policy usually signifies remote, abandoned, declining or underdeveloped in relation to population density. European services industry research (specifically French and British in this study) rarely mentions the term, a fact that may simply reflect a more strictly agrarian meaning of the term in these countries. Of course such areas need not be declining nor lacking in subsidies and regional policy attention. (Indeed, on both sides of the Atlantic, it is often alleged that the opposite is the case.) The term "rural" may therefore simply refer to a pattern of land use that non-agricultural regional policy is not attempting to influence.

Our reading of the literature suggests that current regional disparities among the countries of the European Union transcend any dichotomies of centre-periphery and urban-rural. In the field of industrial development (non-agricultural support), the European Commission is now increasingly turning its attention to pursuing policies that favour lower-level cities in the urban hierarchy (Moulaert and Gallouj 1996). It is here that we find common ground between the regional development approaches sometimes advocated in the United States and Canada on the one hand, and in the United Kingdom and France on the other. In both cases, there is a strong presumption that advanced services industries can play a significant role in reducing regional disparities, the relativity of the term 'rural' notwithstanding.[19]

It is not clear which comes first — industry-specific employment growth or more diffuse regional economic growth — or indeed if either necessarily has to come first. However, there can be little doubt that the strong employment growth observed in advanced services over the past several decades has lent support to policies that attempt to influence the supply of (location) and demand for services (Bailly 1995). Examples of such programs are employment- and investment subsidies, investment in human capital, restrictions on location, government procurement, establishment of high-technology districts or clusters, decentralization of industrial production and promotion of the suburbanization of services activity.

The purpose of this section is to describe some services industry characteristics that may have underpinned the belief in proactive policies in the four countries selected. For this purpose we take the very pragmatic approach that the term 'rural areas' is simply a residual category, containing all territory that is non-core (a concept much easier to define).

UNITED STATES

IN REVIEWING THE ROLE OF SERVICE ACTIVITY in regional development in the United States, Harrington (1995) reflects on aspects facing empirical researchers that are reminiscent of conditions in Canada. He notes that the scant official data available, often of poor quality, have limited detailed empirical research into the locational interdependencies involving more narrowly defined services industries. It is clear that this makes it difficult to evaluate policy initiatives that target specific industries or groups of industries among which significant agglomeration economies may be at play.

Beyers (2003), and Wernerheim and Sharpe (2003) discuss the new problems that face services industry researchers using North American data as a consequence of the recent introduction of the NAICS. Although there is an official concordance between it and the preceding Standard Industrial Classification (SIC), the imprecision that necessarily accompanies conversion to a new taxonomy has implications for the time-series analysis of a number of services industry classifications.

While the NAICS/SIC concordance problem is unique to North America, the problems outlined by Harrington are not: problems in the United Kingdom and France are discussed below. Some researchers have therefore resorted to the use of survey data. Although it can sometimes be difficult to draw general conclusions based on such data, interesting insights are often gained. For example, in a survey of services and manufacturing firms in the states of the upper Midwest (Illinois, Iowa, Michigan, Minnesota and Wisconsin), Porterfield and Pulver (1991) find that 32 percent of services sales were exported beyond a 50-mile (80 km) radius of the firms' location. The corresponding figure for manufacturing was 44 percent. Moreover, 12 percent of services sales were exported beyond the upper Midwest, compared with 20 percent in manufacturing.

In a study that included non-metropolitan areas, Beyers (1992) found locational quotients that were less than unity for all advanced services except banking. The most rapid employment growth was in the fastest growing metropolitan areas. These findings appear to be at variance with the findings by Kirn (1987): for the period 1958-77 he reported much higher employment growth for some advanced services in non-metropolitan and small metropolitan areas than in large metropolitan areas. Kirn's findings, however, agree with our own results for Canada, as reported above. Other authors have considered the impact of externalization (outsourcing) on the emergence of advanced services firms in rural areas, where such services may account for as much as 16 percent of employment (Beyers and Lindahl 1996). Although the net effects of outsourcing on employment appear inconclusive, it stands to reason that outsourcing can be expected to account for part of the growth in producer services employment in rural and non-rural areas alike, at least in the earlier stages of services sector development. If so, the resulting (re)locational decisions by existing firms and investment decisions by new advanced services firms may attract the attention of regional policy makers.

A cursory look at the data shows that even after almost half a century of advanced services growth, the Northeast continues to have the largest share of employment, followed by the West (Table 8). Aggregating recent employment data for the same regions used by Kirn (1987) shows that the highest growth rates occurred in the South and North Central regions, the two areas with the smallest services sectors in 1958. While it is evident from these data that the advanced services sector (as defined in Table 8) now accounts for a substantially greater share of the regional economy than in 1958, there does not appear to have been much change in the spatial distribution of this services activity as far as these aggregated regions are concerned. However, the standard deviation of the shares across regions has fallen by about half over the period, suggesting somewhat less regional disparity in the advanced services sector, all else being equal. A possible explanation for these findings is that large metropolitan areas provide advanced services for extensive hinterlands (Gilmer 1990). At the same time a certain diffusion of firms into non-core areas partly reflects a search for new markets (Harrington and Lombard 1989).

In a recent study, Beyers (2003) estimates the contribution of services industries to the economic base of regional economies in the United States between 1995 and 2000. The spatial basis for the analysis consists of the 172 areas used by the Bureau of Economic Analysis (BEA). Beyers reports a strong but uneven contribution of tradeable services to growth in the economic base of the BEAs under study. This finding is in agreement with that of several previous studies for the United States. Interestingly, sole proprietors make up 16.8 percent of employment. The corresponding figure for Canada is only 6.7 percent.

TABLE 8

PROFESSIONAL AND BUSINESS SERVICES* EMPLOYMENT, UNITED STATES, 1958 AND 2003 SHARES BY REGION (PERCENT)

	REGION				
YEAR	NORTH EAST	NORTH CENTRAL	SOUTH	WEST	SD**
1958	3.4	2.7	2.2	3.3	0.01
2003	13.5	10.9	12.6	12.3	0.00
% Growth in Share	390.0	400.0	570.0	370.0	

Notes: * For 1958 this NAICS sector corresponds to SIC 73 (Business), SIC 81 (Legal), SIC 891 (Engineering and Architectural), and SIC 893 (Accounting etc.).
** SD=standard deviation.

Sources: Kirn (1987), and Bureau of Labor Statistics, United States Department of Labor.

UNITED KINGDOM

ACCORDING TO BRYSON (1997), a key feature of the U.K. economy is the "unequal" distribution of business services firms, with well-known concentrations in Greater London and the rest of the South East where population densities are among the highest. The only exception is the North West which has a slightly higher density than the South East. The rapid growth of advanced services employment and the number of small firms in the 1980s that resulted in this skewed distribution of employment is discussed in detail in Keeble, Bryson and Wood (1991), Wood, Bryson and Keeble (1993) and Daniels (1995a). More recent data (Table 9) indicate that there is still relatively little variation in the industry-specific shares of firms, employment and GDP across regions *outside* London and the South East. Bryson argues that a shortage of land, skilled labour and high-quality office space in the West Midlands are major reasons for the geographical concentrations observed in the services sector. Another factor is undoubtedly the larger consumer markets in the South East (MacKay 2003).[20] While Coe and Townsend (1998) agree that such urbanization economies play an important role in explaining agglomeration behaviour, they see an historical, cumulative causation process underlying the current locational pattern of advanced services.

Allen (1992) maintains that much of this concentration is explained by government-sponsored R&D activity. However, it is not immediately apparent from the data on government R&D spending in services industries that it is driven by regional development imperatives. That is, public spending on R&D is positively related to the other economic variables listed (Table 9). The regional variation in R&D expenditure is somewhat higher than it is for the other economic variables, but it has a similar spatial distribution. The only exception is the East which receives a somewhat higher share than its ranking in terms of either of the other variables would suggest.

The distribution of firm sizes in the United Kingdom is remarkably similar to that in Canada. Fully 90 percent of advanced services firms in the United Kingdom have fewer than 10 employees (Figure 9). All else being the same, one would expect this industry to be similarly competitive.

Others have argued that in the past there has been too much emphasis in both research and policy on firms located in primary cities. Daniels and Bryson (2003) focus on business and professional services and use Birmingham as an example of a city that has not benefited from this emphasis on the urban core. They see the development of an 'economy of expertise and knowledge' as a means of re-invention aimed at meeting Birmingham's needs in the 21st century. The authors argue that this aim is advanced with the creation of 'world-class' clusters of firms with high levels of internationalization. The basic problem with this approach is that the majority of these firms are small and local in orientation: they both think and act locally, instead of thinking globally and acting locally. Such firms fall outside the realm of the proposed strategy, although as the authors stress, they play an important role in the region's economy. They should not and cannot be ignored. This same point resonates with much of the regional policy thinking in Canada as noted above.

TABLE 9

ADVANCED SERVICES INDUSTRIES, VARIOUS YEARS, UNITED KINGDOM REGIONAL SHARES AND CHARACTERISTICS

	FIRMS[a] (LOCAL UNITS AS % TOTAL LOCAL UNITS)	EMPLOYEE JOBS[b] (LOCAL JOBS AS % TOTAL LOCAL JOBS)	GDP[c] (AS % TOTAL LOCAL)	GOVERNMENT SPENDING[d] (ON SERVICE R&D AS % OF TOTAL LOCAL)	POPULATION DENSITY[e] (PERSONS PER SQ KM)
United Kingdom	**76.3**	**19.7**	**21.4**	**16.5**	**243**
North East	78.0	12.6	15.2	8.5	294
North West	78.0	15.9	18.3	5.4	477
Yorkshire and the Humber	75.0	15.2	16.3	11.8	322
East Midlands	71.9	14.3	17.0	7.7	268
West Midlands	73.1	15.5	17.9	11.4	405
East	74.4	19.5	22.4	25.1	282
London	87.9	33.6	31.0	30.9	4572
South East	79.0	22.9	26.7	17.7	420
South West	71.5	16.3	19.4	10.8	207
England	77.6	20.4	22.4	n/a	378
Wales	67.4	12.1	15.0	8.3	140
Scotland	73.9	16.8	16.7	8.2	65
Northern Ireland	58.6	n/a	13.1	20.8	124

Notes: a. All services, 2001.
b. Financial and business services, December 2000.
c. Real estate, renting and business activities, 1998.
d. 2000.
e. 2001.

Sources: Office for National Statistics: Inter-Departmental Business Register; Annual Business Inquiry; General Register Office for Scotland; Northern Ireland Statistics and Research Agency; and Research and Development in UK Businesses, Business Monitor MA14.

FIGURE 9

PROPERTY AND BUSINESSES SERVICES, UNITED KINGDOM, 2003 DISTRIBUTION OF VAT-BASED ENTERPRISES

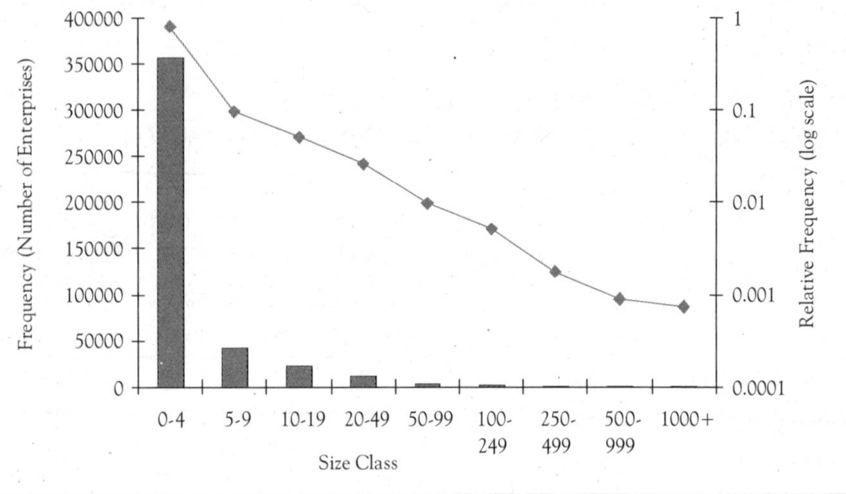

Source: Office for National Statistics, United Kingdom.

FRANCE

A PRELIMINARY SEARCH OF THE LITERATURE on French advanced services with a non-urban orientation turned up few English-language studies. They include Moulaert and Gallouj (1993, 1996) and Shearmur and Alvergne (2002). Although these studies concentrate on inter-urban location and the emergence of 'suburban downtowns,' certain findings may be generalized beyond the metropolis.[21] For example, Moulaert and Gallouj (1996) point to growing evidence that the rise of the multi-locational advanced services firm has a multi-dimensional spatial logic. Proximity to the client is a requirement; firms in the greater Paris region (Île-de-France) are territorially less risk-averse than firms in other centres of the same size; there is a tendency to locate in regions where the services specialization provided complements the demands of the manufacturing sector. In particular, the overt policy of industrial decentralization may have combined with the indirect promotion of services industries (through expansion of social and economic infrastructure) in ways that have bolstered productivity. This in turn has attracted more firms to various regions. However, the underlying relationships are very complex. Moulaert and Gallouj maintain that it is impossible to identify a clear relationship at the national level between the spatial extent of services firms and the nature of the services that they provide. Even within a single region (Île-de-France), locational patterns have been found to be complex and contradictory (Shearmur and Alvergne 2002).

These findings are not inconsistent with those reported for manufacturing (Maurel and Sédillot 1999), although the locational pattern for manufacturing appears more transparent. The authors report that more than one third of manufacturing workers are employed in only two regions, Paris and Lyon, (Île-de-France and Centre-Est in Table 10). Interestingly, while Île-de-France also has the highest proportions of services employment and GDP, Centre-Est ranks fifth in terms of employment, and fourth in terms of both GDP and job seekers. This suggests a spatial pattern where manufacturing and services co-agglomerate in one of the two traditional manufacturing areas (Île-de-France), but not in the other (Centre-Est). This observation agrees with the conclusion reached by Moulaert and Gallouj (1993) who argue that the limits of simple agglomeration economies may have been reached for advanced service industries in France.

TABLE 10

SERVICES INDUSTRIES, FRANCE, 2001
REGIONAL SHARES OF EMPLOYMENT, JOB SEEKERS, AND GDP

ALL SERVICES	EMPLOYMENT (THOUSANDS)	EMPLOYMENT (% OF TOTAL LOCAL)	JOB APPLICANTS[a] (%)	GDP[b] (% OF TOTAL LOCAL)
France	**16,546.1**	**68.6**	**100.0**	**71.9**
Île de France	4,142.9	81.2	20.4	81.3
Bassin Parisien	2,582.8	63.3	14.5	62.9
Nord — Pas-de-Calais	970.0	68.3	7.8	66.8
Est	1,423.0	62.7	7.5	64.6
Ouest	1,973.2	64.0	11.0	66.9
Sud-Ouest	1,750.0	68.8	3.5	71.1
Centre-Est	1,878.4	65.8	10.5	67.2
Méditerranée	1,825.8	78.5	24.8	77.8

Notes: a. Technical, Management, Engineering, and Executive Business Services, 2002.
b. 1999.

Sources: Institut National de la Statistique et des Études Économiques; Eurostat; Office for National Statistics.

CONCLUSIONS

THIS STUDY GIVES A DETAILED SPATIAL DIMENSION to the pattern of employment and establishment location in Canada's PST services sector. We present the results of a descriptive analysis intended to uncover differences between urban and non-urban ('non-core') determinants of location. The fastest growing non-urban employment is identified in terms of both type of geographical area and physical location in the country. The highest employment growth rates occur in the rural fringe and in rural areas. Almost all production takes place in very small firms in the private sector. Self-employed individuals account for a substantial portion of employment only in certain regions of the country.

We identify the 148 CDs that are at least partly urban core (CMA or a CA) as the more likely locations for PST services than the 140 truly rural CDs that have no urban core. Within this set the main concentrations of establishments are found in the principal urban locations in the East (Toronto, Ottawa, and Montreal) and in the West (Vancouver, Edmonton, and Calgary). The remaining metropolitan CDs have much lower concentrations and remarkably similar ratios of establishments in their core and non-core areas. The cores in the remaining 140 metropolitan CDs appear to exert some pull on non-core establishments in both metropolitan and non-metropolitan CDs. However, these metropolitan cores are so small and dispersed that it is unlikely that any such attraction is due to localization economies, or greater need for proximity to the buyer. These firms are generally very small and we conjecture that they are not particularly footloose. Instead, they serve a local market where they may be attached to small-scale manufacturing industries. The 140 non-metropolitan CDs include the largest and remotest in the country. Some have no establishments at all. The rest, on average, have very few establishments which tend to be scattered over large areas.

Using a unique spatial data set derived for this study, consisting of the PST establishments in all non-core areas of the country, we calculate the Herfindahl index of industrial concentration. The result indicates a highly competitive industry in non-core areas. This is consistent with our earlier finding for metropolitan areas reported elsewhere. A stochastic conditional logit framework (Ellison and Glaeser, and Maurel and Sédillot) is then used to test the dartboard theory of firm location. We reject this random location hypothesis and argue that the observed locational pattern is the result of deliberate scattering behaviour in an environment that combines vigorous competition with a spatially-limited output market.

On the face of it, there is nothing to say that this localization pattern, driven as it is by market forces, is not 'optimal' in some sense. Evidence from the services sector and from other industries and countries suggests the importance of traditional agglomeration and localization economies, and the need for face-to-face contact between customer and provider. Given this reality, it is hard to see how localization incentive schemes can be a panacea for rural areas in Canada. Such schemes may nevertheless have a potential in select locations under certain circumstances. The danger here is the temptation to widen the qualifying criteria as a matter of political expediency. Which CDs and which industries might make good candidates? Only a tentative answer to this question can be ventured on the basis of existing research. Before more detailed policy directions can be proposed, further work is needed on the location-specific determinants of plants in more disaggregated industry classifications than the one we have considered here. However, some tentative implications emerge from our present analysis.

One, public policy aimed at broadening the locational base of advanced producer services activity might best be focused on the non-core areas of the 'metropolitan' CDs. It is here, and not in the more remote, and certainly more sparsely populated non-metropolitan CDs that the agglomerative forces that thrive on 'handshakes' and face-to-face contact operate most efficiently.

Two, it should be recognized that while PST firms in rural areas are not numerous and are widely scattered, they are likely an important source of local employment and thus their local economic impact may be disproportionately high. However, attracting advanced services to rural (or non-urban) areas is only half the battle. The other half is making them stay after subsidies run out. Thus, any expenditure of public funds first requires that there be firm evidence for the likelihood of success.

Three, a review of the literature and some recent data on rural service activity for the United States, the United Kingdom and France indicate that, as in Canada, the locational patterns of non-metropolitan advanced services have not attracted much research interest. The reason appears to be much the same as in the case of Canada: non-metropolitan firms are mostly few, small, limited in the range of services they provide, and focused on a local market. While the growth rates of employment outside metro regions are encouraging, it is well to remember that they generally relate to very low base-levels. Non-metropolitan firms undoubtedly provide much needed employment where they are, but the regional development potential of firms in this sector remains connected to agglomeration economies and in particular to the co-location of manufacturing industry. Indeed, the principal similarity between the four countries is the pattern of co-location of advanced services firms and manufacturing firms within easy commuting distance.

At the most general level, locational patterns in Canada and the United States are more similar to each other than they are to the United Kingdom and France. Geography alone probably accounts for most of the differences in the spatial patterns between Canada and the United States on the one hand, and France and the United Kingdom on the other. However, there appear to be remarkable similarities across the Atlantic in terms of industrial organization as manifested in, for example, distribution by firm size, technology and competitive behaviour. Although the spatial economies of the four countries differ in important ways (hence the relativity of the term 'rural'), the features that the location patterns have in common suggest that meaningful international comparisons can be made. This expands the realm of relevant experience in framing domestic regional development policy.

DIRECTIONS FOR FURTHER RESEARCH

OUR SURVEY OF THE LITERATURE indicates that there is a dearth of systematic empirical research on services industry location, particularly in non-metropolitan areas. There is, however, a large literature on firm location in manufacturing industries. Services industries have not been subject to the same statistical tests. This is recognized by Harrington (1995) who is explicit in his call for a coherent theoretical and empirical framework for studying the contribution of services industries to regional development. While there is now a consensus on the appropriate empirical (econometric) techniques for addressing the problem — discrete choice models — several difficulties have hampered research. Some of these difficulties are inherent in empirical location studies. Others help explain why the location and agglomeration of services industries have not received the attention warranted by the importance we think these issues have for regional economic policy.

In order to better explain the *determinants* of the locational pattern identified in this study, we propose to apply geographically-disaggregated, firm-specific data to a deterministic formulation of the conditional logit model. Although well established in the literature since the pioneering work by Carlton (1979, 1983), we know of no attempt to use this model to study services industries.

APPENDIX A

DEFINITION OF NAICS-C 54

541	Professional, Scientific and Technical Services
5411	Legal Services
5412	Accounting, Tax Preparation, Bookkeeping and Payroll Services
5413	Architectural, Engineering and Related Services
5414	Specialized Design
5415	Computer Systems Design and Related Services
5416	Management, Scientific and Technical Consulting Services
5417	Scientific Research and Development Services
5418	Advertising and Related Services
5419	Other Professional, Scientific and Technical Services

Source: Statistics Canada.

APPENDIX B

GEOGRAPHICAL DEFINITIONS

Census Metropolitan Areas (CMA) and *Census Agglomerations* (CA) are centred on large urban areas (known as the urban core) and incorporate urban and rural areas (the urban and rural fringes) which have a high degree of social and economic integration with the urban core. A CMA has a minimum urban core population of 100,000, and a CA of 10,000, based on the previous census.

Urban areas have a minimum population of 1,000 and a minimum density of 400 persons per km^2.

Urban core is a large urban area within a CMA or CA with a minimum population of 100,000 and 10,000 respectively, and a minimum density of 400 persons per km^2.

Urban fringe is an urban area within a CMA or CA that is not contiguous to the urban core.

Rural fringe is all territory within a CMA or CA not classified as urban core or urban fringe.

Small towns are located outside CMAs or CAs and have populations between 1,000-10,000, and a minimum density of 400 persons per km^2.

Rural areas are sparsely populated areas lying outside CMAs and CAs, including small towns, villages and other populated places with populations of less than 1,000, as well as remote areas and agricultural lands.

Sources: Standard Geographical Classification Vols. I & II, 12-571-XPB, 12-572-XPB.

APPENDIX C

DATA SOURCES AND DESIGN

STATISTICS CANADA DEFINES THREE BASIC TYPES of geographical area in an hierarchical system so that census subdivisions (CSDs) aggregate to census divisions (CDs), and CDs to provinces. The 288 CDs which incorporate the entire country, were established under provincial laws to assist in regional planning and the provision of services which can be more effectively delivered to an area larger than a single municipality. CSDs are municipalities (as determined by the appropriate provincial legislation) or their equivalents (i.e. Indian Reserves or settlements, and unorganized territories). In Newfoundland, Nova Scotia and British Columbia, the term also describes areas created by Statistics Canada in cooperation with the province as equivalents to municipalities for the dissemination of statistical data. There are currently 5,600 CSDs of 46 different types.

Determining the number of non-core PST establishments began with a visual inspection of the maps of the Standard Geographical Classification which show the boundaries of all CDs, CSDs, CMAs and CAs. The CSDs incorporated inside a CMA/CA boundary were listed, and those classified as urban areas were identified.[22] This required checking the status of each CSD, since some are constituents of an agglomerated urban area and thus not listed separately, and others are not. Given the Statistics Canada definition of 'urban core', the most critical step was to identify all CSDs contiguous to the central urban area. Contiguity is defined to include boundaries in water areas, as well as on land. Then contiguous CSDs that were not urban areas were excluded from further reclassification.

Any contiguous CSD which had any portion of its population classified as 'urban', regardless of how small that proportion might be, was considered to be part of the urban core. Furthermore, if an urban CSD was contiguous to the urban core of an adjoining CD, it was considered to be part of the urban core, regardless of whether it is contiguous to the urban core in its own CD or whether there is any urban core at all in its own CD[23]. For this reason we have identified 148 'metropolitan' CDs, eight more than the total number of CMAs and CAs. Once the number of establishments located in the urban cores of the metropolitan CDs has been determined, this number is subtracted from the total number of establishments to give us the number we seek, the number of non-core establishments in the 148 metropolitan CDs.

ENDNOTES

1 Synonymous here with services that are knowledge-intensive, high order, high quality or focused on business.

2 Notably, the Atlantic Canada Opportunities Agency in Atlantic Canada; Western Economic Diversification in British Columbia; Canada Economic Development of Quebec Regions in Quebec and FedNor in Northern Ontario.

3 For example, see Rounds (1993). See Martinelli (1991) for a relevant study for Italy.

4 For example, see Luger and Shetty (1985); Moomaw (1988); Coughlin, Terza and Arromdee (1991); Woodward (1992); K. Head, J. Ries and D. Swenson (1995); and Maurel and Sédillot (1999).

5 For example, see Coffey (1996); Shearmur and Alvergne (2002); and Wernerheim and Sharpe (2003).

6 These studies are referenced in Wernerheim and Sharpe (1999). See also Bandt (1991) for a discussion of problems with introducing services into the standard theorems of international trade.

7 See also Wasylenko and McGuire (1985).

8 The CBP data does not allow us to distinguish between firms and establishments. We use these terms interchangeably for the present purpose.

9 See Appendices B and C for definitions and more details.

10 In practice, this process is complicated by contiguity and boundary issues that affect the number of urban cores identified. See Appendix C for more details.

11 For example, see Coffey (1996); and Coffey and Shearmur (1997).

12 The CMA of Quebec, for example, incorporates all or part of 8 CDs; that of Ottawa, 4; Toronto, 7; and Montreal, 16. The larger amount of non-core area in these CDs gives rise to a higher non-core/core ratio.

13 The observations for 1997, 1999 and 2000 that indicate a zero unemployment rate are likely due to missing data.

14 This is the (in)famous independence-of-irrelevant-alternatives assumption (IIA), implying that the effects of unobservable attributes of plants and location choices are uncorrelated.

15 See Ellison and Glaeser (1997: 893-895) for details.

16 The $\{x_i\}$ are taken as exogenous, and the $\{s_i\}$ are taken as endogenously determined by $s_i = \sum_k z_k u_{ki}$ where z_k is the kth plant's exogenously fixed share of the industry's employment, and u_{ki} is an indicator variable equal to 1 if plant k chooses to locate in area i, and zero otherwise. The Herfindahl index is calculated as $H = \sum_k z_k^2$.

17 The trigger values used by Ellison and Glaeser, and Maurel and Sédillot are as follows: $\gamma < 0.02; 0.02 \leq \gamma \leq 0.05; \gamma \geq 0.05$ imply, respectively, low, medium and high concentration (localization).

18 This is consistent with the result for PST establishments in metropolitan areas reported by Wernerheim and Sharpe (2003).

19 For example, metropolitan areas as defined by Statistics Canada include, in addition to an urban core, territories that have rural character.

20 See also Marshall, Damesick and Wood (1987); Begg and Cameron (1988); Daniels (1995b); Coe and Townsend (1998); and Bennet, Graham and Bratton (1999).

21 See Monnoyer and Philippe (1991) and various studies in Bonamy and May (1994).

22 The components of all CMAs and CAs are listed in Table 5, Volume 1 of the Standard Geographical Classification, which also indicates the CSD type and identification number. A comprehensive list of all urban areas, and their constituent parts can be found in Table 8 of the 2001 census publication 93-360-XPB.

23 If it is not, it would normally be considered part of the urban fringe of the CMA.

ACKNOWLEDGMENTS

THIS STUDY REPORTS ON RESEARCH DONE under contract with Industry Canada. The financial assistance is gratefully acknowledged. We are also grateful to Mario Polèse for helpful comments on an earlier version presented at the Industry Canada Conference on Service Industries, Winnipeg, Manitoba, October 16-18, 2003. Thanks are also due Joelle Aucoin for able research assistance, and Alvin Simms of the GEOIDAL Centre at Memorial University of Newfoundland for enthusiastically sharing his cartographic expertise.

BIBLIOGRAPHY

Allen, J. 1992. "Services and the UK Space: Regionalization and Economic Dislocation," *Transaction of the Institute of British Geographers NS*, 17: 292-305.

Bailly, A. 1995. "Producer Services in Europe," *Professional Geographer*, 47 (1): 70-74.

Bandt, J. 1991. "Compétitivité et échanges internationaux dans une économie de service," *Revue d'économie industrielle*, (55): 108-117.

Bartik, T.J. 1985. "Business Location Decisions in the United States: Estimates of the Effects of Unionization, Taxes, and Other Characteristics of States," *Journal of Business and Economic Statistics*, 3 (1): 14-22.

Begg, I.G., and G.C. Cameron. 1988. "High Technology Location," *Urban Studies*, 25: 361-379.

Bennett, R.J., D.J. Graham, and W. Bratton. 1999. "The Location and Concentration of Businesses in Britain: Business Clusters, Business Services, Market Coverage and Local Economic Development," *Transactions of the Institute of British Geographers* NS, 24: 393-420.

Beyers, W.B. 1992. "Producer Services and Metropolitan Growth and Development," in E.S. Mills and J.F. McDonald (eds.). *Sources of Metropolitan Growth*. New Brunswick, NJ: Center for Urban Policy Research, pp. 125-146.

————. 2003. "Trade in Services and Regional Development in the United States," presented to the 13th International Conference of the European Network of Economic and Spatial Service Research (RESER), October 9-10, Facultés Universitaires Catholiques de Mons, Belgium.

Beyers, W.B., and D. Lindahl. 1996. "Lone Eagles and High Flyers in the Rural Producer Services: Is Cost Driven Externalization the Major Force?" *Rural Development Perspectives*, 75: 351-374.

Bonamy, J., and J. May. (eds.). 1994. *Services et mutations urbaines: questionnements et perspectives*. Paris: Anthopos, Economica.

Bryson, J.R. 1997. "Services and Internationalization," Report of the English Team, European Research Network on Services and Space (RESER), http://www.reser.net. Accessed February 1, 2005.

Buss, T.F. 2001. "The Effect of State Tax Incentives on Economic Growth and Firm Location Decisions: An Overview of the Literature," *Economic Development Quarterly*, 15 (1): 90-105.

Canadian Press. 2003. "Atlantic Canada Behind the Times, report states." *Globe and Mail*, Wednesday, October 8.

Carlton, D.W. 1979. "Why Do Firms Locate Where They Do: An Econometric Model," in W. Wheaton (ed.). *Interregional Movements and Regional Growth*. Washington: The Urban Institute, pp. 13-50.

————. 1983. "The Location and Employment Choices of New Firms: An Econometric Model With Discrete and Continuous Endogenous Variables," *Review of Economics and Statistics*, 65 (August): 440-449.

Coe, N.M., and A.R. Townsend. 1998. "Debunking the Myth of the Localized Agglomeration: the Development of a Regionalized Service Economy in South-East England," *Transactions of the Institute of British Geographers NS*, 23: 385-404.

Coffey, William J. 1993. "The Impact of the Growth of Tradeable Services Upon Non-Metropolitan Areas," in R.C. Rounds (ed.). "*Restructuring Industrial Production and Tradeable Services in Rural Canada in the 1990s*," AARG Working Paper Series No. 3. Brandon, Manitoba: The Canadian Agriculture and Rural Restructuring Group.

————. 1996. "The Role and Location of Service Activities in the Canadian Space Economy," in J.N.H. Britton (ed.). *Canada and the Global Economy: the Geography of Structural and Technological Change*. Montreal: McGill-Queen's University Press.

Coffey William J., and Mario Polèse. 1987. "Trade and Location of Producer Services: A Canadian Perspective," *Environment and Planning*, A 19: 597-611.

————. 1989. "Producer Services and Regional Development: A Policy-Oriented Perspective," *Papers of The Regional Science Association*, 67: 13-27.

Coffey, William J., and Richard G. Shearmur. 1997. "The Growth and Location of High Order Services in the Canadian Urban System 1971-1991," *Professional Geographer*, 49: 404-418.

Coughlin, C.C., J.V. Terza, and V. Arromdee. 1991. "State Characteristics and the Location of Foreign Direct Investments Within the United States," *Review of Economics and Statistics*, 73 (November): 675-683.

Daniels, P.W. 1995a. "Producer Services Research in the United Kingdom," *Professional Geographer*, 47 (1): 82-87.

————. 1995b. "The Locational Geography of Advanced Producer Service Firms in the United Kingdom," in F. Moulaert and F. Tödtling (eds.), "The Geography of Advanced Producer Services In Europe," *Progress in Planning*, 43: 123-33.

Daniels, P.W., and J.R. Bryson. 2003. "Business and Professional Services in a Second City Region: Linking Local to Global?" presented to the 13th International Conference of the European Network of Economic and Spatial Service Research (RESER), October 9-10, Facultés Universitaires Catholiques de Mons, Belgium.

Eberts, D., and J.E. Randall. 1998. "Producer Services, Labour Market Segmentation and Peripheral Regions: The Case of Saskatchewan," *Growth and Change*, 29: 401-22.

Ellison, Glenn, and Edward L. Glaeser. 1997. "Geographic Concentration in U.S. Manufacturing Industries: A Dartboard Approach," *Journal of Political Economy*, 105 (5): 889-927.

Feser, E.J. 2001. "A Flexible Test for Agglomeration Economies in Two U.S. Manufacturing Industries," *Regional Science and Urban Economics*, 31: 1-19.

Finney, M. 1994. "Property Tax Effects on Intra-metropolitan Firm Location: Further Evidence," *Applied Economic Letters*, 1: 29-31.

Friedman, J.D., A. Gerlowski, and J. Silberman. 1992. "What Attracts Foreign Multinational Corporations? Evidence from Branch Plant Location in the United States," *Journal of Regional Science*, 32 (4): 403-418.

Gatrell, J.D. 1999. "Re-Thinking Economic Development in Peripheral Regions," *Social Science Journal*, 36: 623-639.

Gilmer, R.W. 1990. "Identifying Service-Sector Exports From Major Texas Cities," *Economic Review*, Federal Reserve Bank of Dallas (July): 1-16.

Gius, M.P., and P. Frese. 2002. "The Impact of State and Personal and Corporate Tax Rates on Firm Location," *Applied Economic Letters*, 9: 47-49.

Glaeser, Edward L., H.D. Kallal, J.A. Scheinkman, and A. Schleifer. 1992. "Growth in Cities," *Journal of Political Economy*, 100: 1126-52.

Glasmeier, A., and M. Howland. 1994. "Service-Led Rural Development: Definitions, Theories, and Empirical Evidence," *International Regional Science Review*, 16: 197-229.

Graham, Stuart. 1998. "The End of Geography or the Explosion of Place? Conceptualizing Space, Place and Information Technology," *Progress in Human Geography*, 22: 165-185.

————. 1999. "Global Grids of Glass: on Global Cities, Telecommunications and Planetary Urban Networks," *Urban Studies*, 36: 929-949.

———. 2001. "Information Technologies and Reconfigurations of Urban Space," *International Journal of Urban and Regional Science*, 25: 405-410.

———. 2002. "Bridging Urban Digital Divides? Urban Polarisation and Information and Communications Technologies (ICTs)," *Urban Studies*, 39: 33-56.

Harrington, J.W. 1995. "Producer Service Research in U.S. Regional Studies," *Professional Geographer*, 47 (1): 87-96.

Harrington, J.W., and J.R. Lombard. 1989. "Producer-Service Firms in a Declining Manufacturing Region," *Environmental Planning* A, 21: 65-79.

Head, Keith, John Ries, and D. Swenson. 1995. "Agglomeration Benefits and Location Choice: Evidence from Japanese Manufacturing Investments in the United States," *Journal of International Economics*, 38: 223-247.

Henderson, J.V. 1983. "Industrial Bases and City Sizes," *American Economic Review*, 73: 164-169.

———. 1986. "Efficiency of Resource Usage and City Size," *Journal of Urban Economics*, 19: 47-70.

Hoover, E.M. 1936. *Location Theory and the Shoe and Leather Industries.* Cambridge, MA: Harvard University Press.

Illeris, S. 1991. *Location of Services in a Service Society* in P. W. Daniels and F. Moulaert (eds.). *The Changing Geography of Advanced Producer Services*. London: Bellhaven Press, pp. 93-107.

———. 1996. *The Service Economy: A Geographical Approach.* Chichester: John Wiley.

Jorgenson, Dale W. 2001. "Information Technology and the U.S. Economy," *American Economic Review*, 91 (March): 1-32.

———. 2003. "Information Technology and the G-7 Economies," Department of Economics, Harvard University, November 4, http://post.economics.harvard.edu/faculty/jorgenson/papers/papers.html. Accessed February 1, 2005.

Keeble, D., A.J. Bryson, and P. Wood. 1991. "Small Firms, Business Services Growth and Regional Development in the United Kingdom: Some Empirical Findings," *Regional Studies*, 25 (5): 439-457.

Kirn, T.J. 1987. "Growth and Change in the Service Sector of the U.S.: A Spatial Perspective," *Annals of the Association of American Geographers, 77* (3): 353-372.

Kitchin, R.M. 1998. "Towards Geographies of Cyberspace," *Progress In Human Geography*, 22: 385-406.

Krugman, Paul. 1991. *Geography and Trade.* Cambridge, MA: MIT Press.

Luger, M.I., and S. Shetty. 1985. "Determinants of Foreign Plant Start-ups in the United States: Lessons for Policymakers in the Southeast," *Vanderbilt Journal of Transnational Law* (Spring): 223-245.

Mackay, R.R. 2003. "Twenty-five Years of Regional Development," *Regional Studies*, 37 (3): 303-317.

Malecki, E.J. 2002. "The Economic Geography of the Internet's Infrastructure," *Economic Geography*, 78: 399-424.

Marshall, A. 1890. *Principles of Economics.* London: Macmillan.

Marshall, N., P. Damesick, and P. Wood. 1987. "Understanding the Location and Role of Producer Services in the United Kingdom," *Environment and Planning* A, 19: 575-596.

Martinelli, F. 1991. "Branch Plants and Service Underdevelopment in Peripheral Regions: the Case of Southern Italy," in P.W. Daniels and F. Moulaert (eds.). *The Geography of Services*. London: Frank Cass.

Maurel, F., and B. Sédillot. 1999. "A Measure of the Geographic Concentration in French Manufacturing Industries," *Regional Science and Urban Economics, 29:* 575-604.

McFadden, D.L. 1974. "Conditional Logit Analysis of Qualitative Choice Behavior," in P. Zarembka (ed.). *Frontiers in Econometrics*. New York: Academic Press.

Monnoyer, M.-C., and J. Philippe. 1991. "Localisation Factors and Development Strategies of Producer Services," in P.W. Daniels and F. Moulaert (eds.). *The Changing Geography of Advanced Producer Services*. London: Bellhaven, pp. 108-117.

Moomaw, R.L. 1988. "Agglomeration Economies: Localization or Urbanization?" *Urban Studies*, 25: 150-161.

Moriset, B. 2003. "The New Economy in the City: Emergence and Location Factors of Internet-based Companies in the Metropolitan Area of Lyon, France," *Urban Studies*, 40: 2165-2186.

Moulaert, F., and C. Gallouj. 1993. "The Locational Geography of Advanced Producer Service Firms: the Limits of Economies of Agglomeration," in P. W. Daniels and F. Moulaert (eds.). *The Geography of Services*. London: Frank Cass.

———. 1996. "Advanced Producer Services in the French Space Economy: Decentralization at the Highest Level," *Progress in Planning*, 43: 139-153.

Nakamura, R. 1985. "Agglomeration Economies in Urban Manufacturing Industries: A Case of Japanese Cities," *Journal of Urban Economics*, 17: 108-124.

O'Farrell, P.N., L.A.R. Moffatt, and D.M.W.N. Hitchens. 1993. "Manufacturing Demand for Business Services in a Core and Peripheral Region: Does Flexible Production Imply Vertical Disintegration of Business Services, *Regional Studies, 27:* 385-400.

Owens, R.E., and P.-D. Sarte. 2002. "Analyzing Firm Location Decisions: Is Public Intervention Justified?" *Journal of Public Economics*, 86: 223-242.

Papke, L.E. 1991. "Interstate Business Tax Differentials and New Firm Location," *Journal of Public Economics*, 45: 47-68.

Perry, M. 1990. "Business Service Specialization and Regional Economic Change," *Regional Studies*, 24: 195-209.

———. 1991. "The Capacity of Producer Services to Generate Regional Growth: Some Evidence From a Peripheral Metropolitan Economy," *Environment and Planning* A, 23: 1331-1347.

Polèse, Mario, and Richard G. Shearmur. 2002. *The Periphery in the Knowledge Economy*. Quebec City: The Canadian Institute for Research on Regional Development, University of Quebec.

Polèse, Mario, and R. Verreault. 1989. "Trade in Information-Intensive Services: How and Why Regions Develop Export Advantages," *Canadian Public Policy*, XV (4): 376-386.

Porterfield, S., and G. Pulver. 1991. "Service Producers, Exports, and the Generation of Economic Growth," *International Regional Science Review*, 14: 41-59.

Rivera-Batiz, F. 1988. "Increasing Returns, Monopolistic Competition, and Agglomeration Economies in Consumption and Production," *Regional Science and Urban Economics*, 18: 125-153.

Rounds, R.C. 1993. (ed.) "*Restructuring Industrial Production and Tradeable Services in Rural Canada in the 1990s*," AARG Working Paper Series No. 3. Brandon, Manitoba: The Canadian Agriculture and Rural Restructuring Group.

Shearmur, Richard G., and C. Alvergne. 2002. "Intra-metropolitan Patterns of High-order Business Service Location: A Comparative Study of Seventeen Sectors in Île-de-France," *Urban Studies*, 39 (7): 1143-1163.

Thrift, N. 1996. "New Urban Areas and Old Technological Fears: Reconfiguring the Goodwill of Electronic Things," *Urban Studies*, 33: 1463-1493.

Wasylenko, M. 1991. "Industry Location, Business Climate and Employment Growth: A Review of the Evidence," in H.W. Herzog and A.M. Schlottmann (eds.). *Industry Location and Public Policy*. Knoxville, TN: University of Tennessee Press.

Wasylenko, M., and T. McGuire. 1985. "Jobs and Taxes: the Effect of Business Climate on State's Employment Growth Rates," *National Tax Journal*, 38: 497-511.

Wernerheim, C. Michael. 2003. "Determinants of Location and Employment of New Advanced Service Firms in Rural and Urban Areas — A Preliminary Analysis," presented to the 13th International Conference of the European Network of Economic and Spatial Service Research (RESER), October 9-10, Facultés Universitaires Catholiques de Mons, Belgium.

————. 2004. "Understanding Regional High-Order Service Growth in Canada: A Cointegration Approach," *Service Industries Journal*, 24 (1): 131-154.

Wernerheim, C. Michael, and Christopher A. Sharpe. 1999. "Producer Services and the 'Mixed Market' Problem: Some Empirical Evidence," *Area*, 31 (2): 123-140.

————. 2003. "'High-Order' Producer Services in Metropolitan Canada: How Footloose Are They?" *Regional Studies*, 37 (5): 469-490.

Windrum, P., and M. Tomlinson. 1999. "Knowledge-intensive Services and International Competitiveness: A Four Country Comparison," *Technology Analysis & Strategic Management*, 11 (3): 391-408.

Wood, P.A. 1998. "Services and Internationalization," British Report, European Research Network in Services and Space (RESER), www.reser.net/gbl.

Wood, P., A.J. Bryson, and D. Keeble. 1993. "Regional Patterns of Small Firm Development in the Business Services: Evidence from the United Kingdom," *Environment and Planning A*, 25: 677-700.

Woodward, D.P. 1992. "Locational Determinants of Japanese Manufacturing Start-ups in the United States," *Southern Economic Journal*, 58 (January): 690-708.

Comment

Mario Polèse
Institut national de la recherche scientifique (INRS)
Urbanisation, Culture et Société

IS THERE HOPE FOR KNOWLEDGE-INTENSIVE SERVICES BEYOND THE CITY?

A FAMILIAR FRENCH CATHOLIC MAXIM, although admittedly somewhat dated, is "Hors de l'église, point de salut" (roughly, all is lost outside of the church). A similar adage might be applied to knowledge-intensive services (defined below) with respect to cities. Knowledge-intensive services do not seem to fare well outside the big city. Wernerheim and Sharpe look at the spatial distribution in Canada of establishments and employment in professional, scientific and technical services (PST).[1] Unsurprisingly, they find that such services are highly concentrated in urban areas. They also point to similar findings for other nations. The spatial concentration of advanced producer services (to use the author's vocabulary) is today well documented in Canada and elsewhere.[2] The evidence that such 'advanced' services are highly sensitive to what economists and economic geographers call agglomeration economies is overwhelming. The case no longer needs to be argued.

How then should one view the future of knowledge-intensive services in rural areas and smaller cities that are far removed from the bright lights of the big city? Is there any evidence, the literature notwithstanding, that such services can develop in less urban environments? With the rise of new information technologies (IT), might we not expect to see an increase in PST activity in less urban locations? In their attempt to answer the question, Wernerheim and Sharpe draw on data that allow them to decompose information for urban areas into three classes ('urban core', 'urban fringe', and the undeveloped 'rural fringe'), and divide the rest of Canada into two classes: 'small towns' and 'rural areas'. The former are towns with populations of 10,000 or less (but more than 1,000). Outside of the urban core, they observe (for 1996-2002) that growth in PST employment was most rapid in the 'rural fringe'. This is not an unexpected result: we would expect high growth in the newly developing parts of cities (even if these are still formally zoned as rural). Rates of growth in 'rural' areas are more rapid than for 'small towns', which leads one to suspect that much of the growth is taking place just beyond the outer limits of the metropolis (a point to which I shall return).

On the whole, the picture is one of continuing spread of the suburbs and somewhat beyond. This is quite different from a 'true' regional dispersion to small towns and outlying regions. The authors are, quite rightly, not very optimistic about the prospects of advanced producer services becoming engines of economic growth for Canada's less urban regions. Their second major finding reinforces this conclusion. Using a modelling technique that allows them to characterize spatial patterns of PST establishments, the authors observe that PST establishments located outside urban cores are, as a rule, small and geographically dispersed (in a quite regular manner). This, again, is not an unexpected result. As the authors quite reasonably infer, this suggests a universe of small establishments, mainly serving local clientele: accountants, lawyers, computer technicians and the like. The authors also cite other sources and data, which reinforce the perception that a high percentage of PST services are not easily tradable and that, on both the production and the delivery side, such services are very sensitive to the need for face-to-face contacts (IT not withstanding) — thus, the continuing pull of agglomeration economies. Unfortunately, their data does not allow them to decompose the PST sector and thus to separate out 'modern' (scientific and technical) tradable services from more traditional professional services, a point to which I shall also return.

In sum, the picture suggested is one of continued concentration of advanced producer services (NAICS 54) in or near Canada's largest urban areas. The spatial dynamics suggest a process of continued suburbanization (now moving slightly further out). Those PST firms that do function in less urban environments, including those in the suburbs, are generally small and restricted to serving local markets. I do not disagree with this general picture. However, I should like to take the analysis one step further. In the Wernerheim and Sharpe study, all 'rural' and 'small town' locations are grouped in a single class, leaving aside considerations of proximity (to large cities). Also, treating PST as a single class excludes the possibility of identifying specific economic sectors that might (hopefully) be flourishing in less urban settings. In the rest of this study, I shall look at knowledge-intensive services in Canada using a different data set, decomposing the PST sector and introducing a distance variable.

A Brief Analysis of the Spatial Dynamics of Knowledge-Intensive Services

Data Base

THE ANALYSIS THAT FOLLOWS draws on an information system, housed at Institut national de la recherche scientifique (INRS) in Montreal, based on special tabulations performed by Statistics Canada using census data and updated after each census since 1971.[3] The geographies have been standardized, meaning that all spatial units (observations) are invariant over time. The information system uses an industrial classification system comprising 136 classes, compatible in principle with both the NAICS introduced in 1997, and with the previous SIC codes.[4] As a result, sector definitions are also invariant over time.

Like Wernerheim and Sharpe, we assume that NAICS class 54 (PST) is a reasonable proxy for the knowledge-intensive services sector, though the latter remains an elastic concept. However, the definition used here is somewhat broader, introducing elements of NAICS 51 (notably, information services) due to the constraints imposed by the need to match NAICS with classes constructed on the basis of the old SIC. In the INRS classification system, the aggregate 'knowledge-intensive services' sector (referred to hereafter as KI services) is composed of two classes, each composed of three additional detailed classes, as shown in Table 1 with NAICS equivalents.

Spatial units are grouped into 12 classes, according to population size and distance from a CMA with a population of 500,000 or more. Those falling within approximately one hour's drive (100 to 150 km depending on road conditions) of a major metropolis of this size are classified as 'central', and all the rest as 'peripheral'. Large urban areas of 500,000 or more are 'central' by definition. Other 'central' and 'peripheral' observations are grouped into five classes, based on size. Those with a population below 10,000 are classified as 'rural' (see Figure 1). The 'rural' class thus combines the 'rural' and 'small town' classes used by Wernerheim and Sharpe.

TABLE 1

KNOWLEDGE-INTENSIVE SERVICES: INRS CLASSIFICATION

CLASS	NAICS CODES
"High-Tech" Services	
Computer Services	514, 5112, 5415
Engineering Consultants, Architects, Industrial Design	5413, 5414, 5417
Management Consultants, Scientific Research and R&D Services	5416
Professional Services	
Accounting, Bookkeeping, and Related Services	5412
Advertising and Marketing Services	5418
Legal Services	5411

The Location of Knowledge-Intensive Services

Figure 1 shows the weight (in percentage) of KI services in total employment in 2001 for the 12 spatial classes. The percentage of KI employment declines systematically with city size, as would be expected. This is a corollary to the concentration of PST employment in urban places that is noted by Wernerheim and Sharpe. Figure 1 tells us that such employment is highly concentrated in the largest urban centres. Two additional inferences can be drawn from Figure 1. First, central rural locations (those close to urban locations) have a visibly higher proportion of KI services employment than those located further away from large urban centres. As suggested earlier, this shows that employment in KI services that is attributed to 'rural' areas is in many cases located just beyond the outer limits of the CMA.[5] Second, for urban areas with populations falling between 25,000 and 500,000 (the three middle columns in Figure 1), values are higher for peripheral than for central observations. This is consistent with what economic geographers call 'central place theory'. In a nutshell, central place theory postulates that one of the primary functions of a city is to act as a services centre for a surrounding hinterland (market area). We would expect cities located far from a major metropolis to play a more active role as regional services centres than similar

Figure 1

% Employment in Knowledge-Intensive [KI] Services by Urban Size and Location, 2001

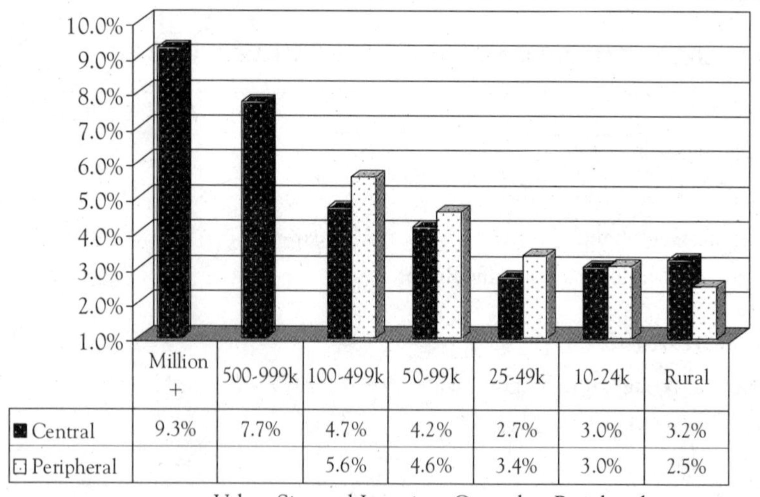

	Million +	500-999k	100-499k	50-99k	25-49k	10-24k	Rural
■ Central	9.3%	7.7%	4.7%	4.2%	2.7%	3.0%	3.2%
□ Peripheral			5.6%	4.6%	3.4%	3.0%	2.5%

sized cities located within the shadow of a major metropolis. This is the difference between, say, Saskatoon or St. John's and Kitchener-Waterloo or St. Catharines, where we would expect the former two to play a more important role as regional services centres. In sum, the relative importance of the KI services sector is not only a matter of city size (although that remains the first consideration), but also of location.

Figure 2 shows the relative weight of what we have called "high-tech" services (recall Table 1) in total KI services employment by spatial class. We may assume that high-tech services are, in general, more tradable and have a higher scientific and technological-knowledge content than the professional services class. Here again, we observe a fairly systematic variation linked with city size, leaving the 'rural' class aside. In other words, the composition of the KI services sector is not the same in small cities as in large urban centres. This result is, yet again, consistent with expectations, confirming that smaller cities are more specialized in locally traded professional services. By the same token, this suggests that within the broad KI services sector, high-tech services are even more sensitive to agglomeration economies than the KI services sector as a whole. This is not necessarily good news for small towns.

However, the results also suggest that the urban size threshold may not be as high as feared. Indeed, the second urban size class (500,000 to 1 million) shows a stronger high tech services specialization than the largest urban

FIGURE 2

"HIGH-TECH" SERVICES AS A PERCENTAGE OF KI SERVICES BY URBAN SIZE AND LOCATION, 2001

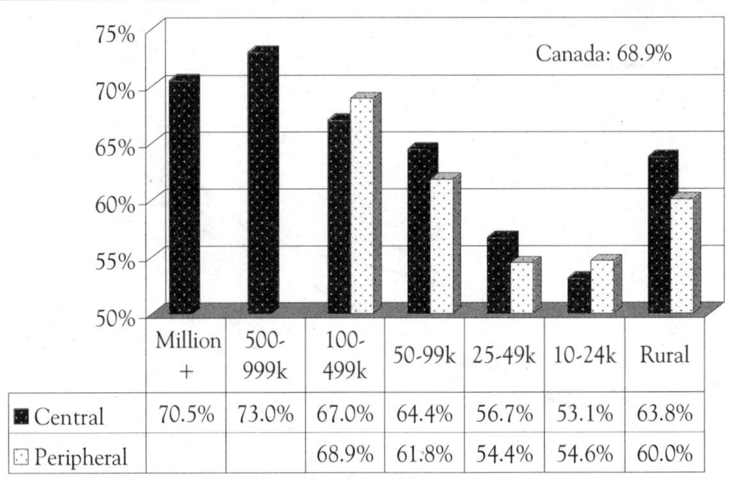

	Million +	500-999k	100-499k	50-99k	25-49k	10-24k	Rural
■ Central	70.5%	73.0%	67.0%	64.4%	56.7%	53.1%	63.8%
☐ Peripheral			68.9%	61.8%	54.4%	54.6%	60.0%

Urban Size and Location: Central or Peripheral

centres. This is partly a reflection of a strong engineering sector in Calgary and in other urban centres with a significant natural resource base, a point to which I shall return. This also provides a partial explanation of the good showing of the largest peripheral urban size class (100-400,000) and of the two rural classes, which partially capture the effects of proximity to these larger 'peripheral' cities and to the largest urban centres, as noted earlier. In other words, not all hope is lost of developing a "high tech" services base in peripheral locations.[6] For the remainder of the analysis, we shall thus concentrate on the high-tech services class as defined in Table 1.

THE EVOLUTION OF EMPLOYMENT IN "HIGH-TECH" SERVICES, 1971-2001

FIGURES 3, 4, AND 5 show the evolution of employment in "high-tech" services from 1971 to 2001 by spatial grouping; in each case, with 1971 set to equal 1.00. Figure 3 tells us that between 1971 and 2001, employment in the

FIGURE 3

EMPLOYMENT IN "HIGH TECH" SERVICES
LARGE URBAN AREAS (500K+) AND THE REST OF CANADA, 1971-2001 (1971=1)

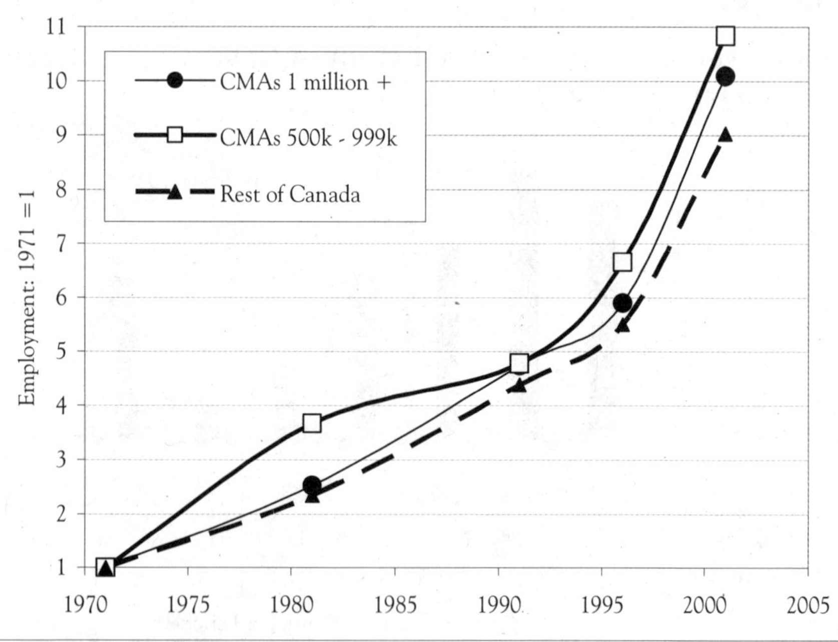

high-tech services class expanded very rapidly in Canada by a factor of about 10, an observation that should come as no surprise.[7] Figure 3 also tells us that high-tech services employment grew more rapidly in the largest urban centres (500,000+) than in the rest of the nation. The trend is thus toward increased spatial concentration, most noticeably since 1991. This mirrors findings in other studies, both in Canada and elsewhere, on the centralizing effects of IT.[8] However, Figure 3 also shows that high-tech services employment grew fastest in the second tier large urban centres, which include Calgary, as is consistent with our comments on Figure 2.[9] In other words, size matters a great deal but a city need not necessarily be a super metropolis to attract high-tech services employment. Again, this is consistent with findings for other nations. Boston and the San Francisco Bay area, arguably the two leading high-tech services poles in the United States, are not the nation's largest metropolitan areas, nor are smaller urban areas such as Seattle or Austin. However, none of these are small towns either.

FIGURE 4

**EMPLOYMENT IN "HIGH TECH" SERVICES IN SMALL TOWNS AND RURAL AREAS, 1971-2001
PERIPHERAL AND CENTRAL LOCATIONS (1971=1)**

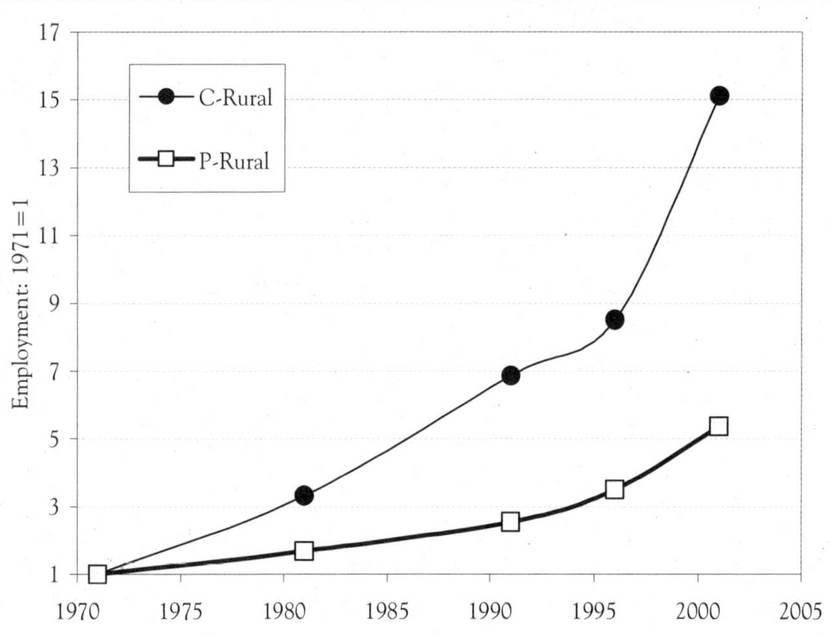

FIGURE 5

**EMPLOYMENT IN "HIGH TECH" SERVICES, 1971-2001
URBAN AREAS WITH POPULATIONS UNDER 500K BY POPULATION SIZE AND DISTANCE FROM LARGER CMAS (1971=1)**

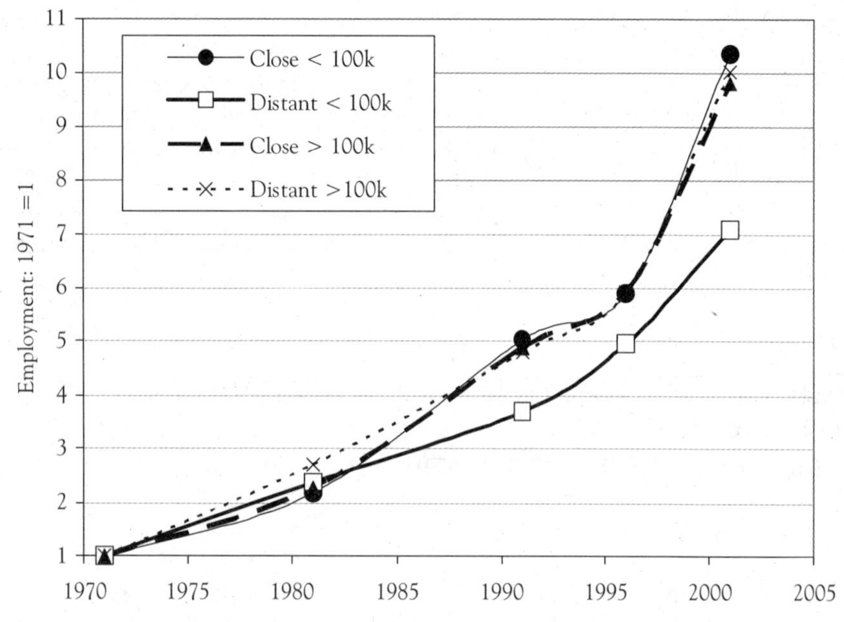

Figure 4 confirms the growing gap between those 'rural' areas that are far from and those that are close to large urban centres. Stated differently, being 'rural' is not necessarily a handicap, but being far from a major urban centre is. And the handicap is growing. The chances of developing a strong high-tech services base in places that are both small and far away remain bleak. However, distance need not be a barrier if it is offset by sufficient size. We already noted that the necessary urban size threshold may not be all that high — perhaps in the order of 100,000 (recall Figure 2). Figure 5 suggests that this may indeed be the case. High-tech services employment has continued to grow rapidly, at rates close to the national average, for 'peripheral' urban areas with populations above this threshold. The locations losing out are those, on average, that find themselves below this threshold and that are located beyond a one-hour driving distance from a major metropolitan area.[10] Before giving up all hope for these smaller, distant places, however, let us take a closer look at the "high-tech" services sector.

There is hope for knowledge-intensive services beyond large cities. It is all bound up with natural resources.

Figure 6 gives the distribution (in percentage) of "high-tech" employment among the following sub-sectors: management consulting and scientific research and R&D services; engineering and related services; and computer services. The difference between the latter class and the first two (especially engineering) is significant. The computer-services class, which encompasses various NAICS codes (see Table 1), arguably comes closest to the commonly perceived notion of modern, high-tech, knowledge-intensive services. More to the point, most activities falling within this class are largely independent of industrial structure and resource endowments. These activities are largely driven by human capital with knowledge externalities playing a major role in locational decisions.[11] In simple language, these activities go where the talent and the brains are. This is less true for the two other classes, although human capital and knowledge externalities remain essential factors. Many research and engineering services are linked to the material world: the object under study or being redesigned must be readily available. For example, oceanographic research requires an ocean and geological research or engineering related to underground; mining requires active mines.

FIGURE 6

DISTRIBUTION OF "HIGH TECH" EMPLOYMENT AMONG THREE SUB-SECTORS, 2001 BY LOCATION AND URBAN SIZE CLASS

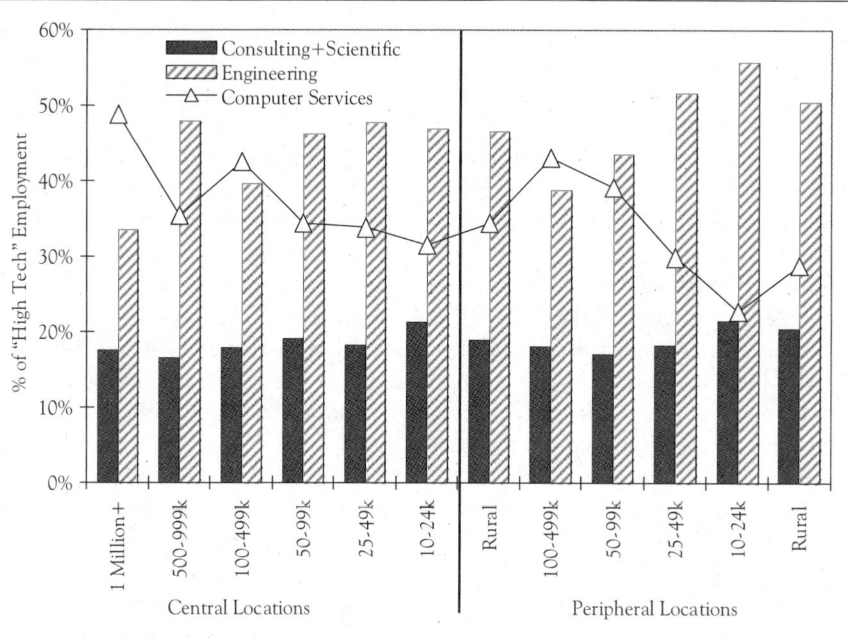

Figure 6 tells us that computer services are the mainstay of the high-tech services economy in large metropolitan areas of more than a million inhabitants. Although important, engineering services play a secondary role. The situation is reversed for small peripheral cities. Indeed, the relationship appears to be systematic: for peripheral locations, the smaller the city, the greater the proportion of engineering and related services in the total. This result is not difficult to interpret. Natural resource exploration and exploitation, the basis of most peripheral small town economies in Canada, is highly dependent on engineering and related research services. Oil drilling and exploration — whether in Alberta or off the shores of Newfoundland — requires an array of engineers, geologists, and other similar specialized labour. The same is true for mining in areas such as Northern Ontario and Northern Quebec. Aluminium smelting is also highly dependent on engineering and related research services. Alcan maintains a major research centre in Chicoutimi. The link between manufacturing and KI services (where there is one) will often manifest itself via the engineering sector. This also helps to explain the high proportion of engineering in smaller, centrally located cities. In sum, the results shown in Figure 6 are consistent with what one would expect: "high-tech" services as a whole are much less present in small peripheral cities (recall Figures 1 and 2), but where they are present, they tend to be concentrated in engineering and other KI services linked to the exploitation or primary transformation of natural resources.

In conclusion, what does this suggest for the possible development of 'tradable' KI services in small towns and cities in peripheral locations? Simply put, engineering consulting firms (and related services firms) will spring up in many places and may end up selling their locally developed expertise abroad. A consulting firm specializing in gold mining in Val d'Or, Quebec may get contracts in Chile, Australia, or South Africa.[12] By the same token, engineering firms in Sudbury specializing in copper and zinc mining (or smelting) may bid on contracts in Zambia; St. John's-based engineering firms working off-shore in Newfoundland may also work in the North Sea. Examples are not difficult to imagine. The point is that such high tech KI services are dependent on the continued existence of the local resource economy. If the mines dry up, the engineers, geologists, and others will eventually leave. The expertise cannot be maintained and developed without a material base to which it can refer. A local KI services export base built on non-renewable resources will necessarily be fragile. In this respect, KI services do not differ from other economic activities derived from natural resources.

Ultimately, long-term growth based (at least in part) on KI services can only be sustained if the area diversifies into other KI services that are not dependent on a natural resource base. This is most likely to occur in urban areas that have attained a certain population threshold (in the order of 100,000), as the results in Figure 6 suggest. For most other peripheral places, the traditional barriers to economic development (i.e. small size and distance) will continue to hamper diversification. The rise of the knowledge-based services economy does not alter the fundamental fragility of small resource-based economies. I began with a French adage. I shall end with another: "plus ça change, plus c'est la même chose" (I leave the joy of translation to the reader).

ENDNOTES

1 Class 54, following the 1997 NAICS.

2 A wide variety of expressions exists to designate information-rich "advanced" services: high-order services; information services; producer services; modern services; etc. Classes and labels can vary from author to author, depending on the subject under study and the nature of available data.

3 This is part of a broader, on-going, research effort on the spatial dynamics of the North American economy, conducted together with Richard Shearmur, William Coffey, and other colleagues at INRS and at the University of Montreal. I should like to thank Richard Shearmur for his help in organizing the data for this paper.

4 However, some caution is in order, which is why 'in principle' is in the sentence. Discrepancies continue to exist between classes built on the old SIC codes and those built on the NAICs codes. However, the differences are sufficiently minor, we believe, so as not to warrant detailed comment. For more information, please contact the author or Richard Shearmur at INRS in Montreal.

5 Note that our information is based on census data for place of residence, which means that it also captures KI services employees who work in the city, but live in 'rural' areas located just beyond the normal commuting shed that defines the CMA. This is one of the shortcomings of our data set but it does not significantly affect our conclusions. An analogous long-distance commuting effect is perceptible for the rural 'peripheral' class with respect to peripheral urban areas (below 500,000), but the impact is necessarily less pronounced.

6 The reader will have guessed by now that much depends on how one defines 'peripheral'. Our definition (a location beyond a one-hour range of a CMA with a population in excess of 500,000) is certainly not the only one possible.

7 For Canada as whole, the precise figure is 9.87, not shown on Figure 3.

8 See, for example, chapter 3 in Polèse and Shearmur (2002), cited in Wernerheim and Sharpe, which also includes references to other studies.

9 Since 2001, Calgary has moved into the first tier. The population of the Calgary CMA passed the million mark in 2003.

10 We say 'on average' because, of course, exceptions exist. However, Red Deer pointed out in the Wernerheim and Sharpe study, would not be an exception in our scheme because of its proximity to both Calgary (84 km) and Edmonton (94 km).

11 The term currently favoured in urban economics is 'knowledge spillovers', which are notoriously difficult to measure. The concept, however, remains appealing. However, I prefer a less technical equivalent heard at a conference; quoting an anonymous speaker: "the knowledge economy is all about *buzz*".

12 This is a real world example, encountered by the authors in the course of the Polèse and Shearmur (2002) study, cited in the Wernerheim and Sharpe paper.

Someshwar Rao
Industry Canada

Andrew Sharpe
Centre for the Study of Living Standards

& *Jianmin Tang*
Industry Canada

14

Productivity Growth in Services Industries: A Canadian Success Story

INTRODUCTION

CANADA'S PRODUCTIVITY AND REAL INCOME increased at a considerably slower pace after 1973 than it had between 1946 and 1973. In addition, Canada lagged behind the United States in terms of aggregate labour productivity growth in the 1990s, particularly when measured in terms of the business sector.[1] As a result, the Canada-U.S. productivity gap has increased over the past decade. There is a general consensus that growth in labour productivity increased significantly in both Canada and the United States in the second half of the 1990s. Given that factors of production and innovation activities are becoming increasingly footloose, it is important that Canada improves its productivity performance vis-à-vis its southern neighbour. Otherwise, a falling relative standard of living may make it difficult to attract and retain capital, skilled workers and higher value-added activities to Canada. This could set in motion a vicious cycle of net out-migration of these internationally mobile resources coupled with weak economic growth. It is thus important to deepen our understanding of productivity trends in both Canada and the United States.

To date, a disproportionate amount of Canadian productivity research has focused on manufacturing industries. In part this is because high quality data on outputs and inputs is available for manufacturing; in part it is because of the dominant role of manufactured products in international trade. Services sector productivity has been neglected because the quality of data for many services industries is poor and because many services are non-traded and thus less subject to international competitive pressures.

Nevertheless, services industries account for more than 70 percent of real gross domestic product (GDP) and employment in Canada and their importance is growing. This means that productivity trends in the services sector and not manufacturing are the real driving force behind aggregate productivity growth and hence real income growth. In addition, services exports, especially business-services exports, are increasing at a healthy pace. Furthermore, interdependence between manufacturing and services industries has been increasing steadily. As a result, productivity improvements in services industries can be crucial for improving the competitive position of Canadian manufacturing industries. It is important, therefore, to perform an in-depth analysis of productivity trends in Canadian services industries, especially business-sector services. This study performs such an analysis with the following objectives:

- to analyze output and employment growth in Canadian services industries, comparing them to the United States;
- to compare and contrast the productivity performance of Canadian services industries with that of manufacturing and primary industries;
- to examine the impact of inter-industry shifts in business-sector services industries on the aggregate growth of services sector productivity;
- to compare and contrast the output and productivity performance of Canadian business-sector services industries with their U.S. counterparts over the past two decades; and
- to analyze possible reasons for relatively strong productivity performance in Canadian business-sector services industries.

DATA SOURCES

THE STUDY USES TWO MAJOR SOURCES OF DATA. The first is the productivity database maintained by the Centre for the Study of Living Standards (CSLS) that is based on input and output data from Statistics Canada, covering the period 1987-2002. A similar database for the United States, covering the period 1987-2001, has been constructed from data collected by the U.S. Bureau of Economic Analysis.

The second data set was constructed as part of a joint project between Industry Canada, Statistics Canada and Harvard University directed by Dale Jorgenson of Harvard University. It focused on the impact of information and communications technologies (ICTs) on productivity growth (Ho, Rao and Tang 2003). This project developed comparable capital, labour, energy, materials and services (KLEMS) estimates for both Canada and the United States in 40 industries for the 1981-2000 period. It used this database to examine sources of economic and productivity growth in the two countries. The appendix to this study discusses some technical details of this database.

There are a number of differences between the two databases. One, the first data set is based on the North American Industry Classification System (NAICS) for Canada and the Standard Industrial Classification (SIC) for the United States, while the second data set uses the SIC for both countries. Two, the first database uses a value-added approach for estimates of output and labour productivity, while the second uses a gross output framework to calculate estimates of labour and multifactor or total factor productivity.

MOTIVATION OF THE STUDY

CANADIAN SERVICES INDUSTRIES and especially business-sector services have performed strongly in recent years. Output and labour productivity growth picked up significantly in the second half of the 1990s, relative to 1981-95. Canadian business-sector services have outperformed U.S. business-sector services in terms of output, labour productivity and multifactor productivity in both the 1981-95 and 1995-2000 periods. This is not well known or recognized for the 1995-2000 period because of the superior productivity performance of the U.S. economy at the aggregate level. However, it is the very strong productivity performance of the U.S. goods sector, particularly manufacturing, rather than services that accounts for the overall superior productivity performance of the U.S. business sector.

Considering Canadian business-sector services as a group, the key research question motivating this study is why has performance been so good in terms of labour and multifactor productivity in recent years, both in absolute terms and relative to the United States. Indeed, it has been so good that it has offset much of the poorer performance of the manufacturing sector (Bernstein, Harris and Sharpe 2002). The many possible explanations include technological convergence toward the best-practice country, that is the United States; greater accumulation of human capital; greater competition in services industries; employment shifts to high productivity level industries; and more effective use of ICTs.

ORGANIZATION OF THE STUDY

THE FIRST PART OF THIS STUDY looks at output and employment shares, and labour productivity levels in the Canadian and U.S. services industries. It is followed by an examination of productivity trends in business-sector services industries in Canada and the United States, and the impact of inter-industry employment shifts on aggregate business-sector services productivity growth. The section after that is based on data from the Jorgenson project on ICT (Ho, Rao and Tang 2003). It examines the sources of output and labour productivity growth in business-sector services industries in Canada and the United States in the 1981-1995 and 1995-2000 periods. Data from the Jorgenson project is then used to analyze the absolute contribution of business-sector services industries to aggregate output, labour productivity and multifactor productivity growth in Canada and the United States, again in the 1981-1995 and 1995-2000 periods. The final section examines the factors that account for the relatively successful productivity performance of the Canadian business-sector services, both in terms of its acceleration in productivity growth relative to the pre-1995 period and its higher productivity growth compared with its U.S. counterpart since 1981. This is followed by a conclusion.

Comparison of Output and Employment Shares and Labour Productivity Levels in the Canadian and U.S. Services Sectors

Before beginning our discussion of services sector trends, it is useful to present a number of caveats that should be kept in mind.

One, the services sector is a very heterogeneous category responsible for the lion's share of the economy's output and employment. It encompasses all non-goods producing industries. Consequently, the characteristics of the different industries that comprise the services sector are very diverse, some well above the overall sector average for productivity growth and some well below. This means that the services sector may only have limited usefulness as a frame of reference for productivity analysis or as an analytical category in general. From the point of view of productivity analysis, it may be more useful to focus at the industry level.

Two, it is important not to confuse two commonly used definitions of services. The first is a broad definition of services that includes all services-producing industries. The second is a narrow definition derived from the SIC definition, which included what were called business, community and personal services (including health and education). This industry is sometimes referred to collectively as "services". This study uses the first, broader definition of services.

Three, measurement problems are generally recognized as severe in services producing industries. This reflects the non-marketed nature of a large proportion of the output of the non-business services (public administration, and most of health and education in Canada). It also reflects difficulties with the conceptual definition of output in certain industries such as insurance and banking as well as difficulties in capturing changes in quality (both improvement and deterioration) in certain sectors.

Real Output

Canada

According to official GDP estimates compiled by Statistics Canada, the largest single sector of the Canadian economy by far is services, defined as the sum of all industries except primary industries, manufacturing and construction. Using NAICS as the basis for calculation, in 2001, the services sector accounted for 70.8 percent of total real (1997$) output as compared to 18.0 percent for manufacturing, 5.9 percent for primary industries, and 5.4 percent for construction (Table 1). Over time, there has been a slight increase in the importance of the services sector for total output. In 1987, it accounted for 69.4 percent of GDP, but by 2001 it was more than one percentage point higher.

TABLE 1

OUTPUT AND EMPLOYMENT SHARES AND LABOUR PRODUCTIVITY OF CANADIAN INDUSTRIES

	OUTPUT (REAL GDP)			EMPLOYMENT			RELATIVE LABOUR PRODUCTIVITY (TOTAL ECONOMY=100)
	1987	1995	2001	1987	1995	2001	2001
Aggregate Services Sector	**69.4**	**71.0**	**70.8**	**71.2**	**74.9**	**75.2**	**94.2**
Utilities	3.7	3.4	2.7	1.0	0.9	0.8	335.4
Wholesale Trade	4.3	5.0	5.7	3.4	3.2	3.7	155.0
Retail Trade	5.6	5.0	5.5	12.8	12.5	12.1	45.1
Transportation and Warehousing	4.7	4.9	4.7	5.2	5.0	5.1	92.2
Information and Cultural Industries	3.0	3.5	4.0	2.6	2.6	2.7	150.0
FIRE	17.8	19.6	19.8	6.1	6.4	5.8	341.3
Professional and Scientific Services	2.9	3.3	4.4	3.9	5.0	6.5	67.4
Administrative and Support Services	1.6	1.9	2.1	2.1	3.0	3.7	57.4
Education Services	5.9	5.3	4.7	6.4	7.0	6.4	72.8
Health Care and Social Assistance	6.9	6.8	5.8	9.3	10.4	10.2	57.2
Arts, Entertainment and Recreation	1.0	0.9	0.9	1.4	1.7	2.0	45.5
Accommodation and Food Services	2.8	2.5	2.4	5.7	6.1	6.5	37.0
Other Services	2.5	2.4	2.4	5.1	4.9	4.5	52.6
Public Administration	6.8	6.6	5.7	6.2	6.2	5.1	111.8
Construction	**6.7**	**5.1**	**5.4**	**6.0**	**5.5**	**5.6**	**95.7**
Primary Industries	**6.8**	**6.9**	**5.9**	**6.3**	**5.4**	**4.1**	**142.9**
Manufacturing Industries	**17.1**	**17.1**	**18.0**	**16.6**	**14.3**	**15.1**	**119.1**
Total Economy	**100.0**	**100.0**	**100.0**	**100.0**	**100.0**	**100.0**	**100.0**

Notes: Real GDP is in 1997 constant (Laspeyres fixed-weight) dollars and labour productivity is real GDP per worker. Industries are based on NAICS. Relative labour productivity levels are calculated by dividing the output shares by the employment shares. FIRE refers to finance, insurance and real estate, leasing and management.

Sources: Unpublished data provided by Statistics Canada, Division of Industry Measures and Division of Labour Statistics, November 2003.

Within the services sector, the finance, insurance, real estate and leasing and management industry (FIRE) was the single most important component, accounting for 28.0 percent of the services sector as a whole and 19.8 percent of Canadian real GDP.[2] All other industrial groups within the services sector industries contributed shares to total GDP that ranged between one and five percent.

United States

According to SIC data from the U.S. Bureau of Economic Analysis (BEA), in the United States in 2001, the services sector accounted for almost four fifths (77.3 percent) of total GDP, up from 75.1 percent in 1987 (Table 2). In comparison, manufacturing real output represented 15.8 percent of total GDP, construction contributed 4.0 percent and primary industries (agriculture, forestry and fisheries and mining) contributed 2.9 percent. The U.S. services sector is classified into six industries: transportation and public utilities, wholesale trade, retail trade, FIRE, services and public administration. The "services" industry in this classification scheme consists of 14 sub-industries including business, health, legal and educational services. As in Canada, FIRE accounted for the largest single component of the aggregated services sector. At 19.6 percent of total economic output, it was tied with the total contribution of the 14 sub-industries of the "services industry" category. Within the latter, health services and business services were the largest sub-industries, contributing 5.3 and 4.9 percent respectively to total economic output in 2001.

Canada-U.S. Comparison

Any comparison between the Canadian and U.S. services sectors is made difficult by the use of different classification systems and different aggregation conventions in the two countries. Statistics Canada adopted the new NAICS as of 2000, while the U.S. statistical agencies have not fully converted to NAICS and are still mostly using the SIC system.[3] It is nevertheless possible to perform a rough comparison of the relative sizes of the different services industries. As noted above, the U.S. services sector is classified into six industries: transportation and public utilities, wholesale trade, retail trade, FIRE, services and public administration. There are 3 sub-industries in the transportation and public utilities industry and 14 sub-industries under the catchall category of services industry. By contrast, the Canadian services sector represents the sum of 14 industries.

To make comparisons possible, some industries have to be aggregated. By adding the real output shares of utilities to the share of transportation and warehousing in Canada, we obtain a combined total of 7.4 percent in 2001, which is comparable in magnitude to the 8.3 percent share of the U.S. transportation and public utilities industry.

A similar procedure can be used to compare the real output shares of public administration. The U.S. SIC does not have a public administration industry. It is rather called government, and it is much larger than the Canadian public administration industry (11.8 percent of total GDP versus 5.7 percent in 2001). This may be due to different treatment of the public goods provided by the state, namely health care, social assistance and education. These account for a large proportion of government expenditure in Canada but these activities are counted under the separate services industries categories of health care and

TABLE 2

OUTPUT AND EMPLOYMENT SHARES AND LABOUR PRODUCTIVITY OF U.S. INDUSTRIES

	OUTPUT (REAL GDP)			EMPLOYMENT			RELATIVE LABOUR PRODUCTIVITY (TOTAL ECONOMY=100)
	1987	1995	2001	1987	1995	2001	2001
Aggregate Services Sector	**75.1**	**75.7**	**77.3**	**75.0**	**77.8**	**79.4**	**97.4**
Transportation and Public Utilities	7.5	8.5	8.3	4.8	4.8	5.1	164.1
Transportation	2.6	3.0	2.9	2.9	3.2	3.3	87.2
Communications	2.2	2.7	3.4	1.1	1.0	1.2	295.0
Electric, Gas and Sanitary Services	2.7	2.8	2.1	0.8	0.7	0.6	360.8
Wholesale Trade	5.8	6.4	8.0	5.2	5.0	4.7	168.9
Retail Trade	8.3	8.6	10.1	17.1	17.2	17.0	59.4
FIRE	19.0	18.6	19.6	6.1	5.6	5.7	344.2
Services	19.2	20.1	19.6	24.8	29.0	31.2	62.9
Hotels and Other Lodging Places	0.8	0.8	0.7	1.3	1.3	1.3	52.2
Personal Services	0.7	0.6	0.6	1.4	1.4	1.4	44.0
Business Services	3.0	4.2	4.9	4.2	5.6	7.0	70.0
Auto Repair, Services, and Parking	0.9	0.9	0.9	1.0	1.1	1.1	81.5
Miscellaneous Repair Services	0.3	0.3	0.2	0.5	0.5	0.4	51.0
Motion Pictures	0.3	0.3	0.3	0.4	0.5	0.5	59.6
Amusement and Recreation Services	0.6	0.7	0.7	0.9	1.2	1.3	54.5
Health Services	6.4	5.9	5.3	6.1	7.4	7.5	71.0
Legal Services	1.6	1.4	1.3	0.9	1.0	0.9	139.4
Educational Services	0.8	0.8	0.7	1.4	1.6	1.8	39.1
Social Services	0.5	0.7	0.6	1.7	2.2	2.4	24.5
Membership Organizations	0.6	0.7	0.5	1.4	1.6	1.7	29.5
Other Services	2.5	2.7	2.8	2.2	2.7	3.1	90.4
Private Households	0.2	0.2	0.1	1.3	0.9	0.8	13.3
Government (Public Administration)	15.3	13.6	11.8	17.1	16.2	15.7	75.2
Construction	**4.5**	**4.0**	**4.0**	**5.4**	**5.1**	**5.7**	**69.7**
Primary Industries	**3.4**	**3.1**	**2.9**	**3.3**	**3.1**	**2.8**	**103.3**
Manufacturing Industries	**17.0**	**17.1**	**15.8**	**16.2**	**14.0**	**12.1**	**130.6**
Total Economy	**100.0**	**100.0**	**100.0**	**100.0**	**100.0**	**100.0**	**100.0**

Notes: Real GDP is in 1996 (Fisher chained-weight) dollars, workers are defined as full time plus part time employees plus the self-employed, and labour productivity is real GDP per worker. Industries are based on SIC. Relative labour productivity levels are calculated by dividing the output shares by the employment shares.

Source: BEA Website, www.bea.gov. Accessed August 17, 2005.

social assistance and education services. Presumably these two industries include both private and public activities, although the former category is likely to be very small relative to the latter. In the United States, the government industry includes all activities of general government and government enterprises, and it appears that the social services, educational services and health services sub-industries of the services industry include only privately funded activities. It is therefore possible to sum the output shares of government, social services, educational services and health services in the United States and public administration, education services and healthcare and social assistance in Canada to determine the proportion of government and all private and public health, education and social services in total economy output. This share was 16.2 percent in Canada and 18.4 percent in the United States in 2001.[4]

Although they have the same names, the trade industries in the two countries have a very different relative importance in terms of real output shares. Retail trade has almost twice the importance in the United States as it has in Canada (10.1 percent compared to 5.5 percent in 2001). Wholesale trade is also much larger in the United States, with a real output share of 8.0 percent of total GDP compared to 5.8 percent in Canada in 2001. However, two factors complicate these comparisons. First of all, food services are included in the U.S. retail trade industry but in Canada they are classified under the accommodation and food services industry. And second, the traditional distinction between wholesale and retail activities has been blurred in recent decades by the increasing tendency for single, vertically integrated firms to have activities in both sectors. This blurring may mean that it is difficult for statistical agencies in the two countries to define activities as taking place within the retail or wholesale sectors in the same way.

The Jorgenson project database (Table 3)[5] offers categories that are easier to use in comparing the relative importance of business-sector services industries output in the aggregate (business) economy in Canada and the United States. This comparison shows major differences in importance for certain sectors, although such differences largely reflect variations in the business/non-business mix in industry activity between the two countries. The most important of these differences is health services: in 2000 it accounted for 14.5 percent of business-sector value added in the United States compared to only 3.2 percent in Canada. Indeed, this difference accounts for the significantly greater size of the services sector in the U.S. business sector relative to the business sector in Canada (69.0 percent compared to 61.2 percent in 2000). Given the slow productivity growth in this sector, a significantly greater weight for health services produces a downward bias in productivity growth figures for the U.S. business sector relative to Canada. FIRE is also more important in the United States than in Canada: 16.6 percent of business sector value added versus 14.2 percent in 2000. In contrast, transportation is more important in Canada (6.2 percent versus 3.3 percent in 2000), as are other services (7.7 percent versus 4.9 percent).

TABLE 3

INDUSTRY SHARES OF VALUE ADDED AND HOURS IN THE BUSINESS SECTOR IN CANADA AND THE UNITED STATES

	CANADA			UNITED STATES		
INDUSTRY	1981	1995	2000	1981	1995	2000
			VALUE ADDED SHARE (%)			
Services Industries	**51.3**	**59.0**	**61.2**	**55.9**	**67.7**	**69.0**
Transportation	6.6	6.1	6.2	4.5	3.9	3.3
Communications	2.9	3.1	2.7	2.7	2.7	2.9
Electric Utilities	3.1	4.0	3.3	2.4	2.4	2.1
Gas Utilities	0.4	0.5	0.4	0.6	0.4	0.3
Wholesale Trade	5.9	7.0	7.2	7.6	7.0	6.7
Retail Trade	7.8	7.2	7.7	9.2	8.5	8.3
FIRE	11.0	13.7	14.2	11.8	15.9	16.6
Business Services	4.2	6.3	8.3	3.4	6.7	8.4
Health Services	2.3	3.3	3.2	9.2	14.5	14.5
Education, Private	0.1	0.1	0.3	0.7	0.9	1.0
Other Services	7.0	7.7	7.7	3.8	4.8	4.9
Construction	**10.1**	**6.7**	**6.8**	**6.8**	**5.2**	**5.3**
Manufacturing	**25.0**	**26.2**	**24.6**	**27.9**	**23.2**	**22.0**
Primary Industries	**13.5**	**8.1**	**7.1**	**9.5**	**4.0**	**3.8**
Business Sector	**100.0**	**100.0**	**100.0**	**100.0**	**100.0**	**100.0**
			HOURS SHARE (%)			
Services Industries	**57.4**	**65.0**	**66.3**	**61.6**	**69.8**	**71.5**
Transportation	6.8	7.0	6.8	3.7	4.2	4.3
Communications	1.5	1.4	1.1	1.6	1.2	1.4
Electric Utilities	0.8	0.8	0.7	0.6	0.5	0.4
Gas Utilities	0.1	0.2	0.1	0.3	0.2	0.1
Wholesale Trade	6.6	7.0	7.8	7.0	6.4	6.2
Retail Trade	14.3	15.0	13.6	17.4	17.8	17.2
FIRE	6.7	7.1	6.6	6.6	6.6	6.7
Business Services	5.5	8.3	11.1	4.2	7.6	9.5
Health Services	1.9	3.5	4.2	12.8	16.8	17.2
Education, Private	0.1	0.1	0.3	1.3	1.5	1.6
Other Services	13.0	14.7	14.0	6.0	6.9	6.9
Construction	**9.7**	**8.7**	**8.8**	**6.4**	**6.8**	**7.7**
Manufacturing	**23.8**	**19.2**	**19.4**	**24.9**	**18.7**	**16.7**
Primary Industries	**9.1**	**7.2**	**5.5**	**7.1**	**4.6**	**4.1**
Business Sector	**100.0**	**100.0**	**100.0**	**100.0**	**100.0**	**100.0**

Source: The KLEMS database from Ho, Rao and Tang (2003).

EMPLOYMENT

Canada

In 2001, the services sector accounted for 75.2 percent of all jobs in Canada, up from 71.2 percent in 1987 (Table 1). Manufacturing was second, accounting for 15.1 percent of all jobs, with construction and primary sectors accounting for 5.6 and 4.1 percent, respectively. Within the services sector, the retail trade industry was the single largest employer: it accounted for 16.1 percent of employment in the services sector and 12.1 percent of all jobs in Canada. Health care and social assistance was the second largest services employer with 10.2 percent of all jobs. Utilities were the smallest employer with 0.8 percent of Canadian jobs, although they contributed 2.7 percent of Canada's GDP in 2001.

United States

In 2001, the U.S. services sector was by far the largest employer in the United States with 79.4 percent of total employment, significantly higher than the Canadian share of 75.2 percent (Table 2). This share was up from 75.0 percent in 1987. The manufacturing sector was the second largest employer with 12.1 percent of all jobs, followed by construction (5.7 percent) and primary industries (2.8 percent). Within the services sector, the catchall services industry accounted for 31.2 percent of services jobs. The health services industry was the most important component of this, representing 7.5 percent of total employment in the U.S. economy in 2001, followed by business services (7.0 percent). Retail trade was the second largest employer, accounting for 17.0 percent of all jobs. The smallest employment share of the six major services industries was in wholesale trade with 4.7 percent of all jobs.

Canada-U.S. Comparison

Although the Canadian and U.S. services sectors account for 75-80 percent of total employment in both countries, the distribution of jobs among services sector industries differs in the two countries. The most notable difference is in the retail trade industry. In 2001, 17.0 percent of U.S. employees worked in that industry compared to only 12.1 percent in Canada. However, this is probably mostly due to a definitional difference: restaurants are included in retail trade in the United States but in accommodation and food services in Canada. On the other hand, the transportation and utilities category (the sum of transportation and warehousing and utilities in the Canadian classification scheme), employs relatively more persons in Canada than in the United States. This industry accounted for 5.1 percent of all jobs in the United States in 2001 compared to 6.0 percent in Canada. The Canadian FIRE industry employs relatively more persons than its U.S. counterpart: 5.8 percent in Canada compared to 5.7 percent in the United States. The wholesale trade industry was larger in the United States: it accounted for 3.7 percent of all jobs in Canada and 4.7 percent in the United States.

The U.S. government industry is larger than its Canadian public administration counterpart. Its employment share in 2001 was 15.7 percent, compared to 5.1 percent in Canada. This large discrepancy is probably the result of different industry definitions in the two countries, as already mentioned previously.

LABOUR PRODUCTIVITY LEVELS

Canada

Though it is the largest sector both in terms of real output and employment, the services sector has a labour productivity level (real output per worker) slightly below average. In 2001, the average worker in the services sector produced only 94.2 percent of the average real output per worker for the economy as a whole (Table 1). At the four-sector level, this represented the lowest relative productivity level. Construction was slightly ahead at 95.7 percent while manufacturing stood at 119.1 percent and primary industries reached 142.9 percent of the total economy average.

Two services industries did record labour productivity levels that were three times higher than the total economy average in 2001. The utilities industry, which accounted for 2.7 percent of GDP and 0.8 percent of employment, had a relative labour productivity level of 335.4 percent of the total economy average. Even this was exceeded by the FIRE industry which had a relative productivity level of 341.3 percent. At the other end of the spectrum, labour productivity was significantly lower in the accommodation and food services industry, where it stood at 37.0 percent of the total economy average.

Table 4 offers a different estimate of labour productivity levels, defined as gross output per hour worked. It compares business-sector services industries with the average for all business industries in Canada in 1981, 1995 and 2000, based on data from the Jorgenson project. Compared against the average for the economy as a whole, services industry productivity levels based on gross output (Table 4) are much lower than levels based on value added (Table 1). Based on gross output, in 2000, the average relative level for the entire business-sector services industry was only 60.0 percent of the average for the business sector as a whole, compared to 107.4 percent for primary industries and 162.1 percent for manufacturing. In other words, the level of labour productivity in manufacturing was 2.7 times greater than that in business-sector services.

TABLE 4

LABOUR PRODUCTIVITY AND CAPITAL INPUT INTENSITY LEVELS IN CANADIAN AND U.S. BUSINESS-SECTOR INDUSTRIES

	CANADA			UNITED STATES		
	1981	1995	2000	1981	1995	2000
	LABOUR PRODUCTIVITY LEVEL (AVERAGE FOR BUSINESS SECTOR=100)					
Services Industries	**64.9**	**60.7**	**60.0**	**82.4**	**75.5**	**71.4**
Transportation	69.9	68.0	64.0	94.4	87.5	77.1
Communications	91.0	134.8	161.7	153.1	191.9	178.0
Electric Utilities	280.1	275.2	244.6	311.4	343.3	382.9
Gas Utilities	236.7	164.5	172.2	632.3	365.9	362.4
Wholesale Trade	54.0	64.0	61.1	61.9	80.8	79.7
Retail Trade	34.7	31.3	34.2	44.0	40.3	39.4
FIRE	137.2	138.1	143.7	162.4	176.9	174.4
Business Services	52.7	48.6	48.8	75.0	60.7	56.5
Health Services	89.4	51.8	41.1	76.6	62.3	56.0
Education, Private	112.2	44.2	49.6	65.4	52.9	43.7
Other Services	47.7	38.6	40.1	67.8	62.5	59.9
Construction	**107.7**	**78.7**	**70.5**	**116.2**	**86.0**	**73.4**
Manufacturing	**146.9**	**166.9**	**162.1**	**122.2**	**153.3**	**170.8**
Primary Industries	**80.6**	**93.7**	**107.4**	**79.2**	**85.2**	**84.4**
	CAPITAL INPUT INTENSITY LEVEL (AVERAGE FOR BUSINESS SECTOR=100)					
Services Industries	**69.1**	**72.5**	**62.9**	**106.5**	**111.3**	**113.7**
Transportation	63.3	57.8	54.9	139.9	78.9	78.5
Communications	204.4	292.0	355.6	265.0	428.3	429.8
Electric Utilities	996.4	920.2	703.6	971.9	1072.0	1056.7
Gas Utilities	676.9	580.0	653.5	419.6	492.2	576.1
Wholesale Trade	63.2	60.5	51.4	44.6	86.6	117.6
Retail Trade	16.9	18.5	18.9	29.3	34.3	34.6
FIRE	198.2	236.2	214.4	430.8	476.5	458.8
Business Services	10.6	25.2	33.9	68.5	76.2	98.7
Health Services	61.1	31.5	21.4	49.1	53.8	59.1
Education, Private	5.0	9.7	4.3	11.2	9.3	8.7
Other Services	23.0	29.2	26.1	70.8	67.7	62.3
Construction	**30.6**	**28.2**	**23.0**	**54.1**	**31.3**	**31.3**
Manufacturing	**125.3**	**123.0**	**105.6**	**116.6**	**133.8**	**139.5**
Primary Industries	**175.0**	**176.3**	**208.5**	**122.8**	**123.7**	**115.5**
	CORRELATION BETWEEN LABOUR PRODUCTIVITY AND CAPITAL INTENSITY LEVELS					
Correlation Coefficient	0.91	0.91	0.88	0.63	0.88	0.93

Notes: Government sector is excluded. Labour productivity is gross output per hour worked and capital intensity is capital input per hour worked (capital including machinery and equipment (M&E), structure, land and inventories).

Source: KLEMS database from Ho, Rao and Tang (2003).

The differences between the gross output and GDP-based measures of relative labour productivity levels are largely due to differences in the intermediate input intensity among industries. For example, the intensity of intermediate inputs in the manufacturing sector in 2000 was almost five times that in business-sector services (Table 5). It should be noted that the labour productivity level comparisons across industries are more meaningful when based on value added per worker than on gross output per worker because of this difference in the intensity of intermediate input use.

Within the business-sector services industries, there was large variation in relative productivity levels. Certain services sectors had well above average levels, including electric utilities (244.6 percent of the business sector average), gas utilities (172.2 percent), communications (161.7 percent), and FIRE (143.7 percent). On the other hand, a number of industries had well below average productivity, including retail trade (34.2 percent), other services (40.1 percent), health services (41.1 percent), business services (48.8 percent) and private education (49.6 percent).

Much of the variation in relative labour productivity levels by industry can be explained by differences in degrees of capital intensity (Table 4). Rates of return on capital tend toward equalization across industries. Consequently,

TABLE 5

INTERMEDIATE INPUT INTENSITY IN CANADIAN AND U.S. BUSINESS-SECTOR INDUSTRIES (AVERAGE FOR BUSINESS SECTOR=100 IN EACH YEAR FOR EACH COUNTRY)

	CANADA			UNITED STATES		
	1981	1995	2000	1981	1995	2000
Services Industries	**41.7**	**41.3**	**42.5**	**55.4**	**52.6**	**51.8**
Transportation	63.7	59.4	55.2	85.9	80.2	70.4
Communications	46.8	69.2	74.0	121.1	153.5	157.1
Electric Utilities	60.1	94.1	95.6	201.5	220.4	230.4
Gas Utilities	46.7	38.6	40.6	733.5	532.2	494.3
Wholesale Trade	37.8	41.8	40.0	50.4	53.9	53.0
Retail Trade	22.7	21.1	24.1	32.4	31.4	29.8
FIRE	94.1	101.8	112.0	92.4	113.3	120.9
Business Services	25.5	29.2	32.0	37.9	32.0	36.0
Health Services	26.8	19.8	18.7	40.1	37.2	36.1
Education, Private	89.2	38.0	26.7	42.3	40.1	34.9
Other Services	32.6	30.4	33.4	49.4	51.2	51.4
Construction	**116.0**	**84.5**	**75.2**	**108.6**	**89.7**	**81.4**
Manufacturing	**167.9**	**201.2**	**197.3**	**144.5**	**175.4**	**189.8**
Primary Industries	**74.4**	**73.0**	**85.0**	**91.5**	**82.3**	**77.0**

Note: Intermediate input intensity is defined as intermediate goods per hour worked.
Source: KLEMS database from Ho, Rao and Tang (2003).

output per worker must be greater in capital-intensive than in non-capital intensive industries to provide a competitive return on the greater amount of capital invested in the industry. It is no surprise that electric utilities, the most capital-intensive industry, have the highest productivity level. Indeed, in 2000, the correlation coefficient between labour productivity, based on gross output and capital intensity levels, was a high 0.88.[6]

United States

The relative productivity level of the U.S. services sector is similar to that of Canada. The services sector had slightly below average labour productivity: 97.4 percent of the level for the total economy in 2001 (Table 2). The manufacturing sector was the most productive with a relative labour productivity level of 130.6 percent, followed by the primary sector (103.3 percent). Labour productivity in the construction sector was well below average (69.7 percent). Of the six major industries in the services sector in 2001, FIRE had by far the highest level of labour productivity at 344.2 percent of the economy average and the retail trade industry had the lowest at 59.4 percent.

Table 4 is based on data from the Jorgenson project. It provides estimates of U.S. labour productivity levels in terms of gross output per hour worked for business-sector services industries relative to the average for the business sector as a whole in the years 1981, 1995 and 2000. In contrast to relative productivity levels based on value added, business-sector services industries tended to have much lower relative productivity levels than do goods industries. The average relative level for the total services sector in 2000 was only 71.4 percent of the average for the business sector. This compared to 170.8 percent for manufacturing though it was still higher than the 60.0 percent recorded in Canada. Once again, as expected, the two measures of relative labour productivity are quite different across industries because of large differences in intensities in intermediate inputs (Table 5).

Within business-sector services industries, there were again large variations in relative productivity levels (Table 4). Certain services industries had levels that were well above average. These included electric utilities (382.9 percent of the average for the business sector), gas utilities (362.4 percent), communications (178.0 percent), and FIRE (174.4 percent). On the other hand industries that were well below average levels included retail trade (39.4 percent), private education (43.7 percent), health services (56.0 percent), business services (56.5 percent), and other services (59.9 percent).

Again, much of the variation by industry in relative labour productivity levels can be explained by differences in the degree of capital intensity. In 2000, the correlation coefficient between labour productivity and capital intensity levels for the United States was 0.93 (Table 4).[7]

TABLE 6

AVERAGE HOURLY LABOUR COMPENSATION IN CANADIAN AND U.S. BUSINESS-SECTOR INDUSTRIES (AVERAGE FOR BUSINESS SECTOR=100 IN EACH YEAR FOR EACH COUNTRY)

	CANADA			UNITED STATES		
	1981	1995	2000	1981	1995	2000
Services Industries	**104.5**	**95.0**	**104.2**	**78.7**	**101.3**	**106.5**
Transportation	97.5	86.0	94.8	109.5	87.8	87.4
Communications	115.3	107.2	104.8	102.0	97.9	125.1
Electric Utilities	155.1	143.0	136.6	140.7	168.5	237.5
Gas Utilities	130.4	105.4	99.4	106.5	85.4	116.6
Wholesale Trade	100.1	102.0	107.7	107.8	117.4	128.7
Retail Trade	61.8	58.0	67.0	55.8	63.2	66.5
FIRE	109.4	121.7	155.5	89.1	137.8	159.4
Business Services	94.8	84.6	96.3	72.3	90.4	95.9
Health Services	189.7	166.0	142.6	78.2	113.4	112.7
Education, Private	169.9	146.8	117.0	66.5	76.5	76.7
Other Services	52.5	55.1	61.2	45.4	53.3	54.7
Construction	**109.3**	**95.4**	**97.5**	**122.5**	**102.7**	**92.4**
Manufacturing	**107.7**	**106.9**	**112.4**	**111.5**	**120.8**	**132.9**
Primary Industries	**78.5**	**102.8**	**85.9**	**87.2**	**75.2**	**68.2**

Note: It is assumed that the self-employed earn the same hourly compensation as paid workers.
Source: KLEMS database from Ho, Rao and Tang (2003).

Canada-U.S. Comparisons

Relative Productivity Levels within a Country

According to Tables 1 and 2, the U.S. services sector had slightly higher labour productivity than the Canadian services sector relative to the total economy. This relationship is not necessarily reflected in individual services industries. In 2001, for the combined transportation and utilities industry, Canada had a relative labour productivity level of 125.4 percent compared to a 165.9 percent in the United States.[8] The relative labour productivity level in FIRE was also higher in the United States: 341.3 percent of the total economy average in Canada and 355.1 percent in the United States.

U.S. trade industries, were relatively more productive than their Canadian counterparts in 2001. Wholesale trade industries' relative productivity level in the United States was 165.8 percent of the total economy average compared to 157.4 percent in Canada. Retail trade industries' labour productivity level was well below average in both countries but it was relatively higher in the United States, at 59.6 percent of the total economy average compared to 45.4 percent in Canada. The remaining services industries had below average labour productivity levels, as is reflected by a level of 65.8 percent in the United States. A similar level characterized all the other Canadian services industries not previously noted, with the exception of information and cultural industries.

Relative Productivity Levels across Countries

Labour productivity levels across countries cannot be compared by converting productivity levels expressed in domestic currencies into a common currency at the market exchange rate. Instead, it is necessary to use purchasing power parity (PPP) exchange rates. However, the GDP PPP is not appropriate as such a PPP may not equalize the price of goods produced in a particular industry across countries. Rather PPPs must be estimated on an industry basis, which is an onerous task. For this reason, there are few reliable estimates of labour productivity levels of Canadian services industries relative to comparable U.S. industries.

Using data from the Jorgenson project, Table 7 estimates labour productivity levels (value added per hour worked) in 2000 for Canadian business-sector

TABLE 7

LABOUR PRODUCTIVITY LEVELS IN CANADIAN INDUSTRIES RELATIVE TO THE UNITED STATES, 2000 (UNITED STATES=100)

INDUSTRY	RELATIVE LABOUR PRODUCTIVITY LEVEL
Services Industries	**83.8**
Transportation	72.7
Communications	135.6
Electric Utilities	96.0
Gas Utilities	115.0
Wholesale Trade	71.3
Retail Trade	98.9
FIRE	63.9
Business Services	90.8
Health Services	99.7
Education, Private	169.1
Other Services	84.1
Construction	**144.9**
Manufacturing	**65.8**
Primary Industries	**86.7**
Business Sector	**84.4**

Notes: Government sector is excluded. Labour productivity is defined as real value added per hour worked, where value added is derived from gross output and intermediate input. For services, construction, and primary industries, industry level value added PPPs in 2000 are derived from the implicit value added PPPs in 1993 from Lee and Tang (2000), using value added deflators from Canada and the United States. Health services and education are mostly private in the United States, while in Canada they are mostly public. The relative labour productivity levels for the manufacturing and business sectors are from Rao, Tang and Wang (2003).

Source: KLEMS database from Ho, Rao and Tang (2003).

services industries relative to their U.S. counterparts. Those estimates are based on PPPs for the specific services industries.

In 2000, the average level of labour productivity for all business-sector services in Canada was 83.8 percent of the U.S. level. The gap in labour productivity is consistent with Canada's lower levels of human capital, lower research and development (R&D) intensity and lower share of ICT capital in total capital (Tables 8, 9 and 10). Even so, this is markedly superior to Canada's manufacturing sector which attained only 65.8 percent of the U.S. level. However, services stood lower than primary industries at 86.7 percent of the U.S. level and construction, which recorded an impressive 144.9 percent of the U.S. level.

Among business-sector services industries, labour productivity levels in three Canadian industries exceeded their U.S. counterparts: private education (169.1 percent of the U.S. level), communications (135.6 percent) and gas utilities (115.0 percent). Private health services had the same labour productivity level in both countries and retail trade was almost identical (98.9 percent). On the other hand, the level of labour productivity in Canada's FIRE industry was only 63.9 percent of the U.S. level. For wholesale trade it was 71.3 percent and 72.7 percent for transportation.[9]

TABLE 8

R&D INTENSITY AND DISTRIBUTION

	CANADA			UNITED STATES		
INDUSTRY	1987	1996	1999	1987	1996	1999
	R&D INTENSITY					
Total Services*	**0.51**	**0.73**	**0.72**	**0.35**	**0.69**	**1.16**
Wholesale and Retail Trade; Repairs	0.20	0.67	0.69		0.49	1.25
Transport and Storage	0.09	0.03	0.05		0.09	0.15
Post and Telecommunications	0.75	0.68	0.35		1.52	
Financial Intermediation	0.59	0.41	0.30		0.23	0.21
Real Estate, Renting and Business Activities	0.80	1.07	1.11			
Electricity, Gas and Water Supply	**1.32**	**0.93**	**0.70**	**0.19**	**0.17**	**0.07**
Construction	**0.01**	**0.07**	**0.06**		**0.09**	**0.16**
Manufacturing	**3.05**	**3.62**	**3.66**	**9.49**	**8.89**	**8.27**
	R&D DISTRIBUTION					
Total Services*	**24.89**	**30.29**	**28.96**	**8.51**	**18.63**	**34.36**
Wholesale and Retail Trade; Repairs	2.88	7.09	7.29		4.42	12.60
Transport and Storage	0.49	0.11	0.24		0.15	0.14
Post and Telecommunications	2.68	1.98	0.86		2.84	
Financial Intermediation	4.39	2.71	1.90		0.90	2.02
Real Estate, Renting and Business Activities	14.45	18.39	18.67			
Electricity, Gas and Water Supply	**5.03**	**2.91**	**1.61**	**0.29**	**0.24**	**0.08**
Construction	**0.09**	**0.32**	**0.25**		**0.20**	**0.12**
Manufacturing	**67.27**	**62.95**	**67.33**	**91.49**	**80.84**	**64.95**

Notes: R&D intensity is defined as R&D expenditure as percentage of value added.
*Total services here includes only the selected services industries in the table.

Sources: OECD BERD and STAN databases.

TABLE 9

HOURS WORKED BY PERSONS WITH A UNIVERSITY DEGREE AND ABOVE (PERCENT OF TOTAL HOURS WORKED)

	CANADA			UNITED STATES		
	1981	1995	2000	1981	1995	2000
Services Industries	**9.86**	**16.97**	**19.48**	**21.92**	**28.15**	**30.34**
Transportation	3.75	6.75	7.24	10.04	16.93	16.99
Communications	10.04	21.30	21.97	18.89	32.80	35.13
Electric Utilities	13.75	20.41	20.74	17.39	28.72	31.66
Gas Utilities	10.15	18.76	19.15	17.05	25.76	28.38
Wholesale Trade	6.12	13.50	14.42	21.03	25.08	24.89
Retail Trade	4.15	8.41	9.26	11.97	13.90	15.42
FIRE	13.43	24.39	25.49	27.47	39.49	41.89
Business Services	33.16	42.20	42.47	37.13	37.60	38.61
Health Services	40.23	31.73	36.85	34.76	40.21	42.80
Education, Private	32.53	44.29	53.66	54.07	63.46	65.09
Other Services	4.69	10.00	11.06	9.73	15.34	17.75
Construction	**4.13**	**5.66**	**6.14**	**8.91**	**10.94**	**10.32**
Manufacturing	**6.49**	**10.98**	**11.78**	**13.17**	**20.01**	**21.61**
Primary Industries	**4.83**	**7.53**	**9.16**	**10.57**	**18.25**	**14.33**
Business Sector	**8.05**	**14.17**	**16.25**	**18.10**	**24.99**	**26.69**

Source: KLEMS database from Ho, Rao and Tang (2003).

TABLE 10

ICT CAPITAL INPUT AS A PERCENTAGE OF TOTAL CAPITAL INPUT (PERCENT)

	CANADA			UNITED STATES		
INDUSTRY	1981	1995	2000	1981	1995	2000
Services Industries	**2.3**	**9.8**	**19.0**	**3.6**	**16.3**	**32.2**
Transportation	1.5	6.8	13.2	2.1	11.3	23.1
Communications	33.3	43.9	51.0	51.5	53.6	60.1
Electric Utilities	0.5	2.2	6.5	1.1	5.9	8.6
Gas Utilities	0.1	1.9	6.5	2.7	16.5	21.1
Wholesale Trade	0.4	5.8	13.8	4.6	31.6	54.0
Retail Trade	0.5	7.5	21.5	0.9	8.9	19.3
FIRE	0.9	6.5	14.6	1.3	9.8	23.6
Business Services	1.7	17.9	30.9	6.8	33.1	58.5
Health Services, Private	0.6	5.4	9.4	1.9	14.7	31.4
Education, Private	5.1	23.4	38.4	2.8	11.7	25.5
Other Services	1.4	10.7	19.4	2.1	6.4	12.8
Construction	**0.2**	**2.5**	**5.5**	**0.1**	**6.0**	**13.7**
Manufacturing	**0.5**	**3.5**	**6.3**	**1.5**	**9.0**	**18.5**
Primary Industries	**0.2**	**0.5**	**1.1**	**0.5**	**2.3**	**4.6**
Business Sector	**1.3**	**6.5**	**12.5**	**2.7**	**13.7**	**27.8**

Notes: Capital input or services equals capital stock multiplied by its user cost. Total capital includes M&E, structure, land and inventories.

Source: KLEMS database from Ho, Rao and Tang (2003).

PRODUCTIVITY GROWTH IN THE BUSINESS-SECTOR COMPONENT OF SERVICES IN CANADA AND THE UNITED STATES

NEXT WE TURN OUR ATTENTION TO the business-sector component of the services sector.[10] According to Table 11, between 1981 and 1995, labour productivity growth in Canadian business-sector services, based on gross output and hours worked, was 1.4 percent per year. This was below manufacturing (2.8 percent) and primary industries (2.9 percent), but above construction (–0.4 percent). U.S. business-sector services experienced even weaker productivity growth at a modest 0.7 percent annual rate, also below that in manufacturing and primary industries, but better than in construction. Within Canadian business-sector services, industries such as communications and wholesale trade did very well with average annual labour productivity growth rates of 4.7 percent and 3.1 percent respectively in 1981-1995. Others, of course, did poorly. The private education, health services and gas utilities industries suffered declines in labour productivity of 4.8 percent, 2.1 percent and 0.8 percent per year, respectively.[11]

TABLE 11

LABOUR PRODUCTIVITY GROWTH IN BUSINESS-SECTOR INDUSTRIES IN CANADA AND THE UNITED STATES (COMPOUND AVERAGE ANNUAL GROWTH RATES)

	CANADA			UNITED STATES		
INDUSTRY	1981-1995	1995-2000	DIFFERENCE	1981-1995	1995-2000	DIFFERENCE
Services Industries	**1.37**	**2.29**	**0.92**	**0.70**	**1.92**	**1.22**
Transportation	1.64	1.33	–0.31	0.79	0.50	–0.29
Communications	4.65	6.18	1.53	2.94	1.54	–1.40
Electric Utilities	1.71	0.17	–1.54	2.02	5.22	3.20
Gas Utilities	–0.76	3.45	4.21	–2.58	2.85	5.43
Wholesale Trade	3.06	1.59	–1.47	3.23	2.78	–0.45
Retail Trade	1.12	4.28	3.16	0.71	2.59	1.88
FIRE	1.88	3.33	1.45	1.94	2.75	0.81
Business Services	1.26	2.61	1.35	–0.19	1.62	1.81
Health Services	–2.06	–2.11	–0.05	–0.16	0.93	1.09
Education, Private	–4.81	4.81	9.62	–0.19	–0.78	–0.59
Other Services	0.34	3.27	2.93	0.74	2.20	1.46
Construction	**–0.40**	**0.33**	**0.73**	**–0.83**	**–0.14**	**0.69**
Manufacturing	**2.75**	**1.95**	**–0.80**	**2.94**	**5.20**	**2.26**
Primary Industries	**2.92**	**5.26**	**2.34**	**1.85**	**2.86**	**1.01**
Business Sector	**1.44**	**1.93**	**0.49**	**1.30**	**2.31**	**1.01**

Notes: FIRE refers to finance, insurance and real estate, and includes leasing and management services. Labour productivity is defined as gross output per hour worked for industries and value added per hour worked for the business sector.

Source: KLEMS database from Ho, Rao and Tang (2003).

Between 1995 and 2000, labour productivity growth in business-sector services industries improved in both Canada and the United States. In Canada, average annual growth increased to 2.3 percent, an acceleration of 0.9 points over the 1981-1995 period (Table 11). This was now better than that experienced in manufacturing (2.0 percent). Labour productivity growth in U.S. business-sector services improved even more, increasing from 1.2 to 1.9 percent, but this advance was not sufficient to catch up to its Canadian counterpart (Exhibit 1). In Canada, the communications industry continued to experience the most rapid labour productivity growth (6.2 percent), followed by private education (4.8 percent) and retail trade (4.3 percent). Health services continued to suffer a decline in labour productivity (–2.1 percent).

Exhibit 2 provides information on the number of business-sector industries that experienced higher labour and multifactor productivity growth in Canada than in the United States in the 1981-95 and 1995-2000 periods. It also shows the number of sectors that experienced greater acceleration between periods and absolute improvement in productivity growth rates between periods.

In terms of labour productivity, 8 out of 11 business-sector services industries experienced higher growth in Canada than in the United States in the 1995-2000 period, up from 5 in the 1981-95 period. This pattern was consistent with overall faster growth in total business-sector services labour productivity.

EXHIBIT 1

LABOUR PRODUCTIVITY GROWTH IN BUSINESS-SECTOR SERVICES INDUSTRIES IN CANADA AND THE UNITED STATES, 1981-1995 AND 1995-2000 (COMPOUND AVERAGE ANNUAL GROWTH RATES)

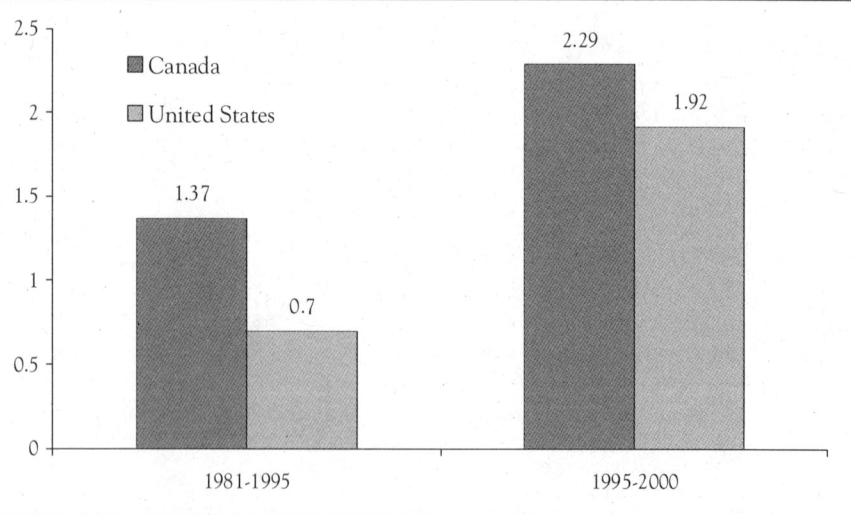

Source: Table 11.

EXHIBIT 2

COMPARISON OF PRODUCTIVITY GROWTH IN BUSINESS-SECTOR SERVICES INDUSTRIES IN CANADA AND THE UNITED STATES

	NO. OF INDUSTRIES (OUT OF 11) WHERE GROWTH IN CANADA EXCEEDED U.S.			INDUSTRIES WITH ABSOLUTE IMPROVEMENT BETWEEN 1981-1995 AND 1995-2000	
	1981-1995	1995-2000	CHANGE 1995-2000 TO 1981-1995	CANADA	U.S.
Labour Productivity	5	8	5	7	7
Multifactor Productivity	6	8	8	8	5

Sources: Table 11 for labour productivity and Table 18 for multifactor productivity.

However, only 5 business-sector services industries had a larger improvement in labour productivity growth between the 1981-95 and 1995-2000 periods in Canada than in the United States. In both countries, there were 7 business-sector services industries that enjoyed an absolute improvement or acceleration in labour productivity growth between periods.

Canada did somewhat better relative to the United States in terms of multifactor productivity. While the number of business-sector services industries that experienced faster multifactor productivity growth in Canada than in the United States was the same or slightly better in the 1981-1995 and 1995-2000 periods, with respect to labour productivity growth (6 and 8 respectively), 8 out of 11 business-sector services industries in Canada had a larger improvement in multifactor productivity growth between periods. Equally, 8 Canadian business-sector services industries experienced faster multifactor productivity growth in the 1995-2000 period relative to the 1981-95 period, compared to only 5 in the United States.

Table 12 provides information on the contribution by industry to labour productivity acceleration in total business-sector services in Canada and the United States between 1981-95 and 1995-2000. In Canada, the largest contribution to the acceleration came from retail trade, which accounted for 44.8 percent of the acceleration, other services (43.4 percent), business services (16.7 percent) and FIRE (9.0 percent). In the United States, the largest industry contribution to acceleration was again from retail trade (44.3 percent), followed by health services (25.7 percent), business services (21.1 percent) and other services (14.0 percent).

TABLE 12

CONTRIBUTION BY INDUSTRY TO THE BUSINESS-SECTOR SERVICES LABOUR PRODUCTIVITY GROWTH ACCELERATION

	CANADA			UNITED STATES		
INDUSTRY	1981-1995	1995-2000	DIFFERENCE	1981-1995	1995-2000	DIFFERENCE
SERVICES INDUSTRIES						
Labour Productivity Growth (percent)	1.37	2.29	0.92	0.70	1.92	1.22
Contribution Distribution (percentage points)						
Transportation	14.4	5.1	–2.7	5.3	1.6	–1.5
Communications	8.6	4.2	0.4	7.2	1.5	–3.3
Electric Utilities	1.7	0.1	–1.3	2.2	1.7	1.3
Gas Utilities	–0.1	0.2	0.6	–1.0	0.3	1.5
Wholesale Trade	26.9	6.6	–10.6	38.2	13.2	–7.8
Retail Trade	21.7	34.2	44.8	22.5	34.3	44.3
FIRE	17.3	12.8	9.0	23.7	14.0	5.9
Business Services	11.3	14.2	16.7	–2.0	10.5	21.1
Health Services	–7.3	–4.5	–2.1	–4.2	12.0	25.7
Education, Private	–0.7	0.7	1.9	–0.5	–0.9	–1.3
Other Services	6.2	26.3	43.4	8.7	11.6	14.0
Total	**100.0**	**100.0**	**100.0**	**100.0**	**100.0**	**100.0**

Notes: Labour productivity is gross output per hour worked. FIRE refers to finance, insurance and real estate, and includes leasing and management services. An industry's contribution is its labour productivity growth multiplied by its average hours share in total services hours.

Source: KLEMS database from Ho, Rao and Tang (2003).

The difference between the two countries in acceleration of labour productivity growth in business-sector services in the post-1995 period (0.3 points greater in the United States) was entirely due to the growing adverse impact of inter-industry shifts in hours among business-sector services industries on the aggregate labour productivity growth in Canadian business-sector services (Table 13). The negative impact increased from –0.1 percent during the 1981-1995 period to –0.4 percent in the post-1995 period. On the other hand, in the United States, the negative impact of the employment shifts on aggregate labour productivity growth was smaller in the latter half of the 1990s, compared to the 1981-1995 period. In other words, the Canada-U.S. productivity growth gap during the 1995-2000 period would have increased from 0.4 percent to 0.6 percent without these employment shifts.

TABLE 13

DECOMPOSITION OF LABOUR PRODUCTIVITY IN TOTAL BUSINESS-SECTOR SERVICES IN CANADA AND THE UNITED STATES

	1981-1995	1995-2000	DIFFERENCES
CANADA			
Annual Labour Productivity Growth Rate	**1.37**	**2.29**	**0.92**
Pure Labour Productivity Growth Effect	1.43	2.64	1.21
Level Effect from Change in Relative Size	–0.06	–0.35	–0.29
UNITED STATES			
Annual Labour Productivity Growth Rate	**0.70**	**1.92**	**1.22**
Pure Labour Productivity Growth Effect	1.00	2.04	1.04
Level Effect from Change in Relative Size	–0.30	–0.12	0.18

Notes: The decomposition is based on a technique drawn from Tang and Wang (2004). An aggregate labour productivity growth can be generally decomposed into three components: the pure labour productivity effect from growth in labour productivity of individual services industries; the relative change size effect from the change in relative hours worked share among services industries; and the interaction term from the first two effects. The level effect in this table includes the relative change size effect and the interaction term. The results are calculated on the basis of 11 services industries as shown in Table 12.

Source: KLEMS database from Ho, Rao and Tang (2003).

SOURCES OF REAL OUTPUT AND LABOUR PRODUCTIVITY GROWTH IN CANADIAN AND U.S. BUSINESS-SECTOR SERVICES INDUSTRIES

SOURCES OF GROSS OUTPUT GROWTH IN CANADIAN AND U.S. BUSINESS-SECTOR SERVICES INDUSTRIES

TABLE 14 LOOKS AT FOUR MAJOR INDUSTRY GROUPINGS in the business sector and 11 business-sector services industries in Canada and the United States over the 1981-95 period, in terms of the average annual growth rate of gross output, percentage point contributions to the growth rate from multifactor productivity (MFP), ICT and non-ICT capital, university and non-university labour and intermediate goods. Table 15 provides estimates for the same categories over the 1995-2000 period. The contributions for capital, labour and intermediate goods are obtained by weighting the growth rate of each variable by its share of total income. MFP is obtained as a residual, being the difference between output growth and input growth. This procedure allows for the identification of what each variable has contributed to gross output growth during a period, based on the assumptions of neoclassical growth accounting.[12] These estimates have been developed as part of the Jorgenson project on the impact of ICT on productivity. The methodology for the estimates is developed in Ho, Rao and Tang (2003) and is described in the appendix to this study.

The following section describes trends in the gross output of business-sector services and its sources in Canada and compares them for each period to other major sectors in Canada and the United States. The four major sectors compared are business-sector services,[13] construction, manufacturing and primary industries.

In Canada, the gross output of business-sector services grew at an average annual rate of 3.4 percent between 1981 and 1995 (Table 14). This was above that for construction (–0.1 percent), manufacturing (2.3 percent) and primary industries (2.3 percent). It was also slightly higher than the U.S. business-sector services industry growth rate of 3.3 percent.

Within the Canadian business-sector services industry, services achieved the highest average annual gross output growth rate at 5.3 percent, followed closely by communications (5.0 percent), and wholesale trade (4.6 percent). The weakest growth occurred in the private education industry (1.8 percent). Gross output growth was faster in Canada than in the United States in only 4 of 11 business-sector services industries (communications, electric utilities, gas utilities and wholesale trade) despite the overall faster total business-sector services growth. The largest difference between growth rates in the two countries was in the gas utilities industry, where gross output advanced 2.3 percent per year in Canada, compared to a 3.7 percent decline in the United States.

Gross output growth was much stronger in the 1995-2000 period than in the 1981-1995 period in both Canada and the United States (Table 15). All four major industry sectors and 9 of the 11 business-sector services industries experienced faster growth in both countries. The exceptions were electric utilities and gas utilities in Canada and transportation and wholesale trade in the United States. Gross output growth in Canada was again faster in the total business-sector services (5.8 percent per year) than in the other three major sectors: manufacturing (5.3 percent), construction (3.6 percent) and primary industries (3.2 percent). This was also the situation in the United States. Canadian business-sector services continued to outpace those in the United States in 1995-2000, with the annual growth differential rising to 1.1 percentage points per year from only 0.1 points in 1981-95. Eight of eleven business-sector services industries experienced faster output growth in Canada than in the United States, the exceptions being communications, electric utilities and FIRE. The private education industry experienced massive output growth between 1995 and 2000 in Canada, with output rising 22.4 percent per year. At the other end of the spectrum, the gross output of electric utilities only grew 0.7 percent.

TABLE 14

SOURCES OF GROSS OUTPUT GROWTH IN CANADIAN AND U.S. BUSINESS-SECTOR INDUSTRIES, 1981-1995

INDUSTRY	GROSS OUTPUT (AVERAGE ANNUAL GROWTH RATES, PERCENT)	CONTRIBUTIONS (PERCENTAGE POINTS)					
		MFP	ICT CAPITAL	NON-ICT CAPITAL	UNIVERSITY LABOUR	NON-UNIVERSITY LABOUR	INTERMEDIATE INPUT
CANADA							
Total Services Industry	**3.36**	**0.09**	**0.33**	**0.59**	**0.48**	**0.56**	**1.31**
Transportation	2.90	0.87	0.10	0.24	0.15	0.38	1.16
Communications	5.04	1.51	1.23	0.70	0.33	0.06	1.22
Electric Utilities	2.69	0.11	0.41	0.74	0.16	0.16	1.10
Gas Utilities	2.30	–1.28	0.29	1.96	0.31	0.55	0.47
Wholesale Trade	4.60	1.67	0.17	0.38	0.45	0.63	1.31
Retail Trade	2.54	0.18	0.14	0.32	0.29	0.74	0.86
FIRE	3.38	–0.21	0.37	1.07	0.39	0.23	1.51
Business Services	5.27	–1.14	0.59	0.85	1.79	1.17	2.01
Health Services	3.35	–0.77	0.12	0.24	1.10	1.52	1.13
Education, Private	1.76	–2.74	0.35	0.12	1.72	1.08	1.23
Other Services	2.32	–0.88	0.39	0.42	0.30	0.74	1.36
Construction	**–0.12**	**–0.33**	**0.03**	**0.08**	**0.05**	**0.13**	**–0.08**
Manufacturing	**2.34**	**0.41**	**0.06**	**0.09**	**0.08**	**–0.07**	**1.77**
Primary Industries	**2.34**	**1.36**	**0.01**	**0.45**	**0.08**	**–0.05**	**0.48**
Business Sector	**2.55**	**0.55**	**0.34**	**0.70**	**0.51**	**0.45**	
UNITED STATES							
Total Services Industry	**3.30**	**–0.20**	**0.46**	**0.60**	**0.61**	**0.54**	**1.29**
Transportation	3.40	0.59	0.12	–0.06	0.45	0.70	1.60
Communications	2.63	–0.11	0.87	0.73	0.29	–0.25	1.11
Electric Utilities	1.78	0.13	0.29	0.68	0.16	–0.12	0.64
Gas Utilities	–3.67	–2.33	0.23	0.09	0.04	–0.09	–1.61
Wholesale Trade	4.33	1.40	0.76	0.53	0.36	0.34	0.95
Retail Trade	2.55	–0.16	0.18	0.38	0.28	0.71	1.17
FIRE	3.69	–0.19	0.58	1.22	0.49	0.09	1.50
Business Services	5.78	–0.45	1.31	0.36	1.36	1.57	1.63
Health Services	3.50	–0.99	0.35	0.54	1.29	0.96	1.35
Education, Private	2.60	–1.06	0.04	0.06	1.74	0.25	1.58
Other Services	3.43	–0.17	0.11	0.52	0.34	0.83	1.80
Construction	**1.33**	**–0.74**	**0.03**	**–0.03**	**0.21**	**0.81**	**1.06**
Manufacturing	**2.61**	**0.92**	**0.13**	**0.15**	**0.15**	**–0.10**	**1.36**
Primary Industries	**0.47**	**1.00**	**0.05**	**0.15**	**0.13**	**–0.31**	**–0.54**
Business Sector	**3.00**	**0.36**	**0.57**	**0.76**	**0.77**	**0.56**	

Note: The gross output and the multifactor productivity (MFP) columns show the growth rates and the five columns of input contributions indicate contributions to growth, defined as the growth rates multiplied by the output share weights.

Source: KLEMS database from Ho, Rao and Tang (2003).

TABLE 15

SOURCES OF GROSS OUTPUT GROWTH IN CANADIAN AND U.S. BUSINESS-SECTOR INDUSTRIES, 1995-2000

INDUSTRY	GROSS OUTPUT (AVERAGE ANNUAL GROWTH RATES, PERCENT)	CONTRIBUTIONS (PERCENTAGE POINTS)					
		MFP	ICT CAPITAL	NON-ICT CAPITAL	UNIVER-SITY LABOUR	NON-UNIVER-SITY LABOUR	INTER-MEDIATE INPUT
CANADA							
Total Services Industry	**5.75**	**0.73**	**0.50**	**0.45**	**0.76**	**0.87**	**2.44**
Transportation	3.78	0.39	0.24	0.65	0.13	0.81	1.55
Communications	5.69	1.71	2.04	0.97	0.01	−0.05	1.01
Electric Utilities	0.67	0.80	0.45	−1.31	0.03	0.06	0.64
Gas Utilities	0.99	−0.95	0.69	1.61	−0.10	−0.34	0.07
Wholesale Trade	6.71	0.85	0.38	0.57	0.56	1.88	2.46
Retail Trade	5.50	1.86	0.39	0.39	0.20	0.46	2.20
FIRE	4.99	0.96	0.59	0.46	0.25	0.32	2.41
Business Services	11.37	0.15	0.65	1.05	2.68	2.20	4.64
Health Services	4.55	−3.78	0.09	0.15	5.00	1.23	1.85
Education, Private	22.35	4.33	0.12	0.03	8.84	4.07	4.96
Other Services	5.38	0.97	0.32	0.19	0.25	0.77	2.88
Construction	**3.62**	**0.19**	**0.04**	**0.16**	**0.14**	**1.11**	**1.97**
Manufacturing	**5.26**	**0.48**	**0.10**	**0.46**	**0.13**	**0.52**	**3.56**
Primary Industries	**3.15**	**−0.12**	**0.05**	**1.61**	**0.08**	**−0.03**	**1.56**
Business Sector	**5.00**	**1.11**	**0.58**	**1.04**	**0.87**	**1.41**	
UNITED STATES							
Total Services Industry	**4.63**	**−0.16**	**0.88**	**0.65**	**0.68**	**0.52**	**2.06**
Transportation	2.81	−0.22	0.40	0.45	0.18	0.67	1.33
Communications	6.41	−1.20	1.84	0.90	0.52	0.59	3.76
Electric Utilities	2.87	2.33	0.22	0.21	0.00	−0.40	0.50
Gas Utilities	−0.65	0.33	0.34	0.34	−0.04	−0.26	−1.36
Wholesale Trade	4.16	0.08	1.41	0.55	0.24	0.43	1.45
Retail Trade	4.17	1.31	0.30	0.44	0.33	0.31	1.47
FIRE	5.26	0.01	1.18	1.00	0.44	0.17	2.45
Business Services	8.15	−1.38	1.76	0.83	1.50	1.87	3.59
Health Services	3.67	−1.07	0.57	0.53	1.37	0.57	1.71
Education, Private	2.87	−1.55	0.09	0.07	2.24	0.41	1.62
Other Services	4.42	0.51	0.23	0.48	0.31	0.49	2.40
Construction	**4.48**	**−0.95**	**0.12**	**0.41**	**0.18**	**1.49**	**3.23**
Manufacturing	**5.18**	**1.69**	**0.28**	**0.32**	**0.12**	**0.01**	**2.75**
Primary Industries	**2.62**	**1.69**	**0.09**	**0.37**	**−0.34**	**0.08**	**0.73**
Business Sector	**4.54**	**0.81**	**1.15**	**0.98**	**0.82**	**0.78**	

Note: The gross output and the multifactor productivity (MFP) columns show the growth rates and the five columns of input contributions indicate contributions to growth, defined as the growth rates multiplied by the output share weights.

Source: KLEMS database from Ho, Rao and Tang (2003).

In Canada's business-sector services industry, growth in non-ICT capital made the largest contribution to the growth of business-sector gross output between 1981 and 1995 except for intermediate inputs. Multifactor productivity (Table 14) played almost no role in gross output growth (0.1 percentage points). In the U.S. business-sector services industry, university labour growth and non-ICT capital growth made the largest contributions (0.6 points each). MFP growth in the United States had a negative impact of 0.2 percent on gross output growth. Out of the 11 services industries that comprise the business-sector services aggregate in Canada, no variable systematically made the largest impact on output growth, but ICT capital had the smallest impact in 6 industries. MFP also had a negative impact on gross output growth in 6 business-sector services industries (Table 14). The largest was in the private education industry, where MFP reduced gross output by 2.7 percentage points per year.

Non-university labour growth contributed the most to gross output growth between 1995 and 2000 in the Canadian business-sector services industry (0.9 points). Non-ICT capital growth on the other hand had the smallest impact (0.5 points). In the U.S. business-sector services industry, ICT capital had the most important impact (0.9 points). The contribution of university labour varied greatly by industry. In 3 of the 11 Canadian business-sector services industries, it had the largest impact on growth of the four types of capital and labour growth, while in 6 industries, it had the smallest impact. MFP growth (Table 15) picked up substantially in the 1995-2000 period to 0.7 percent per year from 0.1 percent in the 1981-1995 period and consequently made a negative contribution to gross output growth in only 2 industries [gas utilities (–1.0 points) and health services (–3.8 points)].

The following are key features pertaining to the sources of real output growth in the total business-sector services industry in Canada and the United States over the past two decades (Exhibit 3):

- Output growth in the business-sector services industry was much faster in Canada in the 1995-2000 period than in the 1981-95 period: 5.8 percent per year versus 3.7 percent.

- Output growth was slightly stronger in Canada than in the United States in the 1981-1995 period and considerably stronger in the 1995-2000 period.

- Multifactor productivity growth was also much faster in Canada in the 1995-2000 period than in 1981-95: 0.7 percent per year compared to 0.1 percent.

- Multifactor productivity growth was slightly stronger in Canada than in the United States in the 1981-1995 period and considerably stronger (0.9 percentage points per year) in the 1995-2000 period.

EXHIBIT 3

SOURCES OF GROSS OUTPUT GROWTH IN THE BUSINESS-SECTOR SERVICES AGGREGATE IN CANADA AND THE UNITED STATES, 1981-95 AND 1995-2000
(AVERAGE ANNUAL RATE OF CHANGE FOR GROSS OUTPUT AND MFP AND PERCENTAGE POINT CONTRIBUTIONS FOR INPUTS)

	Canada			United States		
	1981-1995	1995-2000	Change	1981-1995	1995-2000	Change
Gross Output	3.36	5.75	2.39	3.30	4.63	1.33
MFP	0.09	0.73	0.64	–0.20	–0.16	0.04
Total Capital	0.92	0.95	0.03	1.06	1.53	0.47
ICT Capital	0.33	0.50	0.17	0.46	0.88	0.42
Non-ICT Capital	0.59	0.45	–0.14	0.60	0.65	0.05
Total Labour	1.04	1.63	0.59	1.15	1.20	0.05
University Labour	0.48	0.76	0.28	0.61	0.68	0.07
Non-University Labour	0.56	0.87	0.31	0.54	0.52	–0.02
Intermediate Goods	1.31	2.44	1.13	1.29	2.06	0.77

Sources: Tables 14 and 15.

- The contributions of ICT capital, university labour and non-university labour to output growth were all greater in Canada in the 1995-2000 period than in 1981-1995. The contribution of non-ICT capital however was less.
- The contribution of ICT capital to business-sector services output growth was greater in the United States than in Canada in both periods, with the difference being 0.4 points greater in the 1995-2000 period. The contribution of this factor was greater in the more recent period in both countries.

SOURCES OF LABOUR PRODUCTIVITY GROWTH IN CANADIAN AND U.S. INDUSTRIES

IN THE SAME MANNER THAT GROSS OUTPUT GROWTH was decomposed using growth accounting assumptions to reflect the contribution of growth in inputs and MFP, labour productivity can be decomposed into the contribution of MFP and the changes in the intensity of the four types of capital and labour input use. Capital intensity is defined as the ratio of capital input to labour input. Labour intensity is defined as the ratio of labour input adjusted for quality (i.e. differences in experience based on gender, age and education) to actual hours worked, unadjusted for quality. The percentage point contributions are presented for 4 major industry groupings and 11 business-sector services industries for Canada and the United States in Tables 16 and 17 for the 1981-1995 and 1995-2000 periods, respectively.[14]

The most important contribution to labour productivity growth in the Canadian business-sector services industry between 1981 and 1995 was made by growth in the intensity of intermediate inputs (0.6 points), while the smallest arose from MFP (0.1 percent) and non-university labour intensity (–0.1 points). In the U.S. business-sector services industry, growth in ICT capital intensity made the largest contribution to labour productivity growth, while MFP made a contribution of –0.2 percent.

Intermediate input intensity growth contributed the most to labour productivity growth in Canadian business-sector services as a whole during the 1995-2000 period. This statement was also true for 3 of the 11 individual business-sector services industries for the same period. In 5 of the 11 business-sector services industries, growth in non-university labour intensity was the least important contributor to labour productivity. The story was similar in the United States where growth in intermediate input intensity and non-university labour intensity were respectively the largest and smallest contributors to labour productivity growth. MFP growth had an even larger negative impact on labour productivity growth in the health services industries during the 1995-2000 period than it did in the previous period as it reduced that industry's labour productivity average annual growth rate by 3.8 percentage points per year. MFP also had a negative impact in the gas utilities industry by reducing labour productivity growth by an average of almost one percentage point a year.

The sources of labour productivity growth for aggregated business-sector services in Canada and the United States over the past two decades (Exhibit 4) display the following characteristics:

- Labour productivity growth in the business-sector services was much faster in Canada in the 1995-2000 period than in the 1981-95 period: 2.3 percent per year compared to 1.4 percent, an acceleration of 0.9 percentage points.

- Labour productivity growth was considerably stronger in Canada than in the United States in the 1981-1995 period (0.7 percentage points) and somewhat stronger in the 1995-2000 period (0.4 points).

- As noted under sources of output growth, multifactor productivity growth was also much faster in Canada in the 1995-2000 period than in 1981-95: 0.7 percent per year compared to 0.1 percent. Multifactor productivity growth was slightly stronger in Canada than in the United States in the 1981-1995 period, and considerably stronger (0.9 percentage points per year) in the 1995-2000 period.

TABLE 16

SOURCES OF LABOUR PRODUCTIVITY GROWTH IN CANADIAN AND U.S. BUSINESS-SECTOR INDUSTRIES, 1981-1995

INDUSTRY	LP (AVERAGE ANNUAL GROWTH RATES, PERCENT)	MFP	CONTRIBUTIONS (PERCENTAGE POINTS) ICT CAPITAL INTENSITY	NON-ICT CAPITAL INTENSITY	UNIVERSITY LABOUR QUALITY	NON-UNIVERSITY LABOUR QUALITY	INTERMEDIATE INPUT INTENSITY
CANADA							
Total Services Industry	**1.37**	**0.09**	**0.28**	**0.16**	**0.32**	**–0.09**	**0.61**
Transportation	1.64	0.87	0.08	0.02	0.12	–0.05	0.59
Communications	4.65	1.51	1.14	0.61	0.31	–0.03	1.11
Electric Utilities	1.71	0.11	0.39	0.09	0.13	0.03	0.96
Gas Utilities	–0.76	–1.28	0.25	0.08	0.19	–0.02	0.01
Wholesale Trade	3.06	1.67	0.15	0.07	0.36	–0.01	0.82
Retail Trade	1.12	0.18	0.13	0.13	0.24	0.03	0.40
FIRE	1.88	–0.21	0.34	0.60	0.31	–0.09	0.93
Business Services	1.26	–1.14	0.50	0.43	0.74	–0.09	0.82
Health Services	–2.06	–0.77	0.09	–0.64	–0.95	0.30	–0.09
Education, Private	–4.81	–2.74	0.26	–0.03	0.40	–0.36	–2.34
Other Services	0.34	–0.88	0.35	0.16	0.22	–0.05	0.54
Construction	**–0.40**	**–0.33**	**0.03**	**0.06**	**0.06**	**0.07**	**–0.29**
Manufacturing	**2.75**	**0.41**	**0.06**	**0.11**	**0.10**	**0.02**	**2.06**
Primary Industries	**2.92**	**1.36**	**0.02**	**0.64**	**0.10**	**0.06**	**0.75**
Business Sector	**1.44**	**0.55**	**0.31**	**0.28**	**0.42**	**–0.11**	
UNITED STATES							
Total Services Industry	**0.70**	**–0.20**	**0.38**	**0.10**	**0.23**	**–0.10**	**0.29**
Transportation	0.79	0.59	0.09	–0.39	0.26	–0.09	0.33
Communications	2.94	–0.11	0.90	0.77	0.31	–0.16	1.23
Electric Utilities	2.02	0.13	0.31	0.82	0.19	–0.09	0.67
Gas Utilities	–2.58	–2.33	0.25	0.26	0.06	–0.03	–0.80
Wholesale Trade	3.23	1.40	0.71	0.39	0.19	–0.02	0.57
Retail Trade	0.71	–0.16	0.17	0.19	0.11	0.02	0.39
FIRE	1.94	–0.19	0.54	0.55	0.29	–0.14	0.90
Business Services	–0.19	–0.45	0.90	–0.41	–0.19	0.06	–0.11
Health Services	–0.16	–0.99	0.28	0.09	0.25	0.04	0.17
Education, Private	–0.19	–1.06	0.04	–0.02	0.69	–0.19	0.36
Other Services	0.74	–0.17	0.08	0.16	0.19	–0.13	0.61
Construction	**–0.83**	**–0.74**	**0.03**	**–0.14**	**0.09**	**0.06**	**–0.13**
Manufacturing	**2.94**	**0.92**	**0.13**	**0.18**	**0.16**	**–0.03**	**1.57**
Primary Industries	**1.85**	**1.00**	**0.05**	**0.53**	**0.19**	**–0.12**	**0.20**
Business Sector	**1.30**	**0.36**	**0.50**	**0.24**	**0.41**	**–0.21**	

Note: The labour productivity (LP) and the multifactor productivity (MFP) columns show the growth rates and the five columns of input contributions indicate contributions to growth, defined as the growth rates multiplied by the output share weights.

Source: KLEMS database from Ho, Rao and Tang (2003).

TABLE 17

SOURCES OF LABOUR PRODUCTIVITY GROWTH IN CANADIAN AND U.S. BUSINESS-SECTOR INDUSTRIES, 1995-2000

INDUSTRY	LP (AVERAGE ANNUAL GROWTH RATES, PERCENT)	MFP	CONTRIBUTIONS (PERCENTAGE POINTS) ICT CAPITAL INTENSITY	NON-ICT CAPITAL INTENSITY	UNIVERSITY LABOUR QUALITY	NON-UNIVERSITY LABOUR QUALITY	INTERMEDIATE INPUT INTENSITY
CANADA							
Total Services Industry	**2.29**	**0.73**	**0.40**	**–0.24**	**0.36**	**–0.09**	**1.13**
Transportation	1.33	0.39	0.21	0.24	0.05	0.01	0.43
Communications	6.18	1.71	2.11	1.07	0.05	0.08	1.15
Electric Utilities	0.17	0.80	0.43	–1.62	0.01	0.02	0.53
Gas Utilities	3.45	–0.95	0.73	3.14	0.02	0.04	0.48
Wholesale Trade	1.59	0.85	0.29	–0.25	0.11	0.03	0.55
Retail Trade	4.28	1.86	0.37	0.22	0.12	–0.07	1.77
FIRE	3.33	0.96	0.54	–0.04	0.10	0.03	1.74
Business Services	2.61	0.15	0.46	0.42	0.04	0.02	1.52
Health Services	–2.11	–3.78	0.05	–0.45	2.06	–0.29	0.30
Education, Private	4.81	4.33	–0.02	–0.32	2.31	–0.08	–1.41
Other Services	3.27	0.97	0.27	–0.08	0.13	0.04	1.94
Construction	**0.33**	**0.19**	**0.03**	**–0.08**	**0.05**	**0.06**	**0.07**
Manufacturing	**1.95**	**0.48**	**0.08**	**–0.01**	**0.04**	**0.01**	**1.35**
Primary Industries	**5.26**	**–0.12**	**0.06**	**2.35**	**0.14**	**0.27**	**2.57**
Business Sector	**1.93**	**1.09**	**0.48**	**–0.07**	**0.44**	**0.00**	
UNITED STATES							
Total Services Industry	**1.92**	**–0.16**	**0.76**	**0.15**	**0.23**	**–0.08**	**1.03**
Transportation	0.50	–0.22	0.35	0.16	0.01	0.02	0.18
Communications	1.54	–1.20	1.03	0.17	0.10	–0.11	1.54
Electric Utilities	5.22	2.33	0.29	1.27	0.15	–0.12	1.30
Gas Utilities	2.85	0:33	0.48	0.94	0.06	–0.06	1.08
Wholesale Trade	2.78	0.08	1.32	0.38	0.01	0.03	0.95
Retail Trade	2.59	1.31	0.28	0.25	0.17	–0.22	0.80
FIRE	2.75	0.01	1.05	0.09	0.12	–0.07	1.55
Business Services	1.62	–1.38	1.33	0.11	–0.08	0.03	1.62
Health Services	0.93	–1.07	0.50	0.23	0.47	0.00	0.80
Education, Private	–0.78	–1.55	0.07	–0.01	0.71	–0.07	0.08
Other Services	2.20	0.51	0.20	0.13	0.19	–0.22	1.39
Construction	**–0.14**	**–0.95**	**0.09**	**0.14**	**–0.07**	**0.06**	**0.60**
Manufacturing	**5.20**	**1.69**	**0.28**	**0.33**	**0.13**	**0.02**	**2.77**
Primary Industries	**2.86**	**1.69**	**0.10**	**0.44**	**–0.33**	**0.13**	**0.84**
Business Sector	**2.31**	**0.81**	**1.02**	**0.31**	**0.30**	**–0.13**	

Note: The labour productivity (LP) and the multifactor productivity (MFP) columns show the growth rates and the five columns of input contributions indicate contributions to growth, defined as the growth rates multiplied by the output share weights.

Source: KLEMS database from Ho, Rao and Tang (2003).

EXHIBIT 4

SOURCES OF LABOUR PRODUCTIVITY GROWTH IN THE BUSINESS-SECTOR SERVICES AGGREGATE IN CANADA AND THE UNITED STATES, 1981-95 AND 1995-2000
(AVERAGE ANNUAL RATE OF CHANGE FOR GROSS OUTPUT PER HOUR AND MFP AND PERCENTAGE POINT CONTRIBUTIONS FOR INPUTS)

	CANADA			UNITED STATES		
	1981-1995	1995-2000	CHANGE	1981-1995	1995-2000	CHANGE
Labour Productivity	**1.37**	**2.29**	**0.92**	**0.70**	**1.92**	**1.22**
MFP	**0.09**	**0.73**	**0.64**	**–0.20**	**–0.16**	**0.04**
Total Capital Intensity	**0.40**	**0.16**	**–0.28**	**0.48**	**0.91**	**0.43**
ICT Capital Intensity	0.28	0.40	0.12	0.38	0.76	0.38
Non-ICT Capital Intensity	0.16	–0.24	–0.40	0.10	0.15	0.05
Total Labour Intensity	**0.23**	**0.27**	**0.04**	**0.13**	**0.15**	**0.02**
University Labour Intensity	0.32	0.36	0.04	0.23	0.23	0.00
Non-University Labour Intensity	–0.09	–0.09	0.00	–0.10	–0.08	0.02
Intermediate Goods Intensity	**0.61**	**1.13**	**0.52**	**0.29**	**1.03**	**0.74**

Sources: Tables 16 and 17.

- The contribution to labour productivity growth from ICT capital (relative to labour) was somewhat greater in the 1995-2000 period (0.4 points) than in the 1981-1995 period (0.3 points) in Canada. The contribution of non-ICT capital was less in the more recent period (–0.2 points versus 0.2 points). The contribution of university labour was in the 0.3-0.4 point range in both periods, while that of non-university labour was –0.1 points in both periods.
- In the United States, ICT capital contributed 0.8 points to labour productivity growth in the 1995-2000 period, up from 0.4 points in the 1981-1995 period and accounted for 31 percent of the acceleration in the growth of labour productivity in business-sector services, compared to only 13 percent in Canada. The contribution of the other three inputs was less than that of ICT capital and was virtually unchanged between periods.

CONTRIBUTIONS OF BUSINESS-SECTOR SERVICES INDUSTRIES TO BUSINESS-SECTOR OUTPUT AND PRODUCTIVITY GROWTH IN CANADA AND THE UNITED STATES

IN CANADA AND THE UNITED STATES, output growth (value added) in business-sector services contributed significantly more than the other three sectors to aggregate value added growth in both the 1981-95 (Figure 1) and 1995-2000 periods (Figure 2). This is not surprising given the fact that in 2001 services represented in 61.2 percent of value added and 66.3 percent of hours worked in the business sector. Over the 1981-95 period, the three most important business-sector services industries in terms of their percentage point contribution to business-sector output growth in Canada were FIRE, wholesale trade, and business services. In the United States, they were FIRE, health services and wholesale trade. In the 1995-2000 period, business services had the largest impact in Canada, while FIRE and wholesale trade came second and third. In the United States, FIRE was still the most important contributor, followed by business services and health services.[15]

Business-sector services industries were again the most important contributor to aggregate labour productivity growth between 1981 and 1995 in Canada (Figure 3). This was, perhaps, surprising given its large share of labour input. This was not the case in the United States, where manufacturing made the largest

FIGURE 1

CONTRIBUTIONS TO BUSINESS-SECTOR OUTPUT GROWTH BY SECTOR IN CANADA AND THE UNITED STATES, 1981-1995 (AVERAGE ANNUAL CHANGE, PERCENTAGE POINTS)

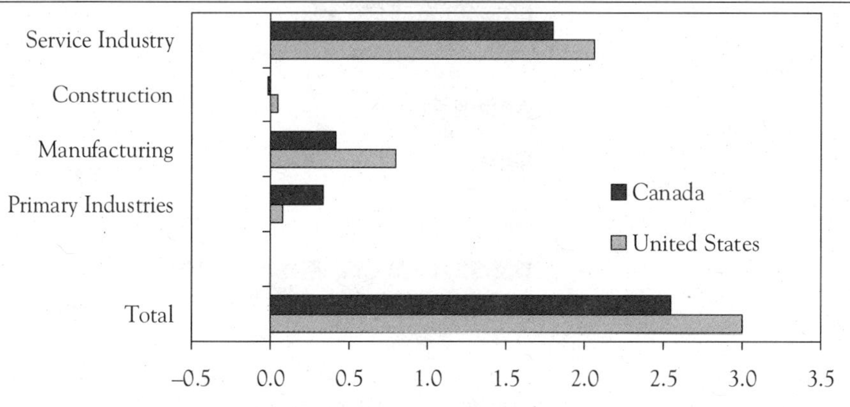

Note: Output is defined as value added.
Source: KLEMS database from Ho, Rao, and Tang (2003).

FIGURE 2

CONTRIBUTIONS TO BUSINESS-SECTOR OUTPUT GROWTH BY SECTOR IN CANADA AND THE UNITED STATES, 1995-2000 (AVERAGE ANNUAL CHANGE, PERCENTAGE POINTS)

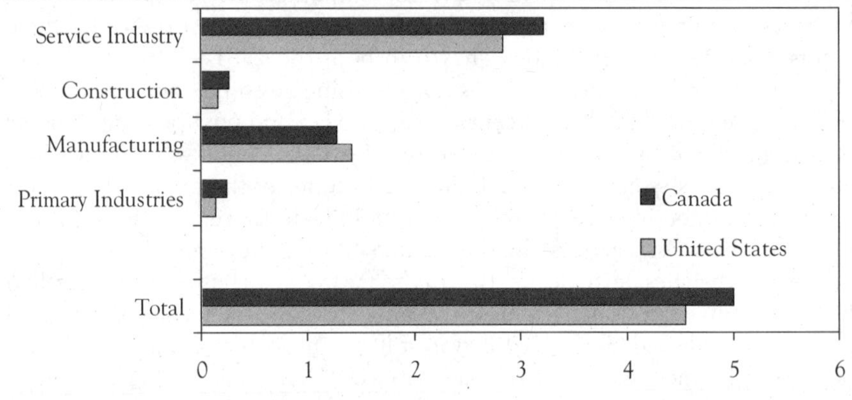

Note: Output is defined as value added.
Source: KLEMS database from Ho, Rao, and Tang (2003).

FIGURE 3

CONTRIBUTIONS TO BUSINESS-SECTOR LABOUR PRODUCTIVITY GROWTH BY SECTOR IN CANADA AND THE UNITED STATES, 1981-1995 (AVERAGE ANNUAL CHANGE, PERCENTAGE POINTS)

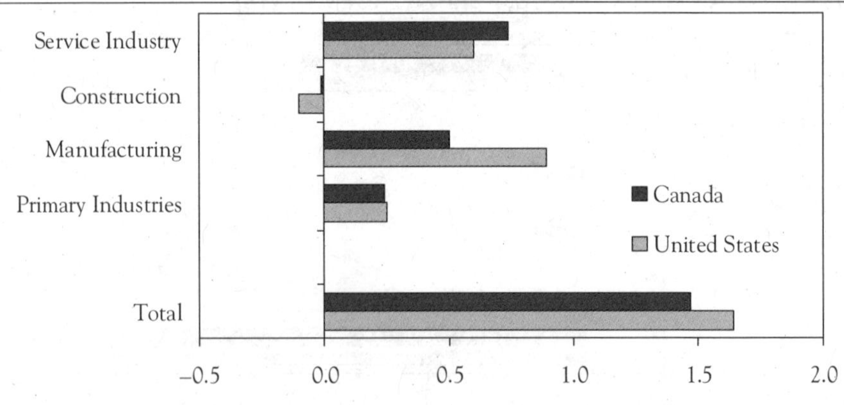

Note: Labour productivity is defined as value added per hour worked.
Source: KLEMS database from Ho, Rao, and Tang (2003).

contribution to labour productivity growth. Very strong labour productivity growth in U.S. manufacturing accounts for this development.[16] In both countries, wholesale trade and FIRE made the largest contributions to aggregate labour productivity among the business-sector services industries. Falling labour productivity in health services had a negative impact on aggregate labour productivity in both countries.

In the 1995-2000 period, the business-sector services industries continued to have the largest impact on aggregate labour productivity growth in Canada, while manufacturing continued to be most important in the United States (Figure 4). FIRE was the most important business-sector services industry in terms of its impact on aggregate labour productivity growth in both countries, followed by retail trade. Health services again contributed negatively to aggregate labour productivity growth in Canada during the period.

There was a major difference between Canada and the United States in the contribution of business-sector services to aggregate (business sector) multifactor productivity growth in both the 1981-95 and 1995-2000 periods. In the first period, business-sector services made a relatively small positive contribution in Canada and a significantly negative contribution in the United States given the negative MFP growth rate (Figure 5). Manufacturing was by far the most important contributor to aggregate MFP growth in both countries, although the contribution was twice as large in the United States. Primary industries were also important in Canada. In terms of business-sector services industries, wholesale trade made a large positive contribution in both countries. Most business-sector services industries in both countries made negative contributions, with health services being particularly important in the United States.

During the 1995-2000 period, business-sector services in Canada made a much larger contribution to aggregate MFP growth than in the previous period (Figures 5 and 6). The contribution also greatly exceeded that of the manufacturing sector. In contrast, business-sector services continued to make a negative contribution to MFP growth in the United States. Manufacturing continued to drive aggregate MFP growth. FIRE made the largest contribution to MFP growth among the business-sector services industries in Canada, closely followed by retail trade. In the United States, retail trade made the most important contribution. Negative MFP growth in health services in both countries had the worst impact on aggregate MFP growth.

FIGURE 4

CONTRIBUTIONS TO BUSINESS-SECTOR LABOUR PRODUCTIVITY GROWTH BY SECTOR IN CANADA AND THE UNITED STATES, 1995-2000 (AVERAGE ANNUAL CHANGE, PERCENTAGE POINTS)

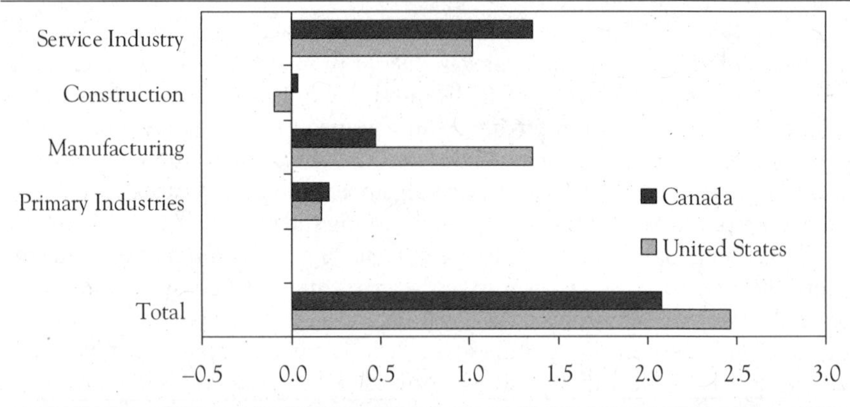

Note: Labour productivity is defined as value added per hour worked.
Source: KLEMS database from Ho, Rao, and Tang (2003).

FIGURE 5

CONTRIBUTIONS TO BUSINESS-SECTOR MFP GROWTH BY SECTOR IN CANADA AND THE UNITED STATES, 1981-1995 (AVERAGE ANNUAL CHANGE, PERCENTAGE POINTS)

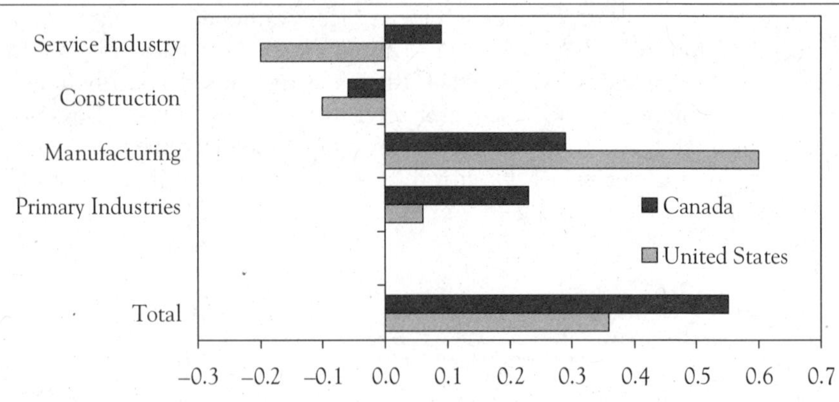

Source: KLEMS database from Ho, Rao, and Tang (2003).

FIGURE 6

CONTRIBUTIONS TO BUSINESS-SECTOR MFP GROWTH BY SECTOR IN CANADA AND THE UNITED STATES, 1995-2000 (AVERAGE ANNUAL CHANGE, PERCENTAGE POINTS)

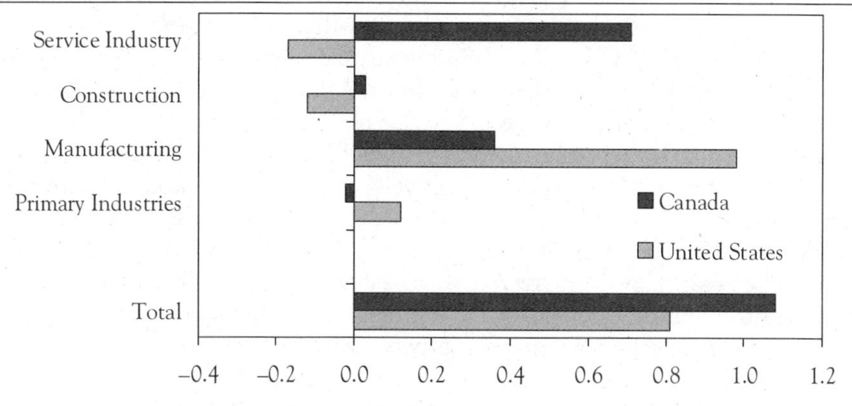

Source: KLEMS database from Ho, Rao, and Tang (2003).

FACTORS ACCOUNTING FOR THE RELATIVE SUCCESS OF BUSINESS-SECTOR SERVICES PRODUCTIVITY GROWTH IN CANADA

THIS STUDY HAS IDENTIFIED AND DOCUMENTED two facts or developments that have been used to argue that the productivity performance of Canadian business-sector services since 1995 represents a relative success story, at least compared to the productivity performance of the Canadian manufacturing sector. The first development is the acceleration in growth of labour and multifactor productivity in business-sector services industries in Canada between 1995 and 2000, relative to 1981-95. This contrasts with the absence of any acceleration in most of the goods-producing sector. The second is the more rapid growth in labour and multifactor productivity in Canadian business-sector services than in their U.S. counterparts in both the 1981-1995 and 1995-2000 periods. The objective of this section is to shed light on the factors underlying these two developments.

Post-1995 Acceleration of Productivity Growth in the Canadian Business-sector Services Industries

As shown earlier in the study, labour productivity growth in Canadian business-sector services industries accelerated by 0.9 percentage points from an average annual rate of 1.4 percent in 1981-95 to 2.3 percent in 1995-2000 (Table 11) and multifactor productivity growth accelerated 0.6 percentage points from 0.1 percent to 0.7 percent per year between the two periods (Table 18). In contrast, labour productivity growth fell in manufacturing from 2.8 percent per year in the 1981-95 period to 2.0 percent in 1995-2000, and labour productivity growth in construction rose only 0.7 points with annual growth of –0.44 percent and 0.33 percent, respectively, over the two periods. In terms of the growth of labour productivity between the two periods, the primary sector showed a strong acceleration of 2.3 percentage points from 2.9 percent to 5.2 percent per year. However, given its small labour share, the primary sector is a small contributor to overall growth in business-sector labour productivity.

The acceleration of labour productivity in business-sector services can be decomposed from the perspective of either sources of growth and growth accounting or industry contribution. In a gross output framework, the approach focusing on sources of growth includes four components: changes in capital intensity, changes in labour quality (labour intensity), changes in the intensity of intermediate goods use and multifactor productivity growth.

Exhibit 4 showed that 0.6 points, or 70 percent, of the 0.9 point acceleration in the labour productivity of Canadian business-sector services in 1995-2000 relative to 1981-95 was accounted for by acceleration in multifactor productivity growth. An additional 0.5 points can be explained by the increased intensity of intermediate goods, although the interpretation of this development is problematic: a value added framework that excluded intermediate goods would intuitively be easier to interpret.

Greater capital intensity and improvements in labour quality were not responsible for the acceleration. Improvements in labour quality made virtually no contribution to acceleration in the labour productivity of business-sector services. Overall, the pace of growth in capital intensity was actually slower in the 1995-2000 period than in 1981-95, so capital intensity actually made a negative contribution of 0.3 points to acceleration. This development was explained by a significant falloff in the growth rate of non-ICT capital intensity, with the contribution falling from 0.2 percentage points per year to –0.2 percentage points between periods. ICT capital intensity grew, however, with the contribution of this input increasing 0.1 points between periods from 0.3 to 0.4 points.

Table 12 shows that four business-sector services industries accounted for the lion's share of the 0.9-point acceleration in the growth of labour productivity in business-sector services between 1981-95 and 1995-2000. In order of importance, they were retail trade, other services, business services and FIRE. Negative contributions to the acceleration were made by wholesale trade and transportation.

TABLE 18

MULTIFACTOR PRODUCTIVITY GROWTH IN BUSINESS-SECTOR SERVICES INDUSTRIES IN CANADA AND THE UNITED STATES (COMPOUND AVERAGE ANNUAL GROWTH RATES)

	CANADA			UNITED STATES		
INDUSTRY	1981-1995	1995-2000	DIFFERENCE	1981-1995	1995-2000	DIFFERENCE
Services Industries	**0.09**	**0.73**	**0.64**	**–0.20**	**–0.16**	**0.04**
Transportation	0.87	0.39	–0.48	0.59	–0.22	–0.81
Communications	1.51	1.71	0.20	–0.11	–1.20	–1.09
Electric Utilities	0.11	0.80	0.69	0.13	2.33	2.20
Gas Utilities	–1.28	–0.95	0.33	–2.33	0.33	2.66
Wholesale Trade	1.67	0.85	–0.82	1.40	0.08	–1.32
Retail Trade	0.18	1.86	1.68	–0.16	1.31	1.47
FIRE	–0.21	0.96	1.17	–0.19	0.01	0.20
Business Services	–1.14	0.15	1.29	–0.45	–1.38	–0.93
Health Services	–0.77	–3.78	–3.01	–0.99	–1.07	–0.08
Education, Private	–2.74	4.33	7.07	–1.06	–1.55	–0.49
Other Services	–0.88	0.97	1.85	–0.17	0.51	0.68
Construction	**–0.33**	**0.19**	**0.52**	**–0.74**	**–0.95**	**–0.21**
Manufacturing	**0.41**	**0.48**	**0.07**	**0.92**	**1.69**	**0.77**
Primary Industries	**1.36**	**–0.12**	**–1.48**	**1.00**	**1.69**	**0.69**
Business Sector	**0.55**	**1.11**	**0.56**	**0.36**	**0.81**	**0.45**

Note: FIRE refers to finance, insurance and real estate, and includes leasing and management services.

Source: KLEMS database from Ho, Rao and Tang (2003).

FASTER PRODUCTIVITY GROWTH IN CANADIAN BUSINESS-SECTOR SERVICES THAN IN THEIR U.S. COUNTERPARTS

A KEY FINDING OF THE STUDY is that there was faster growth of labour and multifactor productivity growth in Canadian business-sector services industries than in the United States (Tables 11 and 18). In the 1981-95 period, growth in labour productivity reached 1.4 percent per year in Canada compared to 0.7 percent in the United States while the figures for multifactor productivity growth were 0.1 percent and –0.2 percent respectively. In the 1995-2000 period, growth in average annual labour productivity was 2.3 percent in Canada compared to 1.9 percent in the United States while the figures for multifactor productivity were 0.7 percent compared to –0.2 percent. This situation contrasts with manufacturing, where labour and multifactor productivity growths were greater in the United States than in Canada, in both the 1981-95 and 1995-2000 periods (Tables 16 and 17).

A key aspect of the strong labour productivity performance of Canadian business-sector services in the post-1995 period was that it was based on very strong multifactor productivity growth and not on increased capital intensity. This has not been the case in U.S. business-sector services, where multifactor productivity growth has been negative and increased capital accumulation or capital intensity has accounted for nearly one half of productivity growth (Exhibit 4), with increased ICT capital intensity responsible for the lion's share of greater overall capital intensity.

As discussed in the third section of this study, inter-industry employment shifts in business-sector services had a negative effect on the growth of labour productivity in Canadian business-sector services in the 1995-2000 period, while they had a positive effect in the United States. Thus, these shifts cannot account for the superior productivity growth performance of Canadian business-sector services relative to their U.S. counterparts. Indeed, when measured by pure productivity effects, Canada's superior business-sector services labour productivity growth was even stronger than when measured by growth in actual productivity that includes shift effects.

A key explanation for faster productivity growth in Canadian business-sector services between 1981 and 2000 is a higher level of productivity in the United States. This gap means that Canadian business-sector services industries had the potential of converging toward U.S. levels through technological catch-up, involving adoption of the best practices used by the world leader, which generally has been the United States.

Table 7 shows that in 2000, the relative labour productivity of Canadian business-sector services industry was 83.8 percent of the U.S. level. The labour productivity of business-sector services grew 0.37 percentage points per year faster in Canada than in the United States between 1995 and 2000, and 0.67 points per year in the 1981-1995 period. This implies that Canada's labour productivity level was 82.0 percent that of the United States in 1995 and 72.6 percent of the U.S. level in 1981. The wider gap in the 1981-95 period, as compared to the more recent period, is consistent with a greater differential in the productivity growth rate during the earlier period. The larger the gap, the greater the potential for catch-up.

Table 7 also shows relative labour productivity levels for specific business-sector services industries. Canadian business-sector services industries with a relative labour productivity gap greater than the average of total business-sector services industries tended to have a larger positive labour productivity growth rate differential compared to their U.S. counterpart in the 1995-2000 period. Canada's transportation, FIRE and other services (which stood at 72.7 percent, 63.9 percent, and 84.1 percent, respectively, of the U.S. labour productivity level) conformed to this pattern. However, wholesale trade, at 71.3 percent of the U.S. productivity level in 2000, experienced slower productivity growth than its U.S. counterpart.

On the other hand, three Canadian business-sector services industries with relative labour productivity levels higher than their U.S. counterparts in 2000 (communications, gas utilities and private education) had labour productivity growth rate differentials with the United States that were greater than the overall business-sector services differential of 0.37 percentage points in 1995-2000. These faster growth rates cannot be accounted for by convergence. These industries are small, however, and make only a limited contribution to the overall superior productivity performance of business-sector services.

In addition to technological convergence, another reason for the faster productivity growth in the Canadian business-sector services industry when compared to the U.S. industry over the past two decades has been a catch-up in the educational attainment of workers in Canadian business-sector services relative to their U.S. counterparts.[17] The proportion of university-educated workers in the total services industry has been and continues to be much higher in the United States, contributing to the Canada-U.S. gap of 16 percent (in 2000) in labour productivity of business-sector services. For example, in 2000, 30.3 percent of employees in U.S. business-sector services industries had completed one university degree or more as compared to only 19.5 percent in Canada (Table 9). But over the 1981-2000 period, the rate of growth in the proportion of university-trained workers advanced at a 2.4 percent average annual rate in Canada, compared to 1.7 percent in the United States, reducing the gap in the proportion of university-trained workers in business-sector services from 12.1 points to 10.9 points.

In his comments on this study, Richard Harris of Simon Fraser University has raised a third possible explanation for higher business-sector services productivity growth in Canada compared to the United States. It is possible that some low-productivity services incidental to manufacturing activities have been outsourced in the United States but not in Canada, with the result that the statistical systems capture this low-productivity activity as taking place within business-sector services in the United States, but within the manufacturing sector in Canada. This would account for the difference between manufacturing and services productivity growth performance between the two countries: the low-productivity manufacturing-related services would be counted in the business-sector services in the United States, boosting manufacturing productivity growth and depressing services productivity growth; while the opposite would hold for Canada.

This implies that the success of Canada's business-sector services relative to the United States and its lagging growth in manufacturing-sector productivity may both be reversed if Canada begins to adopt the same outsourcing procedures as the United States. Unfortunately, this hypothesis cannot be adequately tested without a close examination of the way services activities are classified in both countries at a very detailed level. This is an appealing explanation, however, since it addresses gaps in the growth of both manufacturing and services-sector productivity, and it may prove to be correct if Canadian services-sector productivity growth begins to fall toward that of the United States, while manufacturing productivity growth begins to rise toward that in the United States over the next few years.

CONCLUSIONS

THE OBJECTIVE OF THIS STUDY has been to provide an in-depth analysis of the output and productivity performance of the services industries in Canada, relative to other Canadian industries and to their U.S. counterparts. The main conclusion to be drawn is that Canadian business-sector services have been a relative success story in terms of productivity growth. Both labour and multifactor productivity showed an impressive acceleration in growth between the 1981-1995 and 1995-2000 periods, and the acceleration would have been even greater had the relative labour shares of some lower-productivity services industries not increased between these periods. Retail trade and business services were the largest contributors to this acceleration in labour productivity growth.

The performance of U.S. business-sector services has been somewhat different. Growth in the labour productivity of business-sector services accelerated in the United States between 1981-1995 and 1995-2000 to a greater degree than in Canada. However, Canada outperformed the United States in terms of business-sector services labour productivity growth in both periods. Growth in multifactor productivity of U.S. business-sector services was negative in both periods, with virtually no acceleration in growth between them, in marked contrast to the Canadian experience.

The superior performance of Canadian business-sector services in terms of labour productivity growth relative to U.S. business-sector services contrasts strongly with the dismal relative performance of Canada's manufacturing sector, which has a large and widening labour productivity gap with the U.S. manufacturing sector. Despite Canada's superior business-sector services productivity performance, the level of business-sector services labour productivity in Canada in 2000 was still about 15 percent below that in the United States.

The acceleration in the labour productivity of business-sector services had different origins in the two countries. In Canada, increased growth in multifactor productivity was responsible for 70 percent of the acceleration in labour productivity growth. In the United States, increased intensity of capital and intermediate inputs were the most important contributors to acceleration in the growth in labour productivity of business-sector services. In Canada, the contribution of capital intensity to the growth of business-sector services labour productivity actually fell between 1981-1995 and 1995-2000.

In both the 1981-1995 and 1995-2000 periods, business-sector services were the most important contributor to growth in Canadian business-sector labour productivity. In terms of growth in the multifactor productivity of the whole business sector, business-sector services went from being only the third most important contributor in 1981-1995 — behind both manufacturing and the primary sector but ahead of construction — to being the most important contributor in the 1995-2000 period, with a contribution almost twice that of manufacturing.

The contribution of business-sector services to productivity growth in the U.S. business sector has been smaller than in Canada. The largest contributor to growth in both U.S. business-sector labour productivity and multifactor productivity was manufacturing in both the 1981-1995 and 1995-2000 periods. Although the business-sector services industry was the second most important contributor to growth in U.S. business-sector labour productivity in both periods — ahead of the primary and construction sectors — it made large negative contributions to the growth of multifactor productivity in the business sector, making it the least important contributor in both periods.

The factor driving Canada's superior business-sector services labour productivity growth has been better growth in multifactor productivity, suggesting a productivity convergence with the U.S. level. A faster pace of human capital accumulation relative to the United States, as measured by growth in the proportion of workers with a university degree, fostered the catch-up process of Canadian business-sector services industries.

Further research is needed in several areas. The first is the extent to which the measured superior growth in labour productivity of Canadian business-sector services is due to Canada-U.S. differences in the organization of some production activities between the services and manufacturing sectors. Two other suggestions for future research include extending analysis to the provincial rather than a strictly national level, and investigating any cyclical element in the post-1995 acceleration of labour productivity growth in Canadian business-sector services.[18]

The performance of Canadian business-sector services in terms of productivity growth is a success story both relative to other Canadian industries and relative to U.S. business-sector services. However, to close the remaining Canada-U.S. business-sector services productivity gap, the Canadian side needs to make significant progress in narrowing gaps in human and physical capital intensity.[19] They also need to catch up to their U.S. counterparts in R&D intensity (Table 8) and the share of ICT capital in total capital (Table 10).

APPENDIX

DATA SOURCES AND MEASUREMENT ISSUES

THIS APPENDIX IS BASED ON HO, RAO AND TANG (2003). The KLEMS data for the Canada and U.S. business sectors cover the 1981-2000 period. The business sector does not include imputed rents from owner-occupied dwellings or government. These data include volume indexes of gross output, capital services, labour services, intermediate inputs, the number of hours at work and cost in dollars of each of these inputs. The data source for the U.S. data is Jorgenson, Ho and Stiroh (2002). For their study, they have developed this dataset for 44 industries, which are collapsed into 34 common industries using Törnqvist aggregation indexes. The Canadian data are obtained from the Canadian Productivity Accounts that provide a consistent set of detailed industry data for 122 industries, together with aggregated data on inputs and outputs (current prices and chained Fisher indexes) for productivity measurement and related economic performance analysis.[20] The 122 industries are aggregated into the 34 industries in the same fashion. The Canadian and U.S. data used in this study employ concepts and methods that accord with the Organisation for Economic Co-operation and Development (OECD) productivity manual, to help make comparisons between the two countries.

Gross output and intermediate input values come from a time series of consistent input-output tables. The price indexes for output also are from Statistics Canada and are used to construct prices of intermediate inputs. The input-output tables are generally recorded in a very similar fashion in Canada and the United States. Thus, output and intermediate inputs are fairly comparable. However, our construction of capital and labour inputs is more complicated and some elaboration is needed.

CAPITAL INPUT

THE CAPITAL STOCK FOR EACH TYPE OF ASSET is constructed from investment in constant dollars. The comparability of investment deflators is thus important for comparing capital input in the two countries. This is especially true for ICT assets (computer equipment, communications equipment, and software) that have become increasingly important in total machinery and equipment (M&E) investment.[21] The investment price indexes for those assets diverge significantly across OECD countries due to different methodologies used in estimation.[22] However, Canada and the United States use fairly similar methods to develop the ICT price indexes. Statistical agencies in Canada and the United States have worked very closely and made extensive use of the *hedonic regression technique* and the *matching model technique* in estimating the prices of ICTs.

A detailed documentation of the methodologies used to construct ICT price indexes is given in Ho, Rao, and Tang (2003).

The capital stock for the United States is estimated from investment data in the Tangible Wealth Survey, produced by the Bureau of Economic Analysis (BEA). For Canada, capital stock data are constructed from investment series by asset classes from input-output tables and depreciation rates based on age-price profiles (Harchaoui, Tarkhani, Jackson and Armstrong 2002). There are 28 non-residential asset types in the Canadian classification, and 52 in the United States. The capital stocks are estimated for all types of assets owned by each industry using the perpetual inventory method and geometric depreciation.

On the basis of the translog index, capital stocks of different assets are then aggregated into capital input using user costs as weights, which accounts for differences in quality or marginal productivity for those assets.

Labour Input

IN OUR FRAMEWORK, the labour input for each industry is not a simple sum of hours worked but a translog aggregate over different groups using labour compensation as weights. The labour force categories for the two countries are similar except for education.[23] These include seven age groups, two sexes, two classes of employment and four (for Canada) or six (for the United States) educational attainment groups. Our experiments with the U.S. data show that the difference in education classification has only a small impact on the labour input estimates. A detailed description of the construction of the labour data is provided in Gu and Maynard (2001) for Canada, and Jorgenson, Ho and Stiroh (2002) for the United States.[24]

ENDNOTES

1 From 1989 to 2002, business sector output per hour advanced at an annual average rate of 2.2 percent in the United States compared to 1.7 percent in Canada. Over the same period, total economy output per hour grew at an average annual rate of 1.8 percent in the United States and a 1.5 percent average annual rate in Canada. For a detailed recent discussion of aggregate labour productivity trends in Canada and the United States since 1987, see Smith (2004).

2 Included in FIRE is imputed rent of owner-occupied dwellings and resource royalties, which account for 60 percent of FIRE output but with no associated employment. Consequently, the employment share of FIRE is much smaller than the output share.

3 The Bureau of Labor Statistics mostly completed the transition to NAICS in 2003. The Bureau of Economic Analysis, the source for the data used in this study, will not release data based on NAICS until its release of GDP by industry in June 2004.

4 A brief note of caution is called for in adding the real output shares of U.S. industries. These real output shares are based on output data expressed in chained dollars, which are not additive. Therefore, when real output shares are added for U.S. industries, the result is not expected to be as accurate as the individual shares. In Canada, data for GDP by industry have only recently become available in chained dollars and only as far back as 1997 thus far. Therefore, the data used in this study are based on fixed-weight dollars that are additive.

5 The Appendix discusses the technical details and comparability of these data.

6 There is also a relationship between capital intensity and relative wages, with the most capital-intensive industries tending to have the highest relative wages. Average hourly labour compensation in the Canadian services sector in 2000 was 4.2 percent higher than the business-sector average (Table 6). Average hourly labour compensation was higher in manufacturing, representing 112.4 percent of the average. The construction sector had only 97.5 percent of the average hourly labour compensation of the business sector, and the primary sector had only 85.9 percent. Average hourly labour compensation in the aggregated services sector decreased slightly, relative to the business-sector average between 1981 and 2000. Average hourly labour compensation was highest in FIRE (155.5 percent of the average), health services (142.6 percent), and electric utilities (136.6 percent of the average). The services industries with the lowest average hourly labour compensation were other services (61.2 percent of the average) and retail trade (67.0 percent of the average). Three other services industries had average hourly labour compensation below the business-sector average: gas utilities (99.4 percent), business services (96.3 percent), and transportation (94.8 percent).

7 A strong relationship between capital intensity and wages is also evident in the U.S. data. Table 6 shows that the average hourly labour compensation of the U.S. services sector in 2000, as in Canada, was slightly above the business-sector average (106.5 percent of the average). Average hourly labour compensation rose relative to the business-sector average between 1981 and 2000 starting at 78.7 percent of the average. Only manufacturing average hourly labour compensation was higher in 2000, at 132.9 percent of the average. Average hourly labour compensation also increased relative to the business-sector average in 10 out of the 11 services industries. The three U.S. services industries with the highest average hourly labour compensation in 2000 were electric utilities (237.5 percent of the average), FIRE (159.4 percent) and wholesale trade (128.7 percent). Average hourly labour compensation was lowest in other services (54.7 percent of the average), followed by retail trade (66.5 percent of the average) and private education (76.7 percent of the average).

8 The figure of 125.4 for Canada is obtained by dividing the sum of the output shares for transportation and warehousing and utilities by the sum of the employment shares for the same two industries.

9 A study by van Ark, Monnikhof and Mulder (1999) also provides some estimates of Canada-U.S. relative productivity levels in the services sector based on detailed industry purchasing power parities. They find that in 1990, Canada had a level of value added per hour in the transport and communication sector of 74.1 percent of the United States and in retail and wholesale trade, the figure was 51.1 percent. They also estimated relative productivity levels of 75.4 percent for manufacturing and 89.9 percent for the total economy. This final figure and the much lower relative levels for the other three sectors would imply that certain services industries have relative labour productivity levels above the total economy average.

10 Note that the data discussed from this point forward are from Ho, Rao and Tang (2003). These data refer only to the business sector and the business-sector component of the primary, manufacturing, construction and services sectors. Hereafter, the term services sector is used for the business-sector component of the services sector.

11 Note from Table 11 that several other services industries have displayed negative productivity growth in one or both of the periods examined and in one or both countries. This phenomenon is described in more detail in Sharpe, Rao and Tang (2002), and possible explanations are advanced as well. The explanations focus on measurement error. If the measured negative or near-zero labour productivity growth in the several services industries in Table 11 is indeed due to measurement error, this implies that the services sector would be even more of a success story in terms of productivity growth if the output of these industries were measured accurately.

12 The key assumption is that the income share of a factor of production represents its marginal product and hence its contribution to output. Two conditions for this assumption to hold are that factor and product markets are competitive and that constant returns to scale prevail.

13 The 11 business-sector services industries included are transportation, communications, electric utilities, gas utilities, wholesale trade, retail trade, FIRE, business services, health services, private education and other services.

14 The services sector is the least intensive of the four major sector groupings in intermediate inputs. This is not surprising since services do not involve much material transformation. In 2000, intermediate input intensity in Canadian business-sector services was 42.5 percent of the business-sector average, compared to 75.2 percent in construction, 85.0 percent in primary industries and 197.3 percent in manufacturing (Table 5). The U.S. business-sector services industry was also well below the average in intermediate input intensity at 51.8 percent of the average. Intermediate input intensity was fairly constant relative to the average between 1981 and 2000, but this was not the case in each individual business-sector services industry. In 2000, the three most intensive Canadian services industries in terms of intermediate inputs were FIRE at 112.0 percent of the average, followed by electric utilities and communications industries with intensity levels equal to 95.6 percent and 74.0 percent of the average, respectively. The least intensive industries in terms of intermediate inputs were health services, retail trade and private education with respective relative intensities of 18.7 percent, 24.1 percent and 26.7 percent of the average.

In 2000, among U.S. business-sector services industries, the most intensive industries in terms of intermediate inputs were gas utilities at 494.3 percent of the average, followed by electric utilities and communications industries with relative intensities of 230.4 percent and 157.1 percent of the average. The U.S. utilities were much more intermediate input intensive than manufacturing, which seems strange. The least intermediate input intensive business sector services industries were the same as in Canada. Retail trade had a relative intermediate input intensity of 29.8 percent, while private education had a 34.9 percent relative intensity. Business and health services industries had intermediate input intensity levels equal to 36.0 and 36.1 percent of the average respectively.

15 In Figures 1 through 6, the industry contributions to total business-sector output and labour productivity growth are defined as the given industry's output or productivity growth rate multiplied by its labour share, and are expressed in percentage points.

16 Tang and Wang (2004) have proposed a decomposition of an industry's contribution to aggregate labour productivity growth into 1) the industry's own labour productivity growth; 2) growth in the industry's labour share; and 3) growth in the real price of the industry's output. Based on this decomposition and in contrast to the results reported here, they find that the services sector was the most important contributor to aggregate labour productivity growth by several orders of magnitude in both Canada and the United States.

17 Since 1981, the percentage of persons employed with a university degree has been rising in the business-sector services aggregate in Canada as well as all the industries that comprise it, with the exception of the health services industry (Table 9). The proportion of workers with a university degree was higher in the business-sector services industries than in the good producing sectors. In 2000, 19.5 percent of business-sector services workers had this qualification, compared to 11.8 percent in manufacturing, 9.2 percent in primary industries, and 6.1 percent in construction. In the United States in 2000, the proportion of workers with a university degree was higher than in Canada in all industries, both within and apart from business-sector services. That proportion has also risen in all industries since 1981. The Canadian business-sector services industry with the highest proportion of workers with a university degree in 2000 was private education, with 53.7 percent. Business services and health services industries came second and third with 42.5 percent and 36.9 percent of their workers possessing a university degree. The transportation industry came last with 7.2 percent. In the United States in 2000, private education came first as well with 65.1 percent of its workers having a university degree. Health services followed with 42.8 percent and finance, insurance and real estate with 41.9 percent. Retail trade had the lowest proportion of workers with a university degree at 15.4 percent.

18 Another possible issue to address in future work on the Canadian services sector is how sensitive the conclusions reached thus far are to the particular growth accounting framework utilized. Most of the results discussed here are based on a KLEMS gross output framework, but the differences in the intensity of intermediate input use between Canada and the United States may suggest that some results are not completely comparable across the two countries. It would be interesting for future work to determine if these conclusions also hold with a value-added definition of real output.

19 See Rao, Tang and Wang (2002) for the skill gap, and Rao, Tang and Wang (2003) for the investment gap.

20 The P-level has a total of 123 industries. The present study excludes owner-occupied dwellings (P116).

21 In 2000, ICT investment in Canada was $34 billion, representing 37 percent of M&E investment, compared to less than $6 billion, or 19 percent of the overall M&E investment, in 1981. Similar changes occurred in the United States. In 2000 ICT investment was US$424 billion (39 percent of M&E), compared to US$62 billion (21 percent) in 1981.

22 For instance, the fall in computer prices in European countries in the early 1990s ranged from 10 to 47 percent (Triplett 2001, p.4).

23 Note, however, that the educational classification is not entirely consistent over time in both countries. The educational classification in the Labour Force Survey changed in 1990 in Canada (Gu and Maynard 2001). A similar change also took place in the U.S. Current Population Survey in 1992 and in the Census of Population in 1990 (Jorgenson, Ho and Stiroh 2002).

24 Labour compensation for self-employed workers in an industry is imputed under the assumption that the hourly compensation is the same between paid and self-employed workers.

ACKNOWLEDGMENTS

THIS STUDY WAS PRESENTED at the Industry Canada Conference on Services Industries and the Knowledge-based Economy, Winnipeg, Manitoba, October 16-18, 2003. It represents a preliminary approach and comments are welcome. We would like to thank Richard G. Harris for very useful comments on the study and Renée St-Jacques for comments and support. We would also like to thank Jeremy Smith for research assistance.

BIBLIOGRAPHY

Bernstein, Jeffrey I., Richard G. Harris, and Andrew Sharpe. 2002. "Explaining the Widening Canada-US Productivity Gap in Manufacturing", *International Productivity Monitor*, 5 (Fall): 3-22.

Gu, Wulong, and Jean-Pierre Maynard. 2001. "The Changing Composition of the Canadian Workforce, 1961-95," in Dale W. Jorgenson and Frank C. Lee (eds.). *Industry-level Productivity and International Competitiveness Between Canada and the United States*. Ottawa: Industry Canada Research Monograph.

Harchaoui, Tarek, Faouzi Tarkhani, Chris Jackson, and Philip Armstrong. 2002. "A Comparison of Canada-U.S. Economic Growth in the Information Age, 1981-2000: The Importance of Investment in Information and Communication Technologies," *Monthly Labor Review*, October: 31-47.

Ho, Mun S., Someshwar Rao, and Jianmin Tang. 2003. "Sources of Output Growth in Canadian and U.S. Industries in the Information Age," paper presented at the annual meeting of the Canadian Economics Association, Carleton University, Ottawa, Ontario, May 31-June 2; revised version June 20.

Jorgenson, Dale W., Mun S. Ho, and Kevin J. Stiroh. 2002. "Growth of U.S. Industries and Investments in Information Technology and Higher Education," research paper. Cambridge, MA: Harvard University.

Lee, Frank C., and Jianmin Tang. 2000. "Productivity Levels and International Competitiveness Between Canadian and U.S. Industries," *American Economic Review*, 90 (May): 176-79.

Rao, Someshwar, Jianmin Tang, and Weimin Wang. 2002. "The Importance of Skills for Innovation and Productivity," *International Productivity Monitor*, 4 (Spring): 15-26.

———. 2003. "Canada's Recent Productivity Record and Capital Accumulation," *International Productivity Monitor*, 7 (Fall): 30-45.

Sharpe, Andrew, Someshwar Rao, and Jianmin Tang. 2002. "Perspectives on Negative Productivity Growth in Service Sector Industries in Canada and the United States," Paper presented at Workshop on Service Sector Productivity, May 17, Brookings Institution, Washington, D.C.

Smith, Jeremy. 2004. "Aggregate Labour Productivity Growth in Canada and the United States: Definitions, Trends and Measurement Issues," *International Productivity Monitor*, Spring (8): 47-58.

Tang, Jianmin, and Weimin Wang. 2004. "Sources of Aggregate Labour Productivity Growth in Canada and the United States," *Canadian Journal of Economics*, 37 (2): 421-444.

Triplett, Jack E. 2001. *Handbook on Quality Adjustment of Price Indexes For Information and Communication Technology Products*. Paris: Organisation for Economic Co-operation and Development.

van Ark, Bart, Erik Monnikhof, and Nanno Mulder. 1999. "Productivity in Services: an International Comparative Perspective," *Canadian Journal of Economics*, 32 (2): 471-499.

Comment

Richard G. Harris
Simon Fraser University

THIS IS ANOTHER EXCELLENT STUDY on productivity measurement by three of Canada's best known experts in the area. In a now well-established Industry Canada tradition of productivity research, Someshwar Rao, Andrew Sharpe and Jianmin Tang provide careful and detailed productivity measurements using some of the most recent data available. The current study focuses on the services industries and uses both gross output and value added definitions of output to provide an impressive report on the historical record of services sector growth in the period 1981 through 2000. The study also provides a comparison with productivity growth over the same period in the United States. This complements the earlier work done by Industry Canada on Canada-U.S. manufacturing comparisons.

Before getting into the details of the study, I think it is useful to review why these numbers are important within the overall policy framework. It now seems reasonably clear that most Canadians understand why productivity is important to Canadian living standards. However, beyond this general perception and apart from the economists who worry about such matters, there is little general recognition of some of the more important issues. Most are aware there is a

Canada-U.S. productivity gap, but are not aware as to the exact source of that gap. Studies such as this help to raise the veil of ignorance around this important issue. They also provide important clues as to where policy might have the greatest potential leverage. Even so, this study is primarily devoted to measurement, and in doing so, it adds considerably to our knowledge base.

There is a great deal of scepticism among economists about the reliability of measurements of services-sector output. These problems are particularly acute when making comparisons across countries or over long time-periods. One view is that the deflators used are so ad hoc as to make 'real output' calculations useless. I agree that there are problems, but generally I think that undertaking these comparisons over a few years is still useful. Comparisons of levels are more problematic but these measurement problems are certainly not likely to affect growth rates strongly over shorter time-periods of low inflation.

The basic message of the study is a good news story for Canada — unlike many of the productivity reports we have received over the past few years. Generally, the productivity growth in services industries within Canada has been good and in some cases better than that of the United States. There are a number of results highlighted but probably the most interesting is that labour productivity growth was considerably stronger in Canada than in the United States in the 1981-1995 period (by 0.7 percentage points) and somewhat stronger in the 1995-2000 period (by 0.4 points). By 2000, the level of average labour productivity in Canada was 84 percent of the U.S. level. This is substantially better than the labour productivity gap in manufacturing. The sources of this difference are found in growth in total factor productivity or what the authors refer to as multifactor productivity. Multifactor productivity growth was stronger in Canada than in the United States in the 1981-1995 period and substantially stronger (0.9 percentage points per year) in the 1995-2000 period. There were, however, some productivity negatives in Canada, and I shall return to these shortly.

This study offers a wealth of information on detailed productivity levels and trends. My own interest is in how these particular numbers help resolve some of the as yet unsolved Canadian growth puzzles over the 1980-2000 period, and in particular what it was about the 1990s that seemed to produce relatively poor growth performance in Canada. It is useful to note however that Canada's 'poor' performance is perhaps not so bad after all. In its most recent report on growth, the OECD includes Canada among growth leaders that include Australia, Ireland, Finland, the Netherlands and the United States.[1] Compared to other larger European economies, Canadian growth performance has been above par. Nevertheless, it has not matched that of the United States and this is what remains our major point of reference. My understanding of this study is that if we are to believe the data, the Canadian services sector is not the source of differences in growth levels between Canada and the United States. In fact, strong growth in multifactor productivity suggests that both technological upgrading and catch-up to U.S. levels were at work.

The data do point, however, to one potentially important source of disadvantage. In Exhibit 2, it is reported that from 1995 to 2000, total capital growth contributed 1.53 percentage points to U.S. services output growth, while in Canada the corresponding figure was only 0.95 percentage points. This is all within a gross output KLEMS approach. In Table 4, the intensity of capital input is reported for both countries in terms of capital input per hour worked. These figures are substantially lower for Canada than for the United States. Even by 2000, Canadian capital intensity was less than 60 percent of U.S. levels. Therefore, despite strong growth in multifactor productivity, Canadian growth in labour productivity has been significantly impeded by poor levels of investment, including especially investment in ICT, as is reported in Table 10. This is generally consistent with what has also been found in manufacturing.

The other part of the story concerns the sectors where productivity growth has been high in Canada, as reported in Table 11. These include gas utilities, FIRE, wholesale trade, other services and private education. These sectors also have high growth rates relative to the United States. It is interesting that Canada seems to be similar to Australia in this respect. Australia has had exceptional productivity growth in the late 1990s and that growth has also been concentrated in the services sectors. In both cases, this may represent general catch-up to technological and organizational changes in the services sectors such as Big Box retailing, the adoption of IT and increased competition in many of these sectors. In Canada, for example, the authors report that the largest contribution to accelerated growth in services-sector productivity came from retail trade. Thank you Wal-Mart and Home Depot!

There are some other interesting anomalies in the data. Exhibit 3 shows that 0.52 points of labour productivity growth in Canada can be explained by increased intensity in intermediate goods. This is not the case in the United States. This is rather peculiar and raises some general issues of interpretation. In the Jorgenson KLEMS framework, different countries can have different factor shares or indeed production function parameters beyond the Hicks neutral total factor productivity parameter. It has never been precisely worked out what this is meant to imply, but in this case, we obviously are looking at data drawn from different technologies in Canada and the United States. The differences in the intensity of intermediate inputs may go beyond differences in relative input prices. Instead, they may reflect differences in the degree of outsourcing in the two countries. It would have been useful to see the same numbers (labour productivity and multifactor productivity) reported on a value-added basis in an attempt to sort this out.

The authors attribute the good news on productivity performance in the services sector to a possible convergence with U.S. technology as well as a catch-up in educational attainment. However, one wonders about the possibility that the superior performance of the Canadian services sector, and the poor performance of the manufacturing sector, represents a different mix of activities in the two sectors as captured by the statistical system. If services-sector activities applied to manufacturing and characterized by low productivity growth have been outsourced in the United States but not in Canada, that would tend to shift measured productivity growth toward manufacturing in the United States and toward services in Canada. If outsourcing trends accelerate in Canadian manufacturing, we may start to see the same patterns emerge here as have already occurred in U.S. manufacturing.

There are some obvious questions raised by this study as to timing and patterns of productivity change. First, it would be very instructive to see whether the same patterns emerge in provincial data. There is a general presumption that growth has been stronger in the 1995-2000 period in Central Canada than was the case in the resource-intensive provinces. Do we see a parallel trend in services-sector growth across provinces, or is this simply a manufacturing phenomenon? Secondly, an important cyclical measurement issue can affect the interpretation of these results. The acceleration identified for 1995-2000 relative to the 1981-1995 period may be partly due to cyclical differences between countries. Canada started at a much lower point in the business cycle in 1995 than was the case in the United States and thus there was a much larger output gap. It would be interesting to see the comparisons re-done with some corrections for cyclical differences in the two economies. In the post 2000 period, this issue is even more fascinating given the recent, very strong productivity numbers that have been coming out of the United States.

Despite these problems, this is an interesting and useful study. I expect that it will become the standard reference on comparison of services-sector productivity between Canada and the United States.

ENDNOTES

1 See *The Sources of Economic Growth in OECD Countries.*

BIBLIOGRAPHY

OECD. 2003. *The Sources of Economic Growth in OECD Countries*. Paris: OECD.

W. Erwin Diewert
University of British Columbia

15

Services and the New Economy: Data Needs and Challenges

THE NORTH AMERICAN INDUSTRIAL CLASSIFICATION SYSTEM AND SERVICES SECTOR DATA DEFICIENCIES

IT IS A FACT THAT STATISTICAL INFORMATION on the outputs produced and inputs used by services sector industries has been rather poorly developed in all the Organisation of Economic Co-operation and Development (OECD) countries. The current system of national accounts came into being about 70 years ago when services sector industries played a smaller role in the economy. As the importance of services sector industries grew, however, the statistical system (with some recent exceptions) did not invest resources to improve measurement of that sector.[1]

Statistics Canada (1996) publishes basic information on the productivity performance of 154 industries. Of this total, only 37 are services sector industries. Although services industries account for about 66 percent of Canadian output,[2] only 24 percent of the industries in the Statistics Canada productivity compilation represent this sector.[3] Turning to industry price statistics, Statistics Canada (2001) has a monthly publication on industry price indexes, but the entire publication is devoted to goods prices: the publication contains no output prices for the services sector. Detailed monthly consumer price indexes are available from Statistics Canada (1997) for approximately 160 commodities, of which only about 40 are devoted to services prices.

Canada, the United States and Mexico are in the process of switching from the old Standard Industrial Classification (SIC) system to the North American Industry Classification System (NAICS). Unfortunately, price indexes to deflate the outputs of these new industries will not be available unless some resources are allocated to this task.[4] Without proper price indexes, it will not be possible to measure the real output of these new NAICS industry categories with any degree of accuracy. This, in turn, implies that it will not be possible to measure the productivity of many industries of the new economy with any precision.

In the next section, we attempt to explain why it is important to measure the prices of services industry outputs accurately.[5] This is followed by a section that presents background material on the measurement of industrial net outputs as well as productivity concepts.

Having explained why it is important to collect prices for the outputs of services sector industries, the study then proceeds to take a preliminary look at Canadian services sector industries. The sections of the study that follow systematically go through the 506 NAICS services sector industries, attempting a preliminary classification of these industries according to the difficulties involved in collecting constant quality prices for their outputs. After this analysis, there is a summary of some of the biggest challenges involved in measurement.

The study finishes with an outline of a possible strategy that Statistics Canada could pursue in order to collect price information on Canadian services sector outputs, and a general conclusion.

THE IMPORTANCE OF ACCURATE SERVICES SECTOR PRICE AND OUTPUT MEASUREMENT

FIRST OF ALL, it should be noted that Statistics Canada does provide reasonably accurate measures of the *value* of the outputs produced by the various services sector industries in Canada. What is not provided is an accurate quarterly decomposition of the change in the value of output broken down into an inflation or *price change component*, and a real output growth or *quantity change component*. At this point, the reader may well ask why it is important to provide accurate measures of price change and quantity change for services sector industries. In response, there are at least five reasons for the need to provide accurate information on price and quantity movements in services sector industries.

1. **The provision of basic information on price and quantity movements is a core function of government.**

Nakamura and Diewert (1996) make the case for the importance of the provision of basic data on the economy and the responsibility of the government to provide these data. In a more comprehensive review of government responsibilities, Diewert (2001), following Bates (2001), lists the following *core functions* of a government. These functions include:

- rule of law and security of property rights (internal security including the courts and the police),
- defence (external security),
- *production of national statistical information,*

- foreign relations,
- immigration policy,
- product and workplace safety,
- maintaining macro-economic stability (monetary policy),
- provision of elementary and secondary education,
- infrastructure spending,
- support of scientific research,
- environmental protection,
- regulation of natural monopolies.

A list of *non-core functions* of government might include:[6]

- provision of higher education,
- provision of health services or health insurance,
- provision of pensions,
- provision of income support to the poor,
- provision of unemployment insurance.

The provision of national statistical information is generally regarded by most observers as a core function of government. Measurements of the prices and quantities of two thirds of the economy is pertinent national statistical information.

2. **Services industry outputs form a large proportion of gross domestic product (GDP) and hence price movements within services industries are an important component of the GDP deflator which, in turn, is a key indicator of targets for monetary policy.**

The GDP deflator is probably the second most important indicator of targets for monetary policy. Obviously, if a large proportion of services sector outputs is not being measured adequately, then the GDP deflator could be subject to very significant errors. The most important index used in setting monetary targets is the consumer price index (CPI). However, as was indicated in the first section above, services are inadequately factored into calculating both the CPI as well as the GDP deflator. Hence, increased industrial coverage of services sector output prices would improve coverage of the CPI and enhance its accuracy. In the current period of relatively low inflation, accurate measurement of prices is extremely important for the conduct of monetary policy.

3. In order to measure the productivity of the economy, it is necessary to measure the real output of services sector industries.

Labour productivity is defined as real value added divided by labour input. Total factor productivity is defined as real value added divided by all primary input. Growth of either labour productivity or total factor productivity is key to the improvement of living standards. Both measures of productivity require the accurate measurement of the prices and quantities of all outputs (including services sector outputs) and all intermediate inputs.[7] How can we judge the effectiveness of economic policies designed to improve Canada's productivity performance if we cannot accurately measure the concept of productivity underlying it?

4. In order to measure the contribution of innovations in the economy that either create new goods and services or lower the price of existing goods and services, it is necessary to measure price reductions induced by these innovations.

Since innovations are just as likely to occur in the services industries as in goods-producing industries, it is clear that without accurate measurement of services sector outputs, the efficacy of many innovations cannot be measured.[8] Innovations essentially lead to more real output for the same amount of real input and hence we *must* measure real output if we want to determine the impact of innovations.

5. The accurate measurement of prices and quantities is a necessary input into any kind of general economic model that attempts to capture the effects of changes in economic policies.

Econometric models of the economy are useful for a wide range of policy purposes. Two examples of such uses are the modeling of changes in taxation and the modeling of effects arising from compliance with the Kyoto Treaty.[9] Producer and consumer theory is usually used as a framework for deriving the supply and demand equations for these types of general equilibrium models. However, in order to apply producer or consumer theory, *values must be decomposed into their price and quantity components*. If inaccurate price indexes for services sector outputs are used, most applied econometric models will be inaccurate and could lead to significant errors in policy.

A careful examination of the first four reasons for providing additional information on the prices of services sector outputs reveals that for such purposes, it would not be absolutely necessary to provide price indexes for services products that were pure (domestic) intermediate products, since transactions involving these intermediate products would cancel out as we aggregated over industries. Thus, in order to decompose the components of final demand into price and quantity components, it would not be necessary to obtain price indexes for *purely domestic intermediate products*, such as business services. One might be tempted to think that for many purposes, there is no need for accurate price indexes for outputs and intermediate inputs by industry. There are a number of problems with this line of thought:

- In an open economy such as Canada's, many services sector products are exported or imported and, of course, we require accurate price deflators for these products since they are part of final demand. Thus, there would be little to be gained from following a strategy of measuring only final demand as opposed to systematically providing indexes of services sector prices for all outputs and intermediate inputs, industry by industry.
- Most economic forecasting models have an industrial structure and if they are at all based on production theory, it will be necessary to have accurate industry price deflators for outputs and intermediate inputs. In other words, the fifth reason cited above is still an important consideration in industry price deflators.
- There is great interest in determining exactly where improvements in productivity are taking place. Applied economists have a keen interest in determining the industries that appear to be experiencing the greatest increases in productivity. There is also a tremendous demand to compare the productivity performance of particular industries at home with their counterparts abroad and this cannot be done with any degree of precision without accurate price and quantity information on home industries.[10]
- Many statistical agencies produce economy-wide real input-output tables that seem to have solved all of the deflation problems. However, for most outputs and inputs in the services sector, accurate deflators are not available. Instead, rough and ready proxies are used, which can have substantial errors imbedded in them. Somewhere in their documentation, statistical agencies do warn users that these real input-output tables may not be very accurate, but most users of these tables tend to ignore such warnings and use the numbers as if they were completely accurate. Policy implications are often drawn from studies based on these possibly quite inaccurate tables and such policy recommendations could be quite mistaken.[11] The solution to this difficulty is of course to provide more accurate numbers and that will involve calculating new service sector price indexes.

Before we look at detailed proposals to remedy the measurement shortfall for services industries, we will take a brief look at some of the problems involved in the measurement of productivity.

THE MEASUREMENT OF INDUSTRY OUTPUT AND PRODUCTIVITY

WE BEGIN BY DEFINING VARIOUS PRODUCTIVITY CONCEPTS. *Total factor productivity* is the real output of a production unit (establishment, firm, industry, economy) divided by the real input used over a given time period.[12] *Productivity growth* of a production unit is the rate of growth of its real output divided by the rate of growth of its real input used over two time periods. *Partial productivity measures* are obtained by including only a subset of all of the outputs produced and inputs used by the production unit. For example, *labour productivity* is real output (or real value added) divided by labour input and is a partial productivity measure because it neglects the contributions of other inputs such as capital and land. On the other hand, multifactor productivity (or total factor productivity) includes all outputs produced and inputs used by the production unit.

While labour productivity does have its uses, multifactor productivity seems to be the more useful measure of productivity. Rapid growth in a measure of partial productivity could be due to rapid growth in an omitted input category and thus could be quite misleading. In the remainder of this section, we concentrate on some of the difficulties involved in measuring multifactor productivity.

In order to measure the productivity of a firm, industry or economy, we need information on the outputs produced by the production unit for each time period in the sample along with the average price received by the production unit in each period for each of the outputs. In practice, period-by-period information on revenues received by the industry for a list of output categories is required along with either an output index or a price index for each output. In principle, the revenues received should not include any commodity taxes imposed on the industry's outputs, since producers in the industry do not receive these tax revenues. The above sentences sound very straightforward but many firms produce thousands of products, so the aggregation difficulties are formidable. Moreover, many outputs in services sector industries are difficult to measure conceptually: one need only think of the proliferation of telephone services plans and the difficulties involved in measuring insurance, gambling, banking and options trading.

In addition to information on the prices and quantities of outputs produced by an industry, we require information on all the intermediate inputs used by the industry for each time period in the sample along with the average price paid for each of the inputs. In practice, period-by-period information on costs paid by the industry for a list of intermediate input categories is required along with either an intermediate input quantity index or a price index for each category. In addition, the intermediate input costs paid should include any commodity taxes imposed on the intermediate inputs, since these tax costs are actually paid by producers in the industry.

The major classes of intermediate inputs at the industry level are:

- materials,
- business services, and
- leased capital.

The current input-output framework deals reasonably well with the flows of materials but not so well with real inter-sectoral flows of contracted labour services or rented capital equipment. The input-output system was designed long ago when the leasing of capital was not common and when firms had their own in-house providers of business services. Thus, the input-output system has had a difficult time keeping up with the rapid increase in inter-industry flows of services. Although current flows are modeled reasonably well (at least in terms of broad aggregates) in the input-output tables, real flows are not modeled adequately because there is a lack of appropriate deflators.

This lack of information means the real input-output accounts will have to be greatly expanded to construct reliable estimates of real value added by industry.

It should be noted that at the level of the entire market economy, intermediate inputs collapse down to just imports plus purchases of government and other non-market inputs. This simplification of the hugely complex web of inter-industry transactions of goods and services explains why it may be easier to measure productivity at the national level than at the industry level.

We now turn to a discussion of how difficult it may be to collect price information of consistent quality on the outputs of Canadian services sector industries.

PRELIMINARY CONSIDERATIONS ON MEASURING SERVICES SECTOR OUTPUT PRICES

THERE ARE SOME 926 NAICS INDUSTRIES at the six-digit level. Of these, 381 are goods industries and are out of scope for the present paper, which focuses only on the data needs of services sector industries. A further 29 industries are related to public administration and 10 more pertain to religious, grant-making, civic and professional services. Given the theoretical difficulties involved in measuring the outputs of these public sector and non-profit institutions, and given our focus on measuring and comparing the productivity of private sector industries, we regard these 39 industries as beyond the scope of the present paper. The remaining 506 services sector industries break down as follows:

- education, health and social assistance industries (49 industries);
- wholesale and retail trade (147 industries);

- transportation (51 industries);
- services 1 (communication services consisting of 37 industries: including postal and courier services, warehousing, periodicals and books, software publishers, movies, music, radio and television, telecommunications, news and data processing);
- services 2 (business services consisting of 98 industries: including property leasing, real estate management, car and other rental and leasing, lawyers, accountants, architectural engineering, drafting, design and similar business services, computer services, administrative services, consulting and R&D services, advertising, photography, veterinary services, head office services, employment agencies, telephone call centres, collection agencies, travel agencies, security services, janitorial and cleaning services, and waste collection and disposal services);
- services 3, (personal services consisting of 79 industries: including performing arts, professional sports, museums, parks, zoos, gambling, sports facilities, hotels and other accommodation, food services, drinking places, auto repair, car washes, equipment maintenance and repair, barber shops and beauty salons, funeral homes, laundries, pet care, photo finishing and parking lots);
- finance and insurance (45 industries: including the Bank of Canada, banking and related services, brokerages, exchanges, investment advice, accident, property and life insurance agencies, brokerages and carriers, pension funds and other financial services).

Statistics Canada has very rough and ready price indexes for the wholesale and retail trade industries (147 industries)[13] and more accurate price indexes for the 51 transportation industries.[14] Statistics Canada also has approximately 60 indexes from the consumer price index that it uses to deflate the outputs of some of the remaining services sector industries. This leaves about 250 industries for which we have no deflator at present. In the following sections, we shall list these remaining services sector industries and comment on the difficulties involved in measuring the prices of their outputs.[15]

SERVICES 1: COMMUNICATION, STORAGE, INFORMATION AND ENTERTAINMENT SERVICES

THE 37 INDUSTRIES APPEARING in this class of industries are listed in Box 1. Industries 1-3 are essentially (physical) mail delivery industries and are conceptually straightforward from the viewpoint of pricing products.[16]

Industries 4-7 are storage industries and these industries produce outputs which are also reasonably straightforward to price. Industries 8-10, newspaper, periodical and book publishers, could also be viewed as having outputs that are straightforward to price. The technique would be simply to look at the price of the newspaper or periodical in the base period and compare it with the price in the current period. But what if the quality of the newspaper or periodical has changed? This problem is much more evident with books, since they tend to be relatively unique products and hence, quality may be very difficult to pin down. There is another problem that is particularly acute with newspapers and that may also apply to some periodicals: the newspaper may contain *advertising*. Thus a typical newspaper is an example of a *tied product*: consumers buy it for its non-advertising content but with that content, they are also forced to receive advertising that they may not value at all. Thus the question arises: how do we treat advertising revenues? In other words, what is its price and quantity? This question has not yet been answered in a definitive manner.

The outputs of industries 11 and 12, data base and directory publishers and other publishers, *may* be relatively straightforward to price but the outputs of industry 13, the software industry, are *not*. The problem is that each version of

BOX 1

SERVICES 1 (COMMUNICATION, STORAGE, INFORMATION AND ENTERTAINMENT SERVICES)

1.	Postal Service	19.	Integrated Record Production/Distribution
2.	Couriers	20.*	Music Publishers
3.	Local Messengers and Local Delivery	21.	Sound Recording Studios
4.	General Warehousing and Storage	22.	Other Sound Recording Industries
5.	Refrigerated Warehousing and Storage	23.*	Radio Broadcasting
6.	Farm Product Warehousing and Storage	24.*	Television Broadcasting
7.	Other Warehousing and Storage	25.*	Pay and Specialty Television
8.*	Newspaper Publishers	26.*	Cable and Other Program Distribution
9.*	Periodical Publishers	27.	Wired Telecommunications Carriers
10.*	Book Publishers	28.	Wireless Telecommunications Carriers (except Satellite)
11.	Database and Directory Publishers	29.	Telecommunications Resellers
12.	Other Publishers	30.	Satellite Telecommunications
13.*	Software Publishers	31.	Other Telecommunications
14.*	Motion Picture and Video Production	32.	News Syndicates
15.	Motion Picture and Video Distribution	33.*	Libraries
16.	Motion Picture and Video Exhibition	34.*	Archives
17.	Post-Production and Other Motion Picture and Video Industries	35.	On-Line Information Services
18.*	Record Production	36.	All Other Information Services
		37.	Data Processing Services

Note: *Determined that it would be difficult to measure output and/or collect pricing data.

a software package is generally a unique product and, typically, later versions do more than earlier versions. To deal with this problem of change in quality, it is possible to use either a matched model approach or a hedonic regression approach.[17,18]

Industry 14 listed above, motion picture and video production, is another example of a industry that is difficult to price. The different components of making a movie can be priced reasonably accurately, but the overall output of a movie-making project is typically a *unique product* that cannot be readily compared with previous movies. Moreover, the final value of the movie typically cannot be determined in the period when it is completed and ready to be distributed: returns from an excellent movie can persist for years and even decades. I do not have any good suggestions on how to proceed with pricing the outputs of this industry and this remains a topic for further research!

Industries 15 and 16, motion picture and video distribution and motion picture and video exhibition, are reasonably straightforward. The major products of industry 17, post-production and other motion picture and video industries, may not be easy to define so it may be challenging to determine the difficulty inherent in pricing this industry's outputs.

Industry 18, record production, is similar to movie production, in that the mechanical aspects of record production can be priced with minimal problems but the real challenge is to price the value of the artistic original. The final value of a "hit" song can take years to determine and as is the case with movies, songs tend to be unique commodities that are not readily comparable. Industry 20, music publishers, has similar measurement problems.

Industries 21 and 22, sound recording studios and other sound recording industries, presumably provide straightforward services that can readily be priced.

Industries 23-25, radio broadcasting, television broadcasting and pay and specialty television, have outputs that are difficult to price. Again, the problem stems from advertising revenues. Radio and television stations broadcast programming that households enjoy but do not directly pay for: viewers pay for desirable programming indirectly by consuming the tied product of commercials.[19] As with newspapers, a standard pricing paradigm has not emerged for these industries. In addition to the problem posed by advertising, there are also the challenges of dealing with the qualities inherent in unique programs.[20]

Industries 25 and 26, pay and specialty television and cable and other program distribution, also pose some complex measurement problems. With pay television, there can also be advertising revenues that must be "priced" somehow, and with both industries there are problems posed by the quality of individual stations or by programs changing over time plus complex packages of programming that are not exactly comparable over time.

The five telecommunications industries, 27-31, are reasonably straightforward except for two factors:[21]

- telecommunications services typically consist of two elements: access and minutes of use. It is not always clear how to price these two distinct components; and
- telecommunications firms provide users with a variety of (complex) plans. Until the recent past, statistical agencies have tended to price a plan until it expires and then move to pricing a newer plan, without performing any adjustment in quality between the two plans. This tends to lead to price indexes that do not show the dramatic drops in unit values for telecommunication services that have occurred in recent years.

Industries 32-36, news syndicates, libraries, archives, on-line information services and all other information services, focus on the provision of information. For private-sector firms in these industries, there are often prices for outputs that can readily be collected. For other establishments such as public libraries, outputs will be difficult to measure and prices for services may be nonexistent because of the problem of *subsidized outputs*. For services that are largely subsidized by public transfers, that are not directly related to quantities of services sold, it may be preferable to estimate marginal or average costs for the provision of the service rather than to use a nominal or zero price.

For industry 37, data processing services, it should be reasonably straightforward to collect meaningful prices.

My evaluation of the difficulty of collecting prices for the outputs of the 37 industries in this group suggests that there are 13 industries that are "difficult" to measure and 24 that are relatively "straightforward" to measure. Industries that are difficult to measure are indicated by an asterisk beside their number in the list included in Box 1.

FINANCE AND INSURANCE

SPACE DOES NOT PERMIT a full exposition on how to measure the outputs and intermediate inputs of finance and insurance firms. Virtually all of these industries hold various types of financial assets and it is necessary to work out the costs and benefits to users of these various assets. For material on the user costs of financial assets, see Barnett (1978), Donovan (1978), Hancock (1986), Fixler and Zieschang (1992, 1999), Diewert and Fox (1999, 2001), Hartwick (2000; 17-48), Barnett and Serletis (2000) and Schreyer and Stauffer (2003).

Diewert and Fox (2001) summarize some of the complexities involved in deciding how to price the outputs of the insurance industry:[22]

> The nature of the insurance industry's productive activity requires some discussion. Note that defining the nominal output of the insurance industry as premiums less claims has the rather unpalatable implication that a perfectly

> efficient industry that had no transaction costs would end up contributing nothing to national output. To avoid this unpleasant implication, Denny (1980), Ruggles (1983; 67) and Hornstein and Prescott (1991) suggested that gross premiums paid (rather than net premiums or premiums less claims) is a more appropriate measure of the nominal output of the insurance industry. In this view, consumers are buying protection services rather than forming a club to pool risk. ... This protection services view of insurance services will give rise to a much larger nominal gross output for the insurance industry than the traditional net claims approach, which leads to zero or negative nominal output in years when claims are large.[23]

In addition to accounting complexities, the production decisions of financial and insurance firms take place in an uncertain context because financial firms manage risks of various types. Economic theory has suggested various models to deal with these risk aspects[24] but there are few empirical applications of these rather complicated models within the context of measurements by a statistical agency.[25]

A listing of the 45 NAICS industries in included in Box 2. An asterisk indicates that the outputs and output prices of that industry will be difficult to measure. As can readily be seen, 40 of the 45 industries in this sector have significant conceptual difficulties affecting measurement. Of course, even in the industries where the conceptual problems are thought to be less severe, there can still be problems in following the prices of outputs that are subject to rapid quality change.

BOX 2

FINANCIAL AND INSURANCE SERVICES

1.* Monetary Authorities — Central Bank
2.* Personal and Commercial Banking Industry
3.* Corporate and Institutional Banking Industry
4.* Local Credit Unions
5.* Other Depository Credit Intermediation
6.* Credit Card Issuing
7.* Sales Financing
8.* Consumer Lending
9.* All Other Non-Depository Credit Intermediation
10.* Mortgage and Other Loan Brokers
11. Financial Transactions Processing, Reserve and Clearing House Activities
12.* Other Activities Related to Credit Intermediation
13.* Investment Banking and Securities Dealing
14. Securities Brokerage
15. Commodity Contracts Dealing
16. Commodity Brokerage
17.* Securities and Commodity Exchanges
18.* Miscellaneous Intermediation
19.* Portfolio Management
20.* Investment Advice
21.* Investment Companies
22.* All Other Miscellaneous Financial Investment Activities
23.* Direct Individual Life, Health and Medical Insurance Carriers
24.* Direct Group Life, Health and Medical Insurance Carriers
25.* Direct General Property and Casualty Insurance Carriers

BOX 2 CONTINUED	
26.* Direct, Private, Automobile Insurance Carriers 27.* Direct, Public, Automobile Insurance Carriers 28.* Direct Property Insurance Carriers 29.* Direct Liability Insurance Carriers 30.* Other Direct Insurance (except Life, Health and Medical) Carriers 31.* Life Reinsurance Carriers 32.* Accident and Sickness Reinsurance Carriers 33.* Automobile Reinsurance Carriers 34.* Property Reinsurance Carriers	35.* Liability Reinsurance Carriers 36.* General and Other Reinsurance Carriers 37.* Insurance Agencies and Brokerages 38. Claims Adjusters 39.* All Other Insurance Related Activities 40.* Trusteed Pension Funds 41.* Non-Trusteed Pension Funds 42.* Open-End Investment Funds 43.* Mortgage Investment Funds 44.* Segregated (except Pension) Funds 45.* All Other Funds and Financial Vehicles
Note: *Determined that it would be difficult to measure output and/or collect pricing data.	

SERVICES 2: LEASING SERVICES, REAL ESTATE SERVICES AND OTHER BUSINESS SERVICES

A LISTING OF THE 98 INDUSTRIES IN THIS SECTOR is included in Box 3. Only 25 out of the 98 were regarded as having outputs that are conceptually difficult to measure. However, hedonic regression techniques or model pricing may have to be used to control for quality changes in many of the remaining industries.

BOX 3 **LEASING, SERVICES, REAL ESTATE SERVICES AND OTHER BUSINESS SERVICES**	
1. Lessors of Residential Buildings and Dwellings (except Social Housing Projects) 2. Lessors of Social Housing Projects 3. Lessors of Non-Residential Buildings (except Mini-Warehouses) 4. Self-Storage Mini-Warehouses 5. Lessors of Other Real Estate Property 6. Offices of Real Estate Agents and Brokers 7. Real Estate Property Managers 8. Offices of Real Estate Appraisers 9. Other Activities Related to Real Estate 10. Passenger Car Rental 11. Passenger Car Leasing	12. Truck, Utility Trailer and RV (Recreational Vehicle) Rental and Leasing 13. Consumer Electronics and Appliance Rental 14. Formal Wear and Costume Rental 15. Video Tape and Disc Rental 16. Other Consumer Goods Rental 17. General Rental Centres 18. Construction, Transportation, Mining, and Forestry Machinery and Equipment Rental and Leasing 19. Office Machinery and Equipment Rental and Leasing 20. Other Commercial and Industrial Machinery and Equipment Rental and Leasing

BOX 3 CONTINUED

21. Owners and Lessors of Other Non-Financial Assets
22.* Offices of Lawyers
23. Offices of Notaries
24. Other Legal Services
25.* Offices of Accountants
26. Tax Preparation Services
27. Bookkeeping, Payroll and Related Services
28.* Architectural Services
29. Landscape Architectural Services
30.* Engineering Services
31. Drafting Services
32. Building Inspection Services
33. Geophysical Surveying and Mapping Services
34. Surveying and Mapping (except Geophysical) Services
35. Testing Laboratories
36.* Interior Design Services
37.* Industrial Design Services
38.* Graphic Design Services
39.* Other Specialized Design Services
40.* Computer Systems Design and Related Services
41.* Administrative Management and General Management Consulting Services
42.* Human Resource and Executive Search Consulting Services
43.* Other Management Consulting Services
44. Environmental Consulting Services
45. Other Scientific and Technical Consulting Services
46.* Research and Development in the Physical Sciences and Engineering Sciences
47.* Research and Development in the Life Sciences
48.* Research and Development in the Social Sciences and Humanities
49.* Advertising Agencies
50.* Public Relations Services
51.* Media Buying Agencies
52.* Media Representatives
53. Display Advertising
54. Direct Mail Advertising
55. Advertising Material Distribution Services
56. Specialty Advertising Distributors
57.* All Other Services Related to Advertising
58. Marketing Research and Public Opinion Polling
59. Photographic Services
60. Translation and Interpretation Services
61. Veterinary Services
62.* All Other Professional, Scientific and Technical Services
63.* Holding Companies
64.* Head Offices
65. Office Administrative Services
66. Facilities Support Services
67. Employment Placement Agencies
68. Temporary Help Services
69. Employee Leasing Services
70. Document Preparation Services
71. Telephone Call Centres
72. Business Service Centres
73. Collection Agencies
74.* Credit Bureaus
75.* Other Business Support Services
76. Travel Agencies
77. Tour Operators
78. Other Travel Arrangement and Reservation Services
79.* Investigation Services
80. Security Guard and Patrol Services
81. Armoured Car Services
82. Security Systems Services (except Locksmiths)
83. Locksmiths
84. Exterminating and Pest Control Services
85. Window Cleaning Services
86. Janitorial Services (except Window Cleaning)
87. Landscaping Services
88. Carpet and Upholstery Cleaning Services
89. Duct and Chimney Cleaning Services
90. All Other Services to Buildings and Dwellings

BOX 3 CONTINUED

91. Packaging and Labelling Services	95. Waste Treatment and Disposal
92. Convention and Trade Show Organizers	96. Remediation Services
93. All Other Support Services	97. Material Recovery Facilities
94. Waste Collection	98. All Other Waste Management Services

Note: *Determined that it would be difficult to measure output and/or collect pricing data.

EDUCATION, HEALTH AND SOCIAL ASSISTANCE

A LISTING OF THE 49 INDUSTRIES IN THIS SECTOR is included in Box 4. At least 15 out of the 49 will have outputs for which it will be difficult to obtain comparable and meaningful prices over time. A major problem with many education, health and social service industries is that they are heavily subsidized in a manner that is not directly related to their outputs. Thus the nominal or zero prices for many of their outputs are not meaningful from the viewpoint of developing productivity statistics. In other industries listed in Box 4, it will be difficult to measure outputs. For example, a medical procedure should be judged on *outcomes* and not on the *inputs* to the procedure. But in some cases, it will be difficult to determine whether the patient is "cured" and in other cases, the "quality" of the patient will matter to the outcome; i.e., a physically and mentally fit patient is less likely to die from complications arising from the procedure (but it will be difficult to measure the physical and mental fitness of patients). On the other hand, many of the industries listed in Box 4 are in the private sector and deliver reasonably well-defined services.

BOX 4

EDUCATION, HEALTH AND SOCIAL ASSISTANCE

1.* Elementary and Secondary Schools	14. Offices of Dentists
2.* Community Colleges and C.E.G.E.P.s	15.* Offices of Chiropractors
3.* Universities	16. Offices of Optometrists
4. Business and Secretarial Schools	17.* Offices of Mental Health Practitioners (except Physicians)
5. Computer Training	18. Offices of Physical, Occupational, and Speech Therapists and Audiologists
6. Professional and Management Development Training	19. Offices of All Other Health Practitioners
7. Technical and Trade Schools	20. Family Planning Centres
8. Fine Arts Schools	21.* Out-Patient Mental Health and Substance Abuse Centres
9. Athletic Instruction	22.* Community Health Centres
10. Language Schools	23.* All Other Out-Patient Care Centres
11.* All Other Schools and Instruction	24. Medical and Diagnostic Laboratories
12. Educational Support Services	
13.* Offices of Physicians	

BOX 4 CONTINUED

25. Home Health Care Service	37. Community Care Facilities for the Elderly
26. Ambulance (except Air Ambulance) Services	38. Transition Homes for Women
27. Air Ambulance Services	39. Homes for Emotionally Disturbed Children
28. All Other Ambulatory Health Care Services	40. Homes for the Physically Handicapped or Disabled
29. General (except Pediatric) Hospitals	41. All Other Residential Care Facilities
30.* Pediatric Hospitals	42.* Child and Youth Services
31.*. Psychiatric and Substance Abuse Hospitals	43. Services for the Elderly and Persons with Disabilities
32.* Specialty (except Psychiatric and Substance Abuse) Hospitals	44. Other Individual and Family Services
33. Nursing Care Facilities	45. Community Food Services
34. Residential Developmental Handicap Facilities	46. Community Housing Services
	47.* Emergency and Other Relief Services
35. Residential Substance Abuse Facilities	48. Vocational Rehabilitation Services
36. Homes for the Psychiatrically Disabled	49. Child Day-Care Services

Note: *Determined that it would be difficult to measure output and/or collect pricing data.

SERVICES 3: LIVE ENTERTAINMENT, SPORTS, CULTURAL, RECREATIONAL, TRAVEL, RESTAURANT AND PERSONAL SERVICES

THE 79 INDUSTRIES IN THIS SECTOR are listed in Box 5. Only 18 out of the 79 industries in this services sector were deemed to have major measurement problems and are therefore marked with an asterisk, but this is a rather tentative judgment.

The problem with measuring theatre and other fine arts outputs is that the quality can vary with the chosen play or exhibit and with the cast or staff. If we are willing to ignore this problem, then pricing of commercial theatres or museums is straightforward. However, cultural activities are often subsidized and the subsidy is usually a general subsidy and not one related to the specific cultural products produced from one time period to the next. This creates severe measurement problems.

I have not labeled sports teams and clubs as being hard to measure but a case could be made for quality problems in this context as well. For example, if the Ottawa Senators are doing well, it is likely that more seats will be sold, television revenues will be higher and consumers (in Ottawa) will enjoy their viewing experiences to a greater degree. However, I would say that this type of hedonic adjustment could be left to the distant future.

BOX 5

LIVE ENTERTAINMENT, SPORTS, CULTURAL, RECREATIONAL, TRAVEL, RESTAURANT AND PERSONAL SERVICES

1.* Theatre (except Musical) Companies
2.* Musical Theatre and Opera Companies
3.* Dance Companies
4.* Musical Groups and Artists
5.* Other Performing Arts Companies
6. Sports Teams and Clubs
7. Horse Race Tracks
8. Other Spectator Sports
9.* Live Theatres and Other Performing Arts Presenters with Facilities
10.* Sports Stadiums and Other Presenters with Facilities
11.* Performing Arts Promoters (Presenters) without Facilities
12.* Festivals without Facilities
13.* Sports Presenters and Other Presenters without Facilities
14.* Agents and Managers for Artists, Athletes, Entertainers and Other Public Figures
15.* Independent Artists, Writers and Performers
16.* Non-Commercial Art Museums and Galleries
17.* Museums (except Art Museums and Galleries)
18. Historic and Heritage Sites
19. Zoos and Botanical Gardens
20. Nature Parks and Conservation Areas
21. All Other Heritage Institutions
22. Amusement and Theme Parks
23. Amusement Arcades
24.* Casinos (except Casino Hotels)
25.* Lotteries
26.* All Other Gambling Industries
27. Golf Courses and Country Clubs
28. Skiing Facilities
29. Marinas
30. Fitness and Recreational Sports Centres
31. Bowling Centres
32. All Other Amusement and Recreation Industries
33. Hotels
34. Motor Hotels
35. Resorts
36. Motels
37. Casino Hotels
38. Bed and Breakfast
39. Housekeeping Cottages and Cabins
40. All Other Traveler Accommodation
41. RV (Recreational Vehicle) Parks and Campgrounds
42. Hunting and Fishing Camps
43. Recreational (except Hunting and Fishing) and Vacation Camps
44. Rooming and Boarding Houses
45. Full-Service Restaurants
46. Limited-Service Eating Places
47. Food Service Contractors
48. Caterers
49. Mobile Caterers
50. Drinking Places (Alcoholic Beverages)
51. General Automotive Repair
52. Automotive Exhaust System Repair
53. Other Automotive Mechanical and Electrical Repair and Maintenance
54. Automotive Body, Paint and Interior Repair and Maintenance
55. Automotive Glass Replacement Shops
56. Car Washes
57. All Other Automotive Repair and Maintenance
58. Electronic and Precision Equipment Repair and Maintenance
59. Commercial and Industrial Machinery and Equipment (except Automobile and Electrical) Repair and Maintenance
60. Home and Garden Equipment Repair and Maintenance
61. Appliance Repair and Maintenance
62. Reupholstery and Furniture Repair
63. Footwear and Leather Goods Repair
64. Other Personal and Household Goods Repair and Maintenance
65. Barber Shops
66. Beauty Salons

BOX 5 CONTINUED

67. Unisex Hair Salons	73. Linen and Uniform Supply
68. Other Personal Care Services	74. Other Laundry Services
69. Funeral Homes	75. Pet Care (except Veterinary) Services
70. Cemeteries and Crematoria	76. Photo Finishing Laboratories (except One-Hour)
71. Coin-Operated Laundries and Dry Cleaners	77. One-Hour Photo Finishing
72. Dry Cleaning and Laundry Services (except Coin-Operated)	78. Parking Lots and Garages
	79.* All Other Personal Services

Note: *Determined that it would be difficult to measure output and/or collect pricing data.

SUMMARIZING MEASUREMENT DIFFICULTIES IN THE SERVICES SECTOR

THERE ARE SOME GENERAL THEMES running through the previous sections that make certain types of services products difficult to measure. The following are some general categories of service products that are difficult to measure, with some overlap among categories.

- *Unique products.* This is a pervasive problem in the measurement of the prices of services.
- *Complex products.* Many services products are very complicated, e.g., telephone service plans.
- *Tied products.* Many services products are bundled together and offered as a single unit, e.g., newspapers, cablevision plans, banking services packages. In principle, hedonic regression techniques could be used to price out these first three types of services products.
- *Joint products.* For this type of product, the value depends partially on the characteristics of the purchaser. For example, the value of a year of education depends not only on the characteristics of the school and its teachers but also on the social and genetic characteristics of the student population.
- *Marketing and advertising products.* This class of services sector outputs is dedicated to influencing or informing consumers about their tastes. A standard economic paradigm for this type of product has not yet emerged.
- *Heavily subsidized products.* At the extreme limit, subsidized products can be supplied to consumers free of any explicit charges. Is zero the "right" price for this type of product?

- *Financial products*. What is the "correct" real price of a household's monetary deposits? Somewhat surprisingly, this question has not yet been resolved in a definitive manner.
- *Uncertain products*. What is the correct pricing concept for gambling and insurance expenditures? What is the correct price for a movie or a record original when it is initially released?

What is somewhat surprising is that academics have not been more interested in questions such as these. Hopefully, this study will help stimulate greater interest in these issues.

THE GENERAL STRUCTURE OF A PROPOSAL FOR BETTER SERVICES MEASUREMENT IN CANADA

IT IS NOT FEASIBLE TO MEASURE THE OUTPUTS of all 506 services sector industries listed in NAICS in the near future. Even if the money could be raised to do this, it is obvious from this brief survey of various measurement problems that for many industries, no appropriate methodology has even been developed to undertake such measurements. Moreover, it will not be possible to hire a sufficient number of skilled staff to undertake and supervise surveys for all 506 industries.

It is feasible, however, to initiate a multi-year program in which the relatively easy to measure sectors would be attacked first. At the same time, Statistics Canada should cooperate with other statistical agencies that are faced with the same measurement problems in trying to fill a tremendous gap in our system of business statistics. In particular, the U.S. Bureau of Labor Statistics, under the direction of Irwin Gerduk, is in the process of extending its producer price index to cover services sector industries. Canada should be able to learn from their experience in this area.

The proposed services sector measurement program would involve the collection of producer prices on a quarterly basis and would serve as a direct input into the calculation of real quarterly national accounts. The proposed program would also allow services sector industrial real output to be calculated on a quarterly basis. However, given the extra resources that would be used in the program, it would be useful if some synergies with the CPI program could be developed. In particular, if services sector firms were able to tell what proportion of their sales was sold to the household sector, then those sales could be targeted for representative output prices, which in turn could be fed into the consumer price index.[26] Collection of the price quotes for items that feed into the CPI universe would have to be performed on a monthly rather than quarterly basis. In any case, however, there would be significant advantages to having a monthly rather than quarterly output price collection process.[27]

CONCLUSION

AS OUTLINED IN THE SECOND SECTION OF THIS PAPER, it makes sense to fund better basic economic measurement from a variety of perspectives. This is a core responsibility of the federal government.[28] However, the spill-overs from better economic measurement will be significant. In particular, the conduct of monetary policy should be greatly improved. In addition, if a proposal for better services sector price information is funded, the economic policy community should be able to conduct better analyses and do a better job of managing the economy.

ENDNOTES

1 During the past decade, the Project to Improve Provincial Economic Statistics invested very heavily in the improvement of Canada's annual services sector statistics, although this investment was limited to nominal dollar statistics. Statistics Canada also invested substantial resources into the fuller exploitation of tax data, which are invaluable for measuring the characteristics of small firms that dominate in many services industries. Resources were also put into the expansion and improvement of the business register in the services industries; the manufacturing and mining survey was enhanced to include questions about purchased services inputs; and significant resources were devoted to convert the economic survey system to NAICS, which has a more detailed and up-to-date treatment of the services sector than did the previous classification system. During the 1990s, Statistics Canada also built five new price indexes for particular services industries: consulting engineering, traveller accommodation, accounting, business long distance telecommunications and informatics professional services. In the United States, the Bureau of Labor Statistics has recently embarked on an extensive new program to collect output prices for services sector industries in its PPI program. Also in the United States, the Bureau of Economic Analysis has recently developed deflators for software services.

2 According to Statistics Canada (1998), in 1997, services sector industries accounted for $403,354 million or 66 percent of total Canadian GDP of $691,625 million at factor cost in 1992 prices. The corresponding numbers for 1961 were $124,029 million, accounted for by services industries out of a total GDP of $199,053 million (62 percent of GDP).

3 Not all of the results for the services sector industries are published. In Statistics Canada (1996), there are details on outputs, inputs and productivity for 28 specific industries, of which only 5 are services sector industries. The 5 industries are: (i) transportation and storage industries; (ii) communication industries; (iii) wholesale trade industries; (iv) retail trade industries and (v) community, business and personal services industries.

4 Most of these "new" industries are not really new if the sense of "new" is that they did not exist 10 years ago. They are new in the sense that they have been singled out for disaggregation from a larger grouping of industries.

5 See Baily and Gordon (1988) for a good general discussion of the difficulties involved in measuring services sector outputs.

6 All of the listed "non-core" functions of government are essential today but they are labelled as non-core because it is conceivable that they could be provided privately.

7 Actually, economy-wide measurements of productivity can be calculated from knowing just the price and quantity information for all outputs delivered to final demand sectors. In other words, accurate price and quantity information on intermediate input flows is not required for an economy-wide measurement of productivity. However, there is great interest in Canada in comparing the productivity performance of particular industries with their U.S. or international counterparts. In order to measure industry productivity, we require information on the gross outputs and intermediate inputs by industry. See the following section for a discussion on this topic.

8 One example is fibre optic cable, which has dramatically reduced the price of long-distance telephone communication and led to greater choice for cable television viewers. Other examples are medical improvements and increased choice in larger stores.

9 Econometric models that rely on producer theory are also common in regulatory policy.

10 There is tremendous interest in *benchmarking* the performance of a large number of domestic production units against foreign counterparts. Examples of industries that have been benchmarked in this way include electricity generation, coal mining, electricity distribution, garbage collection, railroads, port operations, airlines telecommunication services, and so on. These benchmarking exercises also require price and quantity decompositions of all inputs used and outputs produced.

11 Zvi Griliches warned me around 1970 that some official statistical agency numbers may not be very accurate. For 15 years, I ignored his warning with the thought that official numbers could not possibly be "wrong." I did finally realize, however, that Zvi's caution was warranted and have been trying ever since to help bring about the improvements required.

12 Real output is simply deflated nominal output.

13 A detailed methodology for pricing the outputs and intermediate inputs of a distribution firm can be found in Diewert and Smith (1994).

14 The methodology for measuring the prices of transportation outputs is generally well developed.

15 The North American Industry Classification System is not yet complete. Hence, we shall have to guess to a certain extent about the nature of the products in each industry.

16 This is probably not entirely accurate; there are no doubt many difficult measurement problems hidden away in this industry as will be the case with every industry. However, everything is relative. Physical mail delivery is much more straightforward to price than the outputs of many of the industries that follow.

17 See Oliner and Sichel (1994) and Abel, Berndt and White (2003).

18 See Seskin (1999) and Grimm and Parker (2000) for the Bureau of Economic Analysis hedonic approach. Hedonic regression techniques date back to Court (1939) and were popularized by Griliches (1971a, b). For a recent comprehensive survey, see Triplett (2002). For recent applications of the technique, see Silver and Heravi (2001, 2002 and 2003).

19 The revenue flows are different for public broadcasters that may receive some or all of their revenues as subsidies. This just makes the price measurement problems more complex.

20 The essence of statistical agency pricing is to compare like with like. This is hard to do in an unambiguous, reproducible manner when products are one of a kind!

21 See the papers on telecommunication services in Woolford (2001).

22 For an additional discussion on pricing concepts for insurance outputs, see Sherwood (1999).

23 Diewert and Fox (2001), p. 186.

24 See for example Arrow (1951, 1984), Bowers, Gerber, Hickman, Jones and Nesbitt (1986) and Diewert (1993, 1995).

25 Yu (2003) offers a recent important empirical study of gambling that takes risk factors into account.

26 This is an ideal situation. An adequate approximation may be just to use the industry output price indexes, adjusting for taxes and transportation if necessary, as direct inputs into the CPI.

27 Monthly prices would be more representative and monthly estimates of real industry product could be provided. Finally, the effects of a missing price quote would not be as severe if prices were collected on a monthly basis.

28 In addition to funding Statistics Canada to collect services sector prices, it would be useful for the Social Sciences and Humanities Council to fund a specific program that would help solve some of the many conceptual problems in defining and measuring services sector outputs.

ACKNOWLEDGMENTS

THE AUTHOR THANKS INDUSTRY CANADA for financial support and Alice Nakamura and Philip Smith for helpful comments on earlier drafts of this paper. None of the above are responsible for opinions expressed in this paper.

BIBLIOGRAPHY

Abel, J.R., E.R. Berndt, and A.G. White. 2003. "Price Indexes for Microsoft's Personal Computer Software Products," Paper presented at the NBER Program on Productivity, July 28, Cambridge, MA.

Arrow, Kenneth J. 1951. "Alternative Approaches to the Theory of Choice in Risk Taking Situations," *Econometrica,* 19, 404-437.

————. 1984. *Individual Choice under Certainty and Uncertainty*. Cambridge, MA: Harvard University Press.

Baily, M.N., and R.J. Gordon. 1988. "The Productivity Slowdown, Measurement Issues and the Explosion of Computer Power," *Brookings Papers on Economic Activity,* 2, 347-420.

Barnett, W.A. 1978. "The User Cost of Money," *Economic Letters*, 1, 145-149.

Barnett, W.A., and A. Serletis. 2000. *The Theory of Monetary Aggregation*. Amsterdam: North-Holland.

Bates, W. 2001. *How Much Government? Do High Levels of Spending and Taxing Harm Economic Performance?* Draft Report commissioned by the New Zealand Business Roundtable, Wellington.

Bowers, N.L., H.U. Gerber, J.C Hickman, D.A. Jones, and C.J. Nesbitt. 1986. *Actuarial Mathematics*. Itasca, Illinois: The Society of Actuaries.

Court, A.T. 1939. "Hedonic Price Indexes with Automotive Examples," in *The Dynamics of Automobile Demand.* New York: General Motors Corporation, pp. 98-117.

Denny, M. 1980. "Measuring the Real Output of the Life Insurance Industry: A Comment," *Review of Economics and Statistics,* 62, 150-152.

Diewert, W. Erwin. 1993. "Symmetric Means and Choice Under Uncertainty," in W. Erwin Diewert and Alice O. Nakamura (eds.). *Essays in Index Number Theory,* Volume 1. Amsterdam: North-Holland, pp. 355-433.

————. 1995. "Functional Form Problems in Modeling Insurance and Gambling," *The Geneva Papers on Risk and Insurance Theory,* 20, 135-150.

————. 2001. "Productivity Growth and the Role of Government," Discussion Paper No. 01-13. Vancouver: Department of Economics, The University of British Columbia, www.econ.ubc.ca/diewert/hmpgdie.htm. (Accessed January 17, 2005).

Diewert, W. Erwin, and Kevin J. Fox. 1999. "Can Measurement Error Explain the Productivity Paradox?" *Canadian Journal of Economics,* 32 (2): 251-280.

————. 2001. "The Productivity Paradox and the Mismeasurement of Economic Activity," in K. Okina and T. Inoue (eds.). *Monetary Policy in a World of Knowledge-Based Growth, Quality Change and Uncertain Measurement.* London: Macmillan Press.

Diewert, W. Erwin, and A.M. Smith. 1994. "Productivity Measurement for a Distribution Firm," *Journal of Productivity Analysis,* 5, 335-347.

Donovan, D. 1978. "Modeling the Demand for Liquid Assets: An Application to Canada," *International Monetary Fund Staff Papers,* 25, 676-704.

Fixler, D.J., and K. Zieschang. 1992. "User Costs, Shadow Prices, and the Real Output of Banks," in Zvi Griliches (ed.). *Output Measurement in the Service Sector.* Chicago: University of Chicago Press, pp. 219-243.

————. 1999. "The Productivity of the Banking Sector: Integrating Financial and Production Approaches to Measuring Financial Service Output," *Canadian Journal of Economics*, 32 (2): 547-569.

Griliches, Zvi. 1971a. "Hedonic Price Indexes for Automobiles: An Econometric Analysis of Quality Change," in Z. Griliches (ed.). *Price Indexes and Quality Change*. Cambridge, MA: Harvard University Press, pp. 55-87.

————. 1971b. "Introduction: Hedonic Price Indexes Revisited," in Z.vi Griliches (ed.). *Price Indexes and Quality Change*. Cambridge, MA: Harvard University Press, pp. 3-15.

Grimm, B., and R. Parker. 2000. "Software Prices and Real Output: Recent Developments at the Bureau of Economic Analysis," paper presented March 17 at the NBER Program on Technological Change and Productivity Measurement, Cambridge, MA.

Hancock, D. 1986. "The Financial Firm: Production with Monetary and Non-Monetary Goods," *Journal of Political Economy*, 93, 859-880.

Hartwick, J.M. 2000. *National Accounting and Capital*. Cheltenham, UK: Edward Elgar, pp. 17-48.

Hornstein, A., and E.D. Prescott. 1991. "Measuring the Real Output of the Life Insurance Industry," *Review of Economics and Statistics*, 59, 211-219.

Nakamura, Alice O., and W. Erwin Diewert. 1996. "Can Canada Afford to Spend Less on National Statistics?" *Canadian Business Economics*, 4 (3): 33-36.

Oliner, S.D., and D.E. Sichel. 1994. "Computers and Output Growth Revisited: How Big is the Puzzle?" *Brookings Papers on Economic Activity*, 2, 273-330.

Ruggles, R. 1983. "The United States National Income Accounts, 1947-1977: Their Conceptual Basis and Evolution," in M. Foss (ed.). *The U.S. National Income and Product Accounts: Selected Topics*. Chicago: University of Chicago Press, pp. F15-96.

Schreyer, P., and P. Stauffer. 2003. "Measuring the Production of Financial Corporations," Draft Final Report, OECD Task Force on Financial Services (Banking Services) in National Accounts, Background Report to the OECD/BSF/SNB (Swiss National Bank) Workshop, August 28-29, Zurich, Switzerland.

Seskin, E.P. 1999. "Improved Estimates of the National Income and Product Accounts for 1959 to 1998: Results of the Comprehensive Revision," *Survey of Current Business*, 79, 15-39.

Sherwood, M.K. 1999. "Output of the Property and Casualty Insurance Industry," *Canadian Journal of Economics*, 32 (2): 518-546.

Silver, M.S., and S. Heravi. 2001. "Scanner Data and the Measurement of Inflation," *The Economic Journal*, 111 (June): F384-F405.

————. 2002. "Why the CPI Matched Models Method May Fail Us," Working Paper 144. Frankfurt: European Central Bank.

————. 2003. "The Measurement of Quality Adjusted Price Changes," in R.C. Feenstra and M. Daniel Shapiro (eds.). *Scanner Data and Price Indexes, Studies in Income and Wealth*, Volume 64. Chicago: The University of Chicago Press, pp. 277-316.

Statistics Canada. 1996. *Aggregate Productivity Measures: 1994*. Ottawa: Minister of Industry.

————. 1997. *Consumer Prices and Price Indexes: October-December 1996*. Ottawa: Minister of Industry.

————. 1998. *Canadian Economic Observer: Historical Statistical Supplement 1997/98*. Ottawa: Minister of Industry.

————. 2001. *Industry Price Indexes: December 2000*. Ottawa: Minister of Industry.

Triplett, Jack E. 2002. *Handbook on Quality Adjustment of Price Indexes for Information and Communication Technology Products*, OECD Directorate for Science, Technology and Industry (Draft). Paris: OECD.

Woolford, K. (ed.). 2001. *International Working Group on Price Indices: Papers and Proceedings of the Sixth Meeting*, April 2-6, Canberra, Australia: The Australian Bureau of Statistics.

Yu, K. 2003. "Measuring the Output and Prices of the Lottery Sector: An Application of Implicit Expected Utility Theory", in *Essays on the Theory and Practice of Index Numbers*, Ph. D. Thesis. Vancouver: University of British Columbia, pp. 95-111.

Comment

Philip Smith
Statistics Canada

FOR THE BENEFIT OF THOSE NOT ALREADY FAMILIAR with the background, Diewert's paper is part of a broad initiative led by Renée St-Jacques and her colleagues at Industry Canada aimed at expanding and improving Canadian statistics related to services sector prices and output. Professor Alice Nakamura is also a proactive player in this undertaking.

The Diewert paper makes a strong case that regular and frequent measurement of services sector price and output trends is very important, noting that the services sector accounts for two-thirds of Canada's GDP and that innovative firm behaviour and productivity advances in the sector cry out for better measurement. I very much agree with him on this, and also on his proposition that Statistics Canada is the right institution to undertake this challenge.

Diewert's framework is quite sensible, as is his suggestion that we initiate a multi-year program as some other countries have done, picking the "low-hanging fruit" first and the more difficult services commodities thereafter. Indeed, Statistics Canada has been working on a draft plan for just such a program.

A key element, of course, will be the necessary funding for the undertaking. It will cost several million dollars to develop a full suite of services price indexes and several million more every year in order to keep the indexes updated. Accordingly, Diewert's paper can best be seen as part of a broader effort to develop and articulate a concrete plan with the ultimate goal of attracting the necessary resources to carry it out.

While a lot more definitely needs to be done, Statistics Canada has already made considerable headway with respect to the measurement of services sector value added at current prices. An ambitious five-year project started in 1996, known as the Project to Improve Provincial Economic Statistics, resulted in a major expansion of Statistics Canada survey-taking in the services sector. Progress has also been made with respect to the measurement of services price indexes, although in this instance the advances have been more modest. The consumer price index includes sub-indexes for a substantial range of personal services commodities. These indexes feed into the calculation of the chain Fisher price and volume GDP indexes. In addition, over the past 15 years or so, the agency has developed price indexes for five types of business services. These indexes cover: (i) consulting engineering services, (ii) informatics professional services, (iii) long distance business telephone services, (iv) accounting services and (v) traveller accommodation services. Work is currently under way to design and implement price indexes for courier services, software publishing, for-hire trucking and non-residential accommodation.

The work done to date has given us valuable experience but as I already acknowledged, much remains to be done. Canada has been falling behind our neighbours in the United States, where the Bureau of Labor Statistics has a US $12 million budget devoted to the development and maintenance of services price indexes. In Canada, we currently spend only about $0.5 million a year.

Resources will always be limited, of course, so it is important that priorities be well established. In this respect, I agree with Diewert that it is wise to begin with those service commodities where good methodologies have already been developed and tested in other countries. Along similar lines, it may be wise to focus on the simplest cases before turning to the more complex ones and in this regard the author's subjective sorting of services categories by degree of complexity is helpful. Another key factor is the relative importance of the various service commodities, both in terms of their individual contributions to GDP and their perceived importance from the policy-maker's perspective. Moreover, in deciding where to focus our resources, we should also be opportunistic, seeking partnerships and exploiting complementarities where they are evident.

In summary, I congratulate the author on an interesting and helpful paper. By writing it, he has highlighted an important issue while at the same time advancing discussions about the shape that a services price index development plan might take. Statistics Canada will be following up on this initiative in the coming months by putting forward a paper of its own on this subject.

Pierre Sauvé
London School of Economics[*]

16

Services Industries in a Knowledge-Based Economy: Summing Up

INTRODUCTION

GAINING A BETTER UNDERSTANDING OF THE SERVICES ECONOMY, identifying the types of policies most likely to sustain the development of a knowledge-based economy, and enhancing the data upon which sound policy decisions must ultimately rest are all goals that are widely seen as holding the key to Canada's longer-term prosperity. Services industries generate close to three quarters of Canadian output and jobs; they have become a source of major product and process innovation; and they are the target of increasing research and development (R&D) spending. Services also rank among the country's most dynamic capital-exporting sectors.

Yet despite the importance of services in the Canadian economy, the sector has tended to receive far less attention than manufacturing or even agriculture in debates on public policy or in the priorities of policy research. The intangible and heterogeneous nature of tertiary activities also means that services tend to receive scant attention in the training of graduates in economics. This is particularly true in the trade field, where the bias toward goods (i.e. manufacturing) continues to dominate much academic output.

This volume, and the conference at which its various chapters were presented, attest to Industry Canada's desire to start redressing such imbalances. The volume provides the academic and policy communities with a very rich, if daunting, agenda for future empirical study. The purpose of this concluding chapter is to take stock of some of the key policy challenges emerging from the research done to-date and to identify a range of issues where further research might be expected to yield strong public-policy dividends, helping Canadians reap the full benefits of a knowledge-based economy.

---

[*] *Author was Director of Studies and Visiting Professor, Groupe d'Économie Mondiale, Institut d'Études Politiques de Paris at the time of writing this summary of proceedings.*

The Services Economy: Salient Facts

WHY, ONE MIGHT ASK, should governments devote greater attention to the services economy? The answer can be found in a number of recent global economic trends that are easy to see within the Canadian context. The following summarizes some of the salient facts of the modern services economy.

- Services are central to overall economic performance: in the Organisation for Economic Co-operation and Development (OECD) they account for close to three quarters of output and employment and in a number of middle-income developing countries, their contribution to output and employment is fast approaching OECD averages.
- They constitute a large and increasing share of intermediate inputs into the production of manufactured goods and the delivery of other services, affecting their cost, price and quality.
- For close to two decades, services have been the most dynamic source of employment creation, export and growth in foreign direct investment (FDI) around the world.
- In recent decades, key services sectors have been subjected to significant experiments in regulatory reform in an effort to stimulate competition.
- Services hold the key to realizing the full benefits of a knowledge economy through the adoption and diffusion of information and communications technologies.
- In response to a globalizing economy, a growing share of labour market adjustments are taking place in services. Such adjustments include outsourcing, moving jobs (increasingly white-collar jobs) off-shore, skills upgrading, life-long learning and the sharply increased participation of women in the labour force.
- Services generally place fewer strains on the global commons and can play a central role in enhancing environmental stewardship.
- Services are where attempts at structural reform typically raise some of the most complex policy challenges and encounter the fiercest political resistance.

Are Services Exceptional?

THE ESSAYS IN THIS VOLUME were first presented at a conference that focused attention on the complex relationship that exists among services, knowledge industries and the innovation process. A theme common to many of this volume's chapters is the extent to which services differ from goods. Simply put, to what extent do services possess features that require us to revisit traditional assumptions about the functioning of markets, measurement techniques and policy prescriptions, all of which have been shaped by our greater and long-standing familiarity with how goods are produced and sold both domestically and across borders? What policy implications arise from the tendency of services to be characterized by greater factor mobility, higher regulatory intensity and a diversity of market failures calling for public-policy responses? Similarly, what is policy to make of the potentially-reduced relevance of time and space (i.e. determinants of location) to products that can be produced, stored and/or delivered through electronic means?

In various ways, all of the essays in this volume test the hypothesis that the services sector is in some way exceptional. They do so in two basic ways. A first set of essays addresses a range of horizontal challenges arising in knowledge-based services. This includes a survey of labour market performance indicators for highly skilled workers (René Morissette, Yuri Ostrovsky and Garnett Picot); a closer look at the locational determinants of services sector activities (Steven Globerman, Daniel Shapiro and Aidan Vining; C. Michael Wernerheim and Christopher Sharpe); the FDI performance of Canadian services sector firms (Walid Hejazi); Canadian and international trends in services sector productivity and outstanding measurement challenges (Someshwar Rao, Andrew Sharpe and Jianmin Tang; Anita Wölfl); sources of services sector innovation and R&D performance (Petr Hanel); as well as the (still mostly unmet) data requirements of a knowledge economy (W. Erwin Diewert).

A second set of papers approaches these issues from a sectoral perspective, focusing attention on the two core groups of infrastructure industries in knowledge-based economies — telecommunications (Zhiqi Chen) and financial services (Edwin H. Neave). A final paper (John Whalley) addressing the effects of China's recent accession to the World Trade Organization (WTO), recalls the important role that trade and investment policy can play both in helping countries reap the benefits of open services markets and in accelerating structural change and the associated international division of labour in key services industries.

What are the main lessons emerging from this research? For starters, the work presented in this conference volume is a useful reminder of how little we still know about the services economy. Compared with the data available for manufacturing, services sector data is of inferior quality and too highly aggregated, even if it is improving. Modeling techniques for the services sector tend to be inadequate and their predictive value lacks credibility, impairing their usefulness for policy-making. It is difficult to measure labour and total factor productivity in fields such as health care and education, where output is intangible. And yet, much as we are far from reaching credible or definitive conclusions on any of the topics taken up by the volume's contributors, conferences such as these go a long way toward helping the academic and policy communities focus on essential questions. For the most part, the answers emerging from the research presented in this volume challenge the traditional view that the services economy is fundamentally distinct from manufacturing. The body of research presented here reflects significant and growing evidence of a services economy characterized by high levels of skill, productivity, innovation and foreign direct investment. However, much as one can derive comfort from growing evidence that services are "unexceptional" in these respects, there is also evidence of a significant gap in services sector labour productivity between Canada and the United States, evidence that leaves little room for policy complacency.

This essay turns first to a more detailed consideration of the conference papers and the discussions they provoked before identifying a list of services-related topics that could usefully command greater attention within the academic and policy research communities.

SUMMING UP WHAT WE KNOW (AND WHAT WE KNOW WE DON'T KNOW)

HORIZONTAL PERSPECTIVES

Labour Market Performance

The labour market is a useful place to gauge the transformative properties of the new economy. Growing technological intensity and the rapid diffusion of information and communication technologies (ICTs) may be expected to exert a strong influence on the demand for new skills, incentives to acquire such skills and the wages they command. Fittingly, the conference opened with a roundtable discussion featuring a presentation by Garnett Picot, describing ongoing work at Statistics Canada on trends in relative wage patterns among the highly educated.

Picot began by noting that, unlike the United States, there had been virtually no increase in the university wage premium in Canada over the past two decades, with rising demand for highly educated workers meeting an equally rapid rise in supply. The supply response was particularly strong among women, whose share of the university-educated labour force had quadrupled in just 20 years, double the level observed for men. He noted that one of the main purposes of ongoing research was to obtain a more disaggregated sense of shifting patterns of supply and demand within the labour market for skilled workers. In particular, it was necessary to probe factors most likely to shape the wage performance of Canadian university graduates: age; sector-specific knowledge-intensity; applied fields of study; and returns to skilled migration.

Picot noted that there was clear evidence of a rising university wage premium among the young on both sides of the 49th parallel, as measured by ratios comparing earnings by university and high-school graduates. Somewhat counter-intuitively, he noted that the data showed only modest evidence for faster growth of the university wage premium in high-knowledge sectors — a trend more pronounced for men than for women — than in sectors that were less skill-intensive. Still, he noted that employment growth had been fastest within the higher-knowledge sectors, both in aggregated terms and within the services economy alone.

Again somewhat counter-intuitively, there was little evidence of changing relative earnings by field of study. Indeed, available data does not support the expectation that in a knowledge-based economy, the earnings of science and engineering graduates should rise relative to those of graduates from other fields. Once more, such results appear to reflect a broad balance between shifts in the demand for, and the supply of, graduates with applied scientific skills.

Among immigrant university graduates, Picot noted that real wages and wages relative to Canadian-born graduates had declined significantly. This, he claimed, could lead to pressures to review Canada's long-standing policy of favouring highly skilled immigration. Moreover, such trends could also dampen prospects for enhanced Canadian offers on trade in the so-called Mode 4 services — services supplied through the temporary entry and stay of mainly highly skilled foreign workers — under the Doha Round of WTO negotiations.

Locational Determinants

An important question arising from the advent of a knowledge-based economy is the extent to which services sector activity may be relatively immune to the influence of geography on the location decisions of firms. This is because of the greater scope such an economy affords for remote supply and its potential to reduce the weight of constraints imposed by time or distance. The answer to such a question has obvious and potentially far-reaching implications for the design of regional development policy.

The conference considered two papers devoted to the question of if and how services differed from goods in terms of the spatial location of production activities. The paper by Steven Globerman, Daniel Shapiro and Aidan Vining (henceforth Globerman et al.), explored the relationship between firm location and performance for information technology (IT) companies in Canada.[1] The second paper, by Michael Wernerheim and Christopher Sharpe, investigated a range of factors that determine the location of firms providing advanced producer services (APS) in rural and urban areas and their agglomeration with firms in related manufacturing industries.[2]

The paper by Globerman et al. sought answers to three important questions. First, do agglomeration and other external economies limit the economic benefits of location to a very few sites in Canada? Second, what initiatives might policy makers undertake to enhance the location benefits of Canadian sites? And third, do Canadian high tech firms enjoy specific spillover benefits from physical proximity to favourable locations in the United States?

The paper's main findings are that IT companies located in Toronto enjoy strong growth advantages (measured in terms of sales volumes) and that growth performance deteriorates with distance from Toronto. While the paper revealed the difficulty of assigning precise advantages to a Toronto location, broad agglomeration economies appear to be at play, including benefits associated with infrastructure related to university research. The paper also finds that it is difficult to identify any possible growth spillover benefits stemming from proximity to the United States.

The authors draw relatively straightforward conclusions from their analysis, though these are clearly controversial in a Canadian context where both the federal and provincial governments are prone to engage in significant industrial policy activism. One, the study suggests that the locational decisions of Canadian IT firms appear sub-optimal: greater concentration in or near Toronto may be warranted from the perspective of growth in sales. Two, the federal and provincial governments should be aware of the limited advantages of most locational incentives targeting IT companies. Three, the study seems to confirm the importance of public research infrastructure, including universities. This might help offset some of the disadvantages resulting from otherwise sub-optimal locations such as Waterloo.

Ajay Agrawal teasingly summarized these results with the observation "there's something really interesting about Toronto, but we're not quite sure what." His discussion of the paper was followed by a lively debate among conference participants. Several participants questioned the paper's methodology on the grounds of sample bias, the fact that the investigation covered the peak of the IT bubble, a period marked by the misallocation of capital that this bubble entailed, as well as the paper's use of sales growth and distance as performance metrics. Others questioned its implications for government conduct.

The Wernerheim-Sharpe paper started by pointing out the dearth of research on location patterns of services industries in non-urban areas relative to the mountain of empirical work devoted to manufacturing. The paper found that for rural APS firms, the forces favouring dispersion tend to dominate those favouring agglomeration. At first glance, such results seem to run counter to those suggested in the paper by Globerman et al. In his comments, Mario Polèse recalled the critical need to properly distinguish between tradable and non-tradable services. Because most services industries produce inputs into manufacturing and other services industries, they tend to be highly sensitive to agglomeration effects. Accordingly, he cautioned against the paper's underlying optimism and the excessive policy activism such optimism might promote. Instead, he noted that the overwhelming majority of services jobs in rural areas were either public or non-tradable in nature. Because most producer services in non-metropolitan areas serve highly localized markets, their greater dispersion might be expected.

Setting aside differences over methodology, the Wernerheim-Sharpe paper usefully recalled why the services sector is increasingly viewed as holding new promise for remote or stagnating regions. The main idea that underpins policies that embed this view is that a number of APS firms can be independent of traditional agglomeration economies, geographical advantages conferred by nature, and physical proximity to a manufacturing sector. Such services can act as their own growth poles to the extent that they are exportable beyond regional and national boundaries. The remarkable growth of the South Indian software industry would be a prime example of this sort of export-led remote supply. This in turn raises the question of the best way of attracting employment to a region. If advanced services firms are sufficiently footloose to locate, relocate or branch out from metropolitan areas into rural areas or areas on the fringes of cities, do the factors that determine such decisions vary across space or sub-sectors? Are firms that locate in non-metropolitan areas less dependent on proximity to manufacturing industries and other factors that have traditionally-conferred locational advantages? Moreover, what types of government intervention targeting APS firms are most likely to generate a sustained positive influence on local growth, employment and rural welfare? The above questions all deserve closer empirical scrutiny across sectors and regions.

Both papers were deemed by discussants and some conference participants to suffer from a number of "first mover" analytical disadvantages. There is little doubt, however, that they shed useful and innovative light on a field where extremely fertile policy enquiries must be conducted. However, in his masterful keynote address, Richard Lipsey reminded participants that governments could not (and should not) be expected to abdicate their support for new economy applications, even outside Ontario!

There is much to be gained from a better understanding of how industrial clusters are created and sustained; of what distinguishes broad versus sector-specific agglomeration effects. It would be helpful to identify the types of knowledge-intensive services activities that are more immune to the constraints of space or distance and hence more likely to allow remote delivery to become a feasible growth strategy. It would be useful to better gauge the payoffs from public investments in higher education and associated research infrastructure. There would be benefit to applying a refined version of the model developed by Globerman et al. incorporating, for instance, elements of the anchor-tenant hypothesis developed by Agrawal and Cockburn to other knowledge sectors.[3] Among these might be professional services, bio-technology or audio-visual services, whose production in Canada manifest significant regional dispersion, as does IT. Doing so would generate useful cross-sectoral information on if and how location matters to the performance of firms and the communities that host them. It would also contribute to the design, distributional consequences and overall effectiveness of regional development policies in Canada.

The FDI Performance of Services Sector Firms

An important distinguishing feature of many services transactions is the pervasive tendency for services to be produced and consumed simultaneously, though IT applications and the growth of e-commerce are beginning to alter this somewhat. It is hard to envisage services trade occurring without the movement of capital and labour either as suppliers or consumers.

Capital is by far the most internationally mobile of the two factors of production, reflecting a policy stance of most host countries that is generally more liberal toward investment than it is toward immigration. This is true despite the fact that the bulk of restrictions on investment continue to be found in services industries. As the recent breakdown of world trade talks in Cancun revealed, at the global level there is considerable sensitivity about investment rules and their effect on the development process and the retention of domestic regulatory sovereignty. It is thus all the more important to get our facts straight.

To date, much attention has been devoted to studying the dynamics of FDI in manufacturing and FDI trends in services, both inward and outward, have hardly been investigated. Walid Hejazi's contribution to closing this knowledge gap in a North American context is therefore particularly welcome.

Hejazi's work confirms a trend that has generally gone unnoticed by observers, including many policy makers. Canada has been transformed from a capital importing economy in the 1970s, with one dollar of outward FDI for every four dollars of inward FDI, into a capital exporting country by the end of the 1990s, with four dollars of outward FDI for every three dollars of inward FDI. Hejazi's paper documents how such a turnaround gathered pace as a result of the integrating forces flowing from the two landmark trade agreements — the 1987 Canada-U.S. Free Trade Agreement (FTA) and the 1994 North American Free Trade Agreement (NAFTA). It further shows that the surge of outward FDI has primarily been a services phenomenon, in contrast to inward FDI, where manufacturing continues to dominate.

Hejazi's findings raise a number of important challenges for the formulation of FDI policy in knowledge-based industries. The first issue is what to make of such changes? Are they necessarily good news? How much do we know about the various forces underlying such a transformation? To what extent have changes in policy, including the negotiation of far-reaching agreements for the protection and liberalization of investment under the NAFTA, contributed to such structural changes? Do the data suggest that the economics of preferential investment liberalization differ from those arising in goods trade? To what extent have inward FDI flows in services been held back by ownership restrictions in telecommunications, transportation and financial services, some of which have only recently been lifted (see the discussion of the Chen paper below)? To what extent can the high degree of market concentration at home explain Canada's strong outward FDI performance in financial services?

Moreover, how broad is the sectoral composition of the changes depicted in Hejazi's analysis? Is Canada's outward FDI performance in services broadly based, and thus indicative of sustained gains in the competitive advantage of Canadian firms? Or does it reflect little more than a few large mergers and acquisitions (notably in financial services) in the U.S. market? To what extent, and in what forms, has the dismantling of the border in goods trade imparted greater substitutability to trade and investment linkages? How was Canada's outward FDI performance in services affected by the relative lack of progress in Canada-U.S. regulatory convergence under the NAFTA? What explains Canada's growing inability to attract third country FDI in manufacturing under NAFTA? To what extent can one correlate such difficulties with the findings of Rao et al., showing continued gaps in labour productivity, R&D and human capital between Canadian and U.S. manufacturing? Why would similar gaps not exert similar effects in services FDI? What cost-effective policies may be employed to influence services sector FDI (tax policy, public investment in research and education, regulatory reform)? More broadly, what do such changes portend for Canada's ability to develop, nurture and retain knowledge-based activities in manufacturing and services?

While advancing answers to several of these questions, the paper leaves many key issues for further enquiry. There is little doubt that significant policy dividends are likely to be reaped through future research directed at dissecting the ownership, locational and internalization advantages that are driving FDI flows into and out of Canada.

Confronting the Productivity Paradox — Did Solow and Baumol Get It Wrong?

In 1987, the Massachusetts Institute of Technology (MIT) economist and Nobel laureate, Robert Solow, famously coined what came to be known as "the productivity paradox" when he quipped that one could see the computer age everywhere but in the productivity statistics! His scepticism toward what would later become a central contention of partisans of the transformational properties of the "new economy" echoed the earlier musings of another famous U.S. economist, New York University's William Baumol. The latter's "cost disease" theory postulated lower productivity levels in services (and especially public services) because of their less intensive use of capital, lower rate of innovation, smaller average firm size and reduced exposure to international competition due to the non-tradability of many services.

Two papers presented at the conference dealt with productivity. The paper by Someshwar Rao, Andrew Sharpe and Jianmin Tang (subsequently Rao et al.), described the recent productivity performance of Canadian services industries; the second, by Anita Wölfl, described broad trends in aggregate labour productivity growth in the services sectors of OECD countries. Both papers suggested that Solow and Baumol had been wrong.

As is true of virtually all topics addressed at this conference, a disproportionate amount of research into Canadian productivity trends has focused on manufacturing industries, partly because of the superior quality and availability of data on inputs, outputs and prices and partly because of the predominance of manufactured goods in international trade. Services industries suffer from significant data limitations (see the paper by Diewert in this volume), yet they account for more than 70 percent of output and employment in Canada and their importance continues to grow. As both papers make clear, it is productivity trends in the services sector, and not in manufacturing, that are and will increasingly be the driving force behind aggregate productivity growth and hence real income growth in Canada. Moreover, because of the growing interdependence between manufacturing and services, productivity improvements in services will loom increasingly larger as a factor in the competitive position of Canadian manufacturing firms.

The above trends explain why it is so crucial to policy that attempts be made at correcting our gaps in knowledge of the sources of productivity growth in services and overcoming what are still acute measurement difficulties in a number of sub-sectors, the output of which tends to be less tangible.

The paper by Rao et al. starts off by noting the widening gap in income levels across the 49th parallel, a gap that the authors ascribe to a widening of aggregate Canada-U.S. labour productivity differentials. Recalling, as Wölfl does, that labour productivity levels vary greatly across services industries, Rao et al. show that U.S. services sector workers were an average of some 16 percent more productive than their Canadian counterparts in 2000. This gap remains even as the Canadian services sector outperformed its U.S. counterpart over the past two decades in terms of both output and labour productivity growth. While Rao et al. conclude that a process of broad convergence towards U.S. productivity levels in services is under way in Canada, their analysis usefully identifies the main parameters of services sector performance where policy can and must make a difference: capital intensity, human capital, the share of ICT capital in total capital, and R&D intensity in services. All four are areas where performance in key Canadian services industries remains lower than in the United States.

An interesting aspect of the paper by Rao et al. is their finding that over the past two decades, retail trade accounted for close to half of the observed growth in services sector labour productivity in both Canada and the United States. Such an outcome suggests that Canada may have benefited strongly from the liberalization of trade and investment in this sector. The paper also reports that in both countries there was negative productivity growth in services industries such as land transportation, audio-visual, health and education services. The authors note that had these industries experienced labour productivity growth of zero or at the average for the services sector as a whole, the boost to economy-wide growth in labour productivity would have been significant. At the same time, they admit that there are difficulties associated with the measurement of real output in such sectors.

Contrary to the popular belief likening the services sector to low-productivity activities, the research by Rao et al. reveals quite unambiguously that the Canadian services sector has been a success story in terms of productivity growth. This is so even as significant further efforts need to be made, notably in narrowing the gaps in human and physical intensity between Canada and the United States. This is needed if real incomes in Canada are to rise to a level approximating those south of the border and thereby mitigate migration pressures among the highly skilled.

The paper by Anita Wölfl looked at cross-country differences in services sector performance in advanced industrial societies. This work is part of ongoing research on the services economy by the Paris-based OECD (see Box 1). It raised a host of important policy and measurement questions relating to the contribution of services to aggregate productivity growth in rich countries. Wölfl's study brought forward a number of salient facts that underscore the central role that services have come to play in knowledge-based economies.

The period 1990-2000 saw manufacturing continue to outperform the services sector in terms of average annual productivity growth rates, and while some services such as health care, education and social work, display low or even negative rates of productivity growth. However, a number of services industries such as finance, storage, post and telecommunications, transport, wholesale and retail trade, produced quite robust productivity figures throughout the period: in a large number of OECD countries, their productivity growth patterns were comparable to those of high-growth manufacturing industries.

Virtually everywhere in the OECD, the contribution of services to aggregate productivity growth is both rising and greater today than ever before. Far from becoming hamburger-flipping nations, OECD countries have seen their services sectors become increasingly intensive users of capital, knowledge and skills, as measured respectively by the ratio of physical capital to total employment; the percentage of services in total business R&D; and the share of highly skilled employment in total employment. What's more, even though services sector firms are generally small in both absolute terms and relative to manufacturing firms, the evidence suggests that small services firms have been among the most innovative, a result that Petr Hanel's findings for Canada appear to contradict (see Box 1).

Decomposing changes in services sector output into its various structural components, Wölfl's paper also usefully documents the extent to which services use and provide intermediate inputs and their increasing exposure to international trade. Long thought of as essentially non-tradable, services have enjoyed export growth that has systematically outpaced that of manufacturing over the past two decades. As a result, services today are on the cutting edge of trade policy. Moreover, a focus on the central role of services as intermediaries has done much to promote regulatory reform and external liberalization in key sectors. This has resulted in associated gains in allocative efficiency and economy-wide performance that have been observed throughout the OECD area.

Box 1

OECD Work on the Services Economy

At the OECD's 2003 ministerial council meeting (MCM), the Japanese Minister for Economy, Trade and Industry (METI) tabled a proposal for work on the services economy, focusing on how economic performance in the services sector can be enhanced.

The proposed research project, to be completed in time for the spring 2005 ministerial meeting, aims to analyze the services economy and the role of public policies in enhancing overall economic performance through the development of services. It will examine the role of different structural policies and provide a synthesis of best practices aimed at growth and employment in the sector. It will seek to update and challenge current thinking by addressing some widely held beliefs about services being unproductive, less innovative, less prone to technological developments and insulated from international trade.

The first section of the report will briefly analyze recent and prospective trends in the services economy, looking at relevant services sectors and noting the relative importance of different modes of services delivery within each sector. It will also compare the importance and impact of the services economy on economic performance. In doing so, it will examine issues of measurement, including the methods of measuring intangible assets of importance to services industries. Finally, it will analyze the interaction between the services and other industries.

The second section will look at the economy-wide factors that allow growth in services industries. This includes policies that facilitate the transfer of resources from declining manufacturing industries, such as an efficient regulatory framework, a flexible labour market and measures to support human resource development. The role of subsidies and taxes that distort market conditions and issues related to privatization and the liberalization of trade and investment flows in the services sector will also be treated, as will the challenges and opportunities facing the services sector as a result of expected demographic changes.

The third section will analyze the role of science, technology and innovation policies, as well as issues related to entrepreneurship, in supporting the development of services. Ways to promote R&D and innovation in the services sector will be examined, as well as ways to boost the overall performance of services sector firms through greater diffusion and application of ICT. Additional work could examine the influence of intellectual property rights (IPRs) on innovation in the services sector — with a particular emphasis on software services — as well as the role of knowledge-intensive services in boosting innovation performance in other services sectors.

Wölfl's paper and the comments on it by Alice Nakamura set the stage for a candid discussion of the pervasive measurement headaches that continue to plague empirical analysis on services, especially with regard to cross-border comparisons of productivity. Nakamura noted how policy conclusions deriving from erroneous measurements could be socially harmful, recalling that nothing was worse than an error passing for a fact. National differences in definitions and data sources used to track employment and hours worked were seen as introducing potentially significant biases into the measurement of labour productivity growth. The discussion also illustrated the policy implications of underestimating labour productivity growth in specific services industries. The problem of measuring the contribution of services to aggregate productivity was deemed most apparent in education, arguably the sector that should occupy the most prominent place in preparing workers for the requirements of a knowledge economy. The productivity of that sector was generally felt to be quite low by traditional measurement standards.

Underestimating productivity growth in key producer services could have significant impacts on the productivity of other user industries. Consequently, it was widely felt that further research efforts should be directed to plugging the measurement gap. The Wölfl paper touches on other issues that deserve closer analytical scrutiny. Effort should be directed toward understanding the influence of innovation, ICT, trade and FDI as well as domestic regulatory conduct, on the performance of product and factor markets. We need to explore the impact of outsourcing on overall services sector performance. And we need to assess the impact of recent trends toward white-collar "offshoring" on wages and income distribution in both sending and receiving countries.

Innovation and R&D in Services

The paper by Petr Hanel confirmed a number of trends identified in the contributions by Rao et al. and Wölfl. His research shows that after many years of neglect, innovation activities in services firms are being increasingly recognized as an important component of national innovation systems. Hanel's survey of the literature shows that a number of dynamic services industries are using and benefiting from ICT more than the rest of the economy. In so doing, the services economy has become a source of significant product and process innovation, contrary to some popular beliefs. In the author's view, this explains why key segments of the services economy have witnessed superior labour productivity performance in recent years.

In exploring various channels of services sector innovation, Hanel cautions against applying to services the conceptual framework that was developed within the context of industrial innovation. The immaterial nature and vast heterogeneity of the services economy complicate attempts at cross-sectoral comparisons. The small size of most services sector firms means that their innovation activities may, to the extent that they exist at all, not be captured by the statistical procedures developed for larger-scale industrial innovation.

While R&D activity is clearly on the upswing in several key services industries, overall, R&D in services remains less important than it is in manufacturing. Its content is typically different and so too is the way it is organized. For example, services rely less on intellectual property rights (IPRs), especially patents which are useful indicators of R&D "output" in manufacturing. This implies that information on R&D in services is often sketchy though improving as IPR use grows in services, notably in ICT-related services. In turn, the paucity of data at the national level significantly lessens the relevance and usefulness of international comparisons.

The organization of R&D in services is not generic, but rather tends to focus specifically on solving a problem or carrying out a development project. It also typically entails — and is indeed often a result of — close interactions between providers and users. The fact that many services are embedded in the expertise of individual services providers underlines the importance of personal contact, training and tacit knowledge in services innovation. An important policy corollary of this is the need to promote or accept greater labour mobility for services providers.

The relative importance of these differences between services and manufacturing warrants closer scrutiny. Even so, Hanel observes a process of convergence in innovation levels between skill-intensive services and manufacturing firms. To some extent, such convergence may result from the blurring of boundaries between services and manufacturing. It may also be related to the growing trend among manufacturing firms toward outsourcing some activities that used to be performed internally to external services-producing firms.

Hanel's overview of innovation in the Canadian services sector highlights how empirical work in this area runs up against significant data constraints. This is so despite the fact that information on Canadian R&D in services ranks among the most complete in the OECD. As things currently stand, the bulk of information on innovation in services dates back only to 1996 and is available for only three dynamic Canadian services industry groups: communications, finance and technical services. Of course, these are not trivial industries: together, they account for close to two-thirds of total value added in the services sector, or roughly a third of Canada's GDP.

Hanel's study of the incidence of product and process innovation within these three services industries shows finance in the lead, followed by communications and technical (or business) services. Recalling Wölfl's findings, his paper reports that innovation rates in Canada's leading services industries (measured as the share of surveyed firms reporting the introduction of product or process innovations) exceeds the average level of innovation found in Canadian manufacturing. Such a level matches that observed in the country's most innovative manufacturing industries: electrical and electronic products, pharmaceuticals, chemicals and machinery.

Hanel found that services sector innovation is strongly associated with firm size. This conclusion may be biased by the large average size of firms in the industries surveyed, especially in finance and communications. Still, his paper cites a range of sources showing that the rate of adoption of both organizational and technological change appears significantly higher in larger services firms than in smaller ones. Size also seems to be a determining factor in explaining the somewhat surprising finding that public-sector organizations introduced organizational and technological change at twice the pace of private-sector firms.

Decomposing the possible sources of services sector innovation, Hanel's study points to the importance of management as a central locus of novel ideas, especially in smaller firms. This is followed by sales and marketing. In all sectors, the crucial innovation input is provided by ICT. The widespread use of computers connected by internal and external high-speed communication networks is the technology that underpins most innovations in services and their diffusion to clients. In his comment, Steven Globerman recalled how much the same influences could be found in leading manufacturing activities. Globerman argued that policy makers should pay closer attention to the various barriers to services sector innovation described in Hanel's paper: its high cost, especially for smaller firms; the critical need for qualified personnel; broadening access to venture capital; promoting pro-competitive regulation (especially in communications); and the need to extend eligibility for public support programs to firms that may be less prone to performing R&D activities. All of these factors were seen as explaining why U.S. firms in services industries were significantly more R&D-oriented than their Canadian counterparts.

The Data Needs of the New Economy

Erwin Diewert performed the Herculean — if somewhat unenviable — task of drawing the attention of conference participants to the current inadequacies of statistical information about the knowledge-based economy. His paper offers an eloquent and informed plea for governments to devote the time, the energy, and above all the resources needed to fill the acute gap in knowledge that is impeding further services sector research and sound policy-making. Conference participants agreed strongly with the author's assertion that the spillovers from better economic measurement of services sector activity would be large, notably in terms of the conduct of monetary policy but also more broadly in terms of general economic policy.

Diewert's paper recalls how the root of the new economy's data problems can be traced to the conceptual underpinnings of the decades-old system of national accounting found throughout the OECD countries. Such a system was devised at a time when the services economy contributed (or was seen as contributing) only marginally to aggregate economic activity. National statistical systems failed quite spectacularly to keep pace with the rapid rise of the modern services economy throughout the post-war period. This had important implications for the quality of economic analysis and of public policy, to say nothing of the credibility of the dismal science and those who practice it!

Diewert illustrates some of the statistical deficiencies affecting services sector analysis in Canada. He notes that while Statistics Canada provides reasonably good measures of the value of services sector outputs, it fails to provide the research and policy-making communities with an accurate decomposition of price and quantity changes affecting the value of output in services.

Of the 154 industries for which Statistics Canada measures productivity performance, only 37, or less than a quarter, are services industries. Detailed consumer price indexes are available for only 40 of the 160 commodity groups which are the focal point of data gathering efforts. And there currently are no monthly output price indexes for the services sector. Diewert goes on to note that governments in North America are switching to a new system of industrial classification. Without price indexes to deflate the outputs of newly disaggregated industries, it will simply be impossible to measure their productivity performance with any degree of accuracy.

Diewert's paper recalls why an investment in reversing our knowledge gap in services data is likely to yield high returns. He cites five main arguments for the development of more extensive and more accurate price and output measurements. He notes, first, that the provision of such basic data is a core function of government. Second, with services being such a large component of output, services price deflators are an important component of the GDP deflator, which in turn is a key indicator used in determining monetary policy. Third, he recalls that no accurate measurement of overall productivity performance is possible without accurately measuring the real output of services industries. Fourth, he notes that measuring the contribution of innovation and new product offerings to overall economic performance depends on the ability to measure the impact of innovation on the price of existing goods and services. Finally, the accurate measurement of prices and quantities is a necessary input into any kind of general economic model that attempts to gauge the effects of changes in economic policies.

Given the scarcity of resources available for data collection in services, Diewert suggests setting out some priorities. He does so by going through the 506 services sector industries of the North American Industrial Classification System (NAICS) with a view to establishing a preliminary classification of services industries according to the difficulties involved in collecting constant quality prices for the outputs. A measure of the challenge at hand is provided by the fact that of the 506 sectors noted above, roughly half currently have no price deflators.

SECTORAL PERSPECTIVES

Telecommunications

Few industries have witnessed as dramatic changes in recent years as the telecommunications industry. The interaction of rapid technological change, product innovation and shifting attitudes toward regulation and competition in the industry have made it the undisputed leader in the diffusion of knowledge in a modern services economy. The paper by Zhiqi Chen places these trends in a Canadian context, comparing the industry's growth in terms of size, infrastructure and productivity relative to a sample of 20 OECD countries. In addition, his study sheds light on two important issues in telecommunications policy: the impact of competition in cellular telephony, for which there has been spectacular gains in market penetration worldwide over the past decade, as well as the spillover effects of telecommunications infrastructure and services across countries.

Chen's overview of Canada's telecommunications industry during the 1990s paints a generally disquieting picture. While the size, infrastructure and labour productivity of Canadian telecommunications have all grown rapidly during the period, the industry's performance was significantly below the OECD average.[4] Chen's paper reports that employment in the industry fell in both absolute and relative terms during the period and that Canada's penetration rate (a proxy measure of infrastructure growth) went from 2nd to 23rd place among OECD countries. Moreover, while Canada remains a world leader in terms of its fixed-line network, the sector's performance in cellular telephony has been laggard by industrial country standards. Chen's econometric analysis suggests that two important factors contributed to this disappointing performance. First, Canada's highly developed fixed-line network and especially its well-developed payphone system, may have dampened demand for cellular mobile services and thus slowed down the industry's growth. Second, relatively high barriers to entry and operation, notably restrictions on foreign ownership, appear to have hindered the growth of cellular telephony. Chen suggests that if such barriers were reduced to the OECD average, Canada's telecommunications penetration rate would stand above the average level for OECD countries.

Turning his attention to the relationship between telecommunications and growth, Chen presents an econometric model covering the period from 1985 to 1998 that includes cellular mobile services and considers the spillover effects from foreign telecommunications infrastructure. His findings show a positive and significant correlation between domestic and foreign telecommunications infrastructure and overall economic growth. Estimates from his analysis show that Canada's GDP per working-age person stands to increase by 1.7 percent over a ten-year period, if Canada were to remove all remaining barriers to foreign direct investment in telecommunications services. The Canadian government refused to contemplate such changes to the industry during both NAFTA negotiations and talks on the Uruguay Round, despite strong pressures from the United States. Given the central role that telecommunications plays in equipping citizens and firms to take full advantage of knowledge-based economies, Chen's depiction of Canada's decline in cellular telecommunications should be a cause for concern within the policy-making community. Prospects are currently bleak for any significant movement either toward a free trade area of the Americas or on the WTO's Doha Round. Consequently, Canadian officials should consider if the time has come to initiate some measure of unilateral liberalization of the country's telecommunications regime.

In his discussion of Chen's paper, Sumit Kundu pondered whether the great diversity of OECD countries in terms of income levels, geography, population and tele-density made them a relevant benchmark to assess Canada's recent performance in telecommunications. He noted that Canada tended to rank higher in other leading comparative studies of IT performance such as the annual World Competitiveness Report of the International Institute for Management Development. He usefully suggested that the author complement his analysis with more firm-level data to enhance measurement of the competitive performance of leading Canadian services providers relative to their U.S. and foreign competitors. He also called for a fuller discussion of the origin and nature of the growth spillover effects of the telecommunications infrastructure described in Chen's paper. For example, he asks if evidence can be found to suggest that the magnitude of spillovers differs for fixed-line and mobile services, as recent studies in developing countries tend to indicate. Finally, Kundu questioned the seemingly counter-intuitive result presented by Chen that barriers to trade and investment did not appear to exert any significant effects on penetration rates in precisely that market segment — fixed services — generally considered the least contestable in Canada.

Finance

If the telecommunications industry is the undisputed leader in diffusing ICT-based applications, the financial sector ranks among the very top users of such applications. Not surprisingly, the financial sector has become an important and ubiquitous source of product and process innovation. The principal input of this industry is information and it has, more than any other sector, played a critical role in advocating the opening of international telecommunications markets, ushering in a spectacular worldwide drop in the cost of handling and trading information. This, in turn, has facilitated the adoption of a dizzying array of new financial products supported by cost-effective means to exchange them within and across countries. Edwin Neave's paper chronicles such changes in a Canadian context, showing how the financial industries' adoption of ICT technologies has improved the operating efficiency of financial institutions while also reducing transaction charges for consumers, whether they are households or businesses. It has also enhanced access to credit by all classes of borrowers through new techniques of risk measurement and growing recourse to securitization.

The competitive pressures arising from such changes are obviously not without an impact on market structures, both at home and abroad. Neave's paper recalls how a process of consolidation through mergers, both domestic and across borders, is becoming common within the banking sector and has now extended to interactions among banking, insurance and securities firms.

Neave describes an industry that has come to manifest almost continuous technological advancement. His paper offers much food for thought to policy makers. ICT-enabled financial innovation has brought e-finance to the retail level, accelerated the gradual disappearance of branch networks, developed new distribution channels and increased the commoditization of financial products. All of these trends raise important new policy challenges in terms of financial supervision, regulation, competition and consumer protection as well as market liberalization which extends to trade. Such changes also call for heightened and novel forms of regulatory cooperation at the international level.

In his discussion of Neave's paper, Eric Santor questioned the extent to which financial markets had become truly global in scope. He agreed however that ICT-enabled innovation was partly responsible for the ongoing blurring of market boundaries in finance which posed formidable challenges to market regulators. Such developments not only rendered the conduct of monetary policy more complex and uncertain, it also raised a host of new policy challenges, notably in distributional terms if some classes of citizens without access to the e-economy were shut out of some market segments. Santor also drew attention to concerns over the offshoring of white-collar back-office software design and management operations to developing countries. Such concerns have in recent years become acute in a number of services industries and are likely to gain in prominence as financial market consolidation proceeds and the technological means to supply such services remotely is enhanced.

A New Eldorado? China's Services Markets After WTO Accession

Few changes in the global economy can match the scale of the transformation implied in the terms of China's recent accession to the WTO. Present at the post-war inception of the General Agreement on Tariffs and Trade, of which it was an original contracting party, but which it left shortly afterwards in light of the political upheavals of 1949, China has agreed to pay a very high price for re-admission to the multilateral trade community. Coming in the wake of two decades of uninterrupted tectonic shifts in the country's economic policy, the process of China's accession to the WTO was extraordinary both in how long it took to complete — some 15 years — and in the level of commitments asked for by China's main trading partners and ultimately accepted by China's reform-minded leadership. Such ambitions are particularly striking in services trade, a comparatively-weaker component of the Chinese economy to which OECD countries and their leading services-supplying firms have long yearned to secure expanded, transparent and non-discriminatory access.

John Whalley's contribution to this volume offers a critical assessment of the path-breaking nature of China's services commitments. Just how broad are these commitments? A quote from Whalley's study brings this out:

> ...over a five-year period from 2002 to 2007, China will open all of its markets to full international competition from foreign service providers in a series of key areas: distribution, telecommunications, financial services, professional business and computer services, motion pictures, environmental services, accounting, law, architecture, construction, and travel and tourism. China will remove all barriers to entry in the form of discriminatory licences to operate and all conduct-related barriers in the form of differential regulations for domestic and foreign entries.

Whalley's essay questions whether China will be able to comply fully with the terms of its accession protocol in services, moving to free trade over what he rightly considers to be an extremely short transition period. He also considers the effects of a likely scenario of non-compliance. Reviewing the literature devoted to assessing the economic impacts of China's services commitments (for itself and the rest of the world), Whalley directs our attention to the paucity of analytical tools and modeling techniques currently at the disposal of the academic and policy communities in the services field. The shortcomings of services trade modeling are compounded in China's case by the paucity of available data.

The current implications arising from available studies suggest that large positive gains will accrue from services liberalization for both China and the global economy. An important caveat however is that for such benefits to materialize, far-reaching changes are required. In China's financial sector, there is a need to lessen the economy's reliance on bank loans as a source of funding, to clean up the problem of the non-performing assets of state banks, and to allow for much-needed consolidation in the banking sector. In the rest of the economy, there is a need to address the problem of loss-making state-owned enterprises in both goods and services producing industries. The sheer scale of such changes and the lessons learned from experience in other transition economies suggests how challenging a five-year implementation period may prove to be. China's ability to make a success of WTO accession in a large range of manufacturing sectors such as textiles and clothing by the end of 2004, will impose an adjustment burden on firms and workers in the rest of the world, including OECD countries. Whalley suggests that China's likely difficulties in implementing its services commitments could place it on a collision course with WTO sanctioned retaliation and heightened judicial activism after 2007. Conflicts have already arisen over anti-dumping duties.

In his discussion of Whalley's paper, John McHale agreed that the magnitude of the challenges facing China was considerable. He argued, however, that there were a number of reasons for measured optimism. He began by recalling that the new political leadership has been unwavering in its support for continued reforms in product and labour markets. He argued that the WTO provided an essential external anchor for pursuing such reforms, especially as regards bringing financial discipline to the state-owned enterprises that are the Achilles heel of the Chinese economy. A short transition period was also useful in preparing China's financial sector for liberalization of capital accounts. Moreover, McHale felt that a booming domestic economy would likely blunt local opposition to reform, both by absorbing surplus labour released during reform of the state-owned enterprises and by encouraging job creation more generally. He cautioned however that the size of the bilateral trade imbalance vis-à-vis the United States could lead to zealous enforcement in services on the part of U.S. trade officials responding to a backlash against the outsourcing of manufacturing jobs to China. McHale nonetheless saw significant opportunities arising from the opening of China's services markets. The country's leadership had fully accepted the crucial contribution that an efficient services infrastructure could make to economy-wide performance. Seen this way, opening the market was likely to be good news for China and its trading partners, including Canada, even though one could not easily document and measure these gains using available computable general equilibrium modeling techniques.

In the general discussion that ensued, conference participants concurred that an improvement in modeling the economic effects of services trade and investment liberalization were important to policy. This is so for three main reasons. One, it would inform Canada's positions and priorities across various negotiating settings at the bilateral, regional and multilateral levels. Two, it would help to anticipate what should come next in services liberalization on the Canada-U.S. front. Three, it would use credible and objective fact-finding to counter the mounting opposition to services trade and investment liberalization that has taken root in various civil society organizations at home and abroad.

A Policy Research Agenda for the Future

MUCH AS WE ARE ALL STILL IN LEARNING MODE when it comes to the services economy, there is little doubt that we know more than we used to as a result of the essays in this conference volume. Despite the rich menu of issues taken up in this conference volume, it by no means exhausts the full range of important policy challenges that governments continue to address in attempting to manage the emerging knowledge-based economy and to help their citizens realize its full promise. Several of the papers in this volume are likely to lead to more detailed investigations. Some will see their methodologies and conceptual insights subjected to critical scrutiny. Some will see them tested out in different sectors. All of this is to be welcomed, for there is a real need to develop a sounder knowledge base on services and the various ways they create wealth, contribute to innovation, affect international trade and investment, and help sustain productivity and hence income levels.

Several topics on which the academic and policy research communities should be seeking answers come to mind as priorities for future research. This essay concludes with a tentative and incomplete list of topics that future Industry Canada conferences might address. While this volume features a down payment of sorts on some of these topics, others have yet to be tackled sufficiently from either a Canadian or international comparative perspective:

- What do we know and what do we need to know: identifying those elements of the services economy and services regulatory policies most in need of enhanced statistical monitoring and measurement. This should include a survey of available information on regulatory environments and regulatory reforms in the services sector.

- Measuring the economy-wide effects of services sector reforms: assessing how services sector policies affect sector and overall economic performance and the impact of such policies on prices, labour and total factor productivity, employment, exports, imports and FDI, including patterns of intra-industry trade and investment in services, innovation and the intensity, nature and organization of R&D activities in services.

- What works best in regulatory reform? What have we learned in two and a half decades of practice in services industries? Distilling the elements of best practices in regulatory reform, both in terms of horizontal policy design (e.g. competition policy) and in key sectors (e.g. finance, telecommunications, energy, transportation, distribution, education and health). Critically appraising earlier mistakes in policy design that led to reform failures.
- How does external liberalization contribute to domestic reform? Developing a methodology for assessing the impact of trade and investment liberalization for use in negotiations around the General Agreement on Trade in Services as well as regional trade negotiations.
- How do labour markets adjust to heightened competition in services markets? Does the path of labour market adjustment in services differ (in time, space, educational profiles and skills of affected workers) from that in manufacturing? Are highly skilled services workers increasingly at risk from sending their jobs offshore? What can be done to facilitate orderly labour market adjustments in services industries?
- Services providers on the move: deepening our understanding of the impact of services sector reform on immigration patterns and policies governing international and inter-provincial labour mobility. Improving recognition of the competencies, experience and educational degrees required in an era of greater mobility.
- Services and the global commons: assessing the environmental impact of the services economy.
- What policy mix holds the key to reaping the full benefits of a knowledge-based services economy?
- How will looming demographic changes affect the optimal design of economic policy and the pace of reform? How can the reform process in services (and particularly in regard to labour market practices) best address the challenges of ageing societies?
- What scope exists for pursuing reform efforts in public and semi-public services such as education, health and environmental services?

- How can reform be made politically viable? What is the packaging of product- or labour-market reform that will meet the least resistance from interest groups? What is the sequencing of labour- and product-market reforms that is most likely to stimulate social consensus in favour of reform policies?

ENDNOTES

1 The study tracked the performance of firms in the following IT sub-sectors: software, wireless software, web development, Internet services providers, applications software providers and diversified services providers.

2 Wernerheim and Sharpe describe advanced producer services as being "synonymous with knowledge-intensive, high order, high quality business services."

3 See Agrawal and Cockburn (2003).

4 Chen measures size in terms of telecommunications sector revenue as a percentage of GDP and in terms of the number of employees in the industry relative to total employment; infrastructure growth is measured in terms of penetration rates; and labour productivity in terms of revenue per employee and access channels (fixed and mobile) per employee.

BIBLIOGRAPHY

Agrawal, Ajay, and Ian Cockburn. 2003. "The Anchor Tenant Hypothesis: Examining the Role of Large, Local, R&D-intensive Firms in University Knowledge Transfer," *International Journal of Industrial Organization*, 21, 1227-1253.

About the Contributors

Ram C. Acharya is an economist in the Micro-Economic Policy Analysis Branch of Industry Canada, where he has conducted research on Canada-U.S. economic integration regarding the impact of trade and technology in factor earnings, specializing in North America, and competition and productivity. He was a policy analyst at the Department of Foreign Affairs and International Trade, where he conducted research on Canada-U.S. regional market integration, and analysis of international trade and investment performance in Canada. He has a Ph.D. in Economics from the University of Ottawa.

Ajay Agrawal is a professor at the University of Toronto's Rotman School of Management where he teaches courses in technology management and innovation policy as well as in corporate strategy. His research interests include the strategic use of intellectual property rights, international labour mobility and knowledge flows, and private-sector competition over public-sector science. His work has appeared in various publications including *Management Science*, the *International Journal of Industrial Organization*, and the *National Bureau of Economic Research Working Paper Series*. Dr. Agrawal received his Ph.D. in Business Economics from the University of British Columbia. In addition, he studied at the London Business School and at the Sloan School of Management at the Massachusetts Institute of Technology as a visiting scholar.

Zhiqi Chen is a professor of Economics at Carleton University. He was the Director of the Carleton Industrial Organization Research Unit from 1996 to 1998, the Director of the Ottawa-Carleton Joint Doctoral Program in Economics from 2001 to 2004. He twice held the T.D. MacDonald Chair in Industrial Economics at the Competition Bureau from 1998 to 1999 and from 2004 to 2005. In 2000, he received a Research Achievement Award from Carleton University. Dr. Chen's main research areas are industrial organization and international trade. His research papers have been published in journals such as the *American Economic Review*, the *RAND Journal of Economics* and the *International Economic Review*.

W. Erwin Diewert is a professor of Economics at the University of British Columbia. He has published over 70 papers in journals and over 70 chapters in books. His main areas of research include duality theory, flexible functional forms, index number theory (including the concept of a superlative index number formula), the measurement of productivity and the calculation of excess burdens of taxation. He has acted as a consultant on measurement and regulatory issues for the International Monetary Fund, the World Bank, the Bureau of Labor Statistics, the Bureau of Economic Analysis, the OECD, Bell Canada and Industry Canada.

Steven Globerman is the Kaiser Professor of International Business and Director of the Centre for International Business at Western Washington University. He is also an adjunct professor at Simon Fraser University. His research interests encompass a range of topics in international economics and industrial organization. He has published extensively in the areas of international trade, foreign direct investment and industrial and regulatory policy. Professor Globerman has consulted for numerous private sector organizations, as well as governments and regulatory agencies, including serving on the research staffs of two Canadian government Royal Commissions.

Petr Hanel is a professor of Economics at the University of Sherbrooke and a member of the Centre interuniversitaire de recherche sur la science et la technologie (CIRST) in Montreal. His previous work includes a book, *La technologie et les exportations canadiennes du matériel pour la filière bois-papier*, and numerous articles and studies on economic aspects of technological change, innovation, industrial and commercial policies and international trade. He is the co-author, with John Baldwin, of *Innovation and Knowledge Creation in an Open Economy-Canadian Industry and International Implications,* published by Cambridge University Press in July 2003.

Richard G. Harris is the Telus Professor of Economics at Simon Fraser University, and a Senior Fellow of the C.D. Howe Institute. His major area of specialization is international economics and, in particular, the economics of integration. During the 1980s, he worked extensively on economic modelling of the impact of the Canada-U.S. Free Trade Agreement and subsequently on the North American Free Trade Agreement (NAFTA). He has served as a consultant to a number of Canadian government departments, international organizations and corporations in the area of international economics. In addition to a number of technical articles, he has published policy-oriented books and articles on Canada-U.S. free trade, international macro-economics, economic growth, the Asia-Pacific region, and Canadian public policy.

Walid Hejazi is an assistant professor of International Business Economics at the University of Toronto's Rotman School of Management and the Division of Management at the University of Toronto at Scarborough. He is also a research associate at the Institute for International Business. His research deals with both international business economics and macro-economics. He has published extensively on issues related to foreign direct investment and international trade. Some of his recent publications include a monograph entitled *Canada and Foreign Direct Investment: A Study of Determinants*, (University of Toronto Centre for Public Management), "Motivations for FDI and Domestic Capital Formation", and "Trade, Foreign Direct Investment and R&D Spillovers", both in the *Journal of International Business Studies*.

Sumit K. Kundu is the Ingersoll-Rand Professor in International Business and an associate professor of Management and International Business in the College of Business Administration at Florida International University. His research interests include internationalization of service industries, theories of multinational enterprise, international entrepreneurship and emerging multinationals. His extensive international teaching experience includes positions at Chulalongkorn University (Thailand), City University of Hong Kong (China), Saint Louis University Madrid Campus (Spain), and the Indian Institute of Management. Dr. Kundu has published several articles in prestigious journals, including the *Journal of International Business Studies, Management International Review*, the *Journal of International Management* and the *Journal of International Marketing*. Dr. Kundu obtained his Ph.D. from Rutgers University.

Richard G. Lipsey is currently Professor Emeritus of Economics at Simon Fraser University and a Fellow of the Canadian Institute for Advanced Research. He is an Officer of the Order of Canada, a Fellow of the Royal Society of Canada and the Econometric Society and a past president of the Canadian Economic Society and the Atlantic Economic Society. He has held a chair in Economics at the London School of Economics and was chairman of the Department of Economics and Dean of the Faculty of Social Science at the University of Essex, England from 1964 to 1970. He was senior economic advisor for the C.D. Howe Institute where he coauthored monographs on Canada's trade options and on the Canada-U.S. Free Trade Agreement, and wrote over a dozen journal articles on various aspects of the free-trade debate. From 1990 to 2002, he was a Fellow of the Canadian Institute for Advanced Research, where he set up and initially directed an international research team studying economic growth and policy. Dr. Lipsey received his Ph.D. from the London School of Economics, and also holds honorary doctorates from the universities of McMaster, Victoria, Carleton, Queen's, Toronto, Guelph, Western Ontario, British Columbia and Essex (England).

John McHale is an associate professor at the School of Business at Queen's University. He has also been an assistant and associate professor in the Department of Economics at Harvard University, where he obtained his Ph.D. in Economics. Dr. McHale's research focuses on the economic effects of highly skilled emigration, international human capital mobility and knowledge flows and international public finance. He has been a consultant to the World Bank on various privatization- and migration-related projects.

René Morissette is Assistant Director of Research in the Business and Labour Market Analysis Division of Statistics Canada. He holds a Ph.D. in Economics from the University of Montreal. He has published several articles on numerous labour market issues such as structural unemployment, earnings and wealth inequality, upward mobility, inter-firm differentials in wages and pension coverage, youth employment and job security. His current research interests include the evolution of family earnings instability in Canada, the impact of job loss on family income and the effect of outsourcing on wages and employment.

Alice O. Nakamura is the Winspear Professor of Business at the University of Alberta. In 1994-95, she served as President of the Canadian Economics Association. She was one of the founders and a former co-chair of the Canadian Employment Research Forum. She is also the founder of www.CareerOwl.ca, an e-recruiting service that was started as a volunteer project of Canadian university faculty members to help employers connect with the talent that their tax dollars helped to train. Her expertise lies in employment, productivity and performance measurement, and econometrics. She has served on numerous federal and provincial task forces and advisory committees, and has been a frequent keynote speaker and presenter at government and business conferences and other events. She has published widely in the areas of labour economics, firm behaviour, econometric methodology, and price and productivity measurement. Dr. Nakamura holds a Ph.D. in Economics from Johns Hopkins University.

Edwin H. Neave is a professor of Finance at the School of Business at Queen's University. Professor Neave's academic work focuses on both financial theory and financial institutions. He is a former departmental editor, Finance, of *Management Science*. He is an author of numerous articles and books focussing on asset pricing and on the theory of financial systems. In the last 10 years, he has presented papers at some 30 international conferences on finance, actuarial science and applied mathematics. Professor Neave is an Honorary Fellow of the Institute of Canadian Bankers. He received his Ph.D. in Business from the University of California, Berkeley.

Yuri Ostrovsky is a research economist at the Business and Labour Market Analysis (BLMA) Division at Statistics Canada. He received his Ph.D. in Economics from York University and, prior to joining BLMA, was a SEDAP Research Fellow in the Department of Economics at McMaster University. His research at BLMA focuses on the issues of family income instability, education wage premium and long-term effects of job losses on family income.

Garnett Picot is Director-General of the Economic and Business Analysis Branch of Statistics Canada. His research interests are in the labour market area, and include topics such as economic outcomes in cities and neighbourhoods, immigrant economic assimilation, worker displacement, job creation and destruction, and firm behaviour. He has written over 30 papers on these and other topics over the past decade. He also has a strong interest in data development, and has worked on the development of longitudinal surveys such as the Survey of Labour and Income Dynamics, and the Workplace and Employee Survey. In addition to other jobs in Statistics Canada, Mr. Picot has held positions at the University of British Columbia, the federal Secretary of State, and Canadian General Electric. Mr. Picot holds degrees in Electrical Engineering and Economics.

Mario Polèse is a professor at the Institut de la recherche scientifique (INRS) in Montreal, and titleholder of the Senior Canada Research Chair in Urban and Regional Studies. Among his books are *The Periphery in the Knowledge Economy*, with Richard G. Shearmur, and *Économie urbaine et régionale*, the principal textbook in French in urban and regional economics (translated into Spanish and Portuguese). Professor Polèse writes regularly on issues of regional and urban development, and frequently acts as a consultant to municipal, provincial and federal governments, and international agencies. He has held teaching and research positions in Latin America, Switzerland and France.

Someshwar Rao is the Director of the Strategic Investment Analysis Directorate, Micro-Economic Policy Analysis Branch, in the Policy Sector at Industry Canada. He is responsible for managing research and analysis associated with issues related to North American linkages, emerging and new economies, commercialization, the services economy, sustainable development, productivity and policy modelling. He is also responsible for the Industry Canada Research Publications Program. Prior to joining Industry Canada in 1992, he worked as a Senior Economist at the Economic Council of Canada for over 15 years. He was actively involved with the preparation of the Council's Annual Reviews and two major reports on the Canada-U.S. Free Trade Agreement and Canada's competitive position. He also served as acting director of the group that was responsible for the development of CANDIDE, a disaggregated model of the Canadian economy. He has published extensively on both micro- and macro-economic issues. He obtained his Ph.D. in Economics from Queen's University.

John Ries holds the HSBC Professorship in Asian Business at the Faculty of Commerce and Business Administration of the University of British Columbia. He teaches courses on international business, international trade policy, government and business, and the Asian business environment. Professor Ries's primary research interests are international trade and business and the Japanese economy. His current research includes assessing the role productivity plays in the FDI versus export decisions of firms and the effects of tariff reductions on Canadian manufacturers. He has published articles in academic journals, including the *American Economic Review*, *Journal of International Economics*, the *Journal of Economics and Management Strategy*, and the *Canadian Journal of Economics*. He has a B.A. from the University of California, Berkeley and received a Ph.D. in Economics from the University of Michigan in 1990.

Eric Santor is a senior economist in the Special Studies Division of the International Department at the Bank of Canada, where he has written on the effects of social capital on the earnings of micro-finance borrowers, financial development, and banking crises and contagion. His research interests also include evaluating the impact of financial development on publicly-traded firms, the integration of Canadian financial markets, and the globalization of finance for Canadian firms. He has presented his research at both academic and central bank venues, including the Econometric Society, Canadian Economics Association, Northern Finance Association, Bank of Spain and the Bank of Guatemala. Dr. Santor holds a Ph.D. in Economics from the University of Toronto.

Pierre Sauvé is a Visiting Fellow of the International Relations Department and a research associate in the International Trade Policy Unit at the London School of Economics. In 2003-04, he was a visiting professor and Director of Studies with the Groupe d'Économie Mondiale at the Institut d'Études Politiques de Paris. He also works as a consultant for the World Bank Institute in Paris. Previously, he served as a senior economist within the OECD Trade Directorate in Paris (1993-2002), and at the GATT in Geneva (1988-1991). He served as services negotiator for the Canadian government during the negotiation of the North American Free Trade Agreement (1991-1993). From 1998 to 2000, he was appointed Fellow and Adjunct Lecturer at Harvard University's John F. Kennedy School of Government, a period during which he was also appointed Non-Resident Senior Fellow at the Brookings Institution in Washington, D.C. He has published widely in the field of trade policy. His most recent books include, *Domestic Regulation and Service Trade Liberalization*, with Aaditya Mattoo, eds., Washington, D.C.: Oxford University Press for The World Bank, 2003, and *Trade Rules Behind Borders: Essays on Services, Investment and the New Trade Agenda*, London: Cameron-May Publishers, 2003.

Daniel M. Shapiro is the Dennis Culver EMBA Alumni Professor in the Faculty of Business Administration at Simon Fraser University. He received his Ph.D. from Cornell University. He was a Director of the Executive MBA program and Associate Dean responsible for executive programs at Simon Fraser University, and has over 20 years experience as a business educator and researcher. He has served as consultant for the Anti-Inflation Board,

Investment Canada, the Bureau of Competition Policy, the OECD, The World Bank and the City of Vancouver. As a consultant, he worked in various sectors, including foreign investment, mergers, competition policy, strategy and industrial policy. He has published books and monographs, and over 40 articles in scholarly journals. His research has been published in periodicals such as the *Academy of Management Journal*, *Journal of International Business Studies* and *Journal of Industrial Economics*.

Andrew Sharpe is founder and Executive Director of the Ottawa-based Centre for the Study of Living Standards (CSLS), a national, independent, not-for-profit economic research organization. He has held a variety of earlier positions, including Head of Research at the Canadian Labour Market and Productivity Centre and Chief, Business Sector Analysis, at the Department of Finance. He holds a Ph.D. in economics from McGill University. He is a founder and past editor (1992-98) of *Canadian Business Economics*, founder and editor of the *International Productivity Monitor* since 2000, and Executive Director of the International Association for Research in Income and Wealth. He is a member of a number of advisory committees, and has served as President of the Canadian Association for Business Economics (1992-94). He has written extensively on labour market, productivity and living standard issues.

Christopher A. Sharpe is a professor of Geography at Memorial University of Newfoundland. His research and teaching interests are in urban geography and planning, and heritage conservation. He holds a Ph.D. in Geography from the University of Toronto.

Philip Smith is Assistant Chief Statistician responsible for the National Accounts and Analytical Studies Field at Statistics Canada. He has experience in national accounting, business financial and production surveys, fiscal policy and international finance. In the past, he has held a number of positions in various management capacities at Statistics Canada and the Department of Finance. He holds a Ph.D. in Economics from Queen's University.

Jianmin Tang is a senior research economist and economic research coordinator in the Micro-Economic Policy Analysis Branch at Industry Canada. His current research interest is in productivity and innovation. Since he joined Industry Canada in 1997, he has published many of his research papers in journals such as the *American Economic Review*, the *Canadian Journal of Economics*, *Canadian Public Policy*, *Environmental and Resource Economics*, *International Tax and Public Finance*, and the *Journal of Productivity Analysis*. He received his Ph.D. in Economics from Queen's University.

Aidan R. Vining is the CNABS Professor of Business and Government Relations in the Faculty of Business Administration at Simon Fraser University. He obtained his Ph.D. from the University of California, Berkeley. He also holds an LL.B (King's College, London), an MBA and a Master's in Public Policy. He teaches and researches in the areas of public policy, policy analysis and business strategy. His research has appeared in academic periodicals such as the *Journal of Policy Analysis and Management*, *Canadian Public Policy*, the *Canadian Journal of Administrative Sciences* and the *Public Administration Review*. He is the co-author of *Policy Analysis: Concepts and Practice* (4th Ed., Pearson Prentice-Hall, 2005) and *Cost-Benefit Analysis: Concepts and Practice* (2nd Ed., Pearson Prentice-Hall, 2001). He is currently the principal investigator of a major Social Sciences and Humanities Research Council grant, examining the strategic behaviour of high-tech firms.

William Watson has taught economics at McGill University since 1977. Educated at McGill and Yale universities, he is a Senior Research Fellow at Montreal's Institute for Research on Public Policy (IRPP) and a Research Fellow at the C. D. Howe Institute in Toronto. In 1997 he took a 21-month leave from McGill and served as editorial pages editor of the *Ottawa Citizen*. From 1998 to 2002 he edited the IRPP's magazine, *Policy Options*. His 1998 book, *Globalization and the Meaning of Canadian Life*, was runner-up for the Donner Prize for best Canadian policy book of the year. He writes on economics and other matters weekly in the *National Post*, bi-monthly in the *Montreal Gazette* and *Ottawa Citizen* and monthly in *Policy Options*.

C. Michael Wernerheim is an associate professor of Economics at Memorial University of Newfoundland. Dr. Wernerheim specializes in industrial and resource economics. He has reviewed manuscripts for a number of internationally circulated journals, and published papers on service industries, taxation, forestry, hydro-electricity production, international trade and public policy. He holds a Ph.D. in Economics from Uppsala University in Sweden.

John Whalley is a professor of Economics at the University of Western Ontario. He is also a research associate with the National Bureau of Economic Research (NBER). He is best known for his contributions to numerical simulation analysis (general equilibrium) of policy issues, work he started in the Tokyo Round (of GATT trade negotiations) and continued through the Uruguay Round (of GATT trade negotiations). He has written extensive policy commentary on trade policy, emphasizing issues confronting developing countries in the trading system. He has written on services trade liberalization, especially as it affects developing countries. He is a Fellow of the Royal Society of Canada and a Fellow of the Econometric Society.

Anita Wölfl is an economist at the Centre d'études prospectives et d'informations internationales (CEPII), France's leading institute for research on the international economy. She received her diploma in Economics from the University of Regensburg and Maastricht, 1996, and holds a postgraduate certificate from the Advanced Studies Programme for International Economic Policy Research, at the Kiel Institute for Economic Research in Germany, 1997. Before joining CEPII in October 2004, she was an economist at the OECD (June 2001-September 2004), in the Economic Analysis and Statistics Division of the OECD-Directorate for Science, Technology and Industry. From July 1997-May 2001, she was an economist at the Halle Institute for Economic Research, one of the six leading institutes for empirical economic research in Germany. Her main fields of research are the analysis of productivity at the micro-, sectoral and macro-economic levels, with a special focus on services industries.